ADDITIONAL COOKBOOKS AND DVD SETS AVAILABLE FROM THE PUBLISHERS OF COOK'S COUNTRY INCLUDE:

The *America's Test Kitchen* Library Series

The How Can It Be Gluten-Free Cookbook

The How Can It Be Gluten-Free Cookbook: Volume 2

The *America's Test Kitchen* Complete Vegetarian Cookbook

The Best Mexican Recipes

The Make-Ahead Cook

The *America's Test Kitchen* Do-It-Yourself Cookbook

Slow Cooker Revolution

Slow Cooker Revolution Volume 2: The Easy-Prep Edition

Healthy Slow Cooker Revolution

Comfort Food Makeovers

From Our Grandmothers' Kitchens

Cook's Country Annual Editions
from each year of publication (2005–2016)

From the Editors of *Cook's Illustrated*

The *Cook's Illustrated* Meat Book

The *Cook's Illustrated* Baking Book

The Science of Good Cooking

Cook's Illustrated Cookbook

The Best One-Dish Suppers

Soups, Stews & Chilis

The New Best Recipe

The Best Skillet Recipes

The Best Slow & Easy Recipes

The Best Chicken Recipes

The Best Make-Ahead Recipe

The Best 30-Minute Recipe

The *Cook's Illustrated* Guide to
Grilling and Barbecue

Best American Side Dishes

Cover & Bake

Steaks, Chops, Roasts, and Ribs

Baking Illustrated

Perfect Vegetables

Italian Classics

The Best American Classics

1993–2016 *Cook's Illustrated* Master Index

Cook's Illustrated Annual Editions
from each year of publication (1993–2016)

America's Test Kitchen

Naturally Sweet

Master of the Grill

Foolproof Preserving

Cook It in Cast Iron

100 Recipes: The Absolute Best Way to Make the True Essentials

Cook's Country Eats Local

Kitchen Hacks: How Clever Cooks Get Things Done

The *America's Test Kitchen* New Family Cookbook

The Complete Cooking for Two Cookbook

The *America's Test Kitchen* Cooking School Cookbook

Pressure Cooker Perfection

The Best of *America's Test Kitchen* (2007–2017 Editions)

Cooking for Two (2009–2013 Editions)

The *America's Test Kitchen* Family Baking Book

The *America's Test Kitchen* Family Cookbook

The *America's Test Kitchen* Healthy Family Cookbook

The *America's Test Kitchen* Quick Family Cookbook

The *America's Test Kitchen* Series Companion Cookbooks

America's Test Kitchen: The TV Companion Cookbook
(2011–2015 Editions)

The Complete *America's Test Kitchen* TV Show Cookbook
(2010–2017 Editions)

America's Test Kitchen: The TV Companion Cookbook (2009)

Behind the Scenes with *America's Test Kitchen* (2008)

Test Kitchen Favorites (2007)

Cooking at Home with *America's Test Kitchen* (2006)

America's Test Kitchen Live! (2005)

Inside *America's Test Kitchen* (2004)

Here in *America's Test Kitchen* (2003)

The *America's Test Kitchen* Cookbook (2002)

The *America's Test Kitchen* Series DVD Sets
(featuring each season's episodes from our hit
public television series)

The *America's Test Kitchen* 4-DVD Set (2002–2015 Seasons)

The *America's Test Kitchen* 2-DVD Set (2001 Season)

The *Cook's Country* TV Series Cookbooks and DVD Sets
(featuring each season's episodes from our hit
public television series)

The Complete *Cook's Country* TV Show Cookbook

The *Cook's Country* 2-DVD Set (Seasons 1–8)

Visit our online bookstore at CooksCountry.com to order any of our cookbooks and DVDs listed above. You can also order subscriptions, gift subscriptions, and any of our cookbooks and DVDs by calling 800-611-0759 inside the U.S., or 515-246-6911 if calling from outside the U.S.

$35.00

To get home delivery of *Cook's Country*, call 800-526-8447 inside the U.S., or 515-247-7571 if calling from outside the U.S., or subscribe online at CooksCountry.com.

2016 Recipe Index

C

Cook's Country

FEBRUARY/MARCH 2016

Crispy Churros

Beef Burgundy

Perfect Pierogi

Bacon-Wrapped Pork Loin
Smoky and Moist

One-Pan Salmon Dinner
with Broccoli and Potatoes

Chicken Scarpariello
Italian American Favorite

Shrimp De Jonghe
Chicago Classic Revived

Alabama Orange Rolls
Citrusy and Sticky-Sweet

Crispy Parmesan Potatoes
Ultimate Super Bowl Snack

Flank Steak in Adobo
Spicy South Texas Stew

Five Easy Pasta Salads
Surprising Pasta Choice

Chocolate Heart Cake
with Raspberry Roses

Cocktail Meatballs
One Bite, Big Flavor

CooksCountry.com
$5.95 U.S./$6.95 CANADA

Churros, flute-shaped fritters dusted in cinnamon sugar and dunked
in chocolate, have become as popular in Southern California as in Latin America.
We brought them into the test kitchen to perfect a light, crispy version. PAGE 14

7 25274 05251 6

03>

Cook's Country

Dear Country Cook,

I grew up working summers on a small-scale dairy farm—20 or so head of Holsteins in a fly-specked barn on the banks of the Battenkill River. The farmer, Charlie Bentley, got to know every moving part in the compressor that powered the milkers, every dent in the tops of the large milk cans, and, of course, the names of every cow and horse on the farm—not to mention the orange tabby that terrorized the mice.

In the days of small farms, there were grocers and wholesalers who knew where things came from—men and women who sorted through the crates and boxes of produce looking for the best carrot, potato, or onion for their customers.

And it wasn't that long ago that the steakhouses of New York would send buyers down to Fourteenth Street to choose specific sides of beef to cut their steaks from. They knew that one beefer wasn't the same as another.

Food was personal. It had a history. It had a place. And when you went shopping, you sorted through to find the very best. That was the definition of shopping.

Maybe it's time to bring back the grocer, the butcher, the baker, the fish-monger, and even the guy who walked the streets sharpening knives. You can ask them for help or for a nice cut of fish or meat or to save you the best sour cherries when they come into season.

We all had friends in the business, and that's what friends are for.

Cordially,

Christopher Kimball
Founder and Editor, Cook's Country

Cook'sCountry

Founder and Editor Christopher Kimball
Chief Creative Officer Jack Bishop
Editorial Director John Willoughby
Executive Editor Tucker Shaw
Deputy Editor Rebecca Hays
Executive Managing Editor, Magazines Todd Meier
Executive Food Editor Bryan Roof
Executive Tastings & Testings Editor Lisa McManus
Managing Editor, Tastings & Testings Scott Kathan
Senior Editors Hannah Crowley, Christie Morrison, Diane Unger
Test Kitchen Director Erin McMurrer
Associate Editor Ashley Moore
Test Cooks Morgan Bolling, Cecelia Jenkins, Katie Leaird
Assistant Editors Lauren Savoie, Kate Shannon
Copy Editors Jillian Campbell, Krista Magnuson
Executive Assistant Christine Gordon
Assistant Test Kitchen Director Leah Rovner
Senior Kitchen Assistants Michelle Blodgot, Alexxa Grattan
Kitchen Assistants Blanca Castanza, Maria Elena Delgado, Ena Gudiel
Executive Producer Melissa Baldino
Co-Executive Producer Stephanie Stender
Associate Producer Kaitlin Hammond

Creative Consultant Amy Klee
Contributing Editors Erika Bruce, Eva Katz, Jeremy Sauer
Consulting Editors Anne Mendelson, Meg Ragland
Science Editor Guy Crosby, PhD
Executive Food Editor, TV, Radio & Media Bridget Lancaster

Managing Editor, Web Christine Liu
Senior Editor, Cooking School Mari Levine
Social Media Manager Jill Fisher
Senior Editor, Web Roger Metcalf
Assistant Editor, Web Terrence Doyle
Senior Video Editor Nick Dakoulas

Design Director, Print Greg Galvan
Photography Director Julie Cote
Art Director Susan Levin
Associate Art Director Lindsey Chandler
Art Director, Marketing Jennifer Cox
Staff Photographer Daniel J. van Ackere
Color Food Photography Keller + Keller
Styling Catrine Kelty, Marie Piraino
Deputy Art Director, Marketing Melanie Gryboski
Associate Art Director, Marketing Janet Taylor
Designer, Marketing Stephanie Cook
Associate Art Director, Photography Steve Klise

VP, Print & Direct Marketing David Mack
Circulation Director Doug Wicinski
Circulation & Fulfillment Manager Carrie Fethe
Partnership Marketing Manager Pamela Putprush
Marketing Assistant Andrea Hampel

Director, Business Systems Alice Carpenter
Manager, Business & Content Systems Dustin Brandt
DAM Systems Manager Ian Matzen
Project Manager Britt Dresser

Chief Digital Officer Fran Middleton
VP, New Product Development Michael Burton
Production Director Guy Rochford
Imaging Manager Lauren Robbins
Production & Imaging Specialists Heather Dube, Dennis Noble
Director, Marketing & Sales Operations Deborah Fagone
Client Services Manager Kate Zebrowski
Sponsorship Sales Associate Morgan Mannino
Senior Controller Theresa Peterson
Customer Loyalty & Support Manager Amy Bootier
Customer Loyalty & Support Reps Caroline Augliere, Rebecca Kowalski, Andrew Straaberg Finfrock

Director, Retail Book Program Beth Ineson
Human Resources Manager Adele Shapiro
Publicity Deborah Broide

ON THE COVER: SO-CAL CHURROS: Keller + Keller, Catrine Kelty
ILLUSTRATION: Greg Stevenson

Follow us on **Pinterest**
pinterest.com/TestKitchen

Follow us on **Twitter**
twitter.com/TestKitchen

Find us on **Facebook**
facebook.com/CooksCountry

Cook's Country magazine (ISSN 1552-1990), number 67, is published bimonthly by Boston Common Press Limited Partnership, 17 Station St., Brookline, MA 02445. Copyright 2016 Boston Common Press Limited Partnership. Periodicals postage paid at Boston, MA, and additional mailing offices. USPS #023453. Publications Mail Agreement No. 40020778. Return undeliverable Canadian addresses to P.O. Box 875, Station A, Windsor, ON N9A 6P2. POSTMASTER: Send address changes to Cook's Country, P.O. Box 6018, Harlan, IA 51593-1518. For subscription and gift subscription orders, subscription inquiries, or change of address notices, visit AmericasTestKitchen.com/support, call 800-526-8447 in the U.S. or 515-248-7684 from outside the U.S., or write to us at Cook's Country, P.O. Box 6018, Harlan, IA 51593-1518. PRINTED IN THE USA.

Contents

EGGS IN PURGATORY, 17

BACON-WRAPPED PORK ROAST, 4

ALABAMA ORANGE ROLLS, 22

Features

Departments

Cook It in Cast Iron

Too many home cooks have a cast-iron skillet but don't use it enough. Our newest book features 120 fail-safe recipes that take advantage of this multitasking pan, from breakfast to dinner to dessert, plus tips on keeping your cast iron in tip-top shape.

America's Test Kitchen is a very real 2,500-square-foot kitchen located just outside Boston. It is the home of Cook's Country and Cook's Illustrated magazines and the workday destination of more than three dozen test cooks, editors, and cookware specialists. Our mission is to test recipes until we understand how and why they work and arrive at the best version. We also test kitchen equipment and supermarket ingredients in search of products that offer the best value and performance. You can watch us work by tuning in to Cook's Country from America's Test Kitchen (CooksCountry.com) and America's Test Kitchen (AmericasTestKitchen.com) on public television.

Ask Cook's Country

BY MORGAN BOLLING

Green Cookies

I substitute sunflower butter for peanut butter in recipes because my son cannot eat peanuts. But recently I made a batch of sunflower butter cookies, and they turned green! Are they safe to eat?
–Joy Stabile, Litchfield, N.H.

This was a new problem to us, so we made a batch of our Soft and Chewy Peanut Butter Cookies, substituting sunflower seed butter to see if we got green cookies. The cookies looked fine, but after two days they started to develop green spots on their interiors, and by six days their insides were forest green.

We reached out to our science editor for insight as to why this was happening. He explained that, while they may be unappetizing to look at, the green cookies are perfectly safe to eat.

Sunflower butter contains chlorophyll, the green pigment present in all green plants. The color is not visible in the jar of sunflower butter because it is being bound by other substances. It's released when it's heated in the presence of alkaline ingredients (ones with low acid and a high pH). Many peanut butter cookie recipes (including ours) call for baking soda, which is alkaline. This combination caused the color to slowly appear, although the green cookies didn't taste any different.

THE BOTTOM LINE Sunflower butter may sometimes create a green color in baked goods. The baked goods taste fine and are perfectly safe to eat—the color comes from the chlorophyll present in sunflower butter.

Slow Starch

I can never get slow-cooker rice to come out properly. Even when the exterior has overcooked and turned mushy, the rice is still crunchy on the interior. Is it just me?
–Diana Lane, Boonton Township, N.J.

Long-grain white rice seems like it would be well suited to the slow cooker. But when we ran some tests (using different heat settings and varying the rice-to-liquid ratios), we had the same poor results as you did: grains with shaggy, blown-apart exteriors and hard insides.

What's the problem? In a word, heat. Rice has a lot of starch, which swells as it cooks. Our science editor explained that rice needs to reach around 212 degrees for its starch to completely gelatinize throughout all of the starch granules and produce evenly cooked rice. The starch in rice cooked at lower temperatures—as in a slow cooker, which typically doesn't get hotter than

190 degrees—may not get hot enough to gelatinize all of the starch granules, resulting in rice that is unevenly cooked.

We tried rinsing, toasting, and microwaving the rice before adding it to the slow cooker to manipulate its starch, but none of these methods resulted in slow-cooker rice with an acceptable texture. In short, there's no good way to cook a big batch of plain rice in the slow cooker. The best option is to add precooked rice to your slow-cooker dish (soup, stew, etc.) at the end of cooking. If you don't like cooking rice on the stovetop, you could use a rice cooker; we highly recommend the Aroma 8-Cup Digital Rice Cooker and Food Steamer, which costs about $30. Or you can use instant rice, which has already been cooked to gelatinize the starch, so it can finish cooking in the slow cooker.

THE BOTTOM LINE Avoid trying to cook long-grain white rice all the way through in the slow cooker. Instead, we suggest precooking the rice on the stove or using instant rice.

Sizing Up a Shallot

You often call for shallots in your recipes. What size of shallots should I be using?
–Andy Bresslin, Lenox, Mass.

Shallots are a sweeter, smaller, milder cousin of onions. We like to use them in recipes where we want a soft onion flavor without much bite. As with most other vegetables (and fruits), we only specify small or large if size is crucial to the success of the recipe. Medium is our default.

But we're more exacting when we're testing recipes in the test kitchen. We use the guideline that one medium-size shallot (which is about the size of a golf ball) yields 3 tablespoons of minced shallot, which translates to 1 ounce (or 28 grams).

THE BOTTOM LINE When cooking our recipes, a medium shallot should yield about 3 tablespoons of minced shallot. You can use part of a large one or multiple small ones as long as you measure after mincing.

Small Shallot	Medium Shallot	Large Shallot
½ ounce (14 grams) Yield: 1 tablespoon minced	1 ounce (28 grams) Yield: 3 tablespoons minced	1½ ounces (42 grams) Yield: 4 tablespoons minced

Naturally Curious

The chicken I buy is labeled "natural," but what exactly does that mean? Is it the same as "organic"?
–Lauren Weddleton, Greenland, N.H.

While the term "natural" sounds nice, it doesn't have much meaning on food packaging. The United States Department of Agriculture (USDA) stipulates that meat or poultry labeled "natural" can have no artificial ingredients added to the raw meat. It doesn't cover how a chicken was raised. So a producer can tack the label on a package even if the animal was fed an unnatural diet, pumped with antibiotics, and/or injected with broth or brine during processing.

On the other hand, "USDA Organic" is a tightly regulated term. It applies not only to the meat itself but also to how the animal was raised. To earn this label, the animals must eat organic feed not containing animal byproducts, be raised without antibiotics, and have access to the outdoors (though not for a specified amount of time).

THE BOTTOM LINE If you see the word "natural" on a poultry or meat label, take it with a grain of salt: The term has very little meaning.

Lard versus Butter

I love using lard to make flaky pie crust. Can I substitute it in place of butter when I make biscuits?
–Jocelyn Jackson, Berkeley, Calif.

Many home cooks swear by lard, which is rendered pork fat (and not vegetable shortening, such as Crisco, as many people think), for pie crusts and biscuits. However, most chefs find supermarket lard to be of subpar quality. To test the validity of this concern, we made two batches of our Buttermilk Drop Biscuits: one with butter as written and one with lard from the supermarket used in place of the butter. The butter biscuits were a clear winner, as our tasters found the biscuits made with supermarket lard dense and gummy, with a slightly sour aftertaste. This wasn't a big surprise since the recipe was developed specifically for butter. But why were the lard biscuits so bad?

Butter's capacity to create flakiness comes from its relatively high water content (15 to 20 percent). This water converts to steam in the oven, producing pockets of air and flaky biscuits. Lard contains no water.

But not all lard is created equal. Higher-quality leaf lard, which is rarely found on supermarket shelves but can be ordered from the butcher, is made from the fat around the pig's kidneys. Our science editor explained that leaf lard has a higher melting point, thereby providing a more effective coating of fat around the other ingredients. This keeps the dough from gumming up in the oven, instead allowing it to bake and set into tender biscuits. Our test confirmed: Leaf lard made incredibly tender biscuits which, if not as flaky as those made with butter, were very tender with a notably rich flavor.

THE BOTTOM LINE You can substitute leaf lard for butter in biscuits for tender, savory results, but they won't be quite as flaky as biscuits made with butter. We don't recommend using supermarket lard for biscuits.

▶ To ask us a cooking question, visit **CooksCountry.com/ask**. Or write to Ask *Cook's Country*, P.O. Box 470739, Brookline, MA 02447. Just try to stump us!

Kitchen Shortcuts

COMPILED BY DIANE UNGER

DOUBLE DUTY
Pan Protector
Elizabeth Brown, Port Huron, Mich.

I make a lot of brownies and bar cookies. Instead of cutting the bars with a knife and scratching the bottom of my pan, I cut the baked items and loosen the edges with my bench scraper. No marks or gouging the pan.

COOL TRICK Spritz It
Peter Spinner, Middletown, Conn.

Sometimes, when making dough for pasta or baked goods, the dough needs a little more water to reach the right consistency. Folding in flour to make it drier is easy. Not so easy is adding water in controlled amounts and folding it in. I discovered that using a spray bottle's fine mist to spray a small amount of water onto the dough allows me to add very small amounts that are much easier to fold in than if I sprinkle by hand.

SMART TIP
A Grate Idea
Buck Evans, Arlington, Mass.

Grating potatoes for hash browns on a box grater can be hazardous because the peeled potatoes are slippery and hard to grip. To make grating easier, I carefully grate a little bit off all the surfaces of each potato so that the roughened spud is easy to hold. I get through my pile of potatoes much more quickly—and more safely—this way.

SMART IDEA
Countdown
Elizabeth Soash, Land O'Lakes, Fla.

I find my eggs stay fresher when I keep them on a shelf in the back of my refrigerator rather than on the door. Each time I use them, I mark how many are left on the end of the container. This way, I only need to look at the carton—and not rummage through everything else on the shelf—to see how many eggs remain.

COOL IDEA
Fro Yo Pops
Francesca Remis, Palo Alto, Calif.

I found an easy way to make healthy Popsicles for my kids. I buy the small "kids" yogurt cups, the kind with foil lids, and then I make a small cut in the top of each lid with a paring knife. I put a clean Popsicle stick through each hole into the center of each cup and freeze them. When they're frozen solid, I run them under hot water for a second and they come right out. *Voilà*: homemade yogurt pops.

CLEVER TRICK
Chicken Rescue
Allison Holmes, Plano, Texas

I often buy rotisserie chickens to make chicken salad for a quick lunch or dinner. The problem is that the meat is most often overcooked, dry, and bland. I've found that I can season some chicken broth (I like to use salt, pepper, and dried thyme), pour it over the chopped-up chicken, and refrigerate the mixture until it's cool. The chicken absorbs the seasoned broth, making the meat much more moist and flavorful.

HOT TIP
Main Squeeze
Robert Mahoney, Westfield, Mass.

I love all things spicy and smoky, especially chipotle chiles in adobo sauce. The problem is, every brand packages their chiles in a can that's way too large to use up in one recipe. And I hate having to get the sauce all over my cutting board when chopping. Instead, I dump the whole can into my blender, buzz it up, and then transfer the pureed mixture to a squeeze bottle that I keep in the fridge. That way, I can put smooth chipotle "ketchup" on anything (everything) I want.

Submit a tip online at CooksCountry.com/kitchenshortcuts or send a letter to Kitchen Shortcuts, *Cook's Country*, P.O. Box 470739, Brookline, MA 02447. Include your name, address, and phone number. If we publish your tip, you will receive a free one-year subscription to *Cook's Country*. Letters may be edited for clarity and length.

Bacon-Wrapped Pork Roast

Wrapping superlean pork loin in bacon does more than impart smoky flavor. It also helps keep things moist. BY CHRISTIE MORRISON

When making bacon for breakfast, we prefer thick-cut. But for wrapping the pork in this recipe, thin-cut bacon is much easier to work with.

BACON MAKES A tasty wrapper for many foods, but when it comes to pork loin, bacon's flavor is just part of its appeal. Pork loin is very lean, so when it overcooks, as it often does, you're left with dry, flavorless meat. Wrapping the pork in (what else?) bacon shrouds this finicky cut in a layer of tasty fat that renders slowly during cooking, basting the roast and protecting it from drying out.

I started with a center-cut pork loin roast (not to be confused with the slimmer, leaner tenderloin), about 5 inches in diameter. At about 3½ pounds, this is just the right size for eight people (or four people and sandwich leftovers) and, conveniently, this was also the perfect size to accommodate a wrapping of packaged bacon slices. Since the meat would be encased in bacon, I removed the roast's thick fat cap.

Of course, even the smokiest bacon can only flavor the exterior of the pork roast. To lock in additional flavor and moisture, I tried both brining the roast (soaking it in a saltwater solution for a period of time) and simply seasoning the roast with salt and letting it sit. Both techniques improved juiciness, but salting worked better. To keep the additional flavorings simple, I sprinkled the pork with pepper and a few teaspoons of aromatic herbes de Provence, a blend of dried herbs including rosemary and thyme, before carefully wrapping it in bacon.

My dilemma presented itself promptly: Lean pork loin cooks best at a relatively low temperature, but bacon needs high heat to render its fat and turn brown and crispy. I tried roasting the wrapped pork at low heat first and then transferring it to the stovetop to sear, but this required another pan and made a greasy mess of the stovetop. Microwaving the bacon before wrapping the pork was also a bust; once the bacon was partially cooked, it would no longer adhere. Broiling after roasting showed some promise, but it cooked the bacon unevenly, leaving large patches of barely rendered bacon on the sides.

Finally, I tried roasting the pork in a low oven before increasing the heat to high for the roast's final minutes of cooking. After a number of tests, I hit on the magic sequence: I roasted the pork in a 250-degree oven until it registered 90 degrees when measured with a meat thermometer. I then removed it from the oven while I jacked the heat up to a sizzling 475 degrees. I returned the roast to the oven and cooked it for another 15 to 20 minutes until it registered 130 degrees. After letting it rest out of the oven for 15 minutes (during which time the roast continued carryover cooking to about 140 degrees, our target for pork loin), I sliced through the beautifully browned, cooked bacon and into the pink, juicy meat. Success.

To round out the dish, I made an easy, fruity sauce with frozen peaches (always perfectly ripe and convenient for a cooked sauce), white wine, sugar, and cider vinegar, with some whole-grain mustard to keep it savory. The thick, glazy sauce gave me an idea: I brushed a few more tablespoons onto the bacon-wrapped roast just before its stint in the 475-degree oven, which created even more browning and a burnished look.

BACON-WRAPPED PORK ROAST WITH PEACH SAUCE Serves 8

Buy a pork loin roast that measures about 9 inches long and is between 4 and 5 inches in diameter. Oscar Mayer Naturally Hardwood Smoked Bacon is our winning thin-sliced bacon. Do not use thick-cut bacon here. The peaches needn't be thawed before making the sauce. The pork needs to cure for at least an hour before cooking.

PORK

Kosher salt and pepper
1 tablespoon sugar
1 (3½-pound) boneless center-cut pork loin roast
2 teaspoons herbes de Provence
10 slices bacon

SAUCE

20 ounces frozen peaches, cut into ½-inch pieces (3 cups)
1 cup dry white wine
½ cup sugar
⅓ cup cider vinegar
4 sprigs fresh thyme
½ teaspoon kosher salt
2 tablespoons whole-grain mustard

1. FOR THE PORK: Combine 4 teaspoons salt and sugar in bowl. Remove fat cap and silverskin from roast. Rub roast with salt-sugar mixture, wrap in plastic wrap, and refrigerate for at least 1 hour or up to 24 hours.

2. FOR THE SAUCE: Bring peaches, wine, sugar, vinegar, thyme sprigs, and salt to simmer in medium saucepan over medium-high heat. Reduce heat to medium and cook at strong simmer, stirring occasionally, until reduced to about 2 cups and spatula leaves trail when dragged through sauce, about 30 minutes. Remove from heat and discard thyme sprigs. Reserve 2 tablespoons of liquid portion of sauce (without peach segments) in small bowl for glazing. Cover and set aside remaining sauce.

3. Meanwhile, adjust oven rack to upper-middle position and heat oven to 250 degrees. Line rimmed baking sheet with aluminum foil and spray with vegetable oil spray. Unwrap roast and pat dry with paper towels. Sprinkle with herbes de Provence and 1 teaspoon pepper.

4. Arrange bacon slices on cutting board parallel to counter's edge, overlapping them slightly to match length of roast. Place roast in center of bacon, perpendicular to slices. Bring ends of bacon up and around sides of roast, overlapping ends of slices as needed.

5. Place bacon-wrapped roast, seam side down, in center of prepared sheet. Roast until center of pork registers 90 degrees, 30 to 40 minutes. Remove roast from oven and increase oven temperature to 475 degrees.

6. Brush top and sides of roast with reserved 2 tablespoons sauce. Once oven reaches temperature, return pork to oven and roast until bacon is well browned and meat registers 130 degrees, 15 to 20 minutes longer. Transfer roast to wire rack and let rest for 15 minutes.

7. Stir mustard into sauce and rewarm over low heat. Transfer roast to carving board and cut into ½-inch-thick slices. Serve with peach sauce.

Ripe and Ready: Turning Frozen Peaches into a Sauce
To whip up a quick sauce that makes a great partner for pork, we start by opening up a bag of frozen peaches. Peaches pair well with pork since their floral sweetness brings out the natural sweetness of the meat. And there's a lot to be said for using frozen peaches instead of fresh. Besides being ripe, frozen peaches are peeled, pitted, and cut into wedges. We mix in dry white wine, sugar, cider vinegar, whole-grain mustard, salt, and a few sprigs of fresh thyme for savoriness and tang.

TEST KITCHEN TECHNIQUE **Wrapping the Roast in Bacon**
To make sure that the roast is completely covered by the bacon strips, we came up with the following method.

Arrange the bacon slices on a cutting board, overlapping them slightly to match the roast's length. Place the roast in the center, perpendicular to the slices, and fold the slices over the roast. As the meat cooks, the bacon slices will fuse together and adhere to the roast.

Bring the ends of the strips up and around the sides of the roast.

Better Peas and Carrots

This classic vegetable combo has fallen out of favor, so we set out to revamp this sleeper of a side dish. BY DIANE UNGER

EVER SINCE CLARENCE Birdseye invented flash-freezing in the early 20th century, people have harvested peas and carrots from the freezer case at the supermarket.

Convenience aside, these freezer foragers are half right. Though freshly shelled peas, if they're available, have bright pea flavor, sweet and tender flash-frozen peas are fine fare. But flash-frozen carrots? Not so much. Thawed and reheated, they tend to be flavorless and mushy. I wanted to reunite these two vegetables, make them equally good, add supporting ingredients to amplify their assets, and still keep the combination a convenient weeknight side dish.

I found many existing recipes to test. Some had flavor problems, others were way too fussy for a simple side, and nearly all suffered from inconsistent doneness—because dense carrots take several minutes to cook completely and peas just need to warm through. I had a balancing act on my hands.

I knew the carrot problem would be trickier to solve, so I decided to tackle it first. I peeled several carrots and cut them into ½-inch pieces. To jump-start their seasoning, I tossed them with ½ teaspoon of salt a few minutes before cooking them in a covered skillet with butter and shallots for just long enough to soften. I added thawed frozen peas, heated them through, and finished the dish with butter, salt, and pepper.

My tasters and I agreed that the carrots were just right, and the process was easy, but while I could see the peas, I couldn't really taste them. I needed to unlock their flavor.

For my next batch, I tossed 1 cup of the thawed peas into a blender with a splash of water and buzzed it to a smooth puree. After the carrots and the remaining 3 cups of peas were nearly cooked through, I stirred in the pea puree to coat the lot, along with butter and 2 teaspoons of minced fresh herbs (we liked chives, mint, or tarragon). The puree tied everything together with vibrant pea flavor, transforming this previously dull side dish.

We puree a portion of the peas to ensure vibrant flavor in every bite.

PEAS AND CARROTS
Serves 4 to 6

For a smooth puree, make sure the peas have thawed completely. A variety of fresh herbs will work here; choose your favorite from the listed options.

3 carrots, peeled, quartered lengthwise, and cut into ½-inch pieces
Salt and pepper
4 cups frozen peas, thawed
½ cup water
5 tablespoons unsalted butter, cut into 5 pieces
2 shallots, minced
2 teaspoons minced fresh chives, mint, or tarragon

1. Combine carrots and ½ teaspoon salt in bowl. Process 1 cup peas, water, and ½ teaspoon salt in blender until smooth, about 1 minute; set aside.

2. Melt 1 tablespoon butter in 12-inch nonstick skillet over medium heat. Add shallots and carrots. Cover and cook until carrots are just softened, 5 to 7 minutes. Add remaining 3 cups peas and cook, uncovered and stirring occasionally, until peas are heated through, 2 to 4 minutes.

3. Stir in pea puree and ½ teaspoon pepper, bring to simmer, and cook, uncovered, until sauce has thickened, about 1 minute. Off heat, stir in remaining 4 tablespoons butter until melted. Season with salt and pepper to taste. Sprinkle with chives and serve.

Pittsburgh Pierogi

We scoured Pittsburgh's Polish Hill neighborhood for the secrets to these popular potato-stuffed boiled dumplings. BY KATIE LEAIRD

WHEN OUR EXECUTIVE food editor, Bryan Roof, returned from a trip to Pittsburgh (see "On the Road"), he was unabashedly enthusiastic about the pierogi he'd eaten in that city's historic Polish American quarter. The tender but chewy dumplings stuffed with potatoes, cheese, and sometimes sauerkraut won him over. I wanted to create a recipe for the rest of us.

Pittsburgh, which rose to prominence as an industrial capital during the late 19th century, attracted thousands of Polish immigrants to work in steel mills and coal mines. By 1920, Polish Americans made up one-third of the city's workforce. Many settled in a steep, winding, hillside neighborhood overlooking the Allegheny River, known as Polish Hill. There, Roof was invited into a Polish American home to make pierogi with Elaine Kitlowski, who generously shared her recipe with us.

It's a simple but exacting recipe, calling for equal parts all-purpose and hard durum semolina flour. Sour cream and egg bind the flours together into a supple dough that's easy to roll out thin, cut into circles, stuff with mashed potato, and seal up into dumplings for boiling. These pierogi had a faint bite, like the al dente quality of properly cooked pasta. They were excellent.

But I wondered about the semolina flour, which isn't always easy to find at the supermarket. Did I need it? I tried making the dough with just all-purpose flour. Unfortunately, the resulting pierogi were a flop.

Flour's protein content is one major factor in a dough's tenderness (water and the amount of kneading are others). Kitlowski's mix of all-purpose (11 grams of protein per cup) and semolina (about 21 grams) clocked in at roughly 16 grams of protein per cup, the same as in commonly available bread flour. Hopeful, I made a batch of pierogi using just bread flour and pitted the results against pierogi made following Kitlowski's recipe. Tasters found both acceptable. Bread flour it would be.

Most Pittsburgh-style pierogi are stuffed with a simple mixture of mashed potatoes and cheddar cheese, plus salt and pepper. The trick lies in thoroughly combining the ingredients. After boiling slices of russet potatoes (chosen for their fluffiness) until soft, I used the stand mixer to quickly and completely incorporate butter and cheese into the still-hot potatoes. Some salt and pepper gave me a well-seasoned filling.

A happy result of all this testing was that it gave me a chance to develop an easy way to cut, fill, and shape the pierogi: I roll the dough thin, to ⅛ inch, and then use a biscuit cutter to cut out 3-inch circles. I drop a tablespoon of potato filling onto each circle and seal the edges up and over the savory mound to form a half-moon shape.

Once the pierogi were boiled, I drizzled a sauce of butter and caramelized chopped onion over the top and offered them up. "Tastes like home," said one Pittsburgh-bred colleague.

POTATO-CHEDDAR PIEROGI

Makes about 30 pierogi

When rolling the dough in step 4, be sure not to dust the top surface with too much flour, as that will prevent the edges from forming a tight seal when pinched.

FILLING
- 1   **pound russet potatoes, peeled and sliced ½ inch thick**
    Salt and pepper
- 4   **ounces sharp cheddar cheese, shredded (1 cup)**
- 2   **tablespoons unsalted butter**

DOUGH
- 2½   **cups (13¾ ounces) bread flour**
- 1   **teaspoon baking powder**
    Salt
- 1   **cup sour cream**
- 1   **large egg plus 1 large yolk**

TOPPING
- 4   **tablespoons unsalted butter**
- 1   **large onion, chopped fine**
- ½   **teaspoon salt**

1. FOR THE FILLING: Combine potatoes and 1 tablespoon salt in large saucepan and cover with water by 1 inch. Bring to boil over medium-high heat; reduce heat to medium and cook at vigorous simmer until potatoes are very tender, about 15 minutes.

2. Drain potatoes in colander. While still hot, combine potatoes, cheddar, butter, ½ teaspoon salt, and ½ teaspoon pepper in bowl of stand mixer. Fit mixer with paddle and mix on medium speed until potatoes are smooth and all ingredients are fully combined, about 1 minute.

Chopped onion caramelized in butter adds a sweet-savory finish to these tender dumplings.

Transfer filling to 8-inch square baking dish and refrigerate until fully chilled, about 30 minutes, or cover with plastic wrap and refrigerate for up to 24 hours.

3. FOR THE DOUGH: Whisk flour, baking powder, and ½ teaspoon salt together in clean bowl of stand mixer. Add sour cream and egg and yolk. Fit mixer with dough hook and knead on medium-high speed for 8 minutes (dough will be smooth and elastic). Transfer dough to floured bowl, cover with plastic, and refrigerate until ready to assemble.

4. Line rimmed baking sheet with parchment paper and dust with flour. Roll dough on lightly floured counter into 18-inch circle, about ⅛ inch thick. Using 3-inch biscuit cutter, cut 20 to 24 circles from dough. Place 1 tablespoon chilled filling in center of each dough round. Fold dough over filling to create half-moon shape and pinch edges firmly to seal. Transfer to prepared sheet.

5. Gather dough scraps and reroll to ⅛-inch thickness. Cut 6 to 10 more circles from dough and repeat with remaining filling. (It may be necessary to reroll dough once more to yield 30 pierogi.) Cover pierogi with plastic and refrigerate until ready to cook, up to 3 hours.

6. FOR THE TOPPING: Melt butter in 12-inch skillet over medium-low heat. Add onion and salt and cook until onion is caramelized, 15 to 20 minutes. Remove skillet from heat and set aside.

7. Bring 4 quarts water to boil in Dutch oven. Add 1 tablespoon salt and

On the Road
In Pursuit of the Perfect Pierogi

Pierogies Plus occupies a renovated gas station just inches from Island Avenue in McKees Rocks, Pennsylvania, about 5 miles from downtown Pittsburgh. Inside, a peg-letter menu board hangs behind the counter for takeout business; the rest of the room is tattooed with newspaper clippings extolling the virtues of owner Helen Mannarino's pierogies, which are famous across Allegheny County.

Mannarino, who immigrated from Poland in 1974, offers a warm greeting before leading me into the small kitchen behind the counter. There, a hulking stove, many years past its prime but still well-loved, anchors the kitchen. Several stockpots of water bubble away on top, and a deep hotel pan of melted butter and softened onions sits to one side. Helen drops pierogies one by one into the water, boils them for several minutes, and then scoops them into a large skillet, where she tosses them with a healthy ladle of the buttery onions before sending them up front for a customer.

Top: Mannarino's crew stretches dough from a laminating machine onto the work table. Bottom: Workers stuff the dough with disks of cold potato filling.

In the next room, six serious-faced women flank a massive flour-dusted table, speaking softly to each other as a giant laminator extrudes sheets of pierogi dough. They cut circles from the supple dough, drop disks of potato filling into their centers, and then fold and crimp them into half-moons with quiet confidence. Like a fingerprint, each cook imparts a slightly different crimp to her dumplings; Helen claims she can trace any broken dumplings—called "angels"—back to the culprit.

A burly cook mans the tilt skillet at the end of the table, where he quickly blanches the dumplings before they are frozen and delivered to area bars and restaurants. He pops the occasional dumpling into his mouth, whole, and then looks around to see if anyone noticed. He likes his job. –BRYAN ROOF

---

half of pierogi to boiling water and cook until tender, about 5 minutes. Using spider or slotted spoon, remove pierogi from water and transfer to skillet with caramelized onion. Return water to boil, cook remaining pierogi, and transfer to skillet with first batch.

8. Add 2 tablespoons cooking water to pierogi in skillet. Cook over medium-low heat, stirring gently, until onion mixture is warmed through and adhered to pierogi. Transfer to platter and serve.

TO MAKE AHEAD
Uncooked pierogi can be frozen for several weeks. After sealing pierogi in step 4, freeze them on baking sheet, about 3 hours. Transfer frozen pierogi to zipper-lock freezer bag. When ready to cook, extend boiling time in step 7 to about 7 minutes.

POTATO-SAUERKRAUT PIEROGI
Omit cheddar and pepper. In step 2, combine 1¼ cups sauerkraut, drained and chopped fine, and ¼ teaspoon white pepper with potatoes.

DON'T MAKE THIS MISTAKE
Ruptured Pierogi
A dumpling that leaks or bursts apart during boiling is lovingly referred to as an "angel." To contain the filling, be sure to pinch the edges of the dough firmly together.

SUPERMARKET SAUERKRAUT: Skip the Cold Stuff

Sauerkraut is made by salting shredded cabbage, packing it in containers, and leaving it to ferment at room temperature for 1 to 6 weeks. During this time, natural bacteria and yeasts eat away at sugars in the cabbage, leaving behind tart lactic acid. To find out which kraut is king, we tried six nationally available sauerkrauts plain, with hot dogs, and in pierogi.

Our tasters detected "off" flavors in three lower-ranked brands. The ingredient labels revealed that these products all added preservatives. With so few other ingredients to mask off-flavors, sauerkrauts with chemical preservatives had a prominent "sulfuric," almost "ammonia-like" quality. Tasters preferred "brighter" products that contained just cabbage, salt, and water. We also liked the "punchy," "zippy" flavor of sauerkrauts with 200 milligrams of sodium or more per 2-tablespoon serving; those with any less just tasted like wet cabbage.

These brighter-tasting krauts were packaged in shelf-stable jars or cans, while lower-ranked products were packed in refrigerated plastic bags. Though we often assume that the products we buy in the refrigerated section are fresher than their shelf-stable counterparts, our science editor explained that unlike jars and cans, plastic bags let in small amounts of air over time, which degrades some of the sauerkraut's pungent flavor. This is also why bagged products are the only ones to add preservatives to prevent the growth of microorganisms.

Canned and jarred sauerkrauts also had a softer, more tender texture. Bagged sauerkrauts were tough and crunchy, which tasters found distracting on hot dogs and in pierogi; we preferred softer krauts with only a hint of crunch to complement a dish. Lower-ranked products also had strands that were large and uneven, while our favorite krauts had small and uniform shreds.

Our favorite was Eden Organic Sauerkraut, a jarred kraut with punchy, tangy flavor and even, delicate shreds. Read the full tasting story and learn about the losers at CooksCountry.com/mar16. –LAUREN SAVOIE

RECOMMENDED

	TASTERS' NOTES
EDEN Organic Sauerkraut **Price:** $4.45 for 32 oz ($0.14 per oz) **Container:** Jar **Ingredients:** Organic cabbage, water, sea salt **Sodium:** 220 mg per 2-tbs serving 	With a "slight sweetness" and subtle notes of "zing" and "funk," this jarred kraut lent a "bright" tanginess that "complemented" but "didn't overpower" the main dish. Tasters thought this product's "smaller" shreds were "soft," with "just a bit of chew," perfect for piling atop hot dogs and stuffing in pierogi.
LIBBY'S Sauerkraut **Price:** $0.87 for 8 oz ($0.11 per oz) **Container:** Can **Ingredients:** Cabbage, water, salt **Sodium:** 200 mg per 2-tbs serving	This canned kraut was "bright" and "almost citrusy," with "good tang" and a "subtle punch" of bitterness. Tasters liked that its "finer," "more tender" shreds provided a "subtle crunch" and "clung nicely" to hot dogs.

RECOMMENDED WITH RESERVATIONS

DEL MONTE Sauerkraut **Price:** $2.09 for 14.5 oz ($0.14 per oz) **Container:** Can **Ingredients:** Sauerkraut, water, salt **Sodium:** 180 mg per 2-tbs serving 	This "finely shredded," "slightly crispy" canned sauerkraut nailed the ideal texture but fell short on flavor. Most tasters found this product "lacking in punch" and a bit "too mild," though a few appreciated its "less pungent" tang.

TEST KITCHEN TECHNIQUE Cutting and Filling Pierogi
After cutting the first batch of circles, gather the scraps, reroll the dough, and cut six to 10 more circles.

1. CUT
Using a 3-inch biscuit cutter, cut 20 to 24 circles from the dough.

2. FILL AND FOLD
Place 1 tablespoon of filling in the center of each dough round. Then, fold the dough over the filling to create a half-moon shape. Pinch firmly to seal.

Steak Diane at Home

Steak Diane is known for fire and flourish. But is this old-school restaurant favorite all smoke and mirrors? BY CECELIA JENKINS

ORIGINALLY CONCEIVED IN the 19th century as an homage to Diana, the Roman goddess of the hunt, Steak Diane was first made with thin cutlets of venison cloaked in a rich, labor-intensive sauce based on veal stock. By the 1950s, the dish had become culinary dinner theater in restaurants from New York to Hollywood; tuxedoed waiters would wheel a cart up to your table, warm up thinly pounded beef filets in a chafing dish of cognac sauce, and set the whole thing aflame. Patrons were thrilled but, more often than not, the show overshadowed the supper. I set out to reclaim the essence of Steak Diane—heavily peppered steaks under a cognac-rich sauce—with a contemporary version I could make at home.

I found many recipes in our cookbook library calling for pricey cuts of meat (rib eyes or New York strips) to be pounded ¼ inch thick, seasoned with salt and coarsely cracked pepper, and cooked quickly in butter before being doused in cognac sauce. I was skeptical. Surely such thin cuts of meat would overcook.

I watched disappointedly as my suspicions bore out: My thinly pounded steaks turned from pink to an unappetizing gray-brown in a matter of seconds in the skillet. I pressed on anyway, removing the steaks to make room to create the sauce, sweating shallots, and then stirring together cognac, beef broth, Worcestershire sauce, and accumulated meat juices to cook down. Once the sauce thickened, I whisked in butter and Dijon to yield a velvety texture.

After balancing out the sauce with lemon juice and a splash of cognac, I stood back and stared at my finished dish. The sauce was excellent. The meat? Leather. Why was I pounding a thick, beautiful steak into an unappealing thin cutlet and sacrificing an opportunity for an attractive brown crust?

I worried at my own flirtation with Steak Diane heresy, but I couldn't help wishing for a thicker cut of meat, one that would develop a flavorful crust. Creating that crust would also allow a fond (flavorful browned bits) to develop in the pan; in turn, this fond would deepen the complexity of the sauce. I tried four 1-inch-thick strip steaks for my next test, but these larger steaks required searing in two batches, leaving the first batch cold by the time the pan sauce was ready.

A switch from strip steaks to filets mignons helps usher this classic into the 21st century.

I followed with a test using four filets mignons gently pounded with a rolling pin to a 1-inch thickness, slightly larger than the traditional ¼-inch thickness, but daintier than the typical 2-inch steakhouse size. This luxurious cut thrilled my tasters. (Since I was already getting out the rolling pin, I also decided to use it to pound and roll the peppercorns into a more authentic coarse crack.)

Ask a panel of people what they think defines Steak Diane, and most will cite the dramatic flambé. But in my research I found several recipes, particularly older ones, that made no mention of torching the cognac. Now, don't get me wrong— I love a dramatic flambé as much as the next person, and the test kitchen has previously shown that this step can

add a subtle depth to similar dishes. But because I was creating a recipe for home kitchens, I wanted to be certain that this eyebrow-singeing step was necessary.

I cooked up a batch of flambéed Diane and a batch of nonflambéed and served them, in a blind side-by-side test, to my tasters. Both got raves. Tasters found both sauces bright and complex. Given Steak Diane's varied history, I was happy to know that skipping this step still produced an excellent dish, one in line with Steak Diane's earliest roots.

With the peppery, boozy Diane flavors intact; a much better cut of meat; and a far easier (and safer) technique, I now had a rewarding home version of Steak Diane that delivered vibrant flavor. No fire extinguisher necessary.

STEAK DIANE Serves 4

Four well-trimmed (9- to 11-ounce) New York strip steaks may be substituted for the filets mignons, if desired. Cook them in two batches with an extra tablespoon of oil. Adding the cognac along with the beef broth helps reduce any potential flare-ups, but still use caution when bringing the sauce to a boil, especially if you have a gas stove.

- 1 teaspoon black peppercorns
- 4 (6- to 8-ounce) center-cut filets mignons, 1½ to 2 inches thick, trimmed
  Salt
- 1 tablespoon vegetable oil
- 5 tablespoons unsalted butter, cut into 5 pieces
- 1 shallot, minced
- ¾ cup beef broth
- ½ cup plus 1 teaspoon cognac
- 1 tablespoon Worcestershire sauce
- 2 tablespoons minced fresh chives
- 1 teaspoon Dijon mustard
- 1 teaspoon lemon juice

1. Place peppercorns in zipper-lock bag, press out air, and seal. Pound and roll peppercorns with rolling pin until coarsely cracked. Pat filets dry with paper towels and season with salt and cracked pepper. Place filets between 2 sheets of plastic wrap and roll and pound lightly with rolling pin to even 1-inch thickness.

2. Heat oil in 12-inch skillet over medium-high heat until just smoking. Place filets in skillet and cook until well browned and registering 120 to 125 degrees (for medium-rare), 5 to 7 minutes per side. Transfer steaks to plate, tent with aluminum foil, and set aside.

3. Reduce heat to low and melt 1 tablespoon butter in now-empty skillet. Add shallot and cook until translucent, about 1 minute. Remove skillet from heat and add broth, ½ cup cognac, Worcestershire, and any accumulated meat juices from plate. Return skillet to medium-high heat and bring to boil, scraping up any browned bits. Cook until reduced to ⅓ cup, 5 to 7 minutes.

4. Off heat, whisk in 1 tablespoon chives, mustard, lemon juice, remaining 4 tablespoons butter, and remaining 1 teaspoon cognac until fully incorporated. Transfer filets to platter, spoon sauce over top, and sprinkle with remaining 1 tablespoon chives. Serve.

Skillet-Roasted Cabbage

Oven-roasted cabbage is sweet and meltingly tender. We wanted the same effect on the stovetop. BY MORGAN BOLLING

THE TEST KITCHEN'S recipe for cabbage wedges roasted in a hot oven has converted many would-be haters into cabbage lovers. In that recipe, the wedges emerge from the oven beautifully (and flavorfully) browned, with a deep, earthy, sweetness and a soft yet firm texture. Could I achieve similar results without turning on the oven?

Six wedges cut from a small head of green cabbage seemed like the right amount to fit in a 12-inch skillet. But when I browned the wedges on each of the two cut sides, the interiors never softened and cooked through. I knew that covering the pan would trap heat and steam to help the wedges soften, but the wedges were too tall to allow a lid to lay flat over the skillet.

Through a series of tests I discovered that if I added salt and a little water to the pan while I cooked the wedges on their first side, they would steam, soften, and shrink enough that I could fit a lid snugly on the skillet. So my method was this: brown the wedges on one cut side with some water in the skillet until the water had evaporated and then flip the wedges onto their second cut side and cover the skillet to finish cooking them. This method produced tender, lightly browned wedges.

To flavor the cabbage, I added pats of butter to the pan and basted the wedges with the melted butter during their final minute of cooking. After trying a range of seasonings, my tasters decided they best liked the combination of caraway seeds, fresh chopped basil, and lemon juice. In about 20 minutes of (largely unattended) stovetop cooking, I had a superstar side dish of lightly browned, tender, satisfying cabbage wedges, just right for a winter meal.

SKILLET-ROASTED CABBAGE
Serves 4 to 6

When slicing the cabbage into wedges, be sure to leave the core intact so the wedges don't fall apart when being flipped in step 3. Be sure not to buy a head of cabbage that weighs more than 2 pounds. If you do, the wedges will not fit in the skillet.

- 1 head green cabbage (2 pounds)
- 6 tablespoons water
- 2 tablespoons vegetable oil
  Salt and pepper
- 4 tablespoons unsalted butter, cut into 4 pieces
- 3 tablespoons chopped fresh basil
- ½ teaspoon caraway seeds
- 1 tablespoon lemon juice

1. Halve cabbage through core. Cut each half into 3 approximately 2½-inch wedges through core, leaving core intact (you should have 6 wedges).

2. Combine ¼ cup water and oil in 12-inch nonstick skillet. Arrange wedges in single layer in skillet, 1 cut side down. Sprinkle wedges with 1 teaspoon salt and cook over medium heat, uncovered, until water has evaporated and wedges are well browned, 16 to 20 minutes.

3. Flip wedges to second cut side, add remaining 2 tablespoons water to pan, and cook, covered, until wedges are tender and second side is well browned, 4 to 6 minutes longer.

4. Evenly scatter butter among wedges and cook, uncovered, until butter is melted and bubbling, about 1 minute. Evenly sprinkle basil, caraway, and ½ teaspoon pepper over wedges. Continue to cook, using large spoon halfway through cooking to baste wedges with melted butter (tilting skillet so butter pools at low point and can be easily scooped into spoon), until fragrant, about 1 minute.

5. Transfer wedges to serving platter. Off heat, stir lemon juice into any remaining butter in skillet, then spoon over wedges. Season with salt and pepper to taste. Serve.

Keeping the core intact helps the wedges hold their shape in the skillet and on the plate.

Chicken Scarpariello

To perfect this Italian American dish, we had to cut back on the grease and keep the heat in check. BY ASHLEY MOORE

CHICKEN SCARPARIELLO IS an Italian American dish of browned chicken and sausage bathed in a spicy, garlicky sauce chock-full of bell peppers, onions, and pickled cherry peppers. When done right, it's a hearty weeknight supper, especially well-suited to folks who love strong flavors.

Its exact origins are murky, but it first became popular stateside in the early 1900s among New York City's burgeoning Italian population, particularly those immigrants from Naples. Some say that the name "scarpariello," which loosely translates to "shoemaker-style," was bestowed upon this dish because it features ingredients inexpensive enough for a poor cobbler to afford. Others say the name came about because, much like a shoe, this dish is something you "cobble" together. Whatever the story, I wanted to perfect my own version.

I spent a few hours gathering chicken scarpariello recipes from our cookbook library and headed into the test kitchen to prepare them for my colleagues. While all the recipes were centered around chicken parts and chunks of uncased sausage in a spicy, tangy sauce, there was some variance in the supporting ingredients: some had potatoes, lemon, and/or fresh hot chiles. None of the recipes was deemed awful (although there was one chile-heavy version that was an adventure in heat tolerance), but there were some problems with the thinness and greasiness of the sauce and with the inclusion of ingredients that led the dish away from its simple nature.

Based on my tasters' feedback, I nixed the fresh chiles and relied solely on the briny heat of pickled cherry peppers to give the dish a consistent, controllable spark; for similar reasons, I opted for sweet Italian sausage, removed from its casing (but fire-eaters should feel free to use hot sausage).

I started by browning chunks of sausage and chicken together in a little oil in a skillet. Then I added chopped onion and bell pepper and let them soften before adding garlic, cherry peppers, oregano, and chicken broth. I brought it to a simmer and moved the skillet to a 350-degree oven to finish cooking the chicken and sausage, which took about 20 minutes. The overall flavor was decent, but the chicken skin was flabby and rubbery, and the sauce was greasy and thin.

The chicken skin wasn't rendering evenly because the skillet was so crowded that not enough of the skin was in contact with the pan; browning the chicken pieces and the sausage separately solved the problem. To fix the greasy sauce, I removed the meats from the skillet after browning and poured off the excess fat before I added the vegetables and sauce ingredients. I also found that positioning the browned chicken on top of the other ingredients, skin side up, prevented the skin from becoming soggy in the oven.

The last big challenge was getting the texture of the sauce just right; I wanted it just thick enough to coat the chicken and sausage without being gloppy. After playing around with ratios for several tests, I ended up with a tablespoon of flour (stirred into the softened vegetables) and ¾ cup of chicken broth. This produced a sauce with the perfect consistency—thick enough to cling but not heavy or sludgy.

Tasters were pleased but wanted just a bit more pizzazz. So I took my scarpariello over the top in two steps: A bit of cherry pepper brine added with the chicken broth brought a sharp tang, and a sprinkle of chopped fresh parsley on the finished dish added brightness. This was a supper any shoemaker (or anyone) could love.

CHICKEN SCARPARIELLO
Serves 4 to 6

We used sweet Italian sausage to balance the spiciness of the cherry peppers. Feel free to substitute hot Italian sausage if you prefer a spicier dish.

- 3 **pounds bone-in chicken pieces (2 split breasts cut in half crosswise, 2 drumsticks, and 2 thighs), trimmed**
  Salt and pepper
- 1 **tablespoon vegetable oil**
- 8 **ounces sweet Italian sausage, casings removed**
- 1 **onion, halved and sliced thin**
- 1 **red bell pepper, stemmed, seeded, and sliced thin**
- ¾ **cup jarred hot cherry peppers, seeded, rinsed, and sliced thin, plus 2 tablespoons brine**
- 5 **garlic cloves, minced**
- 1 **teaspoon dried oregano**
- 1 **tablespoon all-purpose flour**
- ¾ **cup chicken broth**
- 2 **tablespoons chopped fresh parsley**

Jarred cherry peppers, plus a bit of their brine, invigorate this dish with heat and acid.

1. Adjust oven rack to middle position and heat oven to 350 degrees. Pat chicken dry with paper towels and season with salt and pepper. Heat oil in 12-inch skillet over medium-high heat until just smoking. Add chicken to skillet, skin side down, and cook without moving until well browned, about 5 minutes. Flip chicken and continue to cook until browned on second side, about 3 minutes. Transfer chicken to plate.

2. Add sausage to fat left in skillet and cook, breaking up with spoon, until browned, about 3 minutes. Transfer sausage to paper towel–lined plate.

3. Pour off all but 1 tablespoon fat from skillet and return to medium-high heat. Add onion and bell pepper and cook until vegetables are softened and lightly browned, about 5 minutes. Add cherry peppers, garlic, and oregano and cook until fragrant, about 1 minute. Stir in flour and cook for 30 seconds. Add broth and cherry pepper brine and bring to simmer, scraping up any browned bits.

4. Remove skillet from heat and stir in sausage. Arrange chicken pieces, skin side up, in single layer in skillet and add any accumulated juices. Transfer skillet to oven and cook until breasts register 160 degrees and drumsticks/thighs register 175 degrees, 20 to 25 minutes.

5. Carefully remove skillet from oven (handle will be very hot). Transfer chicken to serving platter. Season onion mixture with salt and pepper to taste, then spoon over chicken. Sprinkle with parsley. Serve.

Shrimp De Jonghe

We kept the important things in this Chicago classic—tender shrimp, buttery bread crumbs, and the urge to go back for seconds. BY ASHLEY MOORE

SHRIMP DE JONGHE, a casserole of plump shrimp tossed in garlic and sherry and topped with crunchy herbed bread crumbs, first appeared in the dining room at Chicago's De Jonghe Hotel around the turn of the century. Locals and visitors embraced it wholeheartedly, and it quickly became an iconic Chicago dish.

An iconic dish of seafood? In Chicago? It's an unlikely origin story, but it's true. A confluence of factors led to Shrimp De Jonghe: the need for a signature dish (every hotel had one), the contemporary vogue for gratins, and the rise of refrigerated rail cars, which meant that meat from Chicago's processing plants could be distributed throughout the country—and that the trains coming back could be loaded with seafood.

I found a handful of recipes for Shrimp De Jonghe in the vintage section of our cookbook library and headed into the kitchen to give them a whirl. The results were disappointing: overcooked, overly garlicky shrimp under sandy bread crumbs. And with as much as two sticks of butter per recipe, these dishes were way too rich. I'd have to take the basics as inspiration (shrimp, garlic, sherry, bread crumbs) but otherwise start from scratch.

These initial experiments showed me that using precooked shrimp was a recipe for rubbery disaster, so I began prepping raw shrimp (2 pounds of jumbo shrimp were just right for four servings) by removing their shells and tails. I set them aside in a bowl.

Garlic is a required element of Shrimp De Jonghe, but I wanted to avoid the sharp, raw-tasting garlic I'd encountered in my early tests. This meant cooking it for a few minutes on the stovetop to soften and mellow in flavor before going into the casserole. Some chopped shallot added a subtle sweetness, a bit of cayenne gave a slight kick, and some paprika contributed a vibrant color. I added dry sherry, another irreplaceable element, and a bit of lemon juice for brightness. I tossed this fragrant mixture with the shrimp and carefully shingled it all into a gratin dish. All I needed was a bread-crumb crust on top.

Easier said than done. I auditioned premade supermarket bread crumbs, but these just made a soggy, sandy mess. Fresh bread crumbs, which I made in the food processor and toasted with butter and herbs, absorbed too much liquid from the shrimp (they exude some steam in the oven) and emerged soft, not crunchy.

Would Japanese-style panko bread crumbs be the solution? After toasting them lightly and combining them with softened butter, minced chive and parsley, and a bit of grated lemon zest, I spooned the mixture over the shingled shrimp and slid the casserole into the oven. Sure enough, the bread crumbs, while softening slightly, still delivered a rewarding crunchiness after 15 minutes in the oven.

The garlicky, buttery aroma of my casserole had drawn a crowd of tasters, forks at the ready. "This is from the Midwest?" asked one Gulf Coast native, incredulously, as she held out her bowl for a second serving.

SHRIMP DE JONGHE Serves 4

We prefer untreated shrimp—those without added salt or preservatives like sodium tripolyphosphate. Ask your fishmonger or read the label to see if your shrimp has been treated. (If it has, see "Using Treated Shrimp").

- 1 cup panko bread crumbs, toasted
- 8 tablespoons unsalted butter, softened
- ¼ cup minced fresh parsley
- ¼ cup minced fresh chives
- 1 teaspoon grated lemon zest plus 2 tablespoons juice
   Salt and pepper
   Pinch ground nutmeg
- 2 pounds jumbo shrimp (16 to 20 per pound), peeled, deveined, and tails removed
- 1 shallot, minced
- 6 garlic cloves, minced
- 1 teaspoon paprika
- ⅛ teaspoon cayenne pepper
- ¼ cup dry sherry
   Lemon wedges

1. Adjust oven rack to middle position and heat oven to 375 degrees. Using your fingers, combine panko, 7 tablespoons butter, parsley, chives, lemon zest, ¼ teaspoon salt, ¼ teaspoon pepper, and nutmeg in medium bowl; set aside. Pat shrimp dry with paper towels and transfer to large bowl.

2. Melt remaining 1 tablespoon butter in 10-inch skillet over medium-high heat. Add shallot, ½ teaspoon salt, and ½ teaspoon pepper and cook until softened, about 2 minutes. Add garlic, paprika, and cayenne and cook until fragrant, about 30 seconds.

3. Add sherry and lemon juice and bring to simmer, scraping up any browned bits. Continue to simmer until slightly thickened, about 2 minutes; transfer to bowl with shrimp and toss until shrimp are well coated.

4. Shingle shrimp in 13 by 9-inch baking dish. Scrape any remaining garlic mixture from bowl over shrimp. Sprinkle panko mixture over shrimp. Bake until shrimp are pink and mixture is bubbling around edges, 15 to 17 minutes. Let cool for 5 minutes and serve with lemon wedges.

Panko bread crumbs weren't around way back when, but we love the crunch they give this dish.

Using Treated Shrimp

Much of the shrimp on the market has been treated with sodium tripolyphosphate (STPP) or salt. This treatment promotes moisture retention, which means the shrimp can be soggy. For that reason, we prefer to use untreated shrimp. However, if you can only find the treated kind, here's a way to rid them of the extra moisture: Microwave the shrimp in a covered bowl until they just start to turn pink, about 4 minutes. (Typically, ¼ to ½ cup of liquid will be exuded.) Drain the shrimp in a colander and pat them dry with paper towels before proceeding with the recipe.

Flank Steak in Adobo

It took weeks of kitchen work to unlock the secrets of this remarkable Texas dish. It was worth it.

BY MORGAN BOLLING

ARRACHERA EN ADOBO, a chili-like dish of steak slowly cooked—stewed, really—in a pungent adobo sauce, is a gem of Mexican American cuisine, popular in some corners of Texas but relatively unknown in other parts of the country. Spicy, garlicky, sweet, sour, meaty, fruity, rich—this complex dish, at once comforting and invigorating, is astonishingly good. As soon as I tasted it, I wanted to shout about it from the rooftops—or at least develop a recipe so home cooks across the country could create the dish for themselves.

Ask 10 different cooks what makes an adobo sauce, and you'll get 10 different answers. But an afternoon spent in our cookbook library revealed some common ground across both old and new recipes: garlic, onion, dried chiles, dried herbs and spices (oregano and cumin are particularly common), and citrus juice or vinegar.

I made a half-dozen versions of adobo sauce with wide-ranging results—some were primarily sweet, others spicy; some were thick, some thin. All leaned heavily on the deep, concentrated flavors provided by dried chiles.

Dried chiles are becoming more common in grocery stores across the country (check the international aisle at your supermarket). Our favorites here were anchos (dried poblanos) for their mildly fruity flavor, along with pasillas for their slightly bitter earthiness.

To keep the chiles' unpredictable heat in check, I removed their seeds, where much of that heat lives. And in the same way we toast nuts in the test kitchen for maximum flavor, I found I could coax deep, sweet flavors from the dried chiles by toasting them on a baking sheet in a 350-degree oven for 5 minutes. A rehydrating soak in warm water helped soften them for smooth incorporation into the sauce.

Some chefs use fresh tomatillos to contribute a required sour note to the adobo. We tested this option and loved the flavor it gave our adobo, but fresh tomatillos, which are covered with a papery sheath that must be removed before using them, require extensive preparation. Canned tomatillos were an easy substitution for fresh, but after testing canned *salsa verde*, a green salsa available in most supermarkets that's made with tomatillos, cilantro, and

We usually cook flank steak quickly on the grill or in a skillet, but flank works just as well in this soft, meaty, ultraflavorful stew.

onions, tasters preferred its complex flavors. For sweetness, I stirred in a bit of brown sugar, and for an acidic punch, orange juice.

With my adobo base settled, I turned my attention to the meat. Though flank steak is the traditional choice here, I was still skeptical that such a lean cut was the very best choice.

To find out, I tried it against meats more common in these kind of low-and-slow dishes, like chuck eye and short rib. But whereas the cubes of flank steak softened beautifully, staying just chewy enough even after such a long cooking time, I discovered that the extra fat from the chuck eye and short ribs rendered into the adobo sauce and diluted its bright, spicy impact, muting its flavor and turning it greasy. I should have known.

I went back to flank steak, made one more pot, and topped it with some crumbled *queso fresco* (a mild fresh cheese) to balance out the intensity of the sweet-spicy sauce, as well as chopped cilantro for a note of freshness. When I shared servings with my coworkers, smiles ensued.

"It's just about perfect," one taster said. "But I think you should make a few more batches, just to be sure. Say, around lunchtime tomorrow?"

The American Table
A Brief History of Chili

Is *arrachera en adobo* (flank steak in sauce) a form of chili? The question reveals a culinary quagmire: There is virtually no agreement on the ingredients, techniques, or flavors that constitute "genuine" chili. Even its provenance is debated, save for the relative certainty that chili isn't a Mexican invention. In fact, Mexicans disclaim it: The 1959 edition of the *Diccionario de Mejicanismos* defined chili as "a detestable dish sold from Texas to New York City and erroneously described as Mexican." But chili is no anomaly; similar dishes can be found in cuisines across the globe, including Spanish, Mexican, and Indian.

Many culinary historians claim that the chili tradition as we know it today really took hold in San Antonio, home to the famous "chili queens" of the 19th and early 20th centuries, who sold bowlfuls of the chili to a cadre of customers who'd line up at outdoor stands. The 1893 Columbian Exposition in Chicago replicated a typical San Antonio chili stand, and crowds loved it; soon afterward the dish (and the queens) became popular across the country.

So how does arrachera en adobo fit into the chili family tree? It's one of many similar recipes for chile-based meat stews and sauces from Texas, New Mexico, Arizona, and

The Chili Queens of San Antonio served up stew at food stands and competitions in Texas and points north for decades.

California, all influenced by Spanish and native Mexican cooking. According to Johnny Hernandez, chef and owner of La Gloria restaurant in San Antonio (whose arrachera en adobo inspired our recipe), this style of adobo is one of the more chile-intensive of Mexican stews and can be made with a variety of meats, depending on what is at hand: beef, pork, lamb, mutton, rabbit, and so on. –REBECCA HAYS

FLANK STEAK IN ADOBO
Serves 4 to 6

Salsa verde is a green salsa made from tomatillos and green chiles. Our favorite store-bought brand is Frontera Tomatillo Salsa. You can substitute skirt steak for flank steak here, if desired. If *queso fresco* is unavailable, you can substitute farmer's cheese or a mild feta. This dish is also great served over rice.

ADOBO
- 1½ **ounces dried ancho chiles, stemmed and seeded**
- 1 **ounce dried pasilla chiles, stemmed and seeded**
- ¾ **cup salsa verde**
- ¾ **cup chicken broth**
- ½ **cup orange juice**
- ⅓ **cup packed brown sugar**
- ¼ **cup lime juice (2 limes)**
- 1½ **teaspoons dried oregano**
- 1 **teaspoon salt**
- ½ **teaspoon pepper**

FLANK STEAK
- 2½–3 **pounds flank steak, trimmed and cut into 1½-inch cubes**
  Salt and pepper
- 2 **tablespoons vegetable oil**
- 1 **onion, chopped fine**
- 8 **garlic cloves, minced**
- 1 **tablespoon ground cumin**
- 12 **(8-inch) flour tortillas, warmed**
- 4 **ounces queso fresco, crumbled (1 cup)**
- ½ **cup coarsely chopped fresh cilantro**

1. FOR THE ADOBO: Adjust oven rack to lower-middle position and heat oven to 350 degrees. Arrange anchos and pasillas on rimmed baking sheet and bake until fragrant, about 5 minutes.

Immediately transfer chiles to bowl and cover with hot tap water. Let stand until chiles are softened and pliable, about 5 minutes. Drain.

2. Process salsa verde, broth, orange juice, sugar, lime juice, oregano, salt, pepper, and drained chiles in blender until smooth, 1 to 2 minutes. Set aside.

3. FOR THE FLANK STEAK: Reduce oven temperature to 300 degrees. Pat beef dry with paper towels and sprinkle with ½ teaspoon salt and ½ teaspoon pepper. Heat 1 tablespoon oil in Dutch oven over medium-high heat until just smoking. Add half of beef and cook, stirring occasionally, until well browned on all sides, 6 to 9 minutes. (Adjust heat, if necessary, to keep bottom of pot from scorching.) Using slotted spoon, transfer beef to large bowl. Repeat with remaining 1 tablespoon oil and remaining beef.

4. Add onion and ½ teaspoon salt to now-empty pot. Reduce heat to medium and cook, stirring occasionally, until golden brown, 3 to 5 minutes, scraping up any browned bits. Add garlic and cumin and cook until fragrant, about 30 seconds. Stir in adobo, beef, and any accumulated juices until well incorporated and bring mixture to simmer.

5. Cover pot and transfer to oven. Cook until beef is tender and sauce has thickened, about 1½ hours. Season with salt and pepper to taste. Serve with flour tortillas, sprinkled with queso fresco and cilantro.

TEST KITCHEN TECHNIQUE **Getting the Most Out of Dried Chiles**

TOAST
Toasting dried chiles enhances their deep, sweet flavor. While many recipes recommend toasting them in a skillet, we find that toasting them in the oven is easier and requires less attention. Arrange the chiles on a rimmed baking sheet and bake them until fragrant, about 5 minutes.

HYDRATE
Transfer the toasted chiles to a medium bowl and cover them with hot tap water. Let the submerged chiles stand until they are soft and pliable, about 5 minutes. Remove the chiles from the bowl and discard the soaking water before processing the chiles with the other sauce ingredients.

California Churros

Common wisdom says churro making is better left to *churrerías*.
We view common wisdom as a challenge. BY KATIE LEAIRD

THE KITCHEN WAS stuffy and hot, a pot of oil sizzled on the stove, and dough stuck in clumps to my fingers as I fumbled with a pastry bag. An acrid smell filled the air as one churro started to burn while I was still trying to pipe out the rest of the batch. It was a stressful scene that challenged my will.

Was this the end of my churro trail? Were my California dreams—of breezy Pacific seaside evenings eating fluted, fried fritters coated in sweet cinnamon sugar and dunked in chocolate sauce—at a disappointing end?

No way. I don't go down that easily. I was determined to succeed.

People often think of churros as Latin American doughnuts, but they are actually more closely related to French cream puffs. Both cream puffs and churros start from the same dough, *pâte à choux*. It's a simple affair: A mix of water, flour, and butter is precooked in a saucepan and then enriched with whole eggs before being shaped and cooked. This dough has a high moisture content, so when portions of it hit the heat (in this case, very hot oil), steam forms and puffs up the pastries. The result: delicately crispy exteriors and soft, airy interiors.

I started with a simple dough: 2 cups each of flour and water, a little butter, and an egg. I spooned the stiff stuff into a pastry bag and, employing a fair amount of muscle and a metal star-shaped tip, piped short logs into a Dutch oven filled with oil shimmering at 375 degrees.

In minutes, I had beautiful golden-brown churros. They looked very nice, but once cooled and tasted, they revealed themselves to be one-dimensional: no crispy-soft contrast in textures, no depth of flavor.

I commenced tinkering. I tried an eggless dough, just to see what would happen, but this resulted in crunchy, not crispy, churros. I tried one egg, two eggs, three eggs. Too few and there was no delicate interior; too many and the centers were undercooked and soggy. Two eggs plus 2 tablespoons of butter for richness (without weighing things down) was the right ratio. I added 2 tablespoons of sugar and a teaspoon of vanilla for sweetness and flavor, plus a little salt for balance, and my dough was settled. But it still wasn't easy to squeeze through the bag.

These delicate, crispy, custardy treats are great on their own but are even better when dunked in our rich chocolate sauce.

A *churrería*, a traditional churro-making shop, would, of course, be outfitted with heavy-duty motorized machinery to extrude the stiff dough through grooved cylinders directly into vats of frying oil. I'd been trying to mimic this process by piping cooled dough directly into the oil, using kitchen scissors to snip churros off at the tip. But as each one dropped into the 375-degree oil, it caused a scary splash. I tried to pipe closer to the oil surface, but keeping a steady hand so close to the hot oil was unnerving. Timing was tricky, too: By the time I'd piped in my sixth churro, the first one had burned. What's more, my danger-ridden piping procedure produced inconsistent lengths and shapes.

The string of failures all added to my mounting anxiety (and waning will, as noted earlier).

Churros are meant to be fun, not fraught. I needed to divide and conquer, breaking down the process into smaller, distinct stages. Could I somehow give all of my attention to piping first and then focus on frying?

Warily optimistic, I piped 6-inch lines of prepared and cooled dough onto a parchment-lined baking sheet, taking my time to make each one perfect. To my delight, they held their shape and were easy to just pick up and slip into

1. Stir flour into boiled mixture of water, butter, sugar, vanilla, and salt until no streaks remain.

2. Transfer dough to stand mixer; beat on low speed for 1 minute, then add eggs.

3. Pipe 18 (6-inch) lengths of dough, snipping at tip. Refrigerate 15 minutes to 1 hour.

4. Fry 6 churros at a time in hot oil until dark golden brown, about 6 minutes.

5. Drain, then keep warm in oven. Roll in cinnamon sugar before serving.

---

the hot oil by hand; I could do it quickly enough to ensure that all six finished at about the same time.

But it took a lot of strength to force the cooled dough out of the bag; I pushed so hard in one test that my piping bag split open. I found that if I piped the dough while it was still slightly warm from the saucepan, I could press it out of the bag with relative ease.

This created another minor challenge: When I went to pick up the warm dough logs, they squished in my hands. But this was easily solved by giving the dough time to cool off a bit. Refrigerating the dough logs for 15 minutes helped even more.

Once they were chilled, I could easily slip six churros into the oil at once without rushing or splashing. After 5 minutes in the frying oil, the churros were puffed, crispy, browned, and primed for the final touches: a light coating of sugar tossed with cinnamon and a simple chocolate sauce for dunking. Hold the stress.

SO-CAL CHURROS
Makes about 18 churros

We used a closed star #8 pastry tip, ⅝ inch in diameter, to create deeply grooved ridges in the churros. However, you can use any large, closed star tip of similar diameter, though your yield may vary slightly. It's important to mix the dough for 1 minute in step 2 before adding the eggs to keep them from scrambling.

DOUGH
- **2 cups water**
- **2 tablespoons unsalted butter**
- **2 tablespoons sugar**
- **1 teaspoon vanilla extract**
- **½ teaspoon salt**
- **2 cups (10 ounces) all-purpose flour**
- **2 large eggs**
- **2 quarts vegetable oil**

CHOCOLATE SAUCE
- **¾ cup heavy cream**
- **4 ounces semisweet chocolate chips**
- **Pinch salt**
- **¼ teaspoon vanilla extract**

COATING
- **½ cup (3½ ounces) sugar**
- **¾ teaspoon ground cinnamon**

1. FOR THE DOUGH: Line 1 rimmed baking sheet with parchment paper and spray with vegetable oil spray. Combine water, butter, sugar, vanilla, and salt in large saucepan and bring to boil over medium-high heat. Remove from heat; add flour all at once and stir with rubber spatula until well combined, with no streaks of flour remaining.

2. Transfer dough to bowl of stand mixer. Fit mixer with paddle and mix on low speed until cooled slightly, about 1 minute. Add eggs, increase speed to medium, and beat until fully incorporated, about 1 minute.

3. Transfer warm dough to piping bag fitted with ⅝-inch closed star pastry tip. Pipe 18 (6-inch) lengths of dough onto prepared sheet, using scissors to snip dough at tip. Refrigerate, uncovered, for at least 15 minutes or up to 1 hour.

4. Adjust oven rack to middle position and heat oven to 200 degrees. Set wire rack in second rimmed baking sheet and place in oven. Line large plate with triple layer of paper towels. Add oil to Dutch oven until it measures about 1½ inches deep and heat over medium-high heat to 375 degrees.

5. Gently drop 6 churros into hot oil and fry until dark golden brown on all sides, about 6 minutes, turning frequently for even cooking. Adjust burner, if necessary, to maintain oil temperature between 350 and 375 degrees. Transfer churros to paper towel–lined plate for 30 seconds to drain off excess oil, then transfer to wire rack in oven. Return oil to 375 degrees and repeat with remaining dough in 2 more batches.

6. FOR THE CHOCOLATE SAUCE: Microwave cream, chocolate chips, and salt in bowl at 50 percent power, stirring occasionally, until melted, about 2 minutes. Stir in vanilla until smooth.

7. FOR THE COATING: Combine sugar and cinnamon in shallow dish. Roll churros in cinnamon sugar, tapping gently to remove excess. Transfer churros to platter and serve warm with chocolate sauce.

Do You Think You Need a Piping Set?

A piping bag outfitted with a tip makes easy work not only of decorating cakes but also of many other kitchen tasks. But it's hard to know what to buy: There are hundreds of bags and tips sold in all different sizes, materials, and designs. We wondered if decorating sets—kits that come with pastry bags and a selection of decorating tips—make getting started any easier.

We tried five sets, priced from $11.63 to $29.95, each containing between nine and 12 pastry tips and either cloth or plastic bags. Most sets also came with a large threaded plastic nozzle called a coupler, which adheres the tip to the bag and makes it easier to switch tips in the middle of a project. Professional and novice testers piped buttercream with every tip in each set, and we also decorated cakes, piped out churros, swirled hot duchess potatoes, and filled deviled eggs.

Despite thorough washing, reusable cloth bags either clung to smells or stained (though these smells and stains didn't leach into other fillings). Most were too floppy or too stiff. We preferred disposable plastic bags, which were easier to handle. Unfortunately, the only set with disposable bags lacked a coupler.

Our pro testers determined that there are six essential tips: a small round writing tip, a larger round tip for bigger designs, a large open star tip, a large closed star tip, a leaf tip, and a petal tip. Surprisingly, none of the sets had all the essentials.

The set from Wilton came close to having everything we wanted, but we found its 12-inch bags were too snug. The set also lacked a large closed star tip and a coupler. We knew we could assemble a better kit, so we bought six Wilton tips, a 12-pack of 16-inch bags, and a set of couplers at a craft store. At about $15.00, our à la carte decorating set provides everything you need to perfectly decorate your pastries. Read the full testing story and chart at **CooksCountry.com/mar16**. –LAUREN SAVOIE

HIGHLY RECOMMENDED	CRITERIA		TESTERS' NOTES
TEST KITCHEN À La Carte Decorating Set **Price:** $15.32 **Set Includes:** Twelve 16-inch pastry bags; four plastic couplers; and the following Wilton tips: #4 round, #12 round, #70 leaf, #103 petal, #2D large closed star, #1M open star **Essential Tips:** 6 out of 6	Usefulness Ease of Use Versatility Cleaning Quality of Decorations	★★★ ★★½ ★★★ ★★★ ★★★	This set has all the essentials: six core tips in the right sizes, twelve 16-inch disposable pastry bags, and a set of four reusable couplers. The six tips make topping cupcakes, decorating cakes, piping *pâte à choux*, and filling savory foods effortless. All the components are available at craft stores such as Michael's, Hobby Lobby, or Jo-Ann Fabric and Craft Stores.

RECOMMENDED			
WILTON 20-piece Beginning Buttercream Decorating Set **Price:** $12.20 **Model:** 2104-1367 **Set Includes:** Ten 12-inch disposable plastic pastry bags, 10 stainless-steel decorating tips **Essential Tips:** 5 out of 6	Usefulness Ease of Use Versatility Cleaning Quality of Decorations	★★ ★★ ★★½ ★★★ ★★	This set was almost perfect: It came with five of our essential tips, including a large open star tip for swirls and rosettes. The plastic bags were easy to handle, effortless to clean, and durable. Unfortunately, this set lacked a large closed star tip and a coupler. Some pros also thought the 12-inch bags were too small. Most agreed that this is a great starter set if you buy a few extras to round it out.

Getting to Know Fresh Cheese

Soft, supple fresh cheeses prove what all teenagers think they know: Older isn't always better. Here are a dozen of our fresh, flavorful favorites. BY CHRISTIE MORRISON

Cottage Cheese
FRUIT'S FRIEND

This creamy cow's-milk cheese is curdled and drained but is not pressed like most other cheeses. Cottage cheese has a fresh dairy flavor and little tang. We've found it to be a solid substitute for ricotta in high-heat dishes like baked ziti and lasagna. We also use it as the surprising creamy cheese base in our Breakfast Pizza (**CooksCountry.com/breakfastpizza**).

Cream Cheese
BAGEL SHMEAR

Most commercial varieties of this tangy, spreadable cheese add stabilizers for a supersmooth consistency and to prevent curdling when cooked. We use it to create a velvety texture in the sauce for our Poppy Seed Chicken Casserole (**CooksCountry.com/poppyseedchicken**). To read about our tasting of stabilizer-free artisanal cream cheeses, go to **CooksCountry.com/artisanalcheese**.

Fresh Mozzarella
TOP MELTER

Mozzarella has a creamy, slightly salty milk flavor and melts incredibly well. While originally made from the milk of water buffaloes, most of today's mozzarella is made from cow's milk. Fresh mozzarella is sold in spheres packaged in whey or water or shrink-wrapped. Try fresh mozzarella in our Spicy Sausage Stromboli (**CooksCountry.com/sausagestromboli**).

Ricotta
PASTA STUFFER

Ricotta is made from the liquid (whey) that is discarded when making most other cheeses. The result is fluffy, buttery, and slightly sweet due to the milk sugars; it's no wonder, then, that ricotta is used both in desserts like cheesecake and in savory dishes like our Spinach and Tomato Lasagna (**CooksCountry.com/tomatolasagna**). Our taste-test winner is Calabro Part Skim Ricotta Cheese.

Mascarpone
RICH SCOOP

Mascarpone is the rich, creamy cow's-milk cheese that gives tiramisù its velvety texture. It has a "sweet and fatty" flavor and a texture similar to Greek yogurt. Dollop it on a dish of fresh berries or a tangy fruit pie, or try it atop boiled, roasted, or baked potatoes. Mascarpone is usually sold in small containers due to its short shelf life.

Fresh Goat Cheese
TANGY CRUMBLE

Goat cheese is available fresh or aged, but fresh goat cheese is the soft cheese you often find in a log shape. Fresh goat cheese has a creamy, slightly grainy texture and an unmistakable tang that can veer toward "grassy" or "lemony." Avoid precrumbled cheeses; they tend to be chalky and dry. Our favorite goat cheese is Laura Chenel's Chèvre Fresh Chèvre Log from California.

Boursin
SAVORY SPREAD

Boursin is a garlic-and-herb-flavored triple-cream cheese (meaning it contains more than 75 percent butterfat) developed in France in 1957. It has a spreadable yet slightly grainy consistency. It melts beautifully and makes an easy substitute for a béchamel or Mornay sauce. We use it in our creamy Boursin-Parsley Pan Sauce (**CooksCountry.com/boursinsauce**) for pan-seared steaks.

Feta
BRINED BLOCK

This salty, crumbly cheese often hails from Greece, where it must be made from at least 70 percent sheep's milk by law, but supermarket feta is often made elsewhere with cow's milk or goat's milk. The brine in which the cheese is stored extends its shelf life. Our favorite is Mt. Vikos Traditional Feta, which is made in Greece and contains 80 percent sheep's milk. To keep feta moist and fresh, store it in its brine.

Queso Fresco
ENCHILADA TOPPER

This fresh cheese, called *queso blanco* in its native Mexico, has become widely available in the United States. Made from cow's milk or goat's milk, *queso fresco* is a soft, mild cheese that crumbles easily. It is frequently used as a topping for tostadas, chilaquiles, and other Tex-Mex dishes. Like feta, it holds its shape when warm and resists melting. Feta and farmer's cheese are good substitutes.

Farmer's Cheese
PRESSED CURD

This subtly tangy fresh cheese is pressed into a semisoft texture that is reminiscent of fresh goat cheese. Use it as a stuffing for omelets or blintzes, or try it crumbled over enchiladas or tacos. We love the creamy element it adds to our Watercress and Cucumber Salad with Lemon Vinaigrette (**CooksCountry.com/watercresssalad**).

Haloumi
THICK SLICE

A staple in Mediterranean and Middle Eastern cooking, haloumi has an elastic quality similar to mozzarella, but it's firmer and more dense. It's so sturdy, in fact, that it is frequently sliced and then grilled or fried; instead of melting upon contact with heat, the exterior actually firms and hardens into a crispy shell. Mild and milky in flavor and less salty than feta, it is often packed in brine and sold in blocks.

Paneer
INDIAN STAPLE

You may have had paneer with *saag*, the Indian dish of sautéed spinach and other hearty greens. This mild cheese made from cow's milk or water buffalo's milk is easy to make at home by using buttermilk, lemon juice, or vinegar to curdle steamed milk. The thickened curds are drained to remove excess water. The chilled cheese block can be sliced and sautéed or roasted with vegetables.

CHICKEN POSOLE

CURRIED CHICKEN WITH COUSCOUS

SPAGHETTI WITH MUSHROOMS, KALE, AND FONTINA

**PAN-SEARED SKIRT STEAK WITH
ZUCCHINI AND SCALLION SAUCE**

CURRIED CHICKEN WITH COUSCOUS Serves 4

WHY THIS RECIPE WORKS: Stirring jarred mango chutney, fresh apple, and vinegar into the couscous adds texture and flavor.

- 6 (5- to 7-ounce) bone-in chicken thighs, trimmed
  Salt and pepper
- 1 tablespoon olive oil
- 1 onion, chopped fine
- 2 teaspoons curry powder
- 1½ cups chicken broth
- ¾ cup mango chutney
- 2 tablespoons cider vinegar
- 1 cup couscous
- 1 Granny Smith apple, chopped

1. Adjust oven rack to middle position and heat oven to 450 degrees. Pat chicken dry with paper towels and season with salt and pepper. Heat oil in ovensafe 12-inch skillet over medium-high heat until just smoking. Add chicken skin side down and cook until well browned, 5 to 7 minutes. Transfer skillet to oven and roast until chicken registers 175 degrees, about 15 minutes. Transfer chicken skin side up to platter.

2. Pour off all but 2 tablespoons fat from skillet (skillet handle will be hot). Add onion and cook, covered, over medium-high heat until softened, about 5 minutes. Stir in curry powder and cook until fragrant, about 30 seconds. Stir in broth, ¼ cup chutney, and vinegar and bring to simmer. Stir in couscous, cover, remove from heat, and let stand for 5 minutes.

3. Fluff couscous with fork. Stir in apple and season with salt and pepper to taste. Nestle chicken into couscous. Brush chicken with remaining ½ cup chutney. Serve.

TEST KITCHEN NOTE: Mango chutney is sometimes labeled "Major Grey's."

CHICKEN POSOLE Serves 4

WHY THIS RECIPE WORKS: Stirring some of the brine from the drained chiles into the soup, along with a hefty amount of fresh cilantro, adds a bright finish.

- 2 tablespoons olive oil
- 2 onions, chopped
  Salt and pepper
- 4 garlic cloves, minced
- 1 teaspoon dried oregano
- 6 cups chicken broth
- 2 (15-ounce) cans white hominy, rinsed
- 1 (4-ounce) can diced green chiles, drained, brine reserved
- 1 (2½-pound) rotisserie chicken, skin and bones discarded, meat shredded into bite-size pieces (3 cups)
- ½ cup fresh cilantro leaves

1. Heat oil in Dutch oven over medium heat until shimmering. Add onion and 1 teaspoon salt and cook, covered, stirring occasionally, until softened, about 5 minutes. Stir in garlic and oregano and cook until fragrant, about 30 seconds. Stir in broth, hominy, and chiles and cook until hominy has softened, about 15 minutes.

2. Stir in chicken and cook until heated through, about 1 minute. Off heat, stir in cilantro and 1 tablespoon reserved chile brine. Season with salt and pepper to taste. Serve.

TEST KITCHEN NOTE: Serve this soup with lime wedges.

PAN-SEARED SKIRT STEAK WITH ZUCCHINI AND SCALLION SAUCE Serves 4

WHY THIS RECIPE WORKS: This vibrant, no-cook blender sauce is the perfect accompaniment to quick-cooking skirt steak.

- 1 cup fresh parsley leaves
- 8 scallions, white parts minced, green parts cut into 1-inch pieces
- ½ cup plus 3 tablespoons extra-virgin olive oil
- ¼ cup water
- 4 teaspoons red wine vinegar
- 1 tablespoon Dijon mustard
  Salt and pepper
- 1 (1½-pound) skirt steak, trimmed and cut into 4 equal pieces
- 2 medium zucchini, cut into ½-inch chunks

1. Process parsley, scallion greens, ½ cup oil, water, vinegar, mustard, ½ teaspoon salt, and ½ teaspoon pepper in blender until smooth, about 1 minute. Set aside.

2. Pat steak dry with paper towels and season with salt and pepper. Heat 2 tablespoons oil in 12-inch nonstick skillet over medium-high heat until just smoking. Cook steak until well browned and meat registers 120 to 125 degrees (for medium-rare), about 2 minutes per side. Transfer steak to carving board and tent with foil.

3. Add remaining 1 tablespoon oil and zucchini to now-empty skillet and cook over medium-high heat, without stirring, until zucchini is well browned, about 2 minutes. Stir and continue to cook until softened, about 3 minutes. Off heat, add scallion whites and 2 tablespoons scallion sauce and stir to coat zucchini. Season with salt and pepper to taste. Slice steak thin against grain. Serve with zucchini and remaining scallion sauce.

TEST KITCHEN NOTE: For tender meat, slice the steak against the grain.

SPAGHETTI WITH MUSHROOMS, KALE, AND FONTINA Serves 4

WHY THIS RECIPE WORKS: We partially cook the pasta and then add kale to the pot to steam while the pasta finishes cooking.

- 4 tablespoons unsalted butter
- 1 pound cremini mushrooms, trimmed and quartered
  Salt and pepper
- 6 garlic cloves, minced
- ½ teaspoon red pepper flakes
- 4 cups chicken or vegetable broth
- 1 (14.5-ounce) can crushed tomatoes
- 12 ounces spaghetti, broken in half
- 12 ounces kale, stemmed and chopped
- 6 ounces fontina cheese, shredded (1½ cups), plus extra for serving

1. Melt butter in Dutch oven over medium heat. Add mushrooms and 1 teaspoon salt and cook, covered, until mushrooms release liquid, about 5 minutes. Uncover and cook until well browned, about 5 minutes. Stir in garlic and pepper flakes and cook until fragrant, about 30 seconds.

2. Stir in broth and tomatoes and their juice, increase heat to medium-high, and bring to boil. Stir in spaghetti, reduce heat to medium, and cook, covered, for 6 minutes, stirring occasionally. Place kale on top of pasta and cook, covered, until pasta is al dente and kale is tender, 5 to 7 minutes longer. Stir kale into pasta.

3. Off heat, sprinkle fontina over pasta, cover, and let sit until fontina is melted, about 2 minutes. Stir in fontina until fully incorporated. Season with salt and pepper to taste. Serve, passing extra fontina.

TEST KITCHEN NOTE: Shredded fontina cheese adds both flavor and a creamy texture to the sauce.

**PAN-SEARED SCALLOPS
WITH SUGAR SNAP PEA SLAW**

**ROSEMARY STEAK TIPS
WITH GORGONZOLA POLENTA**

PORK MEDALLIONS WITH RED PEPPER SAUCE

SMOKED TURKEY AND PEPPER JACK PANINI

ROSEMARY STEAK TIPS WITH GORGONZOLA POLENTA

Serves 4

✓ **WHY THIS RECIPE WORKS:** Chunks of blue cheese melt into the hot polenta to make a rich and flavorful side dish for the seared steak.

- 4 cups water
- 1 cup instant polenta
- 4 tablespoons unsalted butter
  Salt and pepper
- 1 tablespoon coarsely chopped fresh rosemary
- 1½ pounds sirloin steak tips, trimmed and cut into 2-inch chunks
- 1 tablespoon vegetable oil
- 10 ounces grape tomatoes, halved
- 4 ounces Gorgonzola cheese, crumbled (1 cup)

1. Bring water to boil in large saucepan over medium-high heat. Whisk in polenta, reduce heat to medium-low, and cook until thickened, about 3 minutes. Off heat, stir in 3 tablespoons butter, 1 teaspoon salt, and ½ teaspoon pepper. Cover and keep warm.

2. Combine rosemary, 1 teaspoon salt, and 1 teaspoon pepper in bowl. Pat steak tips dry with paper towels and sprinkle with rosemary mixture. Heat oil in 12-inch nonstick skillet over medium-high heat until just smoking. Add steak and cook until well browned on all sides and meat registers 125 degrees (for medium-rare), about 7 minutes. Transfer to plate and tent with foil.

3. Melt remaining 1 tablespoon butter in now-empty skillet over medium-high heat. Add tomatoes and ½ teaspoon salt and cook until just softened, about 1 minute. Transfer to plate with steak. Serve steak and tomatoes over polenta, sprinkled with Gorgonzola.

TEST KITCHEN NOTE: You can substitute another mild blue cheese for the Gorgonzola, if desired.

PAN-SEARED SCALLOPS WITH SUGAR SNAP PEA SLAW

Serves 4

✓ **WHY THIS RECIPE WORKS:** For a fresh take on vegetable slaw, we thinly slice snap peas for a sweet and crunchy accompaniment to caramelized scallops.

- 8 ounces sugar snap peas, strings removed and sliced thin on bias
- 1 English cucumber, halved lengthwise, seeded, and sliced thin crosswise
- 6 radishes, trimmed, halved lengthwise, and sliced thin
- ¼ cup mayonnaise
- 2 tablespoons chopped fresh chives
- ¼ teaspoon grated lemon zest plus 2 tablespoons juice
  Salt and pepper
- 1½ pounds large sea scallops, tendons removed
- 2 tablespoons vegetable oil

1. Toss snap peas, cucumber, radishes, mayonnaise, chives, lemon zest and juice, and ¼ teaspoon salt together in bowl until thoroughly combined.

2. Pat scallops dry with paper towels and season with salt and pepper. Heat 1 tablespoon oil in 12-inch nonstick skillet over high heat until just smoking. Add half of scallops in single layer and cook, without moving scallops, until well browned, 1½ to 2 minutes. Flip and continue to cook until sides of scallops are firm and centers are opaque, 1 to 1½ minutes longer (remove smaller scallops as they finish cooking). Transfer to plate and tent with foil. Wipe out skillet with paper towels and repeat with remaining 1 tablespoon oil and remaining scallops. Serve scallops with slaw.

TEST KITCHEN NOTE: We recommend buying "dry" scallops, which don't have chemical additives and taste better than "wet." Dry scallops will look ivory or pinkish; wet scallops are bright white.

SMOKED TURKEY AND PEPPER JACK PANINI Serves 4

✓ **WHY THIS RECIPE WORKS:** The chipotle-flavored mayonnaise gives this sandwich a spicy, smoky kick.

- ⅓ cup mayonnaise
- 2 teaspoons minced canned chipotle chile in adobo sauce
- 2 shallots, sliced thin
- 2 teaspoons lime juice
- ¼ teaspoon salt
- 2 tablespoons unsalted butter, softened
- 8 slices hearty white sandwich bread
- 8 ounces thinly sliced pepper Jack cheese
- 8 ounces thinly sliced deli smoked turkey
- ½ cup cilantro leaves

1. Whisk mayonnaise and chipotle together in bowl. Toss shallots, lime juice, and salt together in separate bowl.

2. Spread butter over 1 side of each bread slice. Place bread, buttered side down, on cutting board. Spread each slice with chipotle mayonnaise. Place 1 slice pepper Jack on each of 4 bread slices, then top each with 2 slices turkey, cilantro leaves, shallot mixture, and 1 of remaining 4 slices pepper Jack. Top with remaining 4 bread slices, buttered side up.

3. Heat grill pan or large nonstick skillet over medium heat for 1 minute. Place 2 sandwiches in pan and weigh down with Dutch oven. Cook sandwiches until golden brown and cheese is melted, about 2 minutes per side. Repeat with remaining 2 sandwiches. Serve.

TEST KITCHEN NOTE: If you have a panini maker, feel free to use it here.

PORK MEDALLIONS WITH RED PEPPER SAUCE Serves 4

✓ **WHY THIS RECIPE WORKS:** Smoky paprika and toasted nuts boost the flavor of this no-cook sauce.

- 1 cup jarred roasted red peppers, rinsed and patted dry
- ¼ cup plus 2 tablespoons slivered almonds, toasted
- ¼ cup water
- ¼ cup extra-virgin olive oil
- 1 tablespoon sherry vinegar
- 2 garlic cloves, chopped
- 1 teaspoon honey
- ½ teaspoon smoked paprika
  Salt and pepper
- 2 (12-ounce) pork tenderloins, trimmed and cut crosswise into 1½-inch medallions

1. Process red peppers, ¼ cup almonds, water, 3 tablespoons oil, vinegar, garlic, honey, paprika, and ½ teaspoon salt in blender until smooth, about 45 seconds. Transfer to bowl; set aside.

2. Pat pork dry with paper towels and season with salt and pepper. Heat remaining 1 tablespoon oil in 12-inch nonstick skillet over medium-high heat until just smoking. Add pork, cut side down, and cook until well browned and meat registers 140 degrees, about 4 minutes per side. Transfer to plate, tent with foil, and let rest for 5 minutes. Serve pork with romesco, sprinkled with remaining 2 tablespoons almonds.

TEST KITCHEN NOTE: To get a good sear on the medallions, thoroughly pat them dry before seasoning and cooking.

Eggs in Purgatory

There were moments in our quest to perfect this classic dish when we weren't sure we'd find our way out. BY CECELIA JENKINS

EGGS IN PURGATORY is a simple dish of quivering eggs poached directly in a spicy red sauce, equally good as a bracing breakfast or a satisfying meatless supper.

At least, I thought this popular Italian American dish would be simple. And indeed, tests of existing recipes showed that making the tomato sauce was a breeze. But achieving eight perfectly poached large eggs (enough to serve four) with set whites and runny yolks? That was a different story.

First, the sauce: In a 12-inch skillet, I cooked some garlic in oil; added grated onions, tomato paste, red pepper flakes, and dried oregano; and cooked it just until the tomato paste started to brown, about 5 minutes. I stirred in a can of crushed tomatoes and a few basil leaves. After a 15-minute simmer, it was ready for eggs.

I cracked eight eggs over the sauce, covered the skillet, and waited 4 minutes. How wrong could things go? Very. I had a skillet full of totally unevenly cooked eggs: The parts of the eggs that had sunk deeper into the sauce were rubbery and tough, while the whites up top were still watery. A mess.

I tried a few work-arounds, including separating the eggs and cooking the whites first before adding the yolks later. This was too complicated. I tried warming the eggs in hot tap water before cracking them; this proved unreliable. I nestled the eggs deeper into the sauce and then covered the pan to reflect heat back onto the floating whites. Nope: The yolks overcooked, and the whites were still watery. I felt as if I were the one in purgatory.

Next, I tried cooking the eggs in groups of two and four, covered and uncovered, and over varying levels of heat. While some methods came close, nothing gave me even results every time.

I turned to a more reliable source of overhead heat: the broiler. After cooking the eggs for just a couple of minutes on the stovetop, I slid the skillet under the broiler to finish. No dice: The whites were overcooked and rubbery.

But salvation was close. By flipping the oven control from "broil" to "bake," I took advantage of the gentler heat that reflected off the oven walls. This coddled, rather than blasted, the eggs, finishing them to tender-but-set whites and perfectly runny yolks in about 5 minutes. Rotating the pan halfway through ensured even cooking.

Victory. I had a bright tomato sauce, fully cooked whites, and silky yolks, plus a reminder that sometimes the simplest recipes are the hardest to nail down.

EGGS IN PURGATORY Serves 4

Our preferred brands of canned crushed tomatoes are Tuttorosso and Muir Glen. Grate the onion on the large holes of a box grater. This dish should be a little spicy, but if you're averse to heat, we've provided a range for the red pepper flakes. When adding the eggs to the sauce, take care to space them evenly so the whites don't run together.

- 8 (¾-inch-thick) slices rustic Italian bread
- 7 tablespoons extra-virgin olive oil, plus extra for drizzling
- 4 garlic cloves, sliced thin
- ¼ cup grated onion
- 1 tablespoon tomato paste
- ¾–1¼ teaspoons red pepper flakes
  Salt and pepper
- ½ teaspoon dried oregano
- 1 cup fresh basil leaves plus 2 tablespoons chopped
- 1 (28-ounce) can crushed tomatoes
- 8 large eggs
- ¼ cup grated Parmesan cheese

1. Adjust oven rack to middle position and heat broiler. Arrange bread slices on baking sheet and drizzle first sides with 2 tablespoons oil; flip slices and drizzle with 2 tablespoons oil. Broil until deep golden brown, about 3 minutes per side. Set aside and heat oven to 400 degrees.

2. Heat remaining 3 tablespoons oil in ovensafe 12-inch skillet over medium heat until shimmering. Add garlic and cook until golden, about 2 minutes. Add onion, tomato paste, pepper flakes, 1 teaspoon salt, and oregano and cook, stirring occasionally, until rust-colored, about 4 minutes. Add basil leaves and cook until wilted, about 30 seconds. Stir in tomatoes and bring to gentle simmer. Reduce heat to medium-low and continue to simmer until slightly thickened, about 15 minutes, stirring occasionally.

3. Remove skillet from heat and let sit 2 minutes to cool slightly. Crack 1 egg into bowl. Use rubber spatula to clear 2-inch-diameter well in sauce, exposing skillet bottom. Using spatula to hold well open, immediately pour in egg. Repeat with remaining eggs, evenly spacing 7 eggs in total around perimeter of skillet and 1 in center.

4. Season each egg with salt and pepper. Cook over medium heat, covered, until egg whites are just beginning to set but are still translucent with some watery patches, about 3 minutes. Uncover skillet and transfer to oven. Bake until egg whites are set and no watery patches remain, 4 to 5 minutes for slightly runny yolks or about 6 minutes for soft-cooked yolks, rotating skillet halfway through baking.

5. Sprinkle with Parmesan and chopped basil and drizzle with extra oil. Serve with toasted bread.

Spicy red pepper flakes add punch to this one-pan breakfast—or supper.

TEST KITCHEN TECHNIQUE
Making Wells for Eggs

For perfectly cooked eggs, be sure to nestle them deep into the sauce. Use a spatula to clear a 2-inch-long well, exposing the skillet bottom. Quickly pour an egg into the well.

Teriyaki Cocktail Meatballs

Packing outsized flavor into these one-bite chicken meatballs was no small task, but we did it. BY CHRISTIE MORRISON

THE PERFECT HAPPY-HOUR meatball is bite-size, packed with flavor, and cloaked in a glossy sauce that clings to the meatball rather than dripping onto your little black dress. It's sweet and salty, complementing any cocktail in the bartender's canon. And it's good enough to make you spoil your dinner. I set out to create a meatball that was worthy of any fancy toothpick I stuck into it.

I targeted teriyaki. Traditionally a glazy Japanese sauce consisting of soy sauce, mirin (cooking wine), and sugar, teriyaki comfortably straddles sweet and savory. At least, it should. But ever since its first widespread flirtation with mid-century American palates, the sauce has taken countless wrong turns, evolving into a sugary, cloying, one-note wonder.

It didn't take much to bring the sauce back into balance. I played with a handful of existing recipes and tinkered with different ratios of the core ingredients (I chose supermarket mirin over more expensive sake and added cornstarch for thickening) until I found the right consistency to properly cling to a simple beef meatball. My colleagues loved the sauce, especially when I added complementary flavors like ginger, garlic, and scallions to the meatball mix. But the beefiness stubbornly overshadowed these additions.

I scoured the meat case for a replacement. Ground pork was sweet and promising, but ground chicken was even better—its neutral flavor and pleasant chew gave the teriyaki space to shine.

A couple of experiments showed me that an all-white-meat grind of chicken was too dry, so I used regular ground chicken (a mix of white and dark meats) fortified with sautéed shiitake mushrooms and green cabbage for added moisture and deep savory flavor. An egg added richness and structure while some panko bread crumbs helped the meatballs keep their shape. And, to amp up the teriyaki presence, I mashed a bit of my sauce into the mix.

Since these meatballs were meant to be bite-size, I kept them small—just 1 tablespoon each—and baked them in a hot oven for about 20 minutes. Chilling them for about an hour before baking ensured they'd bake into balls, not disks, and also meant I could form them the day before serving. The golden meatballs that emerged from the oven were

flavorful in their own right but even better after a roll around the skillet in the glazy teriyaki sauce. These meatballs were ready to party.

TERIYAKI MEATBALLS

Makes 40 meatballs

If you don't have mirin, use an equal amount of dry white wine and increase the sugar to ¼ cup. Toast the sesame seeds in a dry skillet over medium heat until fragrant (about 1 minute), and then remove the pan from the heat so the seeds won't scorch. Plan ahead: The meatballs need to chill for at least 1 hour before baking.

MEATBALLS

- 6 ounces shiitake mushrooms, stemmed and chopped coarse
- 1½ cups chopped green cabbage
- 2 tablespoons vegetable oil
  Salt and pepper
- 3 garlic cloves, minced
- 1 tablespoon grated fresh ginger
- 1 pound ground chicken
- ½ cup panko bread crumbs
- 4 scallions, minced
- 3 tablespoons minced fresh cilantro
- 1 large egg, lightly beaten
- 1 tablespoon toasted sesame oil

SAUCE

- 1 tablespoon cornstarch
- 1 tablespoon unseasoned rice vinegar
- ½ cup mirin
- ⅓ cup water
- ¼ cup soy sauce
- 3 tablespoons sugar
- 2 scallions, green parts only, sliced thin on bias
- 1 tablespoon sesame seeds, toasted

1. FOR THE MEATBALLS: Adjust oven rack to upper-middle position and heat oven to 400 degrees. Line rimmed baking sheet with aluminum foil and spray evenly with vegetable oil spray. Combine mushrooms and cabbage in food processor and pulse until chopped into ¼-inch pieces, about 5 pulses.

2. Heat vegetable oil in 12-inch nonstick skillet over medium-high heat until shimmering. Add mushroom mixture and ½ teaspoon salt and cook, stirring occasionally, until vegetables are lightly browned, 6 to 8 minutes. Add garlic and ginger and cook until fragrant, about 30 seconds. Transfer to large bowl.

3. FOR THE SAUCE: Wipe now-empty

A balance of savory and sweet makes these tiny meatballs just right for cocktail parties.

skillet clean with paper towels. Whisk cornstarch and vinegar in small bowl until combined; set aside. Bring mirin, water, soy sauce, and sugar to boil over high heat. Whisk in cornstarch slurry, reduce heat to medium-low, and simmer until thickened, about 1 minute. Remove pan from heat; transfer 3 tablespoons teriyaki sauce to mushroom mixture. Let mushroom mixture cool completely, about 15 minutes. Cover skillet and set remaining sauce aside.

4. Add chicken, panko, scallions, cilantro, egg, sesame oil, and ½ teaspoon pepper to cooled mushroom mixture and mix with your hands until thoroughly combined. Divide chicken mixture into 40 portions, about 1 tablespoon each. Roll between your wet

hands to form 1¼-inch balls and space evenly on prepared sheet in 8 rows of 5. Cover lightly with plastic wrap and refrigerate until firm, about 1 hour.

5. Uncover sheet and bake until meatballs are firm and bottoms are lightly browned, 15 to 20 minutes, rotating pan halfway through cooking. Rewarm sauce over medium-low heat. Add meatballs to skillet and toss to coat with sauce. Transfer meatballs and sauce to serving dish and sprinkle with scallions and sesame seeds. Serve.

TO MAKE AHEAD

Meatballs and sauce can be prepared through step 4, covered, and refrigerated for up to 24 hours. Add 2 tablespoons water to sauce when reheating.

Crispy Parmesan Potatoes

We'd seen Parmesan potatoes relegated to side-dish status,
but we wanted a spud fit for snacking. BY DIANE UNGER

CRISPY. CHEESY. POTATOES. Three words that, put together, have to mean good, right? While none of the existing recipes we tried were inedible, some produced overcooked potatoes, while others offered cheese that refused to cling to the oily potatoes. I wanted creamy potato slices (rather than thick wedges) with crispy, flavorful Parmesan cheese adhering to each slice.

After my initial tests, I settled on 2 pounds of creamy Yukon Gold potatoes (enough for four people), sliced ½ inch thick and tossed with olive oil, salt, and pepper for maximum flavor. I knew that roasting the potatoes at a high temperature would achieve the best color and flavor: 500 degrees on the lower-middle rack was just right. Two teaspoons of cornstarch added to the preoven toss helped them get crunchy. Now I could turn my attention to the real sticking point with this recipe: the cheese.

I roasted a pan of potatoes for 20 minutes to a golden brown and then took them out of the oven and sprinkled a bit of grated Parmesan cheese onto each slice. I put them back in the oven to melt and crisp the cheese. But I'd been a bit careless in my cheese distribution, covering the pan as well as the potatoes. As I scraped the mess off the baking sheet, I realized I'd created a giant salty, savory, cheesy Parmesan chip, or *frico*. Not great looking but undeniably delicious. If only I could get that frico to stick to the potato and not the pan.

For my next test, I processed the cheese in the food processor for a finer texture. I also added some rosemary and pepper for flavor and a bit more cornstarch, which we've found helps the finely shredded Parmesan distribute evenly. I sprayed the baking sheet with vegetable oil spray to help prevent sticking; then, when the potatoes came out of the oven 20 minutes later, I sprinkled the cheese liberally over the potatoes and baking sheet. I turned each slice over and returned the sheet to the oven until the cheese turned golden, about 5 minutes. I let the potatoes cool for 15 minutes on a wire rack before removing them from the sheet. The interiors were creamy, the upper sides of the slices were golden brown, and the underside of each had a delicious Parmesan crisp firmly stuck to it.

The only improvement? A dipping sauce. I combined sour cream (a natural with potatoes), chives, rosemary, garlic and onion powders, and salt and pepper. Just right.

CRISPY PARMESAN POTATOES
Serves 6 to 8
Try to find potatoes that are 2½ to 3 inches long. Spray the baking sheet with an aerosol (not pump) vegetable oil spray. Use a good-quality Parmesan cheese here. Serve with Chive Sour Cream (recipe follows), if desired.

- 2 pounds medium Yukon gold potatoes, unpeeled
- 4 teaspoons cornstarch
  Salt and pepper
- 1 tablespoon extra-virgin olive oil
- 6 ounces Parmesan cheese, cut into 1-inch chunks
- 2 teaspoons minced fresh rosemary

1. Adjust oven rack to lower-middle position and heat oven to 500 degrees. Spray rimmed baking sheet liberally with vegetable oil spray. Cut thin slice from 2 opposing long sides of each potato; discard slices. Cut potatoes lengthwise into ½-inch-thick slices and transfer to large bowl.
2. Combine 2 teaspoons cornstarch, 1 teaspoon salt, and 1 teaspoon pepper in small bowl. Sprinkle cornstarch mixture over potatoes and toss until potatoes are thoroughly coated and cornstarch is no longer visible. Add oil and toss to coat.
3. Arrange potatoes in single layer on prepared sheet and bake until golden brown on top, about 20 minutes.
4. Meanwhile, process Parmesan, rosemary, ½ teaspoon pepper, and remaining 2 teaspoons cornstarch in food processor until cheese is finely ground, about 1 minute.
5. Remove potatoes from oven. Sprinkle Parmesan mixture evenly over and between potatoes (cheese should cover surface of baking sheet), pressing on potatoes with back of spoon to adhere. Using two forks, flip slices over into same spot on sheet.
6. Bake until cheese between potatoes turns light golden brown, 5 to 7 minutes. Transfer sheet to wire rack and let potatoes cool for 15 minutes. Using large metal spatula, transfer potatoes, cheese side up, and accompanying cheese to platter and serve.

CHIVE SOUR CREAM
Makes about 1 cup
This enhanced condiment makes an excellent topping for potatoes of all kinds.

- 1 cup sour cream
- ¼ cup minced fresh chives
- ½ teaspoon minced fresh rosemary
- ½ teaspoon salt
- ½ teaspoon pepper
- ½ teaspoon garlic powder
- ¼ teaspoon onion powder

Combine all ingredients in bowl. Cover and refrigerate at least 30 minutes to allow flavors to blend.

The best kind of mess: The cheese that covers the pan bakes into a salty, crunchy *frico*.

TEST KITCHEN TECHNIQUE
Flipping for Frico
Using 2 forks, turn each potato slice over and return it to the same spot on the sheet. As the excess Parmesan bakes, it will transform into crispy cheesy bits called *frico*.

Carolina Chicken Mull

Chicken and milk stewed in a Dutch oven? We were hesitant, too. But before long we were converted by this deeply comforting dish. BY MORGAN BOLLING

On the Road
Mulling Over Mull at Midway BBQ

I FOUND MYSELF in a lengthening procession of cars as I traveled down two-lane back roads through one-light towns tucked into swaths of Carolina pines. This was the Piedmont, a mountainous area of South Carolina, and it was uncharacteristically cold, even for February.

I crossed into Buffalo and followed the snaking line of cars into the parking lot of Midway BBQ, already nearly full for the lunchtime rush.

Midway occupies an unremarkable bunker of a building with stained wood slats and a red brick base. Inside, footsteps echo against the polished concrete floors and plywood walls. A faint whiff of smoke fills the air, wafting past cozy communal picnic tables dressed in checkered oilcloth. Regulars mix with the rest of us; there's a certain camaraderie among the customers that says this place brings strangers closer together.

I queue up behind a group of guys in Carhartt jackets and work boots, all looking up at the menu that hangs above the counter. I place an order, find a table, and sit and wait. Soon the cashier looks up to catch my eye; her nod tells me my lunch is ready. I'm new here, but she's already memorized my face.

Later, owner Jay Allen comes out to say hello. He takes me into the back kitchen where the woodsmoke mingles with a heavy, meaty fog emanating from four 60-gallon steel cauldrons bubbling with Midway's famous chicken mull. Allen and his wife, Amy, took over the business from his father-in-law in 1994. Many of their recipes remain unaltered since Midway opened in 1941, and no, Allen won't share details. Still, I ask for the secret to the mull we enjoyed for lunch. He grins. "Butter. A lot of butter." –BRYAN ROOF

The menu at Midway BBQ (top). Top of tray: pineapple casserole, coleslaw, pulled pork, cornbread, barbecue hash. Bottom of tray: lima beans, rice, and chicken mull (middle). Owner Jay Allen in his kitchen (bottom).

I'M FROM NORTH Carolina, but when I first saw a photo of chicken mull, I was skeptical. Was this pale yellow concoction of pulverized bits of chicken floating in a milky, butter-slicked liquid really something we wanted to bring into the test kitchen?

While mull (the word, food historian Robert Moss tells me, is derived from "muddle," a common Southern term for a range of soups and stews) is little known outside small pockets of North and South Carolina, devotees of this dish are dedicated. And competitive: Bear Grass, North Carolina (population: 73), hosts a chicken mull festival every year that swells the town with throngs of mull fans.

Jay Allen of Midway BBQ (see "On the Road") wouldn't divulge many secrets when I called, but after our conversation I managed to cobble together a working recipe. I placed a chicken in a Dutch oven; covered it with water, milk, and chopped onions; and then let it simmer. Once it was cooked, I shredded the meat and added cayenne, salt, and pepper. My stew tasted cozy, but it looked curdled and the shredding took a long time.

I switched to chicken thighs, which were much easier to wrangle. Cooking them with onions, salt, and water allowed me to make a rich chicken-stock base. Instead of adding the milk at the beginning, I held it until the end, just warming it through before serving.

This version tasted much better, but it still lacked richness. Replacing some of the milk with heavy cream and whisking in 4 tablespoons of butter helped, but the stew needed thickening. In my research I'd learned that some Carolina cooks use crushed saltines to do this. It worked brilliantly: Just 15 crushed saltines gave the stew the right heft.

What you can't see: the subtle spice from cayenne pepper that accents this creamy stew.

Beans and Greens

This old-school favorite is a comforting reminder that simpler is better.

BY ASHLEY MOORE

One sticking point remained: the size of the chicken chunks, which were too big. Instead of using two forks, I turned to the food processor. In seven pulses I had the perfect shred.

I whipped up a final batch on a rainy Boston day. Slurping spoonful after spoonful, I realized that my misgivings were gone: I'd been captivated by homey, faintly spicy chicken mull.

CAROLINA CHICKEN MULL
Serves 4 to 6
An equal weight of bone-in split chicken breasts or a combination of breasts and thighs may be substituted. We prefer heavy cream, but half-and-half can also be used. When heating the finished stew in step 4, do not let it come to a boil, or it may break.

- 15 square or 17 round saltines, plus extra for serving
- 1 large onion, coarsely chopped
- 2 pounds bone-in chicken thighs, trimmed
- 4 cups chicken broth
  Salt and pepper
- 2 cups whole milk
- ¼ cup heavy cream
- 4 tablespoons unsalted butter
- ¼ teaspoon cayenne pepper

1. Process saltines in food processor until finely ground, about 30 seconds; transfer to bowl and set aside. Pulse onion in now-empty food processor until finely chopped, 5 to 7 pulses.

2. Arrange chicken, skin side down, in single layer in bottom of Dutch oven. Add broth, 1 teaspoon salt, and onions and bring to boil over medium-high heat. Reduce heat to low, cover, and simmer for 30 minutes.

3. Remove pot from heat and transfer chicken to plate to let cool slightly, about 15 minutes; cover pot to keep stew warm. Discard chicken skin and bones. Tear chicken into large pieces. Transfer chicken to clean food processor and pulse until finely chopped, about 7 pulses.

4. Whisk chopped chicken, saltine crumbs, milk, cream, butter, cayenne, 1 teaspoon pepper, and ½ teaspoon salt into stew. Heat over medium heat until warmed through but not boiling, 3 to 5 minutes. Season with salt and pepper to taste. Serve with extra saltines.

HEARTY GREENS, SUCH as escarole or kale, cooked down until tender in a flavorful broth and tossed with tender white beans—this is beans and greens, a staple menu item in restaurants in and around Pennsylvania's Western Valley. We wanted a version for cooks around the country to make at home.

Before picking up a pan, I picked up the phone. Denese Colangelo, co-owner of Colangelo's Bakery in Pittsburgh, was kind enough to talk me through how she makes her famous beans and greens. She does a quick sauté of olive oil, sliced cooked red potatoes, garlic, and oven-roasted tomatoes. Colangelo then adds white beans (cannellini or great Northern), white wine, baby spinach, salt, pepper, and red pepper flakes. After a brief steam, she piles the warm beans-and-spinach mixture on a heap of mixed greens. Finally, the whole thing gets topped with some grated Pecorino Romano cheese and served.

I found and tried several more existing recipes. Some used escarole, some baby spinach, some broccoli rabe. Escarole was the hands-down winner with our tasting panel. A member of the endive family, it has a fresh, mild, faintly bitter flavor. We also preferred recipes that skipped the mixed greens, and we ditched the potatoes, which made this side dish too filling.

Taking inspiration from these recipes, I sautéed some onions, garlic, and rosemary to create a savory base. I reduced the heat and added some chicken broth and one head of escarole that I'd cut into 2-inch pieces. I covered the pot and cooked the greens until they wilted. I tossed in a can of cannellini beans for just a few minutes to warm through—I didn't want them to cook too long, or they would lose their shape.

The only tricky part was the timing. After tweaking the amount of broth and the time on the stove, we were happy with the silky-yet-firm texture of the wilted escarole and the garlicky flavor of the sauce. I stirred in a bit of grated Parmesan to help thicken the sauce and add an extra savory note. Then I finished off the dish with a drizzle of olive oil and, for good measure, an extra sprinkling of Parmesan.

Escarole's mild bitterness is tempered once the greens are cooked.

BEANS AND GREENS Serves 4
Don't be alarmed by what may seem like the large amount of greens we call for. Once added to the pot, they wilt down significantly within minutes.

- 2 tablespoons extra-virgin olive oil, plus extra for drizzling
- 1 onion, chopped fine
  Salt and pepper
- 3 garlic cloves, minced
- 1 teaspoon chopped fresh rosemary
- ½ teaspoon red pepper flakes
- ½ cup chicken broth
- 1 head escarole (1 pound), trimmed and cut into 2-inch pieces
- 1 (15-ounce) can cannellini beans, rinsed
- 1 ounce Parmesan cheese, grated (½ cup)

1. Heat oil in Dutch oven over medium-high heat until shimmering. Add onion, ½ teaspoon salt, and ½ teaspoon pepper and cook until softened and beginning to brown, 5 to 7 minutes. Add garlic, rosemary, and pepper flakes and cook until fragrant, about 30 seconds.

2. Reduce heat to medium-low. Stir in broth, scraping up any browned bits. Stir in escarole; cover and cook, stirring occasionally, until wilted, 6 to 8 minutes.

3. Add beans and cook, uncovered and stirring occasionally, until escarole is tender, about 5 minutes. Off heat, stir in ¼ cup Parmesan. Season with salt and pepper to taste. Transfer greens to serving dish. Sprinkle with remaining ¼ cup Parmesan and drizzle with extra oil. Serve.

Alabama Orange Rolls

In Cullman, Alabama, people stand in line for these citrusy, sticky-sweet treats. We wanted to let the rest of the country in on the fun. BY KATIE LEAIRD

FOR YEARS, FRIENDS from Alabama have been telling me about the famous orange rolls served at All Steak restaurant in Cullman, Alabama (see "On the Road"). Crowds go crazy for the sweet spirals that deliver an outsized punch of citrus flavor.

Small and spiraled, like baby cinnamon rolls, these glazy rolls filled with orange-flavored sugar and topped with a citrusy icing filled the room with aromas of yeast, butter, and orange. I loved them, but I couldn't help wondering what they'd smell like while baking and what they'd taste like straight out of the oven. I determined right then to create a version to make at home.

Their soft, chewy texture indicated that these rolls were leavened with yeast, like the doughs we use for cinnamon rolls and other similar pastries. I started with one of our in-house cinnamon roll recipes, mixing together flour, sugar, yeast, and salt. Butter was a must, but instead of the milk we normally use, I swapped in orange juice, hoping this would amp up the orange flavor.

After kneading, resting, shaping, and nestling the dough into a cake pan for a second rise, I baked the rolls and gave them a try. The orange juice definitely increased the citrus presence, but maybe too much: This batch took on a distinctly sour flavor. I tried adding dairy back into the mix in various amounts; after testing different combinations, I found that ½ cup of orange juice and ¼ cup of cream was as far as I could go without introducing sourness.

But the reintroduction of cream, while allowing a bit of subtle orange flavor to come through, still muted the full impact of citrus's signature good-morning zing. To bring it back, I grated the zest from a couple of oranges and tossed it with a bit of sugar to fill the rolls. But once this batch baked off, I realized I'd gone too far; now my filling was bitter, not bright.

A few follow-up tests showed me that the line between bold and bitter was very fine; just 2 teaspoons of orange zest (from a single orange) gave me the right level of vibrancy and virtually no bitterness.

Going into the glaze portion of my testing, I assumed that just stirring together powdered sugar and liquid (in this case, orange juice, of course) would settle things. But this method just made

We pack fresh orange juice into the dough and the glaze and fresh orange zest into the filling to maximize the citrus flavor.

a mess. Too much orange juice and the mixture ran off and pooled at the bottom of the pan rather than clinging to the rolls; too much sugar and the glaze was chalky and sickeningly sweet. I'd have to take a new tack.

After testing a wide range of methods, I found the solution in a quickly cooked glaze based on granulated, not powdered, sugar. When heated, granulated sugar liquefies and becomes smooth and free from chalkiness. Boiling sugar and orange juice, plus some heavy cream to hold the sharp citrus in check, for just 4 minutes allowed any excess moisture to evaporate, leaving a thick, syrupy, flavorful glaze that didn't overwhelm the rolls.

Just a couple of tablespoons of the sweet, vibrant glaze brushed on the rolls after they came out of the oven gave them a lovely sheen. I had a winner.

Take the Temp
Kitchen thermometers aren't just for checking meat. We use them when baking, too. The Alabama Orange Rolls are perfectly done when the interior of the center roll reaches 195 degrees. We recommend our favorite instant-read thermometer, the Thermapen Mk4.

ALABAMA ORANGE ROLLS

Makes 8 rolls

Be sure to zest the oranges before juicing them. When zesting the orange, remove just the outer part of the peel—the inner white pith is very bitter. We bake these rolls in a dark-colored cake pan because they brown better. If you only have a light-colored pan, increase the baking time to 45 to 50 minutes. Be aware that the dough needs to rise for a total of 2½ to 3½ hours.

DOUGH

- 3 cups (15 ounces) all-purpose flour
- ¼ cup (1¾ ounces) sugar
- 2¼ teaspoons instant or rapid-rise yeast
- 1 teaspoon salt
- ½ cup orange juice, warm (110 degrees)
- ¼ cup heavy cream
- 6 tablespoons unsalted butter, cut into 6 pieces and softened
- 1 large egg plus 1 large yolk

FILLING

- ½ cup (3½ ounces) sugar
- 2 teaspoons grated orange zest
- 2 tablespoons unsalted butter, softened

GLAZE

- ¼ cup heavy cream
- ¼ cup (1¾ ounces) sugar
- 2 tablespoons orange juice
- 2 tablespoons unsalted butter
- ⅛ teaspoon salt

1. FOR THE DOUGH: In bowl of stand mixer, whisk flour, sugar, yeast, and salt together. Add orange juice, cream, butter, and egg and yolk. Fit mixer with dough hook and knead on medium speed until dough comes together, about 2 minutes. Increase speed to medium-high and continue to knead dough until smooth and elastic, about 8 minutes longer. Dough will be soft.

2. Transfer dough to lightly floured counter and knead until smooth ball forms, about 30 seconds. Place dough in greased large bowl, cover tightly with plastic wrap, and let rise in warm place until doubled in size, 1½ to 2 hours.

3. FOR THE FILLING: Combine sugar and zest in small bowl. Transfer dough to lightly floured counter. Roll dough into 16 by 8-inch rectangle with long side parallel to counter's edge. Spread butter over surface of dough using small offset spatula, then sprinkle evenly with sugar mixture. Roll dough away from you into tight, even log and pinch seam to seal.

4. Grease dark-colored 9-inch cake pan, line bottom with parchment paper, then grease parchment. Roll log seam side down and cut into eight 2-inch-thick slices using serrated knife. Place 1 roll in center of prepared pan and others around perimeter of pan, seam sides facing center. Cover with plastic and let rise in warm place until doubled in size, 1 to 1½ hours. Adjust oven rack to middle position and heat oven to 325 degrees.

5. Discard plastic and bake rolls until golden brown on top and interior of center roll registers 195 degrees, 40 to 45 minutes. Let rolls cool in pan on wire rack for 30 minutes.

6. FOR THE GLAZE: Once rolls have cooled for 30 minutes, combine all ingredients in small saucepan and bring to boil over medium heat. Cook, stirring frequently, until large, slow bubbles appear and mixture is syrupy, about 4 minutes.

7. Using spatula, loosen rolls from sides of pan and slide onto platter; discard parchment. Brush glaze over tops of rolls and serve warm.

Making Alabama Orange Rolls

1. Roll dough into 16 by 8-inch rectangle with long side parallel to counter's edge. Spread butter over surface of dough with small offset spatula, then sprinkle buttered surface evenly with sugar mixture.

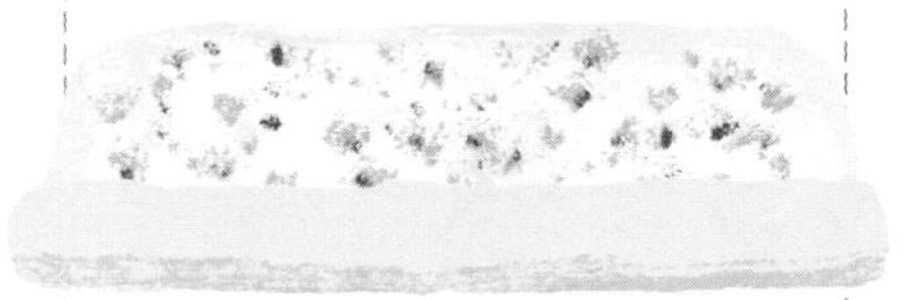

2. Roll dough away from you into tight, even log.

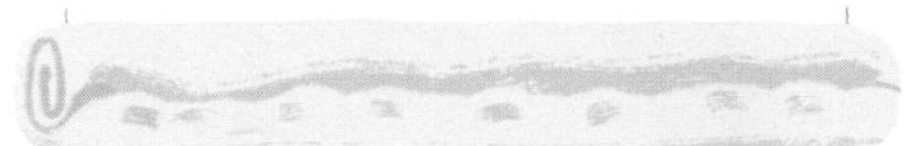

3. Pinch seam between forefinger and thumb along entire length of log to seal tightly.

4. Use serrated knife to cut log into eight 2-inch-thick slices.

5. Arrange slices in cake pan, one roll in center and remaining rolls around perimeter, with seam sides facing inwards.

TECHNIQUE
Removing Zest from Oranges

Citrus zest contains flavorful oils that add a bright vibrancy to recipes, including the filling for our Alabama Orange Rolls. There are a lot of zesting tools out there, but our favorite is the Microplane rasp-style grater. Swipe rinsed and dried fruit along the grater in just one direction—not back and forth—to remove only the flavorful zest and none of the bitter white pith.

On the Road
More to All Steak Than Steak

The color of the sticky roll in my hand is a shocking, almost unnatural day-glo orange, like flames on a speedway race car, but its citrusy-sweet flavor tells me there's nothing fake or fleeting about it. From the first bite, I know I'll remember this roll.

You'd never guess that these orange rolls are a house specialty at All Steak restaurant in Cullman, Alabama, where they are relegated to the very bottom of the menu in type nearly too small to notice. But All Steak has no need to trumpet the rolls, thanks to devotees who've kept this local institution busy for decades. A stubborn stalwart against the march of big chains, All Steak is a survivor; even a 2011 tornado that forced it from its original digs couldn't shut it down.

I arrive for lunch at 10:30 a.m., and it's not too early. A handful of tables are already occupied. And my waiter doesn't flinch when I ask for an orange roll with my steak, though there is a caveat: "I can set you up with either a dozen or half-dozen. That's how they're sold," he says. I opt for the half-dozen, but by noon, when the restaurant's full and I'm driving out of town, I'm wishing I'd ordered all twelve.

—BRYAN ROOF

All Steak's address has changed a few times since it opened in 1934, but a loyal clientele makes sure the famous orange rolls remain the same.

Cooking Class Burgundy Pot Roast

Julia Child's famous Boeuf Bourguignon requires a battery of pots and pans. Ours doesn't. BY CHRISTIE MORRISON

Beef Burgundy 101

Why Chuck-Eye Roast?
Though it has an air of elegance these days, beef braised in wine is at its heart a rustic peasant dish that's best suited to the relatively inexpensive chuck-eye roast (be sure to ask the butcher if you don't find one in the case). This flavorful cut has rich marbling that benefits from long, slow cooking. Its only challenge is the thick line of fat that bisects the meat, which, if left in place, would produce a fatty sauce and inelegant slices. This is easily dealt with: Simply pull the two lobes of meat apart, trim the fat between them, and tie them into two neat roasts.

Use your fingers to find the seam and then pull apart the two pieces.

Look for a well-marbled piece of chuck eye for maximum flavor.

Cooking with Wine
Beef Burgundy gets its name from the region of France where it originated, as well as the namesake wine produced there. French Burgundies are generally expensive wines, though; better to grab a bottle labeled **Pinot Noir**—the grape used to make red Burgundy—even if it's not from France. Pinot Noir tends to be medium-bodied with low tannins and subtle fruit. **Côtes du Rhône** is a good substitute, but stay away from big-bodied reds like **Cabernet Sauvignon** or **Merlot**, which will overwhelm the other flavors in this dish.

EQUIPMENT Pick the Right Vessel
A big, heavy pot with a tightly fitting lid is the perfect vessel for braising. The technique has its own pot—called a brasier—but we think a sturdy Dutch oven works just fine. Our Best Buy is the Lodge Color Enamel 6-Quart Dutch Oven. The cast-iron base effectively conducts and holds heat, while the enameled coating makes the pot nonreactive with acidic ingredients and therefore suitable for all types of foods.

**LODGE COLOR ENAMEL
6-QUART DUTCH OVEN**

Core Techniques

TEST KITCHEN TIPS FOR ANY BRAISED STEW

Add Vegetables in Stages
Braising is a long-cooking method that produces extra-tender meat. What's good for the meat, however, isn't necessarily good for the vegetables; by the time the stew's done, the vegetables are unrecognizable. So it pays to take a two-pronged approach. In this Burgundy Pot Roast, for example, the chopped carrot and onion added to the braise at the beginning contribute tons of flavor, but by the time the meat's done, they've got nothing left to give. We use a strainer to remove these mushy, spent has-beens from our sauce and then cook up a fresh set of vegetables to serve with the finished dish.

VEG PHASE ONE
Chopped carrots and onion contribute flavor before being discarded.

VEG PHASE TWO
Mushrooms and pearl onions are prepared later to serve with the meat.

Skim the Fat
We love fat for the rich body and deep flavor it adds to our stews and braises. But many braising meats, including the chuck-eye roast we use in our Burgundy Pot Roast, release too much fat into the liquid, and if we didn't skim at least some of it, we'd end up with a pot of greasy goo. We've tried many tricks for skimming fat over the years, but we get the best results from the simplest method: After letting the liquid sit for 10 minutes, carefully swipe a wide, shallow spoon across the top of the braising liquid. You won't get all of it, but that's all right. Just removing and discarding the most visible fat will leave behind the perfect amount for a great, not greasy, stew.

STEP BY STEP Ten Steps to Burgundy Pot Roast

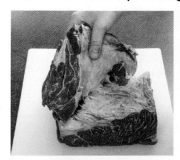

1. MAKE TWO ROASTS
Use a boneless beef chuck-eye roast and pull the roast apart at the seam.
WHY? Two smaller portions cook faster and provide more surface area for browning.

2. TRIM AND TIE
Trim the fat and then tie each roast at 1-inch intervals.
WHY? Trimming away excess fat before cooking staves off a greasy sauce. We secure the roasts with twine to promote even cooking and easier slicing.

3. RENDER BACON
Cook the bacon until it's crispy, remove it from the pan, and reserve 2 tablespoons of the fat.
WHY? Bacon adds depth and salty pork flavor to the dish and renders flavorful fat to use later.

4. BROWN ROASTS
Brown the roasts on all sides in the reserved bacon fat; remove and set aside the meat.
WHY? Browning creates new flavor compounds and adds texture to the roast. The bacon fat infuses more flavor into the meat.

5. BUILD AROMATIC BASE
Sauté the carrots and onion in the bacon and beef fat; then, stir in flour and garlic to combine.
WHY? Sweet carrots, earthy onion, and pungent garlic build a base of flavor. A sprinkling of flour will thicken the sauce.

BURGUNDY POT ROAST Serves 6 to 8

Use a dry red wine, such as Burgundy, Pinot Noir, or Côtes du Rhône.

POT ROAST

- 1 (5- to 6-pound) boneless beef chuck-eye roast, pulled apart at seam into 2 separate roasts, fat trimmed, and roasts tied individually at 1-inch intervals
  Salt and pepper
- 4 slices bacon, halved crosswise
- 4 carrots, peeled and chopped
- 1 onion, chopped
- ¼ cup all-purpose flour
- 3 garlic cloves, minced
- 1 (750-ml) bottle dry red wine
- 2 cups beef broth
- 2 teaspoons minced fresh thyme
- 2 bay leaves

VEGETABLES

- 2 cups frozen pearl onions
- ½ cup beef broth
- 3 tablespoons unsalted butter
- 2 teaspoons sugar
- 1 pound white mushrooms, trimmed and quartered
  Salt and pepper
- 2 tablespoons minced fresh parsley

1. FOR THE POT ROAST: Adjust oven rack to lower-middle position and heat oven to 300 degrees. Pat beef dry with paper towels and season with salt and pepper. Cook bacon in Dutch oven over medium heat until crispy, 6 to 8 minutes. Transfer to paper towel–lined plate. Pour off all but 2 tablespoons fat from pot and heat over medium-high heat until just smoking. Add beef and brown on all sides, 8 to 10 minutes. Transfer to plate.

2. Add carrots and onion to now-empty pot and cook over medium heat until browned, about 5 minutes. Stir in flour and garlic and cook until fragrant, about 1 minute. Whisk in wine and bring to simmer, scraping up any browned bits. Reduce heat to medium-low and cook until reduced by half and slightly thickened, 8 to 10 minutes.

3. Stir in broth, thyme, bay leaves, and bacon. Return beef and any accumulated juices to pot and bring to simmer. Place large sheet of aluminum foil over pot and cover tightly with lid. Bake until fork slips easily in and out of beef, 2½ to 3 hours.

4. FOR THE VEGETABLES: When beef is nearly done, bring pearl onions, broth, butter, and sugar to boil in 12-inch skillet over medium-high heat. Cover, reduce heat to low, and cook until onions are tender, 5 to 8 minutes. Uncover, increase heat to medium-high, and cook until all liquid evaporates, 3 to 5 minutes. Add mushrooms and ¼ teaspoon salt and cook, uncovered, until vegetables are browned and glazed, 8 to 12 minutes. Season with salt and pepper to taste. Cover and set aside until beef is done.

5. Transfer beef to carving board, tent with foil, and let rest for 30 minutes. Let braising liquid settle, then skim any fat from surface with large kitchen spoon. Bring liquid to boil over medium-high heat and cook until reduced to 3 cups and slightly thickened, 15 to 20 minutes.

6. Strain sauce through fine-mesh strainer into 4-cup liquid measuring cup; discard solids. Season with salt and pepper to taste. Reheat vegetables over medium heat, about 3 minutes. Stir parsley into vegetables. Discard twine, slice beef against grain into ½-inch-thick slices, and transfer to platter. Spoon vegetables around beef. Pour 1½ cups sauce over beef. Serve, passing remaining sauce separately.

6. DEGLAZE WITH RED WINE
Whisk the wine into the vegetable mixture and bring it to a simmer, scraping up any browned bits.
WHY? Wine adds rich flavor. Scraping up the browned bits incorporates them into the sauce and keeps them from burning.

7. SEAL POT AND BRAISE MEAT
Return the meat to the pot. Place foil over the opening and cover it tightly with the lid.
WHY? The foil and lid seal in moisture and steam, which causes the roast's connective tissue to melt, leaving the meat fork-tender.

8. SAUTÉ ADD-INS
Sauté the pearl onions and mushrooms in a skillet while the roast braises. Set aside.
WHY? Cooking the pearl onions and mushrooms separately helps them retain their flavor and texture.

9. SKIM AND REDUCE SAUCE
Skim the fat from the braising liquid with a large spoon. Then, simmer to reduce it to 3 cups.
WHY? Skimming the fat ensures a rich, not greasy, sauce. The extra cooking time will thicken the sauce so it clings to the meat.

10. STRAIN AND SERVE
Strain the sauce and discard the solids. Season to taste, and serve over the meat and vegetables.
WHY? Straining removes the spent aromatics from the sauce, leaving the sauce silky and smooth.

Five Easy Recipes Orzo Salads

We wanted to put the emphasis on salad, not pasta.

BY ASHLEY MOORE

Clockwise from top: Arugula and sun-dried tomatoes; cucumber, red onion, and mint; radishes, capers, and anchovy; provolone, capicola, and mortadella; Pecorino, radicchio, and chickpeas.

THE MENTION OF pasta salad brings to mind bland bowls of pasta tossed with bottled salad dressing or mayo and maybe, just maybe, a few sad chunks of vegetables. But why? We love each component, so why shouldn't the sum of these parts be equally great? I set out to make it so with five fresh takes on this oft-neglected dish.

I took nothing for granted, starting with the pasta. The usual suspects of the pasta salad syndicate are elbow macaroni, spiral-shaped rotini, or bow-tie farfalle, but I wanted a more delicate pasta, one that would support other ingredients but not weigh them down. In our test kitchen pantry we keep penne, rigatoni, and spaghetti on hand, but these all seemed too big, too awkward, or too starchy. After a quick discussion with the team, I decided to experiment with orzo, a tiny rice-shaped pasta. The small shape performs its supporting role perfectly, providing just enough bulk to make the salad satisfying but not so much that it becomes too filling. Like most dried pasta, it's a breeze to prepare: I cooked the orzo in salted water, stirring frequently to keep all the pieces separate; when it was al dente (about 8 to 10 minutes later), I drained it and tossed it with a tablespoon of oil to further ensure that it wouldn't clump.

Staring at my bowl of plain, unadorned orzo, I was struck by the endlessness of the possibilities. I could imagine anything in there, from vegetables to meats to nuts to cheese. Choosing a lineup of ingredients was an exercise in restraint. But after a dozen experiments I settled (at least temporarily) on a big pile of chopped peppery baby arugula, a handful of salty grated Parmesan cheese, flavorful chopped sun-dried tomatoes, briny kalamata olives, some pine nuts for a subtle crunch, and some fresh basil for, well, freshness.

To seal the deal, I whisked together a sharp vinaigrette that was almost a 1:1 ratio of vinegar to oil—neutral pasta mutes sharp flavors, so the high proportion of vinegar made sense. I added two minced garlic cloves for extra zing along with plenty of salt and pepper. Rescue mission complete: I had a pasta salad that was bright, colorful, flavorful, and anything but boring. It—and the four others I created—now deserved to be called a salad.

ORZO SALAD WITH ARUGULA AND SUN-DRIED TOMATOES

Serves 4 to 6

We toss the cooked, still-warm orzo with oil to prevent it from clumping.

- 1¼ cups (8 ounces) orzo
  Salt and pepper
- 6 tablespoons extra-virgin olive oil, plus extra for drizzling
- ¼ cup balsamic vinegar
- 2 garlic cloves, minced
- 2 ounces (2 cups) baby arugula, chopped
- 2 ounces Parmesan cheese, grated (1 cup)
- ½ cup oil-packed sun-dried tomatoes, minced
- ½ cup pitted kalamata olives, halved
- ½ cup pine nuts, toasted
- ½ cup chopped fresh basil

1. Bring 2 quarts water to boil in large saucepan. Add orzo and 1½ teaspoons salt and cook, stirring often, until al dente. Drain orzo and transfer to rimmed baking sheet. Toss with 1 tablespoon oil and let cool completely, about 15 minutes.

2. Combine vinegar, garlic, ½ teaspoon salt, and ½ teaspoon pepper in large bowl. Slowly whisk in remaining 5

Is It a Rice or a Grain? Nope.

Confusingly, orzo means "barley" in Italian. Plus, if you look quickly at a small piece of orzo, you might mistake it for a grain of rice. Here in the U.S., the term "orzo" refers to neither a rice nor a grain. It's the name we use to refer to a small pasta made from durum wheat semolina that's great for salads.

RICE, A GRAIN

ORZO, A PASTA

Slow Cooker Split Pea Soup

Make no bones about it, you can still have a tasty slow-cooker split pea soup without a holiday ham. BY DIANE UNGER

tablespoons oil until emulsified. Add arugula, Parmesan, tomatoes, olives, pine nuts, basil, and cooled orzo to dressing and toss to thoroughly combine. Season with salt and pepper to taste.

3. Let salad sit at room temperature for 30 minutes to allow flavors to meld. Serve, drizzled with extra oil. (Salad can be refrigerated for up to 2 days.)

ORZO SALAD WITH CUCUMBER, RED ONION, AND MINT

Omit arugula, tomatoes, olives, and pine nuts. Substitute lemon juice for balsamic vinegar; ½ cup crumbled feta cheese for Parmesan; and chopped fresh mint for basil. Add ½ seedless English cucumber, halved lengthwise and sliced thin crosswise; ½ cup finely chopped red onion; and ¼ cup thinly sliced scallions to dressing in step 2.

ORZO SALAD WITH PECORINO, RADICCHIO, AND CHICKPEAS

Omit arugula, tomatoes, olives, and pine nuts. Substitute Pecorino Romano for Parmesan. Add ½ small head radicchio, cored and chopped fine, and 1 (15-ounce) can chickpeas, rinsed, to dressing in step 2.

ORZO SALAD WITH PROVOLONE, CAPICOLA, AND MORTADELLA

Omit tomatoes, olives, and pine nuts. Substitute red wine vinegar for balsamic vinegar and 2 ounces thinly sliced provolone cheese, cut into ½-inch pieces, for Parmesan. Add 4 ounces thinly sliced hot capicola, cut into ½-inch pieces; 4 ounces thinly sliced mortadella, cut into ½-inch pieces; and ½ cup pepperoncini, drained, stemmed, and sliced thin, to dressing in step 2.

ORZO SALAD WITH RADISHES, CAPERS, AND ANCHOVY

Omit tomatoes and olives. Substitute lemon juice for balsamic vinegar and chopped fresh parsley for basil. Add 1 minced anchovy fillet to lemon juice and garlic in step 2. After whisking in oil, add 4 trimmed and thinly sliced radishes and ¼ cup capers to dressing.

We double up on ham for this meaty, comforting, supersimple soup.

SPLIT PEA SOUP is a cold-weather favorite, appreciated for its stick-to-your-ribs richness, meaty flavor, and frugality. It's typically made a couple of days after a bone-in ham has been served for Sunday supper or a holiday celebration, once the prized slices have been made into sandwiches. The ham bone, with lots of meat still stubbornly clinging to it, is tossed into a pot with aromatics (celery, carrot, onion) and covered with broth or water and a bag of inexpensive dried split green peas. A few hours of simmering later, you're rewarded with a filling pea soup studded with tiny bits of smoky ham. I wanted to put my slow cooker to work and make a hammy split pea soup without the advantage of a leftover ham bone and with minimal up-front work, so I could make it at any time.

I tried a few existing recipes designed for the slow cooker, with varying results. Many turned out watery, while others were so thick you could stand a spoon in them. I knew I could do better.

Since I didn't have a meaty ham bone hanging around, I looked for a decent substitute. After trying ham steak, ham hocks, Canadian bacon, and even smoked pork chops, I settled on the winning combination of a smoked ham hock and a meaty, 1-pound ham steak. The gnarly looking hock boosted the smoky, porky presence throughout the soup, while the ham steak broke down into tender chunks that were easily shredded with two forks at the end of cooking.

For the aromatic component of my soup, side-by-side tests proved that, although traditional, carrot was unnecessary—we preferred soup without its sweetness. I stuck to onion, celery, and garlic, microwaved with 2 tablespoons of butter to soften the garlic's harsh edge. After I'd set the ham steak and hock in the slow cooker, I added the onion mixture and 1 pound of rinsed split green peas.

Some newer recipes for split pea soup call for chicken broth, but I recalled a time when my mother would make split pea soup with just water. I did a three-way test using all broth, all water, and equal parts water and broth. Hands down, my tasters preferred the soup made with just water. The pork's meaty, smoky flavor stood out, and you could really taste the peas.

All that was left was seasoning. To keep it simple, I used only pantry staples: dried thyme and bay leaves for an herby aroma and red pepper flakes for a subtle punch. After about 6 hours on high (or 8 to 9 hours on low), the peas were tender, the ham hock had given up a generous amount of flavor, and the ham steak was perfectly tender, primed for shredding. A quick 30-second stir with a whisk sealed the deal on a velvety texture.

SLOW-COOKER SPLIT PEA SOUP
Serves 6 to 8

Ham hocks add a deep, meaty flavor to soups and other recipes. Cut from the ankle joint of the hog's leg, hocks contain a great deal of bone, fat, and connective tissue, which lend complex flavor and a rich, salimy texture to soups. They can most often be found near the ham and bacon in the supermarket.

- 7 cups water
- 1 pound green split peas (2 cups), picked over and rinsed
- 1 (1-pound) ham steak, rind discarded, quartered
- 1 (12-ounce) smoked ham hock
- 2 bay leaves
- 2 onions, chopped
- 1 celery rib, minced
- 2 tablespoons unsalted butter
- 3 garlic cloves, minced
  Salt and pepper
- ¾ teaspoon dried thyme
- ¼ teaspoon red pepper flakes

1. Combine water, peas, ham steak, ham hock, and bay leaves in slow cooker. Microwave onions, celery, butter, garlic, ¾ teaspoon salt, thyme, and pepper flakes in covered bowl until onions are soft, about 5 minutes. Transfer to slow cooker. Cover and cook until peas are tender, 8 to 9 hours on low or 5 to 6 hours on high.

2. Transfer ham steak pieces to plate. Discard ham hock and bay leaves. Whisk soup vigorously until peas are broken down and soup thickens, about 30 seconds. Using two forks, shred ham steak into bite-size pieces and return to soup. Season with salt and pepper to taste. Serve.

Traditional cassoulet takes days. We wanted a solid stand-in for a weeknight dinner. BY CHRISTIE MORRISON

CASSOULET, THE FRENCH country stew celebrated for its hearty, thick-enough-to-stand-a-spoon-in texture, is a cold-weather favorite in America as well. The dish is typically made with white beans, lots of garlic and other aromatic vegetables, and an endless roster of meats, including garlic sausage, duck confit, pork shoulder, and sometimes game. It's not short on flavor. But the problem with cassoulet is that you have to block off the better part of a week to make it, and then you need to invite over every neighbor in shouting distance to eat it. I wanted a fully flavored cassoulet-inspired dish for two that was easy to pull off for a weeknight dinner.

To get there, I'd need to scale back and focus on just a few flavor-packed proteins. Duck confit had to go; it takes multiple steps and days of cooking. Instead, I substituted meaty chicken thighs. And rather than the traditional Toulouse sausage—a rustic, garlic-laced sausage produced locally in France but tough to find in the United States—I turned to garlicky bratwurst.

I browned the chicken thighs and brats to create flavorful fond (the brown bits that stick to the bottom of the pan) and then removed them to make room for chopped onion and some drained diced tomatoes. I cooked the mixture until the onions were softened and most of the tomatoes' moisture

had been driven off, intensifying their flavor. A few cloves of garlic and some fresh thyme hit the pan for less than a minute before I loosened things with a combination of chicken broth and dry vermouth, scraping the bottom of the pan to incorporate the fond into the broth.

For all its meaty richness, cassoulet really rests on a platform of white beans. Tradition calls for dried beans soaked overnight and cooked for hours with the meat, but that lengthy process just didn't jibe with my abbreviated approach. Canned beans to the rescue. We've proved many times in the test kitchen that canned beans lose their tinny edge if given a chance to simmer in broth, so I stirred them into the pan before adding the chicken and sausage back to cook through. The finished beans were tender, creamy, and rich in flavor from the meat and vegetables.

In the French countryside, cassoulet is usually cooked in a large earthenware casserole dish and covered with crunchy bread crumbs. I was so close to keeping this all in one pan, so for my next test I kicked things off by toasting small pieces of bread in olive oil on the stovetop until they were just crispy. I set them aside and cooked my stew in the same pan. Then, while it was cooling down, I sprinkled it with the crunchy toasted bread. Ah, France.

Crunchy torn-bread croutons take this simple supper over the top.

One Classy Casserole

Cassoulet, which originated in the Languedoc region of southern France, is named for the earthenware vessel, or *cassolle*, that the dish was traditionally prepared in. (The name Languedoc means "language of the Occitan." Both words derive from "oc," which is how that region historically pronounced "oui.") The exact provenance of cassoulet is hotly debated: Toulouse, Castelnaudary, and Carcassonne all lay claim to the dish, and each city—and even each household within it—champions a unique recipe for the dish. Today, cassoulet has an almost cult-like following in France. To wit: the Academie Universelle du Cassoulet, whose mission is to promote and foster knowledge about this "God of Occitan cuisine."

A 1940s French ad for canned cassoulet.

FRENCH-STYLE WHITE BEAN STEW FOR TWO

Canned navy or great Northern beans can be substituted for the cannellini beans. Traditional cassoulet uses Toulouse sausage, a garlicky sausage from France; use it if you can find it.

- 2½ tablespoons olive oil
- 2 slices hearty white sandwich bread, torn into ½-inch pieces
  Salt and pepper
- 2 (5- to 7-ounce) bone-in chicken thighs, trimmed
- 8 ounces bratwurst or garlic sausage
- 1 onion, chopped fine
- ½ cup canned diced tomatoes, drained
- 3 garlic cloves, minced
- 1 tablespoon minced fresh thyme
- 1 cup chicken broth
- ½ cup dry vermouth or dry white wine
- 1 (15-ounce) can cannellini beans, rinsed
- 2 tablespoons minced fresh parsley

1. Heat 1½ tablespoons oil in 10-inch skillet over medium heat until shimmering. Add bread and ¼ teaspoon salt and toast, stirring frequently, until golden and crispy, 5 to 7 minutes. Transfer to bowl and set aside.

2. Pat chicken dry with paper towels

and season with salt and pepper. Heat remaining 1 tablespoon oil in now-empty skillet over medium-high heat until just smoking. Add chicken, skin side down, and sausage and cook, rotating sausage occasionally but leaving chicken undisturbed, until well browned, about 5 minutes. Transfer to plate.

3. Add onion, tomatoes, and ¼ teaspoon salt to now-empty skillet and cook, stirring occasionally, until softened and beginning to brown, 5 to 7 minutes. Stir in garlic and thyme and cook until fragrant, about 30 seconds. Stir in broth and vermouth, scraping up any browned bits. Add beans and stir to combine.

4. Add chicken, skin side up; sausage; and accumulated juices to bean mixture and bring to boil over high heat. Reduce heat to low, cover, and simmer until chicken registers 175 degrees, 10 to 15 minutes.

5. Remove lid, increase heat to medium-low, and continue to simmer until sauce is slightly thickened and liquid falls just below surface of beans, about 10 minutes longer. (Mixture will still be very loose but will continue to thicken as it sits.) Off heat, top stew with toasted bread and sprinkle with parsley. Let rest for 10 minutes before serving.

One-Pan Dinner Roasted Salmon with Broccoli and Red Potatoes

Salmon, broccoli, and red potatoes all require different cooking times. That didn't stop us. BY CECELIA JENKINS

THE PROMISE OF a one-pan dinner is simple: a full meal of protein, starch, and vegetables cooked all together in one pan. But try this with salmon, potatoes, and broccoli, and you're likely to get rubbery fish, undercooked potatoes, and overdone broccoli. I set out to finesse the technique and make it work.

Of the three components, potatoes need the most time in the oven. To find out just how long, I tossed halved small red potatoes in oil, salt, and pepper and then arranged them cut side down on my baking sheet. To maximize browning on the small surface area, I roasted them on the lowest rack (closest to the oven's heating element) to get a ballpark time for how long it took them to achieve tender, creamy interiors and golden-brown exteriors. Answer: about 35 minutes.

To cook everything on the same pan, I looked to existing test kitchen recipes for inspiration. We've found that broccoli with nicely browned edges takes 20 to 25 minutes in the oven, while our recipe for roasted salmon calls for placing fillets on a baking sheet preheated in a 500-degree oven and then roasting for 11 to 15 minutes. Simply adding these ingredients in stages partway through the potatoes' cooking time seemed like a good plan but proved otherwise when I found myself with an overcrowded pan—the surest route to uneven cooking. I searched for a better way.

I needed to be judicious about opening the oven door and letting valuable heat escape, so I aimed to do so as few times as possible. To maximize browning on the broccoli, I started it with the potatoes in the beginning—one side of the pan for spuds, the other for broccoli. After about 20 minutes, the broccoli florets took on good browning and were flavorful but not mushy. The potatoes, though, still needed about 15 more minutes. I swapped the broccoli out for salmon fillets and returned the pan to the oven. The broccoli stayed warm under foil on my platter while the fish cooked and the potatoes finished.

Salmon loves a sauce, so I created one with chopped chives, whole-grain mustard, lemon juice, and olive oil. Tasters loved the vibrancy of the chives but found the sauce too sharp; a dribble of honey rounded out the flavors for a final note to this one-pan supper.

ONE-PAN ROASTED SALMON WITH BROCCOLI AND RED POTATOES Serves 4

Use small red potatoes measuring 1 to 2 inches in diameter for this recipe.

- 4 (6- to 8-ounce) center-cut skinless salmon fillets, 1 to 1½ inches thick
- 2 teaspoons plus 5 tablespoons extra-virgin olive oil
  Salt and pepper
- 1 pound small red potatoes, unpeeled, halved
- 1 pound broccoli florets, cut into 2-inch pieces
- ¼ cup minced fresh chives
- 2 tablespoons whole-grain mustard
- 2 teaspoons lemon juice
- 1 teaspoon honey
  Lemon wedges

1. Adjust oven rack to lowest position and heat oven to 500 degrees. Pat salmon dry with paper towels, then rub all over with 2 teaspoons oil and season with salt and pepper. Refrigerate until needed.

2. Brush rimmed baking sheet with 1 tablespoon oil. Toss potatoes, 1 tablespoon oil, ½ teaspoon salt, and ½ teaspoon pepper together in bowl. Arrange potatoes cut side down on half of sheet. Toss broccoli, 1 tablespoon oil, ¼ teaspoon salt, and ¼ teaspoon pepper together in now-empty bowl. Arrange broccoli on other half of sheet.

3. Roast until potatoes are light golden brown and broccoli is dark brown on bottom, 22 to 24 minutes, rotating sheet halfway through baking.

4. Meanwhile, combine chives, mustard, lemon juice, honey, remaining 2 tablespoons oil, pinch salt, and pinch pepper in bowl; set chive sauce aside.

5. Remove sheet from oven and transfer broccoli to platter, browned side up; cover with foil to keep warm. Using spatula, remove any bits of broccoli remaining on sheet. (Leave potatoes on sheet.)

6. Place salmon skinned side down on now-empty side of sheet, spaced evenly. Place sheet in oven and immediately reduce oven temperature to 275 degrees. Bake until centers of fillets register 125 degrees (for medium-rare), 11 to 15 minutes, rotating sheet halfway through baking. Transfer potatoes and salmon to platter with broccoli. Serve with lemon wedges and chive sauce.

Our sharp stir-together sauce of chopped chives, mustard, and lemon adds a fresh note.

Broccoli-Salmon Switcheroo
To ensure that all three components emerge from the oven well browned and cooked just right, we roast the potatoes the entire time on the baking sheet (they take the longest) but remove the broccoli before placing the salmon fillets on the sheet.

FIRST: JUST THE VEG
Once browned, transfer the florets to a serving platter.

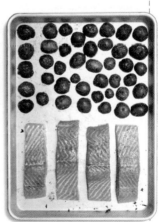

THEN: ADD THE SALMON
Place the fillets skinned side down on the baking sheet.

TEST KITCHEN TECHNIQUE: **When Is Salmon Done?**
We like to serve salmon medium-rare, when the center of the fillet registers 125 degrees.

UNDERCOOKED
Fish is soft and translucent from edge to center.

JUST RIGHT
Fish is moist throughout with a slightly translucent interior.

OVERCOOKED
Opaque flesh means the fish is flaky and dry.

Equipment Review Springform Pans

Have you ever ruined a cheesecake? We've been there, too. But never again: We tested every top-selling springform pan to find the best on the market. BY LAUREN SAVOIE

KEY Good ★★★ Fair ★★ Poor ★

IMAGINE TOILING FOR hours over a cheesecake only to unmold it and find it crumbled, mushy, or cracked due to a faulty springform pan. Springforms consist of two pieces: a round, flat base and a circular collar that latches open and closed, allowing delicate cakes to be unmolded upright. Unfortunately, the two-piece design leaves small gaps where water from a water bath (where the pan is placed in a roasting pan with water to moderate heat) can seep in and butter from the crust can leak out.

Despite a decade of searching, we've yet to find a completely leakproof springform; even our previous winning pan from Nordic Ware leaks a bit. But a number of manufacturers recently redesigned their metal springforms. A few also started making pans out of heat-resistant silicone. We tested eight top-selling models, including our old winner, priced from $13.95 to $49.95—two silicone and six metal options with, variously, glass, ceramic, and nonstick bases. We used each to make no-bake cheesecake, oven-baked cheesecake, and water bath–baked cheesecake.

The silicone pans were disastrous (read our extended story at **Cooks-Country.com/mar16**). Glass bottoms were also problematic: One metal pan with a glass base made pale, pallid crusts that were practically glued into the pan. Darker metal makes for darker baked goods, and one pan's black finish slightly overbrowned crusts (though not enough to affect flavor). We favored pans with light-colored nonstick finishes, which browned slowly and released readily.

A nonstick base wasn't the only factor in how well the pans released cakes: Time after time, cakes tore, crumbled, and cracked when we removed them. Some pans tore cakes along the collar, where a protruding seam clung to fragile swaths of crust. Other pans trapped crust on their bases: Springforms with flat or recessed bases were difficult to maneuver a spatula or knife along, and we often lost parts of the crust when we moved the cake or cut slices. We preferred raised bases, which gave us a full view of the cake and more room to leverage our tools. Compared with the mangled slices we had to dig out from recessed bases, slices cut from raised bases looked picture-perfect. The pans themselves also looked better: Flat and recessed bases had large nicks and knife marks from all the awkward stabbing with our tools, while raised bases showed only small scratches by the end of testing.

Testers also disliked pans with bases that were roughly the same diameter as their collar, which were difficult to handle. The bases of our favorite pans extended at least an inch wider than their collar, giving us something to grab on to before, during, and after baking. Wide bases also tempered leaking. While none of the pans were completely leakproof—every pan leaked butter in the oven—three pans with wide, ridged base troughs contained it. The other pans dripped butter all over the oven.

Though a wide base corralled leaking butter, it didn't stop water from seeping in. We saw this when we baked cheesecakes in a water bath that we dyed blue with food coloring—splotchy blue marks bloomed on the sides and bottom of every single cheesecake (though some were worse than others). To avoid a soggy cake, we always recommend wrapping your springform in foil before baking in a water bath.

We didn't find a perfect pan, but we did find one that improved on our old winner. While both have wide, rimmed bases for better maneuverability and leak-catching, the Williams-Sonoma Goldtouch Springform Pan, 9", also boasts tall sides that give us multiple ways to grip the pan when building a crust, moving a hot cheesecake, or cutting cake slices. Best of all, it upped the ante with even more gorgeously golden crusts thanks to its lighter metallic finish. At nearly $50.00, it's a good investment if you use your springform frequently.

RECOMMENDED

	CRITERIA		TESTERS' NOTES
WILLIAMS-SONOMA Goldtouch Springform Pan, 9" **Model:** 78-2898203 **Price:** $49.95 **Material:** Nonstick metal **Base Width:** 10.65 in 	Design ★★★ Browning ★★★ Release ★★★ Seal ★★ Durability ★★½		This gold-toned pan produced pristine cheesecakes with golden, evenly baked crusts. A ridge along the top was a great guide for leveling batters, and its tall sides gave us something to grab when turning the full or hot pan. While the pan is prone to slight scratching and is not completely leakproof, its wide, raised base easily caught leaking butter and provided support when cutting slices or removing cake.
NORDIC WARE 9" Leakproof Springform Pan **Model:** 55742 (gray ProForm) **Price:** $16.22 **Material:** Nonstick metal **Base Width:** 9.74 in **BEST BUY** 	Design ★★½ Browning ★★½ Release ★★★ Seal ★★ Durability ★★½		Our old favorite, this springform once again made beautiful, evenly browned cheesecakes that were easy to release from the pan. Leaking was minimal, and most butter pooled along its base, though a few drops overflowed onto the oven floor. This pan's base had a few minor scratches after testing.
KAISER LA FORME PLUS 9" Springform Pan **Model:** 70.0637.0200 **Price:** $37.98 **Material:** Nonstick metal **Base Width:** 10.00 in 	Design ★★½ Browning ★★ Release ★★½ Seal ★★ Durability ★★½		The darkest pan of the bunch, this springform slightly over-browned crusts in some spots but not enough to change recipe times or make a big difference in flavor. Cakes were mostly easy to release, and any leaking was corralled along the pan's wide, ridged base.
CALPHALON NONSTICK BAKEWARE 9-in Springform Pan **Model:** 1826048 **Price:** $21.95 **Material:** Nonstick metal **Base Width:** 8.89 in 	Design ★★ Browning ★★★ Release ★★ Seal ★★ Durability ★★½		This pan's lighter finish produced gorgeous, evenly browned crusts. Though cakes were fairly easy to release, its flat base required more finessing and leaked butter onto the oven floor. A few scratches remained after testing.

NOT RECOMMENDED

	CRITERIA		TESTERS' NOTES
ZENKER BY FRIELING Handle-It Glass Bottom Springform with Handles, 9" **Model:** Z3850 **Price:** $34.95 **Materials:** Nonstick metal and glass **Base Width:** 8.92 in 	Design ★★ Browning ★★ Release ★½ Seal ★½ Durability ★		Though handles made this pan easy to maneuver, its small glass bottom was fussy to align with the collar and made unevenly browned crusts. Ridges along the pan's collar crumbled delicate crusts and left an odd pattern on the sides of cakes. By the end of testing, this pan was truly beaten up, with large scratches all along its collar and base.
CUISINART Chef's Classic 9" Springform Pan **Model:** AMB-9SP **Price:** $13.95 **Material:** Nonstick metal **Base Width:** 8.90 in 	Design ★ Browning ★½ Release ★ Seal ★ Durability ★★		This pan's poorly fitting recessed base trapped crust, leaked everywhere, and left us wondering if we had assembled the pan incorrectly (we hadn't). Every cheesecake emerged from the pan mangled, and large scratches remained where we had to dig into the base to remove crust.

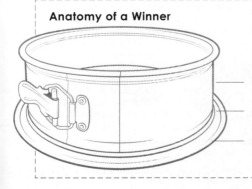

Anatomy of a Winner

These design features helped our favorite pan earn the top spot:

LIGHT FINISH
Allows for controlled, even browning.

TALL SIDES
Let you maneuver pan with potholders.

BASE TROUGH
Catches leaks to help prevent messes.

RAISED BASE
Makes cutting and removing slices easy.

Taste Test Mild Jarred Red Salsa

Piquant jarred salsas can add a little spice to any occasion.
But what do mild salsas have to offer? BY MIYE BROMBERG

SALSA RANKS AMONG America's favorite dips—and nothing beats the jarred varieties for convenience, especially during the winter months when it can be hard to find high-quality fresh tomatoes to make salsa from scratch. But, jarred salsas can often be disappointing: mushy, bland, and overcooked. In the past, we've struggled to find medium and hot versions that we liked, though we've always managed to uncover a few good products. Still, many people prefer their salsa to be less fiery. Could we find a mild salsa that got the ratios of heat, salt, acidity, and sweet tomato flavor just right?

To find out, 21 America's Test Kitchen editors and cooks tasted seven top-selling mild salsas—first plain and then with tortilla chips. One problem emerged almost immediately: Some of the mild salsas weren't mild at all. In fact, two were deemed too hot when eaten on their own. A little heat wasn't entirely unwelcome, though; the very mildest salsas came across as bland. With or without chips, however, tasters preferred salsas that had more moderate heat levels. Our top brand had a bit of a kick but didn't overwhelm more sensitive palates.

Tasters were looking for balance in their salsas. Heat aside, sweetness was critical—brands that had 2 grams of sugar per serving (likely due to the use of tomato concentrate or puree) tended to rate higher than those that had 1 gram or less. But acidity was just as important, if not more so. Six of the seven salsas used vinegar to boost the brightness of their tomatoes; salsas that lacked enough of a sour counterpunch were considered "stale" and "too sweet." Salt levels didn't matter to tasters unless they were significantly low; while the other salsas averaged about 217 milligrams of

sodium per serving, a salsa that had only 65 milligrams was dismissed as "flat." Salsas with flavors that seemed "off" were rejected, as were those overladen with herbs, which imparted a "marinara-like" or "chemically tasting" flavor. Tasters preferred salsas in which the tomato flavor was dominant but still allowed them to "taste the different elements" of the onions and peppers.

The biggest problem was texture. Freshly made salsa weeps vegetable juice as it sits; we found this to be an issue with these jarred salsas, too. To get a better sense of the composition of the salsas, we strained a cup of each overnight in an attempt to separate the solids from the liquids. One jarred salsa that tasters found "runny" shed 17 teaspoons of watery fluid overnight, almost a third of its total volume. Other brands overcompensated for the seepage issue, adding thickeners that kept liquid in but made the salsas "slimy" and "viscous"; one salsa thickened with cornstarch lost only 5 teaspoons of liquid, looking just as gloppy and unnaturally glossy in the morning as it had the night before. Tasters preferred salsas that used either tomato puree or tomato concentrate to give the base full, natural body.

The texture, size, and uniformity of the vegetable chunks were also significant. Our winning salsa boasted even ½-inch onion and pepper pieces that still had some crunch to them. Other salsas featured vegetables that were overcooked, cut into wildly different shapes and sizes, or too big to stay on a chip.

While six of the seven products we tested left us wanting, we did find one that measured up. Better still, it was the cheapest one in our testing. For a salsa that has modest heat, balanced flavor, firm vegetable chunks, and a dip-friendly base consistency, we choose Chi-Chi's.

KEY Truly Mild 🌶 A Little Kick 🌶🌶 Feel the Burn 🌶🌶🌶

RECOMMENDED

CHI-CHI'S Thick & Chunky Salsa
Price: $1.50 for 16 oz ($0.09 per oz)
Sugar: 2 g
Salt: 150 mg
Heat Level: 🌶
Liquid Lost: 8 tsp

Our winning salsa was praised for its "hint of heat," "good balance," and "sweet," "satisfying tomato flavor." But with a "thick," "smooth" base fortified with concentrated crushed tomatoes and studded with "crunchy," "ideal-size chunks" of vegetables, it was the salsa's texture that really won over our panel. Chi-Chi's also produces our favorite medium-heat salsa.

RECOMMENDED WITH RESERVATIONS

TOSTITOS Chunky Salsa
Price: $3.39 for 15.5 oz ($0.22 per oz)
Sugar: 2 g
Salt: 250 mg
Heat Level: 🌶🌶
Liquid Lost: 10 tsp

There was nothing wrong with the salsa—a few tasters thought this "chunky," "balanced," "mellow" salsa with "a decent amount of spice" was "just right." But there was little to distinguish it, either. Overall, we found it "generic," "unremarkable," and "not deeply exciting," especially when eaten with chips. As one taster said: "Solid, but not much X-factor."

LA VICTORIA Thick'n Chunky Salsa
Price: $3.04 for 16 oz ($0.19 per oz)
Sugar: 1 g
Salt: 190 mg
Heat Level: 🌶🌶🌶
Liquid Lost: 9 tsp

"Surprisingly spicy" on its own, this salsa was "better with chips," where tasters generally noted only "a little heat" and found the salsa's "high ratio of chunks to liquid . . . good for dipping." While we liked its "vibrant" color and "very tomato-y" taste, many tasters thought this salsa was "very acidic," marred by a "pickle-y," "vinegary" flavor.

PACE Chunky Salsa
Price: $2.49 for 16 oz ($0.16 per oz)
Sugar: 2 g
Salt: 230 mg
Heat Level: 🌶🌶
Liquid Lost: 10 tsp

This salsa had "nice tomato flavor" and "tang" but a "soft," "soupy," "cooked" base. Worse, tasters consistently found it "too oniony." Indeed, it was the only salsa to use both fresh and dehydrated onions, which may have imparted "canned" or "chemical" overtones—and after straining the salsa, we saw that more than half the solids were unevenly cut onions that our tasters found "tough" and "raw."

NOT RECOMMENDED

HERDEZ Salsa Casera
Price: $2.18 for 16 oz ($0.14 per oz)
Sugar: 1 g
Salt: 220 mg
Heat Level: 🌶🌶🌶
Liquid Lost: 17 tsp

The only product to include serrano peppers (instead of the milder jalapeños favored by the other six companies), this salsa had a heat that "kick[ed] you in the face." Eighteen of our 21 tasters were incredulous: "This is mild?" Although a few liked this salsa's "fresh," "bright" flavor, most disliked its "thin," "runny" base, which made "dipping a challenge."

NEWMAN'S OWN Mild Salsa
Price: $2.99 for 16 oz ($0.19 per oz)
Sugar: 1 g
Salt: 65 mg
Heat Level: 🌶
Liquid Lost: 15 tsp

Although "visually appealing" with large, vegetable chunks, this salsa lost on flavor. Tasters found the cilantro in this salsa to be "weird," "bitter," "harsh," and "chemically," characterized by "a detergent aftertaste." With only 65 milligrams of salt per serving and not enough acidity, this salsa was also deemed "flat" and lacking in "liveliness."

MRS. RENFRO'S Mild Salsa
Price: $3.32 for 16 oz ($0.21 per oz)
Sugar: less than 1 g
Salt: 240 mg
Heat Level: 🌶
Liquid Lost: 5 tsp

Thickened with cornstarch, this salsa had a "slimy," "gelatinous," "viscous" consistency. Flavorwise, the salsa's "bland," "tomato-y," "too sweet" taste prompted comparisons to "baby food," "children's spaghetti sauce," and "Chef Boyardee."

Salt and sugar are listed per 2-tablespoon serving.
Liquid lost represents the volume of liquid shed after draining 1 cup of the salsa overnight.

Separating the Winners from the Losers
Texture played a significant role in our evaluation of jarred salsa. Chi-Chi's Thick & Chunky Salsa lived up to its name with a full-bodied consistency that could be scooped up with a chip. Lower-ranking Herdez Salsa, on the other hand, is so thin and liquidy that dipping was a challenge.

CHI-CHI'S
Thick and dippable

HERDEZ
Runny and watery

Heirloom Recipe

We're looking for recipes that you treasure—the ones that have been handed down in your family for a generation or more; that always come out for the holidays; that have earned a place at your table and in your heart, through many years of meals. Send us the recipes that spell home to you. Visit **CooksCountry.com/magazines/home** (or write to Heirloom Recipes, *Cook's Country*, P.O. Box 470739, Brookline, MA 02447); click on Heirloom Recipes and tell us a little about the recipe. Include your name and mailing address. **If we print your recipe, you'll receive a free one-year subscription to** *Cook's Country***.**

CHIPPED CHOPPED HAM SANDWICHES Serves 8

"Growing up in Pittsburgh, this sweet-salty sandwich was a lunchtime favorite, both at home and in the school cafeteria."
Kendra Johnson, Leetsdale, Pa.

We prefer hearty kaiser or bulkie rolls to soft hamburger buns here because they soak up the sauce without becoming soggy.

- 8 kaiser rolls, split
- 2 pounds thinly shaved low-sodium boiled deli ham
- ½ cup plus 2 tablespoons cider vinegar
- ½ cup tomato paste
- ½ cup ketchup
- ¼ cup light brown sugar
- 2 tablespoons yellow mustard
- 2 teaspoons onion powder
- ½ teaspoon cayenne pepper
- 8 slices American cheese (8 ounces)

1. Adjust oven rack to middle position and heat oven to 375 degrees. Line rimmed baking sheet with parchment paper. Arrange roll bottoms on prepared sheet.

2. Separate layers of ham as much as possible. Whisk vinegar, tomato paste, ketchup, sugar, mustard, onion powder, and cayenne together in Dutch oven until smooth. Bring sauce to simmer over medium heat. Add ham and cook until heated through, about 5 minutes, tossing to coat with sauce.

3. Divide ham among roll bottoms, then top each with 1 slice cheese and roll top. Cover pan with aluminum foil and bake until cheese is melted, about 5 minutes. Serve.

COMING NEXT ISSUE

The sunny skies of California beckon! Next issue, we hit the West Coast for **Garlic Fried Chicken** from Bakersfield and **Dutch Crunch** bread from San Francisco. We also swing through the South for **Brunswick Stew**, **Beef Lombardi**, and **Bananas Foster**; pop into Texas for the ultimate **Chiles Rellenos**; call on Kentucky for **Derby Biscuits**; dip into New England for **Dublin Coddle**; and sweeten the deal with a supereasy **Flourless Chocolate Cake** fit for company (left). Grab a fork and join us.

FIND THE ROOSTER!

A tiny version of this rooster has been hidden in the pages of this issue. Write to us with its location and we'll enter you in a random drawing. The first correct entry drawn will win our winning springform pan, and each of the next five will receive a free one-year subscription to *Cook's Country*. To enter, visit **CooksCountry.com/rooste** by March 31, 2016, or write to Rooster FM16, *Cook's Country*, P.O. Box 470739, Brookline, MA 02447. Include your name and address. Lowell Heine of Minneapo Minn., found the rooster in the October, November 2015 issue on page 24 and won our favorite slicing knife.

WEB EXTRAS

Free for 4 months online at
CooksCountry.com

Boursin-Parsley Pan Sauce
Breakfast Pizza
Chocolate Sheet Cake
Poppy Seed Chicken Casserole
Spicy Sausage Stromboli
Spinach and Tomato Lasagna
Tasting Artisanal Cream Cheese
Tasting Supermarket Sauerkraut
Testing Piping Sets
Testing Springform Pans
Watercress and Cucumber Salad with Lemon Vinaigrette

READ US ON iPAD

Download the *Cook's Country* app for iPad and start a free trial subscription or purchase a single issue of the magazine. issues are enhanced with full-color Cook Mode slide shows that provide step-by-step instructions for completing recipes, plus expanded revie and ratings. Go to **CooksCountry com/iPad** to download our a through iTunes.

Chocolate Raspberry Heart Cake

Give your sweetheart cake and roses—white chocolate–raspberry buttercream roses.

To make this cake, you will need:

- **1** **recipe Chocolate Sheet Cake batter***
- **1½** **cups fresh or thawed frozen raspberries, plus about 20 fresh raspberries**
- **6** **large egg whites**
- **1½** **cups (10½ ounces) sugar**
- **⅛** **teaspoon salt**
- **24** **tablespoons (3 sticks) unsalted butter, cut into 24 pieces and softened**
- **8** **ounces white chocolate, melted and cooled slightly**

FOR THE CAKE: Adjust oven rack to middle position and heat oven to 325 degrees. Grease bottom and sides of one 8-inch square baking pan and one 8-inch round cake pan; line bottom of each with parchment paper. Divide batter evenly between pans. Bake until toothpick inserted into center of each cake comes out clean, 35 to 45 minutes, rotating pans halfway through baking. Let cakes cool in pans for 10 minutes, then run knife around edges of pans and invert cakes onto wire rack. Remove parchment and reinvert cakes. Let cakes cool completely, about 1 hour.

FOR THE FROSTING: Puree 1½ cups raspberries in food processor, about 30 seconds. Strain puree through fine-mesh strainer into bowl; discard solids and set aside puree. Bring 1 inch water to simmer in medium saucepan. Combine egg whites, sugar, and salt in bowl of stand mixer. Place bowl over simmering water and heat, stirring constantly, until mixture reaches 160 degrees, 5 to 8 minutes. Transfer bowl to stand mixer, fit with whisk, and whip on medium-high speed until stiff peaks form, about 5 minutes. Reduce speed to medium-low and add butter, piece by piece. Continue mixing until smooth, about 2 minutes. Add white chocolate and mix until just combined. Slowly add raspberry puree and mix until incorporated.

TO ASSEMBLE: Place 1 corner of square cake against lower edge of large (about 16-inch-diameter) cake plate or pedestal. Using serrated knife, shave domed top from round cake to make it level with square cake; discard top. Cut round cake in half vertically. Place halves, with cut sides facing in, against top 2 edges of square cake to form heart shape. Spread 2½ cups frosting over top and sides of cake in thin, even layer. Place remaining frosting in piping bag fitted with star tip and pipe roses (spiraling from inside out) over top and sides of cake. Place fresh raspberries between roses. Serve.

▶ *Go to CooksCountry.com/chocsheetcake for the recipe for our Chocolate Sheet Cake.

Inside This Issue

Cook's Country

APRIL/MAY 2016

Derby Biscuits

Garlic Fried Chicken

Slow-Cooker Memphis Ribs

Flourless Chocolate Cake
10 Minutes Active Time

Chicken Scaloppini for Two
Quick Caper-Mushroom Sauce

Bananas Foster
New Orleans Classic Revisited

Fluffy Baked Polenta
Local VFW Favorite

Lemon-Braised Chicken
Easy One-Pan Dinner

Bottom Round Roast
Turning Cheap Beef Tender

**Cooking Class:
Eggs Benedict**

Classic Chiles Rellenos
Less Work, All the Flavor

Five Easy Smoothies
We Found Two Secrets

Asparagus Salad
It's All in How You Slice It

CooksCountry.com
$5.95 U.S./$6.95 CANADA

MARYLAND BEATEN BISCUITS

Three pints winter wheat flour, ¼ pound lard, one-half ice water and one-half milk to make a stiff dough, 1 heaping teaspoon salt. Work in the lard, add the liquid and beat with a club for 25 minutes. Make in small biscuits and bake in a hot oven.

This recipe is from Mrs. Charles Sterett Grason, of Cornwalys Cross Manor, the oldest house in Maryland still in the possession of the descendants of the original owner.

–from America Cooks by The Browns

BEFORE TEST COOK Morgan Bolling set to developing her recipe for Derby Biscuits (page 7), we sorted through stacks of ancient recipes, some more than a century old, to find recipes for beaten biscuits. Precursors to the country-style biscuits we all know today, beaten biscuits were leavened not with chemicals but with hardy American muscle.

Among the recipes we studied was the above gem from the hard-to-find Depression-era omnibus *America Cooks* by The Browns—Cora, Rose, and Bob.

It's an elegant little recipe perfectly suited to its time, trusting home cooks of the era to navigate its vague moments ("one-half ice water and one-half milk" is far from exact and would never pass muster with our recipe editors) while giving them an extra hand where required ("beat with a club for 25 minutes" leaves little room for improvisation—except, perhaps, when selecting an appropriate club).

We pride ourselves on precision in the test kitchen. We cherish clarity. We relentlessly pursue innovation, invention, and new ideas to expand the capabilities of contemporary home cooks—and to inspire them.

But our own inspiration? That comes from anywhere and everywhere. Sometimes it comes from experimentation and the happy accidents that occur in the kitchen. Sometimes it comes from farther afield—from an off-road barbecue joint in Alabama, say, or an urban taco stand in Los Angeles. Or even a treasured old cookbook like *America Cooks*. We'll take inspiration anywhere we can get it.

It's a big country.

TUCKER SHAW

Executive Editor

Foolproof Preserving
A Guide to Making Jams, Jellies, Pickles, Condiments & More

Whether you're new to canning or a seasoned pro, make your efforts count with our newest book featuring 75 obsessively tested recipes. Detailed, step-by-step instructions demystify the process, explain the science, and tell you exactly what equipment you need (and don't need) to get started.

 Follow us on **Pinterest**
pinterest.com/TestKitchen

 Follow us on **Twitter**
twitter.com/TestKitchen

 Find us on **Facebook**
facebook.com/CooksCountry

Chief Executive Officer David Nussbaum
Chief Creative Officer Jack Bishop
Editorial Director John Willoughby

Executive Editor Tucker Shaw
Deputy Editor Rebecca Hays
Executive Managing Editor Todd Meier
Executive Food Editor Bryan Roof

Senior Editors Christie Morrison, Diane Unger
Associate Editor Ashley Moore
Test Cooks Morgan Bolling, Cecelia Jenkins, Katie Leaird
Copy Editors Jillian Campbell, Krista Magnuson
Contributing Editors Erika Bruce, Eva Katz
Science Editor Guy Crosby, PhD

Executive Tastings & Testings Editor Lisa McManus
Managing Editor Scott Kathan
Senior Editor Hannah Crowley
Assistant Editors Miye Bromberg, Lauren Savoie, Kate Shannon

Test Kitchen Director Erin McMurrer
Assistant Test Kitchen Director Leah Rovner
Test Kitchen Manager Alexxa Grattan
Senior Test Kitchen Assistant Meridith Lippard
Kitchen Assistants Blanca Castanza, Gladis Campos, Maria Elena Delgado, Ena Gudiel

Design Director, Print Greg Galvan
Photography Director Julie Cote
Art Director Susan Levin
Associate Art Director Lindsey Chandler
Deputy Art Director, Marketing Melanie Gryboski
Associate Art Director, Marketing Janet Taylor
Designer, Marketing Stephanie Cook
Staff Photographer Daniel J. van Ackere
Color Food Photography Keller + Keller
Styling Catrine Kelty, Marie Piraino
Associate Art Director, Photography Steve Klise
Assistant Photography Producer Mary Ball

Design Director, Digital John Torres
Managing Editor, Web Christine Liu
Social Media Manager Jill Fisher
Senior Editor, Web Roger Metcalf
Assistant Editor, Web Terrence Doyle
Test Kitchen Photojournalist Kevin White

VP, Print & Direct Marketing David Mack
Circulation Director Doug Wicinski
Circulation & Fulfillment Manager Carrie Fethe
Partnership Marketing Manager Pamela Putprush
Marketing Assistant Andrea Hampel
Production Director Guy Rochford
Imaging Manager Lauren Robbins
Production & Imaging Specialists Heather Dube, Sean MacDona Dennis Noble, Jessica Voas

Chief Digital Officer Fran Middleton
Chief Financial Officer Jackie McCauley Ford
Senior Controller Theresa Peterson
Director, Business Systems Alice Carpenter
Project Manager Mehgan Conciatori

VP, New Business Development Michael Burton
VP, Strategic Analytics Deborah Fagone
Client Services Manager Kate Zebrowski
Sponsorship Sales Associate Morgan Mannino
Customer Loyalty & Support Manager Amy Bootier
Senior Customer Loyalty & Support Specialist Andrew S. Finfroc
Customer Loyalty & Support Specialists Caroline Augliere, Rebecca Kowalski, Ramesh Pillay
Senior VP, Human Resources & Organizational Development Colleen Zelina
Human Resources Director Adele Shapiro
Director, Retail Book Program Beth Ineson
Retail Sales Manager Derek Meehan
Associate Director, Publicity Susan Hershberg

ON THE COVER: DERBY BISCUITS Keller + Keller, Catrine Kelty
ILLUSTRATION: Greg Stevenson

Departments

AMERICA'S TEST KITCHEN
RECIPES THAT WORK®

America's Test Kitchen is a very real 2,500-square-foot kitchen located just outside Boston. It is the home of more than 60 test cooks, editors, and cookware specialists. Our mission is to test recipes until we understand exactly how and why they work and eventually arrive at the very best version. We also test kitchen equipment and supermarket ingredients in search of products that offer the best value and performance. You can watch us work by tuning in to *America's Test Kitchen* (AmericasTestKitchen.com) and *Cooks Country from America's Test Kitchen* (CooksCountry.com) on public television and listen to us on our weekly radio program on PRX. You can also follow us on Facebook, Twitter, Pinterest, and Instagram.

4 Garlic Fried Chicken
In Bakersfield, California, cooks douse fried chicken with butter and garlic. Puzzled, we paid a visit. Convinced, we fried more than 60 pounds of chicken to perfect our version.

5 Basque Green Beans
To complement a platter of garlicky fried chicken, we turned to this sweet-savory side.

6 Derby Biscuits
Starting with a recipe that dates back centuries, we came up with appetizer biscuits that are hard to beat. And beer cheese, too.
PLUS Testing Biscuit Cutters

8 Bottom Round Roast Beef
This economical cut of roast beef had a bad reputation in the test kitchen. We wanted to give it another chance.

9 Mashed Potato Cakes
Sure, mashed potatoes are good enough. But we never stop at good enough.

10 Fluffy Polenta with Red Sauce
Without knowing his secrets, could we re-create a seasoned veteran's unique Italian American dish of smooth, creamy, but light polenta in a simple red sauce?

11 Asparagus Salad
Raw asparagus? It may sound strange, but it makes a memorable salad.

12 Dublin Coddle
There is no dish more comforting than this savory Irish American classic—if you can get all of its parts to work together.

13 Pecan-Crusted Trout
Our relationship with pecan-crusted fish turned out to be surprisingly one-sided.

14 Chiles Rellenos
Forget the soggy, gloppy versions you've had. This restaurant favorite can be a fresh, vibrant revelation, if you're willing to do a little work. **PLUS** Deep-Frying Lesson

17 Bananas Foster
We wanted to enjoy this New Orleans classic at home, but would that mean singeing our eyebrows?

18 Dutch Crunch
This lightly sweet sandwich bread with a crunchy topping is certainlly unique, but does it have to be unique to San Francisco?

20 Brunswick Stew
This rib-sticking stew is too often the butt of jokes. Our aim was to turn misunderstanding into gushing respect.

21 Beef Lombardi
Ground beef, cheese, sour cream, and egg noodles in one casserole? Sounds like our kind of challenge.

22 Flourless Chocolate Cake
This fancy restaurant dessert is seldom made at home. But after a month in the test kitchen, we had a version that takes just 10 minutes of active time to put together.
PLUS Tasting Whipped Toppings

Cook's Country magazine (ISSN 1552-1990), number 68, is published bimonthly by Boston Common Press Limited Partnership, 17 Station St., Brookline, MA 02445. Copyright 2016 Boston Common Press Limited Partnership. Periodicals postage paid at Boston, MA, and additional mailing offices. USPS #023453. Publications Mail Agreement No. 40020778. Return undeliverable Canadian addresses to P.O. Box 875, Station A, Windsor, ON N9A 6P2. POSTMASTER: Send address changes to Cook's Country, PO Box 6018, Harlan, IA 51593-1518. For subscription and gift subscription orders, subscription inquiries, or change of address notices, visit AmericasTestKitchen.com/support, call 800-526-8447 in the U.S. or 515-248-7684 from outside the U.S., or write to us at Cook's Country, P.O. Box 6018, Harlan, IA 51593-1518. PRINTED IN THE USA.

Ask Cook's Country

BY MORGAN BOLLING

Reusing Parchment

Parchment paper is expensive. Can I reuse sheets for multiple batches of cookies?
–Annette Buck, Beacon, N.Y.

Parchment paper can run upwards of $7 per roll, so we were intrigued by the idea of reusing it to save some money. To test your question, we made five batches of our Perfect Chocolate Chip Cookies and five batches of sugar cookies, baking each batch on the same sheet of parchment (but using cooled baking sheets for each batch). Even after five rounds in the oven, the parchment held up and the cookies didn't have any sticking or spreading issues.

A little common sense goes a long way: Don't reuse parchment that is overly messy (from decorating cookies or anything else), as the mess might burn in the oven, imparting off-flavors. Also, while cookie recipes are usually baked at moderate temperatures that don't significantly degrade the parchment, some bread recipes that call for parchment bake at 450 degrees and above. Higher temperatures can make parchment dry and brittle, so we suggest starting with a fresh sheet.

THE BOTTOM LINE: You can reuse sheets of parchment paper several times for most cookies—but make sure to use a cooled baking sheet.

GOOD TO GO
Ready for the next round

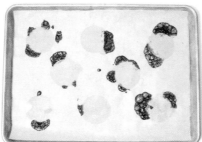

RISKY
Sugary mess may smoke in the oven

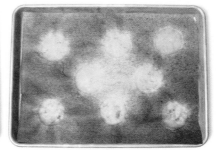

TOSS IT
Too dry and brittle to be reused

Ground Bay Leaves

Why do recipes usually call for whole bay leaves and not ground?
–Barbara Wilson, Hickory, N.C.

Spice producers do sell ground bay leaves, and anyone with a spice grinder could easily grind their own. So why don't more recipes use ground bay leaves?

To find out, we prepared two test kitchen recipes that call for a bay leaf—Cooked Dried Beans and Herbed Rice Pilaf—with no bay leaf, store-bought ground bay leaves, and a whole bay leaf. The versions without any bay leaf were panned as "bland." Those with ground bay leaves felt "more floral but still bland." The ground bay leaves also left the beans and rice visibly speckled an unattractive green. Tasters confirmed that the samples made with a whole bay leaf were "well-rounded" with a notable herb presence.

So what gives? Dried bay leaves, like many other dried herbs, lose their pungency when ground. The oils that are normally protected inside the plant wall can evaporate; plus, the larger surface area causes both light and oxygen to degrade the herb more quickly. Thus, we recommend using whole bay leaves and removing them at the end of cooking. And by the way, we recommend storing your bay leaves in the freezer for optimum flavor.

THE BOTTOM LINE: The flavor of bay leaves deteriorates quickly when they are ground. We suggest sticking with whole bay leaves.

Cruciferous Colors

Besides looking different, is there any flavor difference between red and green cabbage? Can I use them interchangeably?
–Tom DeCelle, North Conway, N.H.

Although both are part of the *Brassicaceae* family, red and green cabbage are two different varieties. However, it's not uncommon for us to use them interchangeably in recipes.

To compare their flavors, we made batches of our Creamy Buttermilk Coleslaw and Braised Red Cabbage recipes with green cabbage and red cabbage and tasted the batches side by side. Tasters didn't notice textural differences. But the green cabbage tasted notably milder in both applications, with tasters commenting on its vegetal flavor while raw. The red cabbage was sweeter and "fruitier" in both recipes, though this was more pronounced in the braised sample.

THE BOTTOM LINE: While they behave similarly and can be used interchangeably in recipes, red and green cabbage have slightly different flavor profiles: Green cabbage is mellower and more vegetal, while red is sweeter and more floral.

Cool Crustaceans

If I buy frozen shrimp and thaw them, can I refreeze a portion of them?
–Jamie McCarthy, Redmond, Wash.

According to the U.S. Food and Drug Administration, as long as the shrimp were thawed properly in the refrigerator or in cold water, it is safe to refreeze and rethaw them. The maximum time they can be held at room temperature is 2 hours, total, over the course of thawing and refreezing. The danger of thawing frozen shrimp at room temperature is that they may sit in the "danger zone" of 40 to 140 degrees Fahrenheit, which is the optimum environment for bacteria growth.

But safe shrimp and good shrimp may be two different things. When shrimp are frozen, the liquid within their cells expands, which can damage the cell walls. When frozen shrimp are thawed, this liquid seeps out, compromising the quality of the shrimp. To find out how greatly the texture and flavor of the shrimp are affected, we prepared sautéed shrimp and shrimp burgers using frozen shrimp that we thawed in the refrigerator and frozen shrimp that we thawed, refroze, and thawed again. In the sautéed shrimp, tasters noted a stark difference, commenting on the mealy and dry texture and off-flavor of the twice-frozen shrimp.

In the shrimp burgers (which feature heavily seasoned chopped shrimp), however, tasters barely noticed a difference. There was a slight preference for those made with shrimp only frozen once, but both were acceptable.

THE BOTTOM LINE: If you're eating the shrimp whole, don't freeze them a second time. However, if you're using them in chopped or minced applications, like shrimp burgers or potstickers, feel free to refreeze the frozen-and-thawed shrimp. And always thaw shrimp in cold water or in the refrigerator.

Leakproofing Springform Pans

In your recent testing of springform pans, you wrote that you recommend wrapping the pans in foil when you use them in a water bath (since none of them are truly leakproof). How do you do this?
–Paul Horton, Ann Arbor, Mich.

It's frustrating to unmold a cheesecake that was baked in a water bath to find that water has seeped in and rendered the crust soggy. To avoid this, we rely on a tried-and-true technique.

THE BOTTOM LINE: With two sheets of aluminum foil, you can create your own leakproof pan.

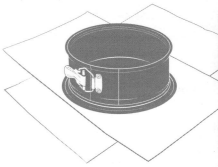

Tear two sheets of 18 by 12-inch heavy-duty foil, stack the sheets perpendicular to each other, and set the springform pan on top.

Carefully fold the edges of the foil against the sides and base of the pan, pressing firmly to seal any gaps.

To ask us a cooking question, visit **CooksCountry.com/ask.** Or write to Ask *Cook's Country*, P.O. Box 470739, Brookline, MA 02447. Just try to stump us!

Kitchen Shortcuts

COMPILED BY DIANE UNGER

SMART IDEA Instant Thickener
Amy Elizabeth, Mendocino, Calif.

We eat roast chicken with gravy twice a week. To streamline the gravy-making, I blend together 1 cup of softened butter and 1 cup of all-purpose flour in my food processor until smooth. Then, using a tablespoon measure, I scoop the mixture onto a parchment paper–lined baking sheet and freeze it. When the butter-flour balls are solid, I put them in a zipper-lock bag in the freezer. It takes 2 tablespoons—two frozen balls—whisked into 1 cup of stock or pan drippings to thicken the gravy perfectly.

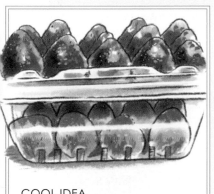

COOL IDEA
Strawberry Storage
Susan Datter, Atlanta, Ga.

Your tip for storing strawberries properly without crushing or bruising (in a single layer on a paper towel–lined plate) works great, but it takes up a lot of room in my refrigerator. To save fridge space, I cut the hinge on the plastic container the strawberries came in and remove the top. I arrange one layer of strawberries in the bottom (stem down to fit the most berries) and then invert the lid and place that back on the container. I set the remaining strawberries in the lid for two tiers of berries.

CLEVER TIP
Keep It Warm
Marjorie French, San Diego, Calif.

I have an easy trick for keeping corn tortillas warm. I wrap a stack of tortillas in a dish towel and microwave them for 2 minutes. Then I wrap them in aluminum foil and slide the foil packet inside the pocket of a square cloth pot holder. I put another pot holder on top and bring them to the table. The tortillas stay warm for a good half-hour.

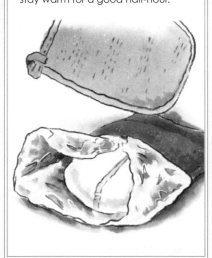

CLEVER IDEA Roll Revival
Sam Bass, Carbondale, Colo.

At my local bakery, the awesome crusty dinner rolls are cheaper if you buy them by the dozen, so I buy 12 at a time and freeze whatever I don't eat in a few days. I found a great way to reheat them that doesn't compromise their texture: Quickly wet the frozen rolls under running water. Then, wrap them in aluminum foil and put them in a 375-degree oven for 10 minutes so the steam defrosts them and heats them through. I then unwrap the rolls and put them back in the oven for 5 minutes or so to crisp the crust. They taste almost fresh-baked.

SMART TIP
Marshmallows to the Rescue
Dorothy Czarnecki, Philadelphia, Pa.

After 50 years of having to deal with rock-hard brown sugar while baking, I found a simple and cheap way to avoid the frustration. I now put two large marshmallows in the container with my brown sugar to keep it soft.

CLEVER TIP
Potato Spin
Ferguson Roundy, Tarrytown, N.Y.

The arthritis in my hands can make peeling potatoes a chore, but I found a trick that really helps make peeling easier (even if you don't have arthritis). I pierce a small end of the potato with a dinner fork and run the peeler down the sides, turning the potato as I go.

SLICK TRICK Ravioli Separator
Stella Allen, Providence, R.I.

My mom taught me to use cornmeal to prevent stacked homemade ravioli from sticking together before cooking or freezing them. I recently discovered that nonstick aluminum foil works just as well, and it leaves no cornmeal mess. I put a sheet of foil in the bottom of a storage container, top it with a layer of ravioli, cover the ravioli with another sheet of foil, and so on. Now my mom uses this trick, too.

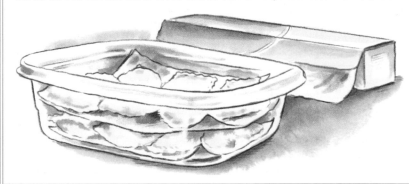

Submit a tip online at CooksCountry.com/kitchenshortcuts or send a letter to Kitchen Shortcuts, *Cook's Country*, P.O. Box 470739, Brookline, MA 02447. Include your name, address, and phone number. If we publish your tip, you will receive a free one-year subscription to *Cook's Country*. Letters may be edited for clarity and length.

Garlic Fried Chicken

In Bakersfield, California, cooks douse fried chicken with butter and garlic. Puzzled, we paid a visit. Convinced, we fried more than 60 pounds of chicken to perfect our version. BY DIANE UNGER

WHEN OUR EXECUTIVE food editor returned from a recent trip to California, he pulled me aside to show me pictures of some fried chicken that he had eaten in Bakersfield (see "On the Road"). "What's that all over the chicken?" I asked. "Butter and garlic. Lots of garlic. And it was amazing." He described moist and tender chicken, permeated with mild garlic flavor, under a crispy coating that was doused with a potent garlic-parsley butter.

I'm a huge fan of fried chicken, any fried chicken. But wouldn't garlic butter sog out the coating? Or mask the flavor of the chicken? But my editor insisted. "You have to figure out how to make this," he said. "You're going to love it."

I searched our test kitchen library to find recipes similar to what he'd described, to no avail. I was flying blind.

In the test kitchen, we often brine or marinate meat and poultry to season it. For my first side-by-side test, I did both. I dunked a cut-up bird in a mixture of buttermilk, granulated garlic, and fresh minced garlic before coating it with a simple mixture of seasoned flour and frying the pieces for 15 minutes in peanut oil heated to 325 degrees. I served this chicken next to a bird that I'd marinated in a mixture of olive oil, fresh and granulated garlic, and salt and pepper before coating and frying it.

Across the board, we preferred the meat that I had marinated. Subsequent tests showed that I could marinate the chicken for just 1 hour or up to 24; in both cases, the chicken was well seasoned and the garlic flavor pronounced. Another series of tests confirmed that, for maximum garlic flavor, I needed both fresh and granulated garlic.

But the coating was still too thin and tended to slip off. A few tests helped me solve this problem with a simple technique: After scraping off any excess marinade, I dipped the chicken pieces in beaten egg white to help the coating stick and then tossed them in the seasoned flour. I let the coated chicken sit on a rack in the refrigerator, uncovered, for at least 30 minutes to give the coating a chance to adhere before frying. Much better. The coating retained its crunch, and it stayed put. I moved on to that saucy garlic topping.

I melted 8 tablespoons of butter in a nonstick skillet on the stovetop, added 6 minced garlic cloves (a garlic press made easy work of that), and cooked the mixture until the garlic was golden brown. I poured it over the fried chicken. But tasters thought the garlic was minced too fine, and it had a bitter flavor because it had gotten too brown.

For the next round, I melted only one tablespoon of butter and added 8 garlic cloves that I'd minced by hand, plus a tablespoon of water to allow the garlic to soften without getting too brown. I let the remaining 7 tablespoons of butter soften before combining them with salt, pepper, and parsley. I poured the hot garlic mixture over the softened butter and whisked it until I had a smooth, emulsified garlic-butter sauce. Success: The chicken was deeply flavorful, and the topping wasn't greasy. I'd fried more than 60 pounds of chicken, but the result was worth it. "Even better than the original," my editor announced.

GARLIC FRIED CHICKEN Serves 4

Use a Dutch oven that holds 6 quarts or more. Mince the garlic with a knife rather than with a garlic press.

CHICKEN

- 3 tablespoons extra-virgin olive oil
- 2 tablespoons granulated garlic
- 5 garlic cloves, minced
   Kosher salt and pepper
- 3 pounds bone-in chicken pieces (split breasts cut in half crosswise, drumsticks, thighs, and/or wings), trimmed
- 2 cups all-purpose flour
- 4 large egg whites
- 3 quarts peanut or vegetable oil

GARLIC BUTTER

- 8 tablespoons unsalted butter, softened
- 2 tablespoons minced fresh parsley
- ¼ teaspoon kosher salt
- ¼ teaspoon pepper
- 8 garlic cloves, minced
- 1 tablespoon water

1. FOR THE CHICKEN: Combine olive oil, 1 tablespoon granulated garlic, minced garlic, 2 teaspoons salt, and 2 teaspoons pepper in large bowl. Add chicken and toss to thoroughly coat with garlic mixture. Cover with plastic wrap and refrigerate for at least 1 hour or up to 24 hours.

2. Set wire rack in rimmed baking sheet. Whisk flour, remaining 1 tablespoon granulated garlic, 2 teaspoons salt, and 2 teaspoons pepper together in separate bowl. Lightly beat egg whites together in shallow dish.

3. Remove chicken from marinade and brush away any solidified clumps of oil with paper towels. Working with 1 piece at a time, dip chicken into egg whites to thoroughly coat, letting excess drip back into dish; then dredge in flour mixture, pressing firmly to adhere. Transfer chicken to prepared wire rack and refrigerate, uncovered, for at least 30 minutes or up to 2 hours.

4. Set second wire rack in second rimmed baking sheet and line with triple layer of paper towels. Add peanut oil to large Dutch oven until it measures about 2 inches deep and heat over medium-high heat to 325 degrees. Add half of chicken

Don't sweat the saucy stuff: The garlicky herb butter is what takes this chicken over the top.

to hot oil and fry until breasts register 160 degrees and drumsticks/thighs register 175 degrees, 13 to 16 minutes. Adjust burner, if necessary, to maintain oil temperature between 300 and 325 degrees. Transfer to paper towel–lined rack, return oil to 325 degrees, and repeat with remaining chicken.

5. FOR THE GARLIC BUTTER: While chicken rests, combine 7 tablespoons butter, parsley, salt, and pepper in bowl; set aside. Melt remaining 1 tablespoon butter in 8-inch nonstick skillet over medium heat. Add garlic and water and cook, stirring frequently, until garlic is softened and fragrant, 1 to 2 minutes. Add hot garlic mixture to butter-parsley mixture and whisk until well combined.

6. Transfer chicken to platter and spoon garlic butter over top. Serve.

Basque Country Cooking—in California

It's a relentless, searingly sunny 103 degrees in Bakersfield, California, so when I enter the Pyrenees Cafe through its heavy, red door, my eyes need a moment to adjust. When they do, I turn left, where a long bar carries the length of the room. On the right, black leather booths sit beneath windows stubbornly shuttered to keep out the heat. Deeper in, the dining room opens up to reveal the first good clue that this is a gathering place for the city's Basque community: long communal tables where patrons sit elbow to elbow.

Though it might seem out of place, Basque food is as comfortable in California as any other cuisine. Immigrants from the Basque lands—primarily the Pyrenees Mountains separating Spain and France—flooded California during the Gold Rush in the mid-19th century; when gold proved elusive, they turned to agriculture and shepherding in and around Bakersfield, which boasts one

of the largest Basque populations in the United States.

A generous handful of Basque restaurants clusters around the Old Town Kern area, each offering takes on the garlicky, peppery, sharp, and soothing flavors of Basque cooking. The deep, earthy, vibrant fare, particularly that created by Pyrenees Cafe chef Gilbert Hernandez, stands firmly against the city's ever-present heat, which strikes like an uppercut from the wide, dusty streets.

After I finish off plates of garlic fried

chicken, Basque-style green beans, cabbage and bean soup dotted with spicy salsa, thin slices of pickled veal tongue, and a glass or two of the chilled house wine, Pyrenees Cafe owners Rod and Julie Crawford invite me to share in the customary Basque dessert: vanilla ice cream doused with red wine. Unusual, yes, but I can think of worse ways to end a meal. –BRYAN ROOF

▶ To see more from our trip to Bakersfield, go to CooksCountry.com/bakersfield.

Above: Pyrenees Cafe proprietor Rod Crawford. Below: Scoops of vanilla ice cream get an atypical but altogether delicious topping—red wine.

Basque Green Beans

To complement a platter of garlicky fried chicken, we turned to this sweet-savory side. BY BRYAN ROOF

IT'S HARD TO imagine a better side dish for garlic fried chicken than the Basque-style green beans served at the Pyrenees Cafe (see "On the Road").

The dish is built on green beans, of course, but finding the perfect texture for them was easier said than done. I wanted fully cooked beans but not mushy beans. I wanted fresh-looking beans but not raw (or even al dente) beans. Twelve minutes with a little liquid in a covered pot over medium heat was the answer.

A few tests showed me that water was better than too-savory chicken stock, and ¼ cup of water was the perfect amount to cook the green beans and leave behind just enough moisture for the right level of sauciness.

The add-ins were easy to settle on: Smoky bacon was a must for its meaty, savory character. Onions offered sweet earthiness, and green and red bell peppers added a bright fruitiness and vibrant color. Some chopped garlic and a cup of canned crushed tomatoes contributed depth, and a healthy dose of sherry vinegar finished it off with a sharp punch.

Bacon, onion, bell peppers, tomatoes, and garlic turn these beans into a memorable side dish.

BASQUE-STYLE GREEN BEANS
Serves 4 to 6

The green beans don't need to be cut into perfect 2-inch pieces; a little variety in length is fine. Red or white wine vinegar may be substituted for the sherry vinegar, if desired.

- 3 slices thick-cut bacon, cut crosswise ¾ inch thick
- 1 large onion, halved and sliced thin
- 1 red bell pepper, stemmed, seeded, and sliced into thin strips
- 1 green bell pepper, stemmed, seeded, and sliced into thin strips
  Salt and pepper
- 4 garlic cloves, sliced thin
- 1½ pounds green beans, trimmed and cut into 2-inch lengths
- ¼ cup water
- 1 cup canned crushed tomatoes
- 1 tablespoon sherry vinegar
  Extra-virgin olive oil

1. Cook bacon in Dutch oven over medium heat until rendered and crispy, 8 to 10 minutes. Add onion, bell peppers, and 1 teaspoon salt. Cover and cook, stirring occasionally, until vegetables are softened, about 7 minutes.

2. Add garlic and cook until fragrant, about 1 minute. Stir in green beans, water, and ½ teaspoon salt. Cover and cook until green beans are just tender, about 12 minutes, stirring occasionally.

3. Stir in tomatoes, cover, and cook until slightly thickened and green beans are fully tender, about 5 minutes. Off heat, stir in vinegar and ½ teaspoon pepper. Season with salt and pepper to taste. Serve, drizzled with oil.

Derby Biscuits

Starting with a recipe that dates back centuries, we came up with appetizer biscuits that are hard to beat. And beer cheese, too. BY MORGAN BOLLING

AMONG LEGENDARY SOUTHERN dishes (fried chicken, collard greens, grits—you know the list), beaten biscuits occupy a place of pride. Dating from before baking powder and baking soda were commercially available (see "Leaveners Through the Ages")—that's right, they are actually modern inventions—these biscuits required the cook to beat the dough as a way of leavening it. By hitting it with a mallet, a rolling pin, or the back of an axe, cooks were trapping air pockets in the tough dough. They were also developing gluten, a protein that trapped the air as the biscuits rose in the oven. The end result was a cross between a biscuit and a cracker, crunchy and firm on the exterior with a flaky, semisoft interior.

The bakers who continue to make beaten biscuits—which, given the work involved, is definitely a labor of love—claim that their simple flavor and sturdy texture make them an ideal vehicle for jam or ham. Intrigued, I decided to try my hand at making them. Not surprisingly, I found that many modern recipes had updated the process, using a stand mixer or food processor in place of hand beating. I decided to try both methods.

Hours and what felt like a full cardiovascular workout later, I gathered my tasters. It was easy to see why these hallowed biscuits had all but disappeared from contemporary cooking. Far from the flaky, buttery biscuits we're accustomed to, these were rock hard and dull.

But some biscuits had qualities we liked. They were pleasantly straightforward in their flavor and, apart from the beating, in their composition. Plus, their size made them ideal for eating as an appetizer with a slice of country ham or a bit of hot pepper jelly, and they were, for lack of a better word, adorable. It seemed well worth figuring out a way to keep these appealing qualities while improving both flavor and texture.

After identifying the qualities I wanted to maintain, I cobbled together a working recipe of flour, salt, water, and butter. Rather than beat the dough by hand, I turned to the food processor and gave it a 5-minute spin. I rolled out the dough, cut out small 2-inch biscuits, and baked them in a 350-degree oven, which is low for standard biscuits but common for beaten biscuits.

Unfortunately, this batch was still too dense. Had I processed it too long?

Tradition suggests serving these bite-size biscuits with country ham, beer cheese, and/or pepper jelly. We agree.

Not long enough? I ran through several technique tests, beating the dough for various times in the mixer, in the food processor, and again by hand for varying lengths. All failed. So I turned to chemistry, trading the beatings for baking powder. Just 2 teaspoons was enough to leaven the biscuits, making them notably suppler and much more tender than what we had sampled in early tests while keeping them pleasantly crunchy.

The 4 tablespoons of butter I was using felt quite lean, so I tried amounts varying from 6 to 12 tablespoons. Too much and the biscuits were too flaky to hold ham; too little and they were dry. Eight tablespoons was the sweet spot. Also, trading milk for the water yielded a more tender biscuit with a sweet, rich flavor, and a single tablespoon of sugar gave sweetness and added more crunch to the biscuits' exteriors.

For a final test, I pan-fried some country ham, split open the biscuits, and nestled the ham inside. What I had was not only charming in appearance but also delicious. While I could no longer claim these as beaten biscuits, they could certainly hold their own. And since ham biscuits are a very common treat at the Kentucky Derby, I decided to call my little gems Derby Biscuits in honor of their Southern heritage.

DERBY BISCUITS

Makes about 28 biscuits

Split a biscuit and fill it with country ham, beer cheese, or hot pepper jelly.

- 2½ cups (12½ ounces) all-purpose flour
- 1 tablespoon sugar
- 2 teaspoons baking powder
- 1 teaspoon salt
- 8 tablespoons unsalted butter, cut into ½-inch pieces and chilled
- 1 cup whole milk, chilled

1. Adjust oven rack to middle position and heat oven to 350 degrees. Line rimmed baking sheet with parchment paper. Pulse flour, sugar, baking powder, and salt in food processor until combined, about 3 pulses. Add butter and pulse until reduced to pea-size pieces, 10 to 12 pulses.

2. Transfer mixture to large bowl. Add milk and stir with rubber spatula until shaggy dough forms. Turn out dough onto heavily floured counter and knead until dough comes together fully and feels smooth, with few small butter flecks still visible, 8 to 10 turns.

3. Roll dough into 11-inch circle about ½ inch thick. Using 2-inch biscuit cutter dipped in flour, cut 22 to 23 rounds from dough. Reroll scraps once to similar thickness and cut out 5 to 6 more rounds to yield 28 biscuits. Space biscuits evenly on prepared baking sheet (7 rows of 4). Prick each biscuit 3 times with tines of fork.

4. Bake until tops are light golden brown, 27 to 30 minutes, rotating sheet halfway through baking. Let biscuits cool on sheet for 5 minutes, then transfer to wire rack. Serve warm or at room temperature.

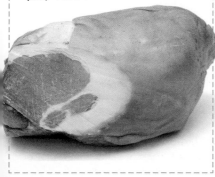
BEER CHEESE Makes about 2½ cups

This spread can also be served as a dip for crudités. Either white or yellow cheddar can be used.

- ½ cup mild lager, such as Budweiser
- 1 pound sharp or extra-sharp cheddar cheese, shredded (4 cups)
- ¼ cup finely chopped onion, rinsed and patted dry
- 2 tablespoons ketchup
- 1 tablespoon Dijon mustard
- 1 tablespoon Worcestershire sauce
- 1½ teaspoons hot sauce
- 1 garlic clove, minced

1. Bring beer to boil in small saucepan over high heat. Reduce heat to medium-low and simmer for 1 minute. Transfer to small bowl and let cool completely.

2. Process cheddar, onion, ketchup, mustard, Worcestershire, hot sauce, and garlic in food processor until smooth, about 1½ minutes. With processor running, slowly drizzle in beer and continue to process until very smooth, about 1 minute longer. Serve immediately, or transfer to bowl, cover with plastic wrap, and refrigerate until firm, about 2 hours.

Do Biscuit Cutters Really Matter?

Crafty home cooks punch out biscuits with old aluminum cans, overturned glasses, and even Mason jar rings. But using a makeshift cutter with rounded edges can compress the sides of dough, leading to misshapen biscuits. We prefer to use biscuit cutters, round cutting tools with sharp edges that make even cuts and thus produce tall, symmetrical biscuits. We tried eight sets, priced from $8.99 to $56.08, all containing between four and 11 different-size rings. We used the cutters on our buttery Derby Biscuits dough, our wetter Cream Biscuits dough, and our elastic Pierogi dough.

Though we tried every cutter in each set, most biscuit recipes call for a 2-, 2½-, or 3-inch biscuit cutter. Oddly, none of the sets in our lineup hit these sizes on the mark when we measured them ourselves, but as long as they came close (within ⅛ inch), we didn't dock them points. One smaller set missed the 3-inch mark by ¼ inch, making pierogi that were far too small and overstuffed—a definite problem.

Sticking wasn't an issue; all the cutters easily relinquished the doughs, especially when we dipped the ring in flour before cutting (as we usually call for in our recipes). Cutting integrity was a bigger concern, especially when working with elastic, stretchy pierogi dough and wet cream biscuits. Flimsier cutters made from thin, malleable metal or plastic easily warped under the pressure of our hands, making lopsided, misshapen biscuits and pierogi. Two sets with handles initially seemed like they'd give us a sturdier grip, but the handles forced testers to grip the cutter with a closed fist, limiting our range of motion and leaving us struggling to turn the cutter in the dough. Double-sided cutters were also out: Their sharp edges pushed painfully into our fingers as we used them. We preferred single-sided sets made from thicker metal or strong plastic, which allowed us to apply sturdy, even pressure for perfectly round biscuits.

Durability proved a high hurdle for some cutters. After just three rounds in the dishwasher, one set's handles broke off. Another set that was made from tin rusted. Our favorite sets were made from stainless steel or tough, durable plastic. In the end, we returned to our old standby, the Ateco 5357 11-Piece Plain Round Cutter Set ($14.95), which is made from tough stainless steel and didn't warp or rust. This set comes with 11 sizes (a bit of overkill, perhaps) nested in a handy storage case and produced biscuits that were tall, even, and perfectly round. Read the full story and see the complete testing chart at **CooksCountry.com/may16**. –LAUREN SAVOIE

HIGHLY RECOMMENDED

	CRITERIA		TESTERS' NOTES
ATECO 5357 11-Piece Plain Round Cutter Set **Model:** 5357 **Price:** $14.95 **Material:** Stainless steel **Number of Cutters:** 11	Usefulness Cutting Handling Durability	★★★ ★★★ ★★★ ★★★	Our old favorite, these stainless-steel cutters once again impressed testers with their crisp, sharp edges and durability. Biscuits made with these cutters were tall and pristine, and the cutters stood up to multiple washes without warping or rusting.

Bottom Round Roast Beef

This economical cut of roast beef had a bad reputation in the test kitchen. We wanted to give it another chance. BY ASHLEY MOORE

PITY THE POOR bottom round roast. Over the years, many cooks (including some of us in the test kitchen) have decried the cut, sometimes called rump roast, as unfit to serve as a special centerpiece—too tough, too liver-y, nothing at all like a tender, melty rib roast or eye round. But I wanted to find a way to serve this less-expensive cut from the usually tough rear leg as the main event—and not to have to apologize for it.

Several years ago, the test kitchen developed a recipe for Slow-Roasted Beef that produced tender meat. To get it, we salted an eye round and set it aside for 18 to 24 hours before searing it in a skillet to jump-start a brown crust. We then slid it into a very low (225-degree) oven for a couple of hours and then turned off the heat, allowing the meat to finish cooking in the cooling oven. This low-and-slow method produced a tender, sliceable eye-round roast. I tried this method with a bottom round roast just to get a baseline for testing and found, much to my surprise, that it wasn't half bad—relatively tender with good beefy flavor. Still, it was a bit difficult to slice evenly and, more important, thinly. I wanted to solve this problem and, while I was at it, dress up the roast with some fresh herbs and streamline the hands-on part of the process.

Cooking this roast to medium makes it much easier to slice paper-thin.

We often sear roasts on the stovetop to build a flavorful exterior before transferring them to the oven. But because I'd be adhering fresh herbs to the surface of the meat, I wondered if I could skip the searing step. After a few tests, I determined that searing the meat first added only a faint note of flavor, which was difficult to pick up among the rosemary and thyme.

We rarely recommend cooking a roast to medium, but after roasting many pounds of bottom round, I found that taking it to medium made a huge difference in my ability to slice it thin, which tasters determined was essential for a tender slice of meat on the plate. I set the oven to 250 degrees and roasted my herb-covered beef to an internal temperature of 120 degrees, which took about 2 hours. I then switched off the oven but left the roast inside until its interior reached 135 degrees, another 20 to 30 minutes. After letting it rest, I had a beautiful, flavorful roast that was easy to slice and looked much more elegant than any of us had expected.

With such a great roast, why not give it a great sauce? After trying several, I landed on a homemade version of herby, flavorful Zip Sauce, a favorite Detroit-area condiment. Our version lives up to the name—it comes together quickly by melting butter in a saucepan and then stirring in Worcestershire sauce, rosemary, thyme, garlic, salt, and pepper; once it comes to a simmer, it's done.

BOTTOM ROUND ROAST BEEF WITH ZIP-STYLE SAUCE Serves 8

We recommend cooking this roast to medium for ease of slicing. Open the oven door as little as possible, and remove the roast from the oven when taking its temperature to prevent dropping the oven temperature too drastically. Because the sauce contains butter, it will solidify as it cools, so it's best kept warm for serving.

BEEF
- 1 (4-pound) boneless beef bottom round roast, trimmed
  Kosher salt and pepper
- 1 tablespoon minced fresh rosemary
- 1 tablespoon minced fresh thyme
- 2 tablespoons vegetable oil

ZIP-STYLE SAUCE
- 8 tablespoons unsalted butter
- ½ cup Worcestershire sauce
- 2 garlic cloves, minced
- 2 teaspoons minced fresh rosemary
- 1 teaspoon minced fresh thyme
- ½ teaspoon kosher salt
- ½ teaspoon pepper

1. FOR THE BEEF: Pat roast dry with paper towels and sprinkle with 2 teaspoons salt. Wrap in plastic wrap and refrigerate for at least 1 hour or up to 24 hours.

2. Adjust oven rack to middle position and heat oven to 250 degrees. Set wire rack in rimmed baking sheet. Combine rosemary, thyme, 2 teaspoons pepper, and 1 teaspoon salt in bowl.

3. Pat roast dry with paper towels. Brush roast all over with oil and sprinkle with herb mixture; place on prepared wire rack. Transfer to oven and cook until meat registers 120 degrees, 1¾ hours to 2¼ hours. Turn off oven and leave roast in oven, without opening door, until meat registers 135 degrees (for medium), 20 to 30 minutes longer. Transfer roast to carving board, tent with aluminum foil, and let rest for 30 minutes.

4. FOR THE ZIP-STYLE SAUCE: Meanwhile, bring butter, Worcestershire, garlic, rosemary, thyme, salt, and pepper to bare simmer in small saucepan over medium heat, whisking constantly. Remove from heat, cover, and keep warm.

5. Slice roast thin against grain and serve with sauce.

Mashed Potato Cakes

Sure, mashed potatoes are good enough. But we never stop at good enough. BY ASHLEY MOORE

MASHED POTATO CAKES—DISKS of soft, fluffy mashed potato coated in bread crumbs and fried up crunchy—are equally welcome at suppertime next to a piece of meat or at breakfast under a poached egg. Thrifty home cooks have long considered them an excellent endgame for leftover mashers. But after testing a handful of existing recipes for this many-textured treat, I found a process riddled with potholes.

Several recipes I tested gave me cakes that were mushy and wet and difficult to form into disks. They refused to hold their shape in the pan. Why? Most of the recipes started with leftover mashed potatoes, so there was quite a lot of dairy (cream and butter) already in the mix, which made it tricky to shape and cook the cakes.

But one promising recipe gave me cakes that were more structurally sound than the rest. The difference? It started with uncooked potatoes and used much less liquid. There were flavor problems, but this recipe showed me that I could get better results if I started with a drier mash. The potato was easier to work with and held its shape much better in the pan and on the plate.

But what kind of potatoes? To find out, I auditioned Yukon Gold, Red Bliss, and russet potatoes. Russets held their shape the best while maintaining soft, fluffy middles.

Eggs proved to be the key for breadcrumb adhesion (dipping the potato rounds in beaten egg before pressing on the panko gave the crumbs a little

something extra to hold on to) and helped with flavor, too (mashing the potatoes with an additional yolk added richness). But I wanted more flavor. I reached for Parmesan, that crowd-pleasing flavor powerhouse. I added it, along with some chopped chives, to the potatoes before mashing them.

One final trick sealed the deal: I found that chilling the mashed potatoes in the fridge for an hour made shaping perfect disks much easier. It wasn't fun to wait, but it made a big difference.

To punctuate the cakes with a touch of tanginess, I served them with a dollop of sour cream.

MASHED POTATO CAKES
Serves 4 to 6

Using two spatulas to flip the cakes helps prevent splattering. We like to change the oil after frying the first batch of cakes because any dark panko remnants left behind will freckle the second batch. You can strain the oil through a fine-mesh strainer if you prefer to reuse it, but be careful because it is very hot. Plan ahead: The cooked mashed potatoes need to chill in the refrigerator for 1 hour, which makes it easier to form the cakes.

- 2½ pounds russet potatoes, peeled, halved lengthwise, and sliced ¼ inch thick
- Salt and pepper
- 1 ounce Parmesan cheese, grated (½ cup)
- ¼ cup chopped fresh chives
- 1 large egg yolk plus 2 large eggs
- 2 cups panko bread crumbs
- 1 cup vegetable oil
- Sour cream

1. Place potatoes in medium saucepan and add water to cover by 1 inch, then stir in 1 tablespoon salt. Bring to boil over high heat. Reduce heat to medium-low and simmer until tip of paring knife inserted into potatoes meets no resistance, 8 to 10 minutes. Drain potatoes and return to saucepan; let cool for 5 minutes.

2. Add Parmesan, chives, egg yolk, ¾ teaspoon salt, and ¼ teaspoon pepper to cooled potatoes. Using potato masher, mash until smooth and well combined. Transfer potato mixture to bowl and refrigerate until completely cool, about 1 hour.

3. Beat remaining 2 eggs together in

shallow dish. Place panko in second shallow dish. Divide potato mixture into 8 equal portions (about ½ cup each) and shape into 3-inch-diameter cakes, about ¾ inch thick. Working with 1 cake at a time, carefully dip cakes in egg mixture, turning to coat both sides and allowing excess to drip off; then coat with panko, pressing gently to adhere. Transfer to plate and let sit for 5 minutes.

4. Line large plate with paper towels. Heat ½ cup oil in 12-inch nonstick skillet over medium-high heat until shimmering. Place 4 cakes in skillet and cook until deep golden brown on first side, about 3 minutes. Using 2 spatulas, carefully flip cakes and continue to cook until deep golden brown on second side, about 2 minutes longer, gently pressing

on cakes with spatula for even browning.

5. Transfer cakes to prepared plate. Discard oil and wipe out skillet with paper towels. Repeat with remaining ½ cup oil and remaining 4 cakes. Serve with sour cream.

BLUE CHEESE AND BACON MASHED POTATO CAKES

Substitute ¾ cup crumbled blue cheese for Parmesan. Stir 6 slices cooked chopped bacon into potato mixture after mashing in step 2.

CHEDDAR AND SCALLION MASHED POTATO CAKES

Substitute 1 cup shredded sharp cheddar cheese for Parmesan and sliced scallions for chives.

TEST KITCHEN TECHNIQUE
Easy Does It

To avoid splattering the hot oil, use two spatulas to carefully flip the cakes.

A bit of beaten egg helps the crunchy bread coating adhere to these soft, creamy potato disks.

Fluffy Polenta with Red Sauce

Without knowing his secrets, could we re-create a seasoned veteran's unique Italian American dish of smooth, creamy, but light polenta in a simple red sauce? BY KATIE LEAIRD

A S I DROVE into Cranston, Rhode Island, the lines in the center of the road changed from yellow to green, white, and red—an homage to the Italian flag. I suspected that following a road literally paved with Italian American pride would lead to excellent food. What I didn't know was that I'd find culinary treasure in a VFW (Veterans of Foreign Wars) dining hall.

Mike Lepizzera has run Mike's Kitchen out of the Tabor-Franchi VFW Post for more than three decades. The restaurant is open for lunch and dinner, except during VFW meetings. There are 125 seats scattered around Formica tables, and the place is so popular that a line of eager diners wraps around the building at peak hours. A large chalkboard posted on the wood-paneled wall between military memorabilia and fading photos of soldiers serves as the menu. Sole Francaise, Gnocchi Sorrentino, Broccoli Rabe, Stuffed Squid . . . I wanted one of each.

I settled into a seat and watched as a waitress wove through the crowded restaurant, doling out dozens of hellos, hugs, and kisses to regular customers on the way to my table. When she arrived, I inquired about the fluffy polenta and red sauce. Was it a side dish? No, she assured me. It's big enough for a meal.

A few minutes later, a 4-inch by 4-inch brick of golden polenta, swimming and smothered in a velvety red sauce, arrived at my table. It was light, airy, intensely flavorful, and substantial—anything but a side. The sauce was smooth, salty, and, while too sweet for my taste when I spooned some directly into my mouth, truly just right when combined with the cheesy polenta.

When I came back to the test kitchen to re-create this dish, I was stumped as to how to get the unique texture of that polenta. I had stealthily asked the waitress if the dish had any eggs in it, confident that this might be Lepizzera's secret ingredient, but her confused shake of the head confirmed that this was not a soufflé. How did he get the polenta so light and fluffy?

Based on the perfectly squared-off profile of the polenta on my plate, it was clear that the slice had been cut out of a larger tray of polenta. It must have had time to set up, probably in the cool environment of a refrigerator, transforming from a creamy porridge to something

For perfect blocks of polenta, we cook it, chill it in a baking pan, and then slice it into rectangles to reheat and lightly brown in the oven.

more solid. Once set, I assumed the cooks would reheat one portion at a time to order. I tried applying this technique to several basic polenta recipes using rich half-and-half. It was not a turn-key solution. Some tests yielded polenta that was too soft, either from too much liquid or too much fat, which just turned into a goopy mess when sliced and baked. Others set up into dense bricks. I needed polenta that

would hold its shape but still stay light.

I started by swapping out the half-and-half for a smaller amount of water, which was easier to control. I also added garlic-infused olive oil and a fair amount of butter. The flavor was much better; it seemed that the dairy had been muting the flavor of the polenta and weighing it down, while the switch to water allowed its corn flavor to stand out while keeping the texture light, not dense. Stirring in a

small amount of half-and-half at the end reintroduced just enough richness.

With that settled, I was ready to start adding cheese. Pecorino Romano, easily identifiable in Lepizzera's polenta, was the obvious choice. While wary that adding too much would weigh down the final product, I was happily surprised to find that I could add 3 ounces (1½ cups) of grated cheese to create a robust flavor without compromising the light and fluffy texture. The cheese also helped fortify the polenta so that once it chilled in an 8-inch square pan, I could slice it neatly into blocks before returning it to the oven to warm through and take on a bit of browning at the edges.

A simple tomato sauce, cooked with a halved onion for just a hint of sharpness and bolstered with a bit of sugar to amplify the polenta's slightly sweet corn flavor (and to mimic Lepizzera's sweeter sauce), plus some grated Pecorino Romano cheese completed the dish.

FLUFFY BAKED POLENTA WITH RED SAUCE Serves 6
We developed this recipe using Quaker Yellow Corn Meal for its desirable texture and relatively short cooking time. We recommend you use the same product for this recipe. The timing may be different for other types of cornmeal, so be sure to cook the polenta until it is thickened and tender. Whole milk can be substituted for the half-and-half. Plan ahead: The polenta needs to be cooled for at least 3 hours before being cut, baked, and served.

POLENTA
- 4 tablespoons unsalted butter
- 2 tablespoons extra-virgin olive oil
- 2 garlic cloves, smashed and peeled
- 7 cups water
- 1½ teaspoons salt
- ½ teaspoon pepper
- 1½ cups cornmeal
- 3 ounces Pecorino Romano cheese, grated (1½ cups)
- ¼ cup half-and-half

RED SAUCE
- 1 (14.5-ounce) can whole peeled tomatoes
- ¼ cup extra-virgin olive oil
- 1 onion, peeled and halved through root end
- 1 (15-ounce) can tomato sauce
- 1 ounce Pecorino Romano cheese, grated (½ cup)
- 1½ tablespoons sugar
- ¾ teaspoon salt
- ½ teaspoon garlic powder

1. FOR THE POLENTA: Lightly grease 8-inch square baking pan. Heat butter and oil in Dutch oven over medium heat until butter is melted. Add garlic and cook until lightly golden, about 4 minutes. Discard garlic.

2. Add water, salt, and pepper to butter mixture. Increase heat to medium-high and bring to boil. Add cornmeal in slow, steady stream, whisking constantly. Reduce heat to medium-low and continue to cook, whisking frequently and scraping sides and bottom of pot, until mixture is

On the Road
Cranston, RI
As you drive into town, the lines in the center of the road give a not-so-subtle hint as to the Italian heritage of many of the residents. To learn more, go to CooksCountry.com/vfw.

thick and cornmeal is tender, about 20 minutes.

3. Off heat, whisk in Pecorino and half-and-half. Transfer to prepared pan and let cool completely on wire rack. Once cooled, cover with plastic wrap and refrigerate until completely chilled, at least 3 hours.

4. FOR THE RED SAUCE: Process tomatoes and their juice in blender until smooth, about 30 seconds. Heat 1 tablespoon oil in large saucepan over medium heat until shimmering. Add onion, cut side down, and cook without moving until lightly browned, about 4 minutes. Add pureed tomatoes, tomato sauce, Pecorino, sugar, salt, garlic powder, and remaining 3 tablespoons oil. Bring mixture to boil, reduce heat to medium-low, and simmer until sauce is slightly thickened, about 15 minutes. Remove from heat, discard onion, cover, and keep warm.

5. Adjust oven rack to middle position and heat oven to 375 degrees. Line rimmed baking sheet with parchment paper, then grease parchment. Cut chilled polenta into 6 equal pieces (about 4 by 2⅔ inches each). Place on prepared sheet and bake until heated through and beginning to brown on bottom, about 30 minutes. Serve each portion covered with about ½ cup red sauce.

Asparagus Salad

Raw asparagus? It may sound strange, but it makes a memorable salad. BY MORGAN BOLLING

GRILLED OR ROASTED asparagus, perfectly tender and browned, is definitely hard to beat. But raw asparagus is equally delicious, mildly sweet and nutty, with a delicate crunch and none of the sulfurous flavors that cooked asparagus sometimes has.

Many recipes call for cut-up lengths of asparagus, but even when I painstakingly peeled the spears, I found these too fibrous. After experimenting, I found that as long as I chose the right spears (bright green, firm, and crisp, with tightly closed tips) and sliced them very thinly on the bias, I could avoid woodiness but still keep things crunchy. This technique worked best with thicker spears, a welcome discovery because they're available year-round.

To complement the fresh asparagus, I wanted an herby dressing. A basil-based vinaigrette reminded me too much of classic pesto, so I turned to mint, keeping basil as a supporting player. I used a high ratio of herbs to oil to create a pesto-style dressing potent enough to enhance but not cover the flavor of the asparagus. A food processor made it easy to chop the herbs along with Pecorino Romano, garlic, lemon, and seasonings before stirring in extra-virgin olive oil.

A few radishes, more Pecorino, and buttery croutons round out the salad.

ASPARAGUS SALAD WITH RADISHES, PECORINO ROMANO, AND CROUTONS
Serves 4 to 6
Parmesan can be substituted for the Pecorino Romano. Grate the cheese for the pesto with a rasp-style grater or use the small holes of a box grater; shave the cheese for the salad with a vegetable peeler. For easier slicing, select large asparagus spears, about ½ inch thick.

CROUTONS
- 2 tablespoons unsalted butter
- 1 tablespoon extra-virgin olive oil
- 2 slices hearty white sandwich bread, crusts discarded, cut into ½-inch cubes (1⅓ cups)
- Salt and pepper

Thinly sliced spears are crunchy, not woody.

PESTO
- 2 cups fresh mint leaves
- ¼ cup fresh basil leaves
- ¼ cup grated Pecorino Romano cheese
- 1 teaspoon grated lemon zest plus 2 teaspoons juice
- 1 garlic clove, minced
- Salt and pepper
- ½ cup extra-virgin olive oil

SALAD
- 2 pounds asparagus, trimmed
- 5 radishes, trimmed and sliced thin
- 2 ounces Pecorino Romano cheese, shaved (¾ cup)
- Salt and pepper

1. FOR THE CROUTONS: Heat butter and oil in 12-inch nonstick skillet over medium heat until butter is melted. Add bread cubes and ⅛ teaspoon salt and cook, stirring frequently, until golden brown, 7 to 10 minutes. Transfer croutons to paper towel–lined plate. Season with salt and pepper to taste.

2. FOR THE PESTO: Process mint, basil, Pecorino, lemon zest and juice, garlic, and ¾ teaspoon salt in food processor until finely chopped, about 20 seconds, scraping down bowl as needed. Transfer to large bowl. Stir in oil until combined and season with salt and pepper to taste.

3. FOR THE SALAD: Cut asparagus tips from stalks into ¾-inch-long pieces. Slice asparagus stalks ⅛ inch thick on bias into approximate 2-inch lengths. Add asparagus tips and stalks, radishes, and Pecorino to pesto and toss to combine. Season with salt and pepper to taste. Transfer salad to platter and top with croutons. Serve.

For two more asparagus salad recipes, go to CooksCountry.com/may16.

Dublin Coddle

There is no dish more comforting than this savory Irish American classic—
if you can get all of its parts to work together. BY CECELIA JENKINS

IT'S LATE, IT'S cold out, and you've just returned home from, say, a long day of work, or perhaps a long night out with friends. All you want is a warm, comforting dish of something. Enter savory, simple Dublin coddle, proof positive that the Irish, both at home and abroad, know their way around rich, restorative meals.

Similar to Irish stew, that famous dish based on lamb and cabbage, coddle instead combines pork sausage, bacon, onions, potatoes, and stock—and rather than stew it all together, it's layered and cooked (or coddled) into a finished dish that's much more than the sum of its parts. Or at least it should be; in my initial research into this dish, I found recipes that boiled the ingredients for hours on end, resulting in a mushy mess of barely identifiable starch-saddled meats. I wanted a flavorful version of this rustic dish that kept its elements intact.

Back in the old country, coddle is built on Irish bangers, a sausage of pork, bread crumbs, and various seasonings. We loved traditional bangers in this dish—but, recognizing that they aren't available in most grocery stores, we developed our version with bratwurst, a more commonly available sausage.

Most recipes I found didn't call for browning any of the meats before simmering them, but I knew I could make

Crisped bacon pieces sprinkled over the top give this simple supper extra crunch.

major inroads into flavor depth by adding a browning step up front. Tests proved this to be true, and further tests helped me nail down the exact process: I cooked 2-inch pieces of thick-cut bacon to render its fat. I set aside these crispy pieces while I browned the sausages and onions in some reserved bacon fat, which not only added flavor to the parts but also left flavorful browned bits, or fond, in the pan. Scraping this fond into chicken stock meant none of it went to waste.

Potatoes are generally a tricky component of braises like this one, as they always seem to take longer to cook than the other components. I twisted myself into pretzels coming up with easy ways to precook the potatoes—microwaving

them, boiling them, roasting them—but ultimately found that I didn't need to. Instead, I cut potatoes into disks (we chose Yukon Golds for their superior flavor), arranged them in the bottom of a baking dish, and covered them with the cooked onions and the fond-bolstered cooking liquid. I then piled the sausages on top and slid the dish into a 350-degree oven. After 45 minutes, the sausages were on the verge of overdone, but the potatoes were still underdone. The fix was simple: I lowered the oven temperature to 325 and cooked the dish for an hour and a quarter, gently coddling the potatoes to a soft, creamy texture.

My coddle was full of flavor, but some testers wanted just a little bit

of brightness. Cider vinegar was the answer: Just 2 tablespoons added to the broth helped cut through the fatty richness, and a final sprinkle of chopped parsley and the reserved bacon finished it off.

DUBLIN CODDLE Serves 4 to 6

An equal weight of traditional Irish bangers can be substituted for the bratwurst. We prefer to use Farmland Thick Sliced Bacon. Serve with crusty bread to soak up the sauce.

- 1¾ **pounds Yukon Gold potatoes, peeled and sliced ¼ inch thick**
  Salt and pepper
- 4 **slices thick-cut bacon, cut into 1-inch pieces**
- 1¼ **pounds bratwurst**
- 2 **onions, sliced into ½-inch-thick rings**
- 1 **tablespoon minced fresh thyme**
- 1¾ **cups chicken broth**
- 2 **tablespoons cider vinegar**
- 2 **tablespoons minced fresh parsley**

1. Adjust oven rack to lower-middle position and heat oven to 325 degrees. Shingle potato slices in bottom of 13 by 9-inch baking dish. Sprinkle with ½ teaspoon salt and ¼ teaspoon pepper; set aside.

2. Cook bacon in 12-inch skillet over medium heat until crispy, 12 to 14 minutes. Using slotted spoon, transfer bacon to paper towel–lined plate.

3. Carefully add sausages to now-empty skillet and cook until lightly browned on tops and bottoms, about 5 minutes. Transfer to paper towel–lined plate.

4. Pour off all but 2 tablespoons fat from skillet and return to medium heat. Add onions, thyme, ½ teaspoon salt, and ½ teaspoon pepper. Cover and cook until onions are softened, 7 to 9 minutes, stirring occasionally and scraping up any browned bits.

5. Add broth and vinegar, scraping up any browned bits, and bring to simmer. Carefully pour onion mixture over potatoes, spreading onions into even layer.

6. Place sausages, browned side up, on top of onions. Transfer to oven and bake until paring knife inserted into potatoes meets little resistance, about 1¼ hours.

7. Remove from oven and let cool for 10 minutes. Sprinkle with parsley and reserved bacon. Serve.

Pecan-Crusted Trout

Our relationship with pecan-crusted fish turned out to be surprisingly one-sided.

BY CHRISTIE MORRISON

PECAN-CRUSTED FISH IS a commonplace item across the American South, where pecans are plentiful and fish like catfish, whiting, and trout are both economical and easy to find. In restaurants, you're likely to encounter a deep-fried version, but to make this easy, multitextured dish at home, I grabbed a nonstick skillet and got ready to pan-fry.

I combed through recipes to find a coating that combined great nut flavor with the perfect crunch. I quickly eliminated those that included only chopped pecans as the crust. Not only did the nuts adhere poorly to the fish, but the coating had a pebbly texture that was unappealing. More promising versions included panko, which added interesting texture and provided better cohesion. My tasters agreed, however, that the higher the ratio of crumbs to chopped pecans, the less they liked the coating. The perfect ratio was just ¼ cup of crumbs for each cup of nuts.

To make short work of chopping, I used the food processor, which pulverized the nuts to a uniform texture. I tried adding the panko to the nuts during chopping and found that the crumbs absorbed some fat and moisture from the nuts, which helped build a more cohesive coating. All it needed was a teaspoon of lemon zest, a bit of cayenne, and some salt and pepper.

I put my coating to the test with lean, mild fish—sole, snapper, flounder, cod, catfish, and trout. Of the bunch, catfish and trout were the top candidates—easy to find (and not just in the South) and sturdy enough to stand up to pan frying (and flipping) without falling apart. Trout worked especially well: Its thin, even fillets cooked in perfect time with the nuts, and its thin skin (boneless, butterflied trout is sold with the skin on) helped it withstand being dunked in egg, coated, and fried without tearing.

My tasters loved the flavor and texture of the trout so much that they complained about the nut crust overwhelming the fish. Up to that point, I had been coating both sides of the fish. For my next test, I coated just the flesh side. The resulting flavor was much more balanced, and I no longer needed to worry about the bottom crusts of the first batch getting soggy while I made the second batch.

The fish was flavorful on its own, but I thought an easy sauce would round out the dish. Traditional tartar sauce and remoulade were too potent. Instead, I mixed lemon zest, lemon juice, parsley, and a little garlic into prepared mayonnaise. The bright, creamy sauce balanced the richness of the pecans with minimal effort.

PECAN-CRUSTED TROUT WITH CREAMY LEMON-GARLIC SAUCE
Serves 4

Only the flesh side of the trout gets coated with the pecan mixture. Note that the lemon zest is divided. If you store your pecans in the freezer, let them come to room temperature before processing for best results.

- ½ cup mayonnaise
- 1 tablespoon minced fresh parsley
- 1½ teaspoons grated lemon zest plus 2 teaspoons juice
- 1 small garlic clove, minced
- 1 cup pecans
- ¼ cup panko bread crumbs
  Salt and pepper
- ⅛ teaspoon cayenne pepper
- 1 large egg
- 1 teaspoon Dijon mustard
- 3 (8- to 10-ounce) headless, boneless, butterflied whole trout
- ¼ cup vegetable oil

1. Combine mayonnaise, parsley, ½ teaspoon lemon zest, lemon juice, and garlic in bowl. Chill until ready to serve. (Sauce can be refrigerated for up to 3 days.)

2. Process pecans and panko in food processor until pecans are finely chopped and mixture resembles coarse meal, 10 to 12 pulses. Transfer to shallow dish. Stir in ½ teaspoon salt, ½ teaspoon pepper, cayenne, and remaining 1 teaspoon lemon zest. Whisk egg, mustard, ¼ teaspoon salt, and ¼ teaspoon pepper together in second shallow dish.

3. Adjust oven rack to middle position and heat oven to 200 degrees. Place wire rack inside rimmed baking sheet. Cut each trout in half lengthwise along natural seam between fillets to yield 2 fillets (you should have 6 fillets in total). Pat trout dry with paper towels and season with salt and pepper.

4. Working with 1 fillet at a time, dredge flesh side of trout in egg mixture, allowing excess to drip off. Dip egg-coated side of trout in pecan mixture, pressing gently to adhere. Transfer trout, pecan side up, to large plate and repeat with remaining fillets.

5. Heat 2 tablespoons oil in 12-inch nonstick skillet over medium heat until shimmering. Place 3 fillets in skillet, pecan side down and in alternating directions to fit. Cook until pecan coating is browned and fragrant, 3 to 4 minutes. Using 2 thin spatulas, carefully flip fillets. Continue to cook until skin is browned and trout flakes easily with fork, 2 to 3 minutes longer. Transfer trout, pecan side up, to wire rack and keep warm in oven.

6. Wipe skillet clean with paper towels. Repeat with remaining 2 tablespoons oil and remaining 3 fillets. Serve with lemon-garlic sauce.

Many recipes call for catfish, but we preferred the cleaner, fresher flavor of trout.

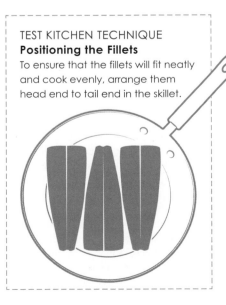

TEST KITCHEN TECHNIQUE
Positioning the Fillets
To ensure that the fillets will fit neatly and cook evenly, arrange them head end to tail end in the skillet.

Chiles Rellenos

Forget the soggy, gloppy versions you've had. This restaurant favorite can be a fresh, vibrant revelation, if you're willing to do a little work. BY MORGAN BOLLING

WHEN I VISIT a Mexican restaurant, I rarely order chiles rellenos (cheese-stuffed chiles). Too many times I've been burned by an overloaded plate of soggy poblanos drowning in canned sauce and gloppy cheese. This saddens me; for as much work as this dish requires (roasting, peeling, seeding, stuffing, battering, and frying chiles, for starters), shouldn't the resulting dish be beautiful and satisfying rather than gloppy and overwrought?

I set out to rescue chiles rellenos with a home version that featured a delicate and crispy coating, a complex sauce, and comforting cheesiness. My first stop was our cookbook library, where I uncovered a handful of existing recipes. But 6 hours and five recipes later, I had little to show for my work other than a sink full of dishes and a stovetop covered in batter, sauce, and cheese. I realized I had quite a task ahead.

Most recipes call for precooking the poblano peppers to ensure that they're tender at the table, and this step proved essential. When I tried to skip it, I had rigid peppers that were difficult to stuff and tasted raw. Setting the peppers on a baking sheet and putting them under the broiler for a few minutes was the best route to peppers with a structure just soft enough to stuff and fry without going mushy. And while most recipes call for the peppers to be peeled after that precook, I found (after a long series of tests) that the peel was a nonissue; tasters didn't mind it at all. And there was an added benefit—leaving the skin on gave the peppers extra stability and made stuffing them easier.

I slit a 3-inch-long opening into the side of each broiled pepper and, using a pair of scissors, snipped out the interior seed bulb. I then used a soupspoon to scrape out any remaining seeds. My poblanos were now ready for cheese.

Recipes vary widely as to the type of cheese to use to fill the chiles, but after testing Monterey Jack, Muenster, and cheddar (and a few other types), my tasters voted for Muenster. The result surprised me, but my concern was assuaged by reading Diana Kennedy, a leading authority on Mexican cooking—soft, mellow, meltable Muenster is her choice of cheese, too.

But while Kennedy calls for long strips of cheese, I used cubes, which

To keep things crispy and light, we dial back just a bit on the cheese and drizzle, not drown, the chiles in sauce.

were easier to stuff into the peppers. I secured the stuffed chiles with wooden skewers and focused on the batter.

I tested an array of batters from the test kitchen arsenal—we have favorite coatings for everything from fried chicken to corn dogs. I settled on a light flour-and-beer-based batter that we use for frying pickles. It creates a light, crispy coating that enhances, rather than cloaks, what's inside.

With a few tweaks (including a prebatter dusting of flour to help the batter adhere), this batter coated the peppers just enough, and when fried in 3 quarts of 375-degree oil on the stovetop, it created a crispy, light, golden-brown coating in the 4 minutes it took for the cheesy interior to melt.

Now for a sauce. I wanted something quick and easy made from pantry staples.

A simple cooked mixture of chili powder, onion powder, granulated garlic, chicken broth, and tomato sauce, bolstered with a teaspoon of the smoky-rich sauce from a can of chipotles in adobo and brightened with lime juice, was just right.

A far cry from the dull and gloppy restaurant dishes I'd encountered in the past, my version was complex, delicate, refined, comforting, and easier than I imagined it would be.

KEY STEPS Making Chiles Rellenos

Before stuffing the poblanos, we broil them until they soften and then peel away any loose skin.

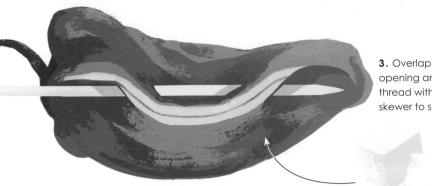

3. Overlap opening and thread with skewer to seal.

1. Cut 3-inch-long vertical slit in poblano, then cut out seed bulb with scissors. (Use spoon to scoop away remaining seeds.)

2. Place 2 cubes of Muenster cheese inside each poblano.

4. Working with 3 poblanos at a time, dredge in flour, shaking gently to remove excess.

5. Holding poblano by stem, dunk in batter to coat.

CHILES RELLENOS Serves 4 to 6

Use a Dutch oven that holds 6 quarts or more. You do not need to remove all of the chile seeds in step 3. Nonalcoholic lagers will also work in this recipe.

SAUCE
- 1 tablespoon vegetable oil
- 1 teaspoon chili powder
- ½ teaspoon onion powder
- ¼ teaspoon granulated garlic
- 1½ cups chicken broth
- 1 (15-ounce) can tomato sauce
- 1 teaspoon adobo sauce from canned chipotle chiles in adobo sauce
- 1 bay leaf
- 1 tablespoon lime juice
- Salt and pepper

CHILES
- 6 (4- to 5-ounce) poblano chiles
- 8 ounces Muenster cheese, cut into 12 (1-inch) cubes
- 6 (4-inch) wooden skewers
- 1½ cups (7½ ounces) all-purpose flour
- 1¼ cups (5 ounces) cornstarch
- 2 teaspoons baking powder
- Salt
- 1½ cups mild lager, such as Budweiser
- 3 quarts peanut or vegetable oil

1. FOR THE SAUCE: Heat oil in medium saucepan over medium-high heat until shimmering. Add chili powder, onion powder, and granulated garlic and cook until fragrant, about 30 seconds. Add broth, tomato sauce, adobo sauce, and bay leaf and bring to boil. Reduce heat to medium and cook at vigorous simmer until reduced to 2 cups, 12 to 15 minutes. Stir in lime juice and season with salt and pepper to taste. Remove from heat, cover, and keep warm. (Discard bay leaf before serving.)

2. FOR THE CHILES: Meanwhile, adjust oven rack 6 inches from broiler element and heat broiler. Line rimmed baking sheet with aluminum foil.

Evenly space poblanos on sheet and broil until skins just begin to blister on first side, 3 to 5 minutes. Flip poblanos and continue to broil until skins are just beginning to blister on second side, about 3 minutes longer. Let poblanos rest on sheet until cool enough to handle, about 10 minutes. Adjust oven temperature to 200 degrees.

3. Peel off any loose skin from poblanos, if desired. Working with 1 poblano at a time, leaving stem intact and starting at top, make 3-inch-long vertical incision down 1 side of chile. Use scissors to cut away interior seed bulb, then use spoon to scoop out and discard bulb and seeds. (Some tearing may occur and is OK.)

4. Place 2 Muenster cubes inside each poblano. Overlap poblano opening and thread with skewer to seal. (Use 1 additional skewer per poblano if necessary.) Allow top of skewer to remain exposed by at least ½ inch for easy removal.

5. Place ½ cup flour in shallow dish. Combine remaining 1 cup flour, cornstarch, baking powder, and 1 teaspoon salt in medium bowl. Whisk lager into flour mixture until smooth.

6. Set wire rack in rimmed baking sheet and line rack with triple layer of paper towels. Add oil to large Dutch oven until it measures 2 inches deep and heat over medium-high heat to 375 degrees.

7. Working with 3 poblanos at a time, dredge poblanos in flour, shaking gently to remove excess. Holding each poblano by its stem, dunk in batter to evenly coat and then transfer to hot oil. Fry until golden and crispy, 4 to 5 minutes, turning frequently for even cooking.

Adjust burner, if necessary, to maintain oil temperature between 350 and 375 degrees.

8. Transfer fried poblanos to prepared wire rack and let drain for 30 seconds. Season poblanos with salt, remove skewers, and transfer sheet to oven to keep poblanos warm. Return oil to 375 degrees and repeat with remaining poblanos and batter. Serve with sauce.

TO MAKE AHEAD

The poblanos can be broiled, seeded, and stuffed 24 hours in advance. The sauce can be made 2 days in advance and microwaved for 2 minutes until hot just before serving.

To see what else we ate in Texas, go to CooksCountry.com/sanantonio.

Taking the Fear Out of Frying

Deep frying doesn't have to be messy or unpredictable if you arm yourself with the right ingredients, tools, and techniques.

Peanut oil is best for deep frying.

Choose the Right Oil

Our top choice for deep frying is neutral-flavored peanut oil. Its high smoke point means it can withstand prolonged heating without breaking down. If you don't have peanut oil, use vegetable oil.

Use a Spider

With its long handle and shallow mesh basket, a wire skimmer, or spider, is the best tool for safely lifting food from oil.

TEST KITCHEN FAVORITE
WMF Profi Plus Skimmer

Monitor the Temperature

Maintaining the proper oil temperature is the key to good results: Oil that's too hot will scorch food; oil that's too cool will yield pale, greasy food. Use a clip-on deep-fry thermometer, and keep in mind that adding food to the pot will cause the temperature to drop. Finally, if the oil starts lightly smoking, remove the pot from the heat and let it cool to the proper temperature. (Oil that is heavily smoking will impart an acrid taste to food and should be discarded.)

TEST KITCHEN FAVORITE
ThermoWorks ChefAlarm

Recycle, Reuse

Unless you fried fish, don't throw away your oil; it's fine to reuse three or four more times. Filter used oil through cheesecloth or a coffee filter, and then store it in an airtight container in a cool, dark spot for up to one month. For longer storage, place the oil in the freezer.

Filter out impurities before storing oil for reuse.

Dispose of Used Oil Properly

Pour cooled oil into a sealable disposable container such as an orange juice jug, and then seal the lid and throw it away.

Getting to Know Coconut Products

While coconuts have been a sought-after food for centuries, today we consume their liquid and meat in a variety of forms. Here's a guide to what's what. BY CHRISTIE MORRISON

Sweetened Flaked Coconut
DESSERT MAKER

To make this light, fluffy, sweet product, coconut meat is boiled, grated, and then partially dried before being soaked in a liquid sugar solution and dried again. The soft, chewy texture helps give coconut macaroons their signature texture; we also use it to adorn our Raspberry Coconut Cloud Cake (**CooksCountry.com/coconutcloudcake**).

Dried Shredded Coconut
NAKED FLAVOR

Also known as desiccated coconut, unsweetened shredded coconut is raw coconut meat that has been boiled, grated, and dried. We preferred dried coconut to sweetened coconut in our French Coconut Pie (**CooksCountry.com/frenchcoconutpie**) so we could pack in extra coconut flavor without going into sugar shock. Our favorite is Now Real Food Organic Unsweetened Coconut.

Coconut Flakes
GRANOLA GO-TO

Coconut flakes (or flaked coconut) are a larger version of dried shredded coconut. Instead of being grated, boiled coconut meat is cut into substantial flakes that are then dried. The larger size makes them less suitable for incorporating into delicate cakes and cookies and better for garnishing salads, stirring into oatmeal, or eating out of hand.

Cream of Coconut
COCKTAIL MAKER

Do you like piña coladas? If so, you've probably already tasted this sweetened coconut product. Not to be confused with coconut cream—the heavy, rich layer of cream that rises to the top of coconut milk after it sits for a while—cream of coconut is a heavily sweetened, emulsified product used in desserts and cocktail mixes. We like it in baked goods like cookies and cakes.

Coconut Milk
CURRY'S COMPANION

This rich, creamy liquid is a staple in Indian and Southeast Asian cooking, where it is used to enrich curries, sauces, and sweets. Coconut milk is made by steeping shredded coconut meat in warm milk or water; the meat is mashed, and then the liquid is strained to ensure a smooth texture. Our taste-test winner is Chaokoh; try it in our Coconut Rice Pudding (**CooksCountry.com/coconutricepudding**).

Fresh Coconut
THE OTHER WHITE MEAT

You'll find two types of coconuts at the market: Young, green ones have more liquid and softer flesh; mature, brown coconuts have less liquid and firmer flesh that is often toasted to bring out its flavor. To access the meat and water inside a coconut, crack it open with a hammer or the back of a cleaver.

▶ See the full story, including information on coconut aminos, at **CooksCountry.com/coconutproducts**.

Coconut Oil
SO REFINED

Made by extracting oil from the meat of coconuts, coconut oil, which is solid at room temperature, comes in "refined" and "unrefined" (or "virgin") versions. We generally prefer to use refined coconut oil in cooking; its coconut flavor is less pronounced than unrefined, which makes it more versatile. It makes a good 1-to-1 substitute for butter or other oils in baking and sautéing.

Coconut Chips
TROPICAL SNACK

Since coconut is rich in natural sugar and oil, it makes a tasty snack when slices of it are baked or fried. Add them to trail mix or granola, or sprinkle them on a bowl of ice cream. Don't be fooled into thinking coconut chips are a low-cal snack, though, as coconut is high in sugar and saturated fats (and some brands of coconut chips have even more sugar added).

Coconut Water
GREEN GOODNESS

This mild, salty-sweet "juice" is the thin liquid harvested from green, immature coconuts (the water inside mature coconuts is less sweet and abundant). Tasters described its flavor as "floral." It has become a popular sports beverage because of its purported hydrating qualities (it contains sodium and potassium as well as some fat). Save it for drinking, not cooking.

Coconut Flour
BETTER BLENDED

Coconut flour is made from dried ground coconut meat. It has a noticeable coconut flavor when used on its own, but it can be used with other flours to provide a more neutral flavor. A popular alternative to wheat flour, it is high in starch and highly absorptive, so it can easily trap liquid during mixing and baking—another reason it's often blended with other flours. Store it in the refrigerator or freezer.

Coconut Sugar
FLOWER POWER

Coconut sugar is made from the sap of coconut palm flower buds rather than from coconuts. It contains less fructose than cane sugar but has a similar calorie count. Coconut sugar has a rich, brown color but is drier than brown sugar. Its caramel-like sweetness tastes nothing like coconut. Because of its large crystal size and moisture content, it cannot be substituted for other sugars.

PORK CUTLETS WITH ARTICHOKES AND GOAT CHEESE

**PAN-SEARED CHICKEN THIGHS
WITH POTATOES AND CHORIZO**

**BEEF TENDERLOIN WITH
CHILES, MINT, AND CUCUMBER**

SHIITAKE AND BOK CHOY LO MEIN

PAN-SEARED CHICKEN THIGHS WITH POTATOES AND CHORIZO Serves 4

✓ **WHY THIS RECIPE WORKS:** Using the rendered fat from the chicken thighs to fry the potatoes imparts great flavor and extra crispiness.

- 8 (5- to 7-ounce) bone-in chicken thighs
   Salt and pepper
- 1 tablespoon extra-virgin olive oil, plus extra for drizzling
- 1½ pounds Yukon Gold potatoes, unpeeled, cut into ½-inch chunks
- 4 ounces chorizo sausage, halved lengthwise and sliced thin crosswise
- 8 ounces (8 cups) baby spinach
   Smoked paprika

1. Adjust oven rack to middle position and heat oven to 375 degrees. Pat chicken dry with paper towels; season with salt and pepper. Heat oil in 12-inch nonstick skillet over medium-high heat until just smoking. Add chicken, skin side down, and cook until well browned, about 7 minutes. Transfer chicken, skin side up, to rimmed baking sheet and roast until meat registers 175 degrees, about 15 minutes.

2. Meanwhile, add potatoes to now-empty skillet and cook, covered, over medium heat until lightly browned, about 5 minutes. Add chorizo and cook, uncovered, until potatoes are tender, about 5 minutes longer. Add spinach and cook until just wilted and liquid has evaporated, about 2 minutes. Serve chicken with potato mixture, sprinkled with paprika.

TEST KITCHEN NOTE: There's no need to peel the potatoes for this dish.

PORK CUTLETS WITH ARTICHOKES AND GOAT CHEESE Serves 4

✓ **WHY THIS RECIPE WORKS:** Lemon and capers give sautéed artichoke hearts a fresh and lively note that pairs well with pork.

- 8 (3-ounce) pork cutlets
   Salt and pepper
- 3 tablespoons extra-virgin olive oil, plus extra for drizzling
- 18 ounces frozen artichoke hearts, thawed and patted dry
- 3 garlic cloves, sliced thin
- 2 tablespoons capers, rinsed and chopped
- 2 tablespoons lemon juice
- 1 tablespoon minced fresh chives
- 2 ounces goat cheese, crumbled (½ cup)

1. Pat pork dry with paper towels; season with salt and pepper. Heat 2 tablespoons oil in 12-inch nonstick skillet over medium-high heat until just smoking. Add half of cutlets and cook until well browned, about 2 minutes per side. Transfer to platter and tent with foil. Repeat with remaining cutlets.

2. Heat remaining 1 tablespoon oil in now-empty skillet over medium heat until shimmering. Add artichokes, 1 teaspoon salt, and ¼ teaspoon pepper and cook until browned, about 3 minutes. Stir in garlic and capers; cook until fragrant, about 30 seconds. Off heat, stir in lemon juice and chives. Serve cutlets with artichokes, sprinkled with goat cheese and drizzled with extra oil.

TEST KITCHEN NOTE: Trim the fat from the cutlets to prevent curling while cooking.

SHIITAKE AND BOK CHOY LO MEIN Serves 4

✓ **WHY THIS RECIPE WORKS:** Cooking the noodles without moving them lets them develop a light, flavorful char.

- 12 ounces fresh Chinese egg noodles
- 2 tablespoons vegetable oil
- 8 ounces shiitake mushrooms, stemmed, halved if small or quartered if large
- 4 heads baby bok choy (4 ounces each), halved and cut into 1-inch pieces
- 1 tablespoon grated fresh ginger
- 3 garlic cloves, minced
- 3 tablespoons hoisin sauce
- 2 tablespoons soy sauce
- 1 tablespoon sesame oil
- 1 teaspoon chili-garlic sauce

1. Bring 4 quarts water to boil in large pot over high heat. Add noodles to boiling water and cook until tender, about 3 minutes. Drain noodles and rinse under cold running water.

2. Heat 1 tablespoon vegetable oil in 12-inch nonstick skillet over medium-high heat until just smoking. Add mushrooms and cook until browned, about 5 minutes. Add bok choy, ginger, garlic, and remaining 1 tablespoon vegetable oil and cook until bok choy begins to soften, about 2 minutes.

3. Add hoisin, soy sauce, and cooked noodles. Stir to combine, then cook for 2 minutes without stirring to develop light char on noodles. Stir noodles again, then cook for 2 more minutes without stirring. Stir in sesame oil and chili-garlic sauce. Serve.

TEST KITCHEN NOTE: For a spicy kick, serve with additional chili-garlic sauce.

BEEF TENDERLOIN WITH CHILES, MINT, AND CUCUMBER Serves 4

✓ **WHY THIS RECIPE WORKS:** The tartness of the lime juice in the dressing is tempered by the salty fish sauce and the sugar's sweetness. We marinate the cucumbers and then use that flavorful marinade to sauce the sliced steaks.

- ¼ cup lime juice (2 limes)
- 3 tablespoons vegetable oil
- 2 tablespoons fish sauce
- 2 tablespoons minced fresh mint
- 1 tablespoon sugar
   Salt and pepper
- 1 seedless English cucumber, quartered lengthwise and sliced thin on bias
- 1 red jalapeño chile, stemmed, halved, seeded, and sliced thin
- 4 (6- to 8-ounce) center-cut filets mignons, 1½ inches thick, trimmed
- 2 heads Bibb lettuce, leaves separated

1. Whisk lime juice, 1 tablespoon oil, fish sauce, mint, sugar, and ½ teaspoon pepper together in bowl. Stir in cucumber and jalapeño; set aside.

2. Pat steaks dry with paper towels and season with salt and pepper. Heat remaining 2 tablespoons oil in 12-inch skillet over medium-high heat until just smoking. Cook steaks until well browned and meat registers 125 degrees (for medium-rare), about 5 minutes per side. Transfer to cutting board and tent with foil.

3. Arrange lettuce leaves on 4 individual plates. Using slotted spoon, divide cucumber mixture evenly among plates. Slice each steak into ½-inch-thick slices and arrange alongside salad. Spoon cucumber marinade evenly over salads and season with salt. Serve.

TEST KITCHEN NOTE: Garnish with chopped salted dry-roasted peanuts, if desired.

PASTRAMI CHEESEBURGERS

PEPPERED PORK CHOPS WITH CELERY ROOT SALAD

PAN-SEARED CHICKEN WITH SPICY PINTO BEANS

LEMONY SHRIMP WITH ORZO, FETA, AND OLIVES

PEPPERED PORK CHOPS WITH CELERY ROOT SALAD Serves 4

✔ **WHY THIS RECIPE WORKS:** Salty capers and a kick of cayenne in the celery root salad provide a nice contrast to the red pepper jelly–glazed pork.

- ½ cup mayonnaise
- 7 tablespoons cider vinegar
- 2 tablespoons capers, rinsed and minced
- 2 tablespoons whole-grain mustard
  Salt and pepper
- ⅛ teaspoon cayenne pepper
- 1 celery root (14 ounces), peeled, quartered, and shredded
- 4 (10-ounce) bone-in pork rib chops, about 1 inch thick, trimmed
- 1 tablespoon vegetable oil
- ½ cup red pepper jelly

1. Whisk mayonnaise, 1 tablespoon vinegar, capers, mustard, ½ teaspoon salt, ½ teaspoon pepper, and cayenne together in large bowl. Add celery root and toss to combine. Pat pork dry with paper towels and season with salt and pepper.

2. Heat oil in 12-inch nonstick skillet over medium-high heat until just smoking. Place chops in skillet in pinwheel formation; cook until golden brown and meat registers 140 degrees, about 6 minutes per side. Transfer chops to plate and tent with foil. Pour off fat from skillet.

3. Add jelly and remaining 6 tablespoons vinegar to now-empty skillet. Cook over medium heat until thick and syrupy, about 3 minutes. Season with salt and pepper to taste. Brush glaze over chops and serve with celery root salad.

TEST KITCHEN NOTE: Use the large holes of a box grater or a food processor fitted with the grating disk to shred the celery root.

PASTRAMI CHEESEBURGERS Serves 4

✔ **WHY THIS RECIPE WORKS:** Sauerkraut, pastrami, Swiss cheese, and a tangy sauce transform an ordinary burger into something special.

- 6 tablespoons mayonnaise
- 3 tablespoons ketchup
- 2 tablespoons sweet pickle relish
  Salt and pepper
- 4 kaiser rolls, split and toasted
- 1 pound 85 percent lean ground beef
- 1 tablespoon vegetable oil
- 6 ounces thinly sliced deli brisket pastrami
- 1½ cups sauerkraut, drained and pressed dry
- 8 slices deli Swiss cheese, folded in half

1. Whisk mayonnaise, ketchup, relish, and ½ teaspoon pepper together in bowl. Spread sauce evenly on roll tops and bottoms; set aside. Gently shape beef into four 4-inch-diameter patties. Season each patty with salt and pepper.

2. Heat oil in 12-inch skillet over medium-high heat until just smoking. Add patties to skillet and cook without moving patties for 2 minutes. Flip patties and cook for 1 minute. Transfer burgers to plate and tent with foil.

3. Add pastrami to now-empty skillet and cook over medium-high heat until lightly browned, about 3 minutes. Stir in sauerkraut and cook until heated through, about 2 minutes. Remove skillet from heat; separate pastrami mixture into 4 portions (still in skillet), then top each portion with 2 slices of cheese. Cover and let sit until cheese melts, about 2 minutes. Transfer burgers to roll bottoms. Top each burger with 1 portion of pastrami mixture. Place roll tops on burgers. Serve.

TEST KITCHEN NOTE: Our favorite sauerkraut is Eden Organic Sauerkraut.

LEMONY SHRIMP WITH ORZO, FETA, AND OLIVES Serves 4

✔ **WHY THIS RECIPE WORKS:** Cooking the orzo pilaf-style gives it extra flavor and allows you to control the slightly creamy consistency.

- 1 tablespoon grated lemon zest plus 1 tablespoon juice
  Salt and pepper
- 1½ pounds extra-large shrimp (21 to 25 per pound), peeled and deveined
- 2 tablespoons extra-virgin olive oil, plus extra for drizzling
- 1 onion, chopped fine
- 2 garlic cloves, minced
- 2 cups orzo
- 4 cups chicken broth
- 1 cup pitted kalamata olives, chopped coarse
- 4 ounces feta cheese, crumbled (1 cup)

1. Mix lemon zest, ½ teaspoon salt, and ½ teaspoon pepper together. Pat shrimp dry with paper towels and toss with lemon-salt mixture to coat; set aside.

2. Heat 1 tablespoon oil in 12-inch nonstick skillet over medium-high heat until just smoking. Add onion and cook until softened, about 4 minutes. Stir in garlic and cook until fragrant, about 30 seconds. Stir in orzo and cook, stirring frequently, until orzo is coated with oil and lightly browned, about 4 minutes. Add broth, bring to boil, and cook, uncovered, until orzo is al dente, about 6 minutes. Stir in olives, ½ cup feta, and lemon juice. Season with salt and pepper to taste.

3. Reduce heat to medium-low, nestle shrimp into orzo, cover, and cook until shrimp are pink and cooked through, about 5 minutes. Sprinkle remaining ½ cup feta over top and drizzle with extra oil. Serve.

TEST KITCHEN NOTE: Garnish with chopped fresh parsley.

PAN-SEARED CHICKEN WITH SPICY PINTO BEANS Serves 4

✔ **WHY THIS RECIPE WORKS:** Mashing the beans gives them an appealing texture, and simmering them with salsa intensifies their flavor.

- 4 (6- to 8-ounce) boneless, skinless chicken breasts, trimmed and pounded to even ½-inch thickness
  Salt and pepper
- ½ cup sour cream
- 3 tablespoons lime juice (2 limes)
- ¼ teaspoon cayenne pepper
- 2 tablespoons vegetable oil
- 2 (15-ounce) cans pinto beans, rinsed
- 1 cup medium salsa
- ¾ cup water
- ½ cup minced fresh cilantro

1. Pat chicken dry with paper towels and season with salt and pepper. Whisk sour cream, 2 tablespoons lime juice, cayenne, ¼ teaspoon salt, and ¼ teaspoon pepper together in bowl; set aside.

2. Heat 1 tablespoon oil in 12-inch nonstick skillet over medium-high heat until just smoking. Add chicken and cook until golden brown and meat registers 160 degrees, about 6 minutes per side. Transfer to plate and tent with foil.

3. Add remaining 1 tablespoon oil and beans to now-empty skillet and cook over medium heat until beans begin to blister, about 2 minutes. Stir in salsa, water, and ¼ teaspoon salt. Using potato masher, mash beans to coarse paste. Simmer until slightly thickened, about 4 minutes. Stir in remaining 1 tablespoon lime juice and ¼ cup cilantro. Divide bean mixture among plates. Slice chicken and arrange over beans. Drizzle sour cream sauce over top and sprinkle with remaining ¼ cup cilantro. Serve.

Bananas Foster

We wanted to enjoy this New Orleans classic at home, but would that mean singeing our eyebrows? BY CHRISTIE MORRISON

ICONIC AMERICAN DISHES come from every corner of the map, but no city's food has more flourish than that of New Orleans. Take Bananas Foster, which chef Paul Blangé of Brennan's restaurant conceived in 1951 for Richard Foster, a regular customer who also happened to be chairman of the New Orleans Crime Commission.

This dessert of bananas sautéed in butter, sugar, cinnamon, banana liqueur, and rum was prepared tableside and then, for a bit of dining room theater, set aflame to mute its boozy edges. Served over vanilla ice cream, it quickly became, and remains, a mainstay at many New Orleans restaurants.

But oh, the crimes it has been subjected to since. In my experiments with existing recipes, I found mushy bananas, harsh alcohol flavors, and greasy, sickly-sweet sauces. My biggest challenge would be balancing the elements to keep the sweetness in check and the butter amount generous but not greasy.

I omitted the banana liqueur right off the bat; my tasters and I thought it unnecessarily sweet, not to mention tough to find. After several tests, I settled on ripe but not too-ripe bananas, which held up nicely without turning to mush. And I chose dark brown sugar over white or light brown; its rich caramel flavor was just right.

With my ingredients settled, I focused on technique. My biggest question concerned the flambé. While dramatic and exciting, it's also tricky and potentially dangerous, so I wanted to know if it was absolutely necessary. In a series of side-by-side tests, tasters detected only a minuscule difference, but when they were pressed to vote, I was surprised but pleased that a majority preferred the nonflambéed version. Courting heresy, I nixed this eyebrow-singeing step.

For my first sans-flambé test, I melted 4 tablespoons of butter in a skillet over medium heat, but I had problems getting all of the sugar dissolved without the butter breaking into a greasy, separated mess, especially after sautéing the bananas and finishing off the sauce. I'd fixed the same problem in other pan sauces, though, so I decided to flip the 65-year-old script and add the butter at the end, off the heat, hoping this would help maintain the butter's creamy emulsion. Would it work?

I set the butter aside and started a fresh batch, whisking together the brown sugar, rum, and cinnamon over medium heat. I also added a couple of tablespoons of water, which loosened the sauce without adding more rum. When the mixture started to steam, I added bananas that I'd quartered into logs and cooked them until they were soft and lightly golden. I moved them to a serving dish and then removed the skillet from the heat and whisked in the butter 1 tablespoon at a time. An extra 2 teaspoons of rum at the end freshened its presence, and a bit of lemon juice offered a burst of brightness.

The resulting sauce was rich, creamy, sweet, buttery, and full of rum flavor. I placed a scoop of vanilla ice cream on top of a few pieces of golden sautéed banana and drizzled the silky sauce over the top. Tasters were too busy gobbling it up to miss the flambé flourish.

To ensure that they hold their shape in the skillet, choose ripe but not mushy bananas.

KEY INGREDIENT Rum Rainbow

The rum-making process starts by fermenting sugar cane juice, sugar cane syrup, or molasses and then distilling the resulting liquid. The clear distillate is then aged—almost always in oak barrels—a process whereby tannins in the wood impart flavor and color. Generally speaking, the longer a rum is aged, the darker it becomes.

LIGHT (AKA WHITE OR SILVER) Typically aged 6 to 12 months; clean, straightforward flavor.

MEDIUM (AKA GOLD OR AMBER) Typically aged about 3 years; nuanced caramel flavor.

BEST FOR BANANAS FOSTER

DARK Typically aged 5 to 7 years; bold molasses flavor.

BANANAS FOSTER Serves 4

Look for yellow bananas with very few spots; overly ripe bananas will fall apart during cooking. We prefer the flavor of gold rum, but you can substitute white or dark rum if desired.

- ½ cup packed (3½ ounces) dark brown sugar
- ¼ cup plus 2 teaspoons gold rum
- 2 tablespoons water
- 1 cinnamon stick
- ¼ teaspoon salt
- 3 ripe bananas, peeled, halved crosswise, then halved lengthwise
- 4 tablespoons unsalted butter, cut into 4 pieces
- 1 teaspoon lemon juice
  Vanilla ice cream

1. Combine sugar, ¼ cup rum, water, cinnamon stick, and salt in 12-inch skillet. Cook over medium heat, whisking frequently, until sugar is dissolved, 1 to 2 minutes.

2. Add bananas, cut side down, to skillet and cook until glossy and golden on bottom, 1 to 1½ minutes. Flip bananas and continue to cook until tender but not mushy, 1 to 1½ minutes longer. Using tongs, transfer bananas to rimmed serving dish, leaving sauce in skillet.

3. Remove skillet from heat and discard cinnamon stick. Whisk butter into sauce, 1 piece at a time, until incorporated. Whisk in lemon juice and remaining 2 teaspoons rum. Pour sauce over bananas. Serve with vanilla ice cream.

Dutch Crunch

This lightly sweet sandwich bread with a crunchy topping is certainly unique, but does it have to be unique to San Francisco? BY KATIE LEAIRD

BACK WHEN I lived in San Francisco, the foundation of my daily lunch was a Dutch crunch roll. A soft, slightly sweet submarine-size roll with a distinctive mottled, crunchy top, it was the basis for nearly every sandwich I ate during those years. Since it was readily available everywhere in the city, I actually had no idea it was a regional specialty until I moved back to the East Coast and suddenly found myself unable to locate it. I realized that I was going to have to create my own recipe.

There are two parts to these sandwich rolls: the dough and the signature craggy topping. I tackled the dough first. While I wanted a soft, chewy crumb inside, the flavor of the bread needed to be unobtrusive, since the roll is merely a backdrop used to showcase sliced meats, cheeses, and other sandwich accoutrements. To achieve the right texture and flavor, I ran a long series of tests. Knowing that different flours have different protein levels that may affect the final texture, I experimented with different varieties before settling on good old all-purpose. I also tried adding an egg to the dough (common in bread recipes), but this made the final product gummy. For liquid, I tested water against milk; water won for its cleaner flavor. A few side-by-side tests led me to choose sugar over honey for a sweet component, and after testing varying amounts of melted butter, I found that 3 tablespoons contributed just the right texture and flavor.

Now that I was happy with the dough, it was time to take on this bread's real distinguishing factor, the crunchy crust. In the Netherlands, Dutch crunch is known as *Tijgerbrood*, or "tiger bread," named for the way the bread's patterned crust resembled the striped cat's coat. In England, fans often refer to it as "giraffe bread."

Regardless of the name, the majority of recipes for Dutch crunch agree on the ingredients for the trademark topping: water, oil, sugar, salt, and—most important—rice flour and yeast. It's these last two ingredients that are the keys to that crunchy, mottled crust.

Just to establish what function the yeast was serving in the topping, I tried baking two batches of Dutch crunch simultaneously, one with the yeasted rice paste topping and the other with an

These rolls get their signature look and crunch from a paste made with water, oil, sugar, salt, rice flour, and rapid-rise yeast.

otherwise-identical topping in which I had left out the yeast. The former had large raised blotches of browned topping in the desired giraffe pattern. The latter had a crackly coating, but it was flush with the bread's surface, and the spots were much smaller and very delicate. So the yeast was definitely in.

I played with the amount of water in the paste until I got the right texture. If the paste was too thick, it weighed

down the bread and inhibited the dough from rising properly; if it was too thin, it ran down the sides of the loaves and pooled into a sticky mess on the baking sheet. I eventually found that 10 tablespoons of water created a paste that could easily be brushed onto the bread.

In the process of making loaf after loaf to test my topping, it occurred to me that the yeasted topping should really be treated, in essence, like a

second bread. So for my next test, instead of just painting the paste onto the rolls and baking them immediately, I let the topping rise before applying it. Sure enough, the resulting loaves had even more dramatic patterns, and their crusts were crunchier and more flavorful than before. Through a series of tests, I settled on a 20-minute rise for the yeasted topping before applying it to the rolls and baking. Perfect.

A San Francisco Treat—via the Netherlands

It's not clear when a Dutch baker first thought to put a rice-paste finish on bread to create a mottled, crackly effect—and rice isn't native to the Netherlands. However, the Dutch had been trading with Asia since the early 1600s via the Dutch East India Company (in Dutch, *Vereenigde Oost-Indische Compagnie*, insignia at right), adding rice to the Dutch pantry along with Asian spices. Dutch immigration to California and the Pacific Northwest surged in the 20th century, as did the popularity of Dutch crunch, as evidenced by newspaper advertisements. In 1947, Schoen's Bakery in Klamath Falls, Oregon, touted it as "That luscious broken crusted bread that your family will call a treat every Tuesday and Wednesday." Today in San Francisco, even supermarkets like Safeway and Whole Foods bake their own Dutch crunch rolls and, of course, you can also find them at smaller bakeries.

DUTCH CRUNCH

Makes 8 sandwich rolls

The topping's consistency is thick (like pancake batter); be sure to use it all. Don't worry if the topping runs down the sides of the rolls (forming a "foot" at the base of each roll) while brushing. Don't use sweet white rice flour in this recipe.

DOUGH

3½	cups (17½ ounces) all-purpose flour
1¼	cups warm water (110 degrees)
3	tablespoons unsalted butter, melted
4	teaspoons sugar
2¼	teaspoons instant or rapid-rise yeast
1	teaspoon salt

TOPPING

½	cup plus 2 tablespoons warm water (110 degrees)
¾	cup (4 ounces) white rice flour
2	tablespoons vegetable oil
2	tablespoons sugar
2¼	teaspoons instant or rapid-rise yeast
½	teaspoon salt

1. FOR THE DOUGH: Using stand mixer fitted with dough hook, mix all ingredients together on low speed until cohesive mass starts to form, about 2 minutes. Increase speed to medium and knead until dough is smooth and elastic, 5 to 7 minutes.

2. Grease large bowl and line rimmed baking sheet with parchment paper. Turn dough onto lightly floured counter and knead briefly to form smooth ball, about 30 seconds. Transfer dough to prepared bowl and turn to coat. Cover with plastic wrap and let rise at room temperature until almost doubled in size and fingertip depression in dough springs back slowly, 1 to 1½ hours.

3. Gently press down on center of dough to deflate. Place dough on clean counter and divide into 8 equal pieces (about 3⅝ ounces each). Form each piece into rough ball by pinching and pulling dough edges under so that top is smooth.

4. Flip each ball onto smooth side and pat into 4-inch circle. Fold top edge of circle down to midline, pressing to seal. Fold bottom edge of circle up to meet first seam at midline and press to seal. Fold in half so top and bottom edges meet and pinch together to form seam. Flip dough seam side down and gently roll into 6-inch log. Arrange rolls in 2 staggered rows of 4 on prepared sheet; set aside to rise at room temperature until almost doubled in size, about 45 minutes. Adjust oven rack to middle position and heat oven to 400 degrees.

5. FOR THE TOPPING: Twenty-five minutes before rolls are finished rising, whisk all ingredients together in medium bowl. Cover bowl and let topping rise until doubled in size, about 20 minutes. Stir risen topping to deflate. Spoon 2 tablespoons topping over each roll and quickly brush to evenly coat top and sides.

6. Transfer sheet to oven and bake until exteriors are golden brown and craggy and centers register 210 degrees, 22 to 25 minutes, rotating sheet halfway through baking. Transfer rolls to wire rack and let cool completely before serving.

Creating the Signature Shape

To form the dough into oblong sandwich rolls, start by dividing it into 8 equal pieces.

1. Form each piece into rough ball by pinching and pulling dough edges under so that top is smooth.

2. Flip each ball onto smooth side and pat into 4-inch circle.

3. Fold top edge of circle down to midline, pressing to seal. Fold bottom edge of circle up to meet first seam at midline and press to seal.

4. Fold in half so top and bottom edges meet and pinch together to form seam. Flip dough seam side down.

5. Gently roll dough into 6-inch log.

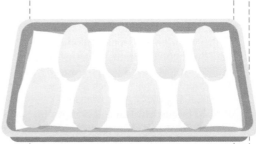

6. Arrange rolls in 2 staggered rows of 4 on prepared baking sheet.

INGREDIENT SPOTLIGHT
Rice Flour

The crackly, mottled crust on Dutch crunch bread is created by brushing the rolls with a thick yeast-and-rice-flour-based paste. As the rolls bake, the rice stays put while the yeast rises, forcing the topping to crack open and form its trademark look.

Rice flour is simply raw long- or medium-grain rice that's been ground to a powdery consistency.

But don't be tempted to grind your own rice flour from raw rice—when we tried to do so using a spice grinder, we couldn't get the rice fine enough. Instead, pick up a bag at the supermarket. Just be aware that some brands are more finely milled than others. The test kitchen likes the fine texture of **Bob's Red Mill White Rice Flour.**

Creating the Signature Crackle

1. Spoon 2 tablespoons of topping over the roll. Be sure to use a full 2 tablespoons; it will look like a lot, but a thick coating is critical to creating the crunchy top.

2. Working quickly, use a brush to evenly coat the top and sides of the roll. Don't worry about letting the excess run down the sides. Continue to spoon and brush the topping onto the remaining rolls.

Brunswick Stew

This rib-sticking stew is too often the butt of jokes. Our aim was to turn misunderstanding into gushing respect. BY MORGAN BOLLING

A SOUTHERN HOG ROAST can be shocking for a first-timer. I learned this at age six as I stood, terrified, staring into the exposed ribs of a whole pig over the fire. I was fresh off *Charlotte's Web*, and the tears gushed. To distract me, my mother turned my attention to the cauldron at the other end of the yard, where a kindly man stood stirring Brunswick stew.

Brunswick stew is a fixture at many Southern barbecues; it's common to find a pot of the rich, tomato-based stew full of assorted (and sometimes unidentifiable) meats and vegetables simmering near the smoking pits. Because there is no definitive Brunswick stew, many cooks and restaurants use it as a kitchen sink dump-all. As writer Roy Blount, Jr., famously said, "Brunswick stew is what happens when small mammals carrying ears of corn fall into barbecue pits."

He was joking, of course, but at the root of the joke is the truth: Brunswick stews vary from town to town and kitchen to kitchen, and they're often awful. I was determined that they didn't have to be.

My first task in developing my own recipe was to try out a few from our cookbook library. I tested a half-dozen from around the South and was struck by how different they were. Stews from Georgia are built on a relatively thin broth with, often, a heavy dose of spice. High in the Appalachians, smoky flavors prevail. And in Virginia, the stew is thick enough to stand a spoon in it.

After trying several versions, I settled on a style from eastern North Carolina,

To take this stew from punch line to punchy, we mixed in our own homemade barbecue sauce.

which was the most popular with my tasters. It's made with barbecue sauce to add complex flavors to the tomato base and also includes potatoes, which add bulk and thicken the broth. The process is simple: You brown the meat, soften the vegetables, add broth and barbecue sauce, and set it to simmer, stirring in this or that additional ingredient along the way. But I couldn't find any recipes that cooked for less than 3 hours. I wanted deep country flavor in much less time.

Eschewing the small mammals, I decided on just chicken and pork for my stew. Tender, forgiving chicken thighs were a no-brainer. For pork, I tried smoky bacon and ham hock, but these imparted too much smoke flavor and not enough meat. Kielbasa, with a broad range of flavors, proved the winner.

Using barbecue sauce for the broth base worked well—up to a point. While I found some brands I liked, others were too sharp or tangy. Because flavors and quality vary so much from brand to brand, I decided to create my own with a few pantry staples: ketchup, mustard, cider vinegar, Worcestershire sauce, and red pepper flakes. At this point, my stew looked beautiful but tasted of raw ketchup. To tame and deepen the flavors, I tried an untraditional method: Before adding the other ingredients, I browned the ketchup, softening its raw edge and creating a rich tomato base.

I added the meats and potatoes to the pot to simmer for a half-hour and then added lima beans and corn for the final

15 minutes. Just before serving, I added a splash of cider vinegar and a final dose of Worcestershire. I had a Brunswick stew my North Carolina relatives could be proud of, and not a single small mammal was harmed.

BRUNSWICK STEW Serves 4 to 6

Our favorite kielbasa is Wellshire Farms Smoked Polska Kielbasa.

- 1 tablespoon vegetable oil
- 1 onion, chopped fine
- ¾ cup ketchup
- 4 cups water
- 2 pounds boneless, skinless chicken thighs, trimmed
- 1 pound russet potatoes, peeled and cut into ½-inch chunks
- 8 ounces kielbasa sausage, sliced ¼ inch thick
- 6–8 tablespoons cider vinegar
- 2 tablespoons Worcestershire sauce
- 1 tablespoon yellow mustard
- 1 teaspoon garlic powder
  Salt and pepper
- ¼ teaspoon red pepper flakes
- 1 cup canned crushed tomatoes
- ½ cup frozen lima beans
- ½ cup frozen corn

1. Heat oil in Dutch oven over medium-high heat until shimmering. Add onion and cook until softened, 3 to 5 minutes. Add ketchup and ¼ cup water and cook, stirring frequently, until fond begins to form on bottom of pot and mixture has thickened, about 6 minutes.

2. Add chicken, potatoes, kielbasa, 6 tablespoons vinegar, 1½ tablespoons Worcestershire, mustard, garlic powder, 1 teaspoon salt, 1 teaspoon pepper, pepper flakes, and remaining 3¾ cups water and bring to boil. Reduce heat to low, cover, and simmer until potatoes are tender, 30 to 35 minutes, stirring frequently.

3. Transfer chicken to plate and let cool for 5 minutes, then shred into bite-size pieces with 2 forks. While chicken cools, stir tomatoes, lima beans, and corn into stew and continue to simmer, uncovered, for 15 minutes. Stir in shredded chicken and remaining 1½ teaspoons Worcestershire and cook until warmed through, about 2 minutes. Season with salt, pepper, and remaining vinegar (up to 2 tablespoons) to taste. Serve.

KEY STEP Browning Ketchup

Ketchup offers a lot of culinary bang for the buck, with sweet, tangy, and savory flavors in a single bottle. For this recipe, we cook the ketchup until it thickens and browns, making it even more complex.

Beef Lombardi

Ground beef, cheese, sour cream, and egg noodles in one casserole?
Sounds like our kind of challenge. BY DIANE UNGER

WHEN I FIRST encountered beef Lombardi—a layered casserole of ground beef, diced tomatoes, and canned chopped green chiles atop a base of egg noodles combined with sour cream, scallions, and lots and lots of cheese—I assumed that the dish came straight out of the midcentury American cookbook. But it turns out this Southern favorite is much younger than that: An enterprising caterer in Cleveland, Mississippi, developed the first recipe in the 1990s. The name? It refers to nothing in particular; she just liked the sound of it.

When I baked up a published version of beef Lombardi in the test kitchen, my tasters thought the recipe showed promise as a one-dish comfort meal, "like Stroganoff meets Tex-Mex," that "reminds me of my childhood."

That said, there were a handful of problems, meaty and otherwise, to solve. The ground beef mixture was too sweet (from 2 teaspoons of sugar) and a bit sludgy (from a 6-ounce can of tomato paste), and even with the green chiles, the dish was a bit bland. Plus, the egg noodles, which I'd boiled up before assembling the casserole, were severely overdone by the time I'd baked it for more than 30 minutes. And while plenty cheesy, the final dish looked like a curdled mess thanks to the sour cream, which often breaks when exposed to sustained heat. I decided this dish was indeed worth an update.

To amp up the flavor in the meat layer, I added onion, a hefty amount of garlic, and plenty of salt and pepper to 90 percent lean ground beef. I cut the sweetness by nixing the sugar and reduced the amount of tomato paste to a restrained 3 tablespoons to improve the texture.

Rather than adding diced tomatoes plus diced green chiles, I turned instead to a single product: Ro-tel Original Diced Tomatoes and Green Chilies, a spicy blend of chopped tomatoes and green chiles. The result: a piquant, well-seasoned, delicious beef mixture. I was ready to move on to the noodle layer.

I doubled the amount of wide egg noodles from a meager 6 ounces to a hefty 12 ounces, and after several rounds of testing, I found that parcooking them for just 3 minutes, instead of the 7 to 8 minutes suggested on the package, would yield tender but not mushy results—they'd finish cooking in the creamy sauce in the oven. To prevent the sour cream from curdling in the oven, I thinned 4 ounces of cream cheese with ½ cup of the hot noodle cooking water and mixed in 1 tablespoon of cornstarch. When I stabilized the sour cream with this mixture, the creamy sauce stayed intact during baking.

I also added another 1½ cups of the noodle cooking water along with the parcooked noodles so that they could fully hydrate and finish cooking in the oven. True to the original, I added some minced scallions to the noodle layer. I settled on 8 ounces of Colby Jack cheese for topping the casserole—just enough to melt down through for a cheesy center while also turning pleasantly golden brown on top.

After a 30-minute bake and a 15-minute rest, my casserole was ready for tasting. Even if its origin story wasn't quite what I'd imagined, I had a comforting, creamy, rich, and satisfying old-fashioned dish.

BEEF LOMBARDI
Serves 6 to 8

We prefer Ro-tel, but other brands of diced tomatoes with chiles can be used. Note the can size, though; if using 14.5-ounce cans, reduce the number of cans to 2. Our favorite egg noodles are Pennsylvania Dutch Wide Egg Noodles. In step 4, the pasta cooking water needs to be hot enough to melt the cream cheese. Colby Jack is a blend of Colby (which is similar to cheddar but with a milder flavor) and Monterey Jack cheeses.

- 1 tablespoon olive oil
- 1 pound 90 percent lean ground beef
- 1 onion, chopped
- Salt and pepper
- 3 tablespoons tomato paste
- 4 garlic cloves, minced
- 3 (10-ounce) cans Ro-tel Original Diced Tomatoes & Green Chilies, drained
- 12 ounces (7¾ cups) wide egg noodles
- 1¼ cups sour cream
- 4 ounces cream cheese, softened
- 1 tablespoon cornstarch
- 4 scallions, sliced thin
- 8 ounces Colby Jack cheese, shredded (2 cups)

1. Adjust oven rack to middle position and heat oven to 350 degrees.

Somewhere between Tex-Mex and stroganoff sits this meaty, cheesy, all-in-one bake.

Grease 13 by 9-inch baking dish. Heat oil in 12-inch nonstick skillet over medium-high heat until just smoking. Add beef, onion, 1 teaspoon salt, and 1 teaspoon pepper and cook, breaking up pieces with spoon, until beef is cooked through, about 8 minutes.

2. Stir in tomato paste and garlic and cook until fragrant, about 30 seconds. Stir in tomatoes and cook until most liquid has evaporated, 3 to 5 minutes. Remove from heat and set aside.

3. Meanwhile, bring 4 quarts water to boil in large pot. Add noodles and 1 tablespoon salt and cook, stirring often, for 3 minutes. Reserve 2 cups cooking water, then drain noodles.

4. Whisk sour cream, cream cheese, cornstarch, and ½ cup reserved cooking water together in now-empty pot until smooth. Stir in scallions, noodles, remaining 1½ cups cooking water, and ¾ teaspoon salt.

5. Spread noodle mixture in even layer in prepared baking dish. Spread beef mixture evenly over noodles. Sprinkle Colby Jack evenly over top. Bake until bubbling around edges and cheese is spotty brown, 25 to 30 minutes. Let cool for 15 minutes. Serve.

TO MAKE AHEAD

The casserole can be fully assembled minus the Colby Jack, cooled completely, covered, and refrigerated for up to 24 hours. To serve, sprinkle with Colby Jack and increase baking time to 45 to 50 minutes.

Flourless Chocolate Cake

This fancy restaurant dessert is seldom made at home. But after a month in the test kitchen, we had a version that takes just 10 minutes of active time to put together. BY ASHLEY MOORE

SWING A CAT in the city of your choice and you're likely to hit a restaurant that serves flourless chocolate cake. Rich, smooth, and dense, with deep chocolate flavor, this once-uncommon dessert is now ubiquitous.

Ubiquitous, that is, except in most home kitchens, where recipes employing complicated techniques keep nonprofessionals away. I set out to create an easy and approachable recipe for flourless chocolate cake that used only straightforward techniques and basic equipment.

I tried making versions using six existing recipes of varying levels of difficulty (one especially easy one was named "Chocolate Idiot Cake"), including our celebrated company recipe from 1998. Some were dense like a brownie, while others reminded us of thick chocolate soup. Since flour was out of contention, some recipes called for ground nuts for structure, but these were deemed too gritty. Others use eggs for structure—and it works beautifully; this cake was delicious, like a soft yet dense chocolate truffle. But this approach, though totally successful, required several bowls and some tricky techniques. I wanted a dump-and-stir version.

I cobbled together a working recipe and hit the kitchen. My first order of business was the easiest: melting the chocolate (we use good-quality bittersweet chocolate) and butter (2 sticks for maximum richness). While most recipes call for a double boiler for this task, I turned to the microwave, where zapping the two ingredients gently in a glass bowl saved me a couple of dirty pots. Letting the combination cool for about 5 minutes allowed me to add it to a mixture of eggs, sugar, cornstarch (for body), and vanilla without curdling the eggs.

Interestingly, a few of my initial recipes called for water in the egg-sugar mixture. Intrigued, I tried one cake with ½ cup added water and one without. The cake with the water was much more moist, while the one without was very chalky and dry. Clearly, the water was helping hydrate the mix and give it a more tender chew. For my next test, I tried incorporating the water in two different ways: with a stand mixer, which incorporates a lot of air into the batter,

This rich, fudgy cake doesn't need dressing up, but who are we to discourage a dollop of whipped cream and some chocolate shavings?

and in a bowl whisked by hand. The results were drastically different: The cake from the stand mixer souffléed so high that it fell over the springform pan and onto the oven floor (a mess I'd be happy never to make again), while the hand-mixed version baked clean and even.

This was welcome news, because it meant I could make this cake from start to finish by hand. But my cake had some minor appearance issues—namely, a small crack and dozens of visible air bubbles on the top. These are minor problems (once you put a bite of this rich, buttery cake in your mouth, the last thing you'll worry about is an imperfect top), but I wanted to minimize them.

Earlier test kitchen experiments showed us that one major culprit in creating cracks in similar cakes (such as cheesecakes) is a high oven temperature—if the cake bakes too quickly or unevenly, it tends to crack. To avoid this, we often set the springform into a larger pan with a couple of inches of water in it; the gentler heat created by this water bath helps the cake come to temperature more gradually without developing cracks. But I wanted to avoid the awkwardness of a water bath. Could I achieve a crack-free cake by simply lowering the oven temperature? As it turned out, I could. After a few experiments, I found that a relatively tame 275-degree oven, with the oven rack smack in the middle, kept cracks at bay.

As for the air bubbles, I found that pouring my fully mixed batter through a strainer and into the springform pan removed much of the trapped air, significantly reducing the number of bubbles on top. It also removed any errant pieces of coagulated egg, further ensuring a supersmooth texture. A gentle tap on the counter followed by a 10-minute rest nudged out even more air. (A few bubbles are inevitable and are a small price to pay for a cake this good.)

After baking it for about 50 minutes and then letting it cool and chill until firmly set (about 6 hours, a major test of patience), I had a great cake. To make sure it wasn't a fluke (and to quiet my still-hungry tasters), I made four more cakes in four different ovens, using the same straining technique. Much to my tasters' delight, all four worked.

FLOURLESS CHOCOLATE CAKE
Serves 10 to 12

Plan ahead: This cake needs to chill for at least 6 hours, so we recommend making it the day before serving. An accurate oven thermometer is essential here. Our preferred bittersweet chocolate is Ghirardelli 60% Cacao Bittersweet Chocolate Premium Baking Bar. Top the cake with chocolate shavings, if desired; to make shavings, simply shave bittersweet bar chocolate with a vegetable peeler.

CAKE

- 12 ounces bittersweet chocolate, broken into 1-inch pieces
- 16 tablespoons unsalted butter
- 6 large eggs
- 1 cup (7 ounces) sugar
- ½ cup water
- 1 tablespoon cornstarch
- 1 tablespoon vanilla extract
- 1 teaspoon instant espresso powder
- ½ teaspoon salt

WHIPPED CREAM

- ½ cup heavy cream, chilled
- 2 teaspoons sugar
- ½ teaspoon vanilla extract

1. FOR THE CAKE: Adjust oven rack to middle position and heat oven to 275 degrees. Spray 9-inch springform pan with vegetable oil spray. Microwave chocolate and butter in bowl at 50 percent power, stirring occasionally with rubber spatula, until melted, about 4 minutes. Let chocolate mixture cool for 5 minutes.

2. Whisk eggs, sugar, water, cornstarch, vanilla, espresso powder, and salt together in large bowl until thoroughly combined, about 30 seconds. Whisk in chocolate mixture until smooth and

DON'T MAKE THIS MISTAKE
Sunken Cake
Baking this cake too quickly at too high of a temperature will cause it to soufflé and subsequently fall and crack. For an even, smooth cake, it is essential to bake it at exactly 275 degrees. To make sure your oven is at the right temperature, place an oven thermometer in the center of the middle rack and heat the oven to 275 degrees. As soon as the oven indicates that it is preheated, check the thermometer reading, then adjust the temperature setting up or down as necessary.

A BAKER'S BEST FRIEND
Our favorite oven thermometer is the CDN Pro Accurate Oven Thermometer ($8.70).

slightly thickened, about 45 seconds. Strain batter through fine-mesh strainer into prepared pan, pressing against strainer with rubber spatula or back of ladle to help batter pass through.

3. Gently tap pan on counter to release air bubbles; then let sit on counter for 10 minutes to allow air bubbles to rise to top. Use tines of fork to gently pop any air bubbles that have risen to surface. Bake until edges are set and center jiggles slightly when cake is shaken gently, 45 to 50 minutes. Let cake cool for 5 minutes, then run paring knife between cake and sides of pan.

4. Let cake cool in pan on wire rack until barely warm, about 30 minutes. Cover cake tightly with plastic wrap, poke small hole in top, and refrigerate until cold and firmly set, at least 6 hours.

5. FOR THE WHIPPED CREAM: Using stand mixer fitted with whisk, whip cream, sugar, and vanilla on medium-low speed until foamy, about 1 minute. Increase speed to high and whip until stiff peaks form, 1 to 3 minutes.

6. To unmold cake, remove sides of pan and slide thin metal spatula between cake bottom and pan bottom to loosen, then slide cake onto serving platter. Let cake stand at room temperature for 30 minutes. Slice with warm, dry knife. Top slices with whipped cream and serve.

Are Supermarket Whipped Toppings Any Good?

We usually make our own whipped cream from heavy cream, sugar, and a little vanilla, but supermarkets are full of premade products. To find the best, we assembled the seven top-selling national whipped toppings; four of them in aerosol cans and three in plastic tubs. Some of the toppings contain cream (or other dairy products); others use water, corn syrup, and oil in lieu of a dairy base. All contain stabilizers and/or emulsifiers. Twenty-one America's Test Kitchen staffers blindly sampled each whipped topping plain and atop flourless chocolate cake.

All three of the tub-style toppings had a textural edge over the aerosols because they're whipped at the factory and then frozen, which, with help from the stabilizers, locks in the air bubbles so the toppings stay fluffy. (You must defrost them before using.) Aerosol cans force their contents through a nozzle with a blast of nitrous oxide, but this often made for unstable toppings that slumped into weepy puddles.

One product stood out from the competition. "Is this real whipped cream?" asked multiple tasters. Although it isn't made with real cream—the first ingredient on the label is skim milk—it duplicated the soft, billowy peaks and rich flavor of homemade whipped cream. It has a relatively high amount of fat, 2 grams per 2-tablespoon serving, which is twice as much as the lowest-scoring whipped topping.

Some of the aerosol whipped toppings were made with cream, but they weren't very good, save one: Land O' Lakes Whipped Heavy Cream, which was our runner-up. It had the same 2 grams of fat per serving as our winner and was one of only two products to specify "heavy cream" (which must be at least 36 percent fat) on its label, compared with the "cream" (which must be 18 percent fat) on other ingredient lists. A few tasters complained that it looked curdled even though it tasted quite good.

Our winner, Cool Whip Extra Creamy, did the best job of mimicking homemade whipped cream, although in a subsequent taste test, no one was fooled. And, at $0.20 per ounce, it was one of the cheapest in our lineup. Read the full story and results chart at **CooksCountry.com/may16.** –HANNAH CROWLEY

RECOMMENDED		TASTERS' NOTES
COOL WHIP Extra Creamy **Price:** $1.59 for 8 oz ($0.20 per oz) **Style:** Frozen **Fat:** 2 g **Sugar:** 2 g		Tasters praised this "thick," "silky," and "luscious" whipped topping for its "excellent, fresh cream flavor" with "just enough sweetness." While a few noted a weird mouth-coating sensation, it seemed "the most like real whipped cream."
LAND O' LAKES Whipped Heavy Cream **Price:** $4.99 for 14 oz ($0.36 per oz) **Style:** Aerosol **Fat:** 2 g **Sugar:** 1 g	REAL CREAM	This product is made with heavy cream, and tasters loved its buttery richness: "Actually tastes like cream!" "Feels like full fat" with "a perfect level of sweetness." The downside: It emerged slightly curdled and chunky from its aerosol nozzle.

RECOMMENDED WITH RESERVATIONS		
TRUWHIP **Price:** $4.49 for 10 oz ($0.45 per oz) **Style:** Frozen **Fat:** 2 g **Sugar:** 2 g		Marketed as a "natural" alternative to Cool Whip, this topping uses tapioca syrup instead of high-fructose and regular corn syrups and contains no actual dairy. It was "fluffy" with "the consistency of homemade" but tasted like marshmallow and almonds.
COOL WHIP Original **Price:** $1.59 for 8 oz ($0.20 per oz) **Style:** Frozen **Fat:** 1.5 g **Sugar:** 2 g		Tasters easily identified this product: "I feel like I'm at a church potluck in Illinois, circa 1998." "Thick" and "fluffy" with an artificial aftertaste and a cooked, marshmallowy flavor, this "kid fantasy" earned a few points for nostalgia.

Fat and sugar are from product packaging and are per 2-tablespoon serving.

Best Supporting Ingredient: Espresso Powder

With decades of collective experience working with chocolate, we in the test kitchen know a few things to be true. One certainty: Coffee, in many forms, makes a great behind-the-scenes addition to all kinds of chocolate desserts. In this recipe, just 1 teaspoon of instant espresso powder sharpens and amplifies the flavor of the chocolate, making it taste deeper, richer, fruitier, and more complex without delivering discernible coffee notes. Some flavor scientists believe that when foods complement each other well, it's because they contain related flavor compounds. Coffee and chocolate are prime examples. They share some of the same flavor compounds (pyrazines) because they are both made from fermented beans.

Cooking Class Eggs Benedict

Eggs Benedict is really two recipes—two finicky recipes. Let us lend a hand. BY CHRISTIE MORRISON

EGGS BENEDICT WITH FOOLPROOF HOLLANDAISE
Serves 4

An instant-read thermometer is essential to this recipe. For an accurate measurement of boiling water, bring a full kettle of water to a boil and then measure out the desired amount. Our favorite English muffins are Bays English Muffins.

HOLLANDAISE
- 8 tablespoons unsalted butter, cut into 8 pieces and softened
- 4 large egg yolks
- ⅓ cup boiling water
- 2 teaspoons lemon juice
  Salt
  Pinch cayenne pepper

EGGS BENEDICT
- 4 English muffins, split
- 8 slices Canadian bacon
- 2 tablespoons distilled white vinegar
- 1 teaspoon salt
- 8 large eggs

1. FOR THE HOLLANDAISE: Place butter and egg yolks in large heat-resistant glass or ceramic bowl. Bring ½ inch water to simmer in medium saucepan. Place bowl over simmering water, making sure that water does not touch bottom of bowl, and whisk constantly until mixture is smooth and homogeneous, about 1 minute.

2. Slowly add boiling water and cook, whisking constantly, until thickened and sauce registers 160 degrees, 7 to 10 minutes. Off heat, whisk in lemon juice, ⅛ teaspoon salt, and cayenne. Remove saucepan from heat (keep bowl over water bath) and season with salt to taste. Cover to keep warm.

3. FOR THE EGGS BENEDICT: Adjust oven rack 6 inches from broiler element and heat broiler. Arrange English muffins split side up on baking sheet and broil until golden brown, 2 to 4 minutes. Place 1 slice bacon on each muffin half and broil until hot and beginning to brown, about 1 minute. Remove sheet from oven and cover loosely with aluminum foil.

4. Fill 12-inch skillet nearly to rim with water. Add vinegar and salt and bring to boil over high heat. Crack 2 eggs into each of 4 cups. Carefully and simultaneously pour eggs into skillet. Cover pan, remove from heat, and poach eggs until whites are set but yolks are still slightly runny, 4 minutes. (For firmer eggs, cook 2 to 3 minutes longer.)

5. Use slotted spoon to transfer eggs from pan to paper towel–lined plate. Arrange 1 poached egg on top of each muffin half. Spoon 1 to 2 tablespoons hollandaise over each egg. Serve, passing remaining hollandaise separately.

Reheating Leftovers
Our sturdy hollandaise can be reheated in the microwave—as long as you warm it gradually so that the emulsion doesn't break. Reheat the sauce at 50 percent power, stirring it every 10 seconds, until warm.

STEP BY STEP Eggs Benedict with Foolproof Hollandaise

1. USE INDIRECT HEAT
Whisk the butter and egg yolks in a bowl set over a saucepan filled with ½ inch of simmering water.
WHY? This gentle heating method gives you more control as you whisk the eggs, allowing them to thicken but not curdle.

2. ADD LOTS OF HOT WATER
Slowly add ⅓ cup of boiling water to the egg mixture, whisking constantly until thickened.
WHY? Adding plenty of hot water makes the sauce less likely to break, since curdling can happen if the mixture is too dry.

3. CHECK TEMPERATURE
It will take 7 to 10 minutes of whisking until the thickening sauce reaches 160 degrees.
WHY? There's a small window between perfectly thickened and curdled; an instant-read thermometer will help you find it.

4. ADD ACID AND SEASONINGS
Off the heat, whisk in the lemon juice, salt, and cayenne, and then season with salt to taste.
WHY? The acidic lemon juice, the cayenne's heat, and salt balance the richness of the sauce and make the flavors pop.

5. BROIL MUFFINS
Broil the English muffins split side up on a baking sheet until they turn golden brown.
WHY? Most toasters can only fit a couple of muffins at a time. This method browns all eight muffins at once.

Good to Know

Use the Right Bowl

A heat-resistant bowl is key for a double boiler setup. We found that glass or ceramic bowls were more forgiving than stainless steel because they tend to be thicker and slower to heat. (Stainless-steel bowls got so hot that it was virtually impossible to keep the yolks from curdling.) We recommend the **Pyrex Smart Essentials Mixing Bowl Set** ($27.98).

Whisk Wisely

Some recipes call for mixing hollandaise with a handheld mixer, but we have found that whisking by hand gives you the best feel for when the sauce starts to thicken. In tests, a side-to-side motion (versus stirring or beating) was easiest to execute quickly and aggressively. Our favorite whisk is the **OXO Good Grips 11" Balloon Whisk** ($9.99).

Extra Water Makes It Foolproof

Hollandaise is notoriously unstable. Like mayonnaise, hollandaise is an emulsion that depends on the proper suspension of fat in liquid. The classic approach is to whisk egg yolks with lemon juice and a small amount of water over a double boiler until thickened and then slowly drizzle in melted butter. It seems easy enough, but things can easily go awry if the mixture overheats. Newer recipes call for using a blender or food processor to ensure a foolproof emulsification without the tedious whisking. These methods usually work, but only if you're serving the sauce immediately (otherwise they will break). To make a reliable sauce with staying power, we add extra water. The sauce turns out a little foamier than a classic hollandaise, yet it's always silky smooth and won't break over time. That's because the extra water dilutes the emulsion, spacing out the oil droplets so they are less likely to combine and separate.

Eggs Benedict Q&A

Who Is the Real Benedict?

Who gets credit for inventing this iconic dish? Food historians point to three popular creation stories:

1894: After a rough night, stockbroker Lemuel Benedict brunches at New York City's Waldorf Hotel and soothes what ails him with two poached eggs, bacon, toast, and a side of hollandaise. The maître d'hôtel trades the bacon for ham and the toast for English muffins, and the dish is born.

1894: Charles Ranhofer, the chef at Delmonico's in New York City, publishes *The Epicurean*, in which he includes a recipe for Eggs à la Benedick, a dish inspired by a patron's long-ago lunch. As the story goes, Mrs. LeGrand Benedict, a regular at Delmonico's in the 1860s, is bored with the usual lunch offerings. Instead of ordering from the menu, she requests the ingredients for the dish and assembles her open-faced creation at the table.

1967: Craig Claiborne receives a recipe for the dish, penned in the late 1800s, from Mr. Edward P. Montgomery. The accompanying letter claims that Commodore Elias Cornelius Benedict, a banker and close friend of President Grover Cleveland, gave the recipe to Montgomery's uncle.

How Do I Avoid Eggs with Raggedy Edges?

Because bubbles will cause delicate egg whites to jostle and fray, don't poach them in simmering water. Instead, slip them into boiling water, cover the skillet, and slide the pan off the heat so they can gently cook through. Adding vinegar to the water helps the proteins set quickly, providing extra insurance against fraying.

DON'T MAKE THIS MISTAKE

Which English Muffins Should I Buy?

In taste tests, **Bays English Muffins** came out on top, with a "fresh, buttery" flavor. Once toasted, these muffins boast plenty of crisp nooks and crannies along with a soft, chewy interior. Look for them in the refrigerated dairy section of your supermarket.

6. LAYER ON MEAT
Place one bacon slice on each toasted English muffin and broil until hot and starting to brown.
WHY? Canadian bacon is precooked, so it just needs to be warmed and browned under the broiler.

7. SEASON WATER
Fill the skillet with water and add the vinegar and salt. Bring the poaching liquid to a boil.
WHY? Salt and vinegar add flavor; vinegar also helps the egg proteins set up with fewer wispy edges.

8. ADD EGGS TOGETHER
Crack two eggs into each of four cups. Carefully and simultaneously pour the eggs into the skillet.
WHY? Sliding the eggs into the water at the same time equalizes the cooking time. Plus, the cups provide a gentle entry.

9. POACH OFF HEAT
Cover the skillet, remove it from the heat, and let the eggs sit until the whites are set but the yolks are still slightly runny.
WHY? This residual heat is gentler than simmering. The upshot? Perfectly formed, round whites.

10. DRAIN THEM WELL
Use a slotted spoon to transfer the eggs to a paper towel–lined plate.
WHY? The paper towel will soak up any excess moisture that might otherwise make the crisp muffins soggy.

Fortunately, cutting this Italian classic down to two servings made it even easier—
and still just as delicious. BY CECELIA JENKINS

SCALOPPINI, WHICH TRANSLATES from Italian as "thin cutlet," consists of just that—thinly pounded chicken breasts that are lightly dredged in flour and quickly sautéed. Served in a vibrant white wine pan sauce enlivened with mushrooms, red bell pepper, garlic, and capers, the cutlets become a dish that's long been a crowd-pleasing favorite in Italian American restaurants. We recently developed a home version that made use of a few timesaving adaptations. I wanted to see whether I could make it even easier, turning it into a good weeknight option for just two people without losing any of its sunny Mediterranean appeal.

I started by slimming the chicken down to just two small boneless breasts, about 6 ounces each. Then, since I needed the breasts to be thin enough to cook quickly in the skillet but didn't want to have to aggressively pound them, which tends to shred the meat, I decided to slice them in half horizontally. But slicing these smaller breasts turned out to be rather tricky. So I decided to adapt a trick we use when slicing beef very thin: I put the chicken in the freezer for 15 minutes, which firmed up the meat just enough to make it easily sliceable. Once cut, the breasts only needed to be lightly pounded to get to the even ¼-inch thickness I was looking for—no need to use excessive force, just even it out.

When I put these scaloppini (now they deserved that name) into the skillet, I was very happy to find that they all fit at the same time. This was a big improvement over the recipe for four people, since I wouldn't have to cook the chicken in batches as you do for that version.

After flouring the cutlets, browning them, and setting them on a plate, I turned to my pan sauce, adding quartered mushrooms, sliced shallots, and red bell pepper strips to the now-empty skillet. Once the vegetables had begun to brown, I added capers and garlic, which made the dish instantly aromatic; poured in the broth and wine and reduced the sauce until slightly thickened; whisked in some butter to yield a rich, velvety finish; spooned it over the cutlets; and dug in—only to discover that the chicken was cold. I'd thought that by eliminating batch cooking I

For superthin chicken, we freeze breasts for 15 minutes before halving and pounding them.

had also eliminated the extra time the chicken had to cool off, but apparently I was wrong.

Heating the chicken through before serving posed a challenge: Typically, finishing a sauce involves taking the pan off the heat and then whisking butter into it. This creates a nice sheen and prevents the butter (an emulsion) from breaking and looking oily, which it easily can if added over heat. I tried adding the chicken to the pan after whisking in butter, covering it and letting it heat up off the heat, but this took too long and didn't seem to get the cutlets hot enough. I couldn't return the chicken to the sauce and then try to whisk in the butter since the chicken got in the way. But, I wondered, what if I turned the heat down very low, whisked in the butter, and then added the chicken to quickly heat through?

Sure enough, the lower heat was gentle enough to keep the butter from breaking but still strong enough to heat the chicken through completely without drying it out.

CHICKEN SCALOPPINI WITH PEPPERS AND MUSHROOMS FOR TWO

Placing the chicken breasts in the freezer for 15 minutes before trimming them firms them up slightly and makes them easier to halve. If the breasts have tenderloins attached, remove them and reserve them for another use.

2 (6- to 8-ounce) boneless, skinless chicken breasts, trimmed
   Salt and pepper
¼ cup all-purpose flour
2 tablespoons vegetable oil
4 ounces white mushrooms, trimmed and quartered
1 red bell pepper, stemmed, seeded, and cut into thin strips
1 shallot, sliced thin
2 tablespoons capers, rinsed
1 garlic clove, minced
¾ cup chicken broth
½ cup dry white wine
2 tablespoons unsalted butter, cut into 2 pieces
1 tablespoon chopped fresh parsley

1. Place breasts on plate, cover with plastic wrap, and freeze for 15 minutes. Working with 1 breast at a time, starting on thick side, cut breasts in half horizontally. Using meat pounder, gently pound each cutlet into even ¼-inch thickness between 2 sheets of plastic wrap. Pat dry with paper towels and season with salt and pepper.

2. Spread flour in shallow dish. Working with 1 cutlet at a time, dredge cutlets in flour, shaking off excess, and return to plate.

3. Heat 1 tablespoon oil in 12-inch nonstick skillet over medium-high heat until just smoking. Add cutlets and cook until lightly golden and cooked through, about 2 minutes per side. Transfer to clean plate.

4. Heat remaining 1 tablespoon oil in now-empty skillet over medium-high heat until shimmering. Add mushrooms, bell pepper, shallot, and ¼ teaspoon salt and cook until liquid has evaporated and vegetables begin to brown, 4 to 6 minutes. Add capers and garlic and cook until fragrant, about 1 minute.

5. Add broth and wine and bring to boil, scraping up any browned bits. Cook until slightly thickened and mixture is reduced to 1½ cups (measured with vegetables), 5 to 7 minutes.

6. Reduce heat to low and whisk in butter. Season with salt and pepper to taste. Return chicken and any accumulated juices to pan to heat through, about 1 minute. Transfer chicken to platter and top with vegetables and sauce. Sprinkle with parsley. Serve.

KEY INGREDIENT Capers

Who would have thought that the unopened flower bud of a shrub (*Capparis spinosa*) would be a mainstay of Mediterranean cooking? Never eaten fresh, the dried buds are preserved either in a salty brine (sometimes with vinegar) or packed in salt. Our favorite product is **Reese Non Pareil Capers** ($2.39 for 3.5 ounces); we enjoy their pungent, salty, and sharp flavors. Look for capers near the pickles in your supermarket.

5 Easy Recipes Smoothies

You'd think making a perfect smoothie would be easy—and it is, as long as you start with the right ingredients. BY ASHLEY MOORE

THE WHOLE POINT of a smoothie is ease (and maybe a little healthfulness). You want to toss a bunch of ingredients—usually fruit, sometimes a vegetable, a bit of liquid, and a nice creamy thickener like yogurt—into a blender, hit "puree," and call it good. And the process is, in fact, more or less that simple.

But oh, the things that can go wrong. One sip is sweet, and the next is sour. Chunks of unincorporated fruit. A too-liquid texture. Chunks of ice. A too-thick cup of concrete that won't budge until you tip it just . . . far . . . enough to slide out and splat on your face. I set out to change all this with a simple smoothie formula that would work with a range of add-ins.

After sending scores of combinations to the blender, I determined that bananas are the secret weapon for smooth smoothies. Blending them creates a substantive (but not stiff) base for smoothies, even those that you don't necessarily want to end up tasting like banana. Pureeing them with honey and a pinch of salt before adding the other ingredients guaranteed an even level of sweetness throughout.

A great smoothie also has a creamy element. Tempted as I was by ice cream, I wanted a smoothie, not a shake. Milk frequently led to a runny smoothie. So I turned to yogurt. Though we love Greek-style yogurt in the test kitchen, a few experiments showed me that it was too thick for smoothies. Low-fat and fat-free yogurts didn't contribute enough creaminess. But whole-milk plain yogurt was just right for a silky, not stiff, smoothie.

I was getting somewhere, but I still had problems to solve. For one, I'd been using crushed ice to keep things cold, but I grew tired of the chunky shards on my tongue. For another, the fresh fruit I was adding (berries, peaches, and so forth) was inconsistent from day to day. But a switch to frozen fruit solved both problems: My smoothies were ice-cold without any ice, and frozen fruit is satisfyingly consistent, no matter the time of year.

▶ Which blender is our favorite? To find out, go to **CooksCountry.com/blendertesting.**

Orange juice added a bright pop of citrusy freshness.

With the basics of smoothie construction locked down, I could focus on flavor. Frozen strawberries and peaches reminded me of midsummer. Mixed berries gave me a vibrant, complex sweetness. Pineapple and kale took things in a more healthful direction (don't worry, it was still sweet), while frozen mango took me to the tropics. And a cherry-almond smoothie, with milk swapped in for the orange juice, was a creamy-sweet success.

STRAWBERRY-PEACH SMOOTHIES
Serves 2
You can substitute low-fat for whole-milk yogurt here, but your smoothies will be much less creamy.

- 1 ripe banana, peeled and halved lengthwise
- 2 tablespoons honey
- ⅛ teaspoon salt
- 1 cup frozen strawberries
- 1 cup frozen peaches
- 1 cup plain whole-milk yogurt
- ¼ cup orange juice

Process banana, honey, and salt in blender until smooth, about 10 seconds. Add strawberries, peaches, yogurt, and orange juice and blend until smooth, scraping down sides of blender as necessary, about 1 minute. Serve.

CHERRY-ALMOND SMOOTHIES
Add ¼ cup almond butter to blender with banana, honey, and salt. Substitute 2 cups frozen cherries for strawberries and peaches. Substitute whole milk for orange juice.

KALE-PINEAPPLE SMOOTHIES
Substitute frozen pineapple chunks for strawberries and 1 cup frozen chopped kale for peaches.

MIXED BERRY SMOOTHIES
Substitute 2 cups frozen mixed berries for strawberries and peaches.

TROPICAL FRUIT SMOOTHIES
Substitute frozen mango chunks for strawberries, frozen pineapple chunks for peaches, and pineapple juice for orange juice.

Above: Strawberry-Peach Smoothies. Below, clockwise from left: Cherry-Almond, Kale-Pineapple, Tropical Fruit, and Mixed Berry Smoothies.

Slow Cooker Memphis-Style Wet Ribs

Slow-cooker ribs can be washed-out and boring.
But not if you use the right technique. BY DIANE UNGER

THE SLOW COOKER is great for things like soups and stews, but when you're trying to replicate a classic outdoor recipe, like Memphis-style ribs, the moist environment of the appliance can be your biggest enemy. I wanted outdoor flavor, but I wanted it from my countertop slow cooker. Unfortunately, after I experimented with a few existing recipes, I had soggy, washed-out meat that was more stew than 'cue: still delicious, but not what I wanted. Had I finally taken on a challenge too big?

Most of the recipes I found called for seasoning the ribs—either with a barbecue rub or by slathering bottled barbecue sauce all over them—and then layering them in the slow cooker and covering them with more barbecue sauce. As the ribs cooked, all the moisture and flavor came out of them; right out of the slow cooker, they looked awful and tasted bland. One recipe called for broiling the ribs to finish them off, which helped with appearance but did very little for flavor. I wanted well-seasoned, tender ribs that tasted and looked as good as their outdoor counterparts, with a sticky, full-flavored sauce and a deep red color.

Memphis-style ribs are always spice-rubbed before cooking and are served either "dry," meaning without sauce and with extra rub added when they come off the grill, or "wet," meaning brushed with a tangy ketchup-and-vinegar-based sauce. I wanted wet ribs, so I turned to

an earlier test kitchen recipe for outdoor Memphis-Style Wet Ribs. I tweaked the rub and sauce quantities to accommodate two racks of St. Louis–style ribs, which we preferred to baby backs for flavor and moisture.

To help the racks fit into the slow cooker, I cut each rack in half and rubbed the four pieces with a simple mixture of paprika, brown sugar, salt, pepper, onion powder, and granulated garlic. (I found that the ribs can be rubbed up to a day ahead of time.)

I stood the ribs up in the slow cooker, with the thinner, exposed bone end up; then, I shifted my focus to cooking liquids. I was torn. I tried barbecue sauce, stock, and water in small amounts to help create steam in the slow cooker. But these tests showed me that I didn't need any liquid at all, because as the ribs cooked, fat began melting away and moisture was created by the ribs themselves. They were cooking low and slow in their own flavorful juices, with no need for anything else in the cooker.

After about 5½ hours on high (or 6 to 7 hours on low), the ribs were tender and perfectly cooked. And because they weren't simmering in tons of liquid, the rub had actually adhered to the meat, making them look much like Memphis dry ribs done outdoors.

While the ribs were cooking, I put together a sauce of ketchup, apple juice, molasses, cider vinegar, Worcestershire, mustard, liquid smoke, and pepper. I simmered the mixture until it was nicely thickened, which only took about 10 minutes. When the ribs were done, I carefully lifted them out of the slow cooker, transferred them to a rack set over a foil-lined baking sheet, and let them rest for about 10 minutes to dry (a dry surface holds sauce better than a moist one). I brushed them liberally with sauce and broiled them until the sugars in the sauce began to caramelize and created a rich, lacquer-like glaze, about 4 minutes.

After a short rest of 20 minutes, I cut up the ribs and gave them a try. They were tender but had a little chew left to them and were flavorful from the spice rub, which had penetrated the meat during cooking. And the slightly smoky glaze added just the right amount of sweetness and tang. Who needs to fire up the grill after all? Not I.

We ditched the water, stock, and barbecue sauce. These ribs cook in their own juices.

TEST KITCHEN TECHNIQUE
A Standing Arrangement
To fit the racks in the slow cooker, cut each one in half and then arrange them vertically with the thick ends pointing down and the meaty side against the interior wall of the slow cooker (the ribs will overlap).

SLOW-COOKER MEMPHIS-STYLE WET RIBS Serves 4 to 6
Try to find ribs of equal shape to ensure even cooking. These ribs should be tender but not falling off the bone.

RIBS
- 2 tablespoons paprika
- 1 tablespoon packed brown sugar
- 1 tablespoon kosher salt
- 2 teaspoons pepper
- 2 teaspoons onion powder
- 2 teaspoons granulated garlic
- 2 (2½- to 3-pound) racks St. Louis–style spareribs, trimmed and each rack cut in half

BARBECUE SAUCE
- ¾ cup ketchup
- 6 tablespoons apple juice
- 2 tablespoons molasses
- 2 tablespoons cider vinegar
- 2 tablespoons Worcestershire sauce
- 1 tablespoon yellow mustard
- 1 teaspoon pepper
- ¼ teaspoon liquid smoke

1. FOR THE RIBS: Combine paprika, sugar, salt, pepper, onion powder, and granulated garlic in bowl. Reserve 1 tablespoon spice rub for sauce. Pat ribs dry with paper towels and coat all over

with remaining 5 tablespoons rub.

2. Arrange ribs vertically with thick ends pointing down and meaty side against interior wall of slow cooker (ribs will overlap). Cover and cook until ribs are just tender, 5 to 6 hours on high or 6 to 7 hours on low.

3. FOR THE BARBECUE SAUCE: Meanwhile, whisk ketchup, apple juice, molasses, vinegar, Worcestershire, mustard, pepper, liquid smoke, and reserved 1 tablespoon spice rub together in medium saucepan. Bring to boil over medium heat, then reduce heat to medium-low and simmer, stirring occasionally, until thickened and reduced to 1 cup, about 10 minutes. (Sauce can be refrigerated for up to 3 days.)

4. Line rimmed baking sheet with aluminum foil and set wire rack in sheet. Using tongs, transfer ribs, meaty side up, to prepared rack. Let ribs sit for 10 minutes to allow surface to dry out.

5. Adjust oven rack 3 inches from broiler element and heat broiler. Liberally brush ribs with ½ cup sauce and broil until sauce is bubbling and beginning to char, about 4 minutes. Remove ribs from oven, brush with remaining ½ cup sauce, tent with foil, and let rest for 20 minutes. Cut ribs in between bones to separate. Serve.

One-Pan Dinner Chicken Thighs with Chickpeas and Fennel

Most braised dishes build flavor through long cooking in a covered vessel. We wanted to get to the flavor faster. BY CHRISTIE MORRISON

BRAISING USUALLY INVOLVES a large—and often tough—cut of meat that cooks very slowly in a moist environment like a Dutch oven or slow cooker. The technique is ideal for breaking down the fat and connective tissue in large, tough cuts. What's more, the long cooking time—say, most of a Sunday afternoon—allows deep flavors to develop.

But braising can happen quickly, too, as with the rich, flavorful dark meat of chicken thighs. The rub, however, is that for a quicker braise, you need bold, powerful ingredients to replace the deep, savory flavor that would otherwise come from slow cooking. I looked to the Mediterranean for inspiration; there, vibrant lemon and briny olives are frequently used to add complexity. Fennel, with its lively, licorice-like flavor, is another ingredient I knew would add a soft but sturdy balance to the dish.

I'd committed to using just one pot, so I started by browning the chicken thighs skin side down in a Dutch oven to build a flavorful base before transferring them to a plate. I added slightly sweet fennel wedges and cooked them until they were just beginning to brown. Next, I added plenty of lemon zest and juice, some citrusy ground coriander, sharp garlic, and hot red pepper flakes to round out the aromatic base, as well as some white wine for flavor and a bit of acidity. Some savory chicken broth and a touch of honey completed my braising liquid. I returned the browned chicken thighs to the pot with a few briny green olives and then baked the dish, covered, until the thighs were cooked through and the fennel wedges were tender.

The dish was full of soothing but energetic flavors, but it lacked the hearty, starchy component that would make it a complete meal. Chickpeas were a natural fit. I added two cans in my next round and, as they braised with the meat, they picked up flavors from the chicken and vegetables. They even contributed some thickening power when I mashed ½ cup of them before adding them to the pot.

The flavors were strong, but the skin on the chicken thighs had turned flabby. Determined to achieve both tender, moist meat and crispy skin in this one-pan meal, I reconsidered my method. Did I really want to finish these in the moist environment of a covered dish if it meant sacrificing the crispy skin I'd so carefully browned earlier? There had to be a way around this. I eyed a large ovensafe skillet and decided to give it a whirl.

This time, after browning the thighs and vegetables and stirring together my braising liquid, I was careful to nestle the chicken into the vegetables so that the skin stayed above the liquid. Then I baked the dish, uncovered, for about 40 minutes.

Was it still a braise? Who cares? The chicken was tender, and the skin was crispier than it had been. But still not crispy enough—until I moved the rack higher in the oven. The reflected heat from the oven ceiling kept the skin impressively crispy and everything else tender. What's more, keeping it uncovered reduced the sauce slightly, deepening its flavors. All that was needed was a baguette to dip into the sauce.

ONE-PAN LEMON-BRAISED CHICKEN THIGHS WITH CHICKPEAS AND FENNEL Serves 4

Only the skin side of the chicken is seared in step 2. Cooking the chicken to an internal temperature of 185 degrees renders the fat and melts the tough connective tissues into rich gelatin. Leave the core in the fennel so the wedges don't fall apart. We prefer briny green olives like Manzanilla, Picholine, or Cerignola in this recipe; look for them in your grocery store's salad bar section or in the pickle aisle.

2 (15-ounce) cans chickpeas, rinsed
6 (5- to 7-ounce) bone-in chicken thighs, trimmed
    Salt and pepper
1 tablespoon olive oil
1 large fennel bulb, stalks discarded, bulb halved and cut into ½-inch-thick wedges through core
4 garlic cloves, minced
2 teaspoons grated lemon zest plus 1½ tablespoons juice
1 teaspoon ground coriander
½ teaspoon red pepper flakes
½ cup dry white wine
1 cup pitted large brine-cured green olives, halved
¾ cup chicken broth
1 tablespoon honey
2 tablespoons chopped fresh parsley
1 baguette, sliced

For inspiration, we looked to Mediterranean cuisine and bolstered our chicken thighs with tart lemon, briny green olives, fennel, chickpeas, and parsley.

1. Adjust oven rack to upper-middle position and heat oven to 350 degrees. Place ½ cup chickpeas in bowl and mash to coarse puree with potato masher; set aside. Pat chicken dry with paper towels and season with salt and pepper.

2. Heat oil in ovensafe 12-inch skillet over medium-high heat until just smoking. Cook chicken, skin side down, until skin is crisped and well browned, 8 to 10 minutes. Transfer chicken to plate, skin side up.

3. Pour off all but 2 tablespoons fat from skillet, then heat fat left in skillet over medium heat until shimmering. Add fennel, cut side down, and sprinkle with ¼ teaspoon salt. Cook, covered, until lightly browned, 3 to 5 minutes per side. Add garlic, lemon zest, coriander, and pepper flakes and cook, uncovered, until fragrant, about 30 seconds. Stir in wine, scraping up any browned bits, and cook until almost evaporated, about 2 minutes.

4. Stir in olives, broth, lemon juice, honey, mashed chickpeas, and remaining whole chickpeas and bring to simmer. Nestle chicken into liquid, keeping skin above surface. Transfer skillet to oven and bake, uncovered, until fennel is tender and chicken registers 185 degrees, 35 to 40 minutes. Sprinkle with parsley and serve with baguette slices.

TEST KITCHEN TECHNIQUE
Fennel Wedges That Don't Fall Apart
Cutting fennel without removing the core will keep its layers intact. Remove and discard the stalks, halve the bulb, and then cut each half into ½-inch-thick wedges through the core.
core

Taste Test Supermarket Black Tea

Which black tea you should buy depends on how you take it—plain or with milk and sugar. BY JENNI WHALEN

COFFEE MAY GET all the buzz, but tea is hot: Americans consumed 3.6 billion gallons in 2014, 84 percent of which was black tea, according to the Tea Association of the United States. Sales of bagged and loose tea have increased by 17 percent in the past five years.

But which affordable, everyday black tea is best? We surveyed the market and chose seven of the most popular and widely available black teas from each of the top-selling national brands, priced from $0.05 to $0.25 per tea bag. Among these teas were English breakfast, British blends, English teatime teas, and black teas. Why the mix? Our tea experts told us that while the names on the packaging might differ, it's mostly just marketing. Unless otherwise noted, supermarket black teas are blends, made by manufacturers who combine leaves grown in different regions to create their desired flavor.

Twenty-one America's Test Kitchen staffers tasted the teas both plain and with milk and sugar, evaluating them for flavor, astringency, complexity, and overall appeal. Once we'd crunched the numbers, we looked at the results and saw an interesting trend: In general, the brands that scored hi gh when tasted plain performed poorly when tasted with milk and sugar; likewise, teas we loved with milk and sugar were at or near the bottom of our plain tasting. Why would

we love a tea plain but not like it with milk and sugar?

Astringency and bitterness in tea are linked to tannins, compounds found in many plants. Tannins are often discussed in relation to red wine; they affect a wine's flavor and tend to dry the mouth as you sip. We had an independent laboratory make tea with one tea bag from each product in our lineup and then measure the tannins in each of the brewed teas; they reported a range of 789 to 1,265 milligrams per liter, which tracked with tasters' preferences: Teas we liked with milk generally had more tannins, and those we liked plain generally had fewer. There were exceptions to this trend, most notably with Lipton, which is high in tannins but came in second in the plain tasting. According to one expert, a huge corporation like Lipton sources and blends teas from dozens of places, meaning that its familiar tea is formulated for balance and consistency—the high tannins are tempered by other flavors for mass appeal.

There's a scientific explanation of why tannins and milk go together so well: The proteins in milk, called caseins, bind with the tannins and smooth out their characteristic astringency. But if a tea isn't tannic enough, the caseins can overwhelm its flavor, which is why most low-tannin teas tasted flat with milk.

We also split open multiple bags of

each tea to weigh and average their contents, which ranged from 1.96 grams to 2.63 grams per bag (a difference of approximately 25 percent). When we compared these weights to our preferences, we noticed a second pattern: Brands that packed more tea into their bags tended to contain more tannins, likely (in part) because more tea in the bag means a stronger, more tannic brew; again, we generally liked these teas with milk and sugar. Those with less tea in their bags were likely to have fewer tannins and were best served plain.

While all of our manufacturers say

that their teas can be served with or without milk and sugar, it does appear that there are two general styles: bolder, more tannic teas designed to stand up to add-ins, and those blended to have fewer tannins and be served plain. So if you prefer to drink your tea with milk and/or sugar, our top choice is Tetley's British Blend. If you're a purist, stick to the milder Twinings English Breakfast Tea.

▶ See the full tasting story and chart at **CooksCountry.com/teatasting.**

If You Like It Plain	
RECOMMENDED	**TASTERS' NOTES**
TWININGS English Breakfast Tea **Price:** $3.49 for 20 bags ($0.17 per bag) **Weight per Tea Bag:** 1.95 g **Tannin Level:** 789 mg per liter	Our tasters crowned this black tea the plain tasting winner because it was "mellow" and "well-balanced" with "honey and floral" notes. It was "a bit sharp but pleasantly so," marked by its straightforward, clean flavors.
LIPTON Black Tea **Price:** $4.99 for 100 bags ($0.05 per bag) **Weight per Tea Bag:** 2.17 g **Tannin Level:** 1,264 mg per liter	Our tasters liked the "floral smell" and "nutty," "toasted" flavors in this black tea blend. While the measured tannins were high, tasters nonetheless found this tea to be "warm" and "pleasant" when tasted plain.
BIGELOW English Teatime **Price:** $2.50 for 20 bags ($0.13 per bag) **Weight per Tea Bag:** 2.33 g **Tannin Level:** 1,061 mg per liter	This black tea fell neatly in the middle of the pack, with "good base flavors" that were not particularly distinctive but had "a hint of bitterness" and a "citrus finish" that made for a pleasant drinking experience.
STASH English Breakfast **Price:** $3.69 for 20 bags ($0.18 per bag) **Weight per Tea Bag:** 2.10 g **Tannin Level:** 941 mg per liter	Our tasters called this reliable tea an "acceptable" blend that "sneaks up on you." It "didn't have much personality," but most agreed that the tea didn't offend the palate either. Summarized one taster: "Your regular ol' tea."

If You Take Milk and Sugar	
RECOMMENDED	**TASTERS' NOTES**
TETLEY British Blend **Price:** $3.99 for 80 bags ($0.05 per bag) **Weight per Tea Bag:** 2.63 g **Tannin Level:** 1,265 mg per liter	With milk and sugar, our tasters preferred this blend's "caramel notes," "pleasant bitterness," and "full, deep, smoky flavors." They also praised its boldness and fruity flavor.
CELESTIAL SEASONINGS English Breakfast Estate Tea **Price:** $4.99 for 20 bags ($0.25 per bag) **Weight per Tea Bag:** 2.41 g **Tannin Level:** 835 mg per liter	When milk and sugar were added, tasters also loved this brand's "strong, true tea taste." It had "appropriate tannins" that made it "interesting" and "balanced" in flavor.
RECOMMENDED WITH RESERVATIONS	
TAZO Awake English Breakfast Tea **Price:** $4.99 for 20 bags ($0.25 per bag) **Weight per Tea Bag:** 2.58 g **Tannin Level:** 1,234 mg per liter	This black tea tasted "nutty" and "woodsy" when we added milk and sugar. While the tea "wasn't thrilling," it did deliver a pleasant aftertaste that tasters preferred to other brands.
LIPTON Black Tea **Price:** $4.99 for 100 bags ($0.05 per bag) **Weight per Tea Bag:** 2.17 g **Tannin Level:** 1,264 mg per liter 	This tea lost some complexity when we added milk and sugar, but it was still "pleasant" and "clean." "My British father-in-law wouldn't approve," one taster noted.

Equipment Review Inexpensive Digital Thermometers

Throw away your old analog dial thermometer: The next generation of inexpensive instant-read thermometers is here. BY HANNAH CROWLEY

THE AXIOM "KNOWLEDGE is power" holds especially true in the kitchen—the more you know about what's going on inside your food as it cooks, the more you can control the result. That's why we're so gung ho about using an instant-read thermometer in the kitchen, as more control means less stress and better results.

In fact, the test kitchen might be described as fanatical when it comes to thermometers. Over the years we've learned that it pays to monitor the temperature not only of meat but also of pies, cakes, breads, poaching water, butter, tea, coffee, caramel, custards, and even baked potatoes. And if you're going to use a thermometer, it should be a digital instant-read model (old dial thermometers are slow and inaccurate in comparison). Our go-to is the Thermapen from ThermoWorks, which is unquestionably the best digital kitchen thermometer on the market.

But at $79 for the basic Thermapen model and $99 for the deluxe, it is an investment. In search of a cheaper alternative, we set out to test inexpensive digital thermometers and find out which model reigns supreme. In selecting our lineup, we capped the price at $35. But as we were narrowing our testing field, we found many thermometers that only read up to about 300 degrees—fine for meat but not much

else. So we added another qualifier to our selection process: Each thermometer had to read up to around 400 degrees so that it could be used when making candy, caramel, and other foods requiring high temperatures.

We ran the thermometers through a battery of tests, including taking the temperature of ice water, boiling water, roasted chicken thighs, and bubbling caramel. Through each test we evaluated every model's accuracy, speed, usability, visibility, comfort, and durability with a mix of lefties, righties, small- and large-handed testers, professional chefs, and lay cooks.

A good digital thermometer needs to be accurate—otherwise, what's the point? Aside from a few buggy models, most thermometers in our lineup were indeed accurate. We next turned to speed and were pleased to find that three-quarters of the thermometers gave accurate readings in under 10 seconds, with the fastest ones clocking in at just over 6 seconds. Most of the thermometers were accurate and reasonably fast, but that doesn't mean they were always easy to use.

Our testers found three major factors that impacted how user-friendly the thermometers were: length, grip, and visibility. Regarding length, the eight thermometers ranged from 5.75 to 8.75 inches long, and we found that longer was better—otherwise, our hands were too close to the heat, and we had to fumble with bulky potholders.

Next up was grip. All of the thermometers have two basic parts, a long metal probe and a head with a digital screen, but only some felt ergonomic and secure in our hands. A few only allowed for dainty two-fingered grips, like a damsel waving a hanky, which simply won't do when you're spearing a chicken thigh that's spitting hot fat.

Lastly, visibility. Larger and clearer displays were best. Testers also preferred screens situated on the side of the thermometer's head as opposed to on top, because they were easier to read from different angles. The best thermometer was lollipop-shaped and had a display that was visible at any angle for both lefties and righties. Said model was also fast, accurate, and easy to use. Manufactured by the same company as the Thermapen, the ThermoWorks ThermoPop ($29) is our top pick for the budget-conscious cook.

Temping 101

Here are a few keys to using instant-read thermometers successfully.

- Go in from the side, and make sure to hit the middle of the thickest part of the food.

- Take the temperature in at least 2 places.

- Wait for the thermometer to settle into a "final" reading.

RECOMMENDED	CRITERIA		TESTERS' NOTES
① THERMOWORKS ThermoPop **Model:** TX-3100-PR (purple) **Price:** $29.00 **Length:** 7.15 in **Average Read Time:** 6.33 sec	Accuracy Speed Ease of Use Visibility Comfort Durability	★★★ ★★★ ★★★ ★★★ ★★½ ★★★	This thermometer was fast, accurate, and easy to hold. It had a few cushy extra features, including a rotating display and a backlight, which came in handy for grilling. The ThermoPop is an excellent inexpensive alternative to the Thermapen.
② POLDER Stable-Read Instant Read Thermometer **Model:** THM-389-90 **Price:** $18.42 **Length:** 8.75 in **Average Read Time:** 6.67 sec	Accuracy Speed Ease of Use Visibility Comfort Durability	★★★ ★★★ ★★★ ★★★ ★★½ ★★½	Testers loved this long thermometer's audible beep when it registered the temperature. It was fast, accurate, and had a handy loop on its end and plenty of room to grip. Our only quibble: It melted when we accidentally rested it on the lip of a saucepan for a moment.
③ LE CREUSET Digital Instant-Read Thermometer **Model:** TR1006 **Price:** $34.95 **Length:** 8.10 in **Average Read Time:** 8.65 sec	Accuracy Speed Ease of Use Visibility Comfort Durability	★★★ ★★½ ★★★ ★★½ ★★½ ★★★	This bright thermometer was quick, accurate, and easy to use. We liked the small loop on the end, but its slim head was a bit small for larger-handed testers to comfortably grip over heat.

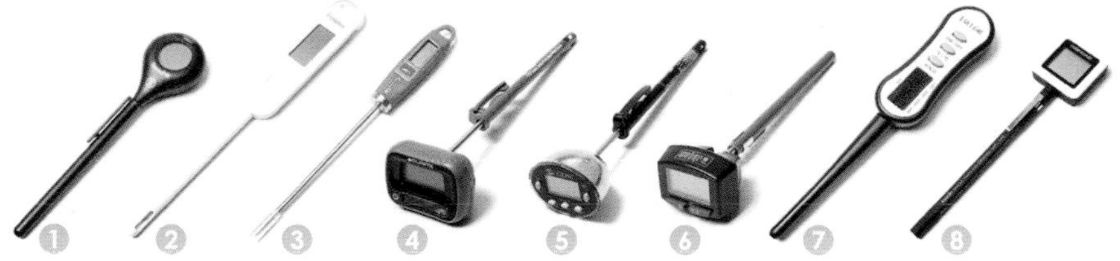

RECOMMENDED WITH RESERVATIONS

	CRITERIA		TESTERS' NOTES
④ ACURITE Digital Instant Read Meat Thermometer **Model:** 295 **Price:** $12.70 **Length:** 5.75 in **Average Read Time:** 9.17 sec	Accuracy Speed Ease of Use Visibility Comfort Durability	★★★ ★★½ ★★★ ★★½ ★½ ★★½	This quick, accurate, and straightforward thermometer had a clear, legible display, but its screen was on top of its head, meaning it was only visible from one often-prohibitive angle. It was also a bit short, and it melted slightly during testing.
⑤ CDN ProAccurate Thermometer **Model:** DTQ450X **Price:** $17.90 **Length:** 6.10 in **Average Read Time:** 8.17 sec	Accuracy Speed Ease of Use Visibility Comfort Durability	★★★ ★★½ ★★½ ★★ ★½ ★★★	This thermometer was accurate and fast, but it was too short. Its face had lots of little buttons that were easy to accidentally press, and we never felt like we had a secure grip on its smooth, round metal head.

NOT RECOMMENDED

	CRITERIA		TESTERS' NOTES
⑥ WEBER Original Instant-Read Thermometer **Model:** 6492 **Price:** $9.99 **Length:** 6.30 in **Average Read Time:** 13.91 sec	Accuracy Speed Ease of Use Visibility Comfort Durability	★½ ★½ ★★½ ★★★ ★★ ★★★	Of our two copies of this thermometer, one was accurate and one was wildly erratic, reporting –7 degrees in a 32-degree ice bath and 153 degrees in a 212-degree pot of boiling water. It was also too short, and its tilting head felt a bit unstable.
⑦ TAYLOR Pro LED Digital Thermometer **Model:** 9835 **Price:** $13.79 **Length:** 8.20 in **Average Read Time:** 26.50 sec	Accuracy Speed Ease of Use Visibility Comfort Durability	★★★ ★ ★½ ★★★ ★½ ★	This thermometer was accurate, but both our testing and backup copies always turned off right when they were about to read the final temperature. They tended to work eventually, but turning them back on a few times took 30 seconds or so—too long to fiddle with over a pot of smoking caramel.
⑧ FARBERWARE Protek Instant Read Thermometer **Model:** 5141007 **Price:** $13.92 **Length:** 6.75 in **Average Read Time:** 18.17 sec	Accuracy Speed Ease of Use Visibility Comfort Durability	★ ★½ ★½ ★★ ★★ ★	Both copies we tested of this thermometer had faulty battery chambers. The small plastic circle that's supposed to lock in place over the lithium battery was loose and would never securely screw in place—one dove right into a boiling pot of water.

Heirloom Recipe

We're looking for recipes that you treasure—the ones that have been handed down in your family for a generation or more; that always come out for the holidays; that have earned a place at your table and in your heart, through many years of meals. Send us the recipes that spell home to you. Visit **CooksCountry.com/recipe_submission** (or write to Heirloom Recipes, *Cook's Country*, P.O. Box 470739, Brookline, MA 02447); click on Heirloom Recipes and tell us a little about the recipe. Include your name and mailing address. **If we print your recipe, you'll receive a free one-year subscription to *Cook's Country*.**

HOT CHICKEN SALAD   Serves 6 to 8

On the first day in our new home, the couple next door brought this casserole over as a welcoming gesture. I knew I'd moved into the right neighborhood. –Terry Callahan, Columbus, Ga.

Go to **CooksCountry.com/poachedchicken** for our recipe for Perfect Poached Chicken Breasts; just increase the amount of chicken in that recipe to 2½ pounds.

- 1 cup sour cream
- 1 cup mayonnaise
- 1 cup slivered almonds, toasted and chopped coarse
- 4 ounces sharp cheddar cheese, shredded (1 cup)
- 4 ounces Gruyère cheese, shredded (1 cup)
- 1 small red onion, chopped fine
- 3 celery ribs, chopped fine
- 2 tablespoons lemon juice
- 1 tablespoon minced fresh chives
- 1 teaspoon salt
- ¼ teaspoon cayenne pepper
- 2½ pounds cooked boneless, skinless chicken breast, cut into ½-inch pieces (6 cups)
- 8 ounces potato chips
- 1 teaspoon paprika

1. Adjust oven rack to middle position and heat oven to 325 degrees. Grease 13 by 9-inch baking dish. Combine sour cream, mayonnaise, almonds, cheddar, Gruyère, onion, celery, lemon juice, chives, salt, and cayenne in large bowl. Fold in chicken until thoroughly combined. Transfer mixture to prepared dish and spread in even layer.

2. Place potato chips and paprika in large zipper-lock bag, press to remove air, and seal. Using rolling pin, crush chips to fine crumbs. Sprinkle chip mixture evenly over casserole. Bake until casserole is bubbling and chips begin to brown, 40 to 45 minutes. Let cool for 10 minutes and serve.

COMING NEXT ISSUE

Summer's coming! Join us at the grill as we show you the secrets to perfect **Pulled Smoked Turkey Sandwiches** and **Texas Thick-Cut Smoked Pork Chops**. We'll cook up some **Best Barbecue Beans** to serve on the side along with **Fried Red Tomatoes**. And to satisfy your sweet tooth, bite into our (truly) amazing Alabama-style **Fried Peach Hand Pies**.

FIND THE ROOSTER!

A tiny version of this rooster has been hidden in the pages of this issue. Write us with its location and we'll enter you a random drawing. The first correct entry drawn will win our winning Inexpensive Instant-Read Thermometer, and each of the next five will receive a free one-year subscription to *Cook's Country*. To enter, visit **CooksCountry.com/rooster** by May 31, 2016, or write to Rooster AM16, *Cook's Country*, P.O. Box 470739, Brookline, MA 02447. Include your name and address. Susan Beasley of Cedar Creek, Texas, found the rooster in the December/January 2016 issue on page 24 and won our favorite small food processor.

WEB EXTRAS

Available online at **CooksCountry.com**
RECIPES FOR:
Asparagus Salad with Grapes, Goat Cheese, and Almonds
Asparagus Salad with Oranges, Feta, and Hazelnuts
Classic Yellow Bundt Cake
Coconut Cloud Cake
Coconut Rice Pudding
French Coconut Pie
Perfect Poached Chicken Breasts
FULL VERSIONS OF:
Biscuit Cutters Testing
Blender Testing
Supermarket Black Tea Tasting
Whipped Toppings Tasting

READ US ON iPAD

Download the *Cook's Country* app for iPad and start a free trial subscription or purchase a single issue of the magazine. All issues are enhanced with full-color Cooking Mode slide shows that provide step-by-step instructions for completing recipes, plus expanded reviews and ratings. Go to **CooksCountry.com/iPad** to download our app through iTunes.

Mint Julep Cake

Place your bets on this lightly boozy Derby-day treat.

To make this cake, you will need:

- ½ **cup bourbon**
- 3 **tablespoons minced fresh mint, plus 10 to 12 leaves for garnish**
- 1 **large egg white**
- 2 **tablespoons granulated sugar**
- ¼ **cup packed (1¾ ounces) light brown sugar**
- 2 **tablespoons water**
- 1 **recipe Classic Yellow Bundt Cake* batter**
- 1 **cup (4 ounces) confectioners' sugar**
- 1 **tablespoon unsalted butter, melted and still warm**
- 2 **drops green food coloring**

FOR THE INFUSED BOURBON AND SYRUP:
Combine bourbon and minced mint in bowl and let sit for 15 minutes. Using brush, paint both sides of remaining mint leaves with thin coat of egg white. Gently press both sides of each leaf into granulated sugar. Shake off excess sugar and place leaves on paper towel–lined plate to dry. Bring brown sugar and water to simmer in small saucepan over medium-high heat, stirring to dissolve sugar; set aside.

FOR THE CAKE:
Adjust oven rack to lower-middle position and heat oven to 325 degrees. Grease and flour 12-cup nonstick tube pan. Strain bourbon-mint mixture through fine-mesh strainer into bowl, pressing on mint to release as much liquid as possible; reserve mint. Add strained mint and ¼ cup infused bourbon to cake batter and stir to combine. Transfer batter to prepared pan. Bake until toothpick inserted in center comes out clean, about 1 hour, rotating pan halfway through baking. Cool cake in pan on wire rack for 10 minutes. Invert cake onto wire rack. Add 2 tablespoons infused bourbon to brown sugar syrup; brush syrup over top and sides of cake. Let cake cool completely, about 2 hours.

FOR THE GLAZE:
Whisk confectioners' sugar, melted butter, food coloring, and remaining 2 tablespoons infused bourbon together in small bowl until smooth. Pour glaze over cake and let sit for at least 10 minutes to set. Garnish cake with sugared mint leaves and serve.

▶ *Go to **CooksCountry.com/yellowbundtcake** for our Classic Yellow Bundt Cake recipe, or use your own.

Inside This Issue

Cook's Country

JUNE/JULY 2016

Citrus-Braised Pork Tacos

We fell for these in Los Angeles and then spent six weeks creating a home recipe.

PAGE 14

Grilled Bourbon Steaks
Extra Char, Extra Flavor

Fried Peach Hand Pies
Peach Perfection

Corn-Poblano Chowder
Creamy, Silky, Flavorful

Backyard Baked Beans
New Approach with Bacon

Cooking Class: Grilled Boneless Chicken Breasts

Fried Red Tomatoes
That's Right, Red

Smashed Potato Salad
Plus: Mayo Showdown

Pulled Turkey Sandwiches
Tennessee Discovery

Taste Test: Hot Dogs
We Ate 300 Dogs

Mississippi Mud Pie
Even More Chocolaty

Texas Smoked Pork Chops
Real Bar-B-Que Flavor

CooksCountry.com
$5.95 U.S./$6.95 CANADA

07>

LETTER FROM THE EDITOR

WHAT KEEPS US going here in the test kitchen, besides the unending intake of calories, is the pervasive sense that everything we think we know for sure is up for reconsideration, retesting, revision, and refinement.

Take, for example, our recipe for Grilled Bourbon Steaks on page 11 of this issue. When this idea first came up for discussion, most of us dismissed it as nonsense. After all, we've grilled thousands of steaks over the years with excellent results. Why would we take something so perfect and simple as a grilled rib eye and clobber it with a boozy, potentially cloying marinade? Balderdash.

But our executive food editor, Bryan Roof, saw possibility. With photographer Steve Klise in tow, Roof made a beeline for Jesse's Restaurant in Magnolia Springs, Alabama, 1,500 miles away from the test kitchen, to sample their signature steak. He returned with good news: Bourbon-marinated steak isn't nonsense. In fact, it's a brilliant idea that should be shared with the world. And after associate editor Ashley Moore (above, right) spent several weeks perfecting our recipe, the rest of us were convinced, too.

Another satisfying reminder that there are no sacred cows in *Cook's Country*. And no sacred steaks.

TUCKER SHAW

Executive Editor

Master of the Grill
742 recipes, techniques, tools, and ingredients that guarantee success when you cook outdoors

Summertime is prime time for cooking over fire. Whether you're a lifelong griller or a new convert, our latest omnibus gives you all the tips and tricks you need to be a backyard pro.

 Follow us on **Pinterest**
pinterest.com/TestKitchen

 Follow us on **Twitter**
twitter.com/TestKitchen

 Find us on **Facebook**
facebook.com/CooksCountry

Photos: Steve Klise

Cook's Country

Chief Executive Officer David Nussbaum
Chief Creative Officer Jack Bishop
Editorial Director John Willoughby
Executive Editor Tucker Shaw
Deputy Editor Rebecca Hays
Executive Managing Editor Todd Meier
Executive Food Editor Bryan Roof
Senior Editors Christie Morrison, Chris O'Connor, Diane Unger
Associate Editors Ashley Moore, Morgan Bolling
Test Cooks Dan Cellucci, Matthew Fairman, Cecelia Jenkins, Katie Leaird
Assistant Test Cook Allison Berkey
Copy Editors Jillian Campbell, Krista Magnuson
Contributing Editors Erika Bruce, Eva Katz
Science Editor Guy Crosby, PhD

Executive Editor, Tastings & Testings Lisa McManus
Managing Editor Scott Kathan
Deputy Editor Hannah Crowley
Associate Editors Lauren Savoie, Kate Shannon
Assistant Editors Miye Bromberg
Editorial Assistant Carolyn Grillo

Test Kitchen Director Erin McMurrer
Assistant Test Kitchen Director Leah Rovner
Test Kitchen Manager Alexxa Grattan
Lead Senior Kitchen Assistant Meridith Lippard
Lead Kitchen Assistant Ena Gudiel
Kitchen Assistants Gladis Campos, Blanca Castanza, Maria Elena Delgado

Design Director, Print Greg Galvan
Photography Director Julie Cote
Art Director Susan Levin
Deputy Art Director Lindsey Chandler
Art Director, Marketing Melanie Gryboski
Deputy Art Director, Marketing Janet Taylor
Associate Art Director, Marketing Stephanie Cook
Staff Photographers Steve Klise, Daniel J. van Ackere
Assistant Photography Producer Mary Ball
Color Food Photography Keller + Keller
Styling Catrine Kelty, Marie Piraino

Senior Director, Digital Design John Torres
Executive Editor, Web Christine Liu
Senior Editor, Web Roger Metcalf
Associate Editor, Web Terrence Doyle
Test Kitchen Photojournalist Kevin White

VP, Print & Direct Marketing David Mack
Circulation Director Doug Wicinski
Circulation & Fulfillment Manager Carrie Fethe
Marketing Assistant Andrea Hampel
Production Director Guy Rochford
Imaging Manager Lauren Robbins
Production & Imaging Specialists Heather Dube, Sean MacDonald, Dennis Noble, Jessica Voas

Chief Digital Officer Fran Middleton
Chief Financial Officer Jackie McCauley Ford
Senior Controller Theresa Peterson
Director, Business Systems Alice Carpenter
Project Manager Mehgan Conciatori
VP, New Business Development Michael Burton
Partnership Marketing Manager Pamela Putprush
Client Services Manager Kate Zebrowski
Sponsorship Sales Associate Morgan Mannino
VP, Strategic Analytics Deborah Fagone
Director of Sponsorship Marketing & Client Services Christine And
Director of Customer Support Amy Bootier
Senior Customer Loyalty & Support Specialist Andrew Straaberg Finfrock
Customer Loyalty & Support Specialists Caroline Augliere, Rebecca Kowalski, Ramesh Pillay
Senior VP, Human Resources & Organizational Development Colleen Zelina
Human Resources Director Adele Shapiro
Director, Retail Book Program Beth Ineson
Retail Sales Manager Derek Meehan
Associate Director, Publicity Susan Hershberg

ON THE COVER: CITRUS-BRAISED PORK TACOS
Keller + Keller, Catrine Kelty
ILLUSTRATION: Greg Stevenson

Contents

AMERICA'S TEST KITCHEN
RECIPES THAT WORK®

America's Test Kitchen is a real 2,500-square-foot kitchen located just outside Boston. It is the home of more than 60 test cooks, editors, and cookware specialists. Our mission is to test recipes until we understand exactly how and why they work and eventually arrive at the very best version. We also test kitchen equipment and supermarket ingredients in search of products that offer the best value and performance. You can watch us work by tuning in to *America's Test Kitchen* (AmericasTestKitchen.com) and *Cook's Country from America's Test Kitchen* (CooksCountry.com) on public television and listen to us on our weekly radio program on PRX. You can also follow us on Facebook, Twitter, Pinterest, and Instagram.

Cook's Country magazine (ISSN 1552-1990), number 69, is published bimonthly by Boston Common Press Limited Partnership, 17 Station St., Brookline, MA 02445. Copyright 2016 Boston Common Press Limited Partnership. Periodicals postage paid at Boston, MA, and additional mailing offices. USPS #023453. Publications Mail Agreement No. 40020778. Return undeliverable Canadian addresses to P.O. Box 875, Station A, Windsor, ON N9A 6P2. POSTMASTER: Send address changes to *Cook's Country*, P.O. Box 6018, Harlan, IA 51593-1518. For subscription and gift subscription orders, subscription inquiries, or change of address notices, visit AmericasTestKitchen.com/support, call 800-526-8447 in the U.S. or 515-248-7684 from outside the U.S., or write to us at *Cook's Country*, P.O. Box 6018, Harlan, IA 51593-1518. PRINTED IN THE USA.

Basting Brush Blues

I saw a chef on TV basting meat on the grill with a brush made of herb bunches tied to a wooden spoon. It looked cool, but does this actually add flavor?
Meg Haber, Lexington, Ky.

To test the effectiveness of a homemade herb brush, we put one together by tying bunches of parsley, sage, rosemary, and thyme to the handle of a wooden spoon using kitchen twine. We brushed butter onto chicken breasts and flank steaks as we grilled them using both the herb brush and a regular silicone basting brush; we also cooked a third sample of each that we didn't baste but instead sauced with herb butter when it came off the grill.

Most tasters could detect only a slight herb presence in the chicken basted with the herb brush. With more flavorful flank steak, however, tasters weren't able to detect a difference in either basted sample. In both tests the meats topped with herb butter had the most herb presence by far.

THE BOTTOM LINE: While an herb basting brush looks impressive, it doesn't contribute much flavor. Serving meat with herb butter gives it much more flavor with less expense and effort.

FLASHY BUT INEFFECTIVE
Skip the herb brush.

Coffee Quandary

When a dessert recipe calls for espresso powder, can I grind my own espresso or dark-roast coffee beans to a fine powder and use that? Or do I have to buy a special espresso powder at the store?
Rene Andersen, Sacramento, Calif.

Pleasantly bitter, ultraconcentrated instant espresso powder can be a baker's secret weapon—just a pinch pumps up chocolate flavor considerably without imparting a coffee flavor. The powder is made by brewing espresso-style coffee, dehydrating it, and grinding the solids into a fine powder.

To test if finely ground espresso beans would work as a substitute, we made two batches of two of our recipes calling for this ingredient, Chocolate Crinkle Cookies and Hazelnut-Mocha Truffles. In one batch we used instant

No Beef About It

What is the best substitute for beef broth when converting a recipe for a vegetarian? I want to maintain rich flavor.
Marjorie Collicutt, Wentworth, N.H.

While you could certainly use vegetable broth instead of beef broth, it's not always the best option. That's because vegetable broth is meant to highlight the light, sweet flavor of vegetables, while beef broth should be rich, meaty, and savory. (Our favorite store-bought beef broth, Better Than Bouillon Beef Base, hits these points.)

We set out to create a meat-free substitute that would match the flavors of beef broth. Our plan was to work with ingredients that build savory flavors, including some that are high in glutamates, the chemical compounds that create umami flavor: soy sauce, tomato paste, miso, Vegemite, Marmite, mushrooms, onions, and liquid smoke. After more than a week of testing, we had a recipe made in a roasting pan that mimics the rich, deep flavors of good beef broth. It requires more than an hour of oven time, so it's not as fast as opening a carton of vegetable broth, but the flavor payoff is worth it. Try this broth in your favorite recipe for French onion soup or vegetable chili.

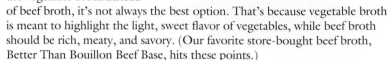

ROASTING BUILDS SAVORY FLAVOR
This vegetarian broth is rich and "meaty."

VEGETARIAN "BEEF" BROTH
Makes about 4 cups

1	pound button mushrooms, sliced thin
1	onion, sliced thin
2	celery ribs, chopped
1	carrot, chopped
2	tablespoons vegetable oil
1	tablespoon tomato paste
3	garlic cloves, unpeeled
8	cups water
2½	teaspoons salt

1. Adjust oven rack to middle position and heat oven to 450 degrees. Combine mushrooms, onion, celery, carrot, oil, tomato paste, and garlic in large roasting pan.

2. Roast until vegetables are tender and very dark in color, 35 to 40 minutes. Add water to pan. Continue to roast until water is reduced by half, about 30 minutes. Strain through fine-mesh strainer and discard solids. Stir in salt and let cool completely. Broth can be refrigerated for 3 days or frozen for up to 1 month.

espresso powder and in the other, freshly ground espresso beans. In the cookies, a few tasters thought the sample with instant powder tasted "more chocolaty" and "complex," but the difference was minor, and tasters thought both were acceptable. The truffles, however, were a different story. The freshly ground espresso did not dissolve, leaving what should have been a creamy truffle with gritty coffee bits.

To make sure we covered all our bases, we repeated these tests using regular ground coffee instead of ground espresso beans. The truffles turned out unacceptably gritty, and the cookies had a clear taste of coffee and left tasters picking bits of grounds from their teeth.

THE BOTTOM LINE: You can use ground espresso beans (but not regular ground coffee) in place of instant espresso powder in most baked goods. But when a recipe requires a smooth texture, like truffles, stick with instant espresso powder.

Saving Squash

My garden is overrun with zucchini. I've heard that it doesn't freeze well but wanted to see if you had any advice.
Patrick Keaton, Mooresville, N.C.

We know that high-moisture vegetables like zucchini (which is about 95 percent water by weight) don't freeze well, but we asked around the test kitchen to see if our cooks had any tips. One suggested we try preparing the zucchini as we sometimes do for zucchini bread or sautéing: grated on the large holes of a box grater and squeezed in a clean dish towel to remove excess moisture. We prepared zucchini this way and froze it. When we defrosted it a few days later, the grated squash was limp and sitting in its own liquid. When we sautéed this frozen and defrosted zucchini, the results were unappealingly mealy and too soft. But when we added the defrosted shreds to our recipe for zucchini bread, tasters were none the wiser.

To freeze zucchini for later use in zucchini bread, grate it on the large holes of a box grater and squeeze it dry. Freeze it in portions in zipper-lock bags, and thaw it before adding it to the batter. If liquid accumulates in the bag with the defrosted squash, add it to the batter. If you don't, the bread will end up being dry.

THE BOTTOM LINE: Because of its high water content, frozen and thawed zucchini turns mushy when sautéed. It's fine, however, to use frozen and thawed grated zucchini in zucchini bread.

Salmon Origins

My grocery store sells frozen "Atlantic salmon," but the package says "product of Chile." What gives?
Julie Morrison, Ardmore, Pa.

The short answer is that "Atlantic salmon" refers to a species of salmon, not to the ocean from which they were caught.

Atlantic salmon did originate in the Atlantic Ocean. But nowadays most Atlantic salmon sold in the United States is raised on farms in Norway, Scotland, Chile, and Canada. Similarly, Pacific salmon—which includes sockeye, coho, and Chinook (also called king)—originated in the North Pacific Ocean. Most Pacific salmon sold in this country is wild-caught in the American Northwest, British Columbia, and Alaska and has a more assertive flavor and a lower fat content than farmed Atlantic salmon.

THE BOTTOM LINE: "Atlantic" and "Pacific" refer to types of salmon, not to the places they were caught. Most Atlantic salmon sold in this country is farm-raised, and most Pacific salmon is wild-caught.

FARMED SALMON
Atlantic salmon has more fat and a mild flavor.

WILD SALMON
Pacific salmon has less fat and more flavor.

▶ To ask us a cooking question, visit **CooksCountry.com/ask**. Or write to Ask Cook's Country, P.O. Box 470739, Brookline, MA 02447. Just try to stump us!

Kitchen Shortcuts

COMPILED BY DIANE UNGER

EASY TRICK Quicker Whipper
Peggy First, Bethesda, Md.

My family loves homemade whipped cream on just about anything, but a full batch is usually too much, and my mixer doesn't do a good job with small amounts. I discovered that I could easily whip cream with my immersion blender. I put about 1 cup of cream in a 4-cup glass measuring cup (a quart takeout container works well, too), add sugar and vanilla, and blend for 30 to 45 seconds. Perfect whipped cream, every time.

TIDY TIP
Stuck on You
Danny Davis, Raleigh, N.C.

To help keep things organized and handy in my kitchen, I glued small magnets to my spice containers. Then I affixed a small metal baking sheet to the inside of my pantry door; I stick all the containers on the sheet, where they stay in plain sight so I can find them easily.

STORAGE SOLUTION
Wrap and Roll
John Weinbaum,
West Hartford, Conn.

I like to take my knives and essential spices with me when I go on vacation, as my wife and I prefer to cook for ourselves. To keep things organized, I use a compartmented small wrench roll (which you can buy at a hardware store). I put my knives safely in one side and my spices in small vials in the other side.

CLEVER TRICK
Stress Reduction
Mary Ellen Wheeler, Warwick, R.I.

I never felt comfortable when a recipe called for a sauce to be reduced by half, as I always felt I was playing a guessing game as to when it was properly reduced. But found a good work-around: I dip a wooden chopstick in the sauce, pull it out, mark the level by cutting a shallow notch with a paring knife, and then make a second notch at the halfway point. Now I have a marker to know exactly when I've hit the proper reduction.

TIMESAVING TIP
Bacon on the Fly
Huldah Taylor, Chalfont, Pa.

I love a few strips of bacon with my morning bagel, but I don't have the time to fry it up before work. Instead, I cook big batches of bacon on the weekends, let them cool, and freeze the strips in plastic containers. On weekday mornings, I quickly reheat a few strips in a skillet or a microwave. The bacon is crispy and tastes as good as fresh.

TIDY TIP
Measure and Tear
Phyllis McConkey,
Palo Alto, Calif.

I've always had a hard time tearing clean sheets of aluminum foil from the roll. To get foil sheets without jagged edges, I pull out a long piece of foil, line a ruler up, and carefully tear the foil against the ruler edge. I get a clean cut every time.

DOUBLE DUTY
Brewing Up Cocktails
Sally Muldoon, Phoenix, Ariz.

My husband and I have date night cocktails at home every Friday night, but we don't own a cocktail shaker. The hubby, clever guy that he is, came up with a great alternative: our French press coffee maker. He loads in the ice and the drink ingredients, gives them a good stir, presses the plunger down, and pours. Cheers!

Texas Thick-Cut Smoked Pork Chops

Was it possible to get that pit-smoked Texas flavor with nothing but a charcoal grill?

BY ASHLEY MOORE

Venison chops aren't on the menu, but the thick pork chops more than suffice.

Big chops demand big flavor; we get it from brining, seasoning, smoking, and saucing these massive chops.

COOPER'S OLD TIME Pit Bar-B-Que in Llano, Texas (see "On the Road"), is famous for the "Big Chop," a massive, 2-inch-thick bone-in pork rib chop seasoned and grilled over mesquite coals before being dunked into a pungent sauce.

Pork chops tend to dry out on the grill, so to prevent this in my recipe, I turned to brining (soaking meat in a saltwater solution). The dissolved salt is drawn into the meat by diffusion, seasoning it and helping it stay juicy.

After a few tests, I knew that a simple saltwater brine was helping keep the meat tender and moist, but I noticed that I was no longer getting much browning on the exterior of the chops. Since sugar helps promote browning, I added 3 tablespoons to the brine. After I had patted the chops dry with a paper towel, they were ready for seasoning.

Cooper's seasoning mix contains salt, pepper, onion powder, and granulated garlic. For my four big chops, I settled on 1½ tablespoons of kosher salt, 2 tablespoons of pepper, and 2 teaspoons each of onion powder and granulated garlic, which I would sprinkle over both sides of the chops just before grilling.

Before dropping the chops on the grill, I did some tinkering in the kitchen to produce a postgrill barbecue sauce reminiscent of Cooper's. I started by rendering whole bacon pieces, which would be easy to remove before serving but would leave deep flavor behind. I stirred in some grated onions and added cider vinegar for acidity.

Chicken broth won out over water as the best liquid. And for a little extra smoky flavor, I stirred in a bit of liquid smoke. Hot sauce gave it kick.

I put my brined, seasoned chops on the cooler side of a hot fire bolstered with soaked mesquite chips for authentic Hill Country flavor. To insulate the meat and keep it from cooking too quickly, I positioned the chops so the bones faced the charcoal. It wasn't long before the mesquite began to smoke, and for 45 minutes, the chops gently cooked through. And sure enough, the sugar in the brine helped them achieve a rich brown crust.

After letting the chops rest for 10 minutes and saucing them, I called my tasters, sliced off chunks of pork, and passed them around.

A chorus of yums ensued, and I knew my meaty, juicy, smoky chops had done Texas proud.

TEXAS THICK-CUT SMOKED PORK CHOPS Serves 8

Each chop can easily serve two people. Grate the onion for the sauce on the large holes of a box grater. Our preferred hot sauce is Frank's RedHot Original Cayenne Pepper Sauce. If you'd like to use wood chunks instead of wood chips when using a charcoal grill, substitute two medium chunks, soaked in water for 1 hour, for the wood chip packet.

PORK
        Kosher salt and pepper
    3   tablespoons sugar
    4   (18- to 20-ounce) bone-in pork rib chops, 2 inches thick
    2   teaspoons onion powder
    2   teaspoons granulated garlic
    2   cups mesquite wood chips

BARBECUE SAUCE
    2   slices bacon
    ¼   cup grated onion
        Kosher salt and pepper
    ¾   cup cider vinegar
    1¼ cups chicken broth
    1   cup ketchup
    2   tablespoons hot sauce
    ½   teaspoon liquid smoke

1. FOR THE PORK: Dissolve 6 tablespoons salt and sugar in 1½ quarts cold water in large container. Submerge chops in brine, cover, and refrigerate for 1 hour. Combine onion powder, granulated garlic, 1½ tablespoons salt, and 2 tablespoons pepper in bowl; set aside.

2. FOR THE BARBECUE SAUCE: Cook bacon in medium saucepan over medium heat until fat begins to render and bacon begins to brown, 4 to 6 minutes. Add onion and ¼ teaspoon salt and cook until softened, 2 to 4 minutes. Stir in vinegar, scraping

up any browned bits, and cook until slightly thickened, about 2 minutes.

3. Stir in broth, ketchup, hot sauce, liquid smoke, and ¼ teaspoon pepper. Bring to simmer and cook until slightly thickened, about 15 minutes, stirring occasionally. Discard bacon and season with salt and pepper to taste. Remove from heat, cover, and keep warm.

4. Just before grilling, soak wood chips in water for 15 minutes, then drain. Using large piece of heavy-duty aluminum foil, wrap soaked chips in 8 by 4½-inch foil packet. (Make sure chips do not poke holes in sides or bottom of packet.) Cut 2 evenly spaced 2-inch slits in top of packet. Remove chops from brine and pat dry with paper towels. Season chops all over with reserved spice mixture.

5A. FOR A CHARCOAL GRILL: Open bottom vent completely. Light large chimney starter three-quarters filled with charcoal briquettes (4½ quarts). When top coals are partially covered with ash, pour evenly over half of grill. Place wood chip packet on coals. Set cooking grate in place, cover, and open lid vent completely. Heat grill until hot and wood chips are smoking, about 5 minutes.

5B. FOR A GAS GRILL: Remove cooking grate and place wood chip packet directly on primary burner. Set grate in place, turn all burners to high, cover, and heat grill until hot and wood chips are smoking, about 15 minutes. Leave primary burner on medium-high and turn off other burner(s). (Adjust primary burner as needed to maintain grill temperature around 325 degrees.)

6. Clean and oil cooking grate. Arrange chops on cooler side of grill with bone ends toward fire. Cook, covered (positioning lid vent over chops if using charcoal), until chops register 140 degrees, 45 to 50 minutes, flipping halfway through cooking.

7. Transfer chops to platter, tent with foil, and let rest for 10 minutes. Brush chops generously with warm sauce and serve, passing remaining sauce separately.

Make It Mesquite
Smoky, peaty mesquite is the wood of choice in Llano, Texas, and its unique flavor is key to these pork chops; hickory is too pungent, apple too sweet, and oak too mild. Mesquite chips are available at most hardware stores and online.

Grilled Broccoli

We wanted tender, not tough. BY CECELIA JENKINS

We quickly precook the spears in a foil packet before browning them over the hot coals.

STEAMING, SAUTÉING, OR microwaving broccoli is fine, but if you want vivid green florets with flavorful charred accents, you can't beat the grill.

Peeling the stalks with a vegetable peeler is key to avoid toughness. I cut the head into spears with 3- to 4-inch-wide florets and ½- to ¾-inch-thick stems: small enough to cook through but large enough to grill easily.

But even after carefully cutting it this way, I couldn't get the broccoli cooked through before it burned. I'd need to precook it. I tried blanching, microwaving, and steaming, and the latter proved best. But could I steam on the grill?

Yes, by using foil "hobo packs." I tossed the spears in an oil mixture, divided them evenly between two sheets of foil, and wrapped them up. Flipping the packs halfway through ensured even cooking. I then removed the spears from the foil and placed them directly on the grill. I had soft, charred florets and sweet, tender stems. A simple squirt of lemon sealed the deal.

GRILLED BROCCOLI WITH LEMON AND PARMESAN Serves 4

To keep the packs from tearing, use heavy-duty aluminum foil. Use the large holes of a box grater to shred the Parmesan. For additional grilled broccoli recipes, go to CooksCountry.com/july16.

    ¼   cup extra-virgin olive oil, plus extra for drizzling
    1   tablespoon water
        Salt and pepper
    2   pounds broccoli
    1   lemon, halved
    ¼   cup shredded Parmesan cheese

1. Cut two 26 by 12-inch sheets of heavy-duty aluminum foil. Whisk oil, water, ¾ teaspoon salt, and ½ teaspoon pepper together in large bowl.

2. Trim stalk ends so each entire head of broccoli measures 6 to 7 inches long. Using vegetable peeler, peel away tough outer layer of broccoli stalks (about ⅛ inch). Cut stalks in half lengthwise into spears (stems should be ½ to ¾ inch thick and florets 3 to 4 inches wide). Add broccoli spears to oil mixture and toss well to coat.

3. Divide broccoli between sheets of foil, cut side down and alternating direction of florets and stems. Bring short sides of foil together and crimp tightly. Crimp long ends to seal packs tightly.

4A. FOR A CHARCOAL GRILL: Open bottom vent completely. Light large chimney starter filled with charcoal briquettes (6 quarts). When top coals are partially covered with ash, pour evenly over half of grill. Set cooking grate in place, cover, and open lid vent completely. Heat grill until hot, about 5 minutes.

4B. FOR A GAS GRILL: Turn all burners to high, cover, and heat grill until hot, about 15 minutes. Turn all burners to medium-high. (Adjust burners as needed to maintain grill temperature around 400 degrees.)

5. Clean and oil cooking grate. Arrange packs evenly on grill (over coals if using charcoal), cover, and cook for 8 minutes, flipping packs halfway through cooking.

6. Transfer packs to rimmed baking sheet and, using scissors, carefully cut open, allowing steam to escape away from you. (Broccoli should be bright green and fork inserted into stems should meet some resistance.)

7. Discard foil and place broccoli and lemon halves cut side down on grill (over coals if using charcoal). Grill (covered if using gas), turning broccoli about every 2 minutes, until stems are fork-tender and well charred on all sides, 6 to 8 minutes total. (Transfer broccoli to now-empty sheet as it finishes cooking.) Grill lemon halves until well charred on cut side, 6 to 8 minutes.

8. Transfer broccoli to cutting board and cut into 2-inch pieces; transfer to platter. Season with salt and pepper to taste. Squeeze lemon over broccoli to taste, sprinkle with Parmesan, and drizzle with extra oil. Serve.

Tennessee Pulled Turkey Sandwiches

Move over, pork. It's turkey time.

BY MORGAN BOLLING

WHEN I GO for barbecue, I typically order my longtime favorite, pulled pork. But when a Tennessee friend recently raved about a local sandwich featuring shreds of juicy turkey breast tossed with a tangy white barbecue sauce, she caught my attention. She spoke of turkey so moist that its juices seeped into the bun, with just enough smokiness to enhance—not overpower—the delicate meat. The rich mayonnaise-based sauce, she said, was an ideal condiment for the lean turkey. I'm a hard sell when it comes to my barbecue routine, but her devotion convinced me to try something new.

I found dozens of recipes online and in the test kitchen library and selected a handful to try. Six turkey breasts and a bag of charcoal later, I was disappointed to find that none of the recipes lived up to the revered sandwich. Most of the sandwiches were overpoweringly smoky or so full of spice that any turkey flavor was lost. The most unsettling part, however, was the texture, which was uniformly cardboard-like. The problem was that most of the recipes had been designed for the low, controlled temperature of a smoker. Since I'd used a charcoal grill (a more accessible option), the turkey had cooked too quickly.

I'd have to create a grill-friendly recipe from scratch. First up: the troublesome anatomy of a bone-in turkey breast. The breastbone juts out in an awkward way, making a portion of the meat sit up high on the grill grate and cook unevenly. I could have removed the bone to make the meat lie flat, but the easier option was to simply purchase boneless split turkey breasts. But without any bones to protect the meat, producing juicy turkey would be even more of a challenge.

Cooking with indirect heat made sense, since it would allow the turkey to slowly heat up on the cooler side of the grill. The problem was that producing a slow, steady fire meant starting with a small amount of coals and periodically lifting the hot grill grate to add more—a procedure that was too precarious for my liking. But getting the meat to reach the target temperature of 160 degrees before a single chimney of charcoal died out meant cooking it relatively quickly. On the plus side, this meant that the breasts were on and off the grill in an hour. The downside? Dry turkey.

I knew that rubbing the turkey with

We salt the turkey a day ahead to ensure juicy, thoroughly seasoned meat. Our Alabama-style white sauce adds even more flavor.

salt and letting it sit overnight would help it retain some of its juices. Sure enough, compared with breasts that had been salted immediately before going on the grill, the turkey that had been salted the previous day was thoroughly seasoned and somewhat moister. A sprinkling of black pepper and cayenne right before grilling added a bit of spiciness.

Things were looking up, but I still wanted the turkey to be more moist.

While more traditional barbecue cuts like fatty pork butt or beef brisket turn meltingly tender as the fat renders during a long stint on the grill, turkey just dries out. With that in mind, I decided to combat the leanness in a direct way: by adding fat. Transferring the turkey to a disposable aluminum pan and smearing it with butter partway through cooking did the trick, adding richness and moisture to the meat. After

testing, I found that cooking the turkey in the pan the whole time shielded it too much from the smoke, whereas moving it to the pan too late made it overly smoky. Making the transfer when the turkey reached 120 degrees delivered the right balance of smoke and moisture.

Speaking of smoke, achieving smoky flavor was simple since most types of smoke are water-soluble, and turkey contains a large amount of water.

I found that 2 cups of soaked wood chips smoldered just enough to give the turkey a substantial but not overpowering level of smoke. Once the meat was done, I shredded it and mixed it with the delicious blend of turkey juices and butter that was left behind in the roasting pan, making it moister still.

The only thing missing was the white barbecue sauce. Unfamiliar in most areas of the United States, this mixture of mayonnaise and vinegar reigns supreme in Alabama and a handful of its border states. Adding some horseradish, Worcestershire sauce, garlic, and both black and cayenne peppers to the sauce gave it a complex kick that complemented my smoky, juicy turkey.

The next time I'm at a barbecue joint, I just might order smoked turkey. But after eating my own succulent creation, I feel that the bar would be high.

TENNESSEE PULLED TURKEY SANDWICHES

Serves 8 to 10

We prefer a natural (unbrined) turkey breast here, but both self-basting and kosher work well. Plan ahead: The salted meat needs to be refrigerated for at least 8 hours. Skip the salting step if you buy a kosher or self-basting breast. Some stores sell only boneless turkey breasts with the skin still attached; the skin can be removed easily with a paring knife. If you don't have ½ cup of juices from the rested turkey, supplement with chicken broth.

TURKEY

- 2 (1¾- to 2-pound) boneless, skinless split turkey breasts, trimmed Kosher salt and pepper
- 2 cups wood chips
- ½ teaspoon cayenne pepper
- 1 (13 by 9-inch) disposable aluminum roasting pan
- 4 tablespoons unsalted butter, cut into 4 pieces

WHITE BARBECUE SAUCE

- 1 cup mayonnaise
- ⅓ cup cider vinegar
- 1 tablespoon prepared horseradish, drained
- 1½ teaspoons kosher salt
- 1 teaspoon Worcestershire sauce
- 1 garlic clove, minced
- 1 teaspoon pepper
- ¼ teaspoon cayenne pepper

- 8 hamburger buns
  Shredded iceberg lettuce

1. FOR THE TURKEY: Pat turkey dry with paper towels, place on large sheet of plastic wrap, and sprinkle with 1 tablespoon salt. Wrap in plastic and refrigerate for at least 8 hours or overnight.

2. Just before grilling, soak wood chips in water for 15 minutes, then drain. Using large piece of heavy-duty aluminum foil, wrap soaked chips in 8 by 4½-inch foil packet. (Make sure chips do not poke holes in sides or bottom of packet.) Cut 2 evenly spaced 2-inch slits in top of packet.

3A. FOR A CHARCOAL GRILL: Open bottom vent completely. Light large chimney starter three-quarters filled with charcoal briquettes (4½ quarts). When top coals are partially covered with ash, pour evenly over half of grill. Place wood chip packet on coals. Set cooking grate in place, cover, and open lid vent completely. Heat grill until hot and wood chips are smoking, about 5 minutes.

3B. FOR A GAS GRILL: Remove cooking grate and place wood chip packet directly on primary burner. Set grate in place, turn all burners to high, cover, and heat grill until hot and wood chips are smoking, about 15 minutes. Leave primary burner on medium-high and turn off other burner(s). (Adjust primary burner as needed to maintain grill temperature between 300 and 350 degrees.)

4. Clean and oil cooking grate. Unwrap turkey and sprinkle with 2 teaspoons pepper and cayenne. Place turkey on cooler side of grill, with thicker parts of breasts closest to fire. Cover grill (positioning lid vent directly over turkey if using charcoal) and cook until breasts register 120 degrees, 30 to 40 minutes.

5. Transfer turkey to disposable pan and top with butter. Cover pan tightly with foil and return to cooler side of grill. Cover grill and continue to cook until breasts register 160 degrees, 25 to 35 minutes longer. Remove pan from grill and let turkey rest in covered pan for 20 minutes.

6. FOR THE WHITE BARBECUE SAUCE: Whisk all ingredients in bowl until smooth.

7. Transfer turkey to cutting board. Using two forks or your hands, shred turkey into bite-size pieces. Transfer to large bowl. Add ½ cup juices from pan to shredded turkey and toss to combine. Season with salt and pepper to taste.

8. Serve turkey on buns with white barbecue sauce and lettuce.

KEY STEP **Top 'em with Butter**
To add richness and help keep the turkey moist, we transfer the partially cooked breasts to a disposable pan and top them with butter before covering the pan with foil.

Should You Buy a Grill Light? It's Complicated.

Grill lights are portable, battery-powered LED lamps that latch onto your grill's handles (or side tables) to illuminate the cooking surface. Looking for the best, we rounded up 14 models, including some designed for camping, to put through their paces.

We tested each light's compatibility with six grills (a mix of gas and charcoal models). Then we took each one into a dark room and used a light meter to measure brightness both in the center of the grill, where each light was aimed, and on the periphery. Finally, we went outside and grilled burgers in the dark, using each of the grill lights as our only illumination.

While every model helped cut through the dark, they all had problems, the biggest of which was the ability to evenly illuminate the entire cooking surface—most could light up only a few burgers on a full grill, making it hard to see char and gauge doneness. Some projected narrow spotlights that washed out the cooks' view of most of the food. Design flaws included flimsy, weak clamps or latches; the inability to attach to some or all grills; long necks that drooped of their own accord; or short, stubby necks that couldn't be positioned to light properly.

Our winning light illuminated the entire grill.

We didn't find a perfect light, but our testing uncovered a few models that do make it easier to grill in the dark. The best of these, from Ivation, attached to every grill and threw a warm spread of light over most of the grill surface. It did not, however, attach as securely as we would have liked. Go to CooksCountry.com/july16 for the full story and testing chart. –LAUREN SAVOIE

RECOMMENDED	CRITERIA		TESTERS' NOTES
IVATION Multipurpose Gooseneck 7-LED Dimmable Clip Light **Model:** IVACLED **Price:** $24.99 **Style:** Clip **Weatherproof:** No	Brightness Coverage Stability Compatibility Ease of Use	★★★ ★★★ ★½ ★★★ ★★	This model was the brightest of the bunch, with an even, wide spread of warm light that allowed us to easily see char and gauge the doneness of the food. While this light stood freely on side tables and clipped effortlessly to handles, it was easily jostled and displaced whenever we moved the grill or lid.
RECOMMENDED WITH RESERVATIONS			
BLACKFIRE Clamplight Waterproof **Model:** BBM905 **Price:** $24.95 **Style:** Clip **Weatherproof:** Yes	Brightness Coverage Stability Compatibility Ease of Use	★★★ ★ ★★★ ★★★ ★★	Testers loved this durable, waterproof camping light's sturdy, simple clamp, which easily attached to all grill handles and didn't budge. It could also be configured to stand freely on a side table for grills without handles. Unfortunately, its brightness was concentrated like a spotlight in the middle of the grill, producing glare and making it hard to get a good look at the food.
CUISINART Grilluminate Extending LED Grill Light **Model:** CGL-330 **Price:** $24.44 **Style:** Screw on **Weatherproof:** No	Brightness Coverage Stability Compatibility Ease of Use	★ ★★★ ★★★ ★½ ★★½	This light, which has two extending light panels, cast a wide spread of soft light that was fine for maneuvering food around the grill but a bit too weak for gauging char and doneness of burgers. It also didn't fit on grills without handles, and its stubby neck had trouble extending past the lid on some larger grills.

TIP **Don't Trust the Pop**
Ignore the pop-up timer that comes with some turkey breasts; the meat will be overcooked long before the popper pops. You should gauge doneness only with an instant-read thermometer. But don't remove the pop-up timer until the meat is done and has rested; otherwise it will leave a hole from which juices will flow, leaving you with a dried-out, totally uninspiring turkey. Our favorite instant-read thermometer is the **ThermoWorks Thermapen Mk4**.

Smashed Potato Salad

Finding the perfect balance of smooth and chunky potatoes for this Southern side was a lesson in restraint. BY CHRISTIE MORRISON

IMAGINE CREAMY MASHED potatoes crossed with tangy, chunky potato salad. This style is nothing new if you're from certain corners of the South, where mashing (or smashing) the potatoes in potato salad is business as usual. But in our Boston-based test kitchen, this was a new approach.

Many recipes advocate using unpeeled potatoes to give the salad a rustic look. Cooking times are loose, as is the nomenclature: The line between "smashed" and "mashed" is vaguely defined, but the goal is a salad with a mix of textures—partly chunky, partly smooth. Potato salads that use a ricer, food mill, or stand mixer to more thoroughly break down the potatoes head squarely into mashed potato territory, a region I wanted to avoid; who wants a whole bowl of cold mashed potatoes?

But developing a smashed potato recipe with varied and—importantly—reproducible texture meant setting some ground rules. Choosing the right potato was the first step. If I wanted to omit peeling the potatoes (and I sure did), Yukon Golds worked best when I tested them against russets and red potatoes. While russets make great mashed potatoes, their starchy flesh became pasty when mixed into a salad. And while red potatoes had decent mashability, their skins were tougher and less appealing in the salad than those of the Yukons. I cooked the Yukons until they were just tender, drained them, and then followed a test kitchen trick, seasoning the still-hot potato chunks with a splash of vinegar for deep flavor.

Getting the best ratio of chunks to mash took some experimenting. Gently smashing an entire bowl of cooked potatoes yielded inconsistent results: Some batches were too smooth, others too chunky. The easiest way to get enough smooth potatoes to bind the salad but enough chunks to give it some texture

Mashing just a portion of the cooked potatoes adds texture to this dish.

was to fully mash a set amount of potatoes and then add the mashed portion to the rest of the salad. I settled on removing about one-third of the total potatoes for smashing. The rest I spread onto a baking sheet to let cool for 15 minutes, which helped them keep their shape.

Southern purists insist that Duke's mayonnaise (see "Mayo Showdown") is the only acceptable mayo for potato salad. Since mail order wasn't in the cards for this recipe, however, I used the test kitchen's favorite nationally available mayo (Hellmann's, or Best Foods

west of the Rockies) and increased the tang with a few tablespoons of yellow mustard. One place I opted for some sweetness was with the pickles: Instead of the dill pickles or dill pickle relish we usually use in potato salad, I opted for bread-and-butter chips (although any type of sweet pickles will work).

A few hard-cooked eggs and some chopped celery added more texture to the mix, while a combination of onion and scallions gave it an edge.

SMASHED POTATO SALAD
Serves 8 to 10

Use the tip of a paring knife to judge the doneness of the potatoes. If the tip inserts easily into the potato pieces, they are done. Hellmann's Real Mayonnaise is our favorite nationally available mayonnaise. Note that the salad needs to be refrigerated for about 2 hours before serving.

- 3 pounds Yukon Gold potatoes, unpeeled, cut into 1-inch chunks
  Salt and pepper
- 2 tablespoons distilled white vinegar
- 1 cup mayonnaise
- 3 tablespoons yellow mustard
- ¼ teaspoon cayenne pepper
- 3 hard-cooked large eggs, chopped
- 3 scallions, sliced thin
- ½ cup chopped sweet pickles
- ½ cup finely chopped celery
- ¼ cup finely chopped onion

1. Combine potatoes, 8 cups water, and 1 tablespoon salt in Dutch oven and bring to boil over high heat. Reduce heat to medium and cook at vigorous simmer until potatoes are tender, 14 to 17 minutes.

2. Drain potatoes in colander. Transfer 3 cups potatoes to large bowl, add 1 tablespoon vinegar, and coarsely mash with potato masher. Transfer remaining potatoes to rimmed baking sheet, drizzle with remaining 1 tablespoon vinegar, and toss gently to combine. Let cool completely, about 15 minutes.

3. Whisk mayonnaise, ½ cup water, mustard, cayenne, 1 teaspoon salt, and 1 teaspoon pepper together in bowl. Stir mayonnaise mixture into mashed potatoes. Fold in eggs, scallions, pickles, celery, onion, and remaining potatoes until combined. (Mixture will be lumpy.)

4. Cover and refrigerate until fully chilled, about 2 hours. Season with salt and pepper to taste. Serve.

Mayo Showdown

Commercial mayonnaise is one of the most hotly debated ingredients out there, with impassioned salad- and sandwich-makers insisting that only their favorite will do. Here are three of the most well-loved mayos.

HELLMANN'S
(sold as Best Foods west of the Rockies) The most popular brand in the U.S., Hellmann's accounts for about half of all mayonnaise sales.

DUKE'S
This spread is made with cider vinegar, which gives it a sharp flavor. It has ardent fans in many Southern states.

BLUE PLATE
The test kitchen's favorite mayo is made with egg yolks, not whole eggs. It must be mail-ordered in most of the country.

Backyard Barbecue Beans

Canned baked beans are not bad.
But with a few additions, they can be so much more. BY DIANE UNGER

A WHILE BACK, I was invited to a cookout, and I asked what I could bring. The host had all the big stuff handled (ribs, brisket, and his secret chicken recipe), so he requested a side dish. "Maybe beans?"

Being a native New Englander, I immediately thought of Boston baked beans. The day before the party, I started my beans soaking. The morning of, I got up at the crack of dawn to get the beans in a low oven to cook for 6 hours. The results were delicious, but I wanted more than just delicious. I wanted showstopping.

I wanted a less sweet, more assertively savory dish, one that would complement a full barbecue spread and serve a crowd. I was inspired by a friend of a friend, Daniel Gruskin of Lexington, Mass., who bolsters his baked beans with add-ins like bacon and garlic. I resolved to do the same . . . and then some.

I decided to save time on the front end by using canned beans rather than dried. This decision freed me up to start with a multifaceted bean base, including pinto beans for their creaminess, cannellini beans for contrast, and traditional Boston-style baked white beans for the slight sweetness I wanted (I chose Bush's for their consistency). I drained the pinto and cannellini beans but left the baked beans clinging to their sauce, which served as the foundation for my savory side dish. Once I'd combined them, it was time to pull out all the stops to transform these canned beans into something special.

I figured I'd bathe the beans in a simple pantry sauce, so I stirred together ketchup, mustard, and bottled barbecue sauce. Apple cider vinegar kept the sweetness in check, granulated garlic and cayenne pepper added a bit of heat, and a tiny touch of liquid smoke gave it an outdoor flavor. I combined my beans with the sauce, transferred everything to a large baking dish, and baked the mixture until it bubbled and turned lightly brown on top. After a 15-minute cooldown, I gathered my tasters for feedback. "Not bad" was one tepid response. "Needs something more" was another. Tough crowd, but they were right.

One of the initial recipes I'd tested included slightly spicy Ro-tel tomatoes in the mix, an idea I loved. It was also topped with 1-inch pieces of bacon. Of course, I thought: bacon.

With beans this good, we made enough to serve a crowd.

I liked the idea of adding a bonus meaty component, not just bacon, to my beans. Sausage and bratwurst were the easiest to find, so I made my next test a side-by-side-by-side sausage showdown: One batch got cooked bulk breakfast sausage, one hot Italian, and one bratwurst stirred in. I also added chopped onion to all three. I topped each batch with bacon (one batch got strips, another got minced, and the third got 1-inch pieces) and baked them until the bacon was rendered and crispy.

Tasters loved the sausage, and when I pressed them to choose a favorite, the consensus was bratwurst for its meaty but not overly intrusive flavor (the Italian was too spicy and the breakfast too breakfasty). As for the bacon, it was hard to go wrong, but for presentation and ease of serving, my tasters preferred the cobblestone effect of the 1-inch pieces arranged on top of the beans.

All that was left to do was hide the can opener and soak in the accolades.

Best for Baking
We tried several varieties of baked beans and found that firm, creamy **Bush's Original Recipe Baked Beans** held their shape best in this recipe. Plus, their meaty flavor is ideal for doctoring.

BACKYARD BARBECUE BEANS
Serves 12 to 16

Be sure to use a 13 by 9-inch metal baking pan; the volume of the beans is too great for a 13 by 9-inch ceramic baking dish, and it will overflow. We found that Bush's Original Recipe Baked Beans are the most consistent product for this recipe. Our favorite supermarket barbecue sauce is Bull's-Eye Original Barbecue Sauce.

- ½ cup barbecue sauce
- ½ cup ketchup
- ½ cup water
- 2 tablespoons spicy brown mustard
- 2 tablespoons cider vinegar
- 1 teaspoon liquid smoke
- 1 teaspoon granulated garlic
- ¼ teaspoon cayenne pepper
- 1¼ pounds bratwurst, casings removed
- 2 onions, chopped
- 2 (28-ounce) cans baked beans
- 2 (15-ounce) cans pinto beans, drained
- 2 (15-ounce) cans cannellini beans, drained
- 1 (10-ounce) can Ro-tel Original Diced Tomatoes & Green Chilies, drained
- 6 slices thick-cut bacon, cut into 1-inch pieces

1. Adjust oven rack to middle position and heat oven to 350 degrees. Whisk barbecue sauce, ketchup, water, mustard, vinegar, liquid smoke, granulated garlic, and cayenne together in large bowl; set aside.

2. Cook bratwurst in 12-inch nonstick skillet over medium-high heat, breaking up into small pieces with spoon, until fat begins to render, about 5 minutes. Stir in onions and cook until sausage and onions are well browned, about 15 minutes.

3. Transfer bratwurst mixture to bowl with sauce. Stir in baked beans, pinto beans, cannellini beans, and tomatoes. Transfer bean mixture to 13 by 9-inch baking pan and place pan on rimmed baking sheet. Arrange bacon pieces in single layer over top of beans.

4. Bake until beans are bubbling and bacon is rendered, about 1½ hours. Let cool for 15 minutes. Serve.

TO MAKE AHEAD
At end of step 3, beans can be wrapped in plastic and refrigerated for up to 24 hours. Proceed with recipe from step 4, increasing baking time to 1¾ hours.

Grilled Bourbon Steaks

Why marinate rib eyes in bourbon? We wondered, too—until we tried it.

BY ASHLEY MOORE

WHAT WOULD POSSESS the cooks at Jesse's Restaurant in Magnolia Springs, Alabama, to marinate perfectly good 16-ounce rib-eye steaks in bourbon whiskey, Worcestershire, and other "secret ingredients"? Aren't rib-eye steaks good enough on their own?

Answer: Yes, rib-eye steaks can be great with just salt. But the Whiskey Steak at Jesse's, which *Cook's Country* executive food editor Bryan Roof tried on a recent trip to Alabama, was something special, with a mild bourbon flavor that enhanced rather than detracted from its essential meatiness and created a lovely char as well. And judging by the fans who return to Jesse's again and again, he's hardly alone in his enthusiasm.

We've developed many recipes in the test kitchen that use a whiskey-based marinade, including a popular recipe for Bourbon Smoked Chicken (August/September 2014), which I used as a starting point. The marinade is a mixture of bourbon, brown sugar, shallots, and garlic (these help add flavor to the exterior of the meat and increase the char), plus soy sauce, which has enough salt to season the meat throughout. Steaks made with this marinade were tasty, but they didn't remind Roof of Jesse's.

Roof approved of the garlic and shallots, but he felt that these steaks were too sweet, so I nixed the brown sugar. I also traded soy sauce for more complex Worcestershire sauce—which also contains enough salt to season the meat deeply. After several tests using whiskey and Worcestershire in varying ratios, tasters preferred a 1:1 partnership (1 cup of each for four steaks).

But which whiskey? In a side-by-side tasting of conventional whiskey versus bourbon (a subset of whiskey), tasters unanimously preferred the subtle caramel and vanilla flavors present in the bourbon. Why? The aging process of the booze. While most whiskey is aged in oak barrels, bourbon is aged in charred new white oak barrels for two to four years. This adds a distinct vanilla note to the bourbon, as well as a lovely chestnut-brown color. And because bourbon is made from a grain mixture that's at least 51 percent corn (see "World of Whiskey"), it has a subtle sweetness that offers a

A simple soak in bourbon, Worcestershire sauce, and seasonings amplifies this steak's sweet-savory flavors and adds extra char besides.

rounder, less harsh, less aggressively alcoholic presence.

My next task was to test marinating times. I found that 1 hour wasn't sufficient for substantive flavor; neither was 2 hours or even 3. Four hours was just right, although marinating for up to 24 hours worked well, too. Any more than that and the texture of the steaks suffered. Dividing the steaks and the marinade between two separate

zipper-lock bags gave the best results—a deep, complex, but not overwhelming whiskey flavor that enhanced rather than overshadowed the meat.

As for a fire, an even, hot charcoal fire made with a full chimney of briquettes gave me an excellent char when the steaks were cooked to medium-rare. On a gas grill, setting all of the burners to high for a 15-minute preheat and then reducing the burners to

medium-high for cooking was ideal.

With all the details settled, I ran through my refined recipe one last time. A few people walked by my grill and commented on how good "whatever that was" smelled. Just a few minutes later, I brought my nicely charred bourbon steaks into the kitchen for tasting, where even the most die-hard rib-eye purists were convinced: Bourbon goes beautifully with steak.

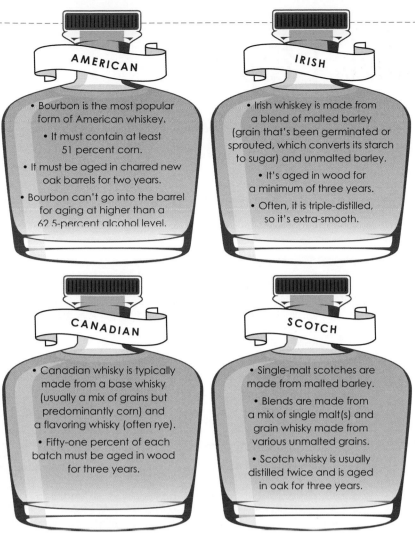

AMERICAN

- Bourbon is the most popular form of American whiskey.
- It must contain at least 51 percent corn.
- It must be aged in charred new oak barrels for two years.
- Bourbon can't go into the barrel for aging at higher than a 62.5-percent alcohol level.

IRISH

- Irish whiskey is made from a blend of malted barley (grain that's been germinated or sprouted, which converts its starch to sugar) and unmalted barley.
- It's aged in wood for a minimum of three years.
- Often, it is triple-distilled, so it's extra-smooth.

CANADIAN

- Canadian whisky is typically made from a base whisky (usually a mix of grains but predominantly corn) and a flavoring whisky (often rye).
- Fifty-one percent of each batch must be aged in wood for three years.

SCOTCH

- Single-malt scotches are made from malted barley.
- Blends are made from a mix of single malt(s) and grain whisky made from various unmalted grains.
- Scotch whisky is usually distilled twice and is aged in oak for three years.

World of Whiskey

The word *whiskey* comes from the Celtic *uisqebaugh* (whis-kee-BAW), meaning "water of life." It is traditionally made from barley, corn, rye, wheat, or oats, but artisanal makers now incorporate everything from buckwheat to farro to spelt. A whiskey's distinct flavor is determined by a number of factors including the type of grain used, the aging time, the type of wood in which it is stored, and the distillation method. There are many types of whiskey, but American, Irish, Canadian, and Scotch are the most widely consumed. (Scotch and Canadian whiskys drop the *e*.)

GRILLED BOURBON STEAKS

Serves 6 to 8

Use a bourbon you'd be happy drinking. Plan ahead: These steaks need to marinate for at least 4 hours before grilling.

- 1 cup bourbon
- 1 cup Worcestershire sauce
- 1 shallot, minced
- 2 garlic cloves, minced
  Kosher salt and pepper
- 4 (1-pound) boneless rib-eye steaks, 1 to 1½ inches thick, trimmed
- 2 tablespoons vegetable oil

1. Whisk bourbon, Worcestershire, shallot, garlic, 2 teaspoons salt, and 2 teaspoons pepper together in bowl. Place 2 steaks in each of two 1-gallon zipper-lock bags and divide bourbon mixture between bags, about 1 cup each. Seal bags, turn to distribute marinade, and refrigerate for at least 4 hours or up to 24 hours, flipping occasionally.

2. Remove steaks from marinade and pat dry with paper towels; discard marinade. Brush steaks all over with oil and season liberally with salt and pepper.

3A. FOR A CHARCOAL GRILL: Open bottom vent completely. Light large chimney starter filled with charcoal briquettes (6 quarts). When top coals are partially covered with ash, pour evenly over grill. Set cooking grate in place, cover, and open lid vent completely. Heat grill until hot, about 5 minutes.

3B. FOR A GAS GRILL: Turn all burners to high, cover, and heat grill until hot, about 15 minutes. Turn all burners to medium-high. (Adjust burners as needed to maintain grill temperature between 350 and 400 degrees.)

4. Clean and oil cooking grate. Place steaks on grill and cook (covered if using gas) until well charred and meat registers 125 degrees (for medium-rare), 6 to 8 minutes per side.

5. Transfer steaks to wire rack set in rimmed baking sheet, tent with aluminum foil, and let rest for 10 minutes. Serve.

What's the Best Worcestershire Sauce?

We use Worcestershire sauce to add salty, punchy kick and depth to all sorts of dishes. This ingredient originated in the English county of Worcester in the early 19th century. As the story goes, a wealthy Brit who had recently returned from India commissioned chemists John Lea and William Perrins to create a sauce reminiscent of those he'd enjoyed abroad. Lea and Perrins made the sauce to his specifications but found it unpalatable, so it sat, forgotten, in a corner of their shop's basement until someone decided to try it a few years later and discovered that fermentation had transformed it into a sauce with incredible depth.

While no manufacturer wants to give up its exact recipe, most Worcestershire sauce today is made with onions, garlic, salt, anchovies, vinegar, spices, tamarind, molasses, and sugar. The sauce is aged for a few weeks to a few months before being strained, diluted with water, and bottled. To find the best version, we sampled four nationally available products plain, in barbecue sauce, and in our recipe for Grilled Bourbon Steaks, which uses a full cup in the marinade.

Texture wasn't important in our findings, but flavor certainly was. Two manufacturers made their sauces vegan by omitting anchovies and substituting ingredients like onion oil, mushrooms, and soy sauce. Unfortunately, these sauces didn't quite match the subtle meatiness and depth of Worcestershire made with anchovies. Tasters also singled out one of the vegan sauces for its overly pungent notes of onion (from the addition of onion oil) when sampled plain and in the steak. We preferred sauces that were balanced, without any one ingredient being too assertive.

Vegan products also tried to compensate by jacking up the sodium: One sauce contained twice as much as our top-ranked sauce. Products with moderate saltiness allowed us better control over the final flavor of the dish. That said, these flaws of balance and salinity didn't matter when we tasted the sauces in barbecue sauce, a recipe that contains a lot of potent ingredients—if you need only a few teaspoons of Worcestershire for a pungent recipe, it's likely any product will do.

Overall, tasters preferred Lea & Perrins Original Worcestershire Sauce for its bright, balanced flavor; remarkable depth; and subtle kick of heat. It's no wonder this product has stuck around for almost 200 years. –LAUREN SAVOIE

RECOMMENDED		TASTERS' NOTES
LEA & PERRINS Original Worcestershire Sauce **Price:** $4.19 for 10 oz ($0.42 per oz) **Sodium:** 65 mg **Ingredients:** Distilled white vinegar, molasses, sugar, water, salt, onions, anchovies, garlic, cloves, tamarind extract, natural flavorings, chili pepper extract		The original Worcestershire sauce, this product "hit all the marks," with "balanced" notes of vinegar, pepper, and tamarind. In a marinade, this sauce was "distinctively punchy" and lent a "bright" tanginess that tasters loved.
FRENCH'S Worcestershire Sauce **Price:** $2.39 for 10 oz ($0.24 per oz) **Sodium:** 65 mg **Ingredients:** Distilled vinegar, water, molasses, corn syrup, salt, sugar, spices, caramel color, anchovies, natural flavors (soy), xanthan gum, dehydrated garlic powder and tamarind extract		This sauce was full of "bold citrusy tang," with a "mild" sweetness and a hint of "fishy" flavor ("in a good way!"). Though a few tasters thought this sauce was "a little hot for Worcestershire," most appreciated its "spicy" heat and "balanced" flavors.
ANNIE'S Organic Vegan Worcestershire Sauce **Price:** $3.59 for 6.25 oz ($0.57 per oz) **Sodium:** 75 mg **Ingredients:** Water, apple cider vinegar, molasses, soy sauce (water, soybean, salt, wheat, alcohol), cane sugar, tamarind, sea salt, cornstarch, xanthan gum, garlic, onion, clove, chili pepper		Tasters liked the "hint of tang" and slightly "fruity" flavor of this organic sauce though, without anchovies, some lamented that this product was "more sweet" and "mild" than other samples. In steak marinade, this sauce was "molasses-forward," with subtle "smoky," "woodsy" notes.

RECOMMENDED WITH RESERVATIONS

THE WIZARD'S Organic Vegan Worcestershire Sauce **Price:** $4.09 for 8.5 oz ($0.48 per oz) **Sodium:** 130 mg **Ingredients:** Apple cider vinegar, molasses, wheat-free tamari (water, soybeans, salt), filtered water, evaporated cane juice, salt, lemon juice concentrate, ginger puree, tamarind, chili pepper, garlic powder, xanthan gum, shiitake mushrooms, allspice, cloves, orange extract, lemon extract, natural smoke flavor, natural onion flavor (onion oil)		While some tasters liked the "funky," "assertive" flavor of this "piquant" and "salty" sauce, many thought this vegan product "lacked the distinguishing flavors of Worcestershire." Instead, these tasters identified "heavy" notes of "salt" and "soy sauce," with a prominent "oniony" smell, likely from the addition of onion oil.

Sodium levels are for a 1-teaspoon serving.

Summery Stuffed Peppers

Traditional stuffed peppers can be heavy, meat-filled meals. We wanted a fresher, lighter version for summertime. BY DIANE UNGER

IT'S THE HEIGHT of summer, and I'm on the lookout for ideas for what to do with the bounty of bell peppers at the market. For years, my go-to recipe has been my grandmother's meat-and-rice-stuffed peppers. But I wanted something fresher, lighter, and easier.

To garner ideas, I gathered five intriguing stuffed pepper recipes and set out a grand tasting for my colleagues. One recipe, from celebrated California chef Alice Waters, featured peppers that were roasted, peeled, and stuffed with crusty bread, creamy sheep's-milk cheese, fresh herbs, lemon zest, and pine nuts. I liked the bright flavors but wanted to simplify the process and use less-expensive alternatives to the pricey pine nuts and sheep's-milk cheese.

Armed with inspiration, I cut the tops off six peppers and seeded them. I set them cut side down in an oiled baking pan, brushed them with extra-virgin olive oil, and roasted them (along with the stemmed pepper tops, which I'd chop and add to the filling later) in a 475-degree oven until they began to blister and soften, which took about 20 minutes. After standing them upright to cool, I turned my focus to the filling.

I cut a small baguette (about 7 ounces) into ½-inch pieces and toasted them in a nonstick skillet with ¼ cup of olive oil. After removing the bread, I added a little more oil to the skillet with some garlic and red pepper flakes and cooked the mixture briefly. I then tossed this with the bread.

I chopped the roasted pepper tops and minced plenty of fresh parsley and basil to toss with the toasted bread. I swapped out sheep's milk cheese in favor of easy-to-find goat cheese—6 ounces was enough to add a creamy, tangy element without overpowering things.

For a bit of substance, I added a can of chickpeas; their nutty flavor complemented the mixture, and mashing them helped hold the stuffing together.

Some lemon zest and juice added freshness, a few capers contributed savory depth, and some sliced scallions provided a nuanced but pungent punch. After about 15 minutes in the oven, I had a lovely summery dish.

STUFFED PEPPERS WITH CHICKPEAS, GOAT CHEESE, AND HERBS Serves 6

Laura Chenel's Chèvre Fresh Chèvre Log is our favorite goat cheese. Note that we bake the peppers in a metal baking pan, not a ceramic baking dish; the metal pan gets hotter.

- ½ cup extra-virgin olive oil, plus extra for drizzling
- 6 (7- to 8-ounce) bell peppers
  Salt and pepper
- 1 (15-ounce) can chickpeas, rinsed
- 7 ounces baguette, cut into ½-inch pieces (4 cups)
- 8 garlic cloves, minced
- ¼ teaspoon red pepper flakes
- 8 scallions, sliced
- ¼ cup minced fresh parsley
- ¼ cup minced fresh basil
- 3 tablespoons capers, chopped
- 1 tablespoon grated lemon zest plus 1 tablespoon juice
- 6 ounces goat cheese, crumbled (1½ cups)

1. Adjust oven rack to upper-middle position and heat oven to 475 degrees. Grease 13 by 9-inch metal baking pan with 1 tablespoon oil. Cut off top ½ inch of bell peppers and reserve; discard stems and seeds. Arrange bell peppers and their tops cut side down in prepared pan. Brush bell peppers and tops with 1 tablespoon oil, then season with salt and pepper.

2. Roast until bell peppers are softened and beginning to blister, about 20 minutes. Flip bell peppers cut side up and let sit until cool enough to handle, about 5 minutes. Season insides with salt and pepper. Adjust oven temperature to 350 degrees.

3. Using potato masher, mash chickpeas coarse in large bowl. Chop bell pepper tops into ¼-inch pieces and add to bowl with chickpeas.

4. Heat ¼ cup oil in 12-inch nonstick skillet over medium heat until shimmering. Add bread and cook, stirring occasionally, until light golden brown and crispy, 5 to 7 minutes. Push bread to 1 side of skillet and add remaining 2 tablespoons oil to empty spot. Add garlic and pepper flakes to oil and cook until fragrant, about 30 seconds. Stir garlic mixture and ½ teaspoon salt into bread to combine. Transfer to bowl with chickpea mixture; let cool completely, about 10 minutes.

5. Stir scallions, parsley, basil, capers, lemon zest and juice, 1 teaspoon salt, and 1 teaspoon pepper into chickpea mixture. Gently fold in goat cheese until combined.

6. Divide filling evenly among bell peppers, mounding slightly. Bake until filling registers between 100 and 120 degrees and begins to brown on top, 15 to 20 minutes. Transfer to platter and drizzle with extra oil. Serve.

Chickpeas help bulk up this summery vegetarian dish, elevating it from a side to a light supper.

Alice Waters, Culinary Pioneer

Alice Waters's early food memories involve tomatoes, rhubarb, and asparagus, all from a backyard "victory garden" kept by her mother. Such gardens were planted during World Wars I and II and produced as much as 40 percent of the vegetables consumed in the U.S. some years. Fast-forward to 1965 when Waters spent her junior year in France and her passion for fresh ingredients surged. Returning to the States and unable to find favorites from abroad such as radishes or sorrel, she opened her now-legendary restaurant, Chez Panisse, with a vision of serving fresh, seasonal, and local ingredients. –REBECCA HAYS

Fried Red Tomatoes

What? Everybody knows it's fried *green* tomatoes, right? Not at this whistle-stop.

BY DIANE UNGER

FRIED GREEN TOMATOES may be the stuff movies are made of, but red, ripe tomatoes deserve a shot at fame, too. But simply swapping red tomatoes into our existing recipe for Fried Green Tomatoes was a total disaster. The coating barely adhered to the tomato slices, leaving me with a steamy, wet mess. It was time to reengineer this recipe for the sweeter, richer red tomato.

I auditioned several varieties of tomatoes: beefsteak, vine-ripened, heirloom, and plum. After many a soggy test, I found that plum tomatoes' compact size and dense flesh made them the ideal choice, as they stayed relatively firm. But they still had too much moisture.

To coax out this excess water, I tried salting them (an old test kitchen trick). It backfired, leaving the tomato flesh mealy. Simply letting the slices sit on paper towels for about 40 minutes worked better. Now for the breading.

I knew I'd need a sticky layer first; after several tests, I settled on ⅓ cup of buttermilk mixed with 1 beaten egg.

From there, I turned to the dry coating. Cornmeal on its own was too gritty and formed a hard, cardboard-like sheet. Cutting it with all-purpose flour did the trick. Adding granulated garlic to the drying tomatoes before coating them boosted flavor, as did some grated Parmesan cheese added to the coating mix. Shallow-fried in hot oil until crunchy on both sides but still tender in the middle, my fried red tomatoes were sure to make the cut.

FRIED RED TOMATOES Serves 4

Use two forks to turn the tomatoes quickly. This recipe can easily be doubled and cooked in two batches; change the oil and wipe out the skillet between batches.

- 8 ounces plum tomatoes, ends trimmed, sliced ¼ inch thick
- ½ teaspoon granulated garlic
- ⅓ cup buttermilk
- 1 large egg
- ⅔ cup cornmeal
- ⅓ cup all-purpose flour
- 1 ounce Parmesan cheese, grated (½ cup)
  Salt and pepper
- ⅛ teaspoon cayenne pepper
- ½ cup vegetable oil
- 2 tablespoons minced fresh basil
  Lemon wedges

1. Line wire rack with triple layer of paper towels. Evenly space tomato slices on rack, sprinkle with granulated garlic, and let drain for 40 minutes, flipping halfway through draining.

2. Line rimmed baking sheet with parchment paper. Whisk buttermilk and egg together in shallow dish. Combine cornmeal, flour, Parmesan, ¾ teaspoon salt, ¼ teaspoon pepper, and cayenne in second shallow dish. Lightly pat tops of tomatoes with paper towels to remove any accumulated liquid. Working with one at a time, dip tomato slices in buttermilk mixture, then dredge in cornmeal mixture, pressing firmly to adhere; transfer to prepared sheet.

3. Heat oil in 12-inch nonstick skillet over medium-high heat until just smoking. Add all tomato slices to skillet and fry until golden brown, 2 to 4 minutes per side. Transfer to platter and sprinkle with basil. Serve with lemon wedges.

A light cornmeal-and-Parmesan-cheese coating gives these flavorful slices a satisfying crunch.

DON'T MAKE THIS MISTAKE
Using the Wrong Tomato

The juicy flesh of beefsteak, heirloom, and vine-ripened tomatoes is so full of moisture that no amount of pretreatment can adequately dry it out for frying. These varieties also contain lots of watery, seedy jelly that prevents a coating from properly adhering and frying up crunchy.

KEYS TO **Firm, Crunchy Fried Red Tomatoes**

Use Plum Tomatoes
More meaty and less watery than other options, plum tomatoes stay relatively firm once coated and fried.

Eliminate Excess Moisture
Evenly space the tomato slices on a paper towel–lined wire rack, and let them drain for 40 minutes.

Double Dip
For a crunchy coating that doesn't slough off, coat the slices with an egg-and-buttermilk "glue" before dredging them in a mix of cornmeal, flour, Parmesan, and seasonings.

Citrus-Braised Pork Tacos

Traditional *cochinita pibil* takes two days and visits to three specialty stores. Unbelievably good, yes, but there had to be an easier way. BY MORGAN BOLLING

COCHINITA PIBIL, THE inspiration for our Citrus-Braised Pork Tacos, is a Mexican dish traditionally made by coating a whole suckling pig in the juice from bitter oranges and a blend of warm spices. It marinates overnight before being swaddled in banana leaves and slowly pit-roasted. The banana leaves impart a mild herby flavor while helping insulate the meat and keep it moist. The result is succulent, multifaceted, and richly flavored. But it's hardly easy to achieve. To make a version suitable for cooking at home, I would have to adjust. A lot. But would I have to compromise?

Figuring out what cut of meat to use would be my first task. Suckling pig is incredibly rich in collagen, which, when cooked, yields delicate, tender meat. Extensive research into existing recipes showed a range of options, from pork ribs to pork loin to pork butt. To be thorough, I cooked through several of these recipes using different cuts of meat and found that pork butt was the way to go. Its rich marbling mimicked suckling pig's ability to become ultratender during a long stint over low heat.

The ingredient that stood out as most problematic for home cooks was, of course, banana leaves. Though we've found substitutions in the past—in our recipe for Kalua Pork (August/September 2011), we substituted green tea for banana leaves—I wasn't sure how critical the leaves would be here. To find out, I ordered some banana leaves and ran a test, bundling one pork butt in the leaves and leaving the other unbundled. Only a few tasters were able to pick up on the aromatic flavor they added, and we saw very little difference in the moisture level. Less authentic, yes. But given the leaves' minor flavor contribution and the difficulty of obtaining them, it was a cut worth making.

My next task was to assemble a cooking liquid that would mimic the traditional cochinita pibil. Garlic was a given, providing a savory flavor base. Cinnamon, cumin, and pepper lent warm spiciness. A teaspoon of oregano and annatto, a spice popular in Mexican cuisine and not always easy to find in the States (more on that in a moment), contributed earthiness. I added orange juice concentrate (more reliable and consistent than orange juice), flavorful

Our slightly sweet, superspicy habanero sauce gets its vibrant orange color from an unexpected ingredient: carrot.

tomato paste, and enough water to keep the meat moist while braising.

Testing revealed that 2 hours, uncovered, in a 300-degree oven (more controlled than the stove) turned the pork into the luscious, fall-apart meat I was after. Shredding by hand and with two forks worked, but mashing the slow-cooked meat with a potato masher got the job done three times as fast.

Back to the annatto. The most common culinary use for annatto in the United States is coloring. In amounts small enough to be undetectable to most tasters, the vibrantly red spice is used to impart an orange color in products from cheddar cheese to breakfast cereals. In Mexican cuisine, however, larger doses of the mild spice offer an herbal, faintly bitter flavor. While we enjoyed the complexity and rusty color the annatto was giving the pork, it's not available in most grocery stores.

I tried a batch without annatto, instead browning the tomato paste. This solved the color issue, but I missed

the flavor. A coworker suggested bay leaves, and she was right. Five bay leaves added a subtle, earthy note that balanced the dish. And a small amount of Worcestershire sauce closed the loop with a meaty, bitter boost.

To assemble my tacos, I put together a dish of quickly pickled red onions and a fiery, bright orange habanero sauce based, in the traditional way, on cooked carrots for structure and sweetness. These tacos were the most popular dish in the test kitchen that week.

Tracking Tacos in East Los Angeles

In 2010, when Armando De La Torre Sr. turned 50 and decided to open a restaurant, he reached back to the comfort food of his youth, the *guisados* (stews and braises) that his mother used to make. "Growing up we didn't come home to carne asada. Like many Mexican families we ate guisados—*tinga, calabacitas, picado*—with beans and tortillas. One-pot meals. I remember sneaking into the kitchen, and my mom would be yelling that it wasn't ready, but I'd run in, grab a tortilla, and make a taco out of whatever she was cooking. That's how I enjoyed her food."

Top, Armando De La Torre Jr. inspects a case of chicharrones. Bottom left, a Guisados employee hand-pats fresh tortillas. Bottom right, one of many guisados (stews) bubbling away in the kitchen.

Scores of brightly colored signs hang above the storefronts and restaurants that pack Cesar Chavez Avenue in the Boyle Heights neighborhood of East Los Angeles. The vibe on the avenue is mildly gritty yet a little tender, and the smiles I encounter are genuinely warm. A few steps inside Guisados, I stop at the counter to take in the large chalkboard menu that climbs to the ceiling; pitchers of aguas frescas sit next to the register. I'm mesmerized by a woman hand-patting tortillas from a bowl of fresh masa and slapping them onto the hot griddle. She moves quickly and flips the hot tortillas with her bare hands. I order several tacos and finish up just as Armando and his son, Armando Jr., arrive to greet me.

We head outside around the back of the building, step down through a low door, and make our way up a flight of stairs to the Guisados prep kitchen. There's a blur of shuffling bodies and bubbling pots, and the aroma of chiles and cumin hangs thick in the air. Armando Sr. dips a spoon into a guisado, clearing the chile-laced oil slick on top, and offers up a taste of the meat and pepper combination from its lower depths. Again, I'm mesmerized. –BRYAN ROOF

CITRUS-BRAISED PORK TACOS

Serves 6

Pork butt roast is often labeled Boston butt in the supermarket. For a spicier sauce, add an extra habanero or two; if you are spice-averse, substitute less-spicy jalapeños for the habaneros.

PORK
- 2 tablespoons vegetable oil
- 1 onion, chopped fine
- 3 garlic cloves, minced
- 1 teaspoon ground cumin
- 1 teaspoon dried oregano
- ½ teaspoon ground allspice
- ½ teaspoon ground cinnamon
- ⅓ cup tomato paste
- 1½ cups water
- ¼ cup frozen orange juice concentrate, thawed
- 3 tablespoons distilled white vinegar
- 1½ tablespoons Worcestershire sauce
- 5 bay leaves
  Salt and pepper
- 1 (2½- to 3-pound) boneless pork butt roast, trimmed and cut into 1-inch chunks

PICKLED RED ONIONS
- 1 red onion, halved and sliced thin
- 1 cup distilled white vinegar
- ⅓ cup sugar
- ¼ teaspoon salt

HABANERO SAUCE
- 1 cup water
- 1 carrot, peeled and chopped
- 1 vine-ripened tomato, cored and chopped

- ¼ cup chopped onion
- ½ habanero chile, stemmed
- 1 garlic clove, smashed and peeled
  Salt and pepper
- 1 tablespoon distilled white vinegar
- 1½ teaspoons lime juice, plus lime wedges for serving

- 18 (6-inch) corn tortillas, warmed

1. FOR THE PORK: Adjust oven rack to lower-middle position and heat oven to 300 degrees. Heat oil in Dutch oven over medium heat until shimmering. Add onion and cook until lightly browned, 4 to 6 minutes.

2. Add garlic, cumin, oregano, allspice, and cinnamon and cook until fragrant, about 30 seconds. Stir in tomato paste and cook, stirring constantly, until paste begins to darken, about 45 seconds. Stir in water, orange juice concentrate, 2 tablespoons vinegar, Worcestershire, bay leaves, 2 teaspoons salt, and 1 teaspoon pepper, scraping up any browned bits.

3. Add pork and bring to boil. Transfer to oven, uncovered, and cook until pork is tender, about 2 hours, stirring once halfway through cooking.

4. FOR THE PICKLED RED ONIONS: Meanwhile, place onion in medium bowl. Bring vinegar, sugar, and salt to simmer in small saucepan over medium-high heat, stirring occasionally, until sugar dissolves. Pour over onions and cover loosely. Let onions cool completely, about 30 minutes. (Onions can be refrigerated for up to 1 week.)

5. FOR THE HABANERO SAUCE: Combine water, carrot, tomato, onion, habanero, garlic, and ½ teaspoon salt in now-empty saucepan. Bring to boil over medium heat and cook until carrot is tender, about 10 minutes. Remove from heat and let carrot mixture cool slightly, about 5 minutes. Transfer carrot mixture to blender, add vinegar and lime juice, and process until sauce is smooth, 1 to 2 minutes. Season with salt and pepper to taste; set aside. (Sauce can be refrigerated for up to 1 week.)

6. Transfer pot to stovetop; discard bay leaves. Using potato masher, mash pork until finely shredded. Bring to simmer over medium-high heat, then reduce heat to medium-low and cook until most of liquid has evaporated, 3 to 5 minutes.

7. Off heat, stir in remaining 1 tablespoon vinegar and season with salt and pepper to taste. Serve on tortillas with pickled red onions, habanero sauce, and lime wedges.

TEST KITCHEN TIP
Safely Handling Habaneros
Take our word for it: Don't handle habaneros with your bare hands. The capsaicin levels are so high that they can irritate your skin (or worse, your eyes). To protect yourself, wear disposable latex gloves. In a pinch, zipper-lock bags can serve as makeshift gloves.

Translating Cochinita Pibil
Authentic *cochinita pibil* is full of hard-to-source ingredients, including ultratender whole suckling pig, fragrant banana leaves for wrapping the pork during cooking, and annatto (pebble-like seeds that contribute color and a mild herbal flavor). We skipped the banana leaves since the flavor contribution is negligible, swapping in substitutes for the rest.

PORK BUTT
Well-marbled, collagen-rich pork is nearly as succulent and tender as suckling pig.

BAY LEAVES
These provide an herbal aroma that's similar to that of annatto.

TOMATO PASTE
Concentrated tomato paste adds saturated color, just as annatto does.

Getting to Know Tomato Products

These versatile pantry items take many shapes and forms. Here's a sampling of the ones we use most often.

BY CHRISTIE MORRISON

Whole Peeled Tomatoes
CLOSEST TO FRESH
We reach for whole peeled tomatoes when making soups, marinara, or Sunday gravy. Their sweet flavor is the closest to that of in-season tomatoes, and they're peeled, so they're ultraconvenient. We reach for our taste-test winner, Muir Glen Organic Whole Peeled Tomatoes, when making our Tomato Casserole (**CooksCountry.com/tomatocasserole**).

Canned Diced Tomatoes
PANTRY STAPLE
Good canned diced tomatoes have a fresh flavor and firm texture that make them one of our top pantry items. Most products are treated with calcium chloride (for a firm texture), salt, and citric acid (for flavor). Try our favorite, Hunt's Diced Tomatoes, in our recipe for One-Minute Tomato Salsa (**CooksCountry.com/oneminutesalsa**).

Fire-Roasted Tomatoes
BRING THE SMOKE
Fire-roasted tomatoes have a sweet, smoky flavor (some are actually charred, others simply smoke-flavored) that adds complexity to a wide range of dishes—from pasta sauces to chilis and stews. We've found that the smoke level varies widely from product to product and that it mellows with longer cooking. We like the "warm, intense" flavor of DeLallo Fire-Roasted Diced Tomatoes.

Tomato Paste
INTENSE CONCENTRATION
Packed with savory-tasting glutamates, tomato paste adds meaty depth, sweetness, and richness to dishes like our Meatballs and Marinara (**CooksCountry.com/meatballsmarinara**). This thick paste is made by cooking skinned, seeded tomatoes until most of their water has evaporated. Our taste-test winner is "bright," "robust" Goya.

Crushed Tomatoes
TEXTURAL ENIGMA
With no U.S. Food and Drug Administration oversight to regulate consistency, crushed tomato products differ greatly—from thick and saucy to chunky and full of seeds. We prefer our crushed tomatoes chunky—not thick like tomato paste or smooth like tomato sauce. Our favorite is Tutto-rosso Crushed Tomatoes in Thick Puree with Basil.

Ketchup
A FRIEND TO FRIES
Supermarket tomato ketchup is sweet, salty, and boldly seasoned with onions, garlic, cloves, cinnamon, allspice, and vinegar. Its thick body and intense flavor make it a powerful ingredient in recipes like cocktail and barbecue sauces, baked beans, meatloaf, and our Sweet-and-Sour Chicken (see page 19). Heinz Organic Tomato Ketchup is our taste-test winner.

Tomato Salsa
NOT JUST FOR DIPPING
You'll find many jarred salsas at the market. You'll also find that the fresh flavors and textures of tomatoes, onion, chiles, and cilantro are missing from most products. In a recent tasting of jarred salsas, we found that Chi-Chi's Medium Thick and Chunky Salsa was "spicy, fresh, and tomatoey" with "pleasant, not overpowering" heat. We use jarred salsa in our recipe for Pan-Seared Chicken with Spicy Pinto Beans (**CooksCountry.com/chickenwithspicybeans**).

Sun-Dried Tomatoes
SHRIVELED GOODNESS
Sun-dried plum tomatoes are valued for their chewy texture and concentrated flavor. Most products are imported from Italy or Turkey and are sold either dry-packed in plastic containers or bags or oil-packed in jars. We prefer oil-packed; the dry-packed variety is often leathery. Try them in our Chicken Baked in Foil with Fennel and Sun-Dried Tomatoes (**CooksCountry.com/sundriedtomatochicken**).

Tomato Puree
SEEDLESS STEWER
Canned tomato puree is fully cooked and strained. It has a thick, even texture that is especially well suited for long-cooked dishes like stews and ragus. We combine tomato puree with diced tomatoes for a blend of textures in our recipe for Slow-Cooker Weeknight Chili (**CooksCountry.com/slowcookerchili**). Our favorite is Muir Glen Organic Tomato Puree.

Tomato Sauce
SEASONED SUPPORTER
Canned tomato sauce is typically tomato paste thinned with water and usually seasoned with garlic and onion. We often use it in combination with other tomato products; a mix of tomato sauce and diced tomatoes creates a sauce with the perfect flavor and texture in our recipe for One-Pot Baked Ziti with Sausage and Spinach (**CooksCountry.com/onepotbakedziti**).

Tomato Juice
BREAKFAST STANDBY
Tomato juice's utility goes far beyond breakfast and Bloody Marys. Use it in place of water or broth in soups, stews, or pan sauces for richer flavor. We love the intensity it brings to our easy Gazpacho (**CooksCountry.com/gazpacho**). Campbell's makes our favorite tomato juice; our tasters praised its "thick, but not too thick" texture and "sweet, bright" tomato flavor.

Cocktail Sauce
POTENT STUFF
This spicy, nose-tingling sauce is a must with shrimp cocktail and raw oysters. Most versions are a combination of ketchup, prepared horseradish, lemon juice, and seasonings; some include Worcestershire, hot sauce, or tomato-based chili sauce. Homemade trumps store-bought—see for yourself with our recipe for Shrimp Cocktail (**CooksCountry.com/shrimpcocktail**).

SKILLET BEEF ENCHILADAS

CRISPY FALAFEL PITA WITH YOGURT SAUCE

**GRILLED PORK TENDERLOIN
WITH TOMATO-ONION SALAD**

**SMOKY BEEF SKEWERS
WITH CORN AND BLACK BEAN SALAD**

CRISPY FALAFEL PITA WITH YOGURT SAUCE Serves 4

✓ **WHY THIS RECIPE WORKS:** Pita bread serves as both the sandwich pocket and the starchy binder for the chickpea patties.

- 2½ (8-inch) pita breads
- 1 (15-ounce) can chickpeas, rinsed
- ¼ cup chopped fresh parsley
- 1 large egg
- 1½ teaspoons ground cumin
- Salt and pepper
- 1 cup plain whole-milk yogurt
- 1 tablespoon lemon juice
- 2 vine-ripened tomatoes, chopped (1 cup)
- ½ cup vegetable oil

1. Tear ½ pita into small pieces and process in food processor until finely ground, about 15 seconds. Add chickpeas, 2 tablespoons parsley, egg, 1 teaspoon cumin, ¾ teaspoon salt, and ½ teaspoon pepper and pulse until chickpeas are coarsely chopped and mixture is cohesive, about 10 pulses. Divide mixture into 16 patties, about 2 inches in diameter.

2. Whisk yogurt, lemon juice, remaining 2 tablespoons parsley, remaining ½ teaspoon cumin, ½ teaspoon salt, and ½ teaspoon pepper together in bowl. Season tomatoes with salt and pepper to taste.

3. Heat oil in 12-inch nonstick skillet over medium-high heat until just smoking. Fry patties until golden brown, about 2 minutes per side. Cut remaining 2 pitas in half and stuff each pocket with ¼ cup tomatoes, 4 falafel, and ¼ cup yogurt sauce. Serve.

TEST KITCHEN NOTE: Our favorite brand of canned chickpeas is Pastene.

SKILLET BEEF ENCHILADAS Serves 4

✓ **WHY THIS RECIPE WORKS:** Frying the tortilla strips keeps them from becoming soggy while they simmer in the sauce.

- 2 tablespoons vegetable oil
- 12 corn tortillas, halved and cut crosswise into 1-inch-wide strips
- 1 pound 90 percent lean ground beef
- 1 onion, chopped fine
- ½ teaspoon salt
- 1 (15-ounce) can enchilada sauce
- 6 ounces Colby Jack cheese, shredded (1½ cups)
- 1 (2.25-ounce) can sliced black olives, drained
- 3 scallions, sliced thin on bias
- Sour cream

1. Heat oil in 12-inch nonstick skillet over medium heat until shimmering. Add tortilla strips and fry until spotty brown, about 7 minutes; transfer to paper towel–lined plate.

2. Cook beef, onion, and salt in now-empty skillet over medium-high heat, breaking up meat with spoon, until browned, about 6 minutes. Reduce heat to medium and stir in enchilada sauce and 2 cups tortilla strips. Simmer until slightly thickened, about 5 minutes. Sprinkle remaining 1 cup tortilla strips, Colby Jack, olives, and scallions over top. Reduce heat to low and cook until cheese is melted, about 3 minutes. Serve with sour cream.

TEST KITCHEN NOTE: For a spicy kick, use pepper Jack cheese.

SMOKY BEEF SKEWERS WITH CORN AND BLACK BEAN SALAD Serves 4

✓ **WHY THIS RECIPE WORKS:** Chipotle powder seasons the meat before it hits the grill and adds smoky heat to the sour cream sauce.

- ½ cup sour cream
- 2 tablespoons extra-virgin olive oil
- ½ teaspoon grated lime zest plus 2 tablespoons juice
- Salt and pepper
- 1 teaspoon chipotle chile powder
- 2 cups fresh or thawed frozen corn
- 1 (15-ounce) can black beans, rinsed
- 2 scallions, sliced thin
- 2 tablespoons chopped fresh cilantro plus 2 tablespoons cilantro leaves
- 1½ pounds sirloin steak tips, trimmed and cut into 1-inch chunks

1. Whisk sour cream, oil, lime juice, ¾ teaspoon salt, ½ teaspoon chile powder, and ⅛ teaspoon pepper together in large bowl; transfer ¼ cup sour cream mixture to small bowl and set aside. Add corn, beans, scallions, chopped cilantro, and lime zest to remaining sour cream mixture and toss to combine; transfer to platter.

2. Pat steak dry with paper towels and sprinkle with ¾ teaspoon salt, ½ teaspoon pepper, and remaining ½ teaspoon chile powder. Thread steak onto four 12-inch metal skewers. Grill skewers over hot fire until meat is browned on all sides, 5 to 7 minutes. Transfer to platter with corn salad and drizzle with reserved sour cream mixture. Sprinkle with cilantro leaves and serve.

TEST KITCHEN NOTE: If using a gas grill, cover while cooking in step 2.

GRILLED PORK TENDERLOIN WITH TOMATO-ONION SALAD Serves 4

✓ **WHY THIS RECIPE WORKS:** Ground fennel adheres well to the pork and imparts more flavor than whole fennel seeds.

- 1 tablespoon ground fennel
- Salt and pepper
- 2 (12-ounce) pork tenderloins, trimmed
- 1 red onion, sliced into ¼-inch-thick rounds
- 3 tablespoons extra-virgin olive oil
- 4 plum tomatoes, cored and sliced ¼ inch thick
- ¼ cup chopped fresh basil
- 2 tablespoons capers, rinsed
- 2 tablespoons red wine vinegar

1. Combine fennel, 1 teaspoon salt, and 1 teaspoon pepper in bowl. Pat pork dry with paper towels and sprinkle with fennel mixture. Grill pork over hot fire, turning occasionally, until well browned and registering 140 degrees, 12 to 15 minutes. Transfer to carving board, tent with foil, and let rest for 5 minutes.

2. Meanwhile, brush onion with 1 tablespoon oil and sprinkle with ¼ teaspoon salt and ¼ teaspoon pepper. Grill onion over hot fire until lightly charred, about 2 minutes per side; transfer to large bowl. Add tomatoes, basil, capers, vinegar, and remaining 2 tablespoons oil to bowl with onion and toss to combine. Season with salt and pepper to taste. Slice pork and serve with salad.

TEST KITCHEN NOTE: You can substitute vine-ripened or heirloom tomatoes for the plum tomatoes.

WHOLE-GRAIN MUSTARD CHICKEN SALAD

SPAGHETTI WITH SAUSAGE AND PEPPERS

**PAN-SEARED PAPRIKA SALMON
WITH SPICY GREEN BEANS**

**PAN-SEARED CHICKEN
WITH WARM MEDITERRANEAN GRAIN PILAF**

SPAGHETTI WITH SAUSAGE AND PEPPERS Serves 4

✓ **WHY THIS RECIPE WORKS:** As the sausage cooks, the fat renders and coats the onion and peppers to add even more meaty flavor.

- 1 pound hot Italian sausage, casings removed
- 2 red bell peppers, stemmed, seeded, and sliced thin
- 1 red onion, halved and sliced thin
- 3 garlic cloves, sliced thin
- 1 (14.5-ounce) can crushed tomatoes
  Salt and pepper
- 1 pound spaghetti
- 2 tablespoons extra-virgin olive oil
  Grated Parmesan cheese

1. Cook sausage, peppers, and onion in 12-inch nonstick skillet over medium-high heat, breaking up meat with spoon, until lightly browned and cooked through, about 12 minutes. Add garlic and cook until fragrant, about 30 seconds. Stir in tomatoes, 1 teaspoon salt, and ¼ teaspoon pepper; bring to boil. Reduce heat to medium and simmer, uncovered, until sauce is slightly thickened, about 5 minutes.

2. Meanwhile, bring 4 quarts water to boil in large pot. Add pasta and 1 tablespoon salt and cook, stirring often, until al dente. Reserve ½ cup cooking water, then drain pasta and return it to pot. Add sauce and oil and toss to combine. Adjust consistency with reserved cooking water as needed. Serve, passing Parmesan separately.

TEST KITCHEN NOTE: If you prefer a less spicy dish, substitute sweet Italian sausage.

WHOLE-GRAIN MUSTARD CHICKEN SALAD Serves 4

✓ **WHY THIS RECIPE WORKS:** Fresh lemon juice brightens this light and summery version of chicken salad, while sugar snap peas and red grapes add a juicy crunch.

- 8 ounces sugar snap peas, strings removed
  Salt and pepper
- ½ cup whole-grain mustard
- 3 tablespoons lemon juice
- 2 tablespoons extra-virgin olive oil
- 1 (2½-pound) rotisserie chicken, skin and bones discarded, meat shredded into bite-size pieces (3 cups)
- 1 cup red grapes, halved
- 3 tablespoons minced fresh chives
- 4 whole red leaf lettuce leaves

1. Bring 6 cups water to boil in large saucepan. Add snap peas and 1 teaspoon salt and cook until slightly tender, about 2 minutes. Fill large bowl halfway with ice and water. Drain snap peas, then transfer to ice bath to cool completely. Drain again, transfer to salad spinner, and spin to remove excess moisture.

2. Whisk mustard, lemon juice, oil, ½ teaspoon pepper, and ¼ teaspoon salt together in large bowl. Stir in chicken, grapes, chives, and snap peas until combined. Season with salt and pepper to taste.

3. Place 1 lettuce leaf on each of 4 plates. Place 1 cup chicken salad on each lettuce leaf. Serve.

TEST KITCHEN NOTE: You can substitute more delicate Bibb lettuce leaves if you prefer.

PAN-SEARED CHICKEN WITH WARM MEDITERRANEAN GRAIN PILAF Serves 4

✓ **WHY THIS RECIPE WORKS:** Deglazing the pan after searing the chicken releases the browned bits and creates a flavorful broth for cooking the bulgur.

- 4 (6- to 8-ounce) boneless, skinless chicken breasts, trimmed
  Salt and pepper
- 3 tablespoons extra-virgin olive oil, plus extra for drizzling
- 1½ cups water
- 1 cup fine-grind bulgur
- 10 ounces cherry tomatoes, halved
- 4 ounces feta cheese, crumbled (1 cup)
- ¾ cup minced fresh parsley
- ½ cup pitted kalamata olives, halved
- 1 tablespoon lemon juice, plus wedges for serving

1. Pat chicken dry with paper towels and season with salt and pepper. Heat 1 tablespoon oil in 12-inch skillet over medium-high heat until just smoking. Cook chicken until golden brown and registering 160 degrees, 6 to 8 minutes per side. Transfer to cutting board and tent with foil.

2. Add water to pan and bring to boil over medium-high heat, scraping up any browned bits. Stir in bulgur and ½ teaspoon salt. Cover, remove from heat, and let rest for 5 minutes. Fluff with fork. Add tomatoes, feta, parsley, olives, lemon juice, and remaining 2 tablespoons oil and stir to combine. Season with salt and pepper to taste. Slice chicken and serve with bulgur salad and lemon wedges, drizzled with extra oil.

TEST KITCHEN NOTE: Do not use coarse- or medium-grind bulgur in this recipe.

PAN-SEARED PAPRIKA SALMON WITH SPICY GREEN BEANS Serves 4

✓ **WHY THIS RECIPE WORKS:** Since the intense heat needed to blister the green beans would burn minced garlic, we smash the garlic cloves instead. The bigger pieces release intense garlic flavor without burning.

- 1¼ teaspoons smoked paprika
  Salt and pepper
- 4 (6- to 8-ounce) skin-on salmon fillets, 1¼ inches thick
- 4 teaspoons extra-virgin olive oil
- 1 pound green beans, trimmed
- 6 garlic cloves, smashed
- 2 tablespoons water
- ½ cup jarred hot banana pepper rings

1. Combine 1 teaspoon paprika, ½ teaspoon salt, and ¼ teaspoon pepper in bowl. Pat salmon dry with paper towels and sprinkle with paprika mixture. Heat 1 teaspoon oil in 12-inch nonstick skillet over medium-high heat until just smoking. Cook fillets until well browned and centers register 125 degrees (for medium-rare), 4 to 5 minutes per side. Transfer to platter and sprinkle with remaining ¼ teaspoon paprika. Wipe out skillet with paper towels.

2. Heat remaining 1 tablespoon oil in now-empty skillet over medium-high heat until just smoking. Add green beans, garlic, ½ teaspoon salt, and ¼ teaspoon pepper and cook, stirring often, until green beans and garlic turn spotty brown, about 6 minutes. Add water, cover, and reduce heat to medium. Cook until green beans are crisp-tender, about 1 minute. Off heat, stir in pepper rings and season with salt and pepper to taste. Serve.

TEST KITCHEN NOTE: For salmon fillets of even thickness, look for center-cut fillets.

Quick Strawberry Jam

Fresh strawberry jam that doesn't take all day and doesn't taste like syrup? Yes, please.

BY LEAH COLINS

STRAWBERRY JAM ADDS fresh, fruity flavor and color to breakfasts, snacks, and desserts, but too often, store-bought varieties can be sticky and cloyingly sweet, tasting more like sugar or corn syrup than strawberries. I wanted a bright homemade jam that tasted like strawberries and didn't take all day or require a battery of canning equipment to make.

Turning fresh berries into a thick jam involves three key components (besides the berries, of course): pectin, acid (in this case, lemon juice), and sugar. Pectin is a natural substance found in varying amounts in fruits and vegetables; when combined with acid, sugar, and heat, the pectin sets into a gel, suspending the fruit in a spreadable jam. Strawberries have some natural pectin but not quite enough. I did some early tests with store-bought pectin but was left with tacky, gloppy results.

Drawing on long-standing test kitchen knowledge, I shredded and added a large Granny Smith apple, which had just enough pectin to help the jam gel and also contributed a welcome tartness without any discernible apple flavor. Two tablespoons of acidic lemon juice helped activate the pectin and amplified the flavor, too.

As sweet as strawberries can be, jam needs sugar. After playing with various amounts, I settled on 3 cups of granulated sugar. This was enough to sweeten the jam and help the pectin gel while not overshadowing the strawberry flavor.

Cooking ingredients into a jam requires a bit of focus and faith. I learned to stay at attention: I found that I had to stir every couple of minutes during the 20- to 25-minute boiling time to keep the frothy mixture from boiling over (especially during the first few minutes of cooking) and to ensure even cooking. An instant-read thermometer made it easy to keep tabs on the mixture; once it registered between 217 and 220 degrees, I removed the pot from the heat. I performed a quick test—I dabbed a spoonful of jam on a chilled plate and put it in the freezer. After a couple of minutes, I dragged my finger through it to see if I left a trail. This gave me a sense of its jamminess; if the jam runs back into the line on the plate, it needs another minute or two on the heat.

Just four basic ingredients produce a thick, spreadable summertime jam.

Just for certainty's sake, I tested this recipe with subpar berries and can now confirm the least surprising thing about this recipe: Fresh berries produce the best jam. Be sure to choose small, fragrant berries that are just ripe, and discard any that are heavily bruised. If possible, use the fruit the same day you bring it home; overly ripe fruit will give you mushy, not gelled, jam. In addition, it won't taste as fresh and delicious as jam made with fresh berries.

Bonus: There's no need to process and can this strawberry jam. It lasts for two months in a tightly covered container in the refrigerator.

CLASSIC STRAWBERRY JAM
Makes 4 cups

Be sure to choose small, fragrant berries that are just ripe, and discard any that are bruised or mushy. Do not try to make a double batch of this jam in a large pot; rather, make two single batches in separate pots. Shred the apple on the large holes of a box grater.

- 3 pounds strawberries, hulled and cut into ½-inch pieces (10 cups)
- 3 cups (21 ounces) sugar
- 1 large Granny Smith apple, peeled and shredded (1¼ cups)
- 2 tablespoons lemon juice

1. Place 2 small plates in freezer to chill. Using potato masher, crush strawberries in Dutch oven until fruit is mostly broken down. Stir in sugar, apple, and lemon juice.

2. Bring to boil over medium-high heat, stirring to ensure sugar is completely dissolved. Continue to boil mixture, stirring and adjusting heat as needed, until thickened and registering 217 to 220 degrees, 20 to 25 minutes. (Jam is very frothy in beginning and requires near-constant stirring to prevent it from boiling over; froth will subside as jam boils.) Remove pot from heat.

3. To test consistency, place 1 teaspoon jam on chilled plate and freeze for 2 minutes. Drag your finger through jam on plate; jam has correct consistency when your finger leaves distinct trail. If jam is runny, return pot to heat and simmer for 1 to 3 minutes longer before retesting. Skim any foam from surface of jam using spoon.

4. Let jam cool completely, about 2 hours. Transfer jam to airtight container and refrigerate until set, 12 to 24 hours. (Jam can be refrigerated for up to 2 months.)

SECRET INGREDIENT
Granny Smith Apple
There's no need to buy commercial pectin: A shredded Granny Smith apple contains just enough natural pectin to help the jam gel.

TEST KITCHEN TECHNIQUE
Consistency Test
Place 1 teaspoon of jam on a chilled plate, freeze it for 2 minutes, and then drag your finger through it. If your finger leaves a distinct trail, the jam is ready. If the trail is blurred, return the pot to the heat and simmer the jam for 1 to 3 minutes longer before retesting.

Roasted Corn and Poblano Chowder

A few simple tricks help us coax satisfying flavor from sweet fresh corn and spicy poblano chiles.

BY ASHLEY MOORE

WE JUST DON'T taste the corn," my tasters said. "Or the poblanos." I was ready to throw in the towel. I had cooked a dozen batches of corn and poblano chowder using every trick I could think of, but the sweet flavor of the corn and the slightly spicy, earthy taste of the poblano chiles weren't coming through.

I was in search of a creamy, silky soup full of these contrasting flavors, shucking ears of corn to roast until browned alongside poblanos before stirring them into a soup—to lackluster results. No matter what I tried, the vegetables always turned soft, steamy, and flat.

I set to tinkering, and my first adjustment was promising: I switched from roasting to broiling. After stripping the corn kernels from the cob, I tossed them with oil, salt, and pepper; spread them over a baking sheet with halved poblanos on the side; and set the whole thing to broil. In just 10 minutes, I had beautiful charred vegetables.

Meanwhile, I sautéed some onion and garlic in a Dutch oven, poured in chicken broth, and then added the corn and poblanos along with some cut-up red potatoes. After 15 minutes of simmering, the potatoes were tender.

Things were finally moving in the right direction, but the chowder's flavor was still a bit flat. Bring on the bacon: I rendered some in the pot, using its fat to cook the onion and garlic before adding the other ingredients.

To add some body, I whirred a few ladles of the simmered soup in the blender and stirred this puree back into the pot. This helped, but the color was murky. For my next try, I kept the roasted poblanos out of the soup until the end, adding them to warm through when the soup was done. This soup had a better color, but even with a bit of half-and-half, it needed more thickness.

I considered a trick I'd seen in a few recipes: adding ground masa (corn flour) to the chowder for deeper corn flavor and some thickening. But I didn't want to hunt down a specialty ingredient, so I used a substitute that was just as flavorful and easier to find—corn tortillas. I tore a couple of tortillas into pieces and added them to the blender. The mixture was decidedly thicker, with even stronger corn flavor. Some fresh chopped cilantro and a few squirts of lime juice added a final flourish.

ROASTED CORN AND POBLANO CHOWDER Serves 6 to 8

Don't substitute frozen corn for fresh. Because it is parcooked, frozen corn won't release the starchy liquid that flavors and thickens the soup. In addition to the usual garnishes, you can serve the chowder with our Fried Corn Tortilla Pieces (recipe follows), if desired.

- 2 poblano chiles, stemmed, halved lengthwise, and seeded
- 1 tablespoon vegetable oil
- 6 ears corn, kernels cut from cobs (5¼ cups)
  Salt and pepper
- 4 slices bacon, chopped fine
- 1 onion, chopped fine
- 2 garlic cloves, minced
- 7 cups chicken broth
- 1 pound red potatoes, unpeeled, cut into ½-inch chunks
- ¼ cup half-and-half
- 2 (6-inch) corn tortillas, torn into 1-inch pieces
- 1 tablespoon minced fresh cilantro, plus leaves for serving
- 1 tablespoon lime juice, plus lime wedges for serving
  Sour cream
  Crumbled queso fresco

1. Adjust oven rack 6 inches from broiler element and heat broiler. Line rimmed baking sheet with aluminum foil. Toss poblanos with 1 teaspoon oil in bowl. Arrange poblanos cut side down in single column flush against short side of sheet.

2. Toss corn, remaining 2 teaspoons oil, ½ teaspoon salt, and ½ teaspoon pepper together in now-empty bowl. Spread corn in even layer on remaining portion of sheet next to poblanos. Broil until poblanos are mostly blackened and corn is well browned and tender, 10 to 15 minutes, flipping poblanos and stirring corn halfway through broiling.

3. Place poblanos in bowl, cover with plastic wrap, and let cool for 5 minutes. Remove skins and chop poblanos into ½-inch pieces; transfer to clean bowl and set aside.

4. Meanwhile, cook bacon in Dutch oven over medium heat until crispy, 5 to 7 minutes. Using slotted spoon, transfer bacon to paper towel–lined plate. Add onion and ¼ teaspoon salt to fat left in pot and cook until onion is softened and beginning to brown,

Bright garnishes like cilantro and lime invigorate this deeply satisfying soup.

5 to 7 minutes. Add garlic and cook until fragrant, about 30 seconds.

5. Add broth, potatoes, browned corn, and ½ teaspoon salt to Dutch oven and bring to simmer, scraping up any browned bits. Cook at vigorous simmer until potatoes are tender, 15 to 20 minutes. Remove from heat and stir in half-and-half.

6. Transfer 2 cups chowder to blender. Add tortillas and process until smooth, about 1 minute. Return pureed chowder to pot and stir in chopped poblanos. Return to medium heat and bring to simmer. Stir in minced cilantro, lime juice, ¾ teaspoon salt, and ¾ teaspoon pepper. Serve, passing bacon, cilantro leaves, lime wedges, sour cream, and queso fresco separately.

FRIED CORN TORTILLA PIECES
Makes about 1 cup

These fried pieces of tortilla make an excellent crispy accompaniment to soups and chowders, including our Roasted Corn and Poblano Chowder.

- ¾ cup vegetable oil
- 4 (6-inch) corn tortillas, cut into ½-inch pieces
  Salt

Heat oil in 10-inch skillet over medium-high heat until shimmering. Add tortillas and cook, stirring occasionally, until golden brown, 3 to 5 minutes. Using slotted spoon, transfer tortillas to paper towel–lined plate. Sprinkle with salt and let cool slightly to crisp.

Sweet-and-Sour Chicken

Puffy chicken fingers smothered in a way-too-sweet sauce? No thanks.
This go-to takeout dish from my childhood needed an update. BY DIANE UNGER

SWEET-AND-SOUR CHICKEN IS a mainstay of American Chinese restaurants. It can be great, but often the sauce is cloying and the chicken squishy. I set out to rescue it by creating crispy chicken in a light sauce.

I gathered several existing recipes and made five of them to help set my course. Most were awful. But I learned a few things: One, chicken fried at 375 degrees was superior to chicken fried at 350. Two, marinating was unnecessary; any flavor gained was lost once the chicken was sauced. Three, a complex and refined sauce was possible.

The trickiest piece of the puzzle was the batter. After many attempts, I settled on a version that uses a mix of flour and cornstarch and, surprisingly, no egg, which I found weighed down the batter. Instead, I added 3 tablespoons of oil and 1¼ cups of water. Our science editor explained that the oil coated the flour and cornstarch particles, preventing them from being wetted by the water and sticking together to allow for a light, airy coating.

For the sauce, I kept it simple: I simmered equal parts water, orange juice, pineapple juice, white vinegar (for the sour component), and sugar along with 3 tablespoons of ketchup and some red pepper flakes. I thickened the sauce with a slurry of cornstarch and water—just enough to help it cling. Some bell peppers and scallions, quickly fried in the same oil, finished the dish.

SWEET-AND-SOUR CHICKEN
Serves 4

Use a Dutch oven that holds 6 quarts or more for this recipe. Be sure to turn off the heat before frying the vegetables; the residual heat is enough to cook them through. Serve with rice.

SAUCE
- ½ cup pineapple juice
- ½ cup orange juice
- ½ cup distilled white vinegar
- ½ cup sugar
- 3 tablespoons ketchup
- ¼ teaspoon red pepper flakes
- ⅛ teaspoon salt
- 1 tablespoon cornstarch

CHICKEN
- 1 pound boneless, skinless chicken breasts, trimmed and cut crosswise on slight bias into ½-inch-wide strips
  Salt and pepper
- 1 cup (5 ounces) all-purpose flour
- 1 cup (4 ounces) cornstarch
- 2 teaspoons baking powder
- ½ teaspoon baking soda
- 1¼ cups water
- 3 tablespoons plus 2 quarts peanut or vegetable oil
- 2 red bell peppers, stemmed, seeded, and cut into 1-inch pieces
- 6 scallions, cut into 1-inch pieces

Cornstarch helps our sauce cling to the chicken without sogging out the coating.

1. FOR THE SAUCE: Combine pineapple juice, orange juice, vinegar, ½ cup water, sugar, ketchup, pepper flakes, and salt in medium saucepan and bring to boil over medium-high heat. Reduce heat to medium and simmer until reduced to 1½ cups, 8 to 10 minutes. Dissolve cornstarch in 1 tablespoon cold water, whisk into sauce, and cook until thickened, about 1 minute. Transfer sauce to 2-cup liquid measuring cup; set aside.

2. FOR THE CHICKEN: Set wire rack in rimmed baking sheet and line half of rack with triple layer of paper towels. Line large plate with triple layer of paper towels. Pat chicken dry with paper towels and season with salt and pepper.

3. Whisk flour, cornstarch, baking powder, baking soda, 2 teaspoons salt, and 1 teaspoon pepper together in large bowl. Whisk in water and 3 tablespoons oil until smooth. Submerge half of chicken in batter, stirring to thoroughly coat.

4. Add remaining 2 quarts oil to large Dutch oven until it measures about 1½ inches deep and heat over medium-high heat to 375 degrees. Working quickly, with 1 piece of chicken at a time, use fork to spear chicken in batter and carefully drop into hot oil. (Use second fork to help release chicken into oil.) Adjust burner, if necessary, to maintain oil temperature between 350 and 375 degrees.

5. Fry, stirring gently to prevent pieces from sticking together, until chicken is golden and cooked through, 2 to 3 minutes. Transfer chicken to paper towel–lined side of prepared rack. Let drain for 30 seconds, then move to unlined side of rack. Return oil to 375 degrees, submerge remaining chicken in remaining batter, and repeat frying with remaining chicken.

6. Turn off heat, add bell peppers to oil, and fry, stirring constantly, until softened, about 1 minute. Transfer to prepared plate. Add scallions to oil and fry until tender, about 5 seconds. Transfer to plate with peppers. Blot vegetables with paper towels to remove excess oil.

7. Microwave sauce until hot, about 1 minute. Gently toss chicken, bell peppers, scallions, and 1 cup sauce in large bowl to combine; transfer to platter. Serve immediately, passing remaining sauce separately.

The American Table
Sourcing Sweet and Sour

The concept of sweet-and-sour anything (protein cloaked in the namesake sauce and gussied up with pineapple and maraschino cherries) was popularized in the post-WWII era when Americans were enamored with "Polynesian," or pseudo-Hawaiian-Chinese, cooking, inspiring Trader Vic's restaurant to put sweet-and-sour chicken on its menu. But the dish doesn't have much of a foothold in true Chinese cuisine, where the sweet-and-sour combo is almost exclusively associated with fish. In fact, in *The Food of China* (1988), author E.N. Anderson writes that "the Cantonese regard the whole business as proof that Westerners are cultureless barbarians."
–REBECCA HAYS

Fried Peach Hand Pies

After sampling this unbelievably delicious Alabama specialty, even the fry-shy wanted in on the act.

BY CECELIA JENKINS

MANY RESTAURANTS IN the South pride themselves on their peach pies. Some even tout their peach hand pies. But the folks at Peach Park in Clanton, Alabama (see "On the Road"), really have something to crow about: *deep-fried* peach hand pies. Golden-brown crescents of tender dough filled with bright, sweet peaches, these popular little treats draw crowds from miles around. I wanted to create a recipe so the rest of us could get in on the action.

The crust in Peach Park's hand pies is not quite stiff or sturdy like tart crust, not quite flaky like pie pastry, and not quite bready like fried dough. Instead, it's somewhere in between—delicate and tender but crumbly, like soft shortbread without the snap. And the filling is pure peach flavor, with none of the spice add-ins that inform other pie fillings (think apple).

I'd tackle the filling first. I knew that to achieve the clearest peach flavor, I had to keep it simple. I tried a batch using just peaches and no sugar, but the result was dull. My next round pitted granulated sugar against brown sugar: Granulated won, boosting the sweet peach flavor without adding any distractions like molasses or caramel, as the brown sugar did. A few method tests helped me settle on my simple process: Peeled, sliced peaches (or frozen—both worked beautifully) joined granulated sugar and a pinch of salt in the saucepan over medium heat. Covered, they began to soften in about 5 minutes (longer for frozen peaches), after which I uncovered the saucepan and gently mashed the peaches, releasing juices that reduced and concentrated the peach flavor. Once the filling thickened, all it needed was a bit of lemon juice for vibrancy.

My bigger challenge was the crust: soft and tender, almost breaking in half under its own weight if held upright, yet just sturdy enough to be portable. To get my bearings and confirm my suspicion that it wouldn't be the right path, I tried a standard pie dough first, cutting chilled fat into flour. But as expected, the resulting fried pies were too flaky. A slightly wetter dough fried up to resemble peach-filled doughnuts, and lard-based doughs tasted too similar to fried dough. These were happy experiments because all were tasty, but none hit the target I aimed for.

Fresh or frozen peaches both work to create this sweet (but not too sweet), peachy pie filling.

I took a hard look at pastry mechanics: Cutting cold butter into flour creates pockets of fat and moisture that give rise to flakiness. What if I instead added melted butter? I pulsed the melted butter with the flour in the food processor, coating every speck of flour in fat. The result? A soft, pliable dough that fried up tender and just sturdy enough.

And while this crust was good—it still wasn't quite right. I wanted a faint, dainty, almost imperceptible crumble. To get it, I deviated even further from traditional pie dough, adding baking powder to the mix and swapping out water in favor of milk. To avoid breadiness, I decreased the amount of milk from ¾ cup to only ½ cup. With that final adjustment, I had a dough that was simple to prepare and, after chilling in the fridge for a spell (as most doughs do), a breeze to work with.

After portioning the dough into eight pieces, I rolled the pieces into rounds, placed a small amount of filling on each, folded them all into half-moon shapes, crimped the edges of each half-moon, and slipped them all gently into the oil. I couldn't believe how satisfying it was to watch them turn a beautiful golden brown, and my tasters couldn't believe how satisfying it was to eat these perfect little pies.

The American Table
Portable Fried Pies

Hand-size, portable fruit pies have been around in America since colonial times, most likely arriving with British settlers. During that era, the individual pies were generally made from dried fruit—usually peaches or apples—and were typically fried, not baked. That's because it was easier for cooks to monitor the doneness of delicate pastry in a pot of boiling lard (or other fat) than it was when the pies were placed at the hearthside to bake. What's more, many homes in those days weren't equipped with the type of three-sided ovens necessary for hearth baking, but they did have pots that could be strategically positioned over a fire for deep frying.

The tradition of frying individual hand pies is one that will likely always have a place in American cookery: Even McDonald's fried its individual apple pies until 1992, when it switched to baking. Just last year, however, in response to public requests, some Southern California outlets of the chain reverted to frying the pies. –REBECCA HAYS

No oven? Just suspend an iron pot over the fire and deep-fry instead.

FRIED PEACH PIES   Makes 8 hand pies

If using frozen peaches, purchase a no-sugar-added product; we prefer Earthbound Farm or Cascadian Farm frozen peaches. There is no need to thaw the frozen peaches, but they will take longer to cook; times for both fresh and frozen are given in step 1. Use a Dutch oven that holds 6 quarts or more for frying. The assembled pies can be refrigerated for up to 24 hours before frying.

- 4 ripe peaches, peeled, halved, pitted, and cut into ½-inch wedges, or 20 ounces frozen peaches
- ½ cup (3½ ounces) sugar
- Salt
- 2 teaspoons lemon juice
- 2 cups (10 ounces) all-purpose flour
- 2 teaspoons baking powder
- 6 tablespoons unsalted butter, melted and cooled
- ½ cup whole milk
- 2 quarts peanut or vegetable oil

1. Combine peaches, sugar, and ⅛ teaspoon salt in medium saucepan. Cover and cook over medium heat, stirring occasionally and breaking up peaches with spoon, until tender, about 5 minutes for fresh peaches and 16 to 19 minutes for frozen peaches.

2. Uncover and continue to cook, stirring and mashing frequently with potato masher to coarse puree, until mixture is thickened and measures about 1⅔ cups, 7 to 13 minutes. Remove from heat, stir in lemon juice, and let cool completely. (Filling can be refrigerated for up to 3 days.)

3. Line rimmed baking sheet with parchment paper. Pulse flour, baking powder, and ¾ teaspoon salt in food processor until combined, about 3 pulses. Add melted butter and pulse until mixture resembles wet sand, about 8 pulses, scraping down sides of bowl as needed. Add milk and process until no floury bits remain and dough looks pebbly, about 8 seconds.

4. Turn dough onto lightly floured counter, gather into disk, and divide into 8 equal pieces. Roll each piece between your hands into ball, then press to flatten into round. Place rounds on prepared sheet, cover with plastic wrap, and refrigerate for 20 minutes.

5. Working with 1 piece of dough at a time, roll into 6- to 7-inch circle about ⅛ inch thick on lightly floured counter. Place 3 tablespoons filling in center of circle. Brush edges of dough with water and fold dough over filling to create half-moon shape, lightly pressing out air at seam. Trim any ragged edges and crimp edges with tines of fork to seal. Return

pies to prepared sheet, cover with plastic, and refrigerate until ready to fry, up to 24 hours.

6. Line platter with triple layer of paper towels. Add oil to large Dutch oven until it measures about 1½ inches deep and heat over medium-high heat to 375 degrees. Gently place 4 pies in hot oil and fry until golden brown, about 1½ minutes per side, using slotted spatula or spider to flip. Adjust burner, if necessary, to maintain oil temperature between 350 and 375 degrees. Transfer to prepared platter. Return oil to 375 degrees and repeat with remaining 4 pies. Let cool for 10 minutes before serving.

Peach Park

The massive, peach-shaped water tower looming over Clanton, Alabama, heralds Peach Park, a roadside retail attraction and restaurant that serves as the spiritual center of Alabama's peach-producing region. Out front, an open-air market sells fresh produce (peaches, mostly) and peach-based pantry products; inside, a long cafeteria case houses meat-and-three fare (preludes, perhaps, to peach ice cream and peach cobbler). Portraits of the reigning Miss Peach and her younger counterparts Junior Miss Peach, Young Miss Peach, and Little Miss Peach honor their regal stone-fruit court.

But the best reason to visit Peach Park is the fried peach hand pies. Rumor has it these sweet, warm pies were created as a way to use up overripe peaches, too soft and ugly to sell as is but still full of peach flavor. I'm a man who rarely finishes his sweets, but at Peach Park, I left no leftovers. –BRYAN ROOF

AT A GLANCE Fried Peach Pies
Fresh or frozen peaches work equally well in these pies. Be careful not to overfill them.

COOK FILLING
Simmer peaches, sugar, and salt until tender, then mash and cook until thickened. Add lemon juice and let cool.

MAKE DOUGH
Pulse flour, baking powder, and salt, then pulse in melted butter. Add milk and process until pebbly.

SHAPE AND ROLL
Divide dough into 8 pieces. Roll each piece into ball, then flatten into round. Refrigerate, then roll each into 6- to 7-inch circle.

FILL AND FOLD
Place 3 tablespoons filling in center of circle. Brush edges with water and fold to create half-moon shape. Crimp edges with fork to seal.

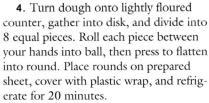

FRY AND FLIP
Deep-fry pies 4 at a time, 1½ minutes per side.

DRAIN AND SERVE
Transfer pies to paper towel–lined platter. Let cool for 10 minutes before serving.

Mississippi Mud Pie

Our approach to Mississippi mud pie was clear: When in doubt, add more chocolate. BY CHRISTIE MORRISON

THE ORIGIN OF Mississippi mud pie is as murky as the depths of the river for which it was (allegedly) named. Close kin to mud pie, a layered dessert of coffee ice cream and chocolate shavings nestled in a chocolate cookie crust that dates back to 1962, Mississippi mud's name is supposedly derived from the layers' resemblance to the silty bottom of the Mississippi River. Beyond that, recipes read like a choose-your-own-adventure book: Pick a crust, build a gooey chocolate layer, and then top it with something cool and creamy.

But know this: Mississippi mud pie is a project. No way around it. My goal was to divide and conquer, making each component as foolproof and simple as possible. As I began to build my own Mississippi mud pie, I imposed only one strict limitation: When in doubt, follow the chocolate current. Why muddy the waters with anything else?

I started with the crust. Most recipes set the chocolate tone with a crumb crust, made from chocolate wafers or sandwich cookies, rather than a pastry crust. I was on board with the crumb crust for its ease and crunch, opting for the mild sweetness of chocolate wafer cookies pulsed in the food processor to a fine crumb. Some melted butter brought it together and made it easy to press into a pie plate for a short parbake in the oven.

Next up: the middle layer, also chocolate. I knew I was after the gooey, fudgy texture of a slightly undercooked brownie, much like a pie that a test kitchen colleague developed a few years ago—Fudgy Tar Heel Pie (August/September 2013). Essentially a brownie baked into a pie, it's made with dark brown sugar (which contains molasses, adding moisture) and both butter and vegetable oil for a perfect chewy texture. Minor tinkering with this recipe, plus underbaking it slightly, gave me just the texture I wanted.

It was the third layer where things started to fishtail. Like mud pie, many Mississippi mud pies are topped with ice cream—usually coffee or vanilla. But for all of ice cream's virtues, its temperature sensitivity made testing, transportation, and storage difficult. Also out: whipped cream (too light) and chocolate pudding (too much work). I set my sights on a mousse. Chocolate, of course.

This dessert takes time and attention. But the payoff—deep, multifaceted chocolate flavor in a striated showstopper—is huge.

Instead of a traditional mousse made with whipped egg whites, I started with something easier: a simple mousse made with milk chocolate, cocoa powder, and whipped cream. After several tests, I found that warming a small portion of the cream slightly was the best, most reliable method to get the cocoa fully incorporated; adding this back to the rest of the cream meant it stayed cool enough to whip effectively. Adding confectioners' sugar before whipping helped stabilize the whipped cream and made folding in the melted, cooled chocolate that much easier.

What wasn't easy was spooning it directly onto the still-warm brownie layer—doing so gave me a soupy mess. The fix was simple, requiring nothing more than patience: I let the brownie layer cool completely and then slid it into the fridge to chill for an hour. The cooler surface held on to the mousse with no soupy side effects.

With a chocolate lily this beautiful, why not gild it—or rather, cover it in more chocolate? I crushed a handful of chocolate wafers into coarse crumbs; tossed them with cocoa powder, confectioners' sugar, and melted butter; and baked them on a baking sheet into a streusel-like crumble to sprinkle over the top for a final chocolaty crunch.

Anatomy of a Slice: Four Layers of Chocolate

Our Mississippi Mud Pie recipe relies on two types of bar chocolate plus cocoa powder and chocolate wafer cookies to hit every chocolate note in the book. The upshot? Deep, complex, and unforgettable chocolate flavor.

COOKIE GARNISH
Toast wafer cookie pieces with melted butter, cocoa, and sugar for a chocolate streusel topping.

FLUFFY TOP
For a simple chocolate mousse, whip cream with sugar and cocoa before folding into melted milk chocolate.

PRESS-IN CRUST
Process chocolate wafer cookies with melted butter to form a crumb crust.

FUDGY MIDDLE
Combine bittersweet chocolate and cocoa in a brownie-like batter, and underbake it slightly to create a chewy middle layer.

MISSISSIPPI MUD PIE Serves 8 to 12

This recipe takes at least 5 hours from start to finish, so plan accordingly. We used Nabisco Famous Chocolate Wafers in this recipe. Be sure to use milk chocolate in the mousse, as bittersweet chocolate will make the mousse too firm. Our favorite milk chocolate is Dove Silky Smooth Milk Chocolate, and our preferred bittersweet chocolate is Ghirardelli 60% Cacao Bittersweet Chocolate Premium Baking Bar. Note that you shouldn't begin making the mousse until the brownie layer is fully chilled.

CRUST
- 25 chocolate wafer cookies (5½ ounces), broken into coarse pieces
- 4 tablespoons unsalted butter, melted

BROWNIE LAYER
- 4 ounces bittersweet chocolate, chopped fine
- 3 tablespoons unsalted butter
- 3 tablespoons vegetable oil
- 1½ tablespoons Dutch-processed cocoa powder
- ⅔ cup packed (4⅔ ounces) dark brown sugar
- 2 large eggs
- 2 teaspoons vanilla extract
- ¼ teaspoon salt
- 3 tablespoons all-purpose flour

TOPPING
- 10 chocolate wafer cookies (2 ounces)
- 2 tablespoons confectioners' sugar
- 1 tablespoon Dutch-processed cocoa powder
- ⅛ teaspoon salt
- 2 tablespoons unsalted butter, melted

MOUSSE
- 6 ounces milk chocolate, chopped fine
- 1 cup heavy cream, chilled
- 2 tablespoons Dutch-processed cocoa powder
- 2 tablespoons confectioners' sugar
- ⅛ teaspoon salt

1. FOR THE CRUST: Adjust oven rack to middle position and heat oven to 325 degrees. Process cookie pieces in food processor until finely ground, about 30 seconds. Add melted butter and pulse until combined, about 6 pulses. Using bottom of dry measuring cup, press crumbs firmly into bottom and up sides of 9-inch pie plate. Bake until fragrant and set, about 15 minutes. Transfer to wire rack.

2. FOR THE BROWNIE LAYER: Combine chocolate, butter, oil, and cocoa in bowl and microwave at 50 percent power, stirring often, until melted, about 1½ minutes. In separate bowl, whisk sugar, eggs, vanilla, and salt until smooth. Whisk in chocolate mixture until incorporated. Whisk in flour until just combined.

3. Pour brownie batter into crust (crust needn't be cool at this point). Bake pie until edges begin to set and toothpick inserted in center comes out with thin coating of batter attached, about 15 minutes. Transfer to wire rack and let cool for 1 hour, then refrigerate until fully chilled, about 1 hour longer.

4. FOR THE TOPPING: Meanwhile, line rimmed baking sheet with parchment paper. Place cookies in zipper-lock bag, press out air, and seal bag. Using rolling pin, crush cookies into ½- to ¾-inch pieces. Combine sugar, cocoa, salt, and crushed cookies in bowl. Stir in melted butter until mixture is moistened and clumps begin to form. Spread crumbs in even layer on prepared sheet and bake until fragrant, about 10 minutes, shaking sheet to break up crumbs halfway through baking. Transfer sheet to wire rack and let cool completely.

5. FOR THE MOUSSE: Once brownie layer has fully chilled, microwave chocolate in large bowl at 50 percent power, stirring often, until melted, 1½ to 2 minutes. Let cool until just barely warm and registers between 90 and 100 degrees, about 10 minutes.

6. Microwave 3 tablespoons cream in small bowl until it registers 105 to 110 degrees, about 15 seconds. Whisk in cocoa until homogeneous. Combine cocoa-cream mixture, sugar, salt, and remaining cream in bowl of stand mixer. Fit mixer with whisk and whip cream mixture on medium speed until beginning to thicken, about 30 seconds, scraping down bowl as needed. Increase speed to high and whip until soft peaks form, 30 to 60 seconds.

7. Using whisk, fold one-third of whipped cream mixture into melted chocolate to lighten. Using rubber spatula, fold in remaining whipped cream mixture until no dark streaks remain. Spoon mousse into chilled pie and spread evenly from edge to edge. Sprinkle with cooled topping and refrigerate for at least 3 hours or overnight. Serve.

WHEN THINGS GO WRONG Loose Mousse
Our first couple of tests produced mousse that was a far cry from the fluffy-yet-sliceable mixture that we ended up with. Two key changes helped us get the right texture. First, we swapped granulated sugar for starchier confectioners' sugar. Second, we made sure to let the chocolate cool to between 90 and 100 degrees before incorporating it—any warmer and the chocolate deflated the mousse.

DEFLATEGATE?
If the chocolate's too hot, the mousse won't set properly.

Cooking Class Grilled Boneless, Skinless Chicken Breasts

Grilled chicken breasts can be a juicy, well-seasoned meal—or a dry, flavorless regret. Here's our guide to success. BY CHRISTIE MORRISON

GRILLED BONELESS, SKINLESS CHICKEN BREASTS Serves 4

This chicken can be served with one of our three sauces (recipes follow) alongside a simply prepared vegetable for a light dinner. The chicken can also be used in a sandwich or sliced and tossed with greens for a salad. The chicken takes longer to cook on a gas grill, so begin checking it at the end of the range in step 4. The chicken should be marinated for no less than 30 minutes and no more than 12 hours.

- 3 tablespoons vegetable oil
- 3 tablespoons water
- 3 garlic cloves, minced
- 1 teaspoon sugar
  Salt and pepper
- 4 (6- to 8-ounce) boneless, skinless chicken breasts, trimmed
- 1 (13 by 9-inch) disposable aluminum roasting pan (if using charcoal)

1. Whisk oil, water, garlic, sugar, 1½ teaspoons salt, and ½ teaspoon pepper together in bowl. Transfer mixture to 1-gallon zipper-lock bag. Add chicken, press out air, seal bag, and turn bag so that contents are evenly distributed. Refrigerate for 30 minutes or up to 12 hours.

2A. FOR A CHARCOAL GRILL: Open bottom vent completely. Light large chimney starter filled with charcoal briquettes (6 quarts). When top coals are partially covered with ash, pour coals evenly over half of grill. Set cooking grate in place, cover, and open lid vent completely. Heat grill until hot, about 5 minutes.

2B. FOR A GAS GRILL: Turn all burners to high, cover, and heat grill until hot, about 15 minutes. Leave primary burner on high and turn off other burner(s).

3. Clean and oil cooking grate. Place chicken on cooler side of grill, skinned side down, with thicker ends facing coals. (Edges of chicken should be no more than 4 inches from center of primary burner if using gas.) Cover with disposable pan if using charcoal (if using gas, close lid) and cook until bottom of chicken just begins to develop light grill marks and is no longer pink, 6 to 9 minutes.

4. Flip chicken and rotate so that thinner ends face coals. Cover as before and continue to cook until chicken registers 140 degrees, 6 to 9 minutes longer.

5. Remove disposable pan and transfer chicken to hotter side of grill. Cook chicken (covered if using gas), until dark grill marks appear, 2 to 4 minutes. Flip chicken and cook, (covered if using gas), until marked on second side and registering 160 degrees, 2 to 4 minutes longer. Transfer chicken to cutting board, tent with aluminum foil, and let rest for 5 minutes. Serve.

STEP BY STEP Grilled Boneless, Skinless Chicken Breasts

1. MAKE BRINERADE
Whisk the oil, water, garlic, sugar, salt, and pepper together in a bowl.
WHY? In addition to thoroughly seasoning the meat, the salt helps keep it moist. The sugar helps brown the chicken's exterior.

2. GIVE IT TIME
Place the chicken and brinerade in a zipper-lock bag and refrigerate it for 30 minutes to 12 hours.
WHY? The longer the chicken remains in the salt-and-oil mixture, the more flavorful it will be. But don't let it sit for more than 12 hours, or it will become too salty.

3. PREHEAT GRILL
Pour the coals evenly over half the grill. Set the cooking grate in place, cover, and heat the grill for about 5 minutes.
WHY? Preheating the grill ensures proper cooking times. Heating the cooking grate also loosens stuck-on debris so it is easy to brush clean.

4. CLEAN AND OIL GRATE
Clean the grill with a grill brush to remove debris; then, rub the grill grate with an oil-soaked paper towel, using long-handled tongs to grip the towel.
WHY? Slicking the grate with oil helps keep the chicken breasts from sticking.

5. PLACE CHICKEN ON COOLER SIDE Place the chicken breasts on the cooler side of the grill with their thicker ends facing the coals.
WHY? Grilling the chicken breasts on the cooler side of the grill over indirect heat helps avoid a tough, leathery exterior.

Need a Sauce?

CLASSIC PESTO

Toast 3 unpeeled garlic cloves over medium heat until exteriors are spotty brown, about 8 minutes; let cool and discard skins. Process garlic, ¼ cup toasted pine nuts, 2 cups fresh basil leaves, 7 tablespoons extra-virgin olive oil, ¼ cup grated Parmesan cheese, and ½ teaspoon salt in food processor until smooth, about 1 minute. Season with salt and pepper to taste. Serve.

PEANUT SAUCE

Heat 1 tablespoon vegetable oil in small saucepan over medium heat until shimmering. Add 3 tablespoons packed dark brown sugar, 2 minced garlic cloves, and 1 tablespoon Thai red curry paste and cook until fragrant, about 30 seconds. Add 1 cup canned coconut milk and bring to boil. Whisk in ⅓ cup chunky peanut butter, 1 tablespoon fish sauce, 1 tablespoon lime juice, and 1 teaspoon soy sauce. Serve.

RED CHIMICHURRI SAUCE

Whisk 1 finely chopped onion, ½ cup minced fresh parsley, ½ cup red wine vinegar, ½ cup extra-virgin olive oil, 3 minced garlic cloves, 1 tablespoon paprika, ½ teaspoon kosher salt, and ¼ teaspoon red pepper flakes together in bowl. Cover and let stand at room temperature for at least 30 minutes. Rewhisk and serve.

Good to Know

TEST KITCHEN TIPS FOR GRILLED CHICKEN

Marinade + Brine = Brinerade

There are two different yet commonly used methods to season meat before throwing it on the grill: a marinade or a brine. The primary goal of soaking meat in a marinade (typically a mixture of oil, herbs, and spices) is to add as much flavor to the exterior of the meat as possible. Conversely, letting meat sit in a brine (a simple solution of salt and water) effectively seasons the interior of the meat as well as helps keep it moist. To get the best of both worlds in this recipe, we combine a brine (a solution of water, salt, and sugar) with a classic marinade (vegetable oil and minced garlic cloves).

Cook First; Sear Second

Most recipes call for searing chicken breasts over hot coals and then moving them to the cooler side of the grill to finish cooking. But we have found that this approach can result in overdone, dry meat and a leathery exterior. To produce perfectly cooked, juicy chicken with substantial grill marks, we use a reverse-sear approach. First, we grill the chicken over the cooler side of the grill, giving it time to slowly cook through via convective heat. Then, when the chicken is just shy of done, we move it to the hotter side of the grill for a quick sear that won't overcook the meat.

Chimney Starters 101

TEST KITCHEN WINNER
The Weber Rapidfire Chimney Starter ($14.99) is a must-have for charcoal grillers.

The Best Tool for the Job

When grilling with charcoal, forget about lighter fluid, which inevitably leaves harsh, acrid flavors in food. Instead, follow the lead of all of our charcoal grilling recipes and use a chimney starter, which lights briquettes safely and efficiently. We like the Weber Rapidfire Chimney Starter; it's easy to control, holds a generous 6 quarts of charcoal, and boasts a heatproof handle. For more info, go to **CooksCountry.com/chimneystarter.**

How to Use It

To light the charcoal, fill the bottom compartment with crumpled newspaper (two sheets are optimal; any more will inhibit airflow and extend the time it takes to light the coals). Set the starter on the bottom rack of the grill, fill the main compartment with as much charcoal as the recipe calls for, and light the newspaper. When the coals are adequately heated, they will be partially covered with a layer of thin, gray ash. This typically takes 30 minutes for a full chimney. You're now ready to dump out the coals onto the bottom grate.

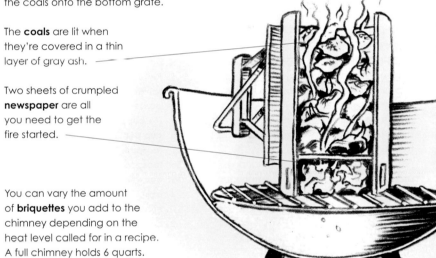

The **coals** are lit when they're covered in a thin layer of gray ash.

Two sheets of crumpled **newspaper** are all you need to get the fire started.

You can vary the amount of **briquettes** you add to the chimney depending on the heat level called for in a recipe. A full chimney holds 6 quarts.

6. COVER CHICKEN

Cover the chicken with a disposable pan if you're using charcoal (if you're using gas, close the lid). **WHY?** Trapping the heat under the pan (or under the lid if using gas) for most of the grilling time ensures that the chicken breasts will cook evenly.

7. FLIP AND ROTATE

Flip the chicken breasts and rotate them so that the thinner ends are facing the coals. **WHY?** The side closest to the coals will cook faster; flipping and rotating the breasts evens out the cooking.

8. UNDERCOOK SLIGHTLY

Cook the chicken until it is firm to the touch and registers 140 degrees. **WHY?** Grilling the chicken breasts until they are slightly underdone means you can sear them directly over the coals without overcooking them.

9. SEAR QUICKLY

Transfer the chicken breasts to the hotter side of the grill and sear them until dark grill marks appear. **WHY?** Placing the chicken directly over the heat at the end of cooking adds appealing grill marks and flavorful char.

10. LET REST

Transfer the chicken breasts to a cutting board, tent them with aluminum foil, and let them rest for 5 minutes before serving. **WHY?** Letting the chicken breasts rest gives the juices time to redistribute before slicing.

Cooking for Two Chicken Parmesan

What's better than a huge batch of chicken Parmesan? A very small batch. BY KATIE LEAIRD

CHICKEN PARMESAN IS a study in contrasts: crunchy cutlets, smooth sauce, and oozy mozzarella. All the elements should shine, individually and together.

For a quick and easy version to serve two, I chose two 6-ounce breasts. And because chicken breasts are often thick at one end and thin at the other, they can cook unevenly; gently pounding just the thick portion evened things out. I seasoned the cutlets with salt and pepper and let them sit for 20 minutes to allow the salt to penetrate the meat.

Usually, there are three steps to coating cutlets for frying. First, the slippery chicken is dredged in flour to create a dry surface. Then, it's dunked in beaten egg—a sort of edible adhesive. Finally, a mixture of bread crumbs and grated Parmesan is pressed into the meat. It works, but I found a faster way: By combining the first two steps into one—whisking the flour and egg together in one bowl—this became a two-step process.

Shallow-frying the breaded chicken breasts produced a crispy exterior with juicy white meat on the inside, and since I was making only two portions, I didn't have to do it in batches. I topped both portions with mozzarella and popped them into the oven to broil. Some sauce and fresh basil completed the dish.

Why Remove the Tenderloin?

Not removing a tenderloin before pounding leaves you with misshapen cutlets.

Boneless, skinless chicken breasts often come with the long, slender tenderloin tenuously attached. To make the cutlets more shapely, we recommend removing the tenderloins before pounding and saving them for another use, such as in soup, stir-fries, or salads. Simply pull the tenderloin off with your hands and then strip out the white tendon that runs through it by grabbing the end of the tendon with a dish towel and pulling.

CHICKEN PARMESAN FOR TWO
This recipe makes enough sauce to top the cutlets and up to a pound of pasta. Any extra sauce can be refrigerated for up to three days or frozen for up to a month. If the cheese browns before the chicken registers 160 degrees, cover the chicken with aluminum foil and continue to broil.

SAUCE
- 2 tablespoons extra-virgin olive oil
- 2 garlic cloves, minced
-     Salt
- ¼ teaspoon dried oregano
-     Pinch red pepper flakes
- 1 (28-ounce) can crushed tomatoes
- ¼ teaspoon sugar

CHICKEN AND PASTA
- 2 (6-ounce) boneless, skinless chicken breasts, trimmed
-     Salt and pepper
- 4 ounces capellini
- 1 large egg
- 1 tablespoon all-purpose flour
- 1 ounce Parmesan cheese, grated (½ cup)
- ½ cup panko bread crumbs
- ½ teaspoon garlic powder
- ½ teaspoon dried oregano
- ⅓ cup vegetable oil
- 2 ounces whole-milk mozzarella cheese, shredded (½ cup)
- 2 tablespoons sliced fresh basil

1. FOR THE SAUCE: Heat 1 tablespoon oil in medium saucepan over medium heat until shimmering. Add garlic, ¾ teaspoon salt, oregano, and pepper flakes; cook, stirring occasionally, until fragrant, about 30 seconds. Stir in tomatoes and sugar and bring to simmer. Reduce heat to medium-low, cover with lid slightly ajar, and simmer until thickened, about 20 minutes. Off heat, stir in remaining 1 tablespoon oil. Cover and keep warm.

2. FOR THE CHICKEN AND PASTA: Remove tenderloins from breasts and reserve for another use. Pound each breast between 2 pieces of plastic wrap to even ½-inch thickness. Season chicken all over with salt and pepper; let stand at room temperature for 20 minutes.

3. Bring 2 quarts water to boil in large saucepan over high heat. Add pasta and ½ tablespoon salt and cook, stirring often, until al dente. Reserve ½ cup cooking water, then drain pasta and return it to pot. Toss pasta with ¾ cup sauce. Cover and keep warm.

4. Meanwhile, whisk egg and flour in shallow dish until smooth. Combine Parmesan, panko, garlic powder, oregano, and ¼ teaspoon pepper in second shallow dish. Pat chicken dry with paper towels. Working with 1 piece at a time, dunk chicken in egg mixture, allowing excess to drip off; then dredge in panko mixture to coat both sides, pressing gently so crumbs adhere. Transfer to plate.

5. Adjust oven rack 4 inches from broiler element and heat broiler. Heat oil in 10-inch nonstick skillet over medium-high heat until shimmering. Carefully place chicken in skillet and cook until deep golden brown, about 3 minutes per side.

6. Transfer chicken to rimmed baking sheet and sprinkle mozzarella evenly over top. Broil until cheese is melted and beginning to brown and chicken registers 160 degrees, 2 to 4 minutes. Transfer chicken to serving plates. Top each piece with 2 tablespoons sauce and sprinkle each with 1 tablespoon basil. Adjust pasta consistency with reserved cooking water as needed and serve with chicken.

Chicken Parmesan without a side of pasta is just lonely.

Streamlined Breading
A classic bound breading process calls for three steps: dipping first in flour, then in egg, and then in bread crumbs. Our abbreviated two-step technique works just as well. Here's how we group the ingredients.

FIRST DIP: EGG AND FLOUR
Instead of dunking into each ingredient separately, we whisk the flour and egg together.

SECOND DIP: PARMESAN AND PANKO
A coating of bread crumbs flavored with Parmesan completes the process.

Five Easy Rice Pilafs

Plain rice has its place at the table. But we'd rather invite something more interesting.

BY ASHLEY MOORE

PLAIN STEAMED RICE is enough for some. But for me, the best role rice can play is serving as a solid base for other flavors. As in, for example, rice pilaf.

The test kitchen's basic method for rice pilaf is simple. First, uncooked long-grain rice is sautéed in butter until the grains begin to become translucent around the edges. This step helps develop rich, nutty flavors and also begins to set the starches in the grains, providing extra insurance against clumping. Next comes water, 2¼ cups for 1½ cups of rice. Once the water boils, the lid goes on the saucepan and the heat's turned down. Twenty minutes of steaming ensue, followed by an off-heat rest of 10 minutes. The result? Flavorful rice that stays in distinct, separate grains.

With something this simple, why not add even more flavor? I toasted the rice in butter with a bit of chopped onion, garlic, and fresh thyme. And rather than water, I cooked my pilaf in chicken broth. The result was deeply savory.

For one variation, I added some vibrant chopped jalapeño at the beginning and a bit of grated lime zest with the chicken broth. For another, I added some curry powder up front and stirred in some crunchy chopped apples and cilantro just before serving. For a bright, herby variation, I introduced lemon zest, tarragon, parsley, and toasted almonds. And for a savory, cool-evening variation, I added some mushrooms and poultry seasoning.

BASIC RICE PILAF Serves 4 to 6
Our preferred long-grain rice is Lundberg Organic Long-Grain White Rice. Allow the rice to cook for the full 20 minutes before lifting the lid to check it.

- 3 tablespoons unsalted butter
- 1 small onion, chopped fine
  Salt and pepper
- 1½ cups long-grain white rice
- 2 garlic cloves, minced
- 1 teaspoon minced fresh thyme
- 2¼ cups chicken broth

1. Melt butter in large saucepan over medium-high heat. Add onion and ¾ teaspoon salt and cook until just softened, about 3 minutes. Add rice and cook, stirring frequently, until edges begin to turn translucent, about 2 minutes. Stir in garlic and thyme and cook until fragrant, about 30 seconds.

2. Stir in broth and bring to boil. Cover, reduce heat to low, and cook until liquid is absorbed and rice is tender, about 20 minutes. Keep covered and remove from heat. Let stand for 10 minutes. Fluff rice with fork. Season with salt and pepper to taste. Serve.

CILANTRO RICE PILAF WITH JALAPEÑO
Omit thyme. Add 1 seeded and minced jalapeño with garlic. Add 2 teaspoons grated lime zest with broth. Stir ¼ cup chopped fresh cilantro into fluffed rice.

CURRIED RICE PILAF WITH APPLES
Omit thyme. Add 1 tablespoon curry powder with onion. Stir 1 peeled and finely chopped apple and ¼ cup chopped fresh cilantro into fluffed rice.

HERBED RICE PILAF WITH ALMONDS
Add 2 teaspoons grated lemon zest with broth. Stir ¼ cup whole almonds, toasted and chopped coarse; ¼ cup chopped fresh parsley; and 2 teaspoons chopped fresh tarragon into fluffed rice.

MUSHROOM RICE PILAF WITH THYME
Add 2 ounces finely chopped cremini mushrooms with onion. Add 1 teaspoon poultry seasoning with garlic. Stir 2 tablespoons chopped fresh parsley into fluffed rice.

Our simple toast-then-steam method brings out rice's nuttier side. Above: Basic Rice Pilaf. Below, clockwise from left: Cilantro with Jalapeño, Curried with Apples, Herbed with Almonds, and Mushroom with Thyme.

Slow Cooker Pasta Genovese

Onions are the surprising key to this dish's rich flavor, but in the slow cooker, they misbehaved. BY KATIE LEAIRD

WARM, MEATY, RAGU-DRESSED noodles are about as comforting as you can get, and pasta Genovese, a 19th-century dish (brought to the States by immigrants from Naples rather than Genoa, though its name suggests otherwise), is a prime example. The peasant-style sauce simmers for hours until the meat becomes fork-tender and the flavors meld into a beefy pasta blanket. It happens to be especially well suited to the slow-cooker—and to the wallet because, despite its beefy profile, the main ingredient is the inexpensive onion.

Besides the rare exception, like French onion soup, onions aren't usually the star of a recipe, perhaps partly because of the intense, sulfuric aroma they emit when raw. But when onions are cooked slowly and carefully in water, this unpleasant aspect becomes an asset (see "Frugal Flavor-Maker").

Our more traditional stovetop recipe for pasta Genovese uses chuck-eye roast, an often-overlooked cut of meat spotted with thick fat deposits. Though too tough for a quick steak, chuck-eye roast thrives in the low-and-slow environment of the slow cooker, where the fat and collagen have time to melt and break down into a velvety sauce. About a pound would be enough for sauce for six to eight servings.

In the old country, this dish would start with kitchen scraps; cooks would mash together scraps of pancetta or leftover salami with some celery and carrot trimmings to make a paste. I did the same in the food processor, using 2 ounces each of the cured meats, one carrot, and one stalk of celery to build a flavorful backdrop for the sauce.

Using our stovetop recipe for inspiration, I combined this paste with 2 pounds of chopped onions, some cut-up chuck eye, a bit of liquid (water and wine), and a few other ingredients in the slow cooker and walked away for a few hours. Disaster. I had a soup instead of a sauce. Because the slow cooker creates a sealed environment, there was no opportunity for evaporation. I'd have to be stricter with my liquid amounts.

I didn't want to nix the wine because it added flavor and acidity, so I tried the sauce without the water. Still soupy. Where was all that liquid coming from?

The onions, of course. Because they are about 90 percent water, 2 pounds of onions just flooded the slow cooker, diluting the sauce. I needed a way to coax out some of the onions' water ahead of time. To do it, I employed two favorite test kitchen techniques: I first tossed the onions with a little bit of salt to draw moisture out of their cells and then microwaved them for 5 minutes. I was amazed at how much pungent, sulfuric water came out of the onions— in some tests, more than a cup.

After discarding their exuded liquid, I added the drained onions and just enough fresh water back into the meaty mixture (along with wine and a bit of tomato paste for even more depth of flavor) and let the slow cooker do the rest. After 5 to 6 hours on high and a gentle mash with a potato masher, the sauce became a ragu instead of *zuppa*.

Onions + Water = Flavor
Usually, creating rich, beefy flavor in a stew or ragu means simmering meat and/or bones to create a potent stock. But we found a cheaper (and easier) approach: Simply cook lots of onions with water. How does it work? When chopped onions are heated, some of the onions' compounds turn into a new compound called MMP (an acronym of its scientific name 3-mercapto-2 methylpentan-1-ol), which tastes like beef broth. Because MMP is water-soluble, we cook the onions with water to enhance their meaty, savory flavor.

TWO POUNDS OF ONIONS. REALLY?
When cooked in water, this mound of onions gives this dish its depth.

Pancetta and salami processed into a paste provide a strong backbone for this satisfying sauce.

SLOW-COOKER BEEF AND ONION RAGU Serves 6 to 8
In step 6, don't be too forceful while mashing the meat; the action of stirring in the pasta will further break it down.

- 1 (1- to 1¼-pound) boneless beef chuck-eye roast, trimmed and cut into 1½-inch pieces
  Salt and pepper
- 2 pounds onions, chopped coarse
- 2 ounces pancetta, chopped coarse
- 2 ounces salami, chopped coarse
- 1 small carrot, peeled and chopped
- 1 small celery rib, chopped
- ⅓ cup dry white wine
- ¼ cup extra-virgin olive oil, plus extra for drizzling
- 2 tablespoons tomato paste
- 1 tablespoon dried oregano
- 1 pound rigatoni
- 2 ounces Pecorino Romano cheese, grated (1 cup), plus extra for serving

1. Sprinkle beef with 1 teaspoon salt and ½ teaspoon pepper. Transfer to slow cooker.

2. Pulse onions in food processor until finely minced, about 15 pulses, scraping down sides of bowl as needed. Transfer to large bowl and stir in ¼ teaspoon salt. Cover and microwave for 5 minutes. Drain onions in fine-mesh strainer, pressing with rubber spatula to extract excess liquid. Return drained onions to now-empty bowl.

3. Process pancetta, salami, carrot, and celery in now-empty processor until ground to paste, about 45 seconds, scraping down sides of bowl as needed. Transfer pancetta mixture to bowl with onions. Stir wine, ⅓ cup water, 2 tablespoons oil, tomato paste, oregano, ¾ teaspoon salt, and ½ teaspoon pepper into onion mixture until thoroughly combined.

4. Pour onion mixture over beef in slow cooker to cover. (Scrape sides of cooker with rubber spatula to remove any onion pieces.) Cover and cook until beef is fully tender, 5 to 6 hours on high or 8 to 9 hours on low.

5. Bring 4 quarts water to boil in large pot. Add pasta and 1 tablespoon salt and cook, stirring often, until al dente. Reserve ½ cup cooking water, then drain pasta.

6. Using potato masher, mash meat until coarsely shredded into bite-size pieces. Stir in Pecorino and remaining 2 tablespoons oil. Transfer pasta to slow cooker and stir to combine with sauce. Adjust consistency with reserved cooking water as needed. Season with salt and pepper to taste. Serve, drizzled with extra oil and sprinkled with extra Pecorino.

One-Pan Dinner Halibut with Potatoes, Corn, and Sausage

The more components, the steeper the challenge. Could we conquer this four-part one-pan supper? BY CECELIA JENKINS

TIMESAVING ONE-PAN SUPPERS can be tricky; all the components need to be cooked evenly and hit the table while they're still hot. For this seaside-style meal, we wanted perfectly cooked fillets of mild, tender halibut with boldly flavored andouille sausage, crispy red potatoes, and juicy corn. But just tossing everything on a baking sheet and cooking it in one visit to the oven produced a mess of overcooked fish, rubbery andouille, rock-hard potatoes, and unevenly cooked corn.

Sorting out this puzzle required first identifying the specific cooking time and temperature for each component. The potatoes needed high heat and the most time to roast. Conveniently, the andouille cooked beautifully along with them in a 500-degree oven, rendering flavorful fat into the pan for the potatoes to soak up.

In contrast to sturdy spuds and sausage, halibut is a delicate fish that needs just a few minutes to reach doneness—any longer and it dries out. I pushed the potatoes and sausage to the side of the pan and added the fish. I immediately dropped the oven to 425 degrees; the fish cooked gently in the declining oven heat, producing soft, tender flesh.

The remaining question mark was the corn. Putting it in to cook with the potatoes and andouille the entire time resulted in raisin-like kernels. But when I added the corn with the fish, the only place I could stick it was atop the potatoes and andouille, where it teetered precariously. The pan was now heavy and unbalanced, a sloppy spill just waiting to happen.

Using small potatoes ensures that all parts of this meal are ready at the same time.

I flipped the script by adding the corn up front with the sausage and potatoes and then swapping it out for the fish. The corn was beautifully cooked, with plump, bright kernels. But would it still be hot at suppertime?

I tossed the corn in a bowl with Old Bay–spiced butter and covered it with foil. It stayed pleasantly warm while everything else finished up.

A few final tweaks: I kept the potatoes cut side down throughout cooking for a deep golden crust. Then, when I took out the pan to remove the finished corn, I moved the andouille on top of the potatoes to make room for the fish. The sausage continued to crisp while its fat trickled onto the potatoes. With a bit more Old Bay butter dolloped on the fish and a sprinkle of fresh parsley, I'd mastered this tricky one-pan challenge.

DIY OLD BAY SEASONING

Makes 2 tablespoons

Store-bought Old Bay seasoning contains a mixture of roughly 18 spices. Our streamlined homemade version features the most prominent spices found in the original.

- 1 tablespoon celery salt
- 1½ teaspoons paprika
- 1⅛ teaspoons ground coriander
- ¼ teaspoon cayenne pepper
- ⅛ teaspoon ground cinnamon

Combine ingredients in small bowl.

One Pan, Two Steps

To ensure even cooking, we start with a baking sheet loaded with potatoes, andouille sausage, and corn (left). We remove the corn to make room for the quick-cooking halibut, which finishes at the same time as the potatoes and sausage.

ONE-PAN HALIBUT WITH RED POTATOES, CORN, AND ANDOUILLE Serves 4

Use small red potatoes measuring 1 to 2 inches in diameter. Note that you need to immediately reduce the oven temperature from 500 to 425 degrees after placing the fish in the oven.

- 4 tablespoons unsalted butter, softened
- 2 teaspoons Old Bay seasoning
- 1 teaspoon lemon juice
- 4 (6- to 8-ounce) center-cut skinless halibut fillets, 1 inch thick
  Salt and pepper
- ¼ cup vegetable oil
- 1½ pounds small red potatoes, unpeeled, halved lengthwise
- 4 ears corn, husks and silk removed, cut into thirds
- 12 ounces andouille sausage, sliced 1 inch thick
- 1 tablespoon minced fresh parsley

1. Adjust oven rack to lowest position and heat oven to 500 degrees. Combine butter, Old Bay, and lemon juice in bowl; set aside. Pat halibut dry with paper towels and season with salt and pepper; refrigerate until needed.

2. Brush rimmed baking sheet with 1 tablespoon oil. Toss potatoes, 2 tablespoons oil, ¼ teaspoon salt, and ¼ teaspoon pepper together in bowl. Arrange potatoes cut side down on half of sheet. Toss corn, remaining 1 tablespoon oil, ¼ teaspoon salt, and ⅛ teaspoon pepper together in now-empty bowl. Arrange corn on empty side of sheet. Nestle andouille pieces around corn.

3. Roast until potatoes and andouille are lightly browned and corn kernels are plump, 20 to 22 minutes, rotating sheet halfway through roasting.

4. Remove sheet from oven, transfer corn and 2 tablespoons Old Bay butter to medium bowl, and toss to combine. Cover bowl tightly with aluminum foil and set aside. Move andouille pieces to side of sheet with potatoes. Arrange halibut fillets evenly on now-empty side of sheet.

5. Return sheet to oven and reduce oven temperature to 425 degrees. Roast until centers of fillets register 130 degrees and flesh is just opaque when checked with tip of paring knife, 8 to 10 minutes, rotating sheet halfway through roasting.

6. Transfer halibut browned side up to serving platter. Portion remaining 2 tablespoons Old Bay butter evenly over halibut. Transfer potatoes, corn, and andouille pieces to platter with halibut and sprinkle with parsley. Serve.

Taste Test All-Beef Hot Dogs

We ate hundreds of hot dogs to unlock the mystery of this classic summertime sausage.

BY LAUREN SAVOIE

RECOMMENDED		TASTERS' NOTES

NATHAN'S FAMOUS
Skinless Beef Franks
Price: $6.99 for 8 hot dogs
($0.87 per hot dog)
Weight of One Dog: 51 g
Width: 0.87 in **Fat:** 15 g
Carbohydrates: 1 g
Sodium: 550 mg

This product emerged as top dog for its "supersmoky" meatiness and "juicy," "snappy" texture. Tasters thought these "plump" hot dogs were the "perfect size" and gave a "nice contrast to the bun." "This is my ideal dog," said one happy taster.

KAYEM
Skinless Beef Hot Dogs
Price: $5.99 for 8 hot dogs
($0.75 per hot dog)
Weight of One Dog: 50 g
Width: 0.87 in **Fat:** 13 g
Carbohydrates: 1 g
Sodium: 440 mg

Another "big and substantial" dog, this "juicy" sausage was "meaty" and "tender," with "just the right amount of smoke." Tasters thought the "mild," "subtle" spice blend used in this product was "classic" and "familiar."

RECOMMENDED WITH RESERVATIONS

BAR-S
Premium Beef Franks
Price: $3.25 for 8 hot dogs
($0.41 per hot dog)
Weight of One Dog: 41 g
Width: 0.77 in **Fat:** 14 g
Carbohydrates: 2 g
Sodium: 536 mg

These dogs were plenty "meaty" and "juicy," with a "firm" texture, though a few tasters noted a "sour" aftertaste. While these dogs were slightly too "small" for some tasters, most agreed that they had a "salty" kick and a "hint of smoke" that stood up against the bun.

HEBREW NATIONAL
Beef Franks
Price: $6.49 for 7 hot dogs
($0.93 per hot dog)
Weight of One Dog: 47 g
Width: 0.76 in **Fat:** 13 g
Carbohydrates: 2 g
Sodium: 459 mg

Tasters liked the "intensely savory" beefiness and "springy" texture of these dogs, but most thought these "slim," "skinny" sausages weren't big enough for a standard bun. Still, many praised this product for its "juicy" tenderness and "slightly spicy" flavor.

OSCAR MAYER
Classic Beef Franks
Price: $5.99 for 10 hot dogs
($0.60 per hot dog)
Weight of One Dog: 41 g
Width: 0.75 in **Fat:** 14 g
Carbohydrates: 1 g
Sodium: 393 mg

These "very skinny" sausages were among the smallest in our lineup, and while tasters liked their "smoky" meatiness, most thought they got "lost in the bun." Some also thought these dogs, which list corn syrup as their third ingredient, were a little too sweet.

NOT RECOMMENDED

BALL PARK
Beef Franks
Price: $4.99 for 8 hot dogs
($0.62 per hot dog)
Weight of One Dog: 50 g
Width: 0.83 in **Fat:** 14 g
Carbohydrates: 4 g
Sodium: 481 mg

"Mush mush mush!" said one taster, complaining about these "spongy," "flabby" sausages, which were likened to "school cafeteria hot dogs." The few tasters that could get past the "creepy soft" texture found these dogs dominated by a "sweet," "bologna-y" flavor.

APPLEGATE
The Great Organic Uncured Beef Hot Dog
Price: $6.49 for 7 hot dogs
($0.93 per hot dog)
Weight of One Dog: 48 g
Width: 0.8 in **Fat:** 7 g
Carbohydrates: 0 g
Sodium: 292 mg

Tasters likened the "odd," "tart" flavors in this hot dog to "cabbage," "broccoli," "sea water," and "low tide." Equally unimpressive was this dog's "crumbly," "mealy" texture, which left a "cottony" dryness in tasters' mouths.

All nutritional information is calculated for a standard 50-gram serving size.

FROM THE "HOT WATER" sausages of Coney Island to the pineapple-topped "puka dogs" of Kauai, you can find a hot dog in nearly every corner of America. While how you dress your dog varies with regional custom (like your hot dogs with ketchup? Don't show your face in Chicago), the sausages themselves remain relatively constant across all 50 states—a mixture of meat trimmings, water, salt, and seasonings is stuffed into casings (sometimes natural but usually made from cellulose) and then smoked and cooked. Cellulose casings are stripped off after cooking, so most supermarket hot dogs are skinless.

Traditional frankfurters—the kind originally brought over by European immigrants in the mid-1800s—are primarily pork-based and can still be found in supermarkets nationwide. But nearly every hot dog manufacturer we talked to told us that all-beef hot dogs now vastly outsell traditional frankfurters because of their punchier meatiness and more straightforward ingredient list. (Pork frankfurters today are often bulked up with added poultry or soy.) With the goal of finding the best supermarket all-beef hot dogs, we cooked up the seven top-selling national varieties of skinless dogs for 21 America's Test Kitchen staffers. To keep everything consistent, we locked away the condiments and served the hot dogs two ways: first boiled and bunless and then grilled and stuffed into buns.

Tasters immediately took issue with thin or skimpy dogs that practically disappeared when we nestled them into standard buns. Almost half the samples were deemed too petite by tasters, so we broke out a scale and calipers to measure the dogs. Top dogs were up to 12 percent plumper than lower-ranked ones, allowing for a higher meat-to-bun ratio in each bite. Our favorite hot dogs were also almost 20 percent heavier than low-scoring products—51 grams per dog versus 41 grams.

But bigger wasn't always better, as some larger dogs had texture issues. Two products were downgraded for their off-putting textures: one was too dry, the other too wet and squishy. The ideal hot dog has a bouncy, snappy texture and a moderate moisture level; from our prior investigating in other sausage stories, we know that this ideal texture is achieved, in part, by a proper balance of fat and protein. So we scrutinized the ingredient labels and compared fat and protein levels. Though they all contained similar amounts of protein, the dog that tasters deemed dry was far too lean, with less than half the fat of our winner—about 7 grams of fat compared with 15 grams of fat in our top-ranked product. We preferred dogs with more fat, which were tender and juicy with just the right amount of bounce and snap.

But what about the wet, squishy dog? While it had fat and protein levels similar to the top-ranked products, it contained twice as many carbohydrates as any of the other samples. While most manufacturers bulk up their hot dogs with added corn or corn syrup for a smoother texture and a sweeter flavor, our science editor explained that this product likely used too much—as evidenced by the high carbohydrate levels—making for a mushy and wet dog.

As for flavor, too much corn or corn syrup also had a big impact. Hot dogs that listed corn products as primary ingredients tended to be too sweet, while our favorites either contained no corn products or reported adding "2% or less" on ingredient lists. Spice was also important: While manufacturers wouldn't tell us exactly what spices they

---

A Peek Inside the Test Kitchen

We do a lot of work before our tasters sit down to evaluate a food like hot dogs. After our preliminary research, we confirm product details and availability with every producer, buy the product locally, pretaste to work out any kinks (like appropriate sample size), print tasting sheets, set the tasting table, cook the samples concurrently, assemble the tasting panel, and bring it all to the table hot. Hot dog, indeed.

Timing is everything—don't use just anything. BY HANNAH CROWLEY

Dog's Best Friend

These days, hot dogs are served in oblong buns, but until the early 20th century, they were typically eaten bunless. Though historians aren't exactly sure how hot dog buns were invented, one version of the story claims that the buns were introduced in 1904 by a clever vendor in St. Louis named Anton Feuchtwanger, who reportedly loaned customers his gloves to hold hot sausages as they ate. Since patrons often wandered off with the gloves, Feuchtwanger asked the family baker to create long rolls that fit the hot dogs—and so the hot dog bun was (supposedly) born. We like to wrap our dogs in **Pepperidge Farm Hot Dog Buns**, which won our previous tastings for their slightly crusty exterior and subtle yeastiness. To read our testing, go to **CooksCountry.com/hotdogbuns**.

THERE'S NOTHING LIKE a spectacular kitchen failure, replete with leathery meat, disintegrated vegetables, or, worse yet, billowing smoke to drive home the importance of timing in cooking. Most every smartphone, tablet, oven, or microwave has a timer these days, so why use a dedicated kitchen timer? Kitchen timers are more durable and moisture-resistant than other electronics, and they're more versatile than appliance timers, with extra features like the ability to track multiple things at once, longer ranges, or the capacity to count up once the timer has sounded to track elapsed time.

When we last tested digital multi-event kitchen timers, the American Innovative Chef's Quad Timer Professional was the winner. But it's not perfect (it's a bit confusing to operate and can't be set for less than 1 minute), and so a slew of new options inspired us to take another look at these products.

We rounded up 12 new digital timers, choosing those that could track between two and four events at once, and pitted them against our old winner. All models were priced between $11.49 and $49.95. We were hard on our timers, because a good kitchen timer should be brutishly durable, unfailingly accurate, and dead easy to use. To see how easy the timers were to use in a hot, busy kitchen, we used them to make pizza dough that required five different timing increments and soft-boiled eggs that cooked for precisely 6 minutes and 30 seconds. We also knocked them off kitchen counters, smeared them with sticky dough and flour, and mopped them up with sopping wet dish towels.

Two factors, accuracy and durability, were nonnegotiable—a broken or inexact timer is about as useful as a mesh umbrella. We tested each unit's timers against the official time kept by the National Institute of Standards and Technology and were pleasantly surprised to find that all the timers were accurate. They also all emerged from our durability testing intact. But that didn't mean we liked them all, as a surprising number of secondary factors decided each timer's fate.

Most important was how easy the timers were to set and reset. We found that some timers had extra "confirming" steps; for example, if you wanted to set the time for 1 minute, you also had to confirm that you wanted zero seconds, instead of just entering 1 minute and pressing "start." The best

---

KEY Good ★★★ Fair ★★ Poor ★

RECOMMENDED

OXO
Good Grips Triple Timer
Model: 1071501
Price: $19.99
Number of Timers: 3
Range: 99 hr, 59 min, 59 sec
Settable for: Hours, minutes, seconds
Dimensions: 3 x 2.5 x 3.75 in
Extra Features: Clock, stopwatch, time elapsed, memory

Intuitiveness	★★★
Ease of Use	★★★
Design	★★½
Versatility	★★★
Display + Alerts	★★½
Cleanup + Durability	★★★

Comments: This sturdy, intuitive triple timer has a dedicated "clear" button and a full 0-to-9 keypad.

MEASUPRO
Digital Timer, Clock, and Stopwatch
Model: CCT400
Price: $14.99
Number of Timers: 4
Range: 23 hr, 59 min, 59 sec
Settable for: Hours, minutes, seconds
Dimensions: 2.8 x 0.75 x 2.4 in
Extra Features: Clock, stopwatch, time elapsed, memory, magnet

Intuitiveness	★★★
Ease of Use	★★½
Design	★★
Versatility	★★★
Display + Alerts	★★½
Cleanup + Durability	★★★

Comments: We liked this timer's clearly labeled, single-purpose buttons; bold display; and small footprint. But it was a little tippy and showed only one timer at a time.

RECOMMENDED WITH RESERVATIONS

MAVERICK
Redi-Check Four Line Timer
Model: TM-09
Price: $14.99
Number of Timers: 4
Range: 99 hr, 59 min, 59 sec
Settable for: Hours, minutes, seconds
Dimensions: 3.6 x 1.25 x 2.75 in
Extra Features: Clock, stopwatch, time elapsed, magnet

Intuitiveness	★★★
Ease of Use	★★½
Design	★★½
Versatility	★★★
Display + Alerts	★★
Cleanup + Durability	★★

Comments: This compact, intuitive timer's audio alerts were a bit shrill, and it showed only one timer at a time.

MARATHON
Large Display 100 Hour
Dual Count Up/Down Timer
Model: TI030017BK (black)
Price: $14.99
Number of Timers: 2
Range: 99 hr, 59 min, 59 sec
Settable for: Hours, minutes, seconds
Dimensions: 3.5 x 0.6 x 3 in
Extra Features: Stopwatch, time elapsed, memory, magnet

Intuitiveness	★★½
Ease of Use	★½
Design	★★
Versatility	★★★
Display + Alerts	★★★
Cleanup + Durability	★★★

Comments: This reasonably intuitive timer had a few nice features (clear digits, volume options), but resetting the time took two hands and too much effort.

---

used, tasters docked lower-ranked products for flavors that seemed out of place. Strong notes of celery salt, paprika, cabbage, or warm spices were no-gos; we preferred dogs with prominent smoky, beefy flavor and strong saltiness. Our favorite hot dogs contained the most sodium of any product—550 milligrams versus as little as 292 milligrams per dog in other samples—and tasters thought these dogs had the punchiest flavor.

In the end, Nathan's Famous Skinless Beef Franks earned the top spot for their robust, meaty flavor and juicy, tender texture. These large, beefy dogs had a substantial heft and a bold, meaty flavor that held its own in a bun. We'll be keeping Nathan's on hand for summer barbecues and easy weeknight dinners.

---

products took three steps: select one of the timers, enter desired time, and press "start." Resetting some timers required us to press multiple buttons simultaneously; others had us hold down one button for a length of time. Testers preferred obvious "clear" buttons that they could hit once with a single finger.

The final factors were small but important design elements that made timers easy to use: legible displays; comfortably audible alerts; compact, stable formats; large, clearly labeled buttons; and displays that showed all of the unit's timers simultaneously.

One model had everything we wanted, plus a unique innovation. Most timers had hours, minutes, and seconds buttons that you press and scroll through to set; better models can reverse so that if you overshoot your

time you don't have to start over, but our new winner was the only timer with a direct-entry keypad with numbers 0 to 9, so users can type in the exact time they want without scrolling.

We have no doubt that technology will continue to develop; at some point, smart devices will be more durable and appliance timers more sophisticated, so we will continue to monitor their development. But until then the accurate, durable, stable OXO Good Grips Triple Timer ($19.99) is the best you can buy. We especially love its direct-entry keypad and smart, simple design that makes time your friend, not your foe.

▶ Visit **CooksCountry.com/july16** to read the full results of our testing and to see the nine lower-rated models that aren't pictured here.

Heirloom Recipe

We're looking for recipes that you treasure—the ones that have been handed down in your family for a generation or more; that always come out for the holidays; that have earned a place at your table and in your heart, through many years of meals. Send us the recipes that spell home to you. Visit **CooksCountry.com/magazines/home** (or write to Heirloom Recipes, *Cook's Country*, P.O. Box 470739, Brookline, MA 02447); click on Heirloom Recipes and tell us a little about the recipe. Include your name and mailing address. **If we print your recipe, you'll receive a free one-year subscription to *Cook's Country*.**

JOE'S SPECIAL

"I enjoyed this dish a long time ago when my parents took me to Original Joe's in San Francisco. This is my version of what I fondly remember as the best breakfast ever." –Valerie Swift, San Jose, Calif.

Serves 4

We like to serve this with toasted sourdough bread and extra hot sauce, such as Frank's RedHot Original Cayenne Pepper Sauce.

- 8 large eggs
- ¼ cup half-and-half
  Salt and pepper
- 4 tablespoons unsalted butter
- 12 ounces cremini mushrooms, trimmed and sliced thin
- 3 garlic cloves, minced
- 1 onion, quartered and sliced thin crosswise
- 12 ounces 85 percent lean ground beef
- 1 tablespoon Worcestershire sauce
- 1 tablespoon hot sauce, plus extra for serving
- 10 ounces (10 cups) baby spinach
- 2 ounces Parmesan cheese, grated (1 cup)

1. Whisk eggs, half-and-half, ½ teaspoon salt, and ¼ teaspoon pepper together in bowl; set aside. Melt 2 tablespoons butter in 12-inch nonstick skillet over medium-high heat. Add mushrooms and ¼ teaspoon salt and cook, covered, until mushrooms release their liquid, about 5 minutes. Uncover and continue to cook until lightly browned, about 5 minutes longer. Stir in half of garlic and cook until fragrant, about 30 seconds. Transfer to bowl, cover with aluminum foil, and set aside.

2. Melt remaining 2 tablespoons butter in now-empty skillet over medium-high heat. Add onion and ¼ teaspoon salt and cook, covered, until onion is softened, about 5 minutes. Stir in beef and cook, uncovered, breaking up meat with spatula, until no longer pink, 5 to 7 minutes. Stir in remaining garlic and cook until fragrant, about 30 seconds. Stir in Worcestershire and hot sauce.

3. Stir half of spinach into beef mixture and cook until just wilted, about 1 minute. Stir in remaining spinach and cook until just wilted, about 1 minute longer. Pour egg mixture into skillet and, using rubber spatula, stir and scrape bottom of skillet, combining beef mixture and eggs, until large curds begin to form and eggs are fully set, 3 to 5 minutes.

4. Off heat, stir in ½ cup Parmesan and season with salt and pepper to taste. Transfer to serving platter and top with reserved mushrooms and remaining ½ cup Parmesan. Serve with extra hot sauce.

COMING NEXT ISSUE

Summer's in full swing! We'll have a slew of backyard recipes perfect for the season, from **Hawaiian Fried Chicken** to **Smoky Stuffed Potatoes** to **South Carolina Smoked Ham**. Follow up with a slice of **Oregon Blackberry Pie**, and wash it all down with one of our **Five Easy Lemonades**.

FIND THE ROOSTER!

A tiny version of this rooster has been hidden in the pages of this issue. Write to us with its location and we'll enter you in a random drawing. The first correct entry drawn will win our winning kitchen timer, and each of the next five will receive a free one-year subscription to *Cook's Country*. To enter, visit **CooksCountry.co** **rooster** by July 31, 2016, or write to Roost JJ16, *Cook's Country*, P.O. Box 470739, Brookline, MA 02447. Include your name and address. Jean Munch of Cincinnati, Ohio, found the rooster in the February/ March 2016 issue on page 8 and won our favorite springform pan.

WEB EXTRAS

Free for 4 months at CooksCountry.com

RECIPES:
Chicken Baked in Foil with Fennel and Sun-Dried Tomatoes
Gazpacho
Grilled Broccoli with Anchovy-Garlic Butt
Grilled Broccoli with Sweet Chili Sauce
Meatballs and Marinara
One-Minute Tomato Salsa
One-Pot Baked Ziti with Sausage and Spinach
Pan-Seared Chicken with Spicy Pinto Bea
Shrimp Cocktail
Single White Cake Round
Slow-Cooker Weeknight Chili
Tomato Casserole
EXPANDED REVIEWS:
Tasting Hot Dog Buns
Testing Chimney Starters
Testing Grill Lights
Testing Kitchen Timers

READ US ON iPAD

Download the *Cook's Country* app for iPad and start a free trial subscription or purchase a single issue of the magazine. All issues are enhanced with full-color Cooking Mode slide shows that provide step-by-step instructions for completing recipes, plus expanded review and ratings. Go to **CooksCountry.com/iP** to download our app through iTunes.

Cracker Jack Ice Cream Cake

Sweeten up the seventh-inning stretch with this home run of a cake.

TO MAKE THIS CAKE, YOU WILL NEED:

- ½ cup caramel topping
- ¼ cup peanut butter
- 1½ quarts vanilla ice cream
- ½ cup unsalted dry-roasted peanuts, chopped
- 1 (9-inch) white cake round*
- 2 (1-ounce) boxes Cracker Jack

FOR THE ICE CREAM CORE: Line 3-cup bowl with plastic wrap, letting ends of plastic overhang bowl by several inches. Combine caramel and peanut butter in small bowl; set aside. Scoop 2 cups ice cream into medium

bowl and mash with wooden spoon until softened. Stir in peanuts until combined. Add ¼ cup caramel mixture and fold until swirled into ice cream. Scrape into plastic-lined bowl and smooth top. Wrap with plastic and freeze until firm, about 6 hours.

TO ASSEMBLE: Line 10-cup bowl with plastic, letting ends of plastic overhang bowl by several inches. Scoop remaining 4 cups ice cream into medium bowl and mash with wooden spoon until softened. Scrape softened ice cream into plastic-lined 10-cup bowl. Working quickly, unwrap caramel-swirled ice

cream, discard plastic, and press, round side down, into softened ice cream until flush with level of ice cream. Place cake round over top, trimming sides as necessary so cake fits inside bowl. Wrap with plastic and freeze until completely firm, about 6 hours.

TO SERVE: When ready to serve, unmold and discard plastic. Place cake side down on plate or pedestal. Drizzle remaining caramel mixture over top, then mound Cracker Jack in center. Serve immediately.

▶ Go to CooksCountry.com/singlewhitecakeround for our Single White Cake Round recipe, or use your own.

Inside This Issue

Cook's Country

AUGUST/SEPTEMBER 2016

Oregon Blackberry Pie

We spent six weeks perfecting this summertime favorite, which features the easiest lattice top ever.

PAGE 22

The Ultimate BLT
Yes, You Need Our Recipe

Slow-Cooker Tomato Sauce
All-Purpose Sauce

Grilled Citrus Chicken
Grill the Fruit, Too

One-Pan Steak Dinner
The Secret Weapon: Coffee

Testing Paper Plates
Avoid Picnic Disasters

**Cooking Class:
English Muffin Bread**

Fettuccine Alfredo
Strong Stirring Is the Key

Hawaiian Fried Chicken
Impossibly Crunchy

Barbecue Coleslaw
Spicy Backyard Favorite

Peach Upside-Down Cake
Easy Skillet Version

Chicken and Rice
Latin Classic at Home

CooksCountry.com
$5.95 U.S./$6.95 CANADA

LETTER FROM THE EDITOR

Senior editor Diane Unger (left) fried dozens of pounds of chicken in pursuit of authentic island flavor. Her secret to a crunchy coating? Potato starch.

W HEN YOU'RE STARING up from your chaise at the palm fronds waving lazily in the tropical breeze, it's hard to imagine you're in the same country as the gray, noisy, traffic-clogged metropolis you may have left behind. But you are. This is Hawaii, our 50th state, and while its natural charms are the stuff of fantasy, it's relatively underappreciated when it comes to food.

Tourists know the luau staples—kalua pork, poi, mai tais—and they have their charms. But the more common (and, frankly, more satisfying) tradition is the omnipresent "plate lunch," often served in a to-go container and including some sort of protein (pork, perhaps, but just as often braised or fried chicken), two scoops of rice, and one scoop of macaroni salad. Sound filling? It is, but then all that outdoor activity—surfing, hiking, poolside lounging—takes energy.

We've covered Hawaiian macaroni salad before (June/July 2009), but this issue marks the first time we've offered a recipe for Hawaiian-style fried chicken, carefully and beautifully developed by our resident fried-chicken expert, senior editor Diane Unger. Learn more about her experience and get her bulletproof recipe on page 11.

TUCKER SHAW

Executive Editor

Foolproof Preserving: A Guide to Small Batch Jams, Jellies, Pickles, Condiments & More

Whether you're bringing in produce from your garden or picking it up at the farmers' market, the bounty of late summer can be overwhelming. Eat as much as you can and preserve the rest! Our indispensable book has tips, ideas, step-by-step instructions, inspiring recipes, and detailed equipment reviews.

Follow us on **Pinterest**
pinterest.com/TestKitchen

Follow us on **Twitter**
twitter.com/TestKitchen

Find us on **Facebook**
facebook.com/CooksCountry

Find us on **Instagram**
instagram.com/cookscountry

Photos: Top, Steve Klise; Middle, iStock; Bottom, Keller+Keller

Cook's Country

Chief Executive Officer David Nussbaum
Chief Creative Officer Jack Bishop
Editorial Director John Willoughby
Executive Editor Tucker Shaw
Deputy Editor Rebecca Hays
Executive Managing Editor Todd Meier
Executive Food Editor Bryan Roof
Senior Editors Chris O'Connor, Diane Unger
Associate Editors Morgan Bolling, Ashley Moore,
Test Cooks Dan Cellucci, Matthew Fairman,
    Cecelia Jenkins, Katie Leaird
Assistant Test Cook Allison Berkey
Copy Editors Jillian Campbell, Krista Magnuson
Contributing Editors Erika Bruce, Eva Katz
Science Editor Guy Crosby, PhD
Director, Creative Operations Alice Carpenter

Executive Editor, Tastings & Testings Lisa McManus
Managing Editor Scott Kathan
Deputy Editor Hannah Crowley
Associate Editors Lauren Savoie, Kate Shannon
Assistant Editors Jason Alvarez, Miye Bromberg
Editorial Assistant Carolyn Grillo

Test Kitchen Director Erin McMurrer
Assistant Test Kitchen Director Leah Rovner
Test Kitchen Manager Alexxa Grattan
Lead Senior Kitchen Assistant Meridith Lippard
Senior Kitchen Assistant Taylor Pond
Lead Kitchen Assistant Ena Gudiel
Kitchen Assistants Gladis Campos, Blanca Castanza,
    Maria Elena Delgado, Heather Ecker

Design Director Greg Galvan
Photography Director Julie Cote
Art Director Susan Levin
Deputy Art Director Lindsey Chandler
Art Director, Marketing Melanie Gryboski
Deputy Art Director, Marketing Janet Taylor
Associate Art Director, Marketing Stephanie Cook
Senior Staff Photographer Daniel J. van Ackere
Staff Photographer Steve Klise
Assistant Photography Producer Mary Ball
Color Food Photography Keller + Keller
Styling Catrine Kelty, Marie Piraino

Senior Director, Digital Design John Torres
Executive Editor, Web Christine Liu
Managing Editor, Web Mari Levine
Senior Editor, Web Roger Metcalf
Associate Editors, Web Terrence Doyle, Briana Palma
Senior Video Editor Nick Dakoulas
Test Kitchen Photojournalist Kevin White

Chief Financial Officer Jackie McCauley Ford
Production Director Guy Rochford
Imaging Manager Lauren Robbins
Production & Imaging Specialists Heather Dube,
    Sean MacDonald, Dennis Noble, Jessica Voas
Senior Controller Theresa Peterson
Director of Business Partnerships Mehgan Conciatori

Chief Digital Officer Fran Middleton
VP, Strategic Analytics Deborah Fagone
Director of Sponsorship Marketing & Client Services
    Christine Anagnostis
National Sponsorship Sales Director Timothy Coburn
Client Services Manager Kate Zebrowski
Client Service & Social Media Coordinator Morgan Mannino
Partnership Marketing Manager Pamela Putprush
Director of Customer Support Amy Bootier
Senior Customer Loyalty & Support Specialist
    Andrew Straaberg Finfrock
Customer Loyalty & Support Specialists Caroline Augliere,
    Rebecca Kowalski, Ramesh Pillay
Senior VP, Human Resources & Organizational
    Development Colleen Zelina
Human Resources Director Adele Shapiro
Director, Retail Book Program Beth Ineson
Retail Sales Manager Derek Meehan
Associate Director, Publicity Susan Hershberg

Circulation Services ProCirc

On the cover: Oregon Blackberry Pie Keller + Keller, Catrine Kelty
Illustration: Greg Stevenson

Contents

Departments

America's Test Kitchen is a real 2,500-square-foot kitchen located just outside Boston. It is the home of more than 60 test cooks, editors, and cookware specialists. Our mission is to test recipes until we understand exactly how and why they work and eventually arrive at the very best version. We also test kitchen equipment and supermarket ingredients in search of products that offer the best value and performance. You can watch us work by tuning in to *America's Test Kitchen* (AmericasTestKitchen.com) and *Cook's Country from America's Test Kitchen* (CooksCountry.com) on public television and listen to us on our weekly radio program on PRX. You can also follow us on Facebook, Twitter, Pinterest, and Instagram.

8

18

27

Cook's Country magazine (ISSN 1552-1990), number 70, is published bimonthly by Boston Common Press Limited Partnership, 17 Station St., Brookline, MA 02445. Copyright 2016 Boston Common Press Limited Partnership. Periodicals postage paid at Boston, MA, and additional mailing offices, USPS #023453. Publications Mail Agreement No. 40020778. Return undeliverable Canadian addresses to P.O. Box 875, Station A, Windsor, ON N9A 6P2. POSTMASTER: Send address changes to *Cook's Country*, P.O. Box 6018, Harlan, IA 51593-1518. For subscription and gift subscription orders, subscription inquiries, or change of address notices, visit AmericasTestKitchen.com/support, call 800-526-8447 in the U.S. or 515-248-7684 from outside the U.S., or write to us at *Cook's Country*, P.O. Box 6018, Harlan, IA 51593-1518. PRINTED IN THE USA.

Ask Cook's Country

BY MORGAN BOLLING

Tea Temperature

I have one friend who swears by bringing the water to a full boil to make a "proper" cup of black tea. But another says that boiling water ruins black tea and the water should be at only a simmer. Is there really a difference?
Natasha Price, Anchorage, Alaska

Different industry experts list the optimal water temperature for brewing black tea as anywhere from 190 to 212 degrees. To see if we could narrow this range a little, we made four batches of black tea (we used Twinings English Breakfast Tea, our favorite plain black tea) using water at 180, 190, 200, and 212 degrees; for each batch, we steeped the tea bags for precisely 4 minutes and then cooled the tea to about 170 degrees before we sampled it plain (no milk or sugar). Our tasters had a distinct preference for the two teas steeped at the higher temperatures, as they found the teas brewed at 180 and 190 degrees to be lacking complexity (because the flavors from the tea weren't fully extracted at lower temperatures). The tasters that preferred the tea brewed with 200-degree water found the tea brewed at 212 degrees to be a little too tannic.
THE BOTTOM LINE: Brew black tea with water that's between 200 and 212 degrees; water in the higher end of this range will produce a stronger, more astringent tea.

Tomato Sizing

When one of your recipes calls for a tomato, what size and type should I use?
Elizabeth Palazzi, Bryn Mawr, Pa.

ONLY ONE OF THESE WILL BOUNCE
A medium tomato is the size of a tennis ball.

The test kitchen uses the guideline that one standard, medium tomato weighs 6 ounces, which translates to ¾ cup of stemmed and chopped tomato. A large tomato weighs 8 ounces. We specify the size and type of tomato only if they are crucial to the recipe's success. Otherwise, we typically default to medium.
THE BOTTOM LINE: When one of our recipes calls for a tomato, generally try to use one that weighs 6 ounces—about the size of a tennis ball. If the recipe is dependent on the type or specific size of the tomato, we'll let you know.

Sheet Shifting

Does it really matter if I switch and rotate my cookie sheets while baking?
Lucy Sammer, Rye, N.Y.

Most of our recipes for cookies, pies, cakes, and tarts call for rotating the baking sheet or pan halfway through baking to ensure even cooking and browning. But we love challenging assumptions, even our own, so to answer your question, we baked our Chewy Sugar Cookies and Thick and Chewy Chocolate Chip Cookies both with and without rotating the sheets. Sure enough, the cookies on the sheets that weren't rotated baked a bit unevenly, with certain cookies darker due to oven hot spots. The difference was minor but noticeable. Since our recipes are designed with that step, which requires opening the oven door and losing heat, the cookies we did not rotate also baked slightly faster.

This effect is more dramatic in recipes that call for baking two sheets of cookies at once on different oven racks and switching and rotating the sheets halfway through baking. When we repeated the test with recipes that called for switching and rotating the sheets of cookies, the cookies from the unrotated sheet on the bottom rack had significantly darker bases and surfaces than those baked on the top rack.

THE BOTTOM LINE: Swapping the locations of the baking sheets in the oven (top rack to bottom rack and vice versa) and rotating the sheets halfway through baking does indeed make for more evenly cooked baked goods.

NOT SWITCHED
The sheet of cookies baked on the bottom oven rack (left) browned more than the sheet of cookies baked on the top rack (right).

NOT ROTATED
The cookies on the lower right are darker than the rest.

Mustard Seeds

Can I use brown and yellow mustard seeds interchangeably in recipes?
Jennifer Gradischer, Marlton, N.J.

Brown and yellow mustard seeds are produced by different species of the mustard plant, which belongs to the same family as broccoli and kale. Brown mustard seeds are smaller than yellow mustard seeds and, as their name implies, are brown. They're more common in African and Asian cooking and are used to make whole-grain and spicy brown mustards. Yellow mustard seeds, more common in the United States, are slightly larger with golden or straw-colored exteriors and are the key ingredient in prepared yellow mustard.

To see how they differed in flavor, we used the seeds to make our Tarragon–Mustard Seed Rub, which we applied to chicken before cooking it, and our Easy Homemade Mustard. In both cases, tasters commented that the brown mustard seeds were "bitter" and "a bit spicy," while the yellow mustard seeds were more "familiar" and "sweet." Tasters noted that the yellow seeds provided more authentic mustard flavor.
THE BOTTOM LINE: We don't recommend using brown and yellow mustard seeds interchangeably—they have distinctly different flavors.

Pulse versus Process

I notice that when you use a food processor to chop something, you "pulse" a certain number of times rather than running the processor for a few seconds. Why?
Valerie Rando, Tallahassee, Fla.

Pulsing food in a processor bowl offers more control than processing it; the food is chopped more evenly because the ingredients are redistributed—akin to stirring—with every pulse. To test this theory, we made two batches of our Five-Minute Fresh Tomato Salsa, which calls for three 1-second pulses. We made one batch as directed and made another batch in which we let the processor run for 3 seconds. We repeated this test with shelled pecans.

The tomato salsa that had been processed was significantly more pureed and like a tomato sauce, while the pulsed salsa was pleasantly chunky, as a salsa should be. The processed pecans featured an uneven mix of very small and large pieces; the pecans that were pulsed for the same amount of time were chopped much more evenly.
THE BOTTOM LINE: Pulsing produces more evenly chopped food than processing does. For that reason, we'll call for pulsing when we want foods to be evenly chopped.

PROCESSED FOR 3 SECONDS
A bad mix of small and large pieces

THREE 1-SECOND PULSES
A nice even chop

▶ To ask us a cooking question, visit **CooksCountry.com/ask**. Or write to Ask *Cook's Country*, P.O. Box 470739, Brookline, MA 02447. Just try to stump us!

Kitchen Shortcuts

COMPILED BY DIANE UNGER

SMART TIP Dust Your Knife
Barbara Blakeson, Annapolis, Md.

My kids love your recipe for Seven-Layer Bars, and I make it at least 10 times a year. I found one trick that makes cutting these sticky treats a bit easier: Once I've removed the uncut bars from the pan using the foil sling, I score the bars to mark where to cut. Then I dust my chef's knife with confectioners' sugar; the sugar adheres to the now-sticky knife. This way the bars don't stick to the knife when I cut them into squares.

DOUBLE DUTY Strain It
Joseph McConkey, Oak Park, Ill.

I love poached eggs, but I hate messy whites, both in the water and on my plate. Thanks to one of your tips, I've learned to crack the eggs into a fine-mesh strainer to let the thin white liquid (the part that gets wispy in the water) drain off. But I found a way to take this tip further: I crack two eggs into a fine-mesh strainer, let the thin liquid drain off, and then place the strainer directly in the poaching water, making sure the eggs stay below the surface. Removing the eggs from the saucepan has never been easier, and they look perfect every time.

HANDY TRICK
Wrench It
Gail Goodman, Glens Falls, N.Y.

I have a heck of a time twisting the small plastic caps off the gallon bottles of water I buy—sometimes they seem cemented on. To solve the problem, I save the fat rubber bands from bunches of broccoli (they're about ½ inch wide) and fit them right over the cap to help me get a better grip. Now I can open the bottles easily, without wrenching the joints in my thumbs.

Submit a tip online at CooksCountry.com/kitchenshortcuts or send a letter to Kitchen Shortcuts, Cook's Country, P.O. Box 470739, Brookline, MA 02447. Include your name, address, and phone number. If we publish your tip, you will receive a free one-year subscription to Cook's Country. Letters may be edited for clarity and length.

CLEVER TRICK
Warm It Up
Agnes Sheehan, Portland, Maine

In my 40 years of cooking, I've learned it's the little things—like warming your bowls for pasta before serving—that really count. On that note, I've found a handy trick for warming bowls (or small plates) for me and my husband before dinner: I heat my toaster oven to 200 degrees and set the bowls inside for about a minute while I'm finishing cooking. This warms the bowls perfectly by the time I'm ready to serve.

HOT IDEA
Diffuse It
Tiffany Moon, Cambridge, Mass.

I have an electric stove with coil burners that heat unevenly; whenever I try to heat milk or cook rice, one side of the saucepan always scorches. Knowing how well and evenly my cast-iron skillet holds heat, I tried putting the skillet on the burner and then my saucepan with milk or rice right in the skillet. This method gives me perfectly even heat and no more scorching.

HANDY TRICK
Marinara Rescue
Dwight Kelton, Sacramento, Calif.

Homemade pizza with store-bought dough is a staple in my house. I used to make my pizza sauce by cooking jarred marinara down until it was thick, but I found that it's easier to dump a jar of marinara into a fine-mesh strainer set over a bowl. By the time I get the dough rolled out, the sauce has drained into a nice thick pizza sauce.

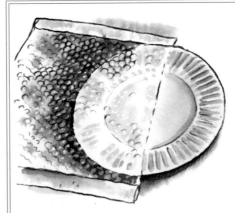

SMART TIP Wrap It Up
Colleen Kelly, Port Townsend, Wash.

I have a lot of china serving plates that are family heirlooms. To protect them from scratches and keep them from sliding around when stacked, I make customized padded envelopes for them. I cut a long piece of bubble wrap, fold it in half, and use duct tape to seal the sides, leaving the top open like an envelope. I slide the plates inside and fold over the top to keep out dust.

Smoked Fresh Ham

This smoke-infused pork nestled in a soft bun gives a whole new meaning to ham sandwich.

BY MORGAN BOLLING

A vibrant mustard sauce adds sharp contrast to this new take on pulled pork.

SHOPPING Fresh Ham

A fresh ham isn't like the cured, smoked, or aged ham most of us are used to. Instead, it's just a large pork roast. For this recipe, we call for a **shank-end roast**, meaning that it is cut from the lower rear leg of the hog. We like this cut because it has more skin than a sirloin-end roast.

KEY STEP Crisp the Skin

The crackly skin is arguably the best part of a fresh ham, but it tends to steam and turn rubbery as the meat roasts. To crisp the skin, we pull it off in one piece once the ham is cooked through and roast it solo until it is dark brown. We then chop it and combine it with the chopped ham.

THE USUAL GO-TO cut of pork for backyard barbecue is the pork shoulder, but in certain corners of the Carolinas, many pitmasters swear by ham (see "On the Road"). I don't mean the smoked, sliced ham you'll find on a holiday table but rather "fresh ham" or "green ham," which is bought uncooked and, with care and attention, can be transformed into a remarkably savory, deeply flavored filling for a summertime sandwich.

Fresh ham, cut from the hindquarters of the hog and sold unsmoked and unseasoned, is leaner than traditional barbecue cuts like shoulder. Cooking it takes a little know-how, but if it's done properly, the payoff is big. The meat is less soft, more chunky, and best of all, the crisp, bacon-like bits of skin are chopped and mixed into it.

To begin my tinkering, I ordered a few hams from my butcher since it's rarely available in the supermarket meat case. He gave me a choice between two cuts: the tapered shank end and the rounded sirloin end. Since the sirloin end, with its many bones, can be hard to carve, I opted for the shank end.

Opinions differ on the "best" way to smoke this cut, even among experts. Some coat the ham liberally with rubs. Others use only salt. Even more surprising, some pros call for cooking the pork to just 145 degrees, while others take it way, way higher to 200 degrees.

To get my bearings, I smoked several fresh hams and made one decision: I'd rub the meat with only salt to keep the flavor pure. Leaving the salt on overnight gave me good flavor plus juicy meat.

I found that hams cooked to 145 degrees had chunks of tender, juicy meat but also featured areas of chewy, unrendered collagen and fat. I experimented with various temperatures, but the roast cooked to 200 degrees was the hands-down favorite. The meat was tender and soft, the fat and collagen having melted over the long, slow cooking process.

But the ham took nearly 5 hours on the grill to reach 200 degrees, and maintaining an outdoor fire for that long is a pain. The easier option was to slowly smoke the ham on the grill for 2 hours to infuse it with smoke flavor and then move it indoors to finish in the controlled environment of the oven. Placing it in a 13 by 9-inch baking pan and covering it tightly with foil helped.

Unfortunately, covering the roast caused the skin to steam and become rubbery. I wanted crackle. I tried removing the skin and baking it alongside the ham, but it turned brittle, with a chewy underside. I opted for a hybrid method: Once the pork reached 200 degrees, I took it out of the oven, removed the skin (using a pair of tongs), and returned the skin to the oven to crisp on a baking sheet. This gave me plenty of crackly skin to chop and add to the ham.

A vinegary mustard sauce, a hallmark of South Carolina barbecue, was just the contrast this sandwich needed. When I set out my final platter of smoked fresh ham sandwiches, I fielded protests from coworkers—not about the quality of the ham but about the fact that I'd served my last smoked ham sandwich, for now.

SOUTH CAROLINA SMOKED FRESH HAM Serves 8 to 10

Plan ahead: The ham must be salted at least 18 hours before cooking. You'll have about 2½ cups of mustard sauce.

HAM

- 1 (6- to 8-pound) bone-in, skin-on shank-end fresh ham
     Kosher salt
- 2 cups wood chips

MUSTARD SAUCE

- 1½ cups yellow mustard
- ½ cup cider vinegar
- 6 tablespoons packed brown sugar
- 2 tablespoons ketchup
- 2 teaspoons hot sauce
- 2 teaspoons Worcestershire sauce
- 1 teaspoon pepper

     Hamburger buns

1. FOR THE HAM: Pat ham dry with paper towels. Place ham on large sheet of plastic wrap and rub all over with 2 tablespoons salt. Wrap tightly in plastic and refrigerate for 18 to 24 hours.

2. Just before grilling, soak wood chips in water for 15 minutes, then drain. Using large piece of heavy-duty aluminum foil, wrap soaked chips in 8 by 4½-inch foil packet. (Make sure chips do not poke holes in sides or bottom of packet.) Cut 2 evenly spaced 2-inch slits in top of packet.

3A. FOR A CHARCOAL GRILL: Open bottom vent completely. Light large chimney starter three-quarters filled

with charcoal briquettes (4½ quarts). When top coals are partially covered with ash, pour evenly over half of grill. Place wood chip packet on coals. Set cooking grate in place, cover, and open lid vent completely. Heat grill until hot and wood chips are smoking, about 5 minutes.

3B. FOR A GAS GRILL: Remove cooking grate and place wood chip packet directly on primary burner. Set cooking grate in place, turn all burners to high, cover, and heat grill until hot and wood chips are smoking, about 15 minutes. Turn primary burner to medium-high and turn off other burner(s). (Adjust primary burner as needed to maintain grill temperature of 300 degrees.)

4. Clean and oil cooking grate. Unwrap ham and place flat side down on cooler side of grill. Cover grill (position lid vent directly over ham if using charcoal) and cook for 2 hours. Thirty minutes before ham comes off grill, adjust oven rack to middle position and heat oven to 300 degrees.

5. FOR THE MUSTARD SAUCE: Meanwhile, whisk all ingredients together in bowl. (Sauce can be refrigerated for up to 1 week.)

6. Transfer ham to 13 by 9-inch baking pan, flat side down. Cover pan tightly with foil. Transfer to oven and roast until fork inserted in ham meets little resistance and meat registers 200 degrees, about 2½ hours.

7. Remove ham from oven and increase oven temperature to 400 degrees. Line rimmed baking sheet with foil. Using tongs, remove ham skin in 1 large piece. Place skin fatty side down on prepared sheet. Transfer to oven and roast until skin is dark and crispy and sounds hollow when tapped with fork, about 25 minutes, rotating sheet halfway through roasting. Tent ham with foil and let rest while skin roasts.

8. Transfer ham to carving board. Strain accumulated juices from pan through fine-mesh strainer set over bowl; discard solids. Trim and discard excess fat from ham. Remove bone and chop meat into bite-size pieces; transfer to large bowl.

9. When cool enough to handle, chop skin fine. Rewarm reserved ham juices in microwave for 1 minute. Add juices and chopped skin to ham and toss to combine. Season with salt to taste. Serve on buns, topped with mustard sauce.

In South Carolina, a Lesson in Old and New

It's a few minutes before 5 a.m., still dark and bitterly cold, when I pull up to a long cinder-block smokehouse in West Columbia, South Carolina. A faint light from inside illuminates a massive pile of split logs that sits in the yard. As I approach the building, a large cargo door slides open and the silhouettes of a man and his dog appear beneath a struggling fluorescent bulb. His breath hangs in the frigid air as he extends a hand and welcomes me to Hite's Bar-B-Que.

David Hite has been on the graveyard shift since 7 p.m. the previous evening, burning fat logs of oak and hickory down to red-hot coals in a weathered brick fireplace and shoveling them under the 25-foot-long barbecue pit where whole hogs, racks of ribs, fresh hams, and slabs of pork skin cook slowly over the dry heat. We huddle around the fire to keep warm; Hite occasionally wanders off to gather more wood for the flames.

Hite, whose family has run the business since 1957, specializes in whole-hog barbecue. The meat is chopped, not shredded, as you might find in other areas of the state; crispy bits of rendered pork skin, aka cracklin', are incorporated into the meat, creating crunchy little jewels in the otherwise soft pork. It's served with a mustardy sauce, a legacy of the mustard-loving German immigrants who settled this part of central South Carolina in the 1700s. Hite uses a massive whisk attached to an electric drill to mix the 10-gallon batches of sauce. He talks at length about the virtues of "new" and "old" pork skins. "Old" skins are those that came with the hogs he's already cooking, but because customers demand these coveted crispy bits in their pork, Hite buys extra sheets of pork skin (aka "new" skins) from the butcher to render down for extra cracklin'. When ordering their barbecue, many regulars specify, "No new skins!" Hite understands—to his mind, old skins have more flavor.

At 7 a.m. Hite opens the pit, pulls some meat and crispy skin from the nearest hog, and drops it on a tattered cutting board. Over the years his thumb has worn down a patch on the wooden handle of the cleaver he uses to chop it. He makes a couple of sandwiches: one for his daughter's school lunch and one for me. –BRYAN ROOF

David Hite (above) carries on a family tradition at Hite's Bar-B-Que, slowly cooking whole hogs, fresh hams, and pork skins over oak and hickory wood. The slow-cooking meats take 10 or more hours to cook, which means that to be prepped for the lunch rush, Hite must start cooking at 7 p.m. the night before. Loyal customers are particular about their orders and don't mind saying so.

▶ To see more images from our trip to South Carolina, go to **CooksCountry.com/southcarolinabbq.**

Grilled Citrus Chicken

To add maximum citrus flavor to the mild-mannered chicken breasts, we grilled the fruit, too.

BY CHRISTIE MORRISON

BONELESS, SKINLESS CHICKEN breasts are often tagged as a boring, easily overcooked substitute for more-flavorful thighs. I disagree. Call me Pollyanna (it wouldn't be the first time), but I think of this lean, mild meat as a blank canvas just waiting for a creative boost.

I love citrus juices—lemon, lime, and orange—but when they're used in a marinade, their acidity can toughen meat. I needed another way to bring these flavors to grilled chicken.

Years of testing have taught us that marinades do most of their work on the surface of the meat, while a solution of salt and water deeply seasons meat and helps keep it moist. By combining the two into a salty marinade, or "brinerade," we season the meat throughout while also adding flavor to the exterior.

I assembled a brinerade of salt, pepper, garlic, sugar (to aid in browning), vegetable oil, and a few tablespoons of water and added equal parts lemon, lime, and orange zest (less acidic than juice) for a balance of sour and sweet. I poured this mixture into a zipper-lock bag, added the chicken breasts, and let them soak for an hour.

Our favorite method for grilling chicken is to build a half-grill fire (piling all the coals on one side of the grill). We cook the chicken on the cooler side, covered with a disposable pan to help trap heat and smoke, until it reaches an internal temperature of 140 degrees. We then transfer it to the hotter side to sear.

Right off the grill, my chicken was juicy and well seasoned, with pronounced citrus flavors—but the orange zest overwhelmed, so I tweaked the ratio (2 parts each lemon and lime zest to 1 part orange).

For one last pop of flavor, I halved the fruit I'd zested and grilled the pieces over direct heat. I used the warm, slightly smoky juices to make a quick citrus-mint sauce, bringing the best bits of summer to this simple dish.

GRILLED CITRUS CHICKEN Serves 4

Plan ahead: The chicken needs to marinate for at least an hour. Do not marinate it longer than 12 hours or it will be too salty. Use a rasp-style grater to zest the citrus. The chicken takes longer to cook on a gas grill, so begin checking it at the end of the range in step 3.

- 1 orange
- 1 lemon
- 1 lime
- 7 tablespoons vegetable oil
- 3 tablespoons water
- 3 garlic cloves, minced
- 2½ teaspoons sugar
   Salt and pepper
- 4 (6- to 8-ounce) boneless, skinless chicken breasts, trimmed
- 1 (13 by 9-inch) disposable aluminum roasting pan (if using charcoal)
- 1 teaspoon mayonnaise
- 1 teaspoon Dijon mustard
- 1 tablespoon minced fresh mint

We grill orange, lemon, and lime halves to create a bracing, bright, lightly smoky citrus sauce.

1. Grate 1 teaspoon zest from orange, 2 teaspoons zest from lemon, and 2 teaspoons zest from lime. Place all citrus zest in bowl. Halve orange, lemon, and lime and set aside. Add 3 tablespoons oil, water, two-thirds of garlic, 2 teaspoons sugar, 1½ teaspoons salt, and ½ teaspoon pepper to citrus zest and whisk to combine. Transfer brinerade to 1-gallon zipper-lock bag. Add chicken, press out air, seal bag, and turn to distribute brinerade. Refrigerate for at least 1 hour or up to 12 hours.

2A. FOR A CHARCOAL GRILL: Open bottom vent completely. Light large chimney starter filled with charcoal briquettes (6 quarts). When top coals are partially covered with ash, pour evenly over half of grill. Set cooking grate in place, cover, and open lid vent completely. Heat grill until hot, about 5 minutes.

2B. FOR A GAS GRILL: Turn all burners to high, cover, and heat grill until hot, about 15 minutes. Leave primary burner on high and turn off other burner(s).

3. Clean and oil cooking grate. Place chicken skinned side down on cooler side of grill, with thicker ends facing coals. (Edges of chicken should be no more than 4 inches from center of primary burner if using gas.) Cover with disposable pan (if using gas, close lid) and cook until bottom of chicken just begins to develop light grill marks and is no longer pink, 6 to 9 minutes.

4. Flip chicken and rotate so that thinner ends face coals. Cover as before and continue to cook until chicken registers 140 degrees, 6 to 9 minutes longer.

5. Remove disposable pan and transfer chicken and citrus halves, cut side down, to hotter side of grill. Cook chicken, uncovered (covered if using gas), until dark grill marks appear, 2 to 4 minutes. Flip chicken and cook, uncovered (covered if using gas), until marked on second side and chicken registers 160 degrees, 2 to 4 minutes longer. Cook citrus halves until lightly charred, about 4 minutes.

6. Transfer chicken to cutting board, tent with aluminum foil, and let rest for 5 minutes. Squeeze 3 tablespoons orange juice, 1 tablespoon lemon juice, and 1 tablespoon lime juice into bowl. Whisk in mayonnaise, Dijon, remaining one-third of garlic, remaining ½ teaspoon sugar, ¼ teaspoon salt, and ⅛ teaspoon pepper. Whisking constantly, slowly drizzle in remaining ¼ cup oil until emulsified. Stir in mint and season with salt and pepper to taste. Slice each breast on bias ¼ inch thick. Serve, drizzled with citrus sauce.

KEY STEP Cover It Up

We've found that covering a charcoal grill restricts oxygen flow to the coals, which can decrease the heat's intensity. In certain recipes we cover food with an overturned disposable aluminum roasting pan to trap heat around the food while still allowing oxygen to reach the coals.

Spicy Barbecue Coleslaw

Slaw is too often relegated to wallflower status. We wanted one that announced itself. BY KATIE LEAIRD

MANY VERSIONS OF coleslaw are nothing more than waterlogged cabbage shreds awash in diluted dressing—no wonder it goes uneaten. I wanted coleslaw with personality that could hold its own amid a full barbecue spread.

Cabbage is 93 percent water, which will thin the dressing, obliterate flavor, and compromise creaminess. I had to get rid of that water.

One popular method is to salt the sliced cabbage, let it drain, and then rinse and dry it before adding it to the slaw. Frustrated with the four-step process, I tried just salting and draining the cabbage, but the results were too briny. I swapped in sugar for some of the salt (sugar also draws out water), but it took 2 hours to fully drain the cabbage. I'm not that patient.

I tried gently heating the salted and sugared cabbage in the microwave for 3 minutes. This released the water from the cabbage and also tenderized the cabbage a bit, taking it from squeaky to semitender, with just enough crunch. A quick squeeze in a dish towel banished the excess water.

I wanted a spicy dressing to cut through those traditional sweet and smoky barbecue flavors. I knew I'd lean on mayonnaise for creaminess, but I wanted this dressing to pack a multi-layered kick, with heat up front, in the middle, and at the finish.

My three-pronged assault started with horseradish. Instead of grating fresh horseradish (a pain), I opted for prepared (not to be confused with its milder sibling, creamed horseradish). Horseradish's signature heat spreads up through the nose with a fiery tingle but then quickly dissipates. My second heat source would be mustard. I auditioned both yellow and Dijon but ultimately settled on dry mustard powder. Though mild on its own, the powder comes alive once activated by the liquid in the dressing, producing a fresher, more potent punch than the jarred stuff. The third heat source is a test kitchen favorite, ground cayenne pepper, which offered a clean, straightforward kick. Instead of traveling into the nasal passages, the capsaicin in cayenne creates lingering heat throughout the mouth and throat. Just ¼ teaspoon turned up the volume one final notch.

With spicy heat hitting multiple targets, from the nose (horseradish and mustard) down to the throat (cayenne), this slaw was far from ho-hum.

SPICY BARBECUE COLESLAW
Serves 8 to 10

To save time, we shred the cabbage in a food processor fitted with a slicing disk. If you don't have a food processor, slice the cabbage wedges crosswise ⅛ inch thick. Shred the carrots on the large holes of a box grater. For an extra spicy kick, up the horseradish to 2 tablespoons. The flavors will intensify as the coleslaw chills.

- 1 head green cabbage (2½ pounds), quartered, cored, and shredded (12 cups)
- 2 tablespoons sugar
  Salt and pepper
- 1 cup mayonnaise
- ⅓ cup distilled white vinegar
- 1 tablespoon prepared horseradish
- 1 teaspoon Worcestershire sauce
- 1 garlic clove, minced
- ½ teaspoon dry mustard
- ¼ teaspoon cayenne pepper
- 2 carrots, peeled and shredded

1. Toss cabbage, sugar, and ½ teaspoon salt together in bowl. Microwave, covered, until just beginning to wilt, about 3 minutes. Let cool slightly, about 5 minutes. Transfer half of cabbage to center of clean dish towel. Gather ends of towel to form bundle and twist to squeeze out excess water. Transfer to clean bowl and repeat with remaining cabbage.

2. Whisk mayonnaise, vinegar, horseradish, Worcestershire, garlic, mustard, cayenne, 1¼ teaspoons salt, and 1 teaspoon pepper in large bowl until smooth. Stir in cabbage and carrots and refrigerate, covered, until chilled, at least 1 hour. Serve. (Coleslaw can be refrigerated for up to 2 days.)

A toss of fresh mozzarella cheese adds a bit of substance to this light, summery side dish.

Watermelon-Tomato Salad

They're neighbors in the garden—could they be friends on the plate?

BY KATIE LEAIRD

WATERMELONS AND TOMATOES are both vibrant in color, exploding with juiciness, and crazily flavorful in the height of summer. When we've experimented with watermelon-tomato salads in the past, we've highlighted the tomato, using the watermelon as a backup element. This time, I wanted the sweet watermelon out front, with tomatoes in the supporting role.

One bugaboo of mixing these two ingredients is the look of it: bright-red components are barely distinguishable from each other. What's more, both release an outsize amount of moisture. Yellow cherry tomatoes solved the color conundrum. As a bonus, the cherry tomatoes released far less liquid than larger varieties did.

But watermelon is so named for a reason: It's full of liquid. And with 4 cups of cut-up watermelon, I had a lot of excess liquid. Patting the watermelon dry with paper towels was insufficient. Weighing down planks of watermelon to press out liquid made a mealy mess.

As it turned out, the best way was the simplest: cutting it into cubes and draining it in a colander. Sprinkling the cubes with salt helped pull out even more moisture but turned the watermelon brackish; a bit of sugar worked just as well, with better flavor results.

To gently balance the melon's sweetness, I added the delicate flavor of a sliced shallot. Fresh basil lent brightness, bits of fresh mozzarella added substance, and a simple vinaigrette brought everything together.

WATERMELON-TOMATO SALAD
Serves 4

This salad benefits from a liberal sprinkling of salt and pepper, so don't be shy when seasoning the mozzarella.

- 4 cups seedless watermelon, cut into 1-inch cubes
- 2 teaspoons sugar
- 12 ounces yellow cherry tomatoes, halved
  Salt and pepper
- 2 tablespoons extra-virgin olive oil, plus extra for drizzling
- 1 tablespoon cider vinegar
- ½ teaspoon grated lemon zest plus 1 tablespoon juice
- 1 shallot, sliced into thin rings
- ¼ cup fresh basil leaves, torn
- 6 ounces fresh mozzarella cheese, torn into 1-inch pieces

1. Gently combine watermelon and sugar in large bowl. Transfer watermelon to colander and set colander in now-empty bowl. Cover colander with plastic wrap and refrigerate for 30 minutes.

2. Toss tomatoes, ¼ teaspoon salt, and ¼ teaspoon pepper together in small bowl; set aside.

3. Whisk oil, vinegar, lemon zest and juice, ½ teaspoon salt, and ¼ teaspoon pepper together in large bowl. Add shallot, basil, drained watermelon, and tomatoes and toss gently to combine. Transfer to platter and evenly scatter mozzarella over top. Drizzle with extra oil and season with salt and pepper to taste. Serve.

Grilled Boneless Short Ribs

We decided to bring this low-and-slow favorite into the fast lane.

BY MATTHEW CARD

LAYERED WITH FAT and ribboned with bands of chewy cartilage, boneless English-style short ribs are not a common choice for grilling in America. We typically use low-and-slow cooking methods, like braising, to unlock this cut's rich flavor.

But in Argentina, where beef is king and grilling is an art form, boneless hunks of short rib are cooked over hardwood coals to a rosy medium-rare. Sliced thin and served with a tangy herb sauce or piquant pepper relish, the ribs often take top billing at the *churrascaria*. I wanted to help us get into the act up here in North America.

I prepared a handful of existing recipes to help set my course and was knocked sideways by the results. The best of the bunch produced juicy ribs with a deep, meaty savor rivaling that of the best—and most expensive—steaks I have tasted. Unfortunately, producing ribs that were an even medium-rare—and weren't scorched by flare-ups—required frequent flipping and steady supervision. There had to be an easier way.

Technically speaking, "short rib" is a vague name applied to ribs taken from three locations along the cow's rib cage, each exhibiting slightly different thickness and attributes. The thickest, leanest, beefiest of the bunch are referred to as "chuck" short ribs, and after grilling all three styles, these chuck ribs won handily. Consult your butcher if necessary; otherwise, look for the thickest ribs available and trim away the exterior membrane and fat before cooking.

I thought it best to treat the ribs like a thick steak, for which there are two prevailing—and opposing—cooking methods: sear quickly on the hotter side of the grill to develop a crust and then finish on the cooler side, or flip the script and cook them through slowly on the cooler side before finishing on the hotter side to develop a crust. In this case, the first method yielded beautifully browned ribs that, once sliced, revealed a band of well-done meat encircling rare meat—and way too much thick, unrendered fat. The latter method came closer but still featured too much fat.

I needed to cook the ribs as slowly as I could, rendering as much fat as possible, before browning them quickly over a very hot fire. To that end, I piled all the coals on one side of the grill and cooked the ribs on the opposite side

We grill the ribs on the cooler side of the grill before moving them to the hotter side to develop rosy interiors and satisfying char.

with the grill covered (essentially, grill roasting) before sliding them over the hot coals to finish. The method produced passable results, but covering the grill quashed much of the coals' heat, making it nearly impossible to create a crust without overcooking the meat.

I turned to a favorite test kitchen trick, capping the ribs with a disposable aluminum roasting pan and waiting patiently for any sign that the meat was cooking. Apparently, there simply wasn't enough heat for this method to work. But after tinkering, it did work when I spread a single thin layer of coals beneath the ribs (piling the majority of coals on the opposite side); the ribs cooked through and rendered their fat, ready for the hot sear.

These ribs were the best to date—evenly cooked, richly browned, and free of gnarly fat chunks—though I wanted a smokier flavor in the meat. This proved easy to do: I slid a foil packet filled with soaked wood chips beneath the ribs during the first step. The disposable pan captured the upwelling smoke, bathing the meat in its flavors. (As an added benefit, the foil packet shielded the coals from the dripping fat, reducing flare-ups).

The ribs tasted terrific on their own, though I still wanted a quick-and-easy accompaniment to cut the richness. An Argentine-style *criolla* sauce of minced raw onion, sweet bell pepper, garlic, olive oil, and vinegar tasted good, albeit a bit raw. I much preferred the blend once I sautéed the ingredients and rounded it out with pungent cumin, fresh cilantro, and spicy cayenne pepper and substituted lemon juice for the vinegar. Welcome to America, grilled short ribs. There's plenty of room at the table.

GRILLED BONELESS SHORT RIBS WITH ARGENTINE-STYLE PEPPER SAUCE Serves 4 to 6

The thickness and marbling of boneless short ribs can vary a good deal. Look for lean ribs cut from the chuck. If in doubt, ask your butcher for the cut by its technical designation: NAMP 130A. If you need to buy bone-in English-style ribs, slice off the ribs, cartilage, and excess fat. If your short ribs are a single slab, cut them into 2- to 3-inch-wide strips. Plan ahead: The salted short ribs need to sit for at least an hour before grilling.

2½–3 pounds boneless beef short ribs, 1½ to 2 inches thick, 2 inches wide, and 4 to 5 inches long, trimmed
Kosher salt and pepper
1½ cups wood chips
½ cup finely chopped red bell pepper
⅓ cup finely chopped red onion
¼ cup extra-virgin olive oil
3 garlic cloves, minced
1 teaspoon paprika
½ teaspoon ground cumin
¼ teaspoon cayenne pepper
⅓ cup minced fresh cilantro
2 tablespoons lemon juice
1 (13 by 9-inch) disposable aluminum roasting pan (if using charcoal)

1. Pat beef dry with paper towels and sprinkle all over with 1 tablespoon salt. Let sit at room temperature for at least 1 hour before grilling. Just before grilling, soak wood chips in water for 15 minutes, then drain.

2. Meanwhile, combine bell pepper, onion, oil, garlic, paprika, cumin, cayenne, and ½ teaspoon salt in small saucepan. Cook over medium-high heat until vegetables are softened, about 5 minutes. Remove from heat and stir in cilantro and lemon juice. Transfer to bowl and set aside.

3A. FOR A CHARCOAL GRILL: Using large piece of heavy-duty aluminum foil, wrap soaked chips in 12 by 10-inch foil packet. (Make sure chips do not poke holes in sides or bottom of packet.) Cut 3 evenly spaced 2-inch slits in top of packet. Open bottom vent completely. Light large chimney starter mounded with charcoal briquettes (7 quarts). When top coals are partially covered with ash, pour two-thirds evenly over half of grill, then pour remaining coals over other half of grill. Place wood chip packet on smaller pile of coals, set cooking grate in place, cover, and open lid vent completely. Heat grill until hot and wood chips are smoking, about 5 minutes.

3B. FOR A GAS GRILL: Using large piece of heavy-duty aluminum foil, wrap soaked chips in 8 by 4½-inch foil packet. (Make sure chips do not poke holes in sides or bottom of packet.) Cut 2 evenly spaced 2-inch slits in top of packet. Remove cooking grate and place wood chip packet directly on primary burner. Set grate in place, turn all burners to high, cover, and heat grill until hot and wood chips are smoking, about 15 minutes. Turn primary burner to medium and secondary burner(s) to medium-high.

4. Clean and oil cooking grate. Season beef with pepper. Place beef on grill directly over foil packet. Cover beef with disposable pan if using charcoal (if using gas, close lid) and cook for 5 minutes. Flip beef and cook 5 minutes longer, covering in same manner.

5. Slide beef to hotter side of grill and cook, covered if using gas, until well browned on all sides and beef registers 125 degrees, 4 to 8 minutes, turning often. Transfer beef to carving board, tent with foil, and let rest for 10 minutes. Slice beef against grain as thin as possible. Serve with pepper sauce.

TEST KITCHEN TIP Going Against the Grain

Cutting meat perpendicular to the grain is essential for creating a tender texture, but the direction of the grain isn't always easy to identify. If the direction of the grain isn't clear, make a test slice. If you see that you've cut parallel to the grain, turn the meat 90 degrees before cutting again.

WRONG WAY
The fibers run parallel to the cut, making each bite stringy.

RIGHT WAY
The fibers run perpendicular to the cut, making each bite tender.

Grilled Button Mushrooms

Portobellos are great on the grill. But what about the little guys? BY MATTHEW CARD

FEW FOODS BENEFIT as much from the high, dry heat of live-fire cooking as mushrooms do. Fire concentrates their sweet, earthy flavor and magnifies their meaty texture. Fans of grilled portobello caps know this already, but what about the smaller, milder white button mushroom?

I tried several recipes for grilled button mushrooms that clearly demonstrated what didn't work. The real duds employed a low fire, corralled the mushrooms in a foil "hobo pack" or disposable pan, or skewered the caps into a stack. In each case, the mushrooms stewed in their own juices and netted no char. It was clear that keeping the heat high was key to drawing out the mushrooms' excess liquid, which allowed them to brown.

I set to figuring out how best to prep the mushrooms. I tried three tacks: leaving the stems intact, completely removing the stems by pulling them out, and trimming the stems flush with the bottoms of the caps. Unsurprisingly, the mushrooms with stems intact browned unevenly. Those with the stem pulled out cooked up tough. But those with the stems trimmed flush? Just right.

A light coating of extra-virgin olive oil and some salt and pepper before grilling added flavor and encouraged even browning. Once the mushrooms had browned, I tossed them with melted butter, soy sauce, garlic, fresh thyme, lemon juice, and parsley in a disposable pan. I set the pan back on the grill and stirred for a few minutes as the mushrooms absorbed the flavors. Result? An easy, surprising side.

GRILLED BUTTON MUSHROOMS
Serves 4 to 6

For even cooking, choose mushrooms of a uniform size. Medium mushrooms (1 to 2 inches in diameter) are best here; large mushrooms take much longer to cook. Season and oil the mushrooms just before grilling, or they will develop a wrinkled appearance and slimy texture.

2 pounds white mushrooms, stems trimmed flush with caps
2 tablespoons extra-virgin olive oil
Salt and pepper
2 tablespoons unsalted butter, softened
2 tablespoons minced fresh parsley
1½ tablespoons soy sauce

A toss in garlicky butter adds deep flavor.

1 tablespoon lemon juice
2 teaspoons minced fresh thyme
1 garlic clove, minced to paste
1 (13 by 9-inch) disposable aluminum roasting pan

1. In large bowl, toss mushrooms with oil, ½ teaspoon salt, and ½ teaspoon pepper. Combine butter, parsley, soy sauce, lemon juice, thyme, and garlic in disposable pan.

2A. FOR A CHARCOAL GRILL: Open bottom vent completely. Light large chimney starter filled with charcoal briquettes (6 quarts). When top coals are partially covered with ash, pour evenly over grill. Set cooking grate in place, cover, and open lid vent completely. Heat grill until hot, about 5 minutes.

2B. FOR A GAS GRILL: Turn all burners to high, cover, and heat grill until hot, about 15 minutes. Turn all burners to medium-high.

3. Clean and oil cooking grate. Place mushrooms gill side up on grill and cook (covered if using gas) until mushrooms have released some liquid and are char-streaked, about 6 minutes. Flip and cook (covered if using gas) until second side is well browned and char-streaked, 4 to 6 minutes longer.

4. Transfer mushrooms to disposable pan and place pan on grill. Cook (covered if using gas), stirring frequently, until butter has melted and mushrooms have absorbed liquid and appear glazed, about 3 minutes. Serve.

Hawaiian Fried Chicken

Just how much flavor can you pack into fried chicken? In Hawaii, the answer is "more."

BY DIANE UNGER

IN HAWAII, FRIED chicken is often served as part of a "plate lunch" with macaroni salad and steamed rice (see "The American Table"). But not all fried chicken in Hawaii is the same. *Mochiko* chicken features boneless, skinless thighs marinated in soy sauce and battered with sweet rice flour. *Katsu*-style chicken is coated in crisp panko crumbs and fried. *Kara-age* chicken is marinated in soy sauce or tamari, brown sugar, sake, and lots of ginger and garlic; coated in potato starch; and then fried and served with a sharp dipping sauce. The common denominator is utter deliciousness.

I made versions of each style and gathered tasters. Each style had its fans, but the flavorful karaage was the most popular; we used it as a primary inspiration. I found a few more recipes to test out the nuances. Some recipes called for marinating the chicken overnight, making for supersalty chicken. Others had so much potato starch that the elements were out of proportion. I wanted the chicken to be seasoned throughout but not too salty. And I wanted the coating to be thin and crispy, with a dipping sauce that united the flavors and balanced the chicken's richness.

> For our recipe for Hawaiian Macaroni Salad, go to CooksCountry.com/hawaiiansalad.

My first decision was to use boneless, skinless chicken thighs, for both ease and maximum flavor. For the marinade, soy sauce (you can substitute tamari if you'd like your chicken gluten-free), brown sugar, and a heavy dose of ginger and garlic were a given, but how to get the biggest bang for the buck was a balancing act. My first tests were too salty, so I decided to dilute the concentration of the soy sauce with another liquid. The easiest and best-tasting option was water, at a ratio of 1 cup water to ½ cup soy sauce.

I used the food processor to make a garlic and ginger paste; doing so let me skip the tedious step of peeling the ginger, as the final result was so finely ground that it didn't matter. Sweetened with 3 tablespoons of brown sugar, the paste adhered nicely to the chicken.

The traditional coating for this chicken is straight-up potato starch, but no matter how many times and techniques I tried (and there were plenty, believe me), I couldn't get an evenly

Our supercrunchy chicken gets its brittle coating from potato starch; a tangy dipping sauce adds even more flavor.

fried, crispy exterior that didn't turn an unsightly blotchy white. I tried combinations of potato starch mixed with rice flour, cornstarch, all-purpose flour, and even tapioca starch, but all left me with blotchy, too-thick, unevenly cooked coatings. I nearly threw in the towel.

But I'm no quitter when it comes to fried chicken, so for my next test I removed the chicken from the marinade, let the excess drip off, and transferred each piece to a mixture of potato starch and baking powder that I'd seasoned with salt, pepper, and sesame seeds. I coated each piece lightly and transferred it to a parchment-lined baking sheet. Once the pieces were coated, I firmly pressed the coating into the meat and then refrigerated it, tightly covered, for at least 30 minutes. This process allowed the potato starch to become fully saturated with absorbed marinade,

allowing it to cook evenly when fried at a temperature of 375 degrees. Finally—perfect, lightly golden chicken pieces.

For a dipping sauce, I combined ½ cup of seasoned rice vinegar and ¼ cup each of fresh lemon juice and soy sauce. I fried up a final batch of chicken, gathered my tasters, and stood back to watch them greedily devour the crispy, crunchy, sweet, sour, salty chicken and then come back for more.

HAWAIIAN-STYLE FRIED CHICKEN

Serves 4 to 6

You will need at least a 6-quart Dutch oven for this recipe. Plan ahead: The chicken marinates for at least an hour before breading. Pressing the chicken after dredging it in the starch ensures a more uniform coating.

CHICKEN

- 1 (3-ounce) piece ginger, unpeeled, cut into ½-inch pieces
- 4 garlic cloves, peeled
- 1 cup water
- ½ cup soy sauce
- 3 tablespoons packed light brown sugar
- 1 tablespoon toasted sesame oil
- 2 pounds boneless, skinless chicken thighs, trimmed and halved crosswise
- 2¼ cups potato starch
- 2 tablespoons sesame seeds
- 1½ teaspoons baking powder
  Salt and pepper
- 3 quarts peanut or vegetable oil

DIPPING SAUCE

- ½ cup seasoned rice vinegar
- ¼ cup soy sauce
- ¼ cup lemon juice (2 lemons)
  Pepper

1. FOR THE CHICKEN: Process ginger and garlic in food processor until finely chopped, about 15 seconds; transfer to large bowl. Add water, soy sauce, sugar, and sesame oil and whisk to combine. Add chicken and press to submerge. Cover bowl with plastic wrap and refrigerate for at least 1 hour or up to 3 hours.

2. FOR THE DIPPING SAUCE: Whisk vinegar, soy sauce, and lemon juice together in bowl. Season with pepper to taste.

3. Line rimmed baking sheet with parchment paper. Set wire rack in second rimmed baking sheet. Whisk potato starch, sesame seeds, baking powder, 1 teaspoon salt, and 1 teaspoon pepper together in large bowl.

4. Working with 1 piece of chicken at a time, remove from marinade, allowing excess to drip back into bowl. Dredge chicken in potato starch mixture, pressing to adhere. Gently shake off excess and transfer chicken to parchment-lined sheet. Coating will look mottled; using your hand, press on chicken to smooth out coating. Cover sheet tightly with plastic and refrigerate for at least 30 minutes or up to 1 hour.

5. Add peanut oil to large Dutch oven until it measures about 2 inches deep; heat oil over medium-high heat to 375 degrees. Carefully add one-third of chicken to pot and fry until deep golden brown and cooked through, about 5 minutes, stirring gently as needed to prevent pieces from sticking together. Adjust burner, if necessary, to maintain oil temperature between 350 and 375 degrees.

6. Transfer chicken to prepared rack. Return oil to 375 degrees and repeat in 2 more batches with remaining chicken. Serve chicken with sauce.

INGREDIENT SPOTLIGHT
Potato Starch

Potato starch is made by peeling potatoes, drying them, grinding them, and then putting them through a wash to remove the starch, which is then dried. We call for potato starch to coat our Hawaiian-Style Fried Chicken because it produced the crunchiest results, besting cornstarch, flour, and a combination of the two in side-by-side tests. That's because potato starch fries up into a crispy, porous coating faster than either cornstarch or wheat starch (flour). This means potato starch can develop into a crunchy coating in the time required to fry the chicken, whereas a cornstarch or flour coating would need to fry longer, resulting in overcooked chicken.

The American Table
Hawaiian Chicken, Japanese Style

Beginning in the mid-1880s, Japanese immigrants arrived in Hawaii by the thousands to work the sugar and pineapple plantations. Influenced by the settlers, the local Hawaiian cuisine evolved to include several recipes for fried chicken: *mochiko, katsu,* and *karaage,* all Japanese adaptations of Chinese or European techniques. Our Hawaiian-Style Fried Chicken recipe takes cues from the *karaage* style, which is a type of "dry" frying (without batter), though it has become shorthand for the recipe. (Our recipe gets its crunch from a dry coating of potato starch.)

Another Hawaiian tradition that takes inspiration from Japan is the ubiquitous "plate lunch," a complete meal usually served in a compartmentalized container, which has an ancestor in the traditional bento box.

–REBECCA HAYS

LUNCH IN A BOX
Hawaii's plate lunch (top) is like Japan's bento box but typically includes fried chicken, macaroni salad, and white rice.

Are All Disposable Plates Created Equal?

A loaded picnic plate suddenly collapses, showering your sandals with potato salad. Been there?

Our longtime favorite disposable plates by Vanity Fair were recently redesigned, so we decided to revisit the category. We stocked up on eight nationally available products priced from $0.11 to $0.54 per plate. Although most come in multiple sizes, we opted for plates around 10 inches wide—roughly the size of a dinner plate.

We put these plates to the test by saddling them with a full 2 pounds of bone-in chicken breast, piping-hot baked beans, coleslaw, and potato salad. Then we walked around the bustling test kitchen, periodically prodding the food with a fork, to simulate plate usage at a barbecue or party. Half the plates buckled, sagged, or cracked from the get-go. But things really took a nosedive when we repeated the test after letting food sit on the plates for 5 minutes: Some plates practically bent in half as we held them, sending baked beans and coleslaw onto the floor. Only a handful of plates—the thickest ones in our lineup—held strong.

But two of the thickest plates, both made from polystyrene (a plastic that can be either hard or flexible), tore and melted when we cut chicken or reheated pizza in a microwave on them. Plates made from thick paper or bagasse (paper made from sugarcane pulp) were better: strong, durable, and microwave-safe. We also preferred plates with close to 8 inches of eating surface (the width of the plate sans rim) and tall, steep sides that helped contain potential spills.

We have a new favorite disposable plate: fully microwavable Hefty Super Strong Paper Plates ($2.99 for 16 plates) were thick, sturdy, and roomy. –LAUREN SAVOIE

▶ To see the complete testing and chart, go to CooksCountry.com/aug16.

KEY   Good ★★★   Fair ★★   Poor ★

HIGHLY RECOMMENDED

HEFTY Super Strong Paper Plates
Price: $2.99 for 16 plates ($0.19 per plate)
Material: 100% bagasse (dried sugarcane pulp)

TESTERS' NOTES

These plates were the roomiest of the bunch, with an 8-inch eating surface and a steep lip to keep food from spilling over. Thanks to their thick bottoms, they were impervious to pizza grease, had no trouble holding up 2 pounds of food, and didn't budge when prodded with a fork or knife (though testers noticed a tiny bit of floppiness after food sat for 5 minutes, food was still safely contained).

Sturdiness ★★½
Containment ★★★

RECOMMENDED

CHINET Classic White Dinner Plates
Price: $6.49 for 32 plates ($0.20 per plate)
Material: 100% preconsumer recycled paper

From afar, these plates look identical to our winning plates and performed nearly as admirably, containing 2 pounds of picnic fare with ease during a loop around the kitchen. Though testers noticed some slouching (slightly more than with our winner) after we let food sit for 5 minutes, these plates were relatively roomy, contained all the food, and kept pizza grease at bay.

Sturdiness ★★
Containment ★★★

DIXIE Ultra Paper Plates
Price: $2.99 for 22 plates ($0.14 per plate)
Materials: Paperboard, printing ink, and a water-based polymer barrier coating

Though slightly thinner than other top products, these plates held piles of food sturdily, with only minor buckling in spots where we pressed with a fork. There were no grease stains when we loaded them with pizza and nary a mark when we cut chicken with steak knives. Some testers thought that the eating surface was a little too cramped when loaded with food.

Sturdiness ★★½
Containment ★★½

Grilled Artichokes

Cooking these vegetables perfectly on the grill took a bit of heart.

BY MORGAN BOLLING

THE CENTER OF the artichoke universe is Monterey County, California, which produces millions of pounds of the vegetable each year. Locals love artichokes' delicate flavor, especially when grilled. Cooking them over an open fire brings out a nutty note.

Artichokes are part of the thistle family and are technically the bud of a flower; the spiky tips of the leaves evolved to protect the bud from predators—except for those with a sharp knife. After experimenting, I found it best to use a vegetable peeler to remove the fibrous outer skin of the stem before snapping off the bottom rows of the remaining tough leaves. Placing each artichoke on its side and lopping off the top quarter got rid of most of the spikes. I pruned the rest of the leaves with scissors (see "Preparing Artichokes").

Early tests proved that precooking the artichokes was essential; if done entirely on the grill, they'd burn before cooking through. Boiling them in a seasoned broth of water, lemon juice, and red pepper flakes softened them just enough. It was easy to cut them in half and scoop out the fuzzy, inedible chokes with a spoon.

Because my artichokes were mostly cooked through, all I needed from the fire was a solid char, which I achieved with just 2 to 4 minutes per side over hot coals.

I wanted a straightforward sauce to highlight the artichokes' flavor. A blend of lemon, garlic, and butter was the answer. It came together in minutes and was perfect for drizzling and dipping.

GRILLED ARTICHOKES WITH LEMON BUTTER
Serves 4 to 6

Look for artichokes that are bright green, with tightly packed leaves; avoid soft artichokes or those with brown splotches. The leaves should not appear feathery or dried out. To eat, use your teeth to scrape the flesh from the inner part of the exterior leaves. The tender inner leaves, heart, and stem are entirely edible.

- 4 artichokes (8 to 10 ounces each)
  Salt and pepper
- ½ teaspoon red pepper flakes
- 2 lemons
- 6 tablespoons unsalted butter
- 1 garlic clove, minced to paste
- 2 tablespoons olive oil

1. Cut off and discard bottom ¼ inch of each artichoke stem. Remove any leaves attached to stems. Using vegetable peeler, peel away outer layer of stems. Pull bottom row of tough outer leaves downward toward stems and break off at base. Cut off and discard top quarter of each artichoke. Using scissors, cut off sharp tips of remaining leaves all around artichokes.

2. Combine 3 quarts water, 3 tablespoons salt, and pepper flakes in Dutch oven. Cut 1 lemon in half; squeeze juice into pot, then add spent halves. Bring to boil over high heat. Add artichokes, cover, and reduce heat to medium-low. Simmer until tip of paring knife inserted into base of artichoke slips easily in and out, 25 to 28 minutes, stirring occasionally.

To ensure their doneness, we parcook the artichokes before throwing them onto the grill.

3. Meanwhile, grate 2 teaspoons zest from remaining lemon; combine with butter, garlic, ½ teaspoon salt, and ¼ teaspoon pepper in bowl. Microwave at 50 percent power until butter is melted and bubbling and garlic is fragrant, about 2 minutes, stirring occasionally. Squeeze 1½ tablespoons juice from zested lemon and stir into butter mixture. Season with salt and pepper to taste.

4. Set wire rack in rimmed baking sheet. Place artichokes stem side up on prepared rack and let drain for 10 minutes. Cut artichokes in half lengthwise. Using spoon, scoop out fuzzy choke, leaving small cavity in center of each half.

5A. FOR A CHARCOAL GRILL: Open bottom vent completely. Light large chimney starter filled with charcoal briquettes (6 quarts). When top coals are partially covered with ash, pour evenly over grill. Set cooking grate in place, cover, and open lid vent completely. Heat grill until hot, about 5 minutes.

5B. FOR A GAS GRILL: Turn all burners to high, cover, and heat grill until hot, about 15 minutes. Leave all burners on high.

6. Clean and oil cooking grate. Brush artichokes with oil. Place artichokes on grill and cook (covered if using gas) until lightly charred, 2 to 4 minutes per side. Transfer artichokes to platter and tent with aluminum foil. Briefly rewarm lemon butter in microwave, if necessary, and serve with artichokes.

TEST KITCHEN TECHNIQUE **Preparing Artichokes**

Trimming before cooking means there's nothing to do at the table but enjoy.

1. Cut off bottom ¼ inch of stem. Remove any leaves attached to stem. Using vegetable peeler, peel stem.

2. Pull bottom row of tough outer leaves downward toward stem and break off at base.

3. Cut off and discard top quarter. Use scissors to cut off sharp tips of remaining leaves.

Smoky Stuffed Potatoes

Traditional twice-baked potatoes are good enough.
But as usual, we wanted something better than that. BY DIANE UNGER

PICTURE A CLASSIC steakhouse favorite, the twice-baked potato: a crisp potato shell filled with fluffy, cheesy mashed potatoes and baked until the top turns golden brown. Now take it to the grill and add smoke. Not a bad idea, if you ask me.

My hopes for creating this dish entirely on the grill were dashed early on; baking potatoes on the grill took forever and gave me subpar, inconsistent results. So I decided to start in the kitchen, fully baking six russets in the oven. I sliced them in half lengthwise, let them cool slightly, and carefully scooped the flesh from all 12 halves into a bowl, leaving about ¼ inch of potato around the interior of each half. I roughly mashed the scooped-out flesh with butter, salt, pepper, half-and-half, and plenty of mild, melty Colby Jack.

I chose eight of the best-looking shells, brushed them with melted butter inside and out, and seasoned them with salt and pepper. (I discarded the remaining four shells.) After dividing the mashed potato mixture equally among the shells, mounding it generously, I scruffed up the tops (the better to hold the extra cheese I'd add later). Then I covered them with plastic and slid them into the fridge to await their visit to the grill. (Bonus discovery: The prepared potatoes can be kept in the refrigerator for up to 24 hours, if you're a make-ahead kind of cook.)

Before grilling, I prepared a wood chip packet by soaking ½ cup of wood chips in water for 15 minutes and then draining them and folding them into a foil packet with 2 small slits in the top.

In the meantime, I started my coals in a chimney starter; once they were ready, I mounded them into a pile on one side of the grill, leaving the other side cool. I set my packet of soaked wood chips directly on the coals, and once they were smoking (about 5 minutes later), I placed the potatoes on the cooler side of the grill, covered it, and crossed my fingers. (See step 5B for gas-grill instructions.)

After about 20 minutes over indirect heat, the exteriors of the potatoes were a deep golden color. I sprinkled a little more grated cheese on top of each and then covered the grill until the cheese melted and browned slightly. A handful of minced chives was the crowning touch, adding a fresh counterpoint to the deep smoke flavor.

My smoky baked potatoes took some time and attention to achieve, but they were adorable. And the smiles on my tasters' faces left no doubt: The extra effort was worth it.

SMOKY BAKED STUFFED POTATOES

Serves 4 to 6

Try to find potatoes of equal size and weight to ensure even cooking. Plan ahead: The potatoes need to bake for about 1 hour and 10 minutes before being prepared for the grill.

- 6 (10- to 12-ounce) russet potatoes
- 2 tablespoons unsalted butter, melted, plus 4 tablespoons softened
  Salt and pepper
- 12 ounces Colby Jack cheese, shredded (3 cups)
- ½ cup half-and-half
- ¼ cup minced fresh chives
- ½ cup wood chips
  Sour cream

1. Adjust oven rack to middle position and heat oven to 450 degrees. Place potatoes on wire rack set in rimmed baking sheet and bake until centers register 205 degrees and potatoes are very soft, about 1 hour 10 minutes.

2. Immediately slice potatoes in half lengthwise; let cool for 5 minutes. Scoop flesh of all potatoes into bowl, leaving ¼-inch layer of potato in each shell. Choose 8 best-looking shells (discard remaining 4 shells); brush interior and exterior of each shell with melted butter and season with salt and pepper. Transfer shells cut side up to rimmed baking sheet.

3. Using potato masher, mash potatoes until smooth. Stir in 1½ cups Colby Jack, half-and-half, 2 tablespoons chives, 1 teaspoon salt, ½ teaspoon pepper, and softened butter until combined. Divide filling among potato shells (about ½ cup each), mounding in center. Scruff up top of filling with tines of fork. (Potatoes can be covered with plastic wrap and refrigerated for up to 24 hours.)

4. Just before grilling, soak wood chips in water for 15 minutes, then drain. Using large piece of heavy-duty aluminum foil, wrap soaked chips in 8 by 4½-inch foil packet. (Make sure chips do not poke holes in sides or bottom of packet.) Cut 2 evenly spaced 2-inch slits in top of packet.

5A. FOR A CHARCOAL GRILL: Open bottom vent completely. Light large chimney starter filled with charcoal briquettes (6 quarts). When top coals are partially covered with ash, pour into steeply banked pile against side of grill. Set wood chip packet on coals. Set cooking grate in place, cover, and open lid vent completely. Heat grill until hot and wood chips are smoking, about 5 minutes.

5B. FOR A GAS GRILL: Remove cooking grate and place wood chip packet directly on primary burner. Set grate in place, turn all burners to high, cover, and heat grill until hot and wood chips are smoking, about 15 minutes. Turn primary burner to medium-high and turn off other burners. (Adjust primary burner as needed to maintain grill temperature between 325 and 350 degrees.)

6. Clean and oil cooking grate. Place potatoes on cooler side of grill. Cover (position lid vent over potatoes if using charcoal) and cook until filling registers 160 degrees and tops of potatoes begin to brown, about 20 minutes. Sprinkle potatoes with remaining 1½ cups Colby Jack, cover, and continue to cook until cheese is melted and lightly browned, 10 to 15 minutes longer. Transfer potatoes to platter and sprinkle with remaining 2 tablespoons chives. Serve with sour cream.

A smoky fire transforms these twice-baked potatoes from good to great.

Arroz con Pollo

Though chicken and rice is a classic combination, creating a single Latin American version was far from simple. BY MORGAN BOLLING

MANY CUISINES AROUND the world have a version of chicken and rice, from Spanish paella to Singaporean chicken rice. But among the most famous, and popular, is Latin American–style arroz con pollo ("rice with chicken"), with fall-off-the-bone chicken nestled in creamy, flavorful rice—a dish you might encounter in Miami, perhaps, or New York City.

Before starting, I spent hours on the phone talking to professional chefs, home cooks, and others who'd grown up with arroz con pollo and make it regularly. They waxed enthusiastically about Puerto Rican versions, Cuban versions, Central American versions, and more. I made six recipes and ordered the dish from a few local restaurants. What I found was that there are as many recipes for arroz con pollo as there are people who cook it. If you grew up with this dish, the version served in your house when you were young remains the only "authentic" version. I set out to make an all-purpose version that nodded to Puerto Rican tradition.

While the common denominators are the chicken and rice, the flavor backbone comes from a *sofrito*, a stable but invigorating base found in many similar dishes. Sofritos vary by the cook but often contain a mixture of onions, peppers, garlic, and herbs. For my sofrito I mixed finely chopped onion, garlic, cumin, cilantro, and a cubanelle pepper (similar to green bell pepper but slightly sweeter and milder). I set the sofrito aside while I browned mixed chicken parts in a Dutch oven. I then removed them and sautéed onion and rice in the chicken fat left behind. Once the rice was nice and toasty, I stirred in chicken broth and the sofrito, added the browned chicken back to the pot, and covered it.

It took about 20 minutes of covered simmering for the rice to become tender and the chicken to cook through, releasing savory aromas into the kitchen. But the rice was unevenly cooked—mushy in certain spots and crunchy in others. And while the chicken's dark meat stayed juicy, the white meat was dry.

One fix was easy: I switched from mixed chicken parts to more-forgiving (and more-flavorful) thighs. I also removed the skin after browning the pieces; the skin added flavor early on but became gummy if I left it on as the chicken finished cooking.

This supersavory comfort-food classic gets a shot of zing from an herby lemon sauce.

The second fix was also easy: I moved the covered Dutch oven from the stovetop to the more-diffuse heat of the oven. I also left the lid on for 15 minutes after removing the pot from the oven to allow the rice to gently finish cooking to a consistent texture.

But it still wasn't perfect; my rice was too sticky. I was using a standard ratio of 3 cups chicken broth to 2 cups rice, but because the chicken was letting off liquid as it cooked, I had rice that was flavorful but mushy. After a couple of tests, I decided to scale back to 2½ cups of broth, just enough to cook the rice through without it feeling stodgy.

Most of the cooks I interviewed told me that medium-grain rice was preferred for this dish. Extensive cross-testing confirmed that medium-grain rice gave me the most creamy, cohesive, evenly cooked result. But I found that long-grain rice worked, too (see "Medium-Grain Rice").

I was already adding capers and olives, sometimes sold together as *alcaparrado*, for a briny flavor and including a couple of bay leaves for earthiness. But something was missing. Some recipes I found called for marinating the chicken in bitter orange juice, but this resulted in mealy meat. Instead, inspired by recipes from home cooks, I chose a different option: *sazón* spice blend.

In the same way Creole seasoning in New Orleans and Old Bay in Maryland are go-to blends, sazón is common in many Latin home kitchens (see Sazón). It's easy to find, available in most international or Latin American food aisles. Just one tablespoon added complexity and brilliant color.

One version of arroz con pollo I found called for a tangy herb sauce on the side. Inspired by this, I stirred together a quick sauce using a couple of tablespoons of my already-made sofrito, which I'd set aside before cooking, along with a little mayonnaise and some lemon juice. Drizzling this over the dish gave it a final punch of freshness.

ARROZ CON POLLO (RICE WITH CHICKEN)
Serves 6

Sazón is a spice blend common in Latin American cooking. We developed this recipe with Goya Sazón with Coriander and Annatto (or *con Culantro y Achiote*). It can be found in the international aisle of most supermarkets; however, other brands will work. (One tablespoon of Goya Sazón equals about two packets.) If you can't find sazón, use our homemade version (recipe follows). You can substitute ¾ cup of chopped green bell pepper for the Cubanelle pepper. Allow the rice to rest for the full 15 minutes before lifting the lid to check it. Long-grain rice may be substituted for medium-grain, but the rice will be slightly less creamy.

- 1 cup fresh cilantro leaves and stems, chopped
- 1 onion, chopped (1 cup)
- 1 Cubanelle pepper, stemmed, seeded, and chopped (¾ cup)
- 5 garlic cloves, chopped coarse
- 1 teaspoon ground cumin
- ½ cup mayonnaise
- 3½ tablespoons lemon juice (2 lemons), plus lemon wedges for serving
  Salt and pepper
- 6 (5- to 7-ounce) bone-in chicken thighs, trimmed
- 1 tablespoon vegetable oil
- 2 cups medium-grain rice, rinsed
- 1 tablespoon Goya Sazón with Coriander and Annatto
- 2½ cups chicken broth
- ¼ cup pimento-stuffed green olives, halved
- 2 tablespoons capers, rinsed
- 2 bay leaves
- ½ cup frozen peas, thawed (optional)

1. Adjust oven rack to middle position and heat oven to 350 degrees. Process cilantro, ½ cup onion, Cubanelle, garlic, and cumin in food processor until finely chopped, about 20 seconds, scraping down bowl as needed. Transfer sofrito to bowl.

2. Process mayonnaise, 1½ tablespoons lemon juice, ⅛ teaspoon salt, and 2 tablespoons sofrito in now-empty processor until almost smooth, about

30 seconds. Transfer mayonnaise-herb sauce to small bowl, cover, and refrigerate until ready to serve.

3. Pat chicken dry with paper towels and sprinkle with 1 teaspoon salt and ¼ teaspoon pepper. Heat oil in Dutch oven over medium heat until shimmering. Add chicken to pot skin side down and cook without moving it until skin is crispy and golden, 7 to 9 minutes. Flip chicken and continue to cook until golden on second side, 7 to 9 minutes longer. Transfer chicken to plate; discard skin.

4. Pour off all but 2 tablespoons fat from pot and heat over medium heat until shimmering. Add remaining ½ cup onion and cook until softened, 3 to 5 minutes. Stir in rice and Sazón and cook until edges of rice begin to turn translucent, about 2 minutes.

5. Stir in broth, olives, capers, bay leaves, remaining sofrito, remaining 2 tablespoons lemon juice, 1 teaspoon salt, and ½ teaspoon pepper, scraping up any browned bits. Nestle chicken into pot along with any accumulated juices and bring to vigorous simmer. Cover, transfer to oven, and bake for 20 minutes.

6. Transfer pot to wire rack and let stand, covered, for 15 minutes. Fluff rice with fork and stir in peas, if using. Discard bay leaves. Serve with mayonnaise-herb sauce and lemon wedges.

HOMEMADE SAZÓN
Makes 1 tablespoon

We add paprika in place of annatto for color. In addition to flavoring our Arroz con Pollo, this blend makes a great seasoning for eggs, beans, and fish. Store it in an airtight container for several months.

- 1 teaspoon garlic powder
- ¾ teaspoon salt
- ½ teaspoon paprika
- ½ teaspoon ground coriander
- ¼ teaspoon ground cumin

Combine all ingredients in bowl.

The American Table
Puerto Rican Flavor

Carmen Aboy Valldejuli (at right) worked with her husband Luis on many of the recipes in *Puerto Rican Cookery*, including a chapter on rum cocktails.

Now in its 38th printing, Carmen Aboy Valldejuli's *Puerto Rican Cookery* (1975) stands as one of the most enduring 20th-century cookbooks focused on that island's complex cuisine.

Why so complex? As Aboy Valldejuli (cousin to Hollywood star José Ferrer) explains it, "One can seldom be exactly sure of how any really ancient dish began, of course. But it is safe to say that our *cocina criolla* [creole cuisine] was initiated by the first human inhabitants of the islands, the Arawaks and the Taínos. For almost five hundred years the basic ingredients the Indians used have been enriched by the culinary skills of newcomers—Spanish, British, French, Danish and Dutch settlers, and slaves brought forcibly from Africa. The delicate blends and innovations of five centuries have developed a genuine cuisine." Also traceable back to Taíno culture? Good old American-style barbecue, based on techniques the original islanders called *barbacoa*.

INGREDIENT SPOTLIGHT Medium-Grain Rice

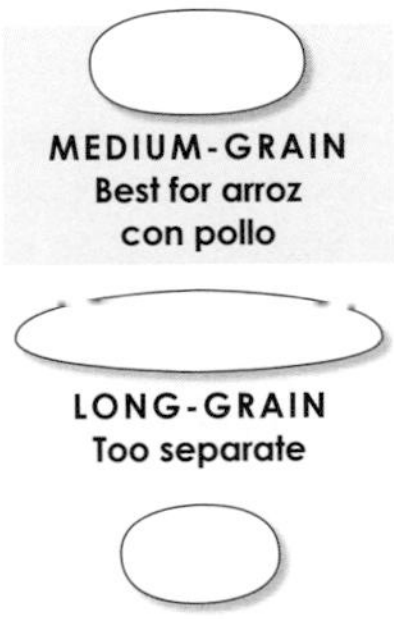

MEDIUM-GRAIN
Best for arroz con pollo

LONG-GRAIN
Too separate

SHORT-GRAIN
Too sticky

After experimenting with long-, medium-, and short-grain rices in our Arroz con Pollo, we decided to call for the medium type, which produced a distinct texture that we preferred. Medium-grain rices (such as Bomba) produced a creamy, cohesive result because their exterior starches thickened the dish while the grains remained firm and distinct. Long-grain varieties like basmati or jasmine will do, but the dish will be less creamy. Finally, short-grain varieties, like Arborio or sushi rice, produced a creamy texture because short-grain rice starts to release its starch (and more of it) at a lower temperature than long-grain rice does.

INGREDIENT SPOTLIGHT Sazón

Sazón (the term means "seasoning" in Spanish) is the signature spice blend of Latino home cooks; it's used in everything from beans and rice to soups, stews, and more. There are many blends (we call for *Culantro y Achiote* in our Arroz con Pollo recipe), and ingredients vary, but sazón traditionally contains ground annatto (or achiote) seeds, which give dishes a rich yellow color. Garlic powder, cumin, and coriander are also often included. Sazón also typically contains monosodium glutamate (MSG), which is what supplies the savoriness. Look for sazón in the Latin American or international section of the supermarket.

SIGNATURE SEASONING
There are many Sazón varieties. Make sure you pick the right one.

Getting to Know Useful Scraps

The best way to eliminate food waste in your kitchen is to take a second look at what you might be discarding. Reconsider some of these gems and their untapped potential.

BY CHRISTIE MORRISON

❶ Cilantro Stems
STRAIGHT SHOOTERS

Most recipes that use fresh herbs call for just the leaves. But cilantro stems are very flavorful and relatively soft; we use finely chopped or minced cilantro stems and leaves in all types of Latin- and Asian-inspired dishes, as well as in dips and dressings. Chopped cilantro stems and leaves add a lot of flavor to our recipe for Arroz con Pollo on page 15.

❷ Corn Cobs
FLAVOR SPONGE

After you've cut all the kernels from a cob, run the back of a knife over the cob to scrape off the flavorful, pulpy "milk" and add it to the corn during cooking. You can use the cobs to flavor vegetable stock or a soup like our Pennsylvania Dutch Chicken and Corn Soup (**CooksCountry.com/chickencornsoup**). Remove the spent cobs before serving.

❸ Hardened Bread
NO LOAFING

You buy a beautiful baguette and enjoy half of it. The next day, it's hard as a brick. Don't throw it away! Remove the crust, tear the bread into rough 1-inch pieces, and blitz it in the food processor. Toast the crumbs (either dry or with butter or oil) and sprinkle them over mac and cheese, pasta dishes, or broiled fish.

❹ Watermelon Rind
SWEET SCRAPS

Southerners traditionally pickle watermelon rind. Simply cut away and discard the bright-green exterior, dice and salt the rind until it softens slightly, and then pickle it in a sugary brine; the resulting sticky-sweet pickles resemble a ripe pear in texture. This classic Southern pickle is a treat straight from the jar, wrapped in bacon or ham for an appetizer, or added to a cocktail. Check out our recipe at **CooksCountry.com/pickledwatermelon**.

❺ Beet Greens
LEAVES NO TRACE

Beet greens will continue to draw moisture and nutrients from the beets as long as they are attached, so be sure to cut the leaves from the beets before storing them. Wash, dry, and store the greens separately as you would kale or lettuce. You can use beet greens in place of collards in our Quick Collard Greens (**CooksCountry.com/quickcollards**).

❻ Chicken Carcass
FLAVOR STOCKED

While store-bought chicken stock is sometimes a necessary convenience, we love the frugality of using the carcasses from a few roasted chickens to make a flavorful stock. The hours of simmering release flavorful marrow from chicken bones and cause collagen to break down into gelatin. Use homemade chicken stock in soups and stews, pan sauces, and gravies.

❼ Vanilla Beans
PERFUMED PODS

Vanilla beans are expensive, so it makes sense to try to get your money's worth. Most recipes call for vanilla seeds, but the spent pods, which contain vanillin—the chemical compound that gives the spice its signature aroma and flavor—can be used to make vanilla sugar: Dry the pods thoroughly, place them upright in an airtight container filled with white granulated sugar, and let the mixture sit for about two weeks, agitating it every few days. Use the vanilla sugar (which will keep at room temperature, tightly covered, for about a month) to sweeten coffee or to add subtle vanilla flavor to custards, cookies, or cakes.

❽ Shrimp Shells
CREOLE BUILDING BLOCKS

Shrimp shells aren't always discarded—Asian recipes for salt and pepper shrimp call for frying shell-on shrimp until the shells become crispy and edible. But when you do peel shrimp, don't throw the shells away. Crustacean shells contain loads of proteins, sugars, and flavor-boosting compounds called glutamates and nucleotides. We brown shrimp shells in butter, add water, and then simmer to make a rich shrimp stock for our Shrimp and Grits (**CooksCountry.com/shrimpandgrits**).

❾ Broccoli Stalks
TOUGH CRUCIFERS

Broccoli stalks are just as edible as the florets, but you'll need to peel away the tough exterior first. The stalks have a wonderful crisp-tender texture when they're cooked properly. We cut the peeled stems into slightly smaller pieces than the florets to ensure that all pieces cook at the same rate in our recipe for Broccoli with Lemon-Oregano Dressing (**CooksCountry.com/microwavebroccoli**).

❿ Ham Bones
PORK INFUSER

A ham bone can imbue a soup or stew with loads of flavor and body and can be wrapped tightly in plastic wrap and frozen (for up to three months) until you're ready to use it. The smoky ham flavor it imparts is a great match for split pea, lentil, or white bean soup or stew, but be aware that a ham bone will add a good bit of saltiness, too.

⓫ Parmesan Rind
SAVORY WRAPPER

Bacteria and mold grow on the rinds of aged Parmesan cheese, creating strong aromas and myriad flavor compounds. That's one reason why many Italian recipes for Sunday gravy and minestrone call for adding a Parmesan rind, which is a good source of glutamates (and umami flavor). Here in the test kitchen, we save our Parmesan rinds for—as well as rinds from other aged cheeses like Pecorino Romano and Gruyère—for this purpose.

QUICK RATATOUILLE

SWEET-AND-SPICY BEEF CHILI

TANDOORI-STYLE CHICKEN WITH GRILLED NAAN

SWORDFISH KEBABS WITH ZUCCHINI RIBBON SALAD

SWEET-AND-SPICY BEEF CHILI Serves 4

✔ **WHY THIS RECIPE WORKS:** Molasses-rich baked beans provide a sweet counterpoint to the smoky heat of chipotles in this quick-cooking chili.

- 1¼   pounds 85 percent lean ground beef
- 1   onion, chopped
-    Salt and pepper
- 2   tablespoons minced canned chipotle chile in adobo sauce
- 4   garlic cloves, minced
- 1   teaspoon ground cumin
- 1   (16-ounce) can Bush's Original Recipe Baked Beans
- 1   (14.5-ounce) can fire-roasted diced tomatoes
- 2   ears corn, kernels cut from cobs
- 4   ounces sharp cheddar cheese, shredded (1 cup)

1. Cook beef, onion, 1 teaspoon salt, and ½ teaspoon pepper in Dutch oven over medium-high heat until meat is no longer pink and onion is softened, about 8 minutes. Stir in chipotle, garlic, and cumin and cook until fragrant, about 30 seconds.

2. Stir in beans, tomatoes and their juice, and corn and bring to boil. Reduce heat to medium-low, cover, and simmer until slightly thickened, about 15 minutes, stirring occasionally. Season with salt and pepper to taste. Serve, sprinkled with cheddar.

TEST KITCHEN NOTE: Serve with diced avocado. We found that Bush's Original Recipe Baked Beans is the most consistent product for this recipe.

QUICK RATATOUILLE Serves 4

✔ **WHY THIS RECIPE WORKS:** Canned crushed tomatoes give this dish long-cooked flavor and texture. We finish the dish with a healthy swirl of olive oil—at least 2 tablespoons—for added richness.

- ¼   cup extra-virgin olive oil, plus extra for drizzling
- 1   pound eggplant, peeled and cut into 1-inch pieces
- 12   ounces yellow summer squash, cut into 1-inch pieces
- 2   red bell peppers, stemmed, seeded, and cut into 1-inch pieces
- 1   onion, chopped
-    Salt and pepper
- 3   garlic cloves, minced
- 1   cup canned crushed tomatoes
- ½   cup fresh basil leaves
- ¼   cup pitted kalamata olives, halved

1. Heat oil in 12-inch nonstick skillet over medium-high heat until shimmering. Add eggplant, squash, bell peppers, onion, 1½ teaspoons salt, and 1 teaspoon pepper. Cover and cook, stirring occasionally, until softened, about 15 minutes. Push vegetables to sides of pan. Add garlic to center and cook until fragrant, about 30 seconds.

2. Stir in tomatoes and basil and cook, uncovered, until mixture has thickened and vegetables are completely tender, about 7 minutes. Season with salt and pepper to taste. Transfer to platter. Stir in olives and drizzle with extra oil before serving.

TEST KITCHEN NOTE: Serve with lemon wedges and crusty bread.

SWORDFISH KEBABS WITH ZUCCHINI RIBBON SALAD
Serves 4

✔ **WHY THIS RECIPE WORKS:** Italian seasoning, an earthy blend of up to six different herbs, is a powerhouse ingredient in our homemade Italian dressing.

- 7   tablespoons extra-virgin olive oil
- ¼   cup lemon juice (2 lemons)
- 1   tablespoon dried Italian seasoning
-    Salt and pepper
- 2   pounds skinless swordfish steaks, 1 inch thick, cut into 1-inch chunks
- 3   zucchini (8 ounces each), shaved into ribbons with vegetable peeler, seeds discarded
- 3   ounces (3 cups) baby kale
- 3   ounces ricotta salata, shaved with vegetable peeler
- 2   tablespoons chopped fresh mint

1. Whisk ¼ cup oil, 2 tablespoons lemon juice, Italian seasoning, ¾ teaspoon salt, and ½ teaspoon pepper together in large bowl. Add swordfish and toss to coat. Thread swordfish evenly onto 4 metal skewers.

2. Whisk remaining 3 tablespoons oil, remaining 2 tablespoons lemon juice, 1 teaspoon salt, and 1 teaspoon pepper together in second large bowl; set dressing aside.

3. Grill skewers over hot fire, turning often, until swordfish registers 140 degrees, 9 to 12 minutes. Transfer to platter. Add zucchini, kale, ricotta salata, and mint to bowl with dressing and toss to coat. Serve with swordfish.

TEST KITCHEN NOTE: To prevent the salad from becoming watery, wait until just before serving to toss the ingredients.

TANDOORI-STYLE CHICKEN WITH GRILLED NAAN Serves 4

✔ **WHY THIS RECIPE WORKS:** Scoring the chicken allows the spiced yogurt marinade to penetrate more deeply into the meat for maximum flavor.

- 1¾   cups plain whole-milk yogurt
- ¼   cup lime juice (2 limes)
- 6   garlic cloves, minced
- 1   tablespoon grated fresh ginger
- 1   tablespoon garam masala
-    Salt and pepper
- 3   pounds bone-in chicken pieces (split breasts cut in half, drumsticks, and/or thighs), trimmed
- 4   naan breads

1. Whisk 1 cup yogurt, 2 tablespoons lime juice, garlic, ginger, garam masala, and ½ teaspoon salt together in large bowl. Pat chicken dry with paper towels and, using sharp knife, cut through skin to make three ½-inch-deep slits across each piece. Season with salt and pepper, transfer to yogurt mixture, and toss to coat.

2. Mix remaining ¾ cup yogurt, remaining 2 tablespoons lime juice, and ½ teaspoon salt in small bowl until smooth; set sauce aside.

3. Grill chicken over medium fire until breasts register 160 degrees and drumsticks/thighs register 175 degrees, about 12 minutes per side. Transfer chicken to platter. Grill naan until warmed through, about 1 minute per side. Serve chicken with naan and sauce.

TEST KITCHEN NOTE: Our favorite garam masala is McCormick Gourmet Collection Garam Masala.

**CARIBBEAN PORK TENDERLOIN WITH
AVOCADO-MANGO SALAD**

**PROSCIUTTO-WRAPPED CHICKEN
WITH ASPARAGUS**

MARGHERITA PIZZA WITH PESTO

**GRILLED CUMIN-RUBBED FLANK STEAK
WITH MEXICAN STREET CORN**

PROSCIUTTO-WRAPPED CHICKEN WITH ASPARAGUS
Serves 4

✔ **WHY THIS RECIPE WORKS:** Wrapping the chicken in salty, flavor-packed prosciutto seasons the poultry and protects the surface from drying out.

- 4 (6-ounce) boneless, skinless chicken breasts, trimmed and pounded to ½-inch thickness
  Salt and pepper
- 8 thin slices prosciutto (4 ounces)
- 2 tablespoons extra-virgin olive oil
- 4 ounces fontina cheese, cut into 4 slices
- 2 pounds asparagus, trimmed
- 2 shallots, halved and sliced thin

1. Adjust oven rack to middle position and heat oven to 350 degrees. Line rimmed baking sheet with parchment paper. Pat chicken dry with paper towels and season with pepper. Wrap each breast with 2 slices prosciutto.

2. Heat 1 tablespoon oil in 12-inch nonstick skillet over medium-high heat until just smoking. Cook chicken until prosciutto is lightly browned, about 2 minutes per side. Transfer to prepared sheet and top each breast with 1 slice fontina. Bake until chicken registers 160 degrees, about 12 minutes.

3. Meanwhile, heat remaining 1 tablespoon oil in now-empty skillet over medium-high heat until shimmering. Add asparagus and cook until just tender and spotty brown, about 4 minutes. Add shallots, ¼ teaspoon salt, and ⅛ teaspoon pepper and cook until shallots are lightly browned, about 2 minutes. Serve.

TEST KITCHEN NOTE: Pound only the thick end of each chicken breast to match the thickness of the thinner end.

CARIBBEAN PORK TENDERLOIN WITH AVOCADO-MANGO SALAD Serves 4

✔ **WHY THIS RECIPE WORKS:** Coating the pork tenderloins in jerk seasoning and brown sugar gives them a spicy-sweet kick.

- 2 (12-ounce) pork tenderloins, trimmed
- 2 tablespoons jerk seasoning
- 2 tablespoons vegetable oil
- ½ cup packed brown sugar
- 2 avocados, halved, pitted, and cut into ½-inch pieces
- 1 mango, peeled, pitted, and cut into ¼-inch pieces
- ½ cup fresh cilantro leaves
- ½ teaspoon grated lime zest plus 3 tablespoons juice (2 limes)
- 1 tablespoon minced shallot
  Salt and pepper

1. Adjust oven rack to middle position and heat oven to 400 degrees. Pat pork dry with paper towels and sprinkle all over with jerk seasoning. Heat 1 tablespoon oil in 12-inch ovensafe nonstick skillet over medium-high heat until just smoking. Cook pork until browned on all sides, 5 to 7 minutes.

2. Off heat, spoon ¼ cup sugar over each tenderloin, pressing to adhere. Transfer skillet to oven and roast until pork registers 140 degrees, 10 to 12 minutes. Transfer pork to carving board, tent with foil, and let rest for 5 minutes.

3. Meanwhile, combine avocados, mango, cilantro, lime zest and juice, shallot, ½ teaspoon salt, ¼ teaspoon pepper, and remaining 1 tablespoon oil in bowl. Slice pork, drizzle with pan juices, and serve with avocado-mango salad.

TEST KITCHEN NOTE: Cut avocados just before serving to avoid discoloration.

GRILLED CUMIN-RUBBED FLANK STEAK WITH MEXICAN STREET CORN Serves 4

✔ **WHY THIS RECIPE WORKS:** Mayonnaise does double duty here, first as a flavorful fat for grilling the corn and then as the base of our sauce.

- 1 tablespoon ground cumin
  Kosher salt and pepper
- ¾ teaspoon chili powder
- ¼ cup mayonnaise
- ¼ cup grated Pecorino Romano cheese
- 2 tablespoons minced fresh cilantro
- 1 tablespoon lime juice, plus lime wedges for serving
- 1 garlic clove, minced
- 1 (1½- to 2-pound) flank steak, 1 inch thick, trimmed
- 4 ears corn, husks and silk removed

1. Combine cumin, 1 tablespoon salt, ½ teaspoon pepper, and ½ teaspoon chili powder in bowl. Combine mayonnaise, Pecorino, cilantro, lime juice, garlic, ½ teaspoon salt, and remaining ¼ teaspoon chili powder in separate bowl.

2. Pat steak dry with paper towels and sprinkle with spice mixture. Grill over hot fire until steak registers 125 degrees (for medium-rare), 4 to 6 minutes per side. Transfer to carving board and tent with foil.

3. Brush corn with half of mayonnaise mixture. Grill corn, turning often, until well browned on all sides, about 12 minutes. Transfer to platter and brush with remaining mayonnaise mixture. Cut corn in half and slice steak on bias against grain. Serve with lime wedges.

TEST KITCHEN NOTE: Morton & Bassett Chili Powder is the test kitchen's favorite chili powder.

MARGHERITA PIZZA WITH PESTO Serves 4

✔ **WHY THIS RECIPE WORKS:** Using prepared pesto is a convenient timesaver. Buitoni Pesto with Basil is the test kitchen's favorite.

- ¼ cup extra-virgin olive oil
- 1 pound pizza dough, room temperature
- 1 (14.5-ounce) can diced tomatoes, drained
- 8 ounces fresh mozzarella cheese, sliced ¼ inch thick and patted dry with paper towels
- ½ teaspoon salt
- ¼ teaspoon pepper
- ¼ cup pesto

1. Adjust oven rack to lowest position and heat oven to 500 degrees. Grease rimmed baking sheet with 1 tablespoon oil. Press and roll dough into 15 by 11-inch rectangle on lightly floured counter. Transfer dough to prepared sheet and press to edges of sheet. Brush edges of dough with 1 tablespoon oil. Bake dough until top appears dry and bottom is just beginning to brown, about 5 minutes.

2. Remove crust from oven and pop any large bubbles with tip of paring knife. Scatter tomatoes over dough, leaving ½-inch border around edge. Arrange mozzarella over tomatoes and sprinkle with salt and pepper. Bake until crust is light golden around edges and mozzarella is melted, about 10 minutes, rotating sheet halfway through baking.

3. Transfer pizza to wire rack and let cool for 5 minutes. Mix pesto and remaining 2 tablespoons oil until smooth and drizzle over pizza. Slice and serve.

TEST KITCHEN NOTE: Be sure to use fresh mozzarella packed in water, not low-moisture mozzarella, in this recipe.

Skillet Peach Upside-Down Cake

Who knew that bright, juicy peaches and cozy, crunchy cornmeal would make such a great pair?

BY STEPHANIE PIXLEY WITH MORGAN BOLLING

THE APPEAL OF a peach upside-down cake lies in its simplicity: You toss butter, sugar, and peaches together in a skillet; pour a basic batter over them; and bake the whole thing until the batter is cooked through. The moment of truth arrives when you invert the skillet onto a plate to reveal (one hopes) beautifully caramelized peaches perched atop a rustic, not-too-sweet cake. But too often the result is overly sweet or, worse, a soggy mess.

When researching peach upside-down cake, I came across several recipes calling for incorporating cornmeal into the cake layer. I loved this rustic, down-home idea and headed into the kitchen to try to make it work.

I employed a simple quick-bread assembly method: Liquid and dry ingredients are mixed separately and then gently stirred together before being spread over the peaches. This process gave me a strong but still tender texture, and toasting the cornmeal first gave it a subtle roasty flavor.

For the sake of ease, I was hoping to be able to leave the peaches raw, simply cutting them into wedges and arranging them in the bottom of the skillet before topping them with batter. It worked, and it made a beautiful cake, but the overall flavor was lacking. I tried increasing the quantity of peaches to ramp up the peach flavor, but the cake became gummy and dense from all the extra liquid the peaches exuded.

Maybe, I thought, I could get more peach flavor by incorporating a portion of the peaches into the cake batter. No dice: The peaches created gummy pockets throughout the cake. Instead I added a bit of fresh orange zest and juice to the cake batter; this brightened up the flavor and meshed well with the cornmeal.

All of these experiments showed me that more peaches wouldn't necessarily get me more peach flavor. I decided to add another layer of flavor to the dish instead, to provide a counterpoint to the peaches. After toasting the cornmeal, I moved it to a bowl. I melted a few tablespoons of butter in the now-empty skillet, whisked in ¼ cup of sugar, and cooked the combination over moderate heat until the sugar turned lightly golden brown, transforming from crystallized clumps to a smooth caramel sauce, a sweet contrasting layer that amplified the peachiness.

I arranged the fruit over the caramel, covered it with the cake batter, put the skillet in the oven, and crossed my fingers. Once the cake was cooked through and allowed to cool slightly, I inverted the pan and knew I'd struck gold: The edges of the cake were golden brown and moist while the peaches held their shape. This cornmeal-peach combination was a winner, with just the right balance of tender cornmeal cake, sweet caramel, and juicy peaches.

PEACH CORNMEAL UPSIDE-DOWN CAKE Serves 8

If using frozen peaches, be sure to thaw and drain them before using; otherwise, they will produce a mushy cake. We like to serve this cake with whipped cream.

- ½ cup (2½ ounces) cornmeal
- 2 tablespoons unsalted butter, plus 6 tablespoons melted and cooled
- ⅓ cup (2⅓ ounces) sugar, plus ¾ cup (5¼ ounces) Salt
- 1 pound peaches, peeled, halved, pitted, and cut into ¾-inch wedges, or 12 ounces frozen sliced peaches, thawed and drained
- 1 cup (5 ounces) all-purpose flour
- 1 teaspoon baking powder
- ⅛ teaspoon baking soda
- ½ cup whole milk
- 2 teaspoons grated orange zest plus ¼ cup juice
- 1 large egg plus 1 large yolk

1. Adjust oven rack to middle position and heat oven to 350 degrees. Toast cornmeal in ovensafe 10-inch nonstick skillet over medium heat until fragrant, 2 to 3 minutes, stirring frequently. Transfer to large bowl and let cool slightly.

2. Wipe skillet clean with paper towels. Melt 2 tablespoons butter in now-empty skillet over medium heat. Add ⅓ cup sugar and pinch salt and cook, whisking constantly, until sugar is melted, smooth, and deep golden brown, 3 to 5 minutes. (Mixture may look broken but will come together.) Off heat, carefully arrange peaches cut side down in tight pinwheel around edge of skillet. Arrange remaining peaches in center of skillet.

3. Whisk flour, baking powder, baking soda, and ½ teaspoon salt into cornmeal. In separate bowl, whisk milk, orange zest and juice, egg and yolk, melted butter, and remaining ¾ cup sugar until smooth. Stir milk mixture into flour mixture until just combined.

4. Pour batter over peaches and spread into even layer. Bake until cake is golden brown and toothpick inserted in center comes out clean, 28 to 33 minutes, rotating skillet halfway through baking.

5. Let cake cool in skillet on wire rack for 15 minutes. Run knife around edge of skillet to loosen cake. Place large, flat serving platter over skillet. Using potholders and holding platter tightly, invert skillet and platter together; lift off skillet (if any peaches stick to skillet, remove and position on top of cake). Let cake cool completely, about 1 hour. Serve.

To amp up the peachiness, we add both fresh orange juice and grated orange zest.

Picking Peaches for Baking

What do peaches, bananas, and avocados have in common? They all belong to a group of fruits referred to as climacteric; they continue to ripen long after they are picked. And even though peaches become sweeter and more aromatic as they ripen, they also become softer. If you've ever tried to peel and pit a peach at its peak ripeness, you know it can be a challenge. For this recipe, we found that slightly firm peaches worked best. They were still sweet and flavorful, but they didn't crush as we peeled and pitted them.

Fettuccine with Butter and Cheese

Once upon a time, Alfredo sauce was velvety and rich, not stodgy and thick. Could we restore its glory?

BY ASHLEY MOORE

FETTUCCINE WITH BUTTER and cheese, aka fettuccine Alfredo, consists of Parmigiano-Reggiano cheese, butter, fettuccine, and a pinch of salt. No cream. No eggs. No black pepper. The cheese and butter should combine to create a creamy sauce that coats each strand of pasta. It is one the world's greatest pasta dishes. But this dish has suffered over the years, mucked up with cream, thickeners, and worse.

Its glory days began in 1914, when Roman restaurateur Alfredo di Lelio needed a high-calorie meal to serve his wife, who was pregnant and having trouble keeping her food down. He created the first version of this cheesy dish, hoping that it would hold her over for a while. Bonus: It was also delicious enough to add to his restaurant's menu.

Cue American silent film stars Mary Pickford and Douglas Fairbanks (see "The American Table"), who visited Rome and made several meals of di Lelio's dish. They brought the recipe home, and in 1928, it was printed in *The Rector Cook Book*. But because American butter and Parmesan-style cheese weren't as rich and creamy as they are in Italy, the dish began its detour into something di Lelio would not recognize. I was determined to return this dish to its simple origins, using only four ingredients.

OK, five ingredients. I'd also add some of the water I'd cooked the pasta in; using this starchy liquid helps create a silky sauce. The rub proved to be determining exactly how much water to boil the pasta in so that the resulting liquid would have just enough starch. Two quarts was too little, 4 quarts too much. Three quarts of water for a pound of pasta gave me the right consistency.

It's essential to use real Italian Parmigiano-Reggiano cheese; facsimiles won't produce the same creaminess. I tested various amounts and grating styles before settling on 4 ounces of cheese grated on a rasp-style grater for ultrasmall (almost feathery) shreds. These melted more smoothly into the sauce than larger shreds, which clumped.

After cooking dozens of batches using a range of techniques, each fussier than the last, I was thrilled to find that the simplest process also produced the best results: After reserving 1 cup of the cooking water, I drained the pasta; returned it to the pot; added 5 tablespoons of butter, a little salt, the

Serving the pasta in heated bowls keeps the sauce soft and silky. Purists say no pepper, but we won't tell if you grind a bit on top.

grated cheese, and the reserved cooking water; and vigorously tossed the ingredients with tongs until the sauce covered the pasta. Then—and this step is important—I covered the pot and let the pasta sit for 1 minute to allow any errant drips of water to absorb. I removed the lid and tossed the pasta again to make sure that all the cheese was incorporated.

I transferred the pasta to heated serving bowls and passed them out to the team. The heat of each bowl helped the sauce stay fluid. Would Alfredo di Lelio recognize my dish? I'm certain he would. And he'd love it.

KEY STEP
Keep on Stirring

When the grated Parmigiano-Reggiano cheese, butter pieces, and reserved pasta cooking water are stirred into the still-hot fettuccine, the dish will appear very watery. But don't fret: After a covered 1-minute rest and a vigorous stir, the sauce will come together, forming a creamy emulsion.

FETTUCCINE WITH BUTTER AND CHEESE

Serves 4 to 6

Be sure to use imported Parmigiano-Reggiano cheese here and not the bland domestic cheese labeled "Parmesan." For the best results, grate the cheese on a rasp-style grater. Do not adjust the amount of water for cooking the pasta. Stir the pasta frequently while cooking so that it doesn't stick together. It's important to move quickly after draining the pasta, as the residual heat from the reserved cooking water and pasta will help the cheese and butter melt. For best results, heat ovensafe dinner bowls in a 200-degree oven for 10 minutes prior to serving and serve the pasta hot. If you are using fresh pasta, increase the amount to 1¼ pounds.

- 1 **pound fettuccine**
  Salt
- 4 **ounces Parmigiano-Reggiano, grated (2 cups), plus extra for serving**
- 5 **tablespoons unsalted butter, cut into 5 pieces**

1. Bring 3 quarts water to boil in large Dutch oven. Add pasta and 1 tablespoon salt and cook, stirring frequently, until al dente. Reserve 1 cup cooking water, then drain pasta and return it to pot.

2. Add Parmigiano-Reggiano, butter, reserved cooking water, and ½ teaspoon salt to pot. Set pot over low heat and, using tongs, toss and stir vigorously to thoroughly combine, about 1 minute. Remove pot from heat, cover, and let pasta sit for 1 minute.

3. Toss pasta vigorously once more so sauce thoroughly coats pasta and any cheese clumps are emulsified into sauce, about 30 seconds. (Mixture may look wet at this point, but pasta will absorb excess moisture as it cools slightly.) Season with salt to taste.

4. Transfer pasta to individual bowls. (Use rubber spatula as needed to remove any clumps of cheese stuck to tongs and bottom of pot.) Serve immediately, passing extra Parmigiano-Reggiano separately.

Which Fettuccine Should You Buy?

Dried fettuccine is a simple product that's been made with two ingredients—flour and water—for centuries. When prepared well, these long, wide noodles are greater than the sum of their short ingredient list, showcasing a clean flavor and a hint of springy chew. To find the best option, 21 America's Test Kitchen staffers tasted four nationally available fettuccines boiled and tossed with neutral-tasting canola oil and in our recipe for Fettuccine with Butter and Cheese.

One product in our lineup, from Ronzoni, was an outlier: Like most fresh—but not dried—fettuccine, it contains eggs and is clearly labeled as "egg fettuccine." (Ronzoni does make an eggless dried fettuccine, but it's not as widely available throughout the United States.) While our tasters liked this pasta, we preferred the cleaner, less-distracting flavor of those pastas without egg. The Ronzoni fettuccine also comes in only a 12-ounce package—an inconvenience for our recipes, which usually call for a full pound.

In the end, we liked all four pastas. Our tasters had a slight preference for wider, thicker noodles, which we found more substantial and chewy. The higher-ranked noodles measure up to 6.9 millimeters wide and 1.9 millimeters thick when cooked, while lower-ranked noodles were 5.4 millimeters wide and 1.6 millimeters thick.

Garofalo Fettucce came out on top. These wide, thick noodles were bouncy and springy, with just the right amount of chew. That said, there wasn't a bad noodle in the bunch. Our advice: Choose pastas with shorter ingredient lists, buy what's cheapest, and take pains to cook it well. Read the full story and results chart at **CooksCountry.com/aug16**.

–LAUREN SAVOIE

WIDEST NOODLE 6.9 MM

NARROWEST NOODLE 5.4 MM

RECOMMENDED	TASTERS' NOTES
GAROFALO Fettucce **Price:** $3.50 for 16 oz ($0.22 per oz) **Average Thickness:** 1.9 mm **Average Width:** 6.2 mm 	These wide, thick noodles cooked up "plump" and "springy," with a "mild," "clean" flavor. When tossed with sauce, this imported Italian pasta retained the "perfect amount of chew" and was "substantial without feeling bulky."
DE CECCO Fettuccine **Price:** $2.99 for 16 oz ($0.19 per oz) **Average Thickness:** 1.6 mm **Average Width:** 6.9 mm 	Imported from Italy, these "big, bouncy ribbons" were the widest we tasted, and tasters loved their "sturdy," "toothsome" snap. Their "neutral" flavor had just "a hint of nuttiness" and provided a "clean," "traditional" backdrop for sauce.
BARILLA Classic Blue Box Fettuccine **Price:** $1.45 for 16 oz ($0.09 per oz) **Average Thickness:** 1.7 mm **Average Width:** 5.7 mm 	"Springy" with just "a touch of chew," this American-made fettuccine won points for its "rustic," "gritty" texture, which helped sauce cling to the pasta. Though tasters found these noodles narrow and "a tad thin," most agreed that these "mild," "neutral" strands made a "good canvas" for sauce.
RONZONI Egg Fettuccine **Price:** $2.45 for 12 oz ($0.20 per oz) **Average Thickness:** 1.6 mm **Average Width:** 5.4 mm 	These narrower noodles were "chewy," with a prominent "springiness." Some tasters picked up on stronger flavors in this American-made product—which, while not unpleasant, distracted slightly from the sauce. Its 12-ounce package was also problematic for our recipes, which usually call for a full pound of pasta.

Mastering Fettuccine "Alfredo"

Our Fettuccine with Butter and Cheese has just a few ingredients and comes together quickly. For the best results, follow these guidelines.

Use the best-quality ingredients you can find, including authentic Italian Parmigiano-Reggiano.

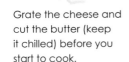

Grate the cheese and cut the butter (keep it chilled) before you start to cook.

Move quickly once the pasta is drained—the hot pasta helps melt the butter.

Heat ovensafe dinner bowls in the oven to help keep the pasta hot at the table.

Have diners ready and waiting for the pasta, not the other way around.

Pletzel

We were latecomers to this old-school deli bread. But now that we've met, we're in love.

BY ASHLEY MOORE

DURING ITS HEYDAY in the 1950s and 1960s, Fritzel's restaurant in Chicago attracted big names: Tony Bennett, Phyllis Diller, Joe DiMaggio, and Marilyn Monroe were just some of the celebrities who ate there. And back then, eating at Fritzel's meant sharing one of its most celebrated dishes: pletzel.

This foccacia-like flatbread (sometimes called "onion board") is not as well-known as other staples of Jewish delis and bakeries (think bagels and rugelach), but those who know pletzel really love pletzel. It took some doing to find existing recipes for pletzel, but persistence paid off, and I found five, including an old recipe from Fritzel's.

The five versions varied widely. One was thin and brittle like a cracker; others were soft and doughy. The one we liked best had a crisp exterior and a chewy, tender interior with lots of air bubbles. It had a very sticky dough that wasn't easy to work with, but this was the version I decided to pursue.

My first fix to the recipe proved to be the best fix: Rather than kneading the wet, sticky dough (a ridiculous mess), I resolved to let the stand mixer deal with it. I attached the dough hook to the stand mixer and combined flour, water, and a bit of salt. I then let it sit for 20 minutes to allow the flour to fully hydrate—a step our resident bread expert recommended to help ensure that chewy interior. At that point, I added the yeast and a bit of sugar for sweetness and browning and set the mixer on high for about 10 minutes until the dough was glossy and began to pull away from the edges of the mixer bowl.

I turned out the dough into a large oiled bowl, covered it with plastic wrap, and set it aside to rise. After about 2 hours, it had tripled in volume. I transferred it to a well-oiled rimmed baking sheet and pressed it flat, nudging it into the corners as best I could. (This sticky task was easier to do with lightly oiled hands.)

But the dough kept springing back, so I stepped away for a moment, hoping that if I let the dough relax for a few minutes, it would be easier to cover the entire baking sheet. I was right. I let the dough rise for 30 more minutes before sliding it into a very hot (500-degree) oven. About 20 minutes

The caramelized onions and poppy seeds give this crisp-chewy flatbread a slightly sweet note.

later, my pletzel came out even and crisp, and the holes in its interior were exactly what I wanted.

Next: Toppings. I put together another pletzel dough. While it was rising on the sheet, I gently cooked chopped onions and a bit of salt in a skillet until they were golden. I then stirred in some poppy seeds and spread the mixture evenly over the risen dough before it went into the oven.

Once the pletzel was baked, I cut it into squares and called over my tasters. It was crispy on the outside and soft and chewy on the inside, with plenty of sweet, oniony topping. Although a celebrity-filled visit to Fritzel's is impossible now (it was shuttered in the early 1970s), I'd re-created a little part of it.

PLETZEL Serves 6 to 8

We found that while kneading the dough in a stand mixer on high speed, the mixer tended to wobble. To prevent this, place a towel or shelf liner under the mixer and watch it during mixing. Handle the dough with your lightly oiled hands and resist flouring your fingers or the dough might stick. Plan ahead: The dough needs to rise for about 3 hours before baking.

- 3 cups (15 ounces) all-purpose flour
- 1⅔ cups water, room temperature Kosher salt
- 1½ teaspoons instant or rapid-rise yeast
- 1¼ teaspoons sugar
- 5 tablespoons olive oil
- 3 onions, chopped fine
- 2 tablespoons poppy seeds

1. Place towel or shelf liner beneath stand mixer to prevent wobbling and fit mixer with dough hook. Add flour, room-temperature water, and 2½ teaspoons salt to bowl and mix on low speed until no patches of dry flour remain, about 4 minutes, occasionally scraping sides and bottom of bowl. Turn off mixer and let dough rest for 20 minutes.

2. Sprinkle yeast and sugar over dough. Knead on low speed until fully combined, about 2 minutes, occasionally scraping sides and bottom of bowl. Increase mixer speed to high and knead until dough is glossy, smooth, and pulls away from sides of bowl, 8 to 10 minutes. (Dough will only pull away from sides while mixer is on. When mixer is off, dough will fall back to sides.)

AT A GLANCE Shaping Pletzel
If the dough resists stretching, let it relax for 5 to 10 minutes and then try again.

Using your oiled fingertips, press dough toward edge of baking sheet. Let it rise, uncovered, for 30 minutes. Stretch again, then poke surface all over with fork.

Brush dough with oil and sprinkle with salt. Distribute onion–poppy seed mixture over dough, leaving ½-inch border around edge.

The Ultimate BLT

Do you really need a recipe for this simple classic? If you want the ultimate version, indeed you do. BY KATIE LEAIRD

3. Using your fingers, coat large bowl and rubber spatula with 1 tablespoon oil. Using oiled spatula, transfer dough to bowl and pour 1 tablespoon oil over top. Flip dough over once so it is well coated with oil; cover bowl tightly with plastic wrap. Let dough rise at room temperature until nearly tripled in volume and large bubbles have formed, 2 to 2½ hours.

4. Meanwhile, heat 1 tablespoon oil in 12-inch skillet over medium heat until shimmering. Add onions and 1 teaspoon salt and cook, stirring occasionally, until onions are golden brown, about 10 minutes. Remove from heat and stir in poppy seeds. Transfer to bowl; set aside. Adjust oven rack to lowest position and heat oven to 500 degrees.

5. Coat bottom and sides of rimmed baking sheet with 1 tablespoon oil. Using oiled rubber spatula, turn dough out onto prepared sheet along with any oil remaining in bowl.

6. Using your oiled fingertips, press dough out toward edges of sheet, taking care not to tear it. (Dough will not fit snugly into corners. If dough resists stretching, let it relax for 5 to 10 minutes before trying to stretch again.) Let dough rise, uncovered, at room temperature for 30 minutes. (Dough will increase but not quite double in volume.)

7. Using your oiled fingertips, press dough out toward edges of sheet once more. Using dinner fork, poke surface of dough 30 to 40 times. Brush top of dough with remaining 1 tablespoon oil and sprinkle with 1½ teaspoons salt. Distribute onion–poppy seed mixture evenly over dough, leaving ½-inch border around edge.

8. Bake until golden brown, 18 to 23 minutes, rotating sheet halfway through baking. Using metal spatula, transfer pletzel to cutting board. Slice and serve.

TO MAKE AHEAD

Once dough has been placed in oiled bowl, flipped to coat in oil, and covered in step 3, it can be refrigerated for up to 24 hours. Let dough come to room temperature, 2 to 2½ hours, before proceeding with step 4.

Doctored mayonnaise and partially toasted bread set this BLT above the rest.

IS THERE A more perfect sandwich than the BLT? Crispy, savory bacon; juicy, ripe tomato; and cool, crunchy lettuce, dressed in tangy mayonnaise and bookended by two pieces of perfectly toasted bread— it's no wonder it's a classic.

But for something so simple, so much can go wrong. The bacon slides free and the tomatoes slink out, leaving just soggy bread and sad lettuce.

I set out to solve these structural snafus. First up: bread. We chose toasted potato bread for its subtle sweetness, but toast can be brittle; soft slices hold on to contents better. So I split the difference, toasting just one side of the bread.

I wanted the bacon to be shatteringly crispy, easier to achieve with standard bacon than with thick-cut. Cooking it all at once on a foil-lined baking sheet in the oven sped things up (no batches). Of the many lettuce options we considered, lightly crunchy Bibb lettuce proved the best choice.

To ensure a bright tomato flavor, even with less-than-perfect tomatoes, I chose to briefly marinate them in red wine vinegar, olive oil, and a bit of salt and pepper. And to elevate my mayonnaise, I stirred in a bit of lemon juice, cayenne, and chopped basil.

Achieving the Ultimate
Easy adjustments go a long way with familiar components.

BREAD Use potato bread, and toast only one side.

MAYO Season it with basil, lemon juice, and cayenne.

BACON Cook it longer so that it's extra-crispy.

LETTUCE Use lightly crunchy Bibb lettuce that stays put.

TOMATO Coat them with vinaigrette for a flavor boost.

With my ingredients rounded up, it was time to optimize the architecture. I grabbed a pencil and sketched a few possibilities. While two layers of bacon were a must, one layer of tomato was plenty. The mayonnaise would serve as an edible adhesive to keep the bacon in place, the lettuce as a shield against soggy bread. My final sketch held the winning design. From top to bottom: bread, mayonnaise, bacon, lettuce, tomato, lettuce, bacon, mayonnaise, bread. With just a little extra attention and effort, I'd transformed the everyday BLT into something so much more.

ULTIMATE BLT SANDWICH
Serves 4

Buy the best tomatoes you can find that are about 2 inches in diameter. If your tomatoes happen to be larger, use only two or three slices per sandwich. Since broiler outputs vary, keep an eye on the toast in step 3. You may need more than one package to get 16 slices of bacon. Do not use thick-cut bacon in this recipe.

- 16 slices bacon
- 3 vine-ripened tomatoes
- 2 tablespoons extra-virgin olive oil
- 1 tablespoon red wine vinegar
  Salt and pepper
- ½ cup mayonnaise
- ¼ cup chopped fresh basil
- 1½ teaspoons lemon juice
  Pinch cayenne pepper
- 8 slices potato sandwich bread
- 1 head Bibb lettuce (8 ounces), leaves separated

1. Adjust oven rack 6 inches from broiler element and heat oven to 400 degrees. Arrange bacon in single layer on aluminum foil–lined rimmed baking sheet, overlapping slightly as needed to fit. Bake until bacon is deeply browned and crispy, 25 to 30 minutes, rotating sheet halfway through baking. Transfer bacon to paper towel–lined plate; discard bacon fat and foil. Heat broiler.

2. Meanwhile, core tomatoes and cut into 16 (¼-inch-thick) slices (you may have some left over). Whisk oil, vinegar, ¼ teaspoon salt, and ¼ teaspoon pepper together in shallow dish. Add tomatoes; turn gently to coat with vinaigrette. Whisk mayonnaise, basil, lemon juice, and cayenne together in bowl.

3. Arrange bread on now-empty sheet. Broil until lightly browned on 1 side only, 1 to 2 minutes.

4. Transfer bread, toasted side down, to cutting board. Spread basil mayonnaise evenly on untoasted sides of bread (use all of it). Break bacon slices in half. Shingle 4 bacon halves on each of 4 bread slices, followed by 2 lettuce leaves, 4 tomato slices, 2 more lettuce leaves, and 4 more bacon halves. Top each sandwich with 1 of 4 remaining bread slices, mayonnaise side down. Cut sandwiches in half, corner to corner. Serve.

Oregon Blackberry Pie

The hallmark of this summertime showstopper is the sturdy blackberry filling.
But getting it right wasn't as easy as pie. BY CECELIA JENKINS

I N HIGH SUMMER, blackberry brambles blanket the Pacific Northwest, and a slice of blackberry pie is never far from reach. In Oregon it's known as marionberry pie, named after the native blackberry variety prized by pie makers. Cut into a good example of this seasonal staple and you'll see what sets it apart from other fruit pies: You won't get a soupy, oozy slice. Instead, the purple filling retains its shape.

But how? Aficionados I spoke with claimed that there are no tricky tricks, no added pectin or gelatin, nothing stranger than a bit of starch. As trustworthy as my sources were, I was skeptical. Could I create a cohesive blackberry filling with tart, clean, fresh summertime flavor? Only one way to find out. I grabbed a handful of existing recipes and got to baking.

Settling on a crust was the easy part. Tasters preferred the flavor of pies with all-butter crusts to crusts that used shortening. After a few quick tests, I settled on the test kitchen's recipe for all-butter pie crust, with 3 tablespoons of sour cream added for a richer dough that was just a bit easier to roll out. Bonus: The acid in the sour cream inhibited the gluten from overdeveloping and becoming tough. And because I knew I'd need to leave open some avenues for evaporation, I chose to follow the example set by blackberry pie pros and use a lattice top.

Now for the filling. Before tackling the puzzle of a thick filling that would hold its shape, I nailed down the flavors. Heavily sweetened pies and added spices confused the blackberry flavor. After baking several pies with different ratios of flavors, I settled on ¾ cup of sugar, a bit of salt, and a good hit of lemon juice for a sweet-enough filling with clear and present blackberry flavor.

But my pies were soupy. A thickener was essential. I needed to take care here; the thickener couldn't influence the flavors, and it also had to help create a smooth, cohesive texture that held its shape without being like Jell-O.

Simply smashing some of the berries should, in theory, release more of the natural pectin found in the berries to help set the pie. But with this technique, the filling felt jammy, and besides, tasters preferred whole berries.

I tried tapioca, a favorite test kitchen

For a cohesive berry filling, we tried a number of thickeners. One option, cornstarch, gave us the best texture—neither gluey nor jammy.

thickener, but this created a gelatin-like texture. Flour turned things gluey. I landed on cornstarch, which gave me a good texture and didn't muck up the flavor. After testing amounts from 1 teaspoon to ½ cup, I learned that 5 tablespoons did the trick.

One final touch made this pie even easier: I developed a quicker, more foolproof lattice top by simply laying four horizontal strips across the pie and

Bake on Parchment-Lined Baking Sheet

Why? Because you never know when a pie made with a buttery pastry and juicy berries will drip. A protective sheet of parchment means there will be no sticky, greasy, or burnt-on mess to clean up.

then four vertical strips over those. This gave the same woven effect without my having to weave the strips together. I had a beautiful, flavorful blackberry pie to be proud of.

OREGON BLACKBERRY PIE Serves 8

Be sure to rinse the berries and dry them thoroughly before using. Do not use frozen berries in this recipe. Freezing the butter for the dough for 15 minutes before processing it in step 1 is crucial to the flaky texture of this crust—do not skip this step. If working in a hot kitchen, refrigerate all the ingredients before making the dough. Plan ahead: The pie dough needs to chill for at least an hour before rolling. When brushing the lattice strips with egg wash, be sure to leave the ends of each strip unbrushed so the wash doesn't impede the crimping process.

PIE DOUGH

⅓ cup ice water, plus extra as needed
3 tablespoons sour cream
2½ cups (12½ ounces) all-purpose flour
1 tablespoon sugar
1 teaspoon salt
16 tablespoons unsalted butter, cut into ¼-inch pieces and frozen for 15 minutes

FILLING

¾ cup (5¼ ounces) sugar, plus 1 teaspoon for topping
5 tablespoons (1¼ ounces) cornstarch
¼ teaspoon salt
20 ounces (4 cups) blackberries
2 tablespoons lemon juice
2 tablespoons unsalted butter, cut into ½-inch pieces

1 large egg, lightly beaten

1. FOR THE PIE DOUGH: Mix ice water and sour cream in bowl. Process flour, sugar, and salt in food processor until combined, about 5 seconds. Scatter butter over top and pulse until butter is size of large peas, about 10 pulses.

2. Pour half of sour cream mixture into bowl with flour mixture and pulse until incorporated, about 3 pulses. Scrape down bowl and repeat with remaining sour cream mixture. Pinch dough with your fingers; if dough feels dry and does not hold together, sprinkle 1 to 2 tablespoons extra ice water over mixture and pulse until dough forms large clumps and no dry flour remains, 3 to 5 pulses.

3. Transfer dough to lightly floured counter. Divide dough in half and form each half into 4-inch disk. Wrap disks tightly in plastic wrap and refrigerate for 1 hour. (Wrapped dough can be refrigerated for up to 2 days or frozen for up to 1 month. If frozen, let dough thaw completely on counter before rolling.)

4. Adjust oven rack to lower-middle position and heat oven to 400 degrees.

TEST KITCHEN TECHNIQUE Foolproof Lattice

A lattice is essential for most berry pies since its open design lets steam escape during baking, preventing a soggy crust. But weaving a lattice from delicate pastry dough can be frustrating, even for seasoned bakers. Our streamlined approach produces a faux lattice that's just as beautiful as the real thing.

1. Cut dough into twelve 1-inch strips. Discard 4 short end pieces. Cover remaining 8 long strips with plastic and refrigerate for 30 minutes.

2. Lay 4 parallel strips about 1 inch apart. Brush with egg, leaving ½ inch at ends unbrushed. Lay remaining 4 strips perpendicular to first layer, about 1 inch apart.

3. Pinch edges of lattice strips and bottom crust firmly together. Trim overhang to ½ inch beyond lip of plate. Tuck overhang under itself. Crimp edge.

The American Table
The Cabernet of Blackberries

With its warm summer days and cool, clear nights, the Pacific Northwest's climate is ideal for growing berries, including a prized variety of blackberry called the marionberry, or Marion blackberry. The berry, which ranges from dark purple to black in color when fully ripe (red berries still need time to ripen and develop flavor), is named for Marion County, the home of Oregon's state capital, Salem. Oregon produces about 30 million pounds of the fruit annually, and 90 percent of commercial marionberries are grown in Marion County. Because the sweet, earthy berries tend to have a little more juice and a sweeter flavor than other common blackberry varieties, they are sometimes referred to as the "Cabernet of blackberries." –REBECCA HAYS

Berries 101

When you're dealing with delicate berries, a little know-how goes a long way toward keeping them fresh.

SHOPPING
Even one moldy berry will encourage the rest of the container to rot. We recommend opening the plastic carton to inspect berries before you purchase them.

WASHING
Washing berries before you use them is always a safe practice, and we think the best way is to place the berries in a colander and rinse them gently under running water for at least 30 seconds.

DRYING
To avoid bruising the delicate fruit, line a salad spinner with a buffering layer of paper towels before adding the berries and spinning them dry.

STORING
Berries are prone to growing mold and rotting quickly. If the berries aren't to be used immediately, we recommend submerging them in a mild vinegar solution (3 cups of water mixed with 1 cup of white vinegar), which will destroy the bacteria, before drying them. Refrigerate them in a paper towel–lined airtight container.

Let chilled dough sit on counter to soften slightly, about 10 minutes, before rolling. Roll 1 disk of dough into 12-inch circle on lightly floured counter. Loosely roll dough around rolling pin and gently unroll it onto 9-inch pie plate, letting excess dough hang over edge. Ease dough into plate by gently lifting edge of dough with your hand while pressing into plate bottom with your other hand.

5. Wrap dough-lined plate loosely in plastic and refrigerate until dough is firm, about 30 minutes. Roll other disk of dough into 12-inch circle on lightly floured counter, then transfer to parchment paper–lined baking sheet. Using pizza cutter, cut dough into twelve 1-inch strips. Discard 4 short end pieces, then cover remaining 8 long strips with plastic and refrigerate for 30 minutes.

6. FOR THE FILLING: Whisk sugar, cornstarch, and salt together in large bowl. Add blackberries and toss gently to coat. Add lemon juice and toss until no dry sugar mixture remains. (Blackberries will start to exude some juice.)

7. Transfer blackberry mixture to dough-lined pie plate and dot with butter. Lay 4 dough strips parallel to each other across pie, about 1 inch apart. Brush strips with egg, leaving ½ inch at ends unbrushed. Lay remaining 4 strips perpendicular to first layer of strips, about 1 inch apart.

8. Pinch edges of lattice strips and bottom crust firmly together. Trim overhang to ½ inch beyond lip of plate. Tuck overhang under itself; folded edge should be flush with edge of plate. Crimp dough evenly around edge of plate using your fingers.

9. Brush lattice top and crimped edge with egg and sprinkle with remaining 1 teaspoon sugar. Set pie on parchment-lined baking sheet. Bake until golden brown and juices bubble evenly along surface, 45 to 50 minutes, rotating sheet halfway through baking. Let cool on wire rack for at least 4 hours before serving.

Cooking Class English Muffin Bread

A good loaf of English muffin bread has the same chewy crumb and porous texture as individual English muffins. It also takes a fraction of the time to make. BY CHRISTIE MORRISON

ENGLISH MUFFIN BREAD Makes 2 loaves

The test kitchen's preferred loaf pan measures 8½ by 4½ inches; if using 9 by 5-inch pans, check for doneness 5 minutes early. English muffin bread is designed to be toasted after it is sliced.

Cornmeal
5 cups (27½ ounces) bread flour
4½ teaspoons instant or rapid-rise yeast
1 tablespoon sugar
2 teaspoons salt
1 teaspoon baking soda
3 cups warm whole milk (120 degrees)

1. Grease two 8½ by 4½-inch loaf pans and dust with cornmeal. Combine flour, yeast, sugar, salt, and baking soda in large bowl. Stir in warm milk until combined, about 1 minute. Cover dough with greased plastic wrap and let rise in warm place for 30 minutes, or until dough is bubbly and has doubled in size.

2. Stir dough and divide between prepared pans, pushing into corners with greased rubber spatula. (Pans should be about two-thirds full.) Cover pans with greased plastic and let dough rise in warm place until it reaches edges of pans, about 30 minutes. Adjust oven rack to middle position and heat oven to 375 degrees.

3. Discard plastic and transfer pans to oven. Bake until bread is well browned and registers 200 degrees, about 30 minutes, switching and rotating pans halfway through baking. Turn bread out onto wire rack and let cool completely, about 1 hour. Slice, toast, and serve.

STEP BY STEP Ten Steps to English Muffin Bread

1. PREPARE PANS
Grease two 8½ by 4½-inch loaf pans and dust them with cornmeal.
WHY? Dusting with cornmeal ensures that the bread releases easily and also produces the iconic gritty crust of English muffins.

2. USE BREAD FLOUR
Add 5 cups of bread flour to a large bowl.
WHY? Bread flour, which has more protein than all-purpose flour, gives the crumb a porous, chewy texture. Using all-purpose flour will make the crumb too tender.

3. ADD TWO LEAVENERS
Combine yeast and baking soda with flour, sugar, and salt.
WHY? Yeast adds flavor and helps small air bubbles develop in the dough; baking soda makes the bubbles grow even larger to create the bread's trademark coarse texture.

4. HEAT MILK
Use 3 cups of whole milk heated to 120 degrees.
WHY? Older recipes call for heating the flour in the oven to jump-start the rise. We found it easier to microwave the milk before stirring it into the flour mixture.

5. GREASE PLASTIC WRAP
Cover the dough with greased plastic wrap and let it rise in a warm place for 30 minutes.
WHY? This dough is sticky and wet, so if you don't grease the plastic, you'll tear the dough when you remove the plastic.

Good to Know

YEAST ONLY
Good rise; small air bubbles

YEAST + BAKING SODA
Good rise; big and small air bubbles

In Search of Nooks and Crannies

We tested a number of English muffin bread recipes—some dating back to the turn of the 19th century—but only those that included baking soda boasted the nooks and crannies we've come to associate with English muffins. That's because while yeast helps the dense dough rise and creates small air bubbles in the dough, baking soda helps those bubbles grow even larger. Here's how it works: During fermentation, yeast breaks down starch into sugars and produces carbon dioxide and alcohol as well as lactic and acetic acids. When baking soda reacts with the acids, it rapidly releases even more carbon dioxide, creating the large bubbles that become the signature nooks and crannies. The large amount of yeast in this recipe—4½ teaspoons—produces more than enough acid to react with the baking soda and cause the bubbles to expand.

The Importance of Bread Flour

While we have found that all-purpose flour often lives up to its name, some breads, including our English Muffin Bread, require a higher-protein flour to achieve the proper texture. All-purpose flour contains about 10 to 12 percent protein; bread flour contains 12 to 14 percent. The higher the protein level, the more structure and chew in the end product. To wit: A rustic Italian loaf made with bread flour will have a sturdy, chewy crumb, whereas a quick bread made with all-purpose flour will be soft and tender.

Bread Bakers' Secrets

A Warm Place to Rise

Since yeast is most active at temperatures between 80 and 90 degrees, dough will rise most successfully in a warm space that is free of drafts. If your kitchen is on the chilly side, microwave 1½ cups of water in a measuring cup until simmering and then place the steaming cup in a turned-off oven or microwave, or even in a cooler, along with the covered bowl of dough. Close the door or lid and let the dough rise according to the recipe.

OVEN (TURNED OFF)   **MICROWAVE (TURNED OFF)**   **COOLER**

How to Keep Bread Fresher Longer

When a local baker recommended storing leftover bread cut side down on a cutting board for up to 24 hours, we were intrigued. Indeed, when we compared this approach with storing the bread in a paper or plastic bag, the countertop loaf remained crisp on the outside and tender on the inside, while the paper-bag and plastic-bag methods were less successful, producing slightly dry or squishy results, respectively.

MAKE A STAND
For short-term storage, stand leftover bread cut side down on a cutting board.

Freeze Some for Later

Leftovers can be sliced (place parchment paper between slices), wrapped in aluminum foil, placed in a zipper-lock bag, and frozen for up to 1 month. We found that letting the slices defrost at room temperature caused them to stale slightly. The best way to thaw frozen slices for toasting is to place the slices on a plate (uncovered) and microwave them on high for 15 to 25 seconds.

6. STIR RISEN DOUGH

Stir the dough and divide it between the prepared pans, pushing it into the corners with a greased rubber spatula.
WHY? Stirring redistributes yeasts and sugars and lightly deflates the batter-like dough, both of which prepare it for a second rise.

7. PROOF DOUGH IN PANS

Cover the pans with greased plastic and let the dough rise in a warm place until it reaches the edges of the pans.
WHY? Allowing the dough to rise a second time produces a consistent, porous crumb.

8. SWITCH AND ROTATE

Switch and rotate the pans halfway through baking.
WHY? Since most ovens don't heat evenly, moving the pans during baking helps ensure even rising and browning.

9. TAKE TEMP

Bake until the bread is well browned and registers 200 degrees, about 30 minutes.
WHY? Beyond looking for a properly browned exterior, the best way to tell if your bread is done is by using an instant-read thermometer.

10. LET COOL COMPLETELY

Turn the bread out onto a wire rack and let it cool completely before slicing it, about 1 hour.
WHY? When the bread is hot, its interior is very moist. As the bread cools, starches inside the loaf dry and firm up, making the bread easier to slice without tearing.

One-Pan Dinner Steak with Sweet Potatoes and Scallions

A nicely cooked steak with a great sear and sides, all ready at once? We doubted it, too. BY KATIE LEAIRD

WHEN WE COOK steaks in the test kitchen, we usually sear them in a hot pan or grill them over a blazing fire to achieve a brown crust around tender, juicy meat. But I wanted to make dinner for four with vegetables as well as strip steaks, dirty only one pan in the process, and have everything ready at the same time. Impossible? We'd see about that.

I started by simply roasting a steak on a rimmed baking sheet. The results were unsurprising: a sad, gray steak without any crust. I missed the intensified flavors that come with searing. But in order to achieve browning, meat requires direct contact with a heating element, which isn't exactly what the oven is built for.

In a bid to simulate the direct, searing heat of a stovetop skillet, I tried preheating the baking sheet in a 450-degree oven. After a half-hour I held my breath, opened the oven, placed the steaks on the hot sheet, and heard a satisfying sizzle. Promising.

The time it took to preheat the sheet was just enough time to jump-start my sides. I began with sweet potatoes—cut into wedges, tossed with olive oil, and seasoned with salt and pepper—which I knew would roast into soft, flavorful fries in about 40 minutes. To have them

finish concurrently with the steak, they'd need a 25-minute head start in the oven, which was plenty of time to also get the baking sheet hot enough to sear the steaks. I contained the sweet potatoes on one side of the sheet so I wouldn't have to move them later. After 25 minutes, I placed the steaks on the empty side of the screaming-hot sheet. After another 15 minutes, the steaks were perfectly medium-rare, and the sweet potatoes were ready to serve. Granted, the steaks were brown on only one side, the "presentation" side, but my tasters liked it.

Not good enough: I wanted them to love it. Could I achieve that by adding a rub for my steak? We tossed out ideas—salt, garlic powder, the usual suspects—until someone mentioned coffee.

Coffee? Yes, coffee. I didn't want to turn my dinner into a cappuccino-flavored novelty, but I hoped coffee's bitter note would accentuate the savoriness of the steak without introducing strong coffee flavor. I mixed some finely ground coffee with chili powder for heat and brown sugar for sweetness and caramelizing properties. This rub gave the steak a gorgeous mahogany color and enhanced the crust even more.

To green up the meal, I tossed scallions with olive oil, salt, and pepper and put them on top of the sweet potatoes, but they shriveled up into a stringy mess after 40 minutes in the oven. I tried waiting to add the scallions at the same time as the steaks. Fifteen minutes in the oven was much kinder to the scallions. Some red radishes, tossed with lime juice and salt, made for a fresh, crunchy finish.

A simple rub of sugar, coffee, and chili powder on the steak helps seal in the sear.

Potatoes First, Steaks Second
Start by roasting the sweet potatoes alone on the sheet. When the potatoes start to soften, arrange the scallions on top of them and place the steaks alongside the potatoes. The upshot? Medium-rare meat and perfectly tender sweet potatoes.

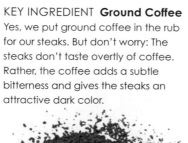

KEY INGREDIENT **Ground Coffee**
Yes, we put ground coffee in the rub for our steaks. But don't worry: The steaks don't taste overtly of coffee. Rather, the coffee adds a subtle bitterness and gives the steaks an attractive dark color.

ONE-PAN STEAK WITH SWEET POTATOES AND SCALLIONS
Serves 4

Don't be afraid to use all of the coffee rub on the steak. It aids in browning as well as adds flavor. The scallions should be left whole; only remove the root hairs.

- 1½ pounds sweet potatoes, unpeeled, cut lengthwise into 1-inch wedges
- 2 tablespoons extra-virgin olive oil
  Salt and pepper
- 16 scallions, trimmed
- 2 tablespoons packed dark brown sugar
- 1 tablespoon finely ground coffee
- 1 tablespoon chili powder
- 2 (1-pound) boneless strip steaks, 1½ to 1¾ inches thick
- 10 radishes, trimmed and sliced thin
- 1 tablespoon lime juice, plus lime wedges for serving

1. Adjust oven rack to lower-middle position and heat oven to 450 degrees. Toss potatoes, 1½ tablespoons oil,

1 teaspoon salt, and 1 teaspoon pepper together in large bowl. Arrange potatoes skin side down in single layer on half of rimmed baking sheet. Roast until potatoes begin to soften, about 25 minutes.

2. Meanwhile, toss scallions with remaining ½ tablespoon oil, ¼ teaspoon salt, and ¼ teaspoon pepper in now-empty bowl. Mix sugar, coffee, chili powder, 1½ teaspoons salt, and 1 teaspoon pepper together in small bowl. Pat steaks dry with paper towels, then sprinkle all over with coffee mixture.

3. Arrange scallions on top of potatoes. Place steaks on empty side of sheet. Roast until potatoes are fully tender and meat registers 125 degrees (for medium-rare), 12 to 15 minutes.

4. Transfer steaks bottom side up to carving board, tent with aluminum foil, and let rest for 5 minutes. Toss radishes, lime juice, and ¼ teaspoon salt together in bowl. Slice steaks thin against grain and serve with potatoes, scallions, radishes, and lime wedges.

We wanted a quick, juicy fruit crisp for any day of the week, at any time of the year.

BY CHRISTIE MORRISON

CHERRY CRISP IS a delightful mix of textures: juicy, vibrant fruit nestled beneath a toasty, crisp streusel topping. But does it need to be a multipan, multidish process? I hoped not.

I decided early on to use sweet, not sour, cherries. They're much easier to find and, of course, they're sweeter (this is dessert, after all). And while I love the flavor and texture of fresh cherries, I wanted this to be a dessert I could make year-round, so I decided to go with frozen cherries. I found that, when mixed with sugar, lemon juice, and vanilla extract, they tasted just as good as fresh. Plus, they don't need to be pitted. A 10-ounce bag was just right for two servings and cut the prep time dramatically. To keep this recipe quick, I resolved to keep it on the stovetop.

Even cherries straight from the freezer cooked quickly on the stovetop, releasing their juice and softening to a luxurious texture in less than 10 minutes. For added punch, I buoyed the frozen cherries with a few dried cherries, which delivered intense flavor and just a bit of chewiness. I found that just ½ teaspoon of cornstarch, which I'd tossed with sugar to help keep it from clumping, was sufficient to thicken the filling.

For a simple topping that would stay crisp even when it hit the cherry filling, I gathered the usual ingredients—old-fashioned rolled oats, brown sugar, cinnamon, and butter—and mixed them together. I toasted this mixture in a small skillet, breaking it into small clumps. The pieces browned nicely but didn't have the crunchy bite I'd hoped to achieve.

Well, nuts are crunchy, and since almonds complement cherries particularly well, I replaced the rolled oats in my topping with ¼ cup of sliced almonds. The added texture was a boon to the streusel, but the almonds didn't have time to brown before the rest of the topping began to burn. So I tried toasting the almonds slightly before adding the remaining ingredients. This step evened out the browning, yielding a fragrant, toasty topping in no time at all. What's more, I was so taken with the almond flavor that I added just a bit of almond extract to the filling, too.

As I looked over my recipe, I realized that I could save a step (and a pan to wash) if I toasted the topping first and set it aside to cool while I cooked the cherry filling in the same skillet. Once the filling had thickened, I scattered the topping from edge to edge and returned the pan to the heat until the filling began to bubble. Served right from the skillet after a short cooldown, the results were spot-on.

CHERRY-ALMOND CRISP FOR TWO

There's no need to thaw the cherries. Serve with vanilla ice cream.

TOPPING
- ⅓ cup (1⅔ ounces) all-purpose flour
- 1 tablespoon packed light brown sugar
- 1 tablespoon granulated sugar
- ¼ teaspoon vanilla extract
  Pinch ground cinnamon
  Pinch salt
- 2 tablespoons unsalted butter, melted
- ¼ cup sliced almonds

FILLING
- 1½ tablespoons granulated sugar
- ½ teaspoon cornstarch
- 10 ounces frozen sweet cherries
- ¼ cup water
- 2 teaspoons lemon juice
- ¼ teaspoon vanilla extract
- ¼ teaspoon almond extract
- ⅛ teaspoon salt
- ¼ cup dried cherries

1. FOR THE TOPPING: Combine flour, brown sugar, granulated sugar, vanilla, cinnamon, and salt in bowl. Stir in melted butter until mixture resembles wet sand and no dry flour remains.

2. Toast almonds in 8-inch skillet over medium-low heat until just beginning to brown, about 4 minutes. Add flour mixture and cook, stirring constantly, until lightly browned, about 4 minutes; transfer to plate to cool. Wipe skillet clean with paper towels.

3. FOR THE FILLING: Combine 1½ teaspoons sugar and cornstarch in small bowl; set aside. Combine sweet cherries, water, lemon juice, vanilla, almond extract, salt, and remaining 1 tablespoon sugar in now-empty skillet. Cook, covered, over medium heat until cherries thaw and release their juice and mixture starts to simmer, about 5 minutes, stirring halfway through cooking. Stir in dried cherries and simmer, uncovered, until plumped and tender, about 2 minutes.

4. Stir in cornstarch mixture and cook, stirring constantly, until mixture is thickened, about 30 seconds. Remove skillet from heat and sprinkle topping evenly over filling. Return skillet to medium-low heat and cook until filling is bubbling around edges, about 1 minute. Remove from heat and let cool for at least 15 minutes. Serve warm.

For this simple stovetop recipe, we rely on a mixture of frozen cherries (no need to thaw) and dried cherries. Both are readily available year-round and don't require pitting.

INGREDIENT SPOTLIGHT
Dried Cherries
Frozen sweet cherries are the backbone of our Cherry-Almond Crisp, providing mild sweetness and lots of juiciness. But to really punch up the cherry flavor, we add a handful of dried cherries to the mix. They offer a pleasant chewy texture, concentrated sweetness, and intense fruitiness.

VERY CHERRY
Dried cherries deliver an intense pop of flavor to our crisp.

One Dessert, Two Sugars
The ingredient list for our crisp's cherry filling calls for granulated sugar—its clean, unobtrusive sweetness bolsters the fruit while letting its flavor (augmented by lemon juice and vanilla and almond extracts) shine. The ingredient list for the topping, however, calls for a 50/50 mixture of granulated and brown sugars. Brown sugar is simply cane sugar with molasses added, which contributes flavor and moisture. In our topping, the brown sugar offers complexity and helps keep the topping from getting brittle.

Five Easy Lemonades

Homemade lemonade is refreshing, invigorating, and much better than store-bought. It's also easier to make than you might think. BY CECELIA JENKINS

IT'S TEMPTING TO reach for bottled lemonades in the grocery store beverage case—what could be more convenient? Unfortunately, many of these cheek-sucking versions are packed with sugar, flavorings, and colorings—and not much else (often they don't even contain real lemon juice). They pale in comparison with homemade, in which lemons add dimension and freshness you just can't find in the supermarket. I wanted a simple recipe for refreshing lemonade that balanced sweetness and tartness—a reward worth all the squeezing.

Lemonade requires sweetening. Many recipes call for doing so with simple syrup (a boiled mixture of sugar and water) to help the sugar dissolve easily. While simple syrup is indeed simple to make, it needs to cool back to room temperature before it's added—a speed bump I wanted to avoid.

I decided to start off by simply whisking sugar, lemon juice, and water together. I was happy to find that it worked just fine (the sugar dissolved without falling out of suspension), but then I took a sip. For fresh lemonade, it was dull. No zing. I began to see the appeal of using the peel called for in some recipes.

A past test kitchen recipe for lemonade took a cue from bartenders, who often mash (or muddle) herbs or fruit with sugar to make flavorful cocktails. Mashing lemon slices with sugar to extract the oils from the zest (prior to whisking in the juice and water) seemed easy enough. I worried that the lemon's white pith would impart bitterness,

but I grabbed a potato masher and made a batch anyway. Bingo. I got the fragrant, bright, fresh boost I wanted, with no bitterness.

I tried a few more tweaks to see if further improvement was possible. Muddling more lemons only made the lemonade more sour. Adding lemon zest to the lemonade made it gritty. One muddled lemon was just right.

With a refreshing glass of lemonade in hand (refrigerated for an hour to help keep the ice cubes from diluting it), I began to think about flavor variations. Raspberries' sweet and tart flavor, a classic addition to lemonade, worked beautifully. A strawberry-lime version gave a nod to margaritas. A cucumber-mint version tasted like a day at the spa. And if there's anything more summery than watermelon lemonade, I can't picture it.

LEMONADE
Serves 6 to 8

When purchasing lemons, choose large ones that give to gentle pressure; hard lemons have thicker skin and yield less juice. Lemons are commonly waxed to prevent moisture loss, increase shelf life, and protect from bruising during shipping. Scrub them with a vegetable brush under running water to remove wax, or buy organic lemons. Don't worry about the seeds in the extracted juice; the entire juice mixture is strained at the end of the recipe. Serve poured over ice, if desired. Note that we recommend chilling the lemonade for 1 hour prior to serving.

1½   cups sugar
2   lemons, sliced thin, seeds and
    ends discarded, plus 2 cups juice
    (12 lemons)
7   cups cold water

1. Using potato masher, mash sugar and half of lemon slices in large bowl until sugar is completely wet, about 1 minute.

2. Add water and lemon juice and whisk until sugar is completely dissolved, about 1 minute. Strain mixture through fine-mesh strainer set over large bowl or pitcher, pressing on solids to extract as much juice as possible. Discard solids.

3. Add remaining lemon slices to strained lemonade and chill for at least 1 hour. Serve.

Clockwise from top: Lemonade, Raspberry Lemonade, Cucumber-Mint Lemonade, Strawberry-Lime Lemonade, and Watermelon Lemonade.

KEY TOOL
Getting Every Last Drop
Our favorite manual citrus juicer is the Chef'n FreshForce Citrus Juicer, which extracts far more juice from a supermarket lemon than any other manual juicer we tried.

Slow Cooker All-Purpose Tomato Sauce

Does a simple tomato sauce have to be a supervised stovetop affair? No.

BY KATIE LEAIRD

CUCUMBER-MINT LEMONADE
Mash 1 peeled, thinly sliced cucumber and 1 cup fresh mint leaves along with sugar and half of lemon slices in step 1, increasing mashing time to 3 minutes. Add 1 peeled, thinly sliced cucumber and ½ cup fresh mint leaves to strained lemonade with remaining half of lemon slices in step 3.

RASPBERRY LEMONADE
Mash 2 cups raspberries along with sugar and half of lemon slices in step 1.

STRAWBERRY-LIME LEMONADE
Substitute 2 thinly sliced limes for thinly sliced lemons. Add half of lime slices and 1 cup sliced strawberries to large bowl and mash with sugar in step 1. Add remaining lime slices and 1 cup sliced strawberries to strained lemonade in step 3.

WATERMELON LEMONADE
Mash 4 cups coarsely chopped seedless watermelon with sugar and half of lemon slices in step 1, increasing mashing time to 3 minutes. Reduce water to 6 cups.

IT'S A ROMANTIC scene: a pot of tomatoes simmering on the stove, filling the kitchen with an aroma promising saucy suppers for weeks to come. But stovetop tomato sauce requires constant monitoring to stave off scorching. I wanted a convenient way to make tomato sauce without peeling the tomatoes first and without the messy task of removing the seeds at the end. I looked to the slow cooker.

In the closed chamber of the slow cooker, I thought, contents can simmer at a consistent low temperature for long periods of time unchaperoned—with no threat of scorching.

To get my bearings, I cut a bunch of plum tomatoes in half, placed them in the slow cooker, and let them stew. A few hours later, I had a fleet of seeds bobbing in a sea of watery sauce. As steam had condensed inside the slow cooker, it had beaded on the bottom of the lid and dripped back into the tomatoes rather than evaporating away. And while we don't mind the seeds in quicker stovetop sauces because the gel around the seeds is packed with flavor, they do contain a bitter compound that is slowly extracted during longer cooking times, eventually permeating the sauce with an unpleasant flavor that overwhelms any benefit gleaned from the gel.

So for an all-day slow-cooker sauce, the seeds had to go, and when the seeds go, so does the gel. I held a sliced tomato half in each hand and squeezed out the seeds and gel. While this step may appear wasteful, remember that in the traditional stovetop method, most of this extra liquid would be cooked off anyway. By squeezing the raw tomatoes up front, you do the dirty work first. Bonus: It's kind of fun.

I left the lid slightly ajar so some steam could escape. This helped concentrate the flavors. After they had spent a few hours in the slow cooker, I ladled the tomatoes into a colander and let the excess water drain away. I then moved them to the blender to whiz into a thick, ruby-red sauce.

I decided to keep this all-purpose tomato sauce unadorned, allowing me to use it later for anything from marinara sauce to a bloody Mary mix (it freezes beautifully for up to two months). Did I sacrifice romance? Perhaps. But this simple sauce has its own charms.

Make a big batch: This sauce keeps for a week in the fridge or two months in the freezer.

SLOW-COOKER ALL-PURPOSE TOMATO SAUCE Makes 7 cups
Be sure to leave the lid slightly ajar—about ½ inch—to allow steam to escape and help concentrate the flavor. Use this versatile sauce as a base for marinara sauce or tomato soup or in place of crushed tomatoes in our Chicken Parmesan for Two (June/July 2016).

- 8 pounds plum tomatoes, cored and halved crosswise
- 1½ teaspoons salt
- ¼ cup extra-virgin olive oil

1. Working over bowl, squeeze each tomato half to remove seeds and excess juice. Discard seeds and juice. Transfer tomatoes to slow cooker; add salt and stir to combine. Leaving lid about ½ inch ajar, cook tomatoes until very soft, 8 to 10 hours on low or 5 to 7 hours on high.

2. Transfer tomatoes to colander and let excess liquid drain (do not press on tomatoes).

3A. FOR A BLENDER: Working in batches, process tomatoes in blender until smooth, about 1 minute. Transfer sauce to clean bowl.

3B. FOR AN IMMERSION BLENDER: Return tomatoes to slow cooker. Submerge blender in slow cooker and process tomatoes until smooth, 1 to 2 minutes.

4. Stir oil into sauce until incorporated. Let sauce cool completely, then refrigerate for up to 1 week or freeze for up to 2 months.

KEY STEP A Big Squeeze
Working over a bowl, squeeze each tomato half to remove the seedy jelly. Why? The seeds would turn the sauce bitter if cooked long enough, and the moisture in the jelly would need to be cooked off anyway.

Equipment Review Dry Measuring Cups

Could we find a perfect set to sweep the competition? BY AMY GRAVES

KEY **Good** ★★★ **Fair** ★★ **Poor** ★

SUCCESS IN BAKING starts with careful measuring. And while a good scale is the most accurate tool, dry measuring cups are often more practical for the home cook. Lots of new models have come on the market since we last tested measuring cups eight years ago, so we decided to revisit the category. We rounded up 12 sets, priced from $5.99 to $44.95 and including our prior winner (from Amco), and headed into the test kitchen to see which ones measured up.

Our preferred measuring method for dry ingredients is the "dip and sweep": We dip the cup into the container of flour or sugar, scoop out a heaping cupful, and then sweep the top of the measure level with the back of a knife. Models with handles that extend out on the same plane as the top of the cup best accommodate this, so we chose a combination of metal and plastic cups with this basic shape. We also limited our selection to sets that included at least the four essential sizes: 1 cup, ½ cup, ⅓ cup, and ¼ cup.

First we evaluated the cups for their most important quality: accuracy. We carefully filled each cup to its maximum capacity with both water and granulated sugar and weighed it on a calibrated lab-quality scale; then, knowing how much a cup of both water and sugar should weigh, we did the math to determine accuracy and scored the cups accordingly. Three sets were off by as much as 6 percent, sending them tumbling in the rankings. Our top performers were either spot-on or off by just a fraction of a percentage point.

Next we turned to ease of use. We asked a range of test cooks and editors to dip and sweep a cup of flour with the 1-cup measure from each of the 12 sets. Even with our carefully vetted lineup of straight-handled cups, our testers found problems with several models—those with rims slightly higher than the handles created a jarring catch to the

> Visit **CooksCountry. com/aug16** to read the full results of our testing and to see the three lower-rated models not pictured here.

sweeping motion that was at best awkward and at worst jostled the cup and required us to start anew. We preferred cups that were perfectly even with the handles for seamless sweeping.

The measurement markings on some cup sets were large and well placed on the handles, where they were easily identifiable. Cups with tiny or hidden markings were irksome, as we had to double-check to see which cup we were using. The downfall for some plastic cups was the impermanence of their measurement markings; those that were printed in ink came off with very little scrubbing. Almost all the stainless-steel sets have markings that are etched on; no amount of scrubbing was going to take those off. One outlying stainless-steel set had markings in ink on plastic handles—markings that came right off.

An additional problem: When we filled cups with flour and placed them on the counter, some smaller ones with long handles tipped over and spilled, causing them to lose points.

To test their durability, we used the cups to repeatedly scoop up wet, heavy sand to simulate years of hard use. Most plastic cups flexed with the motion and went right back into place, although a few smaller cups bent permanently. Many of the stainless-steel handles bent when we used great force; others bent immediately, with very gentle scooping. The most durable sets, including the winner, have shorter handles that are part of the cup mold (rather than riveted on) and didn't bend or flex at all.

Our winning measuring cups, from OXO, are made of sturdy, durable stainless steel and are accurate and easy to use. They have handles perfectly flush with the cup rims for seamless dipping-and-sweeping and laser-etched markings that don't scrub off; plus, they have the handy bonus feature of magnetic tabs to keep the stacked cups tidy in a drawer or cabinet (their short handles also make them more compact and easy to store). These cups are an intelligent improvement on the classic design.

	CRITERIA	TESTERS' NOTES
HIGHLY RECOMMENDED		
OXO Good Grips Stainless Steel Measuring Cups **Model:** 11132000 **Price:** $19.99 **Number of Cups:** 4 **Material:** Stainless Steel	**Accuracy** ★★★ **Durability** ★★★ **Ease of Use** ★★½	Accurate and extremely durable, this set snaps together for compact storage. The handles are seamless with the cups themselves, making them easy to level off.
NORPRO Grip-EZ Set of 6 Measuring Cups **Model:** 3018 **Price:** $6.87 **Number of Cups:** 6 **Material:** Plastic	**Accuracy** ★★★ **Durability** ★★★ **Ease of Use** ★★	This set had a high degree of accuracy in every size, and it was the most durable plastic set we tested. Long handles flush with the rims aided scooping and sweeping.
RECOMMENDED		
OXO Good Grips 6-Piece Plastic Measuring Cups **Model:** 11110901 **Price:** $7.99 **Number of Cups:** 6 **Material:** Plastic	**Accuracy** ★★★ **Durability** ★★½ **Ease of Use** ★★	This accurate six-cup set's matte plastic finish gave the handles a good, tacky grip, but some testers found the handles too short. A few cups tipped over when empty.
NORPRO Grip-EZ Set of 5 Stainless Steel Measuring Cups **Model:** 3067 **Price:** $27.88 **Number of Cups:** 5 **Material:** Stainless Steel	**Accuracy** ★★★ **Durability** ★★ **Ease of Use** ★★½	This accurate, shovel-shaped set felt cup-heavy and unbalanced to some, but plastic tabs on the handles made them easy to hold. The handles bent a bit when we scooped wet sand.
AMCO Houseworks Professional Performance 4-Piece Measuring Cup Set **Model:** 864 **Price:** $15.99 **Number of Cups:** 4 **Material:** Stainless Steel	**Accuracy** ★★½ **Durability** ★★ **Ease of Use** ★★★	Our previous winner, still solid, was surpassed by sets that were slightly more accurate and more durable. The handles bent quickly when we scooped wet sand (but they easily bent back).
RSVP Endurance Measuring Cup Set **Model:** DMC-10 **Price:** $36.95 **Number of Cups:** 7 **Material:** Stainless Steel	**Accuracy** ★★★ **Durability** ★★ **Ease of Use** ★★	This set of seven cups was very accurate. But the handles bent immediately when the cups were dragged through wet sand, and the thin handles dug into some testers' hands.
RECOMMENDED WITH RESERVATIONS		
PREPWORKS by Progressive 6 Piece Measuring Cup Set **Model:** BA-3518 **Price:** $5.99 **Number of Cups:** 6 **Material:** Plastic	**Accuracy** ★★★ **Durability** ★★½ **Ease of Use** ★	Its handles were slippery and too short for most testers, but this set was reasonably durable and very accurate. The handle on the smallest cup bent when scooping sand.
MIU France Stainless Steel Set of 7 Measuring Cups **Model:** 91688 **Price:** $37.28 **Number of Cups:** 7 **Material:** Stainless Steel	**Accuracy** ★★★ **Durability** ★★ **Ease of Use** ★	This accurate seven-cup set has long, uncomfortable, heavy handles that bent when scooping sand and made some cups tip over when empty.
LE CREUSET Stainless Steel Measuring Cups **Model:** SSA2530 **Price:** $44.95 **Number of Cups:** 4 **Material:** Stainless Steel	**Accuracy** ★★ **Durability** ★★ **Ease of Use** ★★	Wide and shallow, like miniature skillets, these heavy, slightly awkward cups seemed sturdy—until we used them to scoop wet sand, which bent the handle on the 1-cup measure.

Taste Test Bagged Popcorn

Bagged popcorn is selling like crazy these days; does it deserve the hype? BY LAUREN SAVOIE

AMERICANS HAVE BEEN crazy about popcorn since the Great Depression, when it became popular as a cheap, filling, and nutritious snack. These days, popcorn comes in all shapes, sizes, and flavors—from kernels you pop on the stovetop to buttery microwavable products and even mail-order heirloom varieties. But we've had our eye on a different category that's exploded over the past few years: bagged popcorn.

While sales of microwave and kernel popcorn have slowly declined, bagged popcorn sales have increased 60 percent since 2012. We rounded up seven top-selling, nationally available varieties of bagged popcorn to see if we could find a favorite. Though most brands offer multiple flavors, we stuck with basic salt-and-oil varieties. Twenty-one America's Test Kitchen staffers sampled the popcorns side by side in a blind, randomized tasting.

Though all the products consisted of just oil, salt, and popcorn kernels, tasters noted clear differences between samples: Some were toasty, nutty, and slightly sweet, while others tasted bland, flat, or even a bit burnt. Examining ingredient labels, we saw no trend in type or amount of oil or type of popcorn (all labels just listed "popcorn").

But the salt was another story. The top products contained a moderate amount of sodium—about 110 milligrams per 1-ounce serving—compared to the 220 milligrams in middle-of-the-pack popcorns and as little as 75 milligrams in the lowest-ranked samples. Products with too little salt were deemed "muted," while those with too much lacked nuanced toasted-corn flavor. We preferred those with moderate levels of sodium, which allowed the subtleties of the popcorn to shine.

Tasters cared about texture and showed a clear preference for certain samples, so we went in search of answers. All popcorn pops the same way. As the kernels are heated, water inside them begins to steam, building up pressure and causing starch in the kernels to gelatinize. Once enough pressure builds up, the foamy starch bursts through the tough outer layer of the kernels and solidifies as it hits the air—that's the whitish, billowy part of popped kernels.

To learn more about the factors that affect how popcorn pops, we reached out to food scientists at the University of Nebraska–Lincoln (UNL). They told us that a number of factors could impact pop: a kernel's size, moisture content, or breed; how the kernels are stored; and how they're heated. Unfortunately, manufacturers weren't willing to disclose specifics about their processes or kernels.

Looking for more clues, we scrutinized the popcorn pieces. Tasters preferred round, hearty pieces. UNL scientists told us that the popcorn industry categorizes popped kernels into three different shapes: unilateral (pieces that expand in one direction), bilateral (pieces that expand in two directions), or multilateral (pieces that expand in three or more directions). Unilateral popcorn pieces are the easiest to spot; they can resemble little octopuses, with dense, round bodies and appendages extending from the bodies on one side. Bilateral pieces are long, flat, and often symmetrical. Multilateral pieces are large and airy, with at least three appendages stemming from the bodies. Using a visual guide provided by David Jackson, a researcher at UNL, we counted out 100 pieces from each popcorn in our lineup and sorted them according to shape.

The result: Top-ranked popcorns contained more than 50 percent unilateral pieces, while the lowest-ranked sample had a paltry 4 percent. Tasters perceived products with a high percentage of unilateral pieces to be crunchier and more substantial, while they commented that those with fewer unilateral pieces were "spongy."

The results mirror one UNL study, which found that consumers preferred unilateral pieces in microwave popcorn, rating them as being crispier than other shapes. While researchers are still exploring consumer popcorn preferences, our tasters strongly preferred the dense, crunchy texture of unilateral pieces.

Our favorite was Cape Cod Sea Salt Popcorn. Tasters found this popcorn, which is made up of half unilateral pieces, crisp and substantial, with a balanced, fresh flavor. In fact, when we tasted it against homemade popcorn, tasters found the two surprisingly similar. You will pay for the convenience of bagged popcorn: Our winner costs $0.72 per ounce compared to $0.08 per ounce of kernels for home-popped. But it's a great no-cook shortcut that's surprisingly similar to homemade.

UNILATERAL
Less expansion makes a denser, crunchier texture.

BILATERAL
A double blow-out makes for a "squishier" texture.

MULTILATERAL
Too much expansion weakens the crunch.

TEST KITCHEN DISCOVERY Popcorn Shapes

The popcorn industry categorizes popped kernels into three basic shapes: Unilateral (pieces that expand in one direction), bilateral (pieces that expand in two directions), and multilateral (pieces that expand in three or more directions). The best popcorns have the highest percentage of unilateral pieces, which are perceived as crunchier and more substantial. In the photos above, picture the raw kernel in the center of each popped piece.

RECOMMENDED | TASTERS' NOTES

CAPE COD Sea Salt Popcorn
Price: $3.15 for 4.4 oz ($0.72 per oz)
Sodium: 110 mg
Percentage Desirable Unilateral Pieces: 50%

This popcorn won tasters over with its "nutty," "toasty" corn flavor and "well-calibrated salt." Its "hearty," "puffy" kernels were "crisp" and "crunchy" up front, with a tender interior that "almost melted" in tasters' mouths as they ate. "This is pretty ideal popcorn," summarized one taster.

SMARTFOOD DELIGHT
Sea Salt Popcorn
Price: $3.99 for 5.5 oz ($0.73 per oz)
Sodium: 115 mg
Percentage Desirable Unilateral Pieces: 63%

Tasters loved this familiar popcorn's "round," "bubbly," "cartoon-y fluffy" pieces, which were "plump" and "meaty," with "good crunch." It also had a nice subtle saltiness and a "toasty" flavor. "Reminds me of the movies," said one taster.

KETTLE Sea Salt Popcorn
Price: $3.29 tor 3 oz ($1.10 per oz)
Sodium: 240 mg
Percentage Desirable Unilateral Pieces: 38%

Though many tasters liked this product's "toasty" notes and "crisp" exterior, some thought the popcorn tasted "slightly burnt." Still, most loved these "airy," "fluffy" kernels, which had a subtly "sweet corn flavor."

POPCORN INDIANA
Sea Salt Popcorn
Price: $3.79 for 4.75 oz ($0.80 per oz)
Sodium: 220 mg
Percentage Desirable Unilateral Pieces: 18%

With a "natural sweetness" and "toasty," almost "buttery" notes, this product was deemed similar to "movie popcorn." Unfortunately, some tasters were disappointed with the "less substantial" shape and size of the kernels, which were "soft" and "lacked crunch."

RECOMMENDED WITH RESERVATIONS

479 Sea Salt Popcorn
Price: $3.59 for 4 oz ($0.90 per oz)
Sodium: 80 mg
Percentage Desirable Unilateral Pieces: 38%

While this popcorn had an "interesting mix of white and yellow pieces" and a "buttery" flavor, a few tasters deemed it too "bland" due to its lower salt content. Despite its high proportion of unilateral pieces, some tasters found the pieces "tough" and "chewy."

BOOMCHICKAPOP
Sea Salt Popcorn
Price: $3.09 for 4.8 oz ($0.64 per oz)
Sodium: 90 mg
Percentage Desirable Unilateral Pieces: 34%

With less salt than most other products, this popcorn was "inoffensive" and "mild," if not "a little bland." Though some tasters did pick up on subtle "toasty," "corn-y" notes in these kernels, many were distracted by their "rubbery," "cardboard-y" texture.

SKINNYPOP Popcorn Original
Price: $3.79 for 4.4 oz ($0.86 per oz)
Sodium: 75 mg
Percentage Desirable Unilateral Pieces: 4%

These smaller, angular pieces lacked structure and shape, compressing between tasters' teeth like "spongy," "stale" bits of "Styrofoam." Flavor was "muted" from lack of salt, though a few salt-conscious tasters appreciated the "purity" of this "mild" popcorn.

Heirloom Recipe

We're looking for recipes that you treasure—the ones that have been handed down in your family for a generation or more, that always come out for the holidays, and that have earned a place at your table and in your heart through many years of meals. Send us the recipes that spell home to you. Visit **CooksCountry.com/recipe_submission** (or write to Heirloom Recipes, *Cook's Country*, P.O. Box 470739, Brookline, MA 02447) and tell us a little about the recipe. Include your name and mailing address. **If we print your recipe, you'll receive a free one-year subscription to *Cook's Country*.**

PEPPER VINEGAR

Kimberley Johnston of Little Rock, Ark., writes, "This vinegar gets better the longer it sits and is great on just about everything, especially pulled pork sandwiches. And don't forget the chiles: I like to chop or mince a few to add a vinegary kick to chili, burgers, and tacos."

Makes about 3 cups
Pepper vinegar is spicy. For a milder vinegar, remove the seeds and ribs from the chiles.

- 6 ounces tabasco, red Fresno, or red jalapeño chiles, halved lengthwise
- 3 cups distilled white vinegar
- 4 teaspoons sugar
- 2 teaspoons salt
- 1 teaspoon black peppercorns
- ¼ teaspoon red pepper flakes

Pack chiles in clean 1-quart glass jar with tight-fitting lid. Combine vinegar, sugar, salt, peppercorns, and pepper flakes in medium saucepan and bring to boil over medium-high heat. Pour brine into jar, making sure chiles are fully submerged. Let cool completely. Affix jar lid and refrigerate for at least 3 weeks before serving. Pepper vinegar will keep, refrigerated, for up to 3 months.

COMING NEXT ISSUE

We've got your holiday season covered in our October/November issue with a comprehensive cooking class on **Roast Turkey**, side dishes like **Brussels Sprouts with Bacon**, appetizers like **Devils on Horseback**, and unexpected desserts including **Apple Pandowdy** and **Rum Pumpkin Pie**. We'll tell you which canned **pumpkin puree** to use and which **nonstick skillet** is the best on the market. We have ideas for easy suppers on those "in between" nights during that busy time of year, including **Meatloaf Burgers**, **Skillet Roast Chicken with Garlic Smashed Potatoes**, and **Pasta with Sausage Ragu**. Finally, we'll pay a visit to North Carolina, where we'll uncover the secrets to that state's famous **Fish Stew**. Join us.

FIND THE ROOSTER!

A tiny version of this rooster has been hidden in the pages of this issue. Write to us with its location and we'll enter you in a random drawing. The first correct entry drawn will win our winning dry measuring cups, and each of the next five will receive a free one-year subscription to *Cook's Country*. To enter, visit **CooksCountry.com/rooster** by July 31, 2016, or write to Rooster AS16, *Cook's Country*, P.O. Box 470739, Brookline, MA 02447. Include your name and address. Constance Conomikes of Williamsburg, Va., found the rooster in the April/May 2016 issue on page 12 and won our favorite inexpensive digital thermometer.

WEB EXTRAS

Free for 4 months online at
CooksCountry.com
Broccoli with Lemon-Oregano Dressing
Hawaiian Macaroni Salad
Pennsylvania Dutch Chicken and Corn Soup
Pickled Watermelon Rind
Quick Collard Greens
Shrimp and Grits
Tasting Fettuccine
Testing Disposable Plates
Testing Dry Measuring Cups
White Layer Cake Rounds

READ US ON iPAD

Download the *Cook's Country* app for iPad and start a free trial subscription or purchase a single issue of the magazine. All issues are enhanced with full-color Cooking Mode slide shows that provide step-by-step instructions for completing recipes, plus expanded reviews and ratings. Go to **CooksCountry.com/iPad** to download our app through iTunes.

Blueberry Jam Cake

TO MAKE THIS CAKE, YOU WILL NEED:

- ½ cup (3½ ounces) granulated sugar
- 2 tablespoons low- or no-sugar-needed fruit pectin
  Pinch salt
- 15 ounces (3 cups) fresh or thawed frozen blueberries
- 1 tablespoon lemon juice
- 8 tablespoons unsalted butter, softened
- 1½ cups (6 ounces) confectioners' sugar
- 8 ounces cream cheese, cut into 8 pieces and softened
- 2 teaspoons vanilla extract
- 3 (8-inch) White Layer Cake Rounds*

FOR THE JAM FILLING: Process granulated sugar, pectin, and salt in food processor until combined, about 3 seconds. Add blueberries and pulse until chopped coarse, 6 to 8 pulses. Transfer blueberry mixture to medium saucepan and bring to simmer over medium heat, stirring occasionally, until mixture is bubbling and just starting to thicken, 6 to 8 minutes. Off heat, stir in lemon juice. Transfer 1⅓ cups jam to small bowl, cover, and refrigerate until firm, about 3 hours. Strain remaining jam through fine-mesh strainer, cover, and set aside at room temperature. (You should have at least ¼ cup.)

FOR THE FROSTING: Using stand mixer fitted with paddle, beat butter and confectioners' sugar on medium-high speed until light and fluffy, about 3 minutes. Add cream cheese, 1 piece at a time, and beat until no lumps remain. Add vanilla and 2 tablespoons strained jam and mix until incorporated. Transfer ⅓ cup frosting to each of 2 small bowls. Add 1 teaspoon strained jam to first bowl and 1 tablespoon strained jam to second bowl, stirring well to combine. (You should have 3 shades of frosting.)

TO ASSEMBLE: Place 1 cake round on cake turntable. Spread ⅔ cup chilled jam in even layer over top. Place second cake round on top of jam and repeat with remaining chilled jam. Place third cake round on top. Spread small amount of lightest-colored frosting in even layer over top and sides of cake. Using small offset spatula, spread darkest-colored frosting over bottom third of sides of cake; medium-colored frosting over middle third; and remaining lightest-colored frosting over top third. While spinning cake turntable, run spatula from bottom to top of side of cake to blend frosting colors. While spinning cake turntable, run spatula over top of cake, working from outside in to create spiral. Serve.

▶ *For our recipe for White Layer Cake Rounds, go to **CooksCountry.com/whitecakerounds**, or use your own recipe.

Inside This Issue

Cook's Country

OCTOBER/NOVEMBER 2016

Pasta with Sausage Ragu

We wanted all-day flavor without spending all day. After a few weeks of work in the test kitchen, we got it.

PAGE 11

Rum Pumpkin Chiffon Pie
Perfect Holiday Dessert

Sticky Chicken
Sweet-Salty Glaze

Cooking Class: Easy Herb-Roasted Turkey

Rating Nonstick Skillets
5 of 7 Failed Our Tests

Meatloaf Burgers
Hemingway Inspired Us

Smothered Pork Chops
Alabama Version

Skillet Chicken Dinner
with Garlic Mashed Potatoes

Leek and Potato Gratin
Easy, Elegant Holiday Dish

Mozzarella Sticks
Gooey and Crunchy

Apple Pandowdy
Down-Home Favorite

CooksCountry.com
$5.95 U.S./$6.95 CANADA

LETTER FROM THE EDITOR

Cook'sCountry

Chief Executive Officer David Nussbaum
Chief Creative Officer Jack Bishop
Editorial Director John Willoughby
Executive Editor Tucker Shaw
Deputy Editor Rebecca Hays
Executive Managing Editor Todd Meier
Executive Food Editor Bryan Roof
Senior Editors Christie Morrison, Chris O'Connor, Diane Unger
Associate Editors Morgan Bolling, Ashley Moore
Test Cooks Daniel Cellucci, Matthew Fairman, Cecelia Jenkins, Katie Leaird
Assistant Test Cooks Allison Berkey, Mady Nichas
Copy Editors Jillian Campbell, Krista Magnuson
Contributing Editors Erika Bruce, Eva Katz
Science Editor Guy Crosby, PhD
Director, Creative Operations Alice Carpenter
Hosts & Executive Editors, Television Bridget Lancaster, Julia Collin Davison

Executive Editor, Tastings & Testings Lisa McManus
Managing Editor Scott Kathan
Deputy Editor Hannah Crowley
Associate Editors Lauren Savoie, Kate Shannon
Assistant Editors Jason Alvarez, Miye Bromberg
Editorial Assistant Carolyn Grillo

Test Kitchen Director Erin McMurrer
Assistant Test Kitchen Director Leah Rovner
Test Kitchen Manager Alexxa Grattan
Lead Senior Kitchen Assistant Meridith Lippard
Senior Kitchen Assistant Taylor Pond
Lead Kitchen Assistant Ena Gudiel
Kitchen Assistants Gladis Campos, Blanca Castanza

Design Director Greg Galvan
Photography Director Julie Cote
Art Director Susan Levin
Deputy Art Director Lindsey Chandler
Art Director, Marketing Melanie Gryboski
Deputy Art Director, Marketing Janet Taylor
Associate Art Director, Marketing Stephanie Cook
Senior Staff Photographer Daniel J. van Ackere
Staff Photographer Steve Klise
Assistant Photography Producer Mary Ball
Color Food Photography Keller + Keller
Styling Catrine Kelty, Marie Piraino

Senior Director, Digital Design John Torres
Executive Editor, Web Christine Liu
Managing Editor, Web Mari Levine
Senior Editor, Web Roger Metcalf
Associate Editors, Web Terrence Doyle, Briana Palma
Senior Video Editor Nick Dakoulas
Test Kitchen Photojournalist Kevin White

Chief Financial Officer Jackie McCauley Ford
Production Director Guy Rochford
Imaging Manager Lauren Robbins
Production & Imaging Specialists Heather Dube, Sean MacDonald, Dennis Noble, Jessica Voas
Senior Controller Theresa Peterson
Director of Business Partnerships Mehgan Conciatori

Chief Digital Officer Fran Middleton
VP, Analytics & Media Strategy Deborah Fagone
Director of Sponsorship Marketing & Client Services Christine Anagnostis
National Sponsorship Sales Director Timothy Coburn
Client Services Manager Kate Zebrowski
Client Service & Social Media Coordinator Morgan Mannino
Partnership Marketing Manager Pamela Putprush
Director of Customer Support Amy Bootier
Senior Customer Loyalty & Support Specialist Andrew Straaberg Finfrock
Customer Loyalty & Support Specialists Caroline Augliere, Rebecca Kowalski, Ramesh Pillay

Senior VP, Human Resources & Organizational Development Colleen Zelina
Human Resources Director Adele Shapiro
Director, Retail Book Program Beth Ineson
Retail Sales Manager Derek Meehan
Associate Director, Publicity Susan Hershberg

Circulation Services ProCirc

On the cover: Pasta with Sausage Ragu Keller + Keller, Catrine Kelty
Illustration: Greg Stevenson

I T'S GOT RUM in it," I said. "For flavor. Just a little bit."

Gram looked at me and blinked. "More than just a little bit, I hope," she said, employing the signature deadpan delivery she's spent nearly 99 years perfecting. "It's supposed to be for a holiday."

We were talking about the Rum Pumpkin Chiffon Pie that test cook Katie Leaird developed for this issue of *Cook's Country*. It's a lighter, fluffier take on the traditional Thanksgiving pumpkin pie, and while to our palates it tastes fresh and contemporary, the pie has rather old roots. Nearly as old as Gram herself (see "Fashions in Food" on page 22).

Our mission in *Cook's Country* magazine is to tell our American culinary story, taking as many twists, turns, and unexpected detours as we can along the way. Sometimes we hit the road to find ideas from hidden corners of the map (see page 7 for our take on North Carolina–style fish stew), and sometimes we hit the books to find ideas from hidden corners of our history.

Happily, both the map and the history books harbor endless inspiration to match our endless curiosity—and our endless appetites.

TUCKER SHAW
Executive Editor

Test cook Katie Leaird, above, took inspiration for her Rum Pumpkin Chiffon Pie recipe from this 1929 cookbook published by the Beverly Hills Women's Club. While she was busy in the kitchen, food editor Bryan Roof was scouring eastern North Carolina for another recipe in this issue: fish stew.

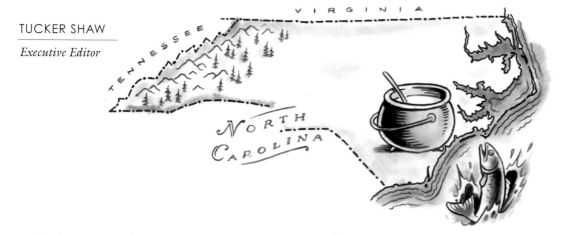

Naturally Sweet

120 revolutionary recipes for great-tasting baked goods and desserts that rely on only natural, less processed sweeteners.

Cooking and baking with less sugar requires creative techniques and thoughtful solutions. Enter America's Test Kitchen. We've developed this collection of must-have recipes to carry you through every special occasion with 30 to 50 percent less sugar.

Order at AmericasTestKitchen.com/NaturallySweet

 Follow us on **Pinterest**
pinterest.com/TestKitchen

 Follow us on **Twitter**
twitter.com/TestKitchen

 Find us on **Facebook**
facebook.com/CooksCountry

 Find us on **Instagram**
instagram.com/cookscountry

Photography: Steve Klise (top left). Andrea Tarwater/Sorrythankyou79 (book jacket); Illustration: Ross MacDonald

AMERICA'S TEST KITCHEN
RECIPES THAT WORK®

America's Test Kitchen is a real 2,500-square-foot kitchen located just outside Boston. It is the home of more than 60 test cooks, editors, and cookware specialists. Our mission is to test recipes until we understand exactly how and why they work and eventually arrive at the very best version. We also test kitchen equipment and supermarket ingredients in search of products that offer the best value and performance. You can watch us work by tuning in to *America's Test Kitchen* (AmericasTestKitchen.com) and *Cooks Country from America's Test Kitchen* (CooksCountry.com) on public television and listen to us on our weekly radio program on PRX. You can also follow us on Facebook, Twitter, Pinterest, and Instagram.

Cook's Country magazine (ISSN 1552-1990), number 71, is published bimonthly by America's Test Kitchen Limited Partnership, 17 Station St., Brookline, MA 02445. Copyright 2016 America's Test Kitchen Limited Partnership. Periodicals postage paid at Boston, MA, and additional mailing offices. USPS #023453. Publications Mail Agreement No. 40020778. Return undeliverable Canadian addresses to P.O. Box 875, Station A, Windsor, ON N9A 6P2. POSTMASTER: Send address changes to *Cook's Country*, P.O. Box 6018, Harlan, IA 51593-1518. For subscription and gift subscription orders, subscription inquiries, or change of address notices, visit AmericasTestKitchen.com/support, call 800-526-8447 in the U.S. or 515-248-7684 from outside the U.S., or write to us at *Cook's Country*, P.O. Box 6018, Harlan, IA 51593-1518. PRINTED IN THE USA.

Ask Cook's Country

BY MORGAN BOLLING

Bundt Pan Chicken

I recently saw a recipe online that called for cooking chicken in a Bundt pan. I'm intrigued. Is there something to it, or is it just a gimmick?
Diane Stapleton, Bloomington, Ind.

We did a little digging and found a load of recipes online for Bundt pan chicken. All call for propping the chicken up vertically by placing its cavity over the center tube of the Bundt pan. (Some call for covering the hole with foil to prevent a mess in the oven). Vegetables, which are scattered around the base of the chicken in the bottom of the pan, soak up the flavorful drippings as the bird cooks.

The benefit of roasting a chicken in a Bundt pan is similar to roasting one suspended over a beer can or a vertical roaster—crispy skin. The vertical position allows the oven heat to circulate more evenly around the body of the chicken than it would in a skillet or roasting pan, where the lips of the pans shield the legs.

But the chickens we cooked in Bundt pans came out funny-looking, with two-toned coloring featuring bronzed breasts and pale legs. Why? Just as the lips of a roasting pan would, the walls of the Bundt pan shielded the bottom half of the bird from the direct heat that causes browning. This also meant that the dark leg meat—which needs to be cooked to a higher temperature than lean breast meat—cooked more slowly, which gave us overcooked breast meat by the time the legs were cooked through.

THE BOTTOM LINE: While it's a fun idea, we decided that the Bundt pan isn't an ideal vessel for cooking chicken because the legs are shielded by the walls of the pan. Chickens roasted this way don't cook evenly. For a primer on how to cook a perfect roast chicken, visit **CooksCountry.com/chickenclass**.

UNEVEN SUNSCREEN APPLICATION?
Nope. The pan's sides prevented even browning.

Getting Skin-Deep

Can I brine a frozen turkey while it thaws to kill two birds with one stone?
John Joiner, La Jolla, Calif.

The easiest way to thaw a frozen turkey is to stick it in the fridge and let it sit, but this takes about 3 days for a 12-pound turkey. In the test kitchen, our quicker method involves submerging the bird in a bucket of cold water for 6 to 8 hours, changing the water every 30 minutes to guard against bacteria.

We were intrigued by your idea for combining brining with this quick-thaw method. So we added salt to the cold water and dropped in a frozen bird. But after changing out the brine a dozen times, we'd run through 3 pounds of salt and grown weary of the process.

We also tried a hybrid method, placing a frozen turkey in a bucket, covering it with brining solution, and placing the bucket in the fridge for 3 days, but this gave us an overbrined exterior and no seasoning within, as the solution couldn't penetrate the frozen flesh. What's more, we had to completely clear out the fridge to make room—not ideal at holiday time.

THE BOTTOM LINE: Unfortunately there's no easy, safe way to combine brining and thawing steps for turkey. For more tips on preparing Thanksgiving turkey and gravy, see "Easy Herb-Roasted Turkey with Gravy" on page 24.

Heirloom Rice

My grocery store recently started carrying both Carolina Gold and Charleston heirloom rice—will they work in your recipes for regular long-grain rice?
Bob Richard, Houston, Texas

Any produce billed as heirloom is simply an older variety that is not associated with large-scale commercial production. The smaller yields often mean that more care is taken in growing, harvesting, and packaging, and you pay more for that. We tasted the two varieties of heirloom rice you spotted, Carolina Gold and Charleston Gold, next to our winning long-grain white rice, Lundberg Organic Long-Grain White Rice. We tried all of these in our recipes for White Rice, Rice Pilaf, and Old-Fashioned Rice Pudding.

In all three applications, both heirloom varieties cooked at similar rates to the long-grain rice. They did, however, have different flavors and textures. Tasters noted that the Carolina Gold rice tasted "nutty" and "sweet," with notes of barley and popcorn; it also had more of an al dente chew than our winning long-grain rice. The Charleston Gold

ACORN SQUASH
One medium acorn squash yields 3 cups when peeled and cut into ½-inch cubes.

BUTTERNUT SQUASH
One medium butternut squash yields 7 cups when peeled and cut into ½-inch cubes.

Squash Servings

I never know how much acorn or butternut squash to buy for my family—do you have any guidelines?
Robin Wilson, Poughkeepsie, N.Y.

As we're sure you've seen when shopping for produce, acorn and butternut squash can vary greatly in size. When we're developing recipes that call for acorn or butternut squash, we follow the guideline that one medium acorn squash weighs about 1½ pounds and yields approximately 3 cups of cubed squash—about three servings. For butternut squash, we follow a similar guideline: A medium squash weighs between 2 and 2½ pounds and yields roughly 7 cups—about seven servings—of cubed squash. By the way, if you have trouble getting your knife through the flesh of dense, hard winter squash, use a rubber mallet to tap on the back of the knife to help get it started.

THE BOTTOM LINE: When we call for these squash varieties in our recipes, we adhere to the following guidelines: A medium acorn squash yields about three 1-cup servings, and a medium butternut squash yields about seven 1-cup servings.

---

rice had smaller kernels, and some tasters commented that it was more "sticky" in texture, with a "perfumed" flavor similar to that of basmati rice. Our winning white rice tasted "plain" in comparison.

THE BOTTOM LINE: Carolina Gold and Charleston Gold heirloom rices have unique flavors and textures and cook at a similar rate to long-grain white rice. They're both worth trying.

Sticking Point

My grocery store sells nonstick aluminum foil. How does it differ from regular foil?
Sarah Jenkins, Franklin, Ohio

Some recipes for baked goods (like brownies) or cheesy casseroles call for greasing the foil you use to cover the baking pan. The shiny side of nonstick aluminum foil is supposed to be non-stick, but it can be difficult to distinguish between the two. This coating supposedly lets the cook skip greasing the foil in recipes that call for it. Nonstick foil is more expensive than regular foil; we

paid $8.21 per 75-square-foot roll, as opposed to $5.21 for the same-size roll of regular aluminum foil.

To test it, we made two batches each of a cheesy pasta bake and our Chocolate Cherry Brownies, lining the pans with regular foil greased with vegetable oil spray (as called for in the recipe) for one batch and with nonstick foil for the other. Both foils released easily from the pasta, but the release from the brownies was a different story. The brownies baked on the standard greased foil released more easily and more cleanly; we had to pick small bits of the nonstick foil off the brownies before serving.

THE BOTTOM LINE: We didn't find nonstick foil to be worth the extra cost; it didn't perform as well as regular foil that we greased ourselves.

▶ To ask us a cooking question, visit **CooksCountry.com/ask**. Or write to Ask Cook's Country, P.O. Box 470739, Brookline, MA 02447. Just try to stump us!

Kitchen Shortcuts

COMPILED BY DIANE UNGER

DOUBLE DUTY
Standard Measure
Sandra Wilson, Lancaster, Pa.

A lot of baking recipes call for rolling dough to a certain length. If I don't have a ruler handy in the kitchen (I never seem to), I use my bench scraper as a guide. The blade is exactly 6 inches long, so I can easily measure and then use the bench scraper to help me transfer my dough.

HOT TRICK Double It Up
Will Hogan, Portland, Maine

When a skillet is moved straight from the oven to the stovetop, the hot handle can be an accident waiting to happen—a lesson I've learned the hard way. To prevent burns, I slip a potholder over the hot handle, fold it over, and secure it with a rubber band. It's much safer.

GOOD THINKING
Splatter Cover
Melissa Staples, Mikanda, Ill.

I often need a lid for my skillet, but the only lidded pots I own are smaller saucepans. I've discovered that I can use my splatter guard, wrapped in aluminum foil, as a makeshift lid for skillets of different sizes. It doesn't make the world's tightest seal, but it works well enough.

SMART TIP E-Z Peel Oranges
Sarah Muldoon, Oswego, N.Y.

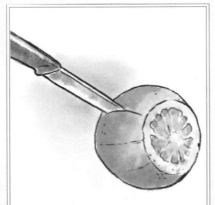

I like to send my kids to school with oranges in their lunches, but they find peeling them messy and frustrating (and a prepeeled orange can dry out). I found a way to prep the oranges that solves the problem: Cut ½ inch off the top and bottom of the fruit. Use a paring knife to score the flesh from top to bottom through the peel and pith about every inch. When you're ready to eat, just pull the peel off each section.

CLEVER IDEA
Helpful Heat
Celeste Walsh, Aurora, Colo.

Whenever I have to measure a sticky ingredient like honey, corn syrup, or molasses, it's hard to get it all off the spoon or out of the measuring cup. To solve this sticky situation, I heat my metal measuring spoon or glass measuring cup under hot tap water, dry it off, and then measure. The sticky stuff comes out easily for accurate measuring.

SMART IDEA
Pineapple Juice Squeeze
Tirzah Peterson, Milwaukee, Wis.

I make several recipes that call for pineapple juice, and I prefer to use fresh—the canned stuff never tastes right to me. I discovered that a handheld citrus juicer works great for juicing pineapple! Just put chunks of ripe pineapple (I get them from my supermarket's salad bar) in the hopper and squeeze them over a measuring cup.

CLEVER THINKING Instant Measuring
Cheryl Curry, Springtown, Texas

Ever notice that a baking powder container, with its plastic lid and lip for leveling, is easier to use when measuring than the cardboard box that some brands of baking soda come in? I took this matter into my own hands by repurposing an empty baking powder container for baking soda—the key is to label it clearly so there's no confusion. Now it's much easier to measure baking soda.

Submit a tip online at CooksCountry.com/kitchenshortcuts or send a letter to Kitchen Shortcuts, Cook's Country, P.O. Box 470739, Brookline, MA 02447. Include your name, address, and phone number. If we publish your tip, you will receive a free one-year subscription to Cook's Country. Letters may be edited for clarity and length.

Roast Chicken with Garlic Smashed Potatoes

Could we infuse smashed potatoes with savory chicken drippings?
Only one way to find out. BY MORGAN BOLLING

ONE OF MY favorite ways to roast chicken is on top of a bed of potatoes. The chicken's skin becomes crackly-crisp while the potatoes slowly steep in the savory juices. And while the test kitchen has mastered this method, we have yet to take it to the next logical place: infusing every bite of potato with comforting chicken flavor by smashing them. I set out to change that.

I started by nestling some cubed potatoes (Yukon Golds, which we love for their buttery flavor) under a 4-pound chicken in a skillet and sending it to the oven. Once the chicken was done, I zeroed in on the potatoes—and found myself disappointed. Those peeking out around the edges of the chicken were deeply browned and bordering on overdone, but the potatoes directly under the chicken were underdone. When I tried to smash them all together, I got nothing but lumps and leather.

I needed a way to even things out and protect the potatoes, allowing them to cook evenly without taking on those dry edges. I decided to create a "lid" for the potatoes by butterflying the chicken—a simpler-than-it-sounds process of removing the backbone and then opening and flattening the chicken. The best tool here is a pair of kitchen shears (also called poultry shears); you just snip from tip to tail along the backbone, flip the chicken, and push down with your palms to flatten it. (See "How to Butterfly a Chicken.")

Cooking the potatoes under the butterflied chicken gave me better results, but there were still some uneven spots. I knew I'd need to add liquid to the potatoes at some point for a successful smash, so why not add it early on and use it to even out the cooking? Rather than cut the spuds into chunks, I sliced them into disks, which stayed fully submerged in the water (1¾ cups was just enough to cover them) and prevented those dark, leathery edges from forming. Bringing the water and potatoes to a boil on the stovetop (which took only 5 minutes) before transferring the skillet to the oven kept things in the fast lane.

But in fixing one problem, I found

A simple stir-together parsley sauce with capers and lemon gives this satisfying one-pan dinner vibrant flavor.

another. The potatoes should have been supple, creamy, and full of chicken flavor when smashed. But instead, they were soupy due to the abundant amount of cooking liquid. Returning the skillet to the stovetop, I cranked up the burner and cooked off much of the excess liquid before smashing them.

Tasters found the spuds a little watery, though, and a bit washed-out. Simply swapping chicken stock

for the water added savoriness but maybe too much. So I stuck with water but also turned to dairy for flavor and richness. After trying buttermilk, sour cream, whole milk, half-and-half, and heavy cream, I settled on half-and-half. Just ½ cup, stirred into the potatoes right after smashing, gave them a bit of extra flavor and plenty of luxurious creaminess without weighing things down.

What's better than smashed potatoes? Smashed garlic potatoes. Six cloves tossed in with the potatoes added sweet, not sharp, garlic flavor to the already-deep chicken flavor. Fresh chives perked them up even more.

To seal the deal on this one-pan wonder, I stirred together a simple sauce of chopped parsley, briny capers, and bracing lemon juice to pass at the table for a final note of freshness.

▶ Get our free recipe for Grilled Butterflied Lemon Chicken at CooksCountry.com/grilledlemonchicken.

BUTTERFLIED CHICKEN WITH GARLIC SMASHED POTATOES

Serves 4

Take care when cooking the potatoes on the stovetop in step 4, as the skillet handle will be very hot. The parsley sauce can be made up to two days in advance.

CHICKEN AND POTATOES

- 1 (4- to 4½-pound) whole chicken, giblets discarded
- 1 tablespoon extra-virgin olive oil
  Kosher salt and pepper
- 2 pounds Yukon Gold potatoes, peeled and sliced ¼ inch thick
- 1¾ cups water
- 6 garlic cloves, peeled and smashed
- ½ cup half-and-half
- 2 tablespoons minced fresh chives

PARSLEY SAUCE

- ½ cup minced fresh parsley
- 6 tablespoons extra-virgin olive oil
- 2 tablespoons capers, minced
- 1 small shallot, minced
- 1½ tablespoons lemon juice
  Kosher salt and pepper

1. FOR THE CHICKEN AND POTATOES: Adjust oven rack to middle position and heat oven to 450 degrees. Place chicken breast side down on cutting board. Using kitchen shears, cut through bones on either side of backbone; discard backbone. Flip chicken over and press on breastbone to flatten. Tuck wingtips behind back. Pat chicken dry with paper towels. Rub skin side of chicken with oil and sprinkle with 1 teaspoon salt and ½ teaspoon pepper.

2. Combine potatoes, water, garlic, 1¼ teaspoons salt, and ¼ teaspoon pepper in 12-inch ovensafe skillet. Place chicken breast side up on top of potato mixture. Bring potato mixture to boil over medium-high heat. Once boiling, transfer skillet to oven and roast until breast registers 160 degrees and thighs register 175 degrees, 50 minutes to 1 hour 5 minutes, rotating skillet halfway through roasting.

3. FOR THE PARSLEY SAUCE: Meanwhile, combine parsley, oil, capers, shallot, and lemon juice in bowl. Season with salt and pepper to taste; set aside.

4. Return skillet to stovetop. Transfer chicken to carving board and let rest for 15 minutes. Bring potato mixture to simmer over medium-high heat (skillet handle will be hot). Cook until potatoes are fully tender and all liquid has evaporated, 8 to 10 minutes.

5. Off heat, use potato masher to coarsely smash potatoes, leaving some chunks intact. Stir in half-and-half and chives. Season with salt and pepper to taste. Carve chicken and serve with potatoes and parsley sauce.

TEST KITCHEN DISCOVERY A Flattened Chicken Makes a Good Lid
The chicken cooks on top of the potatoes and water, trapping steam to cook the spuds evenly. When the chicken is done, we remove it from the pan to rest. We then move the skillet to the stovetop, gently driving off excess liquid and leaving the potatoes tender and ready for smashing.

TEST KITCHEN TECHNIQUE How to Butterfly a Chicken
A butterflied (or spatchcocked) chicken looks impressive but is simple to create. Kitchen shears make this task easy.

1. Place chicken breast side down and cut through bones on either side of backbone. Trim any excess fat or skin at neck.

2. Flip chicken over and use heel of your hand to flatten breastbone.

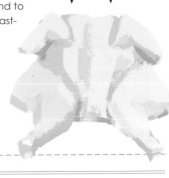

What Makes a Great Potato Masher?

If you don't love your potato masher, maybe it's time for an upgrade. Traditional mashers have long, solid handles attached to either a wavy wire or a perforated disk, but we've seen a number of innovative designs such as a coil shape or spring-loaded handles. Could any of these new products make mashing easier?

We rounded up 15 different mashers priced from $6.99 to $29.99—five wavy, five perforated, and five innovative— and started with an elimination round (mashing 2 pounds of boiled Yukon Golds in a large saucepan). Products that bent or warped, were painful to hold, or took more than 50 passes to mash the potatoes (the best took around 30) were out. This included most of the innovative products with uncomfortable handles and inefficient mashing plates.

That left us with nine mashers, which we tested with starchy russets, softer sweet potatoes, and more Yukon Golds in 2- and 4-quart saucepans and an 8-quart Dutch oven. We had different testers (men and women, lefties and righties) try each masher on boiled potatoes. We muscled through 150 pounds of potatoes to find that perforated mashers were more efficient. We also liked a mashing footprint that was neither too large (awkward) nor too small (inefficient) and a long handle to keep our hands away from hot steam. Our favorite product was the Zyliss Stainless Steel Potato Masher ($12.99), a traditional perforated masher with a long, curved plastic handle and a circular plate. It was maneuverable, comfortable, and easy to use. Read the full story and see the complete testing chart at **CooksCountry.com/oct16**. —LAUREN SAVOIE

INEFFICIENT MASHER

BEST DESIGN

KEY **Good ★★★ Fair ★★ Poor ★**

HIGHLY RECOMMENDED	CRITERIA		TESTERS' NOTES
ZYLISS Stainless Steel Potato Masher **Model:** E980044U **Price:** $12.99 **Style:** Perforated **Number of Holes:** 50	Mashing Comfort Durability Compatibility	★★★ ★★★ ★★★ ★★★	This tall tool has a sturdy mashing plate supported by a long, curved, comfortable handle. The small holes on its mashing plate made an ultrasmooth mash. Its round mashing plate eased effortlessly along the edges of every pan and made quick work of mashing all types of potatoes.

RECOMMENDED			
PREPARA Flip Masher **Model:** PP02-FM100 **Price:** $14.79 **Style:** Innovative, Perforated **Number of Holes:** 73	Mashing Comfort Durability Compatibility	★★★ ★★ ★★ ★★★	This innovative masher's convex plate promoted a gentle rocking motion, allowing us to build momentum as we mashed. Its 73 holes produced very smooth potatoes, and its curved plastic handle was comfortable for all except the largest hands to hold. One qualm: While this masher folds flat for storage, the folding mechanism trapped food and triggered once during mashing.
WMF Profi Plus Potato Masher **Model:** 18.7138.6030 **Price:** $19.69 **Style:** Perforated **Number of Holes:** 34	Mashing Comfort Durability Compatibility	★★ ★★ ★★½ ★★★	Our past favorite made relatively smooth potatoes and easily navigated around the edges of pans, but a few testers lamented its shorter handle and smaller footprint. Its handle had a slight bend after extensive mashing, but it didn't affect performance.

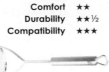

North Carolina Fish Stew

Locals have loved this hearty, bacon-infused Sunday stew for decades. Time to take it outside the Tar Heel State. BY MORGAN BOLLING

WHEN CAST-IRON STEW pots come out in Lenoir County, North Carolina, the safe bet is that a fish stew is nigh (see "On The Road").

Here's how it goes down: First, the host renders bacon or salt pork in a large pot. He or she then layers in sliced onions, sliced potatoes, and chunks of whitefish and adds water, tomato, and red pepper flakes—and then walks away for a bit (it's essential to not stir the stew as it cooks to keep the fish from breaking up). When the stew's nearly done, the cook cracks eggs into it to poach until just cooked through. The stew is ladled into bowls and served with sliced white bread to mop up the spicy broth.

Wait. Eggs?

Yes, eggs.

The origins of this egg addition are murky, so I reached out to Vivian Howard, a chef from Kinston, North Carolina. She speculated, "A frugal farmer probably went fishing and wanted to stretch the fish he got." Note to self: Next time I have a disappointing catch, stop by the grocery store for eggs.

To find a starting point for my own fish stew, I cooked five recipes—two authentic versions from born-and-bred Carolinians and three similar-but-different stews from acclaimed chefs like Craig Claiborne. What I found was this: The simplest stews were the best. Adding all sorts of vegetables and other spices distracted from the simple yet comforting and restorative flavor built from bacon, tomato, fish, and heat.

While most local recipes called for adding the uncooked potatoes, onions, and fish all at once to let them cook together, I found it more effective to do things in stages: After rendering the bacon, I cooked the onions and then added the tomato paste and potatoes. Adding the delicate fish last helped protect it and kept it from breaking down too much.

▶ To see more photos from our trip, go to CooksCountry.com/northcarolina.

Most Carolinians use bone-in chunks of firm, flavorful, locally caught fish like striped bass, sheepshead, or redfish. I wanted a fish that was widely available at any time of year, so I tried cod, halibut, hake, and haddock. I was happy to learn that any mild, firm whitefish

The basic building block of this hearty fish stew is bacon; its flavor (and fat) infuse the stew with deep savory notes. No one knows for sure when cooks began cracking whole eggs directly into the pot, but locals speculate that they were originally added so that a small day's catch could still feed a large crowd.

worked as long as it was cut into chunks of similar thickness.

I cracked eight eggs into several pots of stew—with mixed results. In one batch, gelatinous eggs floated (and wobbled) atop the stew; in another, they boiled into rubber balls. The best approach turned out to be covering the pot and setting it over medium-low heat, which produced eggs with a silky texture. That frugal farmer was onto something.

At a final test kitchen tasting on a very cold winter day, a coworker called it "a bouillabaisse with love from a Southern grandma." She was right.

Fishing for Stew in Deep Run

EASTERN NORTH CAROLINA FISH STEW

Serves 8

Any mild, firm-fleshed whitefish, such as bass, rockfish, cod, hake, haddock, or halibut, will work well in this stew. Our favorite bacons are Farmland Thick Sliced Bacon and Plumrose Premium Thick Sliced Bacon. Serve this rustic stew with soft white sandwich bread or saltines.

- 6 slices thick-cut bacon, cut into ½-inch-wide strips
- 2 onions, halved and sliced thin
  Salt
- ½ teaspoon red pepper flakes
- 6 cups water
- 1 (6-ounce) can tomato paste
- 1 pound red potatoes, unpeeled, sliced ¼ inch thick
- 1 bay leaf
- 1 teaspoon Tabasco sauce, plus extra for serving
- 2 pounds skinless whitefish fillets, 1 to 1½ inches thick, cut into 2-inch chunks
- 8 large eggs

1. Cook bacon in Dutch oven over medium heat until crispy, 9 to 11 minutes, stirring occasionally. Add onions, 1½ teaspoons salt, and pepper flakes and cook until onions begin to soften, about 5 minutes.

2. Stir in water and tomato paste, scraping up any browned bits. Add potatoes and bay leaf. Increase heat to medium-high and bring to boil. Reduce heat to medium and cook at vigorous simmer for 10 minutes.

3. Reduce heat to medium-low and stir in Tabasco. Nestle fish into stew but do not stir. Crack eggs into stew, spacing them evenly. Cover and cook until eggs are just set, 17 to 22 minutes. Season with salt to taste. Serve, passing extra Tabasco separately.

And on the side . . .

North Carolina fish stew is a hearty, satisfying meal in itself, but tradition calls for serving it with slices of soft white bread, such as Wonder bread. Use it to soak up all the flavorful broth at the bottom of your bowl.

"Throwing a fish stew" is what they say in Deep Run, North Carolina, and it's as good an excuse as any for a low-key gathering. They usually happen in the fall, during vest season.

I walk behind the main house on a thick cushion of centipede grass. I spot Greg Smith and his father, Emmett, gathering supplies outside their party shack (formerly a tobacco packhouse). To one side sits a large, black iron kettle.

Emmett found this cauldron years ago in a "manure field," as he describes it, and this gets a rise out of the guests, all longtime friends who grew up together in the small town. He clarifies: It was technically a cow pasture, but you can see the connection. The pot was nearly completely buried when he unearthed it, but with determination and muscle, he scrubbed it back to life. Emmett estimates that his pot has held more than 500 stews.

Emmett and Greg fire up the propane burner under the pot and then drop in a pound and a half of chopped bacon to cook until its fat has rendered. Guests emerge from the kitchen in a procession, each bearing an offering for the stew: 10 pounds of sliced potatoes, 5 pounds of sliced onions, and 7 pounds of local rockfish. Emmett layers it all into the pot. One guest spoons in a couple of cans of tomato paste—his only job, but he performs it with authority.

Emmett throws in a heavy handful of red pepper flakes and stands guard as the stew simmers away. He eventually adds the final, and most unusual, ingredient: four dozen eggs, cracked and dropped one by one into the stew—just enough for 20 people.

–BRYAN ROOF

Clockwise from top: Greg Smith converted his tobacco packhouse into a neighborhood party shack. The 275-mile-long Neuse River is the longest river contained completely in North Carolina. Smith, cocktail in hand, tastes the stew for seasoning before serving it up. Emmett Smith, Greg's father, keeps careful watch over the stew as it simmers slowly in a huge cast-iron pot.

Southern Smothered Pork Chops

Pork chops in gravy should be extra-comforting. It just took a while to get them right.

BY DIANE UNGER

To "SMOTHER" MEAT (usually chicken or pork) is to cook it low-and-slow in rich gravy until the meat is ridiculously tender. Unfortunately, that gravy is often just a cloak to mask subpar meat or, worse, a barrier obscuring perfectly good meat. What I wanted was thick, meaty, ultratender chops nestled in a rich, well-seasoned gravy made lightly nutty by a golden-brown roux.

To find the best chop for smothering, I started by testing rib, loin, and blade chops. Both the rib and loin chops cooked up tough and dry, no matter how gentle the heat. But blade chops have more fat and connective tissue and stand up really well to aggressive browning (which you need for good flavor) and long braising (for tenderizing).

Margaret Boyd of Mrs. B's Home Cooking in Montgomery, Alabama, is famous for her chops, and she generously explained her cooking process to me over the phone. Following her lead, I started by making a spice blend to season the chops. Her secret ingredient? Not so secret: It's Lawry's Seasoned Salt (see "One Entrée, Special Salt"). I mixed some with onion powder, granulated garlic, paprika, and pepper and made enough of it to season the chops, the flour I'd use to coat them before frying, and the gravy.

Although Boyd dredges her chops in flour and deep-fries them before braising, I opted to shallow-fry them in just ½ cup of oil, two at a time, until the exteriors were a deep golden brown. I then transferred them to a wire rack to await the gravy.

It's important to use blade-cut pork chops, which cook up ultratender.

The American Table
One Entrée, Special Salt

Lawrence L. Frank opened Lawry's The Prime Rib restaurant in Beverly Hills in 1938. His novel concept? Offer only one entrée: whole standing ribs of beef, which were wheeled around the dining room on a 5-foot-long, 700-pound silver art deco cart and carved to order. Servers offered a "third shaker" of Frank's special salt mixture, which included sugar and spices. Lawry's began selling the salt in retail outlets, and the rest is seasoned salt history.

All great gravies start with a roux, a cooked mixture of flour and fat; Boyd cooks hers until it is the color of peanut butter. I poured off all but ¼ cup of fat from the skillet before stirring in ½ cup of flour and cooking the mixture, stirring, until the kitchen started to smell like popcorn and the roux achieved the correct color (I kept a jar of Skippy handy). This took about 3 minutes. I then added the rest of the spice mixture and two sliced onions and cooked it all for 2 minutes before stirring in 3 cups of water (surprisingly, my tasters preferred water to broth, which was deemed too savory). I poured the gravy over the browned chops in a baking dish and covered the dish tightly with aluminum foil before transferring it to the oven.

I tested oven temperatures ranging from 250 to 400 degrees before settling on 350 degrees. In 1½ hours of hands-off time, the chops were supertender.

I carefully transferred the chops to a big platter while I finished my gravy by skimming some of the accumulated fat from the surface with a spoon and adding a splash of vinegar to brighten the flavor. I set a pot of cooked rice next to my steaming platter of pork chops and called over my tasters. The pork chops were so tender you could cut them with a thought. The gravy was thick, rich, silky, and packed with flavor. "I just want to curl up with these chops," said one taster.

SOUTHERN-STYLE SMOTHERED PORK CHOPS
Serves 4

Try to find chops of the same thickness for even cooking. For proper sauce consistency, it's important to measure the amount of fat left in the skillet before making the roux. Serve the chops and gravy with plenty of steamed white rice.

- 2 tablespoons Lawry's Seasoned Salt
- 1 tablespoon onion powder
- 1 teaspoon granulated garlic
- 1 teaspoon paprika
  Pepper
- 4 (8- to 10-ounce) bone-in blade-cut pork chops, ¾ to 1 inch thick, trimmed
- 1 cup all-purpose flour
- ½ cup vegetable oil
- 2 onions, quartered through root end and sliced thin crosswise
- 3 cups water
- 1 tablespoon cider vinegar

1. Adjust oven rack to middle position and heat oven to 350 degrees. Set wire rack in rimmed baking sheet. Combine seasoned salt, onion powder, granulated garlic, paprika, and 1 teaspoon pepper in bowl. Pat chops dry with paper towels and sprinkle each chop with 1 teaspoon spice mixture (½ teaspoon per side).

2. Combine ½ cup flour and 4 teaspoons spice mixture in shallow dish. Dredge chops lightly in seasoned flour, shake off excess, and transfer to prepared rack.

3. Heat oil in 12-inch skillet over medium-high heat until just smoking. Add 2 chops to skillet and fry until deep golden brown, 3 to 5 minutes per side. Let excess oil drip from chops, then return chops to rack. Repeat with remaining 2 chops.

4. Transfer fat left in skillet to liquid measuring cup. Return ¼ cup fat to skillet and stir in remaining ½ cup flour. Cook over medium heat, stirring constantly, until roux is color of peanut butter, 3 to 5 minutes. Add onions and remaining 4 teaspoons spice mixture and cook, stirring constantly, until onions begin to soften slightly, about 2 minutes.

5. Slowly stir water into roux mixture until gravy is smooth and free of lumps. Bring to simmer and cook until gravy begins to thicken, about 2 minutes.

Chow-Chow

Don't toss your unripened tomatoes at first frost. We have a better idea.

BY ANNE WOLF

N THE ROAD

A Soul Food Standout

You might pass by Mrs. B's Home Cooking if you're driving too fast, and that would be a shame. Housed in a bright yellow bungalow in Montgomery, Alabama, Mrs. B's has a billboard out front advertising "hot and ready" fare; inside, cooks like Bertha Seawright (above) deliver. A cafeteria-style "hot line" is set up in the homey dining room, with red plastic lunch trays stacked at one end, begging to be filled with smothered chicken or pork chops, collard greens that smack of smoky ham hocks and sugar (cuts their bitterness, I'm told), creamy fried corn, and macaroni and cheese. Everything comes with tender muffin-tin cornbread on the side—lightly crisp on the edges and freckled with kernels of corn. They say you can judge the worth of a Southern eatery by the quality of its cornbread; I use one piece to mop up the extra gravy on my tray, and I slip another into my pocket on the way out. To see more photos from our trip to Alabama, go to **CooksCountry.com/alabama**.

–BRYAN ROOF

Pour half of gravy into 13 by 9-inch baking dish. Nestle browned chops in dish, overlapping slightly as needed. Pour remaining gravy over chops and cover dish tightly with aluminum foil. Bake until chops are fully tender, about 1½ hours.

6. Carefully transfer chops to serving dish. (Chops will be delicate and may fall apart.) Use wide spoon to skim fat from surface of gravy. Add vinegar to gravy and season with pepper to taste. Pour gravy over chops. Serve.

ONE SURE SIGN of autumn is a tomato plant full of unripened fruit. You'll be tempted to throw them out, but we've got a better idea: chow-chow. This relish of tart green tomatoes, vegetables, and spices is best known in the South but is also found as far afield as New Mexico and Pennsylvania. You'll see it alongside dishes as diverse as roast chicken, burgers, boiled potatoes, and crab cakes. Versions vary from kitchen to kitchen—some contain cabbage, some cauliflower, and others squash or hot peppers. One might be sweet, and another might be spicy. But green tomatoes are a constant.

I wanted to straddle the line between sweet and spicy, with complex flavor, a bit of tanginess, and vibrant colors. For inspiration, I took a virtual trip across the country. From the South, I took fruity red and slightly bitter green bell peppers. From the Southwest, jalapeños. Up North, I found crunchy cabbage. And along the way, I grabbed add-ins including celery seeds, turmeric, mustard seeds, sugar, and cayenne.

Achieving a crisp texture was not easy with vegetables minced into ¼- to ½-inch pieces. I started by simply simmering them with vinegar, sugar, and spices. The outcome was simple, all right—simply soupy. I needed to eliminate some of this moisture.

Salt coaxes moisture out of vegetables, so I tossed the chopped tomatoes, cabbage, and peppers with salt and set them in the fridge for 3 hours. I then squeezed the vegetables in a dish towel. The water was gone, but the treatment was too rough for the cabbage, leaving it limp, not crisp. A colander worked better.

Next, I cooked the vinegar with the spices and sugar for 5 minutes to create a pickle brine before taking it off the heat and stirring in the vegetables. This off-heat technique kept the cabbage crisp and the peppers and tomatoes firm. My chow-chow was just right, and with colors and flavors as invigorating as these, I'd just extended summer.

Serve this flavorful relish with chicken, fish, potatoes, or hot dogs.

CHOW-CHOW Makes about 3 cups

To double the recipe, double the amounts of all the ingredients, pulse the vegetables in step 1 in 6 batches, increase the simmering time in step 2 to about 8 minutes, and cook the mixture in a Dutch oven instead of a large saucepan.

- 18 ounces green tomatoes, cored and chopped coarse
- 1 cup coarsely chopped green cabbage
- 1 cup coarsely chopped green bell pepper
- ½ cup coarsely chopped red bell pepper
- ½ cup coarsely chopped onion
- 1 jalapeño chile, stemmed, seeded, and chopped coarse
- 1½ tablespoons salt
- ½ cup distilled white vinegar
- ½ cup sugar
- 1¼ teaspoons yellow mustard seeds
- ½ teaspoon celery seeds
- ¼ teaspoon ground turmeric
- ¼ teaspoon cayenne pepper

1. Combine tomatoes, cabbage, bell peppers, onion, and jalapeño in bowl. Working in 3 batches, pulse vegetables in food processor until pieces measure ¼ to ½ inch, 4 to 6 pulses; transfer to separate bowl. Stir in salt, cover, and refrigerate for 3 hours.

2. Transfer vegetables to colander set in sink and let drain for 20 minutes. Bring vinegar, sugar, mustard seeds, celery seeds, turmeric, and cayenne to boil in large saucepan over high heat. Reduce heat to medium-low and simmer until slightly thickened, about 5 minutes. Off heat, stir in drained vegetables.

3. Let relish cool completely, then refrigerate until ready to serve. (Relish can be refrigerated for up to 6 months.)

Relish Roundup
Cities across the country brighten things up with their own signature relishes. Here are a few:

PEPPER HASH
Philadelphia
Cabbage, bell pepper, vinegar, and sugar. Used on fish and "combo" dogs (hot dogs and fish cakes).

GIARDINIERA
Chicago
A sweet to hot mix of carrot, cauliflower, olives, bell pepper, and gherkins.

OLIVE RELISH
New Orleans
The classic olive-based topper for muffuletta sandwiches.

RUTT'S HUT RELISH
New Jersey
A mix of cabbage, carrots, onion, and mustard. Tops the "Ripper," a hot dog fried long enough for the skin to tear.

Classic Chicken Curry

American home cooks have been dishing up chicken curry for centuries.
We wanted a quick weeknight version. BY CECELIA JENKINS

CURRY HAS DEEP roots in America. It enjoyed its first stateside vogue during the 19th century, when East Coast seaports from Charleston to Portland found themselves suddenly favored with new spices from Asia. Many cookbooks from that era, including *Mrs. Rorer's Philadelphia Cook Book* (1886) and *Mrs. Lincoln's Boston Cook Book* (1884), included recipes for chicken flavored with curry powder.

Curry powder was and still is a complex blend of spices (see "Curry Powder"). Many home cooks create their own blends, but we've had great success with store-bought mixes (our favorite is Penzeys Sweet Curry Powder). Simply tossing chicken with the stuff and cooking it off produces a good dish.

But good isn't good enough; I wanted something great. What's more, I wanted to round out my curry with traditional ingredients including potatoes, cauliflower, and peas to create a one-pot meal.

I started with the curry powder, which, as we know from many years of test kitchen work, benefits (as most spices do) from a quick cooking in fat to "bloom," or release its oils and aromas. Just 10 seconds in the bottom of a Dutch oven does the trick. Because I wanted savory onion flavor to infuse the entire dish, I tossed onions in next, cooking them until just soft. Garlic, ginger, and jalapeño, three curry staples, completed this flavor base.

I wanted my final curry to feature shredded chicken, but I also knew that cooking bone-in, skin-on chicken would give more flavor to the dish. So I added two split chicken breasts to the pot with the onions and curry, followed by a few cut-up Yukon Gold potatoes (we liked their flavor), half a head of cauliflower that I had cut into florets, and a couple of cups of water. I set everything to simmer and came back a while later to have a taste. But my hopes for an all-in-one method were dashed when I found rubbery chicken, mushy cauliflower, and underdone spuds. I'd have to use a staggered approach.

For the next go-round, I added chicken to the pot with 1½ cups of water (enough to braise it and then the potatoes). I brought the water to a simmer, covered the pot, and cooked the chicken for about 20 minutes before transferring it a plate. While the chicken

Chunks of Yukon Gold potatoes, cauliflower florets, and a handful of frozen peas help turn this one-pot dish into a complete meal.

cooled, I added the potatoes to the liquid in the pot and cooked them for 8 minutes before tossing in the cauliflower. Fifteen minutes later, the vegetables were tender. By now I'd taken the chicken off the bone and tossed the skin, and the meat was cool enough to tear into shreds. I stirred the meat (and the juices that had accumulated on the plate) back into the pot with a cup of frozen peas. Once everything was warmed through, it was ready to serve.

Or so I thought. While my curry was hearty and aromatic, it lacked a signature characteristic: tangy creaminess. A cup of whole-milk yogurt stirred in off the heat, plus a scattering of cilantro over the top, sealed the deal on this old-school classic.

CLASSIC CHICKEN CURRY
Serves 4

Do not substitute low-fat or nonfat yogurt for the whole-milk yogurt called for in this recipe or the finished dish will be much less creamy. The curry is best served with white rice.

- 3 tablespoons unsalted butter
- 2 tablespoons curry powder
- 2 onions, chopped
- 1 jalapeño chile, stemmed, seeded, and minced
  Salt and pepper
- 3 garlic cloves, minced
- 1 tablespoon minced fresh ginger
- 2 (10- to 12-ounce) bone-in split chicken breasts, trimmed
- 1½ cups water
- 8 ounces Yukon Gold potatoes, peeled and cut into ½-inch chunks
- ½ head cauliflower (1 pound), cored and cut into 1-inch florets
- 1 cup frozen peas
- ¼ cup minced fresh cilantro
- ¾ cup plain whole-milk yogurt

1. Melt butter in Dutch oven over medium heat. Add curry powder and cook until fragrant, about 10 seconds. Add onions, jalapeño, 1¼ teaspoons salt, and ¼ teaspoon pepper and cook until vegetables are softened, about 5 minutes. Stir in garlic and ginger and cook until fragrant, about 30 seconds.

2. Add chicken and water to pot. Increase heat to medium-high and bring mixture to boil. Reduce heat to low, cover, and simmer until chicken registers 160 degrees, 22 to 24 minutes, flipping chicken halfway through cooking. Transfer chicken to plate and let cool for 5 minutes. Once chicken has cooled, use two forks to shred meat into approximate 2-inch pieces; discard skin and bones.

3. Meanwhile, stir potatoes and ¼ teaspoon salt into curry, cover, and cook until potatoes are slightly tender, about 8 minutes. Stir in cauliflower and continue to cook, covered, until potatoes are fully cooked and cauliflower is tender, about 15 minutes longer, stirring occasionally.

4. Stir in peas, cilantro, and shredded chicken and cook until curry is warmed through, about 1 minute. Off heat, stir in yogurt. Season with salt and pepper to taste, and serve.

Pasta with Sausage Ragu

We wanted to pack all-day flavor into this sauce without spending all day on it.

BY ASHLEY MOORE

COMMON WISDOM SAYS that sausage ragu, hearty Sunday night staple, requires hours of cooking. But I wanted to capture the long-cooked flavor of this Italian American sauce in less than 90 minutes. Goose chase? I set out to see.

The first question to answer was, "What does long-cooked sauce taste like?" After cooking a handful of recipes calling for extended simmering and tasting them against quicker versions, we knew right away: The slow-simmered sauces were deep, savory, and meaty, while the fast ones were less complex and more acidic. Using flavorful sausage gave me a bit of an advantage, but I still had a long way to go.

Every great sauce needs a flavor base of vegetables; in Italian, it's called a *soffritto*. After a test using the usual suspects—chopped onion, carrot, and celery—I realized that the carrot and celery weren't doing much. Just half an onion, plus half a fennel bulb and a tablespoon of fennel seeds, pulsed in the food processor gave me better-defined flavor. But I had other problems to solve.

For example, what kind of sausage should I use? After a few tests, I settled on sweet Italian. I then tested processing it like the vegetables versus breaking it up with a wooden spoon; we preferred using the processor, which helped evenly disperse the sausage throughout the finished dish.

I also had to decide on a tomato product. After experimenting with crushed tomatoes and whole peeled tomatoes (which I processed in the food processor), I found that the whole peeled tomatoes had a far silkier texture.

Ingredients settled, I set out to find long-simmered flavor without the long simmering. The answer was simple, but it took just a small measure of up-front patience: careful browning. By deeply browning the sausage and then adding the soffritto to cook thoroughly with the browned meat (scraping up the browned bits as I went), I was able to amplify the deep flavor of the sauce and add a subtle sweetness, too, thanks to the lightly caramelized sugars in the onions. I added the remaining ingredients and, after just 45 minutes of simmering, tossed the sauce with pasta and a bit of the pasta cooking water to help it achieve the perfect consistency. Tasters swore my sauce had been on the stove all day.

PASTA WITH SAUSAGE RAGU

Serves 4 to 6

For a spicier sauce, substitute hot Italian sausage for sweet. You will have 3 cups of extra sauce, which can be used to sauce 1 pound of pasta.

- ½ fennel bulb, stalks discarded, bulb cored and chopped coarse
- ½ onion, chopped coarse
- 1 tablespoon fennel seeds
- 1 (28-ounce) can whole peeled tomatoes
- 2 pounds sweet Italian sausage, casings removed
- 1 tablespoon extra-virgin olive oil, plus extra for drizzling
    Salt and pepper
- 2 tablespoons tomato paste
- 4 garlic cloves, minced
- 1½ teaspoons dried oregano
- ¾ cup red wine
- 1 pound pappardelle or tagliatelle
    Grated Parmesan cheese

1. Pulse fennel, onion, and fennel seeds in food processor until finely chopped, about 10 pulses, scraping down sides of bowl as needed; transfer to separate bowl. Process tomatoes in now-empty processor until smooth, about 10 seconds; transfer to second bowl. Pulse sausage in now-empty processor until finely chopped, about 10 pulses, scraping down sides of bowl as needed.

2. Heat oil in Dutch oven over medium-high heat until shimmering. Add sausage and cook, breaking up meat with spoon, until all liquid has evaporated and meat begins to sizzle, 10 to 15 minutes.

3. Add fennel mixture and ½ teaspoon salt and cook, stirring occasionally, until softened, about 5 minutes. (Fond on bottom of pot will be deeply browned.) Add tomato paste, garlic, and oregano and cook, stirring constantly, until fragrant, about 30 seconds.

4. Stir in wine, scraping up any browned bits, and cook until nearly evaporated, about 1 minute. Add 1 cup water and pureed tomatoes and bring to simmer. Reduce heat to low and simmer gently, uncovered, until thickened, about 45 minutes. (Wooden spoon should leave trail when dragged through sauce.) Season with salt and pepper to taste; cover and keep warm.

5. Bring 4 quarts water to boil in large pot. Add pasta and 1 tablespoon salt and cook, stirring often, until al dente. Reserve 1 cup cooking water, then drain pasta and return it to pot. Add 3 cups sauce and ½ cup reserved cooking water to pasta and toss to combine. Adjust consistency with remaining reserved cooking water as needed. Transfer to serving dish. Drizzle with extra oil, sprinkle with Parmesan, and serve. (Remaining 3 cups sauce can be refrigerated for up to 3 days or frozen for up to 1 month.)

Wide noodles like pappardelle or tagliatelle stand up best to this meaty sauce.

FLORENCE FENNEL
A vegetable grown for its edible bulb, stems, and fronds

INGREDIENT SPOTLIGHT Fennel

The vegetable that we slice and eat raw or cooked is **Florence fennel**, or finocchio; its bulb, stems, and feathery fronds boast a mildly sweet, faint anise flavor. Fennel seeds, which are a key part of the flavor profile of Italian sausage, come from a perennial herb called **common fennel** (also referred to as herb, sweet, or wild fennel) that has no bulb.

COMMON FENNEL
A perennial herb grown for its ornamental fronds and aromatic seeds

Meatloaf Burgers

Ernest Hemingway was an acclaimed writer. But his culinary skills needed help.

BY CHRISTIE MORRISON

ERNEST "PAPA" HEMINGWAY had an appetite for deep-sea fishing, bullfighting, and drinking. But I recently learned that he also had an appetite for a meatloaf-like hamburger. The JFK Presidential Library in Boston released the recipe for Papa's Favorite Wild West Hamburgers to the public in 2013 in a collection of Hemingway's papers. The beef patty, cooked on the stovetop until it was, in his words, "crispy brown," included a pantry-clearing array of ingredients: capers, garlic, scallions, dried sage, Beau Monde seasoning, India relish, egg, and a healthy pour of wine in which the beef could sit, "quietly marinating." He shaped this meatloaf-like mix into a burger and fried it until it was "juicy." What makes this a "Wild West" burger? We're not sure.

But while Papa knew prose, he was mistaken about protein; when I tried his recipe in the kitchen, all that liquid and acid yielded a mealy and wet—not juicy—burger. Still, for all its shortcomings, I saw the promise of a soft, flavorful, crispy-on-the-edges meatloaf burger.

Hemingway wasn't the only one to have the idea. I tested a range of other existing recipes for "meatloaf burgers." Some showed promise, but it wasn't until I turned to the test kitchen's collected meatloaf knowledge that I started to get my bearings.

I opted for 85 percent lean ground beef instead of a pork-and-beef combo. I mixed in ketchup and other potent stalwarts: Dijon mustard, Worcestershire sauce, parsley, and an egg for cohesion. While most of our meatloaf recipes call for sautéed onion, I substituted 1 teaspoon of onion powder.

To achieve the slightly soft, moist texture of meatloaf, I'd need to incorporate a panade—a matrix of starch (usually bread crumbs or crackers) and liquid—to trap moisture in the burger.

Like Hemingway, I wanted my burgers to have a crispy brown exterior; searing both sides of the burgers in a hot skillet accomplished this quickly. I transferred the browned burgers to the oven to gently cook to 160 degrees (our usual temperature for meatloaf).

One question remained: To have or have not? (A glaze, I mean.) We usually glaze our meatloaves with a ketchup, brown sugar, and cider vinegar mixture, but it covered up the crispy brown crust I'd just achieved. Instead, I mixed ketchup and vinegar with mayonnaise for a creamy spread that tasted both new and familiar.

The finished meatloaf burger had the slightly soft yet juicy texture we expect from meatloaf and that signature crispy crust. I think Papa would be proud.

MEATLOAF BURGERS Serves 4

Ian's makes the test kitchen's favorite panko bread crumbs.

- ½   cup panko bread crumbs
- 2   tablespoons Worcestershire sauce
- 6   tablespoons ketchup
- ¼   cup minced fresh parsley
- 1   large egg
- 1   tablespoon Dijon mustard
- 1   teaspoon onion powder
-      Salt and pepper
- 1½ pounds 85 percent lean ground beef
- 1   tablespoon vegetable oil
- ¼   cup mayonnaise
- 2   teaspoons cider vinegar
- 4   hamburger buns, toasted

1. Combine panko and Worcestershire in large bowl until panko is thoroughly moistened. Stir in 2 tablespoons ketchup, parsley, egg, mustard, onion powder, ¾ teaspoon salt, and ¼ teaspoon pepper. Add beef and knead with your hands until just combined.

2. Shape beef mixture into four ¾-inch-thick patties, about 4½ inches in diameter. Press center of each patty down with your fingertips until about ½ inch thick, creating slight divot in patty. (Patties can be covered and refrigerated for up to 24 hours.)

3. Adjust oven rack to middle position and heat oven to 350 degrees. Set wire rack in aluminum foil–lined rimmed baking sheet. Heat oil in 12-inch nonstick skillet over medium-high heat until just smoking. Transfer patties to skillet and cook without moving them until browned on first side, about 3 minutes. Flip patties and cook without moving them until browned on second side, about 3 minutes. Transfer patties to prepared rack and bake until meat registers 160 degrees, 15 to 20 minutes.

4. Meanwhile, whisk mayonnaise, vinegar, ¼ teaspoon pepper, and remaining ¼ cup ketchup together in bowl.

5. Transfer burgers to plate and let rest for 5 minutes. Serve on buns with sauce.

Like Hemingway, these juicy burgers have a crusty exterior, which we achieve with a hot sear.

The American Table
Hemingway's Appetites

In Cuba, Hemingway was probably more well-known for the number of cocktails named for him than for the burger recipe he developed. A barfly at the El Floridita bar in Havana in the 1930s, Hemingway nurtured a passion for daiquiris. His preferred method? Hold the sugar and double the rum. Legend has it that a bartender at El Floridita named the "Papa Doble" daiquiri in Hemingway's honor. Another cocktail at the same bar—the "Hemingway Special"—was a variation on that daiquiri that included maraschino liqueur, grapefruit juice, and less rum.

Sticky Chicken

Moist and tender chicken with a sweet-salty sheen sounds tricky, but we made it easy.

BY DIANE UNGER

STICKY CHICKEN ISN'T just a great recipe name, it's a great dish, too—deeply flavored roasted chicken with a sticky, slightly sweet, lacquered exterior. It wasn't hard finding existing recipes for this dish—but good recipes? That was a steeper hill to climb.

Most of the recipes I found called for marinating chicken pieces in a mixture of soy sauce, ketchup, and some sort of sweetener (such as brown sugar or honey) for at least 30 minutes; searing them on the stovetop to begin crisping the skin; and then covering the pan or transferring the pan to the oven to finish cooking the chicken. In some cases the chicken was dry and unevenly cooked, and in others it was inedibly salty. I wanted a happy medium: well-seasoned meat, nicely rendered skin, and a sweet and sticky sauce. And it had to be easy and fast enough for a weeknight meal.

My first big decision was to switch from chicken parts to just bone-in chicken thighs, which rarely dry out. Eight would be enough to serve four people. I also took marinating off the table (no time for that). But I did want the chicken to be packed with flavor. So I whisked together a braising liquid of cider vinegar, honey, soy sauce, and ketchup—all pantry staples—tasting the sauce as I went along to ensure the right balance of sweet and salty. I added granulated garlic and red pepper flakes for a punch of flavor.

I assumed that searing the chicken skin side down on the stovetop before adding the braising liquid would give me wonderfully crispy skin (initially), but I could fit only six thighs in my skillet in order to get even browning. What's more, I'd be dousing them with braising liquid anyway, so why bother chasing crispiness? I decided to ditch this step.

Instead, I laid eight chicken thighs skin side down in my cold skillet. My idea was to cook the chicken slowly in my flavorful sauce to begin rendering the fat from the skin. Then I'd turn the chicken skin side up to finish cooking with the skin above the level of the cooking liquid, presumably drying it out a bit and browning it in the process. My coworkers were skeptical, but I was determined.

I set the skillet in a 425-degree oven. After about 20 minutes skin side down and 20 minutes skin side up, my chicken had reached an internal temperature

For a sweet, sour, salty, and sticky glaze, we use cider vinegar, honey, soy sauce, and ketchup.

of 175 degrees. But it looked awful. I kept cooking the chicken for a few more minutes until the skin turned an appetizing brown (chicken thighs can withstand longer cooking, and they actually get more tender when cooked to a higher temperature). Satisfied with the appearance of the skin, I transferred the chicken to a platter and turned my attention to finishing the sauce.

What had started as 1¾ cups of sauce had swelled to 3 cups of liquid from the addition of the chicken's juices. I ran the liquid through a fat separator, returned the defatted liquid to the skillet along with a small amount of cornstarch, and reduced it to ¾ cup, at which point it was just thick enough to coat the chicken and give it the shiny glaze I was looking for.

I gathered my tasters for servings of chicken with some extra sauce for dipping and a sprinkling of toasted sesame seeds. Thumbs up all around. The chicken was tender, and the sauce was balanced and just sweet enough. Mission accomplished: Sweet, savory sticky chicken in less than an hour.

STICKY CHICKEN Serves 4

Trim any fatty pockets from the edges of the chicken thighs to ensure well-rendered skin. Cooking the thighs to 195 degrees melts the tough connective tissues while keeping the meat moist. This dish is best served with white rice.

- 8 (5- to 7-ounce) bone-in chicken thighs, trimmed
  Pepper
- ¾ cup cider vinegar
- ½ cup honey
- ¼ cup soy sauce
- ¼ cup ketchup
- 1 teaspoon granulated garlic
- ¼ teaspoon red pepper flakes
- 1 teaspoon cornstarch
- 1 teaspoon water
- 2 teaspoons toasted sesame seeds

1. Adjust oven rack to upper-middle position and heat oven to 425 degrees. Season chicken with pepper and arrange skin side down in 12-inch ovensafe skillet. Whisk vinegar, honey, soy sauce, ketchup, granulated garlic, and pepper flakes together in bowl and pour over chicken. (Skillet will be full.)

2. Bake chicken for 20 minutes. Flip chicken skin side up and continue to bake until skin is spotty brown and meat registers 195 to 200 degrees, 20 to 25 minutes longer. Transfer chicken to serving platter. Carefully pour pan juices into fat separator (skillet handle will be hot) and let settle for 5 minutes.

3. Dissolve cornstarch in water in small bowl. Return defatted juices to skillet and whisk in cornstarch mixture. Bring sauce to boil over high heat and cook until syrupy and spatula leaves trail when dragged through sauce, 7 to 9 minutes. (You should have about ¾ cup sauce.) Season with pepper to taste.

4. Off heat, return chicken to skillet and turn to coat with sauce. Flip chicken skin side up and sprinkle with sesame seeds. Serve.

Keys to Tender, Flavorful Sticky Chicken

GET THE TEMPERATURE RIGHT
We cook the chicken thighs to 195 degrees (well beyond the temperature at which they're safe to eat) to melt their tough connective tissues while keeping the meat moist.

THICKEN THE GLAZE
For a sticky, shiny glaze that is sure to cling tightly to the cooked chicken, we reduce the cornstarch-thickened sauce until it's syrupy and a spatula leaves a trail when dragged through it.

Mozzarella Sticks

We wanted to enjoy this warm, crunchy, gooey restaurant favorite at home.

BY ASHLEY MOORE

WHEN WORD GOT out that I was working on a recipe for mozzarella sticks, a restaurant favorite that few people make at home, I quickly became the most popular cook in the test kitchen.

I started by testing five existing recipes. The results ranged from exploded sticks of cheese with barely any bread crumbs to chunky, bread-heavy spears with hardly any cheese. But while the results were disappointing, I learned a trick or two.

For one thing, a handful of these recipes called for freezing the coated mozzarella sticks before frying—frozen sticks proved less likely to explode during frying. And while some recipes call for string cheese, my tasters and I preferred sticks cut from a block of actual mozzarella. For the breading, standard bread crumbs proved dusty and prone to sogginess; panko-style crumbs provided the most rewarding crunch. I stitched together a working recipe and hit the kitchen.

I cut the mozzarella into ½-inch-wide planks and cut each plank into three "sticks." I coated each stick using our standard breading procedure (dredge in flour, dip in beaten egg, and press on bread crumbs) and placed the breaded sticks in the freezer. After an hour, I fried them. The panko, though pleasantly crunchy, was too coarse to make a solid coating and left gaps where the cheese could leak out. I decided to give the bread crumbs a spin in the food processor until they were finely ground, hoping they'd form a more cohesive coating. This did the trick.

I dropped one last batch of mozzarella sticks into the frying oil. After just 1 minute in the 400-degree oil, they were a lovely shade of golden brown. I used a spider to remove the sticks, set them on paper towels to let them cool slightly, called down my team, and waited for feedback. It was positive, and it came not in words but in smiles.

MOZZARELLA STICKS
Serves 4 to 6

Do not use fresh or part-skim mozzarella in this recipe; their high moisture content can cause the sticks to rupture in the hot oil. This recipe was developed with Sorrento Galbani Whole Milk Mozzarella, which is the test kitchen's favorite. We do not recommend using string cheese. Use a Dutch oven that holds 6 quarts or more for this recipe.

- 1 pound whole-milk mozzarella cheese
- ½ cup all-purpose flour
- 2 large eggs
- 2 cups panko bread crumbs
- ½ teaspoon salt
- ½ teaspoon pepper
- ¼ teaspoon dried oregano
- ¼ teaspoon garlic powder
- 2 quarts peanut or vegetable oil
- 1 cup jarred marinara sauce, warmed

1. Set wire rack in rimmed baking sheet and line half of rack with triple layer of paper towels. Slice mozzarella crosswise into six ½-inch-wide planks. Cut each plank lengthwise into 3 equal sticks. (You will have 18 pieces.)

2. Spread flour in shallow dish. Beat eggs in second shallow dish. Pulse panko, salt, pepper, oregano, and garlic powder in food processor until finely ground, about 10 pulses; transfer to third shallow dish.

3. Working with 1 piece at a time, coat sticks with flour, shaking to remove excess; dip in eggs, allowing excess to drip off; and dredge in panko mixture, pressing to adhere. Transfer to plate. Freeze sticks until firm, at least 1 hour or up to 2 hours.

4. Add oil to large Dutch oven until it measures about 1½ inches deep and heat over medium-high heat to 400 degrees. Add 6 sticks to hot oil and fry until deeply browned on all sides, about 1 minute. Adjust burner as necessary to maintain oil temperature between 375 and 400 degrees.

5. Transfer sticks to paper towel–lined side of prepared rack to drain for 30 seconds, then move to unlined side of rack. Return oil to 400 degrees and repeat frying in 2 more batches with remaining 12 sticks. Serve with marinara.

Freezing the breaded sticks for an hour before frying keeps the coating intact.

TO MAKE AHEAD
Mozzarella sticks can be prepared through step 3 and frozen in zipper-lock bag or airtight container for up to 1 month. After frying (do not thaw sticks), let sticks rest for 3 minutes before serving to allow residual heat to continue to melt centers.

PROBLEM SOLVING **Mozzarella Sticks Gone Wrong**

PROBLEM
Coarse coating doesn't fully cover cheese and leaves gaps.
SOLUTION
Process panko in food processor until finely ground.

PROBLEM
Sticks explode and create gooey mess.
SOLUTION
Use whole-milk mozzarella cheese and briefly freeze sticks after breading them.

PROBLEM
Cheese sticks are greasy and soggy.
SOLUTION
Fry in 400-degree oil for crispy—not greasy—results.

Devils on Horseback

This retro appetizer is easy to love. We wanted it to be easy to make, too.

BY CECELIA JENKINS

DEVILS ON HORSEBACK are dates or prunes stuffed with cheese and wrapped in bacon. Alone, each ingredient—supersweet dates, pungent blue cheese, and salty, meaty bacon—is capable of an intense cocktail-hour performance. But when they play together, they have the potential to be transformative. Or disastrous.

Making this appetizer can be tedious, time-consuming, and messy, and you run the risk of ending up with burnt or flabby bacon, grease-soaked dates, and cheese that oozes onto the pan to burn. I set out to create a quick and effective assembly process that would keep all the parts in the right places.

After trying a range of recipes, I found prunes too difficult to work with, and my tasters balked at the ropey texture of larger Medjool dates. I settled on more common pitted Deglet Noor dates for their manageable size, tender texture, and ample room for stuffing.

But stuffing cheese into the dates' small holes gave me a headache. Splitting the dates open with a paring knife proved to be the answer (their natural stickiness helped them seal back up nicely), but portioning the creamy blue cheese was a pain. Using a ¼-teaspoon measure to scoop portions of it left more on my fingers than in the dates, and trying to cut the wedge into pieces gunked up my knife and turned my cutting board into a sticky disaster zone. A coworker suggested freezing the cheese. Exasperated, I threw the chunk of cheese in the freezer and walked away. We both needed to chill out.

I returned a bit later to take another swing and, happily, found the fresh-out-of-the-freezer cheese much easier to work with. It was easy to crumble the cold cheese, and the crumbles fit perfectly in the dates and stayed put.

Wrapping the filled dates in bacon slices and securing each with a tooth pick, I placed them directly on a baking sheet and baked them at 450 degrees, assuming that the high temperature and direct contact with the hot sheet would quickly crisp the bacon. Reaching into a smoky oven to flip them, I found nothing but burnt devils swimming in grease.

I needed to slow the cooking and get the devils out of the grease. I reduced the oven temperature to 400 degrees and grabbed a wire rack, setting it in my baking sheet to elevate the devils and allow them to shed grease. And rather than use a full slice of bacon for each date, I cut the slices in half crosswise. They overlapped just a bit but rendered beautifully nonetheless, with no residual gumminess. And with the rack in play, I didn't need to individually flip each devil over halfway through baking.

Since I was opening, stuffing, wrapping, and skewering 32 devils, I was looking for just one step fewer. Hopeful, I assembled another batch (omitting the toothpick skewering step) and positioned them seam side down on the rack. To my satisfaction, as the bacon cooked, it closed tightly around the dates, making the toothpicks superfluous. I instead placed toothpicks on the serving platter for my tasters to use to spear and eat the devils—which they devoured in mere minutes.

One last discovery: I found that you can freeze the fully assembled devils and bake them straight from the freezer for a holiday crowd-pleaser in minutes.

DEVILS ON HORSEBACK
Makes 32 pieces

Use tender dates that measure at least 1¼ inches in length; smaller, drier dates are difficult to stuff. Do not use Medjool dates or thick-cut bacon in this recipe. Freezing the blue cheese for 20 minutes makes it easier to crumble. Our preferred supermarket blue cheese is Stella Blue.

- 4 ounces blue cheese
- 32 pitted Deglet Noor dates, about 1¼ inches long
- 16 slices bacon

1. Adjust oven rack to middle position and heat oven to 400 degrees. Set wire rack in aluminum foil–lined rimmed baking sheet. Freeze blue cheese until firm, about 20 minutes.

2. Cut through 1 long side of each date and open like book. Crumble blue cheese and divide evenly among dates. Close dates around blue cheese and squeeze lightly to seal (dates should be full but not overflowing).

3. Lay bacon slices on cutting board and halve each slice crosswise. Working with 1 date at a time, place blue cheese–filled date on end of 1 halved bacon slice and roll to enclose date. Place wrapped dates seam side down on prepared rack.

4. Bake until bacon is browned, 27 to 30 minutes, rotating sheet halfway through baking. Let cool for 10 minutes. Serve with toothpicks.

TO MAKE AHEAD

Devils on Horseback can be assembled through step 3 and frozen seam side down on rimmed baking sheet. Frozen pieces can be transferred to zipper-lock bag and frozen for up to 1 month. Increase baking time by 8 to 10 minutes.

Assembling Devils on Horseback

Rather than building one devil at a time, we prefer an assembly-line approach, completing each step for all 32 devils before moving on.

1. Cut through one long side of each date.

2. Stuff each date with blue cheese and squeeze the opening to seal it. (To make the cheese easier to work with, freeze it for 20 minutes and then crumble it.)

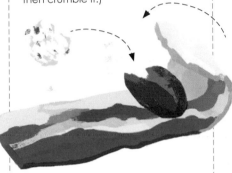

3. Place the date on the end of a half-slice of bacon. Roll to enclose the date.

4. Bake the devils seam side down on a wire rack so that the bacon fuses while cooking, making sealing them with toothpicks unnecessary.

Elevating the devils on a wire rack while baking gives us crisp, not soggy, results.

Getting to Know Dried Herbs

Dried herbs can be more complex and flavorful than fresh. We use them in many dishes—and not just in a pinch.

BY CHRISTIE MORRISON

Oregano
DUAL IDENTITY

Most of the oregano found in U.S. stores is native to Europe, but you can also find Mexican oregano. The two plants are from different genuses, but both contain carvacrol, the essential oil that gives oregano its characteristic flavor. We found European oregano earthy, slightly sweet, and milder than robust Mexican oregano, but the two can be used interchangeably.

Rosemary
PINEY NEEDLES

Dried rosemary isn't a bad substitute for fresh in terms of flavor, but the hard dried needles work best in long-cooked dishes like soups, stews, and braises, where they can soften during cooking. Dried rosemary flavors our Montreal Seasoned Salt Blend (**CooksCountry.com/montrealsalt**) and goes well with most grilled meats. Use it sparingly.

Turkish Bay Leaves
LAUREL AND HEARTY

When a recipe calls for bay leaves, it generally means Turkish bay, with its tea-like (with a hint of menthol) flavor. Bay leaves don't play a leading role but contribute to the overall savory flavor of stocks and soups. We particularly like them in our Arroz con Pollo (**CooksCountry.com/arrozconpollo**). To maintain potency, freeze bay leaves in a zipper-lock bag.

Dill
RANCH HAND

Dried dill is a signature flavor in Eastern European and Scandinavian cuisines, where it lends bright, lemony, and grassy notes to all kinds of dishes. It's also one of the classic flavors in ranch dressing; we use it in our Buttermilk-Ranch Pita Chips (**CooksCountry.com/ranchpitachips**). Dried dill also works well with eggs, vegetables, poultry, and seafood.

Thyme
LESS IS MORE

Thyme's pungent, floral flavors make it well suited to red meat and poultry dishes. It's also common in blends like herbes de Provence, bouquet garni, and za'atar. Use a third as much dried thyme when substituting for fresh; its flavor is much more intense. Dried thyme contributes to the bold herb flavor of our Smoked Roast Beef (**CooksCountry.com/smokedroastbeef**).

Sage
THERE'S THE RUB

Sage leaves are sold whole, rubbed, or ground. To produce rubbed sage, the dried leaves are crumbled, while ground sage may include both finely ground leaves and stems. We prefer sage in its whole leaf form, but rubbed sage is a solid substitute for whole. Ground sage is dusty and bland, so we don't recommend it. When substituting for fresh sage, increase the amount called for by half.

California Bay Leaves
BOLD IMPOSTOR

These large, aromatic leaves are harvested from an evergreen tree native to California. Much more difficult to come by than Turkish bay leaves, dried California bay leaves have a potent, eucalyptus-like flavor that our tasters registered as medicinal, "like something you'd put in a cough drop." We advise against using California bay leaves unless specified in a recipe.

Tarragon
LICORICE LEAF

Tarragon, with its signature licorice flavor, is an herb we often use in its fresh form, but we've found that dried tarragon is a great addition to rubs, spice blends, and dressings, notably our recipe for Romaine Salad with Green Goddess Dressing (**CooksCountry.com/romainegoddess**). Be sure to store all dried herbs in a cool, dark, dry place; heat, light, and moisture can shorten their shelf life.

Marjoram
UNSUNG HERO

This pungent herb is especially good in bean, lamb, and beef dishes. A core ingredient in poultry seasoning and Bell's seasoning, marjoram is related to both oregano and mint, but its earthy, slightly musty flavor is more like that of oregano. Like other dried herbs, marjoram's flavor will fade over time; to test for freshness, rub some between your fingers. If it still smells bright, use it; otherwise, trash it.

Herbes de Provence
FRENCH MELANGE

This herb mix includes rosemary, marjoram, thyme, lavender, and fennel. We use it in our Slow-Cooker Ratatouille (**CooksCountry.com/slowratatouille**). If you can't find herbes de Provence, replace it with 2 teaspoons dried marjoram, 2 teaspoons dried thyme, 1 teaspoon dried basil, 1 teaspoon dried rosemary (crumbled), 1 teaspoon dried sage, ⅛ teaspoon ground fennel, and a pinch of lavender.

Italian Seasoning
POWER PLAYER

This blend combines all the characteristic flavors of Italy in a single jar. It typically contains oregano, marjoram, rosemary, basil, sage, thyme, and savory. These hearty flavors work best in long-cooking dishes, but you can add Italian seasoning to roasted potatoes or vegetables for a Mediterranean twist. Substitute Italian seasoning for oregano in our Mozzarella Sticks (page 14) for more complex flavor.

DON'T DO IT

Delicate leafy herbs such as basil, cilantro, and parsley become bland and musty when dried. Since they're generally used to finish a dish, substituting a dried version is texturally problematic; dried versions also lack the intensity of their fresh counterparts. If you can't use fresh, consider a different flavor profile.

CARAWAY PORK WITH SAUERKRAUT AND APPLES

TOMATILLO CHICKEN TOSTADAS

PAN-SEARED HADDOCK WITH BROCCOLI
AND OREGANO VINAIGRETTE

PASTA WITH CHICKEN SAUSAGE,
SWISS CHARD, AND WHITE BEANS

TOMATILLO CHICKEN TOSTADAS Serves 4

✓ **WHY THIS RECIPE WORKS:** By using jarred tomatillo (green) salsa, you can put this satisfying supper together in minutes.

- 1 tablespoon vegetable oil
- 1 (2½-pound) rotisserie chicken, skin and bones discarded, meat shredded into bite-size pieces (3 cups)
- 1 onion, chopped
- 2 cups tomatillo salsa
- 1 (16-ounce) can refried beans
- 8 (5-inch) corn tostadas, warmed
- 2 cups shredded iceberg lettuce
- 2 tomatoes, cored and chopped
- ½ cup sour cream
- ¼ cup chopped fresh cilantro

1. Heat oil in 12-inch nonstick skillet over medium-high heat until shimmering. Add chicken and onion and cook until onion is softened, about 5 minutes. Add salsa and cook until thickened, about 5 minutes. Cover and keep warm.

2. Place beans in bowl and microwave until hot, about 3 minutes, stirring halfway through microwaving. Divide beans among tostadas. Top each tostada with chicken mixture, lettuce, tomatoes, sour cream, and cilantro. Serve.

TEST KITCHEN NOTE: Our favorite jarred tomatillo salsa is made by Frontera.

CARAWAY PORK WITH SAUERKRAUT AND APPLES Serves 4

✓ **WHY THIS RECIPE WORKS:** Searing the caraway-coated pork toasts the seeds and brings out their full flavor and aroma.

- 2 (12- to 16-ounce) pork tenderloins, trimmed
- 1 tablespoon caraway seeds
  Salt and pepper
- 2 tablespoons vegetable oil
- 2 apples, cored, halved, and cut into ¼-inch-thick slices
- 1 onion, chopped fine
- 1 pound sauerkraut, rinsed and drained
- 2 tablespoons packed light brown sugar
- 2 tablespoons minced fresh dill

1. Adjust oven rack to middle position and heat oven to 475 degrees. Pat pork dry with paper towels and sprinkle with caraway seeds, 1 teaspoon salt, and ½ teaspoon pepper, pressing lightly to adhere. Heat 1 tablespoon oil in 12-inch skillet over medium-high heat until just smoking. Cook pork until browned on all sides, 5 to 7 minutes; transfer to plate.

2. Add remaining 1 tablespoon oil, apples, onion, ⅛ teaspoon salt, and ⅛ teaspoon pepper to now-empty skillet and cook over medium heat until softened, about 5 minutes, scraping up any browned bits. Stir in sauerkraut and sugar. Place pork on top of sauerkraut mixture. Bake until pork registers 140 degrees, about 13 minutes.

3. Transfer pork to cutting board, tent with foil, and let rest for 5 minutes. Stir dill into sauerkraut mixture and serve with pork.

TEST KITCHEN NOTE: There's no need to peel the apples for this dish; we prefer red-skinned Fujis or Galas to give the dish more color, but any sweet apple will do.

PASTA WITH CHICKEN SAUSAGE, SWISS CHARD, AND WHITE BEANS Serves 4

✓ **WHY THIS RECIPE WORKS:** The bean liquid thickens the sauce.

- 8 ounces spaghetti
  Salt and pepper
- 12 ounces Swiss chard, stems chopped fine, leaves sliced into ½-inch-wide strips
- 1 tablespoon extra-virgin olive oil, plus extra for drizzling
- 12 ounces cooked chicken sausage, halved lengthwise and sliced ½ inch thick
- 3 garlic cloves, minced
- 1 (15-ounce) can cannellini beans
- ½ cup chicken broth
- 2 ounces Pecorino Romano cheese, grated (1 cup)
- 1½ tablespoons lemon juice

1. Bring 4 quarts water to boil in large pot. Add pasta and 1 tablespoon salt and cook, stirring often, until just al dente. Add chard and cook until tender, about 1 minute. Drain pasta and chard and return to pot.

2. Meanwhile, heat oil in 12-inch skillet over medium heat until shimmering. Add sausage and cook, stirring occasionally, until well browned, about 8 minutes. Add garlic, ¼ teaspoon salt, and ¼ teaspoon pepper and cook until fragrant, about 30 seconds. Add beans and their liquid and broth and bring to boil, scraping up any browned bits.

3. Add ½ cup Pecorino, lemon juice, and sausage-bean mixture to pasta and toss to combine. Season with salt and pepper to taste. Serve, drizzled with extra oil and passing remaining ½ cup Pecorino separately.

TEST KITCHEN NOTE: Our favorite canned cannellini beans are from Goya. For a spicy kick, add a pinch of red pepper flakes with the Pecorino.

PAN-SEARED HADDOCK WITH BROCCOLI AND OREGANO VINAIGRETTE Serves 4

✓ **WHY THIS RECIPE WORKS:** Mayonnaise adheres the bread crumbs to the haddock without a messy breading process.

- 1 pound broccoli florets, cut into 2-inch pieces
- ½ cup extra-virgin olive oil
  Salt and pepper
- 2 tablespoons minced fresh oregano
- 2 tablespoons minced fresh parsley
- 1 tablespoon lemon juice, plus lemon wedges for serving
- 1 small garlic clove, minced
- ½ cup panko bread crumbs
- 4 (6- to 8-ounce) skinless haddock fillets, 1 inch thick
- 4 teaspoons mayonnaise

1. Adjust oven rack to lowest position and heat oven to 450 degrees. Toss broccoli with 2 tablespoons oil, ¼ teaspoon salt, and ¼ teaspoon pepper on rimmed baking sheet. Roast until browned and tender, 14 to 16 minutes.

2. Meanwhile, combine oregano, parsley, lemon juice, garlic, ¼ cup oil, ¼ teaspoon salt, and ¼ teaspoon pepper in bowl; set aside. Place panko in shallow dish. Pat haddock dry with paper towels and season with salt and pepper. Spread 1 teaspoon mayonnaise on 1 side of each fillet. Press mayonnaise-coated sides of fillets into panko.

3. Heat remaining 2 tablespoons oil in 12-inch nonstick skillet over medium heat until shimmering. Place fillets panko side down in skillet and cook until browned, about 7 minutes. Flip fillets and cook until fish registers 140 degrees, about 2 minutes. Serve with broccoli, vinaigrette, and lemon wedges.

TEST KITCHEN NOTE: The vinaigrette will separate after 5 to 10 minutes; rewhisk before serving. If you can't find haddock, you can use cod here.

**PECAN-STUFFED PORK CHOPS WITH
MASHED SWEET POTATOES**

MEATBALL SUBS

CREAMY GNOCCHI WITH MUSHROOMS

STEAK WITH DIJON GREEN BEAN–POTATO SALAD

MEATBALL SUBS Serves 4

✓ **WHY THIS RECIPE WORKS:** From making the meatballs to heating the sauce and melting the cheese, this entire recipe happens in the oven, avoiding stovetop splatter.

- 1 tablespoon olive oil
- 1¼ pounds 85 percent lean ground beef
- ¾ cup dried bread crumbs with Italian seasonings
- 2 large eggs, lightly beaten
- 1 teaspoon garlic powder
- 1 teaspoon salt
- ½ teaspoon pepper
- 4 (6-inch) Italian sub rolls, split lengthwise
- 1⅓ cups jarred marinara sauce
- 4 thin slices deli provolone cheese (4 ounces)

1. Adjust oven rack to middle position and heat oven to 400 degrees. Grease rimmed baking sheet with oil. Mix beef, bread crumbs, eggs, garlic powder, salt, and pepper in bowl until well combined. Form mixture into twelve 2-inch meatballs, place on prepared sheet, and bake until browned and meat registers 160 degrees, about 15 minutes. Transfer meatballs to plate; discard accumulated grease on sheet.

2. Carefully line now-empty sheet with parchment paper. Place rolls on sheet and lay 3 meatballs inside each roll. Top meatballs on each sandwich with ⅓ cup marinara sauce and 1 slice provolone. Bake until cheese is melted and sauce is heated through, about 5 minutes. Serve.

TEST KITCHEN NOTE: Our favorite premium jarred sauce is Victoria Marinara Sauce.

PECAN-STUFFED PORK CHOPS WITH MASHED SWEET POTATOES Serves 4

✓ **WHY THIS RECIPE WORKS:** Garlicky Boursin is a good stuffing base.

- 4 (6- to 8-ounce) boneless pork chops, ¾ to 1 inch thick, trimmed
- ½ (5.2-ounce) package Boursin Garlic & Fine Herbs cheese
- ¼ cup pecans, toasted and chopped fine
  Salt and pepper
- 3 tablespoons unsalted butter
- 2 pounds sweet potatoes, peeled and cut into ½-inch pieces
- 1½ cups water
- ¼ cup heavy cream
- ⅛ teaspoon cayenne pepper
- 2 tablespoons minced fresh chives

1. Using paring knife, cut 2-inch opening in side of each chop and create pocket. Mash Boursin and pecans together in bowl. Stuff pockets evenly with cheese mixture, then seal pockets with toothpicks. Pat chops dry with paper towels and season with salt and pepper.

2. Melt 1 tablespoon butter in 12-inch nonstick skillet over medium heat. Add chops and cook until well browned on first side, about 6 minutes. Flip chops, cover, and cook until meat registers 140 degrees, about 6 minutes. Transfer chops to plate, discard toothpicks, and tent with aluminum foil.

3. Combine potatoes, water, remaining 2 tablespoons butter, 1 teaspoon salt, and ½ teaspoon pepper in now-empty skillet. Cover and bring to simmer over medium-high heat. Cook until potatoes are tender, about 10 minutes. Uncover and continue to cook until almost dry, about 2 minutes longer. Off heat, stir in cream and cayenne; mash with potato masher until smooth. Serve potatoes with chops, sprinkled with chives.

TEST KITCHEN NOTE: You will need four sturdy, plain toothpicks.

STEAK WITH DIJON GREEN BEAN–POTATO SALAD Serves 4

✓ **WHY THIS RECIPE WORKS:** To ensure that the potatoes and green beans effectively absorb the vinaigrette, we dress them while they are still hot.

- 1½ pounds small red potatoes, unpeeled, halved
  Salt and pepper
- 8 ounces green beans, trimmed and cut into 1½-inch lengths
- 6 tablespoons extra-virgin olive oil
- ¼ cup chopped fresh parsley
- 2 tablespoons Dijon mustard
- 2 tablespoons white wine vinegar
- 1 small shallot, minced
- 2 (1-pound) boneless strip or rib-eye steaks, about 1 inch thick, trimmed and halved crosswise

1. Bring 2 quarts water to boil in large saucepan over medium-high heat. Add potatoes and 1½ tablespoons salt; return to boil and cook for 10 minutes. Add green beans and cook until both vegetables are tender, about 5 minutes. Drain.

2. Whisk 5 tablespoons oil, parsley, mustard, vinegar, shallot, and ½ teaspoon pepper together in large bowl. Add hot vegetables to bowl with dressing and toss gently to combine. Season with salt and pepper to taste.

3. Pat steaks dry with paper towels and season with salt and pepper. Heat remaining 1 tablespoon oil in 12-inch skillet over medium-high heat until just smoking. Cook steaks until well browned and meat registers 125 degrees (for medium-rare), 3 to 5 minutes per side. Serve steaks with salad.

TEST KITCHEN NOTE: Use small red potatoes measuring 1 to 2 inches in diameter.

CREAMY GNOCCHI WITH MUSHROOMS Serves 4

✓ **WHY THIS RECIPE WORKS:** Combining vegetable broth with Parmesan and just a touch of cream makes a velvety sauce that doesn't weigh down the gnocchi.

- 1¼ cups vegetable broth
- 2 ounces Parmesan cheese, grated (1 cup)
- ¼ cup heavy cream
- ⅛ teaspoon ground nutmeg
  Salt and pepper
- 3 tablespoons unsalted butter
- 1 pound vacuum-packed gnocchi
- 1 pound cremini mushrooms, trimmed and quartered
- 2 garlic cloves, minced
- ¼ cup fresh basil leaves, torn

1. Whisk broth, Parmesan, cream, nutmeg, and ½ teaspoon pepper together in bowl; set aside. Melt 2 tablespoons butter in 12-inch nonstick skillet over medium-high heat. Add gnocchi and cook until lightly browned, about 5 minutes; transfer to plate.

2. Melt remaining 1 tablespoon butter in now-empty skillet over medium-high heat. Add mushrooms and ¼ teaspoon salt and cook until golden brown, about 10 minutes. Stir in garlic and cook until fragrant, about 30 seconds. Add broth mixture and gnocchi and bring to simmer. Cook, stirring occasionally, until sauce has thickened, 5 to 7 minutes. Sprinkle with basil and serve.

TEST KITCHEN NOTE: The partially cooked, vacuum-packed gnocchi found in the pasta aisle work best here, but refrigerated or frozen gnocchi can also be used.

Marinated Beet Salad

Could we bring people together over these divisive roots? BY KATIE LEAIRD

BEETS CAN BE a tough sell. Haters say they taste like dirt and are a pain to prepare. But my Estonian-American mother loves beets, and I know in my Baltic heart that they have the potential to be sweet, earthy jewels.

Much of beets' baggage lies in their skins, which must be removed. Just taking a peeler to them will work, but it will also dye your hands a semipermanent purple. What's more, when I peeled and roasted a few beets (I chose roasting to concentrate their sweetness), the outside layer became tough and leathery.

It turns out that beet skins do a bang-up job of protecting the insides while the beets are in the oven, yielding deeply sweet, evenly cooked vegetables. And as the beets' juice converts to steam in the oven, the skins loosen their grip, making them easy to remove. I found that wrapping the skin-on beets in foil with a little water made things even easier; while the beets were still warm, I easily slipped the skins off without using any tool other than my hands.

What makes beets so beautiful is also what makes them such a mess: the vibrant red-hued juice, which stains hands and clothes (and cutting boards). To minimize staining, I held each warm beet in one hand with a paper towel and used another paper towel to rub off its skin. I did this over the foil I'd just unwrapped to catch any juice dribbles and keep my cutting board clean.

Once they were skinned, I cut up the still-warm beets and tossed them with sherry vinegar, olive oil, and fresh thyme. The dressing's vinegar balanced the vegetable's sweetness, and the thyme played perfectly with the beets' earthy flavors.

To create a sturdy framework for these rubies, I laid down a bed of peppery arugula. I drizzled the remaining marinade (whatever the beets hadn't soaked up) over the greens and scattered the beets over top. Just before serving, I added orange segments, Pecorino Romano cheese, and chopped walnuts. Hate away, beet foes. More salad for me.

> ▶ Beets are not the only root. Learn about other options at **CooksCountry. com/rootveg.**

MARINATED BEET SALAD WITH ORANGES AND PECORINO Serves 6

To ensure even cooking, look for beets of similar size—roughly 2 to 3 inches in diameter. Red or golden beets work equally well in this recipe. Peel the cooked beets over the leftover foil packet to minimize mess.

- 1 **pound beets, trimmed**
- ½ **cup water**
- ¼ **cup sherry vinegar**
- 2 **tablespoons extra-virgin olive oil, plus extra for drizzling**
- 1 **teaspoon fresh thyme leaves Salt and pepper**
- 2 **oranges**
- 4 **ounces (4 cups) baby arugula**
- 2 **ounces Pecorino Romano cheese, shaved with vegetable peeler**
- ½ **cup walnuts, toasted and chopped coarse**

1. Adjust oven rack to middle position and heat oven to 400 degrees. Place 16 by 12-inch piece of aluminum foil on rimmed baking sheet. Arrange beets in center of foil and lift sides of foil to form bowl. Add water to beets and crimp foil tightly to seal. Roast until beets can be pierced easily with fork, 1¼ to 1½ hours.

2. Once beets are cool enough to handle, rub off skins with paper towels. Halve each beet vertically, then cut into ½-inch-thick wedges.

3. Whisk vinegar, oil, thyme, ½ teaspoon salt, and ¼ teaspoon pepper together in large bowl. Add beets and toss to combine. Cover and refrigerate for at least 30 minutes or up to 24 hours.

4. Cut away peel and pith from oranges. Holding fruit over bowl, use paring knife to slice between membranes to release segments; set aside. Arrange arugula on serving platter. Spoon beets over arugula and drizzle with remaining marinade. Arrange orange segments over salad and top with Pecorino and walnuts. Season with salt and pepper to taste. Drizzle with extra oil and serve.

MARINATED BEET SALAD WITH PEAR AND FETA

Substitute 1 halved, cored, and thinly sliced pear for oranges; ¾ cup crumbled feta for Pecorino; and 2 tablespoons toasted pistachios for walnuts.

MARINATED BEET SALAD WITH RASPBERRIES AND BLUE CHEESE

Substitute ⅔ cup raspberries for oranges, ¾ cup crumbled blue cheese for Pecorino, and skinned hazelnuts for walnuts.

Shaved Pecorino Romano cheese adds a salty, creamy element to this vibrant salad.

TEST KITCHEN TECHNIQUES
How to Segment an Orange

Using a paring knife, cut toward the center, between the pulp and the membrane of each segment.

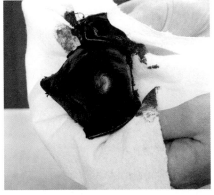

How to Peel Beets

Peel roasted beets by rubbing them with paper towels. The skins should slide right off. For easy cleanup, do this over the foil used for roasting the beets.

Potato and Leek Gratin

There's nothing wrong with your standard potato gratin.
But we wanted something a bit more elegant. BY ASHLEY MOORE

AN IDEAL POTATO gratin is soft and creamy inside and cheesy, crunchy, and crispy on top. Throw some tender leeks into the mix and you'll get their mild, slightly grassy, onion-like flavor in every bite. Seems easy enough, right? Not so fast.

I surrounded myself with stacks of French cookbooks full of potato gratin recipes and selected five that varied in method and ingredients. In one mad afternoon I cleaned dozens of leeks, sliced pounds of potatoes, grated massive blocks of cheese, baked five gratins, and set them out for my tasters. One looked like mashed potatoes. Another had dark, woody leek shards poking out around the perimeter. One featured a broken, stodgy sauce. And despite all those leeks, none had any leek flavor to speak of; it was especially lacking in the gratins with the most cream. So I learned at least one thing: Broth would be my primary base, and if I was going to use any cream, it wouldn't be much.

Back at my workstation, I cut up another 2 pounds of potatoes and thinly sliced an equal amount of leeks. I thoroughly soaked and cleaned my sliced leeks before cooking them in a skillet with white wine, chicken broth, and a bit of cream to create a leeky sauce. I tossed the potatoes and leeks together in a baking dish, sprinkled the top with shredded Gruyère cheese, and then baked the gratin until the potatoes were tender. My gratin looked promising straight out of the oven, but as I spooned portions out of the dish, I was struck by the unpleasant color—a light green, slightly yellow hue that looked more like a mistake than a triumph. What's more, the leeks were unappealingly slimy.

To help avoid slippery leeks in my next test, I tried cutting them into bigger pieces, about ½ inch thick. And rather than stir the sauce into the leeks on the stovetop, I simply softened the leeks in the skillet by themselves (with a bit of garlic for punch) and then transferred them to a bowl. I then cooked my sauce—wine, broth, and cream—in the now-empty skillet.

I layered half the softened leeks on the bottom of my baking dish, topped them with half the sliced potatoes, repeated the process, and poured the sauce over the top. I topped it all with a generous sprinkling of Gruyère

and baked it until the potatoes were tender and the cheesy top was covered in lovely brown spots. After letting it cool for 15 minutes, we dug in: perfect potatoes, vibrant and flavorful leeks, a luxurious sauce—and not a bit of slime to be found.

POTATO AND LEEK GRATIN
Serves 6 to 8

Do not prepare the potatoes ahead of time or store them in water; the potato starch is essential for thickening the sauce. A mandoline makes quick work of slicing the potatoes.

- 2 tablespoons unsalted butter
- 2 pounds leeks, white and light green parts only, quartered lengthwise, sliced ½ inch thick, and washed thoroughly
  Salt and pepper
- 4 garlic cloves, minced
- ½ cup dry white wine
- 1 cup chicken broth
- ½ cup heavy cream
- 2 pounds large Yukon Gold potatoes, peeled and sliced ⅛ inch thick
- 2 teaspoons minced fresh thyme
- 4 ounces Gruyère cheese, shredded (1 cup)

1. Adjust oven rack to middle position and heat oven to 350 degrees. Grease 13 by 9-inch baking dish. Melt butter in 12-inch skillet over medium-high heat. Add leeks and ¾ teaspoon salt and cook, stirring occasionally, until softened, 5 to 7 minutes. Add garlic and cook until fragrant, about 30 seconds; transfer to bowl.

2. Return skillet to medium-high heat, add wine, and cook until nearly evaporated, about 2 minutes, scraping up any browned bits. Add broth and cream and bring to simmer; cook until slightly thickened and reduced to 1¼ cups, 3 to 5 minutes.

3. Toss potatoes, thyme, 1 teaspoon salt, and ½ teaspoon pepper together in separate bowl. Spread half of leeks evenly in prepared dish. Arrange half of potatoes over leeks. Spread remaining leeks over potatoes. Arrange remaining potatoes evenly over leeks. Pour broth-cream mixture over potatoes and sprinkle with Gruyère.

4. Bake until potatoes are tender and cheese is spotty brown, about 45 minutes. Let cool for 15 minutes. Serve.

Cooking the leeks and the sauce separately before combining the components to bake is key.

TEST KITCHEN TECHNIQUE Preparing Leeks

Only the white and pale green parts of a leek are tender. Save the tough, dark green leaves in the freezer for making stock.

FIRST CHOP
Cut away the dark green leaves. Quarter the white and pale green portions lengthwise. Slice ½ inch thick.

THEN WASH
Place the leeks in a salad spinner full of water, swishing to wash. Lift the basket to drain the leeks, leaving any dirt behind. Spin dry.

Rice and Sausage Casserole

Is it a stuffing? A dressing? This surprising dish is neither, but it belongs on the Thanksgiving table.

BY MORGAN BOLLING

THOUGH I HAVE a large and varied repertoire of rice-based side dishes—a fortunate result of my Carolina childhood—I wanted to create a new one that was versatile, flavorful, and easy enough to slide into a Thanksgiving lineup. I pored over recipes ranging from old family favorites to recipes from Southern-cuisine stalwarts like Nathalie Dupree and John Folse.

My tests illuminated two things: Tasters liked simple recipes that mirrored the flavors of Thanksgiving dressing. And some loved the meatiness in recipes like dirty rice, a New Orleans favorite that includes sautéed chicken livers or giblets (some, of course, did not love this direction—giblets can be divisive). I decided to pursue a hybrid version.

My first hurdle was the rice, which I assumed I'd have to precook. For such a simple ingredient, rice can be a headache—even some of the pros in the test kitchen have trouble (I've seen the scorched pots to prove it). One option was to cook the rice using the standard absorption method. Another was to boil the rice in water and drain it like pasta. Both vexed me. So when a coworker suggested I assemble my casserole with raw rice and plenty of liquid, I was game but doubtful.

I combined 4 cups of water, 2 cups of raw rice, some browned sausage, and some celery and onions that I had sautéed with garlic, sage, and seasonings in a baking dish, covered the dish, and slid it into a 350-degree oven for an hour.

The results were promising—nicely steamed rice and plenty of flavor. Some grains were uncooked, and the flavor was inconsistent, but a few adjustments solved these bugaboos: First, I swapped the water for 3 cups of chicken broth, which gave the dish a more savory backbone. I then added a little white wine for acidity and sweetness and some cream, which helped the overall texture. Boiling this liquid before pouring it over the rice-and-sausage mixture helped even out the cooking and shortened the time as well—from more than an hour to 40 minutes. To freshen everything up before serving, I used a fork to fluff up the rice and incorporate some chopped parsley.

A Thanksgiving stuffing? Not quite. But I have no doubt that this flavorful, satisfying, and multitextured side dish will be front and center on my table.

RICE AND SAUSAGE CASSEROLE
Serves 8 to 10

Lundberg Organic Long-Grain White Rice is the test kitchen's favorite long-grain rice. To minimize the loss of liquid through evaporation, transfer the broth mixture to the rice as soon as it comes to a boil.

- 2 cups long-grain white rice
- 8 ounces bulk pork sausage
- 2 onions, chopped fine
- 1 large celery rib, minced
  Salt and pepper
- 2 tablespoons minced fresh sage
- 3 garlic cloves, minced
- 3 cups chicken broth
- ½ cup dry white wine
- ½ cup heavy cream
- ¼ cup chopped fresh parsley

1. Adjust oven rack to middle position and heat oven to 350 degrees. Spread rice in 13 by 9-inch baking dish.

2. Cook sausage in large saucepan over medium-high heat until no longer pink, 4 to 6 minutes, breaking up meat with spoon. Add onions, celery, 1¼ teaspoons salt, and ½ teaspoon pepper and cook until vegetables are softened, 5 to 7 minutes, scraping up any browned bits. Add sage and garlic and cook until fragrant, about 30 seconds.

3. Stir in broth, wine, and cream and bring to boil. Once boiling, immediately pour over rice in baking dish. Cover dish tightly with double layer of aluminum foil. Bake until rice is tender, 40 to 45 minutes. Remove from oven and let stand, covered, for 10 minutes. Fluff rice with fork and stir in parsley. Season with salt and pepper to taste. Serve.

Brussels Sprouts with Bacon

Roasted sprouts are satisfying on their own; savory bacon and sweet onion only make them better.

BY DIANE UNGER

MY GO-TO METHOD for roasting Brussels sprouts is to toss halved sprouts with olive oil, throw them on a baking sheet, and roast them cut side down at 475 degrees for about 15 minutes. The bottoms caramelize, the insides soften, and even sprout haters admit to enjoying them. But for the holidays, I pictured my roasted sprouts surrounded by crispy bacon and caramelized onions. I just needed to work out the details.

I tossed ¼-inch pieces of thick-cut bacon and a sliced onion with the halved sprouts, transferred the mix to a baking sheet, and put the sheet in the oven. At the 15-minute mark, the sprouts were tender, but the bacon was still flabby and the onion still crunchy. I let them continue to roast until the bacon and onion were where I wanted them to be, but by that point, my sprouts were way overcooked. Clearly, the bacon and onion had to have a jump start before I added the sprouts.

For my next test, I arranged the bacon pieces on one half of the sheet and then scattered the oil-coated onion over the other half. I slid the sheet into the oven for about 8 minutes, until the bacon was starting to brown, and then added the sprouts to the sheet. I stirred everything together, being careful to nestle the sprouts down onto the sheet to ensure contact. After 15 more minutes in the oven, the bacon was crispy, the onion was tender, and the sprouts were perfectly cooked—pleasantly brown and coated in flavorful bacon fat. A perfect holiday side dish.

ROASTED BRUSSELS SPROUTS WITH BACON AND ONION
Serves 4 to 6

Choose Brussels sprouts that are similar in size to ensure even cooking. To keep the sprouts' leaves intact, be sure to trim just a small amount from of the stem before halving the sprouts.

- 1½ pounds Brussels sprouts, trimmed and halved
- 2 tablespoons olive oil
- 1 onion, halved and sliced ¼ inch thick
- 3 slices thick-cut bacon, cut into ¼-inch pieces
- ¼ teaspoon salt
- ¼ teaspoon pepper

1. Adjust oven rack to lowest position and heat oven to 475 degrees. Spray rimmed baking sheet with vegetable oil spray. Toss sprouts and 1 tablespoon oil together in large bowl and set aside. Toss onion and remaining 1 tablespoon oil together in small bowl. Arrange onion in even layer on half of prepared sheet. Arrange bacon in even layer on other half of sheet. Cook until bacon begins to brown and onion begins to soften, 7 to 9 minutes.

2. Remove sheet from oven and transfer to wire rack. Add sprouts to sheet and stir to combine bacon, onion, and sprouts. Flip sprouts cut side down and nestle into sheet. Return sheet to oven and continue to cook until sprouts are deep golden brown and bacon is crispy, 15 to 17 minutes longer. Sprinkle with salt and pepper. Transfer to platter and serve.

Apple Pandowdy

Say bye-bye to pie (for now) and howdy to Apple Pandowdy.

BY CECELIA JENKINS

ONE OF MANY old-school New England desserts with funny names (slumps, grunts, etc.), an apple pandowdy is pie or biscuit dough casually laid atop a pan of apple filling and baked. It's similar to a skillet pie, but during baking, the crust is pressed or slashed into the filling so the juices flood over the top crust and caramelize in the oven. That's right, you purposefully mess up the top of your dessert, a process called "dowdying," which leaves a dowdy-looking but eminently delicious result.

The inventor's name is lost to history, but way back in the colonial era (and even before), this counterintuitive process helped soften tough dough to make it easier to eat. The happy side effect was a dessert with layers of texture (some crisp, some soft) and an unexpected range of deep, sweet flavors.

These days, using modern kitchen equipment and more-standardized ingredients, we can easily create delicate crusts, so softening the dough is no longer an urgent goal. But I did want that caramelized top—along with perfectly cooked apples and a thick, syrupy sauce to drizzle over a side of vanilla ice cream.

Existing recipes confused me. Some called for dowdying the dough before baking and others halfway through, while still others instructed you to wait until after baking. But reading through them made it clear that I'd have to nail down my filling first. I started with Granny Smith apples, which held their shape during baking but turned unpleasantly acidic once cooked. Golden Delicious apples, however, remained sweet and buttery and just firm enough. And while many old recipes called for molasses as a sweetener, I found it far too intense. Instead, I chose brown sugar (for gentler molasses flavor) and a bit of tart apple cider and lemon juice for balance. I knew I'd have to precook the apples briefly; doing so helps set their pectin, allowing them to hold their shape while concurrently softening as they cook. Done. I was back to the dough.

Placing a round of homemade all-butter dough (to which I added just a tablespoon of sour cream for tang) over the cooked apples and pressing it into the filling raw before baking it off was a disaster—I ended up with

Sweet Golden Delicious apples create a flavorful syrup that goes beautifully with vanilla ice cream.

cardboard. Dowdying the crust after it was fully baked only made it soggy. So I tried dowdying halfway through baking. This was the ticket; it first allowed the crust time to set up and then gave the flooded juices time to caramelize. I was onto something.

But my excitement was short-lived. Digging deeper, I found a mess of mushy apples. My dough, though dowdied, had resealed itself over the filling, leaving no escape for moisture and turning my filling into, essentially, applesauce. Simply slashing ventilation holes in the top wasn't enough either;

there was still too much moisture.

For my next test I cut my dough into 2½-inch squares and arranged them in a rough overlapping pattern. When I opened the oven halfway through baking to do my dowdying, I felt a jolt of excitement. The partial coverage and overlapping squares of dough appeared to be promoting ventilation, allowing the apples to keep their shape and not overcook. Plus, this new setup gave the crust even more textural contrast: sticky caramelization, flaky pastry, and a few soft spots. The juices were still too thin, but a simple cornstarch slurry fixed that

in my next round of testing, giving me a luxuriously syrupy sauce.

I'm always looking for shortcuts, so I decided to try the pandowdy using a store-bought pie crust. The results were totally disappointing, gummy and dull. A naturally denser product, store-bought crust turned gluey and didn't produce pandowdy's hallmark textures.

On my last day of testing, I scooped portions of pandowdy and served them with vanilla ice cream, drizzling a little extra syrup over top. I asked my tasters for feedback, but they were too busy licking their spoons to respond.

APPLE PANDOWDY Serves 6

Disturbing the crust, or "dowdying," allows juices from the filling to rise over the crust and caramelize as the dessert continues to bake. Removing the skillet from the oven allows you to properly press down on the crust. Do not use store-bought pie crust in this recipe; it yields gummy results.

PIE DOUGH

- 3 tablespoons ice water
- 1 tablespoon sour cream
- ⅔ cup (3⅓ ounces) all-purpose flour
- 1 teaspoon granulated sugar
- ½ teaspoon salt
- 6 tablespoons unsalted butter, cut into ¼-inch pieces and frozen for 15 minutes

FILLING

- 2½ pounds Golden Delicious apples, peeled, cored, halved, and cut into ½-inch-thick wedges
- ¼ cup packed (1¾ ounces) light brown sugar
- ½ teaspoon ground cinnamon
- ¼ teaspoon salt
- 3 tablespoons unsalted butter
- ¾ cup apple cider
- 1 tablespoon cornstarch
- 2 teaspoons lemon juice

TOPPING

- 1 tablespoon granulated sugar
- ¼ teaspoon ground cinnamon
- 1 large egg, lightly beaten

  Vanilla ice cream

1. FOR THE PIE DOUGH: Combine ice water and sour cream in bowl. Process flour, sugar, and salt in food processor until combined, about 3 seconds. Add butter and pulse until size of large peas, 6 to 8 pulses. Add sour cream mixture and pulse until dough forms large clumps and no dry flour remains, 3 to 6 pulses, scraping down sides of bowl as needed.

2. Form dough into 4-inch disk, wrap tightly in plastic wrap, and refrigerate for 1 hour. (Wrapped dough can be refrigerated for up to 2 days or frozen for up to 1 month. If frozen, let dough thaw completely on counter before rolling.)

3. Adjust oven rack to middle position and heat oven to 400 degrees. Let chilled dough sit on counter to soften slightly, about 5 minutes, before rolling. Roll dough into 10-inch circle on lightly floured counter. Using pizza cutter, cut dough into four 2½-inch-wide strips, then make four 2½-inch-wide perpendicular cuts to form squares. (Pieces around edges of dough will be smaller.) Transfer dough pieces to parchment paper–lined baking sheet, cover with plastic, and refrigerate until firm, at least 30 minutes.

4. FOR THE FILLING: Toss apples, sugar, cinnamon, and salt together in large bowl. Melt butter in 10-inch skillet over medium heat. Add apple mixture, cover, and cook until apples become slightly pliable and release their juice, about 10 minutes, stirring occasionally.

5. Whisk cider, cornstarch, and lemon juice in bowl until no lumps remain; add to skillet. Bring to simmer and cook, uncovered, stirring occasionally, until sauce is thickened, about 2 minutes. Off heat, press lightly on apples to form even layer.

6. FOR THE TOPPING: Combine sugar and cinnamon in small bowl. Working quickly, shingle dough pieces over filling until mostly covered, overlapping as needed. Brush dough pieces with egg and sprinkle with cinnamon sugar.

7. Bake until crust is slightly puffed and beginning to brown, about 15 minutes. Remove skillet from oven. Using back of large spoon, press down in center of crust until juices come up over top of crust. Repeat four more times around skillet. Make sure all apples are submerged and return skillet to oven. Continue to bake until crust is golden brown, about 15 minutes longer.

8. Transfer skillet to wire rack and let cool for at least 20 minutes. Serve with ice cream, drizzling extra sauce over top.

TEST KITCHEN TECHNIQUE **Assembling Apple Pandowdy**

ROLL AND CUT
Using pizza cutter, cut dough into 4 strips, then make 4 perpendicular cuts. Transfer pieces to parchment-lined baking sheet, cover with plastic, and refrigerate for 30 minutes.

SHINGLE PIECES
Working quickly, shingle dough pieces evenly over cooked filling until mostly covered, overlapping pieces as needed. (Arrangement doesn't need to be perfect.)

BRUSH WITH EGG
Using pastry brush, coat dough pieces with lightly beaten egg and then sprinkle with cinnamon sugar.

"Dowdy" is a verb meaning to gently press the crust into the filling with the back of a spoon. It sounds messy, but this step brings juices up over the crust to caramelize in the oven.

SCIENCE **Preventing Mushy Apples**

When raw apples are baked into a dessert like pandowdy, they often turn overly soft and applesauce-like. The solution to the problem sounds counterintuitive, but precooking the apples actually helps them hold their shape once they are baked. Here's how it works: When apples are gently heated, their pectin is converted to a heat-stable form that helps the apples stay intact and hold their shape as they soften further in the oven.

Rum Pumpkin Chiffon Pie

Pumpkin pie is great. But this year, we were in the mood for something exceptional.

BY KATIE LEAIRD

PUMPKIN CHIFFON PIE—A lighter, more elegant, and (as we found out) incredibly delicious version of the old Thanksgiving standard—consists of a gelatin-stabilized pumpkin custard lightened by meringue and sometimes whipped cream. The result is a fluffy, mousse-like, flavor-packed pie that, in my opinion, makes an elegant finale to a heavy Thanksgiving feast. The healthy glug of rum makes it an even happier holiday closer.

I know. I just used a big list of red-flag chef words: "chiffon," "gelatin-stabilized," "custard," "meringue." But my real operative word for this pie was "ease." I set out to dial this dessert back from scary to simple and create an accessible but still showstopping pie that my relatives would ask for year after year.

After studying various existing recipes (see "Fashions in Food"), I learned that the first step in most pumpkin chiffon pie recipes is to separate the eggs. You gently cook the yolks with sugar and pumpkin puree to make a custard base, taking care not to scramble the eggs. Then you mix in melted gelatin for extra stability. After chilling the warm mixture, you can finally fold in whipped egg whites and whipped cream. I tried this routine a few times in the test kitchen and found my head spinning as I tried to juggle the pies' various heating, cooling, whipping, and folding needs.

I began to question whether cooking a custard base was really necessary. Pumpkin puree has plenty of body and flavor, so maybe I didn't need to go to the trouble. I simply microwaved the pumpkin puree before combining it with cream, brown sugar, cinnamon, and salt and stirring in warmed gelatin and rum—without the egg yolks, there was no need to heat the mixture further. True, the pumpkin mixture was slightly fibrous, but pureeing the filling in the food processor took care of that, leaving it silky-smooth. Next up, an airy meringue to fold into it.

There's a limit to how much air egg whites can hold. Once that line is crossed, the resulting meringue will become dry and deflate. But for this recipe, I wanted my egg whites to hold as much air as possible. To make this goal easier to achieve, I added sugar, which dissolves in the egg white, forming a more stable film surrounding the air bubbles, halfway through whipping.

Eliminating the egg yolks from the filling streamlines the cooking process, and a quick spin in a food processor makes the filling as smooth as silk.

Once my mixture tripled in volume, transformed from transparent to opaque white, and held its shape, I carefully folded it into my pumpkin base. I transferred this mixture to a prebaked graham cracker crust and placed the pie in the refrigerator, where it would chill and set—the whole thing was done without any time on the stovetop.

A few hours later, the filling had shed its jiggle and was cleanly sliceable. A layer of whipped cream spread over the domed pie intensified its dramatic look, and a handful of crumbled gingersnap cookies sprinkled over the top gave it some playful decoration and a bit of contrasting crunch.

Removing the custard-making step made this a pretty simple dessert, one that delivered outsize flavors and left my tasters humming happy songs for the rest of the day.

One Pie, Two Cookies

We love the flavor combination of gingersnap cookies and pumpkin, but we found that a crust made with crushed gingersnaps overpowered the delicate filling. Instead, we make a traditional graham cracker crust and garnish the pie with crumbled gingersnaps.

RUM PUMPKIN CHIFFON PIE

Serves 8 to 10

If you prefer to use pasteurized egg whites in the filling, use ½ cup and increase the whipping time in step 4 to 5 to 6 minutes. For a well-mounded pie, be sure to fully whip the egg whites to glossy, stiff peaks in step 4. Plan ahead: This pie needs to be chilled for at least 4 hours before serving.

CRUST

- 9 whole graham crackers, broken into 1-inch pieces
- 3 tablespoons granulated sugar
- ½ teaspoon ground ginger
- 5 tablespoons unsalted butter, melted

FILLING

- 1 tablespoon unflavored gelatin
- ¼ cup dark rum
- 1 (15-ounce) can unsweetened pumpkin puree
- ⅓ cup packed (2⅓ ounces) dark brown sugar
- 1 teaspoon ground cinnamon
- ¾ teaspoon salt
- ½ cup heavy cream
- 4 large egg whites
- ⅓ cup (2⅓ ounces) granulated sugar

TOPPING

- 1 cup heavy cream, chilled
- 1 tablespoon granulated sugar
- ½ teaspoon vanilla extract
- 4 gingersnap cookies, crushed into ¼-inch pieces

The American Table
Fashions in Food

One of the earliest recipes for pumpkin chiffon pie appears in *Fashions in Food*, a cookbook published in 1929 by the Beverly Hills Women's Club. In the book's foreword, Roy Rogers declared that "When you have helped to raise the standard of cooking, you have helped to raise the only thing in the world that really matters anyhow." With recipes like A Palatable Dish (a casserole of beef, potato, and tomato), Dependable Digestible Dumplings, and Bestest Cake, the cookbook surely did just that.

–REBECCA HAYS

Club members show off winning bouquets after a flower show.

1. FOR THE CRUST: Adjust oven rack to middle position and heat oven to 325 degrees. Process graham cracker pieces, sugar, and ginger in food processor until finely ground, about 30 seconds. Add melted butter and pulse until combined, about 8 pulses. Transfer crumbs to 9-inch pie plate. Using bottom of dry measuring cup, press crumbs into bottom and up sides of plate. Bake until crust is fragrant and beginning to brown, 14 to 16 minutes. Let crust cool completely on wire rack, about 30 minutes.

2. FOR THE FILLING: Sprinkle gelatin over rum in large bowl and let sit until gelatin softens, about 5 minutes. Microwave until mixture is bubbling around edges and gelatin dissolves, about 30 seconds. Let cool until slightly warm, about 110 degrees. (It will be syrupy.)

3. Meanwhile, microwave pumpkin until heated to 110 degrees, 30 to 60 seconds. Process pumpkin, brown sugar, cinnamon, and salt in food processor until completely smooth, about 1 minute. Scrape down sides of bowl and process until no streaks remain, 10 to 15 seconds. Transfer pumpkin mixture to bowl with gelatin mixture and stir to combine. Stir in cream.

4. Using stand mixer fitted with whisk, whip egg whites on medium-low speed until foamy, about 1 minute. Increase speed to medium-high and whip whites to soft, billowy mounds, about 1 minute. Gradually add granulated sugar and whip until glossy, stiff peaks form, 2 to 3 minutes. Whisk one-third of meringue into pumpkin mixture until smooth. Using rubber spatula, fold remaining meringue into pumpkin mixture until only few white streaks remain.

5. Spoon filling into center of cooled crust. Gently spread filling to edges of crust, leaving mounded dome in center. Refrigerate pie for at least 4 hours or up to 24 hours.

6. FOR THE TOPPING: Using stand mixer fitted with whisk, whip cream, sugar, and vanilla on medium-low speed until foamy, about 1 minute. Increase speed to high and whip until soft peaks form, 1 to 3 minutes. Spread whipped cream evenly over pie, following domed contours. Sprinkle gingersnap pieces over top. Serve.

What's the Best Canned Pumpkin?

Americans rely on canned pumpkin to add a subtle sweetness and bright orange color to pumpkin pie and pumpkin bread. But does it really matter which canned pumpkin you choose? To find out, we picked three widely available products and had 21 test kitchen staffers sample each plain, baked into pumpkin cake, and whipped into our no-bake Rum Pumpkin Chiffon Pie. In the plain tasting, tasters noted the differences in color: Two samples were orange, as expected, but one was pale yellow. Tasters also noted textural differences. The yellow puree was pulpy and made an oddly thick pie filling and an overly dense cake. Another product was prominently fibrous and turned out a gritty pie. We preferred the smoothness of the less-fibrous pumpkin, which made tender cakes and a smooth pie filling.

Tasters described the flavor of the two lower-ranked purees as metallic and bitter, while the top-rated product was deemed pleasantly sweet. Here, sugar was the culprit: While the lower-ranked options contained 14 grams of sugar per can, our top-ranked pumpkin had 17.5 grams of sugar per can and was lightly sweet, with minimal bitterness. Clearly, some products were relying on pumpkins with more natural sugar. In fact, every product had just one ingredient: pumpkin. So what accounted for the color, texture, and flavor differences?

As it turns out, the U.S. Department of Agriculture doesn't have strict guidelines for what can be labeled as pumpkin. Since botanists define pumpkin as any squash with a firm shell, round body, and golden flesh, there are many pumpkins from which to choose. We reached out to manufacturers and learned that our top-ranked product uses Dickinson pumpkins cultivated in Illinois, while the poorest-performing product is made from Golden Delicious pumpkins harvested in Oregon. And though our runner-up is also made from Dickinson pumpkins, each brand uses a proprietary variety unique to its product.

Our favorite was Libby's 100% Pure Pumpkin, which tasters praised for its silky consistency and subtle sweetness that makes moist, rich cakes and fluffy, delicate pies. Fortunately it's also the easiest to find: Libby's makes 85 percent of the world's canned pumpkin. –JASON ALVAREZ

RECOMMENDED

LIBBY'S
100% Pure Pumpkin
Price: $2.55 for 15 oz ($0.17 per oz)
Sugar: 17.5 g
Fiber: 10.5 g
Pumpkin Variety: Dickinson

TASTERS' NOTES

Tasters praised our top pick, which is made from pumpkins grown in Illinois, for its "smooth" consistency, "slightly sweet" notes, and "prominent pumpkin flavor." This puree made pies and cakes that tasted the "most classic" of the bunch, and tasters loved its "bright orange color" and "subtle" squashiness.

SMOOTH, SWEET, AND "PUMPKINY"

RECOMMENDED WITH RESERVATIONS

ONE-PIE Pumpkin
Price: $2.20 for 15 oz ($0.15 per oz)
Sugar: 14 g
Fiber: 14 g
Pumpkin Variety: Dickinson

Most tasters thought this New England–based product's "muted pumpkin" notes "balanced" well with other ingredients. The cake made with this puree was perfectly "tender," but tasters noticed a slightly "gritty" texture in the pie. A few tasters also picked up on a "metallic" off-flavor.

TEXTURE AND FLAVOR A LITTLE OFF

NOT RECOMMENDED

FARMER'S MARKET Organic Pumpkin
Price: $3.10 for 15 oz ($0.21 per oz)
Sugar: 14 g
Fiber: 14 g
Pumpkin Variety: Golden Delicious

This product's "unappealing," alarmingly pale color was an immediate no-go for tasters, who noted that its "squash-y" color "looked nothing like pumpkin." It didn't taste much better either: Tasters complained of "bitter," "starchy," and "vegetal" notes and a "foamy," "chalky" texture.

BITTER, STARCHY, AND CHALKY

Sugar and fiber amounts are per 15-ounce can.

Cooking Class Easy Herb-Roasted Turkey with Gravy

We give you all the tools you need to make a moist, juicy herb-rubbed turkey and a rich gravy from start to finish. Our motto? Slow and steady wins the race. BY CHRISTIE MORRISON

EASY HERB-ROASTED TURKEY WITH GRAVY
Serves 10 to 12

We recommend using a self-basting turkey for this recipe (Butterball makes our favorite self-basting bird). Butterballs are "prebrined," meaning that they're injected with a salt solution that helps them stay moist.

TURKEY
- 2 onions, chopped
- 1 carrot, peeled and chopped
- 1 celery rib, chopped
- 4 cups chicken broth
- 1 cup dry white wine
- 5 fresh sage leaves, plus 1 tablespoon minced
- 1 sprig fresh rosemary, plus 1 tablespoon minced
- 1 sprig fresh thyme, plus 1 tablespoon minced
- 8 tablespoons unsalted butter, softened
- 4 garlic cloves, minced
- 1 tablespoon grated lemon zest
- 1 teaspoon salt
- 1 teaspoon pepper
- 1 (12- to 14-pound) prebrined turkey, neck and giblets discarded

GRAVY
- 4 tablespoons unsalted butter
- ⅓ cup all-purpose flour
- 2 tablespoons minced fresh parsley
  Salt and pepper

1. FOR THE TURKEY: Adjust oven rack to lowest position and heat oven to 325 degrees. Scatter onions, carrot, and celery in bottom of large roasting pan; add broth, wine, sage leaves, rosemary sprig, and thyme sprig to pan. Set V-rack over vegetables in roasting pan.

2. Combine butter, garlic, lemon zest, salt, pepper, minced sage, minced rosemary, and minced thyme in bowl and mix until smooth. Pat turkey dry inside and out with paper towels. Using your fingers, gently loosen skin covering breasts and leg quarters, being careful not to tear skin. Spoon half of butter mixture under skin, directly on meat. Using your hands, rub remaining butter mixture over outside of turkey. Tuck wings behind back and tie legs together with kitchen twine.

3. Transfer turkey, breast side up, to V-rack. Roast until breast registers 160 degrees and thighs register 175 degrees, 2½ to 3 hours. Transfer turkey to cutting board and let rest for 30 minutes.

4. FOR THE GRAVY: Meanwhile, carefully strain contents of pan through fine-mesh strainer into fat separator; discard solids and let liquid settle for at least 5 minutes.

5. Melt butter in medium saucepan over medium heat. Add flour and whisk constantly until honey-colored, about 2 minutes. Gradually whisk in 4 cups defatted pan juices (if necessary, add enough water to equal 4 cups) and bring to boil. Reduce heat to medium-low and simmer, stirring occasionally, until thickened, about 5 minutes. Off heat, stir in parsley and season with salt and pepper to taste. Carve turkey and serve with herb gravy.

STEP BY STEP Easy Herb-Roasted Turkey with Gravy

  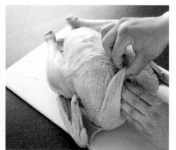  

1. BUILD GRAVY BASE
Scatter the onions, carrot, and celery in a large roasting pan. Add the broth, wine, and herbs.
WHY? The aromatic vegetables and herbs infuse the pan drippings with deep, complex flavor while broth and wine form the base of the gravy.

2. MAKE HERB BUTTER
Combine the butter, garlic, lemon zest, salt, pepper, and minced herbs in a bowl and mix until smooth.
WHY? This herbaceous and citrusy compound butter adds bright, fresh flavor to the bird.

3. SEASON UNDER SKIN
Using your fingers, gently loosen the skin covering the breasts and leg quarters without tearing it. Spoon half the butter mixture under the skin, onto the meat.
WHY? The salty butter mixture seasons the meat and helps keep it moist during cooking.

4. SEASON EXTERIOR
Using your hands, rub the remaining butter mixture over the outside of the turkey.
WHY? The fat in the butter helps crisp the skin while the sugars in the milk solids aid in browning.

5. TUCK AND TIE
Tuck the wings behind the back of the bird and tie the legs together with kitchen twine.
WHY? Tucking the wings keeps them from burning. Tying the legs makes the bird easier to maneuver and makes for an attractive presentation.

Shopping and Thawing

A Note About Size

We typically recommend roasting a 12- to 14-pound bird. Larger birds can be difficult to locate except at Thanksgiving; plus, they're hard to handle and to fit in a roasting pan.

KOSHER

Koshering employs salt to help draw blood from the bird. This seasons the meat, improves its texture, and keeps it moist.

FRESH VERSUS FROZEN

Most store-bought "fresh" turkeys have previously been frozen. We recommend buying a frozen turkey, since the freezing process results in a more consistent, moist texture than store-bought "fresh" turkeys have.

ORGANIC AND HERITAGE

These birds taste great, but they require brining or salting to keep them from drying out during cooking.

Thawing a Frozen Turkey

To defrost a turkey in the refrigerator, plan on one day of defrosting for every 4 pounds. If it won't fit in the fridge, use a big cooler and ice packs (changing the ice packs as needed to keep things cool). For quicker thawing, fill a large bucket with cold water. Place the turkey, still in its original wrapper, in the bucket for 6 to 8 hours for a 12-pound bird (30 minutes per pound). Change the water every half-hour to guard against bacteria. Refrigerate the thawed bird until you are ready to roast.

TEST KITCHEN TECHNIQUE Taking the Temperature of a Turkey

1. Insert the thermometer in the neck end, holding it parallel to the bird. The breast should reach 160 degrees. Confirm the temperature in both sides of the bird.

2. Insert the thermometer between the breast and drumstick and into the thickest part of the thigh, staying away from the bone. The thigh should reach 175 degrees. Confirm the temperature in the other thigh.

Good to Know

ESSENTIAL EQUIPMENT For Roasting Whole Poultry

For successful turkey roasting, make sure you're armed with the right equipment.

ROASTING PAN

The **Calphalon Contemporary Stainless Roasting Pan with Rack ($99.99)** is big enough to accommodate a turkey and has roomy, secure handles to facilitate lifting.

FAT SEPARATOR

With its long, comfortable handle and a wide, tall-sided strainer that contains splashes and is easy to pour into, the **Cuisipro Fat Separator ($33.95)** consistently produces fat-free pan drippings.

KITCHEN TWINE

We like **Librett Cotton Butcher's Twine ($8.29)**. This 100 percent cotton twine conveniently releases string from the ball's center and ties and holds foods without burning, fraying, or breaking.

THERMOMETER

The **ThermoWorks Thermapen Mk4 ($99.00)** registers quickly, which is important when you are opening the oven to check the bird.

Getting the Roux Right

A roux is a cooked mixture of flour and fat that thickens and adds flavor to gravy. The darker the roux, the more pronounced its flavor will be. Here we use a light roux to let the flavor of the turkey shine. Cook the roux, whisking it constantly, until it is the color of honey.

▶ Cooking for a crowd? We've got you covered. Go to **Cooks-Country.com/guide** for our Thanksgiving Survival Guide.

6. ELEVATE BIRD

Transfer the turkey to a V-rack set inside the roasting pan.
WHY? Elevating the turkey allows air to circulate around it, resulting in more even cooking.

7. USE LOWER HEAT

Roast the turkey at 325 degrees for 2½ to 3 hours.
WHY? A relatively low oven temperature helps the white and dark meat cook more evenly and allows the skin to brown without scorching.

8. LET IT REST

Transfer the turkey to a cutting board and let it rest for 30 minutes.
WHY? Resting allows the juices to redistribute throughout the turkey, keeping it moist.

9. STRAIN PAN JUICES

Strain the contents of the roasting pan through a fine-mesh strainer into a fat separator.
WHY? Straining and defatting removes the spent vegetables and excess fat from the gravy.

10. THICKEN THEM

Gradually whisk the defatted pan juices into a roux.
WHY? The roux will thicken and enrich the pan juices into a flavorful gravy that clings lightly to the turkey.

One-Pan Dinner Pork Loin Roast with Barley, Squash, and Swiss Chard

Most meats cooked *en cocotte* fly solo. Not this time.

BY CHRISTIE MORRISON

PORC EN COCOTTE may sound highbrow, but it couldn't be simpler: Brown a pork roast in a Dutch oven (the cocotte) and then cover the pot tightly and bake it in a low oven. Adding vegetables and barley makes it a complete one-pot dinner.

The low-heat, trapped-moisture method guards against overcooking the pork. Meanwhile, the barley and vegetables could cook in the liquid. Neither long-cooking hulled barley nor instant barley fit the timeline, but pearl (or pearled) barley—hulled barley with the outer coating polished off—cooks in the right time frame.

After rinsing a cup of barley (otherwise its dusty surface might burn), I browned the pork in my Dutch oven. Then, following the method we use for rice pilaf, I cooked the barley with some chopped onion in the fat left in the pot, allowing it to toast a bit. Some garlic, fresh thyme, and a glug of white wine added a heady aroma to the mix. I stirred in 4 cups of chicken broth and nestled the pork on top.

I slipped the covered pot into the oven for about 40 minutes, at which point the pork hit 135 degrees (it would increase to serving temperature, 140 degrees, as it rested on a carving board). The barley wasn't quite tender, but I had time to finish the barley on the stovetop. I stirred in cubed butternut squash and chopped Swiss chard to cook just until tender and brilliantly colored.

A bit of Parmesan cheese was the final touch. The result was chewy and stick-to-your-ribs satisfying—the perfect complement to rosy slices of tender pork.

PORK LOIN ROAST WITH BARLEY, BUTTERNUT SQUASH, AND SWISS CHARD Serves 4 to 6

Arrowhead Mills and Quaker pearl barley yield the most consistent results in this recipe. If you use a different brand, you may need to extend the cooking time in step 5, adding water as necessary. Use a large Dutch oven with a tight-fitting lid. Look for a 3-pound pork loin roast that is 7 to 8 inches long and 4 to 5 inches wide.

- 1 (3-pound) boneless pork loin roast
  Salt and pepper
- 2 tablespoons minced fresh thyme
- 3 tablespoons vegetable oil
- 1 onion, chopped
- 1 cup pearl barley, rinsed
- 3 garlic cloves, minced
- ¼ cup dry white wine
- 4 cups chicken broth
- ½ small butternut squash, peeled, seeded, and cut into ½-inch pieces (2½ cups)
- 8 ounces Swiss chard, stems chopped, leaves cut into 1-inch pieces
- 1 ounce Parmesan cheese, grated (½ cup)
- 2 teaspoons cider vinegar

1. Adjust oven rack to lowest position and heat oven to 250 degrees. Trim pork, leaving ¼-inch-thick layer of fat on top. Pat pork dry with paper towels, then tie with kitchen twine at 1-inch intervals. Season pork with salt and pepper and sprinkle with 1 tablespoon thyme. Heat 2 tablespoons oil in Dutch oven over medium-high heat until just smoking. Brown pork on all sides, 7 to 10 minutes, reducing heat if pot begins to scorch. Transfer pork to plate.

2. Reduce heat to medium and add remaining 1 tablespoon oil, onion, barley, and ¼ teaspoon salt to now-empty pot. Cook until onion is softened, about 5 minutes. Stir in garlic and remaining 1 tablespoon thyme and cook until fragrant, about 30 seconds. Stir in wine, scraping up any browned bits, and cook until evaporated, about 30 seconds. Stir in broth and bring to simmer.

3. Off heat, return browned pork and any accumulated juices to pot. Place large sheet of aluminum foil over pot and press to seal, then cover tightly with lid. Transfer pot to oven and cook until center of pork registers 135 degrees, 25 to 35 minutes.

4. Remove pot from oven. Transfer pork to carving board, tent with foil, and let rest while barley and vegetables finish cooking.

5. Meanwhile, transfer pot to stovetop and simmer over medium-low heat, covered, until barley is just cooked through but still somewhat firm in center, 10 to 15 minutes. Stir in squash and chard stems and cook, covered, until vegetables are tender, 10 to 15 minutes. Stir in chard leaves, increase heat to medium, and cook, uncovered, until leaves are tender and mixture is thickened to risotto-like consistency, 2 to 5 minutes. Off heat, stir in Parmesan and vinegar. Season with salt and pepper to taste.

6. Discard twine and slice pork. Serve with barley and vegetables.

The barley is not fully cooked when the pot comes out of the oven, but it has time to cook through on the stovetop once we add the squash and chard.

Cooking Pork, Barley, and Vegetables in Just One Pot

START ON STOVETOP
Brown pork in oil, then set pork aside. Add oil, onion and barley and sauté until onion softens. Add garlic and thyme.

ADD PORK
Stir in wine and chicken broth, then return browned pork and any accumulated juices to barley mixture.

TRANSFER TO OVEN
Cover pot tightly with sheet of aluminum foil and lid and transfer pot to oven. Cook until pork registers 135 degrees.

FINISH ON STOVETOP
Remove pork. Simmer barley, covered, until somewhat firm before adding squash and chard.

Cooking for Two Grilled Cheese with Tomato Soup

Grilled cheese is a snap, but soup? Believe it: Ours is so easy and so much better than opening a can.

BY CECELIA JENKINS

GRILLED CHEESE AND tomato soup are a classic combination, but too often, people reach for the familiar red can. Store-bought has its charms, but I wanted a simple homemade tomato soup for two to pair with a couple of golden-brown, crispy, creamy grilled cheese sandwiches. I wanted it to happen fast and to make just enough soup, not an overwhelming vat.

I started the soup in a saucepan, sweating onions and garlic with a bay leaf and a pinch of red pepper flakes. I opened a can of whole peeled tomatoes (we prefer them to other canned tomato products for their deeper tomato flavor) and added them along with chicken broth and a pinch of sugar to balance the tomatoes' acidity. I poured the warm mixture into the blender to puree. It was flavorful, but it was also watery.

Many tomato soup recipes call for finishing the blended soup with cream to create a silky texture. But cream muted the tomatoes' brightness. I turned to a traditional Spanish technique for gazpacho, adding half a piece of torn white sandwich bread to the pot; once the bread was saturated, I blended it into the soup. The bread lent body without compromising the tomato flavor. My soup was done in 15 minutes.

After assembling the sandwiches with plenty of American cheese, I brushed melted butter on top (this provided easier and better coverage than spreading soft butter with a knife). I placed my sandwiches in a conventional skillet, turned the heat to low (to prevent burning and allow time to melt the cheese), and waited. And waited. After more than 10 minutes, the bread had barely browned. Clearly I needed a hotter pan and more enveloping heat.

Preheating the pan and covering the skillet with a lid helped, but low heat still took too long. I jumped to medium-low heat, waiting until the bread on the bottom was golden brown before flipping the sandwiches over to finish. This time, the sandwiches were brown on the bottom in 4 to 8 minutes.

I dunked my sandwich into my soup and gobbled down the most comforting meal of the week. Next time I consider reaching for the can, I'll kick it down the road instead.

GRILLED CHEESE WITH TOMATO SOUP FOR TWO

For this recipe, we prefer the creamy texture and smooth melting ability of American cheese, but you can substitute cheddar or Gruyère cheese, if desired. Our favorite sliced deli American cheese is Boar's Head American Cheese. Because we don't recommend preheating an empty nonstick skillet, we call for a conventional skillet here.

4½ slices hearty white sandwich bread
1 tablespoon unsalted butter, plus 2 tablespoons melted
¾ cup chopped onion
1 garlic clove, minced
1 bay leaf
Salt and pepper
Pinch red pepper flakes (optional)
1 (14.5-ounce) can whole peeled tomatoes
1 cup chicken broth
1½ teaspoons packed light brown sugar
4 slices deli American cheese (4 ounces)
1 tablespoon minced fresh chives

1. Tear ½ slice bread into 1-inch pieces; set aside. Melt 1 tablespoon butter in medium saucepan over medium-low heat. Add onion, garlic, bay leaf, ¼ teaspoon salt, and pepper flakes, if using. Cover and cook until onion is softened, 3 to 5 minutes, stirring occasionally.

2. Add tomatoes and their juice, broth, sugar, and bread pieces to saucepan, breaking up tomatoes with wooden spoon. Cook, uncovered, until bread pieces break down, about 5 minutes, stirring occasionally. Remove from heat; discard bay leaf.

3A. FOR A BLENDER: Transfer soup to blender jar and process until smooth and creamy, about 2 minutes. Return soup to saucepan and season with salt and pepper to taste.

3B. FOR AN IMMERSION BLENDER: Place blender directly in saucepan so blades are submerged (you may need to tilt saucepan slightly) and blend until smooth and creamy, about 3 minutes, scraping down sides of saucepan as needed. Season with salt and pepper to taste.

4. Using remaining 4 slices bread, make 2 sandwiches with 2 cheese slices each. Preheat 12-inch skillet over medium-low heat for 3 minutes. Brush 1 side of sandwiches with half of melted butter. Place sandwiches buttered side down in skillet. Brush tops of sandwiches with remaining melted butter. Cover and cook until sandwich bottoms are golden brown, 4 to 8 minutes, moving sandwiches as needed for even browning.

5. Using metal spatula, flip sandwiches and continue to cook, covered, until golden brown on second side and cheese is melted, about 3 minutes.

6. Bring soup to simmer over medium heat. Ladle into bowls, sprinkle with chives, and serve with sandwiches.

It's hard to beat easy-melting American cheese, but this sandwich is great with cheddar or Gruyère, too.

TWO KEYS
Perfecting Soup and Sandwich

For golden sandwiches with evenly melted cheese, preheat the skillet over medium-low heat before slowly toasting the sandwiches. For a velvety soup that retains its bright flavor, we give it body not with cream but with half a piece of torn bread.

The American Table
Dynamic Duo

This soup and sandwich have been linked since the 1940s, when they were paired as a school cafeteria lunch. At the time, teachers were often charged with preparing lunch for their students, and canned tomato soup was recommended by the government as an easy way to provide children with a dose of vitamin C. And, in the words of a 1960 Campbell's ad, tomato soup and a sandwich is a "wholesome, nourishing 4-minute meal."

–REBECCA HAYS

Five Easy Granolas

Life's too short for dry, dusty, flavorless supermarket granola. BY ASHLEY MOORE

WE ALL KNOW those promising-looking boxes of granola that line the shelves in the grocery store, pasted with pictures of chunky golden-brown clusters, crunchy nuts, and bits of tender dried fruit. But when you bring them home and reach into the box, too often you come up with a sad mixture of pale oats, dried-out nuts, and a few raisins at the bottom of the bag. I knew I could create a recipe for better granola. But could I create an easy recipe? How about five? I set off to find out.

I started out with a company recipe (Almond Granola with Dried Fruit, *Cook's Illustrated*, April/May 2012) that calls for whisking together maple syrup, brown sugar, vanilla extract, salt, and vegetable oil. I tossed old-fashioned rolled oats and chopped almonds into the sticky mixture before spreading and packing it into a rimmed baking sheet and taking it to the oven. After 40 to 45 minutes, the granola baked into a solid mass. Once I let the granola cool to room temperature, I was able to easily break it into smaller pieces and add the dried fruit—in this case raisins—which I chopped to help them evenly distribute throughout the mixture.

It's an excellent recipe, but granola is a very personal experience and I prefer slightly lighter oats, so I shortened the cooking time to 35 to 40 minutes. Everything else I kept the same. The next order of business was to decide on a few different variations with easy, flavorful add-ins. For apricot-orange granola, I packed the mixture with

We mastered a recipe for Almond-Raisin Granola (above) before developing variations that include other dried fruits and nuts, chocolate chips, honey, caramel sauce, or orange zest.

pepitas, dried apricots, and orange zest. In a second variation, I left the almonds in for crunch and added crowd-pleasing mini chocolate chips and chopped dried cherries. For another, I substituted some honey for the sugar and buttery pecans

for the almonds; plus, I added ground cinnamon with the honey mixture. My final variation, salted caramel and peanut, meant swapping in caramel for the brown sugar and subbing peanuts for the almonds.

ALMOND-RAISIN GRANOLA
Makes about 9 cups

Do not use quick oats here. We prefer to chop the almonds by hand for even texture and superior crunch. (A food processor will chop whole nuts unevenly.) You can substitute an equal amount of slivered or sliced almonds, if desired.

- ½ cup vegetable oil
- ⅓ cup maple syrup
- ⅓ cup packed (2⅓ ounces) light brown sugar
- 4 teaspoons vanilla extract
- ½ teaspoon salt
- 5 cups (15 ounces) old-fashioned rolled oats
- 2 cups (10 ounces) raw almonds, chopped coarse
- 2 cups (10 ounces) raisins, chopped

1. Adjust oven rack to upper-middle position and heat oven to 325 degrees. Line rimmed baking sheet with parchment paper. Spray parchment with vegetable oil spray.

2. Whisk oil, maple syrup, sugar, vanilla, and salt together in large bowl. Fold in oats and almonds until thoroughly combined.

3. Transfer oat mixture to prepared sheet and spread across entire surface of sheet in even layer. Using stiff metal spatula, press down firmly on oat mixture until very compact. Bake until lightly browned, 35 to 40 minutes, rotating sheet halfway through baking.

4. Transfer sheet to wire rack and let granola cool completely, about 1 hour. Break cooled granola into pieces of desired size. Stir in raisins and serve. (Granola can be stored in airtight container for up to 2 weeks.)

APRICOT-ORANGE GRANOLA
Substitute 1 cup raw pepitas, chopped coarse, for almonds and dried apricots for raisins. Add 1 tablespoon grated orange zest to oil mixture in step 2.

CHERRY–CHOCOLATE CHIP GRANOLA
Substitute dried cherries for raisins. Add 1 cup mini semisweet chocolate chips to mixture with dried cherries in step 4.

HONEY-PECAN GRANOLA
Substitute honey for sugar and pecans for almonds. Add 1 tablespoon ground cinnamon to oil mixture in step 2.

SALTED CARAMEL–PEANUT GRANOLA
Omit raisins. Increase salt to 1½ teaspoons. Substitute ¾ cup jarred caramel sauce for sugar and unsalted dry-roasted peanuts for almonds.

Slow Cooker Tuscan White Bean Stew

This rustic Italian dish can take all day to prepare, so we outsourced it to the slow cooker.

BY KATIE LEAIRD

I KNEW THAT this hearty, restorative autumn stew of creamy cannellini beans, savory pancetta, sweet garlic, and healthful kale would need time to develop its deep flavors. I didn't, however, want to stand at the stove and stir the pot for hours on end. So I turned to the slow cooker, an appliance built for long, hands-off simmering. But even when loaded up with assertively flavored pancetta, garlic, and rosemary—iconic Italian ingredients—slow cookers have a tendency to produce a washed-out result. My challenge was to keep the flavors intact and keep the stew in balance.

I decided early on to use dried, rather than canned, beans. Besides being even cheaper than the canned variety, dried beans are a better choice for the slow cooker because they are less likely to overcook—and because they're in the cooker for several hours, they don't need a presoak. Lucky for us, slow cookers expertly handle beans with a gentle heat that prevents rupturing and toughening.

But during a few tests, I noticed that the beans were cooking inconsistently—a handful or so of each batch floated to the top of the stew and remained crunchy. For an easy fix, I used a cartouche, a piece of parchment paper carefully cut to just cover the food while it simmers. This kept all the beans submerged for even cooking.

Pancetta, the Italian bacon, gives Tuscan bean soup smoky, meaty notes. But after stewing for 6 to 7 hours, the meat tasted spent. To preserve its flavor and texture, I sautéed the pancetta first to render its fat and then removed the meat and set it aside to stir into the stew just before serving. I then cooked chopped onion, celery, carrots, and smashed garlic cloves in the fat, ensuring bacony flavor evenly distributed throughout.

Rosemary is a fickle herb; its pinelike pungency can turn bitter if stewed for too long. Adding it just 30 to 45 minutes before the stew was done kept its flavor in check. I also added chopped kale and a small can of diced tomatoes at the same time; stirring them in at this late stage helped ensure vibrant color and guarded against sliminess.

Once the stew was ready (after about 8 to 9 hours on low or 6 to 7 on high),

I roughly mashed a few of the beans with the back of a spoon and gave it a final stir for extra creaminess. A healthy swirl of good olive oil over the top finished it off.

SLOW-COOKER TUSCAN WHITE BEAN STEW
Serves 6 to 8
We prefer the color and texture of Lacinato kale in this stew, but you can substitute curly kale or 6 ounces of bagged, chopped kale. We top the stew with a cartouche (an oval piece of parchment paper that sits directly on the food) during cooking to trap moisture and help the beans cook evenly.

- 3 tablespoons extra-virgin olive oil, plus extra for drizzling
- 6 ounces pancetta, cut into ¼-inch pieces
- 1 onion, chopped fine
- 2 celery ribs, cut into ½-inch pieces
- 2 carrots, peeled and cut into ½-inch pieces
- 8 garlic cloves, smashed and peeled
- 1 pound (2½ cups) dried cannellini beans, picked over and rinsed
- 4 cups chicken broth
- 4 cups water
- 2 bay leaves
- 2 teaspoons salt
- ½ teaspoon pepper
- 8 ounces kale, stemmed and cut into 1-inch pieces
- 1 (14.5-ounce) can diced tomatoes, drained
- 1 sprig fresh rosemary

1. Trace lid of slow cooker on parchment paper and cut just inside of outline; set aside. Heat oil in 12-inch nonstick skillet over medium heat until shimmering. Add pancetta and cook until crispy, 6 to 8 minutes. Using slotted spoon, transfer pancetta to small bowl and let cool completely; cover and refrigerate until needed.

2. Add onion, celery, and carrots to fat in skillet and cook, stirring occasionally, until vegetables are lightly browned, about 10 minutes. Stir in garlic and cook until fragrant, about 1 minute. Transfer vegetable mixture to slow cooker.

3. Add beans, broth, water, bay leaves, salt, and pepper to slow cooker; stir to combine. Gently press parchment

Canned beans turn to mush after hours in a slow cooker, so for this recipe we start with dried beans. The gentle, steady heat of the slow cooker renders the beans tender, not tough.

cutout onto surface of stew. Cover and cook until beans are tender, 6 to 7 hours on high or 8 to 9 hours on low.

4. Discard parchment. Stir in kale, tomatoes, and rosemary sprig. Cover and cook until kale is fully tender, 30 to 45 minutes on high.

5. Discard bay leaves and rosemary sprig. Use back of spoon to mash some beans against side of slow cooker to thicken stew, if desired. Stir in pancetta. Serve, drizzled with extra oil.

INGREDIENT SPOTLIGHT
Lacinato Kale
For this recipe, we prefer the robust, rich flavor and tender texture of Lacinato kale (also called black, dinosaur, *cavolo nero*, or Tuscan).

TEST KITCHEN TECHNIQUE
Making a Cartouche
A cartouche (a rounded piece of parchment paper) has a fancy name, but it's very simple to make. Simply trace the lid of the slow cooker on the parchment paper and cut just inside the outline. Gently press the cartouche onto the surface of the stew to keep the beans submerged during cooking.

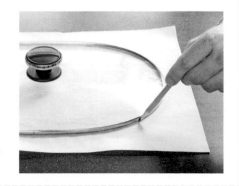

We demanded our contenders clear a slew of sticky hurdles.

BY HANNAH CROWLEY

KEY Good ★★★ Fair ★★ Poor ★

THE TEST KITCHEN GAUNTLET
7 skillets,
9 tests

There are numerous factors to consider when testing cookware. These are the tests we subjected each skillet to:

1. Fry consecutive eggs with no fat until they stick—up to 50 eggs
2. Brown layer of flour to observe heating patterns and evenness
3. Cook pork and broccoli stir-fry
4. Pan-fry sole fillets
5. Cook, slice, and serve frittata using metal utensils
6. Wash by hand 10 times; wash in dishwasher five times
7. Bang on concrete ledge
8. Heat and then shock in cold water
9. Fry consecutive eggs with no fat until they stick—up to 50 eggs—a second time to evaluate durability

WINNING TRAITS
Shape and Color Matter

What makes one skillet better than another? Here are three common characteristics of our top-rated pans.

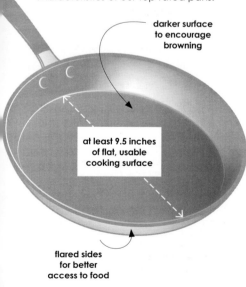

darker surface to encourage browning

at least 9.5 inches of flat, usable cooking surface

flared sides for better access to food

▶ Visit CooksCountry.com/oct16 to view the entire results chart and get tips on keeping your nonstick skillet in tip-top shape for the long haul.

HIGHLY RECOMMENDED

OXO GOOD GRIPS
Non-Stick 12-Inch
Open Frypan
Model: CW000957-003
Price: $39.99
Layers of Nonstick Coating: 3
Ovensafe to: 390°F
Weight: 2.35 lb
Diameter: 12.25 in
Usable Surface Area: 9.75 in

Nonstick Ability	★★★
Food Quality	★★★
Maneuverability	★★★
Capacity	★★★
Durability	★★½

This pan came slick and stayed that way—we stopped both fried egg tests after 50 eggs. It cooked and released food perfectly, thanks to its darker finish and excellent nonstick coating. Its gently flared sides and lightweight design made it easy to load, unload, and move. Its grippy, stay-cool handle was flawless and its cooking surface vast. It showed some light knife marks but otherwise emerged from testing unscathed.

RECOMMENDED

T-FAL Professional
Non-Stick Fry Pan
Model: E9380884
Price: $32.02
Layers of Nonstick Coating: 5
Ovensafe to: 400°F
Weight: 2.5 lb
Diameter: 12.4 in
Usable Surface Area: 9.5 in

Nonstick Ability	★★★
Food Quality	★★½
Maneuverability	★★★
Capacity	★★★
Durability	★★

Thanks to five layers of nonstick coating, our old winner emerged from our slicing tests virtually unmarked. It cooked and released food well, was light and comfortable, and had flared sides for easy access. Unfortunately, its surface domed slightly, so oil and egg yolks pooled around the edges. It also dented during abuse testing.

NOT RECOMMENDED

ZWILLING
Madura Plus 11" Nonstick
Fry Pan
Model: 66299-286
Price: $59.99

This pan was just too small— fish fillets rode up its sides. Its handle was jarred loose during testing.

FARBERWARE
High Performance
Stainless Steel 12-inch
Nonstick Skillet
Model: 77227 **Price:** $32.99

This product offered only two layers of coating, and its raised surface wasn't nonstick.

CUISINART
Chef's Classic Non-Stick
Stainless 12" Skillet
Model: 722-30HNS
Price: $52.95

A small disk bottom led to overcooking around the perimeter of this skillet, and it just wasn't very nonstick.

CIRCULON
Symmetry 11-inch
Open Skillet
Model: 82894 **Price:** $37.31

This small pan's imprinted bull's-eye pattern wasn't very nonstick. Its handle was uncomfortable.

BIALETTI
Triply 12" Saute Pan
Model: 7472 **Price:** $59.99

This heavy pan released only five eggs before mangling its sixth, and at the end of testing: zero. Plus, its pale surface resulted in pale frittatas.

NONSTICK SKILLETS ARE big business: According to Hugh Rushing of the Cookware Manufacturers Association, 70 percent of all skillets sold in this country are nonstick. In the test kitchen, we reach for our nonstick skillets when we're cooking delicate foods that stick, like eggs or fish. We also like these pans for stir-fries because the brown bits (or fond) don't stick to the pans as much, so there's less chance of their burning.

Our ideal nonstick skillet is easy to handle, is durable, has great release, and cooks food evenly with appropriate browning. We evaluated the market and chose the top seven pans from major manufacturers, including our past winner from T-fal. We prefer 12-inch skillets, but we included two 11-inch models because they were the largest skillets offered by two major manufacturers. We set a $60 price limit because nonstick pans wear faster than other pans, so we don't think they're worth a major investment.

We started by cracking eggs into each preheated pan—with no fat added—to assess their nonstick ability. We kept cooking consecutive over-easy eggs in each pan until they started to stick; we repeated this test at the end of testing (after cooking fish fillets, stir-fries, and frittatas in each pan) to gauge how the nonstick coatings held up over time. Along the way, we intentionally broke every rule we could think of for nonstick pans. We cut food in the skillets with knives, used metal spatulas and abrasive sponges, stacked the skillets, repeatedly shocked them in cold water, and washed them in a dishwasher. We also took them outside and banged them on a sharp concrete ledge to simulate years of rough handling.

What did we learn? First of all, size, shape, and design matter. The two smaller pans were a bust. While we looked at each pan's rim-to-rim diameter (the metric used by manufacturers and retailers) initially, it was the diameter of their flat bottoms— their cooking area—that proved more important; we needed at least 9.5 inches of flat surface or fish fillets rode up the sides and cooked unevenly and anything we sautéed was crowded and browned poorly.

Heavy pans were taxing to move and maneuver, as were pans with sharp han-dles or handles that got hot. We preferred lightweight pans with rounded, grippy handles that stayed cool. We also preferred lower, flared sides to taller or straighter ones; their more open design made it easier to maneuver the food in and out of the pan.

As for the nonstick coatings, most cookware manufacturers purchase them from large chemical companies. They choose from a range of options, from cheap to premium. The composition of the coating, how well it's applied, and

---

EQUIPMENT UPDATE
Chemical Concerns

There has been a recent big change in nonstick cookware. Due to health concerns, the Environmental Protection Agency asked chemical companies to remove perfluorooctanoic acid (PFOA), one of the concerning chemicals used by manufacturers, from processing by 2015. Every manufacturer we researched has complied, and all of the nonstick skillets in our lineup are now PFOA-free.

Taste Test Apple Cider Vinegar

Mellow, punchy, sweet, subtle: Could we find a cider vinegar that has it all? BY LAUREN SAVOIE

how many layers are applied all affect performance and durability.

Two pans we tested had raised patterns, ostensibly for durability and better heat transfer, but they weren't very nonstick and mangled eggs. Only two pans (both with smooth surfaces) aced all of our nonstick tests, culminating with flawlessly releasing 50 eggs in a row after weeks of testing. By contrast, one low-ranked pan failed to flip a single egg at the end of testing.

The skillets in our lineup had from two to five layers of nonstick coating; the top performers had at least three. The pan with five layers was our past winner from T-fal; the extra layers offered superior durability in the coating, but this skillet had other construction issues. It dented readily when we struck it on the concrete ledge and domed slightly in the center of its cooking surface when it was heated. This meant that oil ran to the pan edges, so the fish fillets browned irregularly and the eggs were misshapen—they sprouted legs where the whites had leaked toward the edges. We still think it's a good pan, but it's no longer best in show.

Of the seven pans we tested, we can recommend only two. Our top pan, from Oxo Good Grips, had a broad, smooth, flat surface that cooked and released food perfectly. It had a darker finish for better browning and was light and maneuverable, with an excellent grippy, stay-cool handle. Its flared sides allowed us to easily move food in and out of the pan. It's a little more expensive than our past winner, but it was the only skillet that earned our "highly recommended" rating.

JUST AS ITALY is known for balsamic vinegar and Spain for sherry vinegar, America has a vinegar to lay claim to: apple cider vinegar. Cider vinegar is a natural byproduct of apple cider—left to sit long enough, the sugar in the apples will convert to alcohol and then to acetic acid. Cider vinegar has been around since at least 2500 BC, and it has been produced in the United States since the colonial days. Before the advent of refrigeration, most American homes kept cider vinegar on hand for preserving, cooking, and cleaning.

These days, we use apple cider vinegar for a comparatively mellow, slightly sweet kick of acidity in glazes, slaws, and sauces. We're particularly keen on using it in fall dishes, where the apple notes complement other seasonal ingredients. Since we last tasted apple cider vinegar, our former winning product by French manufacturer Maille has become hard to find in the United States. We wanted to see if there was a better, more widely available option.

We rounded up six American-made cider vinegars and asked 21 America's Test Kitchen staffers to sample the products plain, cooked into a pan sauce, stirred into coleslaw, and mixed into a barbecue sauce. Every vinegar we tried worked fine. That said, tasters zeroed in on some characteristics that separate vinegar that's "fine" from vinegar that's really good.

Cider will convert naturally to vinegar with time, but manufacturers typically speed up the process by adding a "mother," which is bacteria from an established vinegar. Once all the alcohol is converted to acid (there's no measurable alcohol in vinegar), the vinegar is either filtered to remove the cloudy sediment of leftover mother or bottled unfiltered. In the plain tasting, testers could visually identify the unfiltered vinegars by their darker, hazier appearance and small floating particles. While tasters didn't notice any difference in consistency when tasting filtered and unfiltered products, many thought the unfiltered vinegars were slightly more complex—fruity, floral, and appley—when sampled straight.

These nuances were still prominent when we tasted the vinegars in a subtle pan sauce, where tasters preferred the fruitiness and slightly funky liveliness of unfiltered products. But the lines between filtered and unfiltered started

to blur when we tried the vinegars in barbecue sauce and slaw, punchy foods with lots of competing flavors. In these applications, tasters wanted a bright, bold kick of tartness and preferred products they perceived as more acidic—regardless of whether they were filtered or unfiltered.

But more acidity wasn't always a good thing. One product was slightly too tangy and overwhelmed the mellow pan sauce with its harsher tartness. To get a better read on acidity, we sent the vinegars to an independent lab for analysis. There was no clear correlation between acidity and whether the vinegars were filtered or not. All the products contained between 5.0 percent and 5.3 percent acid, with tasters giving the edge to products that fell in the middle, at around 5.1 percent acid. Though this may seem like a relatively small range, our science editor confirmed that it's actually pretty significant when measuring acidity. Products with any less acid lacked brightness in more flavorful recipes, while vinegars that were more acidic overpowered delicate dishes. Products that met in the middle worked well in every recipe we tried, lending a lively bite to edgier dishes without washing out the mellower ones.

The one exception was our runner-up, which, at 5.3 percent acid, was the most acidic product in the lineup. Lab tests showed, however, that this was the only vinegar we tasted that was also measurably sweet, at 1.4 percent sugar compared with 0 percent in every other product. Manufacturers don't add sugar to vinegar; instead, this product's manufacturer likely started with a sweeter cider and stopped fermentation before all the sugars were converted to acid. Tasters thought the extra sugar in this vinegar helped amplify its apple flavor and temper its higher acidity.

Our favorite was a well-rounded, versatile vinegar that worked well in every recipe. Fortunately, it's also the one you're most likely to encounter at the supermarket. Heinz Filtered Apple Cider Vinegar enlivened pan sauce, tempered sweet slaw, and balanced barbecue sauce with its bright, moderate acidity and clear apple notes. At $0.17 an ounce, it's also one of the cheapest cider products we found, proving that you don't have to shell out extra for great apple cider vinegar.

RECOMMENDED

HEINZ Filtered Apple Cider Vinegar
Price: $2.79 for 16 fl oz ($0.17 per fl oz)
Style: Filtered **Acidity:** 5.1% **Sugar:** 0%

With just the right amount of acidity, this familiar supermarket vinegar was "sharp" and "punchy," with a subtle "floral" fruitiness. "I'd let this enliven my barbecue any day," said one taster.

WHITE HOUSE Apple Cider Vinegar
Price: $1.59 for 16 fl oz ($0.10 per fl oz)
Style: Filtered **Acidity:** 5.3% **Sugar:** 1.4%

With a "bright" punch of acidity and just a hint of sugar, this filtered vinegar had a "juicy," "almost drinkable" sweetness and "vibrant" notes of "green apple." It was also the cheapest vinegar in the bunch.

BRAGG Organic Apple Cider Vinegar
Price: $3.99 for 16 fl oz ($0.25 per fl oz)
Style: Unfiltered **Acidity:** 5.1% **Sugar:** 0%

This unfiltered vinegar emerged at the top of the pack in pan sauce, where its "boozy," "zesty" apple flavor lent a complex "zing." While these "slightly funky" notes were lost in slaw and barbecue sauce, most tasters appreciated this product's "lively" acidity and "sweet apple finish."

SPECTRUM NATURALS Organic Unpasteurized Apple Cider Vinegar Filtered
Price: $3.99 for 16 fl oz ($0.25 per fl oz)
Style: Filtered **Acidity:** 5.0% **Sugar:** 0%

This "very pale" vinegar had a "mellow" flavor. Though tasters thought this product was "clean" and "bright," some lamented that it "lacked complexity." Still, it worked decently in every recipe we tried.

SPECTRUM NATURALS Organic Unpasteurized Apple Cider Vinegar Unfiltered
Price: $3.49 for 16 fl oz ($0.22 per fl oz)
Style: Unfiltered **Acidity:** 5.0% **Sugar:** 0%

When sampled plain and in pan sauce, this unfiltered vinegar had delicate hints of "melon" and "sweet apple." These nuances were much subtler in punchy recipes like slaw and barbecue sauce. This vinegar won't ruin your recipes, but there are better choices.

EDEN Organic Apple Cider Vinegar
Price: $3.59 for 16 fl oz ($0.22 per fl oz)
Style: Unfiltered **Acidity:** 5.2% **Sugar:** 0%

This unfiltered vinegar had plenty of acidity but no sweetness to balance it out. While its "bold" tartness was deemed "bright" in barbecue sauce, tasters found it a tiny bit "harsh" in pan sauce. Tasters were also mixed about its "boozy," "fermented" notes.

Heirloom Recipe

We're looking for recipes that you treasure—the ones that have been handed down in your family for a generation or more, that always come out for the holidays, and that have earned a place at your table and in your heart through many years of meals. Send us the recipes that spell home to you. Visit CooksCountry.com/recipe_submission (or write to Heirloom Recipes, *Cook's Country*, P.O. Box 470739, Brookline, MA 02447) and tell us a little about the recipe. Include your name and mailing address. **If we print your recipe, you'll receive a free one-year subscription to *Cook's Country*.**

OLD-FASHIONED COCONUT-PECAN SQUARES

"When I was in college, my mother would send a box of these to me every semester, just before exams." –Trina Drysdale, Eugene, Ore.

Makes 24 bars
Use a fine-mesh strainer to evenly distribute the confectioners' sugar.

- 12 tablespoons unsalted butter, softened
- 2½ cups packed (17½ ounces) light brown sugar
- 1½ cups (7½ ounces) all-purpose flour Salt
- 5 large eggs (3 separated, 2 whole)
- 1 tablespoon vanilla extract
- 1 cup pecans, toasted and chopped fine
- 1 cup (3 ounces) sweetened shredded coconut, toasted and chopped fine
- 1 tablespoon confectioners' sugar

1. Adjust oven rack to lower-middle position and heat oven to 350 degrees. Grease 13 by 9-inch baking pan. Using stand mixer fitted with paddle, beat butter and ½ cup brown sugar on medium speed until smooth, about 1 minute. Add flour and ½ teaspoon salt and continue to beat until dough begins to form, about 2 minutes longer. Press dough evenly into bottom of prepared pan. Bake until light golden brown, 12 to 15 minutes. Transfer pan to wire rack and let cool for 15 minutes.

2. Using clean, dry mixer bowl fitted with whisk, whip 3 egg whites on medium-low speed until foamy, about 1 minute. Increase speed to medium-high and whip until stiff peaks form, 1 to 2 minutes. Transfer whites to separate bowl; set aside.

3. Return now-empty bowl to mixer still fitted with whisk and whip vanilla, remaining 2 cups brown sugar, 2 whole eggs, remaining 3 egg yolks, and ½ teaspoon salt on medium-high speed until thick, about 2 minutes, scraping down bowl as needed. Fold in pecans, coconut, and reserved whipped egg whites by hand until fully incorporated.

4. Spread mixture evenly over cooled crust. Bake until top is deep golden brown, 24 to 26 minutes. Transfer pan to wire rack and let cool completely. Run paring knife around edges of pan to release bars. Cut into 2-inch squares and dust with confectioners' sugar. Serve.

COMING NEXT ISSUE

Our festive December/January issue features holiday favorites from **Boneless Rib Roast with Yorkshire Pudding** to **Soft and Chewy Gingerbread Cookies** and **Classic Eggnog**. Then we visit Pittsburgh for **Transylvanian Goulash** and **Haluski**, drop by the Connecticut coast for **Lighthouse Inn Potatoes**, and hop over to Hawaii for a slice of **Chocolate Haupia Pie**. Come along for the ride!

FIND THE ROOSTER!
A tiny version of this rooster has been hidden in the pages of this issue. Write to us with its location and we'll enter you in a random drawing. The first correct entry drawn will win our winning nonstick 12-inch skillet, and each of the next five will receive a free one-year subscription to *Cook's Country*. To enter, visit CooksCountry.com/rooster by November 30, 2016, or write to Rooster ON16, *Cook's Country*, P.O. Box 470739, Brookline, MA 02447. Include your name and address. Stephanie Sharp of Omaha, Nebraska, found the rooster in the June/July 2016 issue on page 14 and won our favorite kitchen timer.

WEB EXTRAS
More recipes and expanded reviews are available for free for 4 months at
CooksCountry.com
Arroz con Pollo
Buttermilk-Ranch Pita Chips
Classic Yellow Bundt Cake
Grilled Butterflied Lemon Chicken
Herb Roast Chicken
Lightly Sweetened Whipped Cream
Montreal Seasoned Salt Blend
Romaine Salad with Green Goddess Dressing
Slow-Cooker Ratatouille
Smoked Roast Beef
Testing Nonstick Skillets
Testing Potato Mashers

READ US ON iPAD
Download the *Cook's Country* app for iPad and start a free trial subscription or purchase a single issue of the magazine. All issues are enhanced with full-color Cooking Mode slide shows that provide step-by-step instructions for completing recipes, plus expanded reviews and ratings. Go to CooksCountry.com/iPad to download our app through iTunes.

Cranberry-Pear Stack Cake

Ripe pears and tart cranberries make a fine filling for buttery cake layers.

TO MAKE THIS CAKE, YOU WILL NEED:

- 10 ounces (2½ cups) fresh or frozen cranberries
- ½ cup (3½ ounces) sugar
- ¼ cup water
- 2 pounds Bartlett or Bosc pears, peeled, halved, cored, and cut into 1-inch pieces
- 2 teaspoons grated orange zest
- 1 teaspoon ground cinnamon
- ⅛ teaspoon salt
- 1 recipe Classic Yellow Bundt Cake batter*
- 1½ cups Lightly Sweetened Whipped Cream*

FOR THE FILLING: Combine cranberries, sugar, and water in large saucepan and cook over medium heat until cranberries are just starting to burst, about 5 minutes, stirring frequently. Remove 2 tablespoons cranberries and set aside in refrigerator. Add pears, orange zest, cinnamon, and salt to remaining cranberries in saucepan and cook over medium heat until pears are very soft and almost all liquid has evaporated, about 45 minutes, stirring frequently and reducing heat as needed if bottom begins to scorch. Transfer fruit mixture to food processor and process until smooth, 30 to 45 seconds (you should have 2½ cups puree). Transfer to bowl, press parchment paper on top, and refrigerate until completely cool, about 4 hours.

FOR THE CAKE: Adjust oven rack to middle position and heat oven to 350 degrees. Spray two 8-inch round cake pans with baking spray with flour and line with parchment. Pour 8 ounces (about 1 cup) batter into each pan and spread into even layer. Bake until tops are set and edges are just starting to brown, 12 to 14 minutes. Let cakes cool in pans for 10 minutes, then remove cakes from pans and let cool completely on wire rack (leaving parchment on cakes). Wipe pans clean and repeat process twice more, for a total of 6 cake layers.

TO ASSEMBLE: Gently remove parchment and place 1 cake round on cake plate or pedestal. Spread ½ cup puree in even layer over cake. Repeat with remaining cake layers and remaining puree, leaving top of cake plain. Spread whipped cream in even layer over top of cake. Garnish center with reserved cranberries. Serve.

▶ *Go to **CooksCountry.com** for our recipes for Classic Yellow Bundt Cake and Lightly Sweetened Whipped Cream or use your own. Be advised that if you use your own Bundt cake recipe, you will need at least 6 cups of batter.

Inside This Issue

Cook's Country

DECEMBER/JANUARY 2017

CooksCountry.com
$5.95 U.S./$6.95 CANADA

7 25274 05251 6

01>

THE RESPONSES AROUND the test kitchen to the announcement that we'd be developing a recipe for eggnog fell into two distinct camps: pro and con. Folks either loved eggnog or hated it. There was no in between.

Test cook Morgan Bolling had her work cut out for her—not just to create a perfect recipe for eggnog but to win over the naysayers. (Spoiler alert: She did. See the recipe on page 17.)

I'll admit my bias: I was in the pro camp. For most of my life I was . . . well, I was just fine with eggnog. I liked it, but I didn't crave it. But then I watched the classic screwball comedy *The Awful Truth*. In one early scene, Cary Grant stands behind a gargantuan punch bowl, spooning out servings of eggnog to a group of friends while awaiting the return of Irene Dunne and her apparent paramour. He did it with so much élan (he was Cary Grant, after all) that I, previously relatively ambivalent about eggnog, fell head over heels in love with it.

Funny how the context surrounding a thing can influence how you feel about the thing itself. We think about that a lot here at *Cook's Country*. Our core mission is to produce great recipes and great ideas for food that you'll like. But through travel, history, and culture, we also strive to find stories that will make you fall in love.

TUCKER SHAW

Executive Editor

Associate editor Morgan Bolling (top) was not a fan of eggnog until she developed a recipe for it. The process involved tasting several existing recipes (above) before setting goals for a fresh, rich eggnog. For inspiration, we watched *The Awful Truth*, the 1930s movie in which Cary Grant (left) commandeered the punch bowl to ladle out nog for his guests.

Photo: The Awful Truth © 1937, 1965 CPII; Kitchen photography: Kevin White

Bread Illustrated
Demystifying the art and science of bread baking
We show bakers of all skill levels how to make crisp-crusted, chewy-crumbed loaves, rolls, sweet breads, and more. *Bread Illustrated*—our first cookbook devoted solely to bread baking—is a fully illustrated handbook with more than 100 meticulously tested recipes that will enable you to bake artisan bakery–quality bread at home.
Order online at americastestkitchen.com/breadillustrated

Follow us on **Pinterest**
pinterest.com/TestKitchen

Follow us on **Twitter**
twitter.com/TestKitchen

Find us on **Facebook**
facebook.com/CooksCountry

Find us on **Instagram**
instagram.com/cookscountry

Cook's Country

Chief Executive Officer David Nussbaum
Chief Creative Officer Jack Bishop
Editorial Director John Willoughby
Executive Editor Tucker Shaw
Deputy Editor Rebecca Hays
Executive Managing Editor Todd Meier
Executive Food Editor Bryan Roof
Senior Editors Christie Morrison, Chris O'Connor, Diane Unger
Associate Editors Morgan Bolling, Katie Leaird, Ashley Moore
Test Cooks Allison Berkey, Daniel Cellucci, Matthew Fairman, Cecelia Jenkins
Assistant Test Cook Mady Nichas
Senior Copy Editor Krista Magnuson
Copy Editor Jillian Campbell
Contributing Editors Erika Bruce, Eva Katz
Science Editor Guy Crosby, PhD, CFS
Director, Creative Operations Alice Carpenter
Hosts & Executive Editors, Television Bridget Lancaster, Julia Collin Davison

Executive Editor, Tastings & Testings Lisa McManus
Managing Editor Scott Kathan
Deputy Editor Hannah Crowley
Associate Editors Lauren Savoie, Kate Shannon
Assistant Editor Miye Bromberg
Editorial Assistant Carolyn Grillo

Test Kitchen Director Erin McMurrer
Assistant Test Kitchen Director Leah Rovner
Test Kitchen Manager Alexxa Benson
Lead Senior Kitchen Assistant Meridith Lippard
Senior Kitchen Assistant Taylor Pond
Lead Kitchen Assistant Ena Gudiel
Kitchen Assistants Gladis Campos, Blanca Castanza

Design Director Greg Galvan
Photography Director Julie Cote
Art Director Susan Levin
Designer Maggie Edgar
Art Director, Marketing Melanie Gryboski
Deputy Art Director, Marketing Janet Taylor
Associate Art Director, Marketing Stephanie Cook
Senior Staff Photographer Daniel J. van Ackere
Staff Photographer Steve Klise
Assistant Photography Producer Mary Ball
Color Food Photography Keller + Keller
Styling Catrine Kelty, Marie Piraino

Senior Director, Digital Design John Torres
Executive Editor, Web Christine Liu
Managing Editor, Web Mari Levine
Senior Editor, Web Roger Metcalf
Associate Editors, Web Terrence Doyle, Briana Palma
Senior Video Editor Nick Dakoulas
Test Kitchen Photojournalist Kevin White

Chief Financial Officer Jackie McCauley Ford
Production Director Guy Rochford
Imaging Manager Lauren Robbins
Production & Imaging Specialists Heather Dube, Sean MacDonald, Dennis Noble, Jessica Voas
Senior Controller Theresa Peterson
Director, Business Partnerships Meghan Conciatori

Chief Digital Officer Fran Middleton
VP, Analytics & Media Strategy Deborah Fagone
Director, Sponsorship Marketing & Client Services Christine Anagnostis
National Sponsorship Sales Director Timothy Coburn
Client Services Manager Kate Zebrowski
Client Service & Social Media Coordinator Morgan Mannino
Partnership Marketing Manager Pamela Putprush
Director, Customer Support Amy Bootier
Senior Customer Loyalty & Support Specialists Rebecca Kowalski, Andrew Straaberg Finfrock
Customer Loyalty & Support Specialist Caroline Augliere

Senior VP, Human Resources & Organizational Development Colleen Zelina
Human Resources Director Adele Shapiro
Director, Retail Book Program Beth Ineson
Retail Sales Manager Derek Meehan
Associate Director, Publicity Susan Hershberg

Circulation Services ProCirc

On the cover: Double-Crust Chicken Pot Pie
Keller + Keller, Catrine Kelty
Illustration: Greg Stevenson

Contents

AMERICA'S TEST KITCHEN
RECIPES THAT WORK®

America's Test Kitchen is a real 2,500-square-foot kitchen located just outside Boston. It is the home of more than 60 test cooks, editors, and cookware specialists. Our mission is to test recipes until we understand exactly how and why they work and eventually arrive at the very best version. We also test kitchen equipment and supermarket ingredients in search of products that offer the best value and performance. You can watch us work by tuning in to *America's Test Kitchen* (AmericasTestKitchen.com) and *Cook's Country from America's Test Kitchen* (CooksCountry.com) on public television and listen to us on our weekly radio program on PRX. You can also follow us on Facebook, Twitter, Pinterest, and Instagram.

Cook's Country magazine (ISSN 1552-1990), number 72, is published bimonthly by America's Test Kitchen Limited Partnership, 17 Station St., Brookline, MA 02445. Copyright 2016 America's Test Kitchen Limited Partnership. Periodicals postage paid at Boston, MA, and additional mailing offices. USPS #023453. Publications Mail Agreement No. 40020778. Return undeliverable Canadian addresses to P.O. Box 875, Station A, Windsor, ON N9A 6P2. POSTMASTER: Send address changes to Cook's Country, P.O. Box 6018, Harlan, IA 51593-1518. For subscription and gift subscription orders, subscription inquiries, or change of address notices, visit AmericasTestKitchen.com/support, call 800-526-8447 in the U.S. or 515-248-7684 from outside the U.S., or write to us at Cook's Country, P.O. Box 6018, Harlan, IA 51593-1518. PRINTED IN THE USA.

Ask Cook's Country

BY MORGAN BOLLING

What's in a Name?

What's the difference between broccoli rabe, broccolini, and broccoli?
Jerry Schutz, Hopewell, Va.

Most Americans are familiar with broccoli, but not the other two. Broccoli, broccolini, and broccoli rabe are all cruciferous vegetables, but broccoli rabe is more closely related to turnips, another member of the *Brassicaceae* family. Broccolini is a cross between broccoli and Chinese broccoli, and it looks like broccoli stretched into a long, skinny form.

Broccoli rabe has a bitter bite that can be polarizing: People who love dark leafy greens are typically fans, while others can be turned off by its pungent flavor. In a recent tasting, our tasters lauded its "sharp" and "minerally" flavor and spicy finish. Broccolini is a bit sweeter than broccoli, with a flavor some tasters likened to a cross between spinach and asparagus.

THE BOTTOM LINE: Broccoli rabe is bitter and a bit spicy; broccolini is sweeter.

BROCCOLI
Supermarket staple

BROCCOLINI
Sweet, vegetal flavor

BROCCOLI RABE
Pleasantly pungent bite

Sizing up Carrots

Can you advise me on the weight or volume equivalency when you call for a single carrot in recipes?
Ellen Darrah-Schenk, Elkhart, Ind.

In the test kitchen, we specify vegetable size only if it's crucial to the success of the recipe. But we are as precise as possible in our recipe testing and development, so we do have an answer for you. Our default carrot size is "medium." What does that mean? We use the guideline that six medium carrots equal 1 pound, so one medium carrot weighs 2⅔ ounces. When peeled and chopped into ½-inch pieces, one medium carrot should yield a scant ½ cup.

THE BOTTOM LINE: One medium carrot should yield slightly less than ½ cup of chopped carrot.

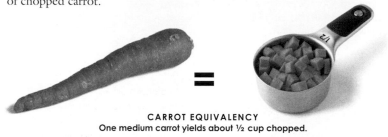

CARROT EQUIVALENCY
One medium carrot yields about ½ cup chopped.

Sugar Swap?

I love the test kitchen's Brown Sugar Cookies and make the recipe several times a year. I recently made it using organic dark brown sugar, and the cookies came out a bit tough. What gives?
Meghan Sheehan, South Tuscon, Ariz.

Intrigued by your results, we used regular brown sugar and organic brown sugar (either light or dark, per each recipe) to make batches of three of our recipes: Brown Sugar Cookies, Bourbon–Brown Sugar Whipped Cream, and Ultranutty Pecan Bars.

In the Bourbon–Brown Sugar Whipped Cream (which calls for light brown sugar), tasters barely noticed a difference. But in both the Brown Sugar Cookies (made with dark brown sugar) and the Ultranutty Pecan Bars (made with light brown sugar), the difference was clear: The cookies made with organic brown sugar were crispier and tougher. The pecan bars, which should be pleasantly chewy, were brittle and toffee-like when made with the organic sugar. And both samples made with the organic sugar felt grittier.

Why? Because most organic brown sugars are minimally processed, their crystals tend to be larger than those of regular brown sugar. We think of sugar as a dry ingredient, but it melts in the heat of the oven and thus provides baked goods with moisture. Larger crystals don't dissolve as readily when heated, which means that they are more likely to result in drier, grittier, crunchier treats.

THE BOTTOM LINE: Most organic brown sugars have larger crystals than standard brown sugar; these large crystals don't dissolve as readily in baked goods. Because of this, we do not recommend organic brown sugar for baking unless a recipe specifically calls for it.

Refreezing Pie Dough

I love the convenience of store-bought pie dough. The product I buy comes with two crusts—one for the bottom and one for the top of the pie. When I don't use both crusts in a pack, is it okay to refreeze the one that's already been thawed?
Alex Donovan, Mount Holly, N.J.

To find out if we could refreeze the extra roll of dough that often comes in packages of store-bought pie dough, we bought three varieties of prepared pie dough, including our taste-test winner, Wholly Wholesome 9" Certified Organic Traditional Bake at Home Rolled Pie Dough.

We tested frozen pie doughs that had been thawed for 24 hours in the refrigerator, refrozen, and thawed again (all in their original packages) and compared them with freshly thawed doughs. We sampled them baked without a filling, in our Lemon Chess Pie, and in our French Coconut Pie. While a few tasters noticed that the twice-thawed shells were slightly tougher than the fresh shells, most could not distinguish between the samples.

THE BOTTOM LINE: Go ahead and refreeze that extra roll of pie dough, preferably in its original packaging. If you opened the dough and took it out of its packaging, wrap it tightly in plastic before refreezing.

Mixed Bag

I recently bought one of those mesh bags of purple, yellow, and red baby potatoes. But when I roasted them all together, I found that the purple ones took longer to cook than the other two. Is there a reason?
Frank Gordon, Keokuk, Iowa

Raina Pape-Boone, a produce expert from Boston-area specialty grocer Sid Wainer and Sons, explained to us that most likely the three potatoes in your mesh bag are Purple, Yukon Gold, and Red Bliss potatoes.

Purple potatoes are a high-starch, low-moisture variety, similar to russets; when cooked, they become dry and fluffy. Red Bliss are low-starch potatoes that cook up firm, dense, and waxy. Yukon Golds are the middle ground, with a medium starch content.

When we bought a few bags of mixed-color potatoes and roasted them in a 450-degree oven, our results mirrored yours—the purple spuds took longer to cook. After a few more tests, we found that we could mitigate the problem by covering the pan with foil for the first 20 minutes of roasting. Purple potatoes contain less moisture than Red Bliss and Yukon Gold potatoes, meaning there's less moisture available to gelatinize the starch as the Purple potatoes cook and it takes them longer to cook. The foil traps steam and heat, which helps gelatinize the starch so the potatoes cook faster.

THE BOTTOM LINE: Small potatoes of different colors vary in starch and moisture contents, so they cook at dissimilar rates. If you want to roast them together, make sure to cover the roasting pan with foil. The foil traps steam and heat that speeds the cooking of the starchier potatoes and help equalize the cooking times.

A COLORFUL CONUNDRUM
Spuds of different hues cook at different rates.

▶ To ask us a cooking question, visit **CooksCountry.com/ask**. Or write to Ask *Cook's Country*, P.O. Box 470739, Brookline, MA 02447. Just try to stump us!

Kitchen Shortcuts

COMPILED BY DIANE UNGER

NEAT IDEA
Organize It!
Beth Haber, Colorado Springs, Colo.

Frosting and decorating holiday cookies can turn into a huge mess—especially if my kids are involved. To keep things neat and orderly, I use a 12-cup muffin tin to hold the sprinkles, glitter, and candy. This way all the decorations are contained in one place.

SMART TIP
Grate Idea for Brown Sugar
Mike Harrison, Palmyra, Va.

I've found myself with rock-hard brown sugar on many occasions; the kind that's too hard to salvage with any of the well-known tricks. Unwilling to pitch it in the trash, I've found that I can grate the sugar using a rasp-style grater and use the dry, granular sugar for sprinkling on oatmeal, berries, or buttered toast. Waste not, want not.

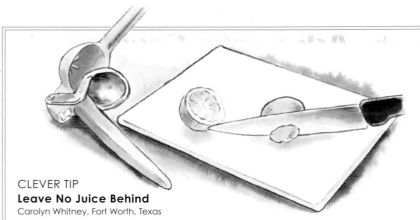

CLEVER TIP
Leave No Juice Behind
Carolyn Whitney, Fort Worth, Texas

Hinged handheld citrus juicers are great for squeezing small amounts of juice. But very often I find lots of juice left after squeezing. To extract the most juice with the least effort, I cut the ends off the lemon, halve it through the equator, and put the interior side facing down in the hopper. Then I squeeze, flip the fruit, and squeeze again. Cutting the ends off makes a world of difference.

SMART PREP
Skewering Line
Donald Barrows, Vernon, Conn.

I've come up with a trick to assemble kebabs quickly and with military precision. I cut everything into chunks, and then I slice a large potato in half lengthwise and set the halves cut side down on my cutting board. I insert three or four wooden skewers into each potato half and slide on the meat and vegetables in assembly-line fashion. When I'm done with the potatoes, I slice them up and either add them to the last skewers or grill them on the side.

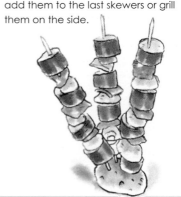

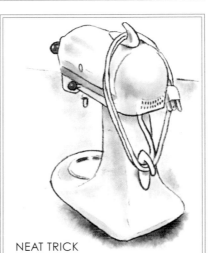

NEAT TRICK
Wrap it Up
Mary Prestidge, Tow Harbors, Minn.

I'm kind of a neatnik in the kitchen, especially when it comes to my kitchen appliances. I found an easy trick to keep straggling cords from my mixer or food processor in place. I use adhesive plastic hooks (the kind you might use for towels on your bathroom door) affixed to the back of the machines to wrap up cords and keep them out of the way.

GREEN CLEAN
Citrus Scent
Bob Ellis, Salem, Mass.

My wife and I aren't big fans of chemical-laden store-bought household cleaning products, so we make our own from vinegar and citrus peel. We just fill a spray bottle about ⅔ full with distilled white vinegar and add the peels of two lemons or oranges to the bottle. This cleaning solution works great on the stove, counters, etc., and the citrus helps cover the vinegar smell.

DOUBLE DUTY
Neater Mincing
Rosemary Mansfield, Amherst, Mass.

I add minced anchovy to a lot of different dishes: dressings, pizza, stews, and even tomato sauce. But as much as I appreciate the deep flavor, I hate getting the anchovy smell on my hands or my cutting board. I've discovered that I can easily mince anchovies in my garlic press. I just fill the hopper with anchovy filets, press, and scrape the minced anchovies off with the back of a knife. No mess or lingering odor.

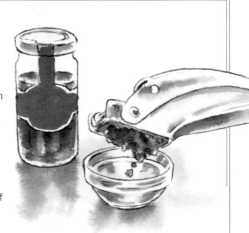

Submit a tip online at CooksCountry.com/kitchenshortcuts or send a letter to Kitchen Shortcuts, *Cook's Country*, P.O. Box 470739, Brookline, MA 02447. Include your name, address, and phone number. If we publish your tip, you will receive a free one-year subscription to *Cook's Country*. Letters may be edited for clarity and length.

Double-Crust Chicken Pot Pie

Patience is more than just a virtue. It's also the key to a perfect pot pie.

BY KATIE LEAIRD

I T'S HARD TO imagine anything more comforting than a traditional pot pie: savory chicken and vegetables suspended in a velvety cream gravy and topped with a flaky pie crust. That is, unless you imagine a perfect slice of this rich, savory pie, standing tall on a plate, with a second buttery crust underneath.

I started with a favorite test kitchen pie dough, which I bolstered with a beaten egg for richness (and to make it easier to work with), as well as a healthy dose of sour cream to lend it a slightly tangy flavor. The dough came together easily in the food processor and, after a quick knead to bring it all together and an hour-long chill in the fridge, it rolled out easily and neatly on my very lightly floured counter. I was ready to tackle the filling.

I wanted the pie's filling to be savory and satisfying but also just as simple to make as the crust. I sautéed vegetables (onion, carrots, and celery) with butter in a large saucepan, thickened this mixture with a generous sprinkling of flour, and whisked in some chicken broth and half-and-half. I cut a potato into tiny cubes and added them to the sauce, where they cooked through in just 8 minutes. After stirring in fresh thyme for an herbal boost and some salt and pepper for thorough seasoning, I had a flavorful base ready for cooked chicken.

In the past, we've used many methods for cooking chicken before adding it to pie filling, including poaching, sautéing, and baking. But all of these required additional pots and pans and quite a bit of time—and since this pie is already a project, I wanted an easier route. So I grabbed a grocery store rotisserie chicken, shredded the already-cooked meat—both light and dark—and stirred it into my filling. Not only was this a timesaver (and a dirty dish saver), but my filling turned out flavorful and moist.

I spooned the filling into the bottom crust and topped it with the rolled-out top crust before carefully crimping the edges, cutting four slits in the top for ventilation, and baking the pie for about 20 minutes at 450 degrees and 15 minutes longer at 375, until the crust was a gorgeous golden brown.

By now, the only trouble I was having was with serving. Whenever I sliced into the pie and lifted out a piece, the piping-hot filling just flowed out. I needed to thicken things up.

Brushing the top crust with beaten egg ensures a shiny, lacquered finish. Vent holes slit into the top help keep the crust crisp and the filling cohesive.

I was hesitant to increase the amount of flour for fear of turning the silky sauce into glue. I was equally wary of cornstarch. While I considered my options for a spell, the answer revealed itself: Simply letting the fully baked pie rest for 45 minutes gave it time to tighten up and become satisfyingly sliceable. And my crust didn't sog out at all. (Don't worry, it was still warm enough to eat.)

The hardest part of this recipe is waiting for the filling to firm up before slicing and serving the pie. I have no advice to offer other than "Good luck with that."

STEP BY STEP Double-Crust Chicken Pot Pie
Sour cream and egg bolster the dough so it's easy to roll out and stays crisp on the bottom.

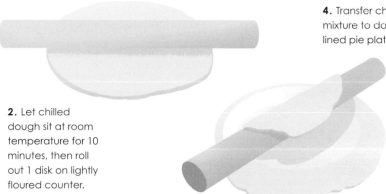

1. Prepare dough in food processor, knead briefly on counter, divide into 2 disks, and refrigerate for 1 hour.

2. Let chilled dough sit at room temperature for 10 minutes, then roll out 1 disk on lightly floured counter.

3. Loosely roll dough around pin, unroll onto pie plate, and gently press in. Roll out second disk and refrigerate.

4. Transfer chicken mixture to dough-lined pie plate.

5. Unroll top crust onto filling, trim and pinch edges, and tuck overhang. Crimp edge, cut slits in top, and brush with egg.

DOUBLE-CRUST CHICKEN POT PIE
Serves 6 to 8

The pie may seem loose when it comes out of the oven; it will set up as it cools. You can substitute 3 cups of turkey meat for the chicken, if desired.

CRUST
- ½ cup sour cream, chilled
- 1 large egg, lightly beaten
- 2½ cups (12½ ounces) all-purpose flour
- 1½ teaspoons salt
- 12 tablespoons unsalted butter, cut into ½-inch pieces and chilled

FILLING
- 4 tablespoons unsalted butter
- 1 onion, chopped fine
- 2 carrots, peeled and cut into ¼-inch pieces (⅔ cup)
- 2 celery ribs, cut into ¼-inch pieces (½ cup)
- ½ teaspoon salt
- ½ teaspoon pepper
- 6 tablespoons all-purpose flour
- 2¼ cups chicken broth
- ½ cup half-and-half
- 1 small russet potato (6 ounces), peeled and cut into ¼-inch pieces (1 cup)
- 1 teaspoon minced fresh thyme
- 1 (2½-pound) rotisserie chicken, skin and bones discarded, meat shredded into bite-size pieces (3 cups)
- ¾ cup frozen peas

- 1 large egg, lightly beaten

1. FOR THE CRUST: Combine sour cream and egg in bowl. Process flour and salt in food processor until combined, about 3 seconds. Add butter and pulse until only pea-size pieces remain, about 10 pulses. Add half of sour cream mixture and pulse until combined, 5 pulses. Add remaining sour cream mixture and pulse until dough begins to form, about 10 pulses.

2. Transfer mixture to lightly floured counter and knead briefly until dough comes together. Divide dough in half and form each half into 4-inch disk. Wrap disks tightly in plastic wrap and refrigerate for 1 hour. (Wrapped dough can be refrigerated for up to 2 days or frozen for up to 2 months. If frozen, let dough thaw completely on counter before rolling.)

3. Let chilled dough sit on counter to soften slightly, about 10 minutes, before rolling. Roll 1 disk of dough into 12-inch circle on lightly floured counter. Loosely roll dough around rolling pin and gently unroll it onto 9-inch pie plate, letting excess dough hang over edge. Ease dough into plate by gently lifting edge of dough with your hand while pressing into plate bottom with your other hand.

4. Roll other disk of dough into 12-inch circle on lightly floured counter, then transfer to parchment paper–lined baking sheet; cover with plastic. Refrigerate both doughs for 30 minutes.

5. FOR THE FILLING: Meanwhile, adjust oven rack to lowest position and heat oven to 450 degrees. Melt butter in large saucepan over medium heat. Add onion, carrots, celery, salt, and pepper and cook until vegetables begin to soften, about 6 minutes. Add flour and cook, stirring constantly, until golden, 1 to 2 minutes. Slowly stir in broth and half-and-half and bring to boil over medium-high heat.

6. Stir in potato and thyme. Reduce heat to medium and simmer until sauce is thickened and potato is tender, about 8 minutes. Off heat, stir in chicken and peas.

7. Transfer filling to dough-lined pie plate. Loosely roll remaining dough round around rolling pin and gently unroll it onto filling. Trim overhang to ½ inch beyond lip of plate. Pinch edges of top and bottom crusts firmly together. Tuck overhang under itself; folded edge should be flush with edge of plate. Crimp dough evenly around edge of plate using your fingers. Cut four 2-inch slits in top of dough.

8. Brush top of pie with egg. Place pie on rimmed baking sheet. Bake until top is light golden brown, 18 to 20 minutes. Reduce oven temperature to 375 degrees, rotate sheet, and continue to bake until crust is deep golden brown, 12 to 15 minutes longer. Let pie cool on wire rack for at least 45 minutes. Serve.

TO MAKE AHEAD
At end of step 6, transfer filling to bowl and refrigerate until fully chilled, about 1½ hours. Continue with step 7, then wrap pie tightly in plastic wrap and then aluminum foil. Freeze for up to 1 month. When ready to bake, unwrap frozen pie, cover with foil, and place on rimmed baking sheet (do not thaw). Place sheet on middle rack of cold oven and set oven to 375 degrees. Bake for 1¼ hours. Uncover pie and brush with egg. Rotate sheet and continue to bake until crust is golden brown and filling is beginning to bubble up through slits and registers at least 150 degrees, 55 minutes to 1¼ hours longer. Let cool for 45 minutes before serving.

Let It Cool Before Slicing It
Don't be tempted to eat the pot pie straight out of the oven. We tried it, and the piping-hot filling ran all over our plates. Letting the pie cool on a wire rack for at least 45 minutes gives the filling time to firm up just enough to hold together during slicing. (Don't worry, it will still be plenty hot.)

The American Table
Chicken Run

Until the 1920s, chickens were common enough, though they were raised primarily for eggs and not for meat. But in 1923, Delaware farmer Celia Steele was mistakenly sent 500 chicks instead of the 50 she'd ordered, and rather than send them back, she decided to raise them in her barn. Within weeks, she had a squawking surplus of "broilers," which she sold at a tidy profit, unknowingly kicking off a factory-farming boom. Enterprising entrepreneurs saw that chicken meat was (and still is) vastly less expensive to raise than beef or pork, and customers loved it.

By 1932, chicken was ubiquitous enough that President Herbert Hoover was reported to have promised "a chicken in every pot and a car in every garage" in an earlier campaign advertisement. He lost his reelection bid, but chicken was well on its way to being the most widely consumed meat in the country.

Transylvanian Goulash

No vampires were consulted in the making of this Pittsburgh favorite, but we did get some tips from a goulash master. BY CHRISTIE MORRISON

AMONG THE MOST popular dishes served at Alexander Bodnar's tiny restaurant in the Hazelwood neighborhood of Pittsburgh (see "On The Road") is his signature Transylvanian goulash. Like its Hungarian counterpart, Transylvanian goulash (named for the picturesque area in central Romania, Hungary's next door neighbor) is a flavorful stew made of browned meat, aromatic vegetables, and a heavy dose of paprika. But while most Hungarian goulash is made with beef, Bodnar's version features pork and tangy sauerkraut.

To re-create the dish, I started with a boneless pork butt roast that I cut into chunks. I knew that this cut has good marbling and was therefore well suited to a prolonged braise that would result in tender meat and deep flavor. Browning the pork in batches built up a flavorful fond in the bottom of the pot. I consulted Bodnar on the vegetables he uses to add complexity: onion, celery, green bell pepper, and a single tomato. I cooked these in the rendered pork fat for about 8 minutes to soften them before adding spices.

The dish's trademark red color and subtle earthy, slightly fruity flavor come from 3 tablespoons of sweet Hungarian paprika (not to be confused with sweet smoked paprika—a different beast entirely). I loved the addition of caraway seeds, another staple in Eastern European cooking; though sharp and assertive in rye and pumpernickel breads, the seeds' flavor mellows over the long cooking time into a subtle, almost citrusy presence.

While we often add chicken stock in the test kitchen to boost savory depth in all sorts of stews, Bodnar insisted that water would better allow the complex flavors of the different ingredients to shine. Tasters agreed: The stew was intensely flavored and deeply savory, especially after the addition of sauerkraut two-thirds of the way through cooking. But the sauerkraut was too sour to all but one of my tasters—a professed sauerkraut lover. At Bodnar's suggestion, I rinsed the sauerkraut to remove some of the excess brine and soften the flavor before adding it to the stew.

Once the pork was fully cooked and the stew was ready to serve, I took another cue from Bodnar and served it with a dollop of tangy sour cream and a sprinkling of fresh minced dill (a family tradition inspired by its abundance in his mother's garden).

The textures and flavors were in sync: The pork was perfectly tender but still held its shape, its richness balanced by the sturdy backbone of paprika and the faintly sharp sauerkraut. I had a satisfying, entirely comforting stew, full of flavors from Pittsburgh—and Transylvania, too.

Creamy, tangy sour cream adds character to this dish; a final toss of minced dill freshens it up.

INGREDIENT SPOTLIGHT Paprika

Some think of paprika as merely a coloring agent for soups and stews or a garnish for deviled eggs. With its deep reddish hue and rich, earthy flavor, paprika is an essential element of goulash. It's made by grinding dried sweet red chile peppers, a different variety than is used to make hot or smoked paprika.

TEST KITCHEN FAVORITE Our winning sweet paprika—The Spice House Hungarian Sweet Paprika—bested the competition with its "earthy," "fruity" flavors.

TRANSYLVANIAN GOULASH

Serves 6 to 8

Pork butt roast is often labeled Boston butt in the supermarket. Since paprika is vital to the success of this recipe, it is best to use a fresh bottle. Do not substitute hot or smoked Spanish paprika for the sweet paprika called for here. Eden Organic jarred sauerkraut is the test kitchen's favorite sauerkraut. Rinsing the sauerkraut reduces its sharp flavor and bite; if you prefer sharper sauerkraut flavor, omit this step. Serve with white rice, if desired.

- 1 (3½-pound) boneless pork butt roast, trimmed and cut into 1½-inch pieces
   Salt and pepper
- 1 tablespoon vegetable oil
- 1 onion, chopped fine
- 1 green bell pepper, stemmed, seeded, and chopped fine
- 2 celery ribs, chopped fine
- 1 plum tomato, chopped
- 3 tablespoons sweet paprika
- 1 tablespoon caraway seeds
- 2 garlic cloves, minced
- 3 cups water
- 2 cups sauerkraut, rinsed and drained
   Sour cream
   Minced fresh dill

1. Adjust oven rack to lower-middle position and heat oven to 325 degrees. Pat pork dry with paper towels and sprinkle with 1 teaspoon salt and ½ teaspoon pepper.

2. Heat oil in Dutch oven over medium-high heat until just smoking. Add half of pork and cook, stirring occasionally, until brown on all sides, about 8 minutes; transfer to bowl. (Reduce heat if bottom of pot begins to scorch.) Repeat with remaining pork.

3. Reduce heat to medium. Add onion, bell pepper, celery, tomato, and ½ teaspoon salt to now-empty pot and cook until vegetables are softened and liquid has evaporated, 8 to 10 minutes, scraping up any browned bits.

4. Add paprika, caraway seeds, and garlic and cook until fragrant, about 1 minute. Stir in water and pork and any accumulated juices and bring to simmer, scraping up any browned bits. Cover, transfer to oven, and cook for 1 hour. Stir in sauerkraut, cover, return pot to oven, and continue to cook until pork is fully tender, about 30 minutes longer.

5. Using wide spoon, skim off any surface fat. Season with salt and pepper to taste. Serve, garnished with sour cream and dill.

▶ Go to CooksCountry.com/pittsburgh to learn more about the food we ate in Pittsburgh and to see pictures of our trip.

ON THE ROAD

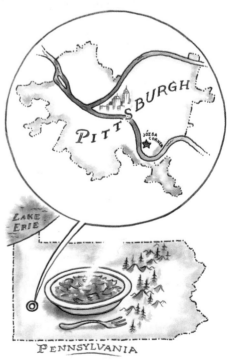

Alexander Bodnar, top, welcomes regulars and newcomers alike to his literal hole in the wall at Józsa Corner. Elbow to elbow, patrons use plastic cutlery and paper plates to devour the traditional Eastern European fare. The restaurant is located in Pittsburgh's Hazelwood neighborhood.

A Big, Strong Pittsburgh Belly

There's something very satisfying about finding a diamond in the rough. Hazelwood, a neighborhood a few minutes from downtown Pittsburgh, can accurately be described as "the rough"—a fact my cabbie was sure to reinforce—and the unassuming Hungarian restaurant Józsa Corner as "the diamond." It occupies a distressed whitewashed building along the railroad tracks where the owner, Alexander Józsa Bodnar, a veteran of the Hungarian Revolution of 1956, rules the kitchen.

One Friday a month, Bodnar hosts "Hungarian Night." You step through the main entrance directly into the kitchen, where Bodnar is feverishly preparing the coming meal. He welcomes everyone warmly. You then pass from the kitchen to the dining room through a sledgehammered opening in a weathered brick wall, which looks like the Hulk himself busted through one night in search of *paprikash*. Guests cozy up, elbow to elbow, at long tables in a converted living room where an ancient red velvet sofa and an old piano rest quietly unused.

Bodnar enters the dining room through the hole in the wall with a plate of yeasted fry bread called *lángos* and a bowl of mushroom paprikash to be spooned over the top, chanting "Egyetek, vegyetek, hadd n jön a begyetek," a saying that promotes the virtues of eating for a "big, strong belly." What follows is a simple meal with a personality as big as our host: peasant soup (so called for the many bones it contains), *haluska*, chicken paprikash, and goulash.

Although I'm dining with strangers, the mood transforms into one of a familiar dinner with close friends. Hours later, I leave, patting my own full, strong belly. –BRYAN ROOF

Grapefruit-Avocado Salad

A midwinter salad using in-season ingredients? Challenge accepted.

BY KATIE LEAIRD

Just ¼ cup of blanched hazelnuts, toasted in a skillet and chopped, adds crunch.

PALE GREEN AVOCADO and vibrant pink grapefruit, both in season during winter's bleakest months, make a handsome couple. At the fruits' best, the buttery and nutty notes of the soft avocado play well with the grapefruit's invigorating tang. But if assembled carelessly, the combination can be bitter and wet. I wanted a salad that showcased the natural beauty and best flavors of each fruit.

Grapefruit peel is intensely bitter, as is the pith—the soft white layer between the fruit and its skin. I tried simply cutting away these two offending layers and then slicing the exposed fruit into rounds. This method was quick and easy, but the result still retained too much membrane and was tricky to eat. The better method was to cut each segment away from its membranes, leaving pure, sweet bites of grapefruit.

Tossing cut-up avocado with the other salad ingredients made for a muddy result, so I had to assemble this salad less roughly. I dispensed with the idea of arranging the components on a platter in an alternating pattern of green and pink—too fancy and precious. Instead, I arranged a single layer of grapefruit segments over the avocado slices. Attractive and simple.

I considered incorporating salad greens, but these obscured the colors of the avocado and grapefruit. Instead, I went for herbs: Whole cilantro leaves and torn mint leaves packed plenty of flavor without becoming overwhelming, and they looked pretty, too. Toasted hazelnuts added a little crunch.

I needed a carefully crafted dressing with a strong olive oil presence and a little sugar to enhance the grapefruit's sweetness and temper its tang. I used a shallot for its subtle onion flavor and some Dijon for both its zip and its emulsifying properties. For brightness, I added juice left over from segmenting the grapefruits, along with a teaspoon of white wine vinegar.

GRAPEFRUIT-AVOCADO SALAD

Serves 4 to 6

A ripe avocado will yield slightly to a gentle squeeze when held in the palm of your hand.

- 3   red grapefruits
- 2   ripe avocados, halved, pitted, and sliced ¼ inch thick
- ¼   cup fresh mint leaves, torn
- ¼   cup fresh cilantro leaves
- ¼   cup blanched hazelnuts, toasted and chopped coarse
- 3   tablespoons extra-virgin olive oil
- 1   tablespoon minced shallot
- 1   teaspoon white wine vinegar
- 1   teaspoon Dijon mustard
- 1   teaspoon sugar
- ½   teaspoon salt

1. Cut away peel and pith from grapefruits. Holding fruit over bowl, use paring knife to slice between membranes to release segments. Reserve 2 tablespoons grapefruit juice.

2. Arrange avocado in single layer on large platter. Distribute grapefruit evenly over top. Sprinkle mint, cilantro, and hazelnuts over top.

3. Whisk oil, shallot, vinegar, mustard, sugar, salt, and reserved grapefruit juice together in bowl. Drizzle dressing over salad. Serve immediately.

TEST KITCHEN TIPS **Prepping the Main Ingredients for the Salad**

Grapefruit: Peel and Segment
Using a paring knife, trim away the peel and pith. Cut toward the center between the pulp and the membrane to remove each segment.

Avocado: Remove Pit and Scoop
Strike the pit sharply with a chef's knife. Twist the blade to remove the pit and use a dish towel to pull the pit off the blade. Insert a spoon between the skin and the flesh to separate the two.

Hazelnuts: Toast and Chop
Place the nuts in a dry skillet set over medium heat and stir frequently until they're fragrant and have darkened slightly, 3 to 5 minutes. To corral the nuts during chopping, place a cutting board inside a rimmed baking sheet.

Braised Leeks

A simple technique brings out the best in this often-neglected vegetable.

BY SARAH GABRIEL WITH MORGAN BOLLING

TOO OFTEN, FRESH and flavorful leeks end up as supporting players in soups—or worse, they never leave the grocery store produce aisle. I wanted to treat this underrated vegetable a little more carefully, braising it slowly to bring out its mild flavors in a warm dish suitable for still-brisk springtime nights.

I gathered a variety of existing recipes, and after much slicing, washing, browning, braising, whisking, and dressing, I called my tasters. We agreed on a few things: One, cutting the leeks lengthwise, leaving the root ends intact, made for the best presentation. Two, browning the leeks and then braising them in broth yielded the deepest flavor. And three, it had to be easy.

Back in the kitchen, I halved and washed 3 pounds of leeks, seasoned them with salt and pepper, and browned them in a skillet with olive oil. I then added a cup of chicken broth, covered the pan, reduced the heat, and braised the leeks for 30 minutes. The flavor was lovely—subtle and sweet—but the leeks were mushy and had begun to discolor. After experimenting with various cooking times, I found that about 10 minutes brought out plenty of sweetness and yielded tender, not mushy, leeks.

They were delicious, but they needed a dressing. I combined some white wine vinegar, Dijon mustard, minced garlic, oil, salt, and pepper in a jar; screwed on the lid tightly; and shook the jar vigorously. I then drizzled the vinaigrette over the leeks. It was good, but it overshadowed, rather than amplified, the bright flavor of the leeks.

Maybe instead of discarding the now-flavorful liquid I'd used for braising the leeks, I could use it to bolster the flavor of my dish. I had about ⅔ cup left in the skillet, but simply adding a bit of this liquid did not contribute much flavor. If I used more, the dressing was watery. I found success by simmering the liquid, still in the skillet, down to 2 tablespoons and adding it to the other dressing ingredients (leaving out the salt because the concentrated stock was salty). Chopped fresh tarragon added a subtle licorice-like note.

Finally, I had tender leeks and a flavorful, balanced vinaigrette—not to mention a simple new vegetable dish to spruce up my side-dish repertoire.

BRAISED LEEKS

Serves 4 to 6

We prefer to use leeks measuring 1 inch or less in diameter for this recipe because they're more tender than larger leeks. Larger leeks will work, but discard their first two outer layers because they tend to be fibrous. Orienting the leeks in one direction makes them easier to transfer in and out of the skillet. When trimming the leeks, be careful to leave the root ends intact so that the layers stay together when the leeks are halved. If you don't have a small jar with a lid, whisk the vinaigrette together in a bowl.

- 3 pounds small (1-inch-diameter) leeks, white and light green parts only
  Salt and pepper
- 6 tablespoons extra-virgin olive oil
- 1 cup chicken broth
- 1 tablespoon white wine vinegar
- 1 teaspoon Dijon mustard
- 1 small garlic clove, minced
- 1 tablespoon chopped fresh tarragon

1. Trim roots from leeks, leaving ends intact so layers stay together when halved. Halve leeks lengthwise, wash thoroughly between layers to remove any dirt, and pat dry with paper towels. Season cut sides with salt and pepper.

2. Heat 1 tablespoon oil in 12-inch nonstick skillet over medium-high heat until shimmering. Add half of leeks to skillet, with root ends pointed in same direction, and cook until browned, about 2 minutes per side. Transfer to plate. Repeat with 1 tablespoon oil and remaining leeks.

3. Return all leeks to skillet, facing same direction. Add broth and bring to boil. Cover, reduce heat to medium-low, and simmer until leeks are tender when poked with tip of paring knife, 10 to 12 minutes. Using slotted spatula, transfer leeks to shallow serving platter, leaving braising liquid in skillet.

4. Increase heat to medium-high and bring braising liquid to boil; cook until reduced to about 2 tablespoons, 2 to 4 minutes. Transfer braising liquid to small jar and add vinegar, mustard, garlic, remaining ¼ cup oil, ¼ teaspoon salt, and ¼ teaspoon pepper. Affix lid and shake jar vigorously until vinaigrette is emulsified, about 15 seconds. Spoon vinaigrette over leeks. Sprinkle with tarragon and serve.

We use a bit of reserved braising liquid to add deep leek flavor to the simple dressing.

Prepping Leeks for Braising

For this recipe, choose leeks that measure 1 inch or less in diameter. If you can find only larger leeks, remove the first two fibrous outer layers.

Carefully trim roots from leek bottoms, keeping ends intact so layers stay together when halved.

Halve each leek lengthwise, then rinse each half under cool running water, gently fanning out leaves to rinse between layers. Pat dry.

Pork Marsala

Could we use pork in this sweet-savory weeknight supper without it drying out?

BY ASHLEY MOORE

VEAL MARSALA, THIN cutlets or medallions of meat served with mushrooms and sweet Marsala wine, is a ubiquitous menu item at Italian American restaurants. You'll find pork Marsala, too, but it tends to be dry and disappointing.

I knew I'd have to choose the right cut of pork, one that's easy to work with but also tender and quick-cooking. Pork loin proved too tough, but pork tenderloin, cut into slices, worked better. After pounding the slices into thin cutlets, however, I found that they too easily overcooked. Instead, I settled on 1½-inch-thick medallions. I could cut 12 from two tenderloins, enough to serve four people heartily or six less-hungry people.

I was happy to find that my medallions all fit into a single 12-inch skillet. They developed a pleasantly brown crust after about 4 minutes on each side, by which time the meat registered 140 degrees inside—perfect. That is, except for the uneven end pieces, which cooked too quickly and got tough. The best solution was to trim off the narrow ends of the tenderloins before I portioned the rest into equal medallions.

I let the cooked pork rest while I made the rest of the dish. Seeing how some of the mushrooms turned soggy in my initial five-recipe test, I turned to cremini mushrooms rather than regular button mushrooms, since they have a meatier texture and would hold up better. I also found that cooking the mushrooms first, until they were brown and tender, and then removing them from the skillet to cook the pork, gave me more consistent results, both in the meat and the mushrooms.

With the pork and mushroom sequence locked down, I moved on to the defining element of this dish: the Marsala sauce. I drew on a test kitchen recipe we've used in the past for chicken Marsala that achieves a fine balance of sweetness from Marsala wine, savoriness from chicken broth, and slight acidity from lemon juice. A tablespoon of flour for thickening, some aromatic shallots, and a final stir-in of cold butter gave me the ideal consistency—just thick enough to coat the meat without being overly sweet.

Cancel your reservation at the Italian restaurant—dinner tonight comes from your own kitchen.

Because we use medallions rather than cutlets, our pork stays tender and moist.

INGREDIENT SPOTLIGHT
Marsala

Marsala, which comes from Sicily, is a fortified wine. This means that brandy or a neutral spirit has been added to it. It can be found in both sweet and dry styles, a classification based primarily on the residual sugar content of the wine. Aside from the obvious—sweet Marsala tasted sweeter than dry—the dry type features raisin and prune flavors balanced by sharp acidity and savory, nutty notes. Sweet Marsalas possess those same dried-fruit flavors but also offer hints of molasses and caramel. For this recipe, be sure to use the dry type.

TECHNIQUE

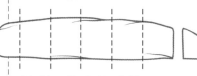

Making Pork Medallions

Cut away about 1 inch from tail of each tenderloin; reserve for another use. Cut each tenderloin crosswise into 6 equal medallions, about 1½ inches thick. Press medallions lightly to even thickness.

PORK MARSALA Serves 4 to 6

We trim off the narrow tail portions of the tenderloins to ensure evenly sized (and cooked) pork medallions. Reserve the trimmed pieces for another use. Be sure to buy dry Marsala, not sweet.

- 2 (12- to 16-ounce) pork tenderloins, trimmed
  Salt and pepper
- ¼ cup olive oil
- 12 ounces cremini mushrooms, trimmed and sliced thin
- 1 shallot, minced
- 3 garlic cloves, minced
- 1 tablespoon all-purpose flour
- 1 cup chicken broth
- ¾ cup dry Marsala
- 4 tablespoons unsalted butter, cut into 4 pieces and chilled
- 1 tablespoon lemon juice
- 1 tablespoon minced fresh parsley

1. Cut 1-inch piece from tail end of each tenderloin; reserve for another use. Cut each tenderloin crosswise into 6 equal medallions, about 1½ inches thick. Press medallions lightly to even thickness, then pat dry with paper towels and season with salt and pepper.

2. Heat 1 tablespoon oil in 12-inch nonstick skillet over medium-high heat until shimmering. Add mushrooms, ¼ teaspoon salt, and ¼ teaspoon pepper and cook, stirring occasionally, until liquid has evaporated and mushrooms are well browned, about 10 minutes. Transfer to bowl; cover to keep warm.

3. Add 2 tablespoons oil to now-empty skillet and heat over medium-high heat until just smoking. Add pork and cook until well browned and centers register 140 degrees, about 4 minutes per side. Transfer pork to platter and tent with aluminum foil.

4. Heat remaining 1 tablespoon oil in now-empty skillet over medium-high heat until shimmering. Add shallot, garlic, flour, ¼ teaspoon salt, and ¼ teaspoon pepper and cook until shallot is softened, about 1 minute. Stir in broth and Marsala and bring to boil. Cook until reduced to 1 cup and slightly thickened, about 5 minutes.

5. Reduce heat to low and whisk in butter, 1 piece at a time, until emulsified. Stir in lemon juice, parsley, mushrooms, and any accumulated pork juices. Season with salt and pepper to taste. Spoon sauce over pork and serve.

Crispy Skillet Turkey Burgers

A juicy, flavorful turkey burger would be good enough—but we wanted crispy edges, too.

BY KATIE LEAIRD

SO MUCH CAN go wrong with a turkey burger. Even when made with care, it can be dry, dense, or totally lacking in flavor. We've cracked the code before in the test kitchen, but our process involved grinding our own turkey meat. I wanted a moist, flavorful turkey burger using store-bought ground turkey. And what's more, I wanted slightly crispy edges.

First I had to rectify the pitfalls of most turkey burgers—dryness and denseness—without changing the culprits: the relative lack of fat and the need to cook turkey to 160 degrees.

To fight dryness, you can add moisture, which usually means adding fat. Using fattier ground turkey (usually a blend of white and dark meat and about 93 percent lean) instead of ground turkey breast (white meat only and up to 99 percent lean) made a difference. So did adding a bit of mayonnaise to the mix, which was easy to incorporate.

But in the end it was the density of bad turkey burgers that clued me in to the most transformative fix: a panade. We often add a panade of bread crumbs and dairy to our meatloaf mixture to create juicy pockets within the ground meat and keep it from coagulating too tightly when cooked. Much like meat loaf, my turkey burgers needed a bit of internal physical disruption to keep them from being so dense.

After several experiments, I settled on a combination of panko bread crumbs and shredded cheese; with the mayonnaise, this served as a panade. The cheese—just 2 ounces for four burgers—also added a delicate savory flavor. And the exposed cheese on the tops and bottoms of the burgers crisped up into a browned, *frico*-like crust—a crispy, savory foil to the tender juiciness inside.

Talk about easy: All four burgers could be cooked together in a nonstick skillet over medium heat until deeply browned and crunchy. Flipping the burgers just once made the process a snap. My final recipe required no more than 10 minutes and one skillet.

Since the flavors of the mayonnaise and cheese are subtle, these burgers are great canvases for any additional flavors. Standards like ketchup, mustard, lettuce, and tomato dress up the turkey burgers in a classic style. If you like southwestern flavors, try layering some pickled jalapeños on the patties and a smear of mashed avocado on the buns. Or give the burgers a smoky slant with some barbecue sauce and a couple of slices of bacon.

CRISPY SKILLET TURKEY BURGERS
Serves 4

Be sure to use 93 percent lean ground turkey, not 99 percent fat-free ground turkey breast, in this recipe or the burgers will be tough. Serve with your favorite burger toppings, including Pickled Onions (recipe follows).

- 1 pound ground turkey
- 1 cup panko bread crumbs
- 2 ounces Monterey Jack cheese, shredded (½ cup)
- ¼ cup mayonnaise
-    Salt and pepper
- 1 tablespoon vegetable oil
- 4 hamburger buns, toasted and buttered

1. Combine turkey, panko, Monterey Jack, mayonnaise, ½ teaspoon salt, and ½ teaspoon pepper in bowl. Using your hands, pat turkey mixture into four ¾-inch-thick patties, about 4 inches in diameter. Season patties with salt and pepper.

2. Heat oil in 12-inch nonstick skillet over medium heat until shimmering. Add patties and cook until well browned and meat registers 160 degrees, about 5 minutes per side.

3. Place burgers on buns and serve.

PICKLED ONIONS
Makes about 2 cups

- 1 small red onion, halved and sliced thin
- 2 jalapeño chiles, stemmed and sliced into thin rings
- 1 cup white wine vinegar
- 2 tablespoons lime juice
- 1 tablespoon sugar
- 1 teaspoon salt

Combine onion and jalapeños in medium bowl. Bring vinegar, lime juice, sugar, and salt to boil in small saucepan. Pour vinegar mixture over onion mixture and let sit for at least 30 minutes. (Pickled onions can be made in advance and refrigerated for up to 1 week.)

Sure, they're juicy, but what made these burgers the talk of the kitchen was their crispy exteriors.

KEY INGREDIENTS
Panko, Mayo, and Cheese

Most supermarket ground turkey is very lean and has a tendency to cook up dry. Our three key mix-ins—bread crumbs, mayonnaise, and cheese—help solve this problem, creating a burger that's juicy on the inside and crispy on the outside.

When shopping for ground turkey, look for 93 percent lean meat—not 99 percent lean. (Fat content is indicated on the label but is not always listed prominently.) Your best bet? Ask the butcher to grind it for you. The coarser grind of store-ground meat will give you the most tender, most juicy burger of all. Mayonnaise adds fat to the lean meat, and panko bread crumbs prevent it from becoming too dense. Shredded Monterey Jack cooks up into a well-browned, crispy, cheesy crust.

TERRIFIC TRIO
Panko prevents the meat from becoming dense as it cooks. Mayonnaise adds fat for juiciness. And grated Monterey Jack creates a crispy, cheesy crust.

Cast Iron Calzone

Handheld calzones are great. But we wanted something bigger.

BY RUSSELL SELANDER

THE CALZONE, SIMILAR to pizza, has been a mainstay in America since the dish traveled here with Italians in the late 19th and early 20th centuries. These half-moon-shaped hand pies were popular midday meals, often sold from carts and eaten on the run. I set out to reinvent the calzone as a shareable meal serving several people.

Step one: I ruled out the half-moon pies in favor of a single large, circular calzone. To keep it easy, I started with store-bought pizza dough (though homemade worked just as well).

I knew that a cast-iron skillet would be an ideal vessel because I could use it first to cook the meat and then again as the perfect baking vessel. Its high sides would allow for easy assembly and keep this massive calzone contained while also conducting heat directly onto the crust, producing a crisp-chewy texture.

For my filling, I settled on two cheeses: creamy ricotta for richness and melty mozzarella for gooeyness. Crumbled Italian sausage and sliced pepperoni, seared in the skillet and drained on a paper towel–lined plate to remove excess grease, made this a meat lover's dream. Marinara sauce was a must, and fresh basil added just a bit of freshness.

Next, it was time for construction. I kneaded 2 pounds of pizza dough and split it into two portions, using the bigger portion (two-thirds of the dough) for the larger bottom crust. I rolled this out and nestled it into the pan. Atop, I sprinkled a cup of mozzarella and then about ½ pound of sausage and pepperoni, which I'd stirred together with the ricotta and basil. Next came marinara sauce and another cup of mozzarella. I laid the remaining dough over the top, sliced in some air vents, sealed the edges with an egg wash, and pinched the sides together.

Nailing the best oven temperature and placement took some experimentation. Too cold and the crust didn't crisp up; too hot and the crust just overcooked. I settled on 450 degrees and the lower-middle rack, which kept the top from getting too dark while the filling got hot. After about 30 minutes, I pulled out a golden-brown, aromatic calzone.

But there was too much dough for the amount of filling. So for my next test, I doubled the filling to include more than a pound of meat, 8 ounces of ricotta, and a full pound of mozzarella. Once the calzone was baked, I let it cool for about 30 minutes before effortlessly popping the entire calzone out of the pan. I was delighted to find that I could easily slice it into wedges, with strings of gooey mozzarella forming as I pulled the first piece away. Perfect.

CAST-IRON SKILLET CALZONE
Serves 8

Room-temperature dough is much easier to shape than cold dough, so pull the dough from the fridge about 1 hour before you plan to start cooking. Use low-sodium marinara sauce to prevent the calzone from becoming overly salty.

- 2 teaspoons extra-virgin olive oil
- 1 pound sweet or hot Italian sausage, casings removed
- 4 ounces thinly sliced pepperoni, quartered
- 2 garlic cloves, minced
- 2 (1-pound) balls pizza dough, room temperature
- 1 pound mozzarella cheese, shredded (4 cups)
- 8 ounces (1 cup) whole-milk ricotta cheese
- 2 tablespoons chopped fresh basil
- 1 teaspoon pepper
- 1 cup low-sodium marinara sauce, plus extra for serving
- 1 large egg, lightly beaten with 2 tablespoons water
- 2 teaspoons toasted sesame seeds

1. Adjust oven rack to lower-middle position and heat oven to 450 degrees. Heat 12-inch cast-iron skillet over medium heat for 3 minutes. Add oil and heat until shimmering. Add sausage and pepperoni and cook, breaking up meat with wooden spoon, until sausage is no longer pink, 5 to 7 minutes. Stir in garlic and cook until fragrant, about 30 seconds. Using slotted spoon, transfer meat mixture to paper towel–lined plate. Wipe skillet clean with paper towels.

2. Knead dough balls together on lightly floured counter to create 1 large ball, 8 to 10 turns. Divide dough ball into two-thirds and one-third (one 22-ounce piece and one 10-ounce piece).

3. Press and roll larger piece of dough into 16-inch round. (Keep remaining dough covered with greased plastic wrap.) Loosely roll dough around rolling pin and gently unroll it onto now-empty skillet, letting excess dough hang over edge. Ease dough into skillet by gently lifting edge of dough with your hand while pressing into skillet bottom with your other hand. Some dough will overhang edge of skillet; leave in place.

4. Sprinkle 2 cups mozzarella over surface of dough. Combine ricotta, basil, pepper, and meat mixture in bowl. Dollop ricotta mixture over mozzarella and press into even layer. Spread marinara over top, then sprinkle with remaining 2 cups mozzarella.

5. Brush overhanging dough with some of egg wash. Press and roll remaining dough piece into 14-inch circle; loosely roll dough around rolling pin and gently unroll it onto skillet.

Trim overhang to ½ inch beyond edge of skillet. Pinch edges of top and bottom crusts firmly together. Tuck overhang under itself; folded edge should be flush with edge of skillet. Crimp dough with tines of fork.

6. Brush top of calzone with remaining egg wash and sprinkle with sesame seeds. Using paring knife, cut eight 1-inch vents in top of dough in circular pattern. Transfer skillet to oven and bake until crust is golden brown, about 30 minutes, rotating skillet halfway through baking.

7. Transfer skillet to wire rack and let calzone cool for 30 minutes. Using spatula, slide calzone onto cutting board. Slice into wedges and serve, passing extra marinara separately.

Store-bought pizza dough and marinara take this from an all-day project to a weeknight supper.

Stovetop-Roasted Chicken

Crispy-skinned chicken pieces on top of the stove, with no mess and no fuss?
An unconventional method makes it easy. BY DIANE UNGER

BONE-IN CHICKEN PARTS, from kid-friendly drumsticks to parent-pleasing breasts and thighs, are one of my favorite weeknight suppers. Bone-in pieces are juicier and more economical than boneless. But they are usually relegated to the oven, and they take time to cook. I wanted roast-chicken flavor with crispy skin in one skillet on the stovetop, with delicious browned bits left in the skillet to make a pan sauce.

The variables: which pan to use and at what temperature, if and when to flip the pieces, and if and when to cover them. I tested a variety of techniques, but none was easy or foolproof enough. Then I came across a method that intrigued me: chicken arranged skin side down in a cold nonstick skillet.

Why not? I nestled the pieces in the skillet and then turned the heat to high. Once the skin had browned, I covered the skillet to help the chicken cook through. I was sure the chicken was going to stick to the skillet, or worse, turn out steamy and greasy. But to my surprise, the skin was golden and crispy and the meat supertender. The stove, however, was a mess, splattered with chicken grease from corner to corner.

So for my next test, I again placed the chicken in a cold nonstick skillet, but this time I covered the pan before browning the chicken over a more moderate medium heat, hoping that covering the skillet the whole time would trap the mess and keep the chicken moist. After about 15 minutes, I cranked the heat to medium-high and cooked the chicken 10 to 15 minutes longer. Bingo: The skin was deep golden brown, and every piece was cooked through and juicy.

TEST KITCHEN TRICK
Browning Like You've Never Seen
Placing the chicken in a cold nonstick skillet and covering it before turning on the heat gives the fatty skin time to slowly render and turn deeply browned and crispy.

The gorgeous browned bits in the pan were perfect for a quick sauce. I cooked rosemary and garlic until they were fragrant and added lemon juice and water. Off heat, I whisked in butter and chives. Adding capers, sun-dried tomatoes, or cornichons with other herbs made easy, flavorful variations.

STOVETOP-ROASTED CHICKEN WITH LEMON-HERB SAUCE
Serves 4

For even cooking, it's important to buy chicken pieces within the specifications given. If you prefer all dark meat, this recipe will work with a total of eight bone-in thighs or drumsticks; if you prefer all white meat, you can use four bone-in breasts. Note that the chicken is started in a cold skillet to give the fat time to render.

CHICKEN
- 2 (10- to 12-ounce) bone-in split chicken breasts, trimmed
- 4 (5- to 7-ounce) bone-in chicken thighs or drumsticks, trimmed
  Salt and pepper
- ½ teaspoon minced fresh rosemary

HERB SAUCE
- 2 garlic cloves, minced
- ½ teaspoon minced fresh rosemary
- 2 tablespoons water
- ½ teaspoon grated lemon zest plus 1 tablespoon juice
- 6 tablespoons unsalted butter, cut into 6 pieces
- 1 tablespoon minced fresh chives
  Salt and pepper

1. FOR THE CHICKEN: Pat chicken dry with paper towels. Place breasts on cutting board, bone side down, and cover with plastic wrap. Using meat pounder, pound thick ends of breasts to ¾- to 1-inch thickness. Season all chicken pieces with salt and pepper. Place chicken, skin side down, in cold 12-inch nonstick skillet and sprinkle with rosemary.

2. Cover skillet and place over medium heat. (If using electric stove, preheat burner for 3 minutes over medium heat.) Cook chicken, without moving it, until skin is light golden brown, about 15 minutes.

3. Increase heat to medium-high and continue to cook, covered, until skin is deep golden brown and crispy and breasts register 160 degrees and

Our bright pan sauce, made with fresh rosemary and chives, gives this dish a vibrant finish.

thighs/drumsticks register at least 175 degrees, 10 to 15 minutes longer, rotating skillet halfway through cooking. (If using drumsticks, flip them during last 5 minutes of cooking.) Transfer chicken, skin side up, to platter and tent with aluminum foil.

4. FOR THE HERB SAUCE: While chicken rests, pour off all but 2 teaspoons fat from skillet. Add garlic and rosemary and cook over medium heat until fragrant, about 30 seconds, scraping up any browned bits. Off heat, stir in water and lemon zest and juice. Whisk in butter, 1 piece at a time, until smooth and emulsified.

5. Stir in chives and any accumulated chicken juices; season with salt and pepper to taste. Spoon sauce over chicken and serve.

STOVETOP-ROASTED CHICKEN WITH LEMON-CAPER SAUCE
Add 2 tablespoons minced capers to skillet with garlic in step 4. Substitute ½ teaspoon minced fresh thyme for chives.

STOVETOP-ROASTED CHICKEN WITH LEMON-CORNICHON SAUCE
Add 2 tablespoons minced cornichons to skillet with garlic in step 4. Substitute 2 teaspoons minced fresh tarragon for chives.

STOVETOP-ROASTED CHICKEN WITH LEMON–SUN-DRIED TOMATO SAUCE
Add ¼ cup oil-packed sun-dried tomatoes, chopped, to skillet with garlic in step 4. Increase rosemary in sauce to 1 teaspoon and omit chives.

Chocolate Haupia Cream Pie

The name takes some sounding out, but once we'd settled the recipe,
this Hawaiian pie was the talk of the test kitchen. BY CECELIA JENKINS

THE FIRM PUDDING made with coconut milk and customarily served in chilled cubes is known as haupia (pronounced how-PEE-ah) in Hawaii. Though it's wonderful on its own, why not put it in a pie? And for that matter, why not put it in a two-tone pie with melted chocolate added to one layer? This is not just a good idea—it's a delicious reality at Hawaiian bakeries such as Ted's, located on Oahu. I wanted to bring it home to my kitchen.

Rather than the rich, ploppable stuff you usually think of as pudding, haupia is firmer. Experiments with existing recipes gave me haupia that resembled bouncy Jell-O and was far too sweet. I wanted stable yet delicate pudding, balanced but insistent coconut flavor, and measured sweetness.

I also wanted my pie to be easy, so I decided up front to use a store-bought pie crust, which I baked until it was golden brown and flaky. I then set it aside to cool and got to work on the filling.

Haupia's key ingredient is coconut milk. To ensure a thick pudding, I knew I'd need a product with plenty of fat (our favorite is Chaokoh). I whisked a 13.5-ounce can of coconut milk together with 1 cup of water, ½ cup of sugar, and 3 tablespoons of cornstarch and cooked the lot in a saucepan over medium heat until it began to thicken, about 6 minutes.

Next, I melted 4 ounces of chopped semisweet chocolate in the microwave and stirred it together with half the pudding. I spread this chocolaty mixture into the cooled pie shell and rewhisked the remaining coconut pudding in the saucepan to smooth out any lumps that had formed while it sat. I then poured it on top of the chocolate layer, spreading it evenly with a spatula. I chilled the pie in the fridge until I was certain it had set up completely, about 4 hours.

Slicing into this first attempt, my heart sank. The knife mushed the layers together, leaving me with a droopy, sad blob that ran all over the plate—not the perfect, semifirm, two-tone slice I'd imagined. And my layers were uneven, with the chocolate layer much too thick.

To address the consistency of the pudding, I increased the amount of cornstarch to 5 tablespoons, but this gave me a too-firm filling that I could bounce a nickel off (true story; I tried). Decreasing

A blanket of whipped cream stars is traditional, but we won't tell if you prefer simpler dollops.

the cornstarch to 4 tablespoons proved best for creating clean slices.

One ingredient was bugging me: water. I knew I needed the liquid to dissolve the cornstarch and achieve the consistency I sought, but I wondered: Would a more flavorful liquid give me a better pie? To find out, I made three pies: one with water, one with milk, and one with an additional cup of coconut milk.

The pie with the extra coconut milk tasted chalky and a bit sour; the pie with water was too lean. But the pie with milk had rich, round coconut flavor. Further testing showed me that both whole milk and 2 percent low-fat milk worked fine, but skim milk was a bust.

I looked over my method for more ways to streamline it, and found that I could ditch the microwave and simply pour the hot pudding over the chopped chocolate to let its residual heat do the work. After a few more experiments, I determined that rather than dividing the pudding equally and adding chocolate to one portion, dividing it slightly unevenly and mixing the chocolate with just a cup of the hot pudding created perfectly equal layers.

To finish things off, I piped sweetened whipped cream on top of the pie. I then sliced it and stood back while coworkers dove in like surfers along Waikiki Beach.

CHOCOLATE HAUPIA CREAM PIE
Serves 8 to 10

We prefer Chaokoh or Thai Kitchen coconut milk for this recipe. Do not use "lite" coconut milk or any coconut milk that has less than 12 grams of fat and/or greater than 3 grams of sugar per ⅓-cup serving. If you do, the pudding will be too runny and sweet. While we prefer whole milk in this recipe, 2 percent low-fat milk will also work. We use a pastry bag outfitted with a star tip to decorate the pie with whipped cream. Our favorite piping set is the Wilton 20-Piece Beginning Buttercream Decorating Set.

CRUST
- 1 (9-inch) store-bought pie dough round

FILLING
- 4 ounces semisweet chocolate, chopped
- 1 (13.5-ounce) can unsweetened coconut milk
- 1 cup whole milk
- ½ cup (3½ ounces) sugar
- ¼ cup (1 ounce) cornstarch
- ⅛ teaspoon salt

TOPPING
- 1 cup heavy cream, chilled
- 1 tablespoon sugar

1. FOR THE CRUST: Adjust oven rack to lower-middle position and heat oven to 375 degrees. Roll dough into 12-inch circle on lightly floured counter. Loosely roll dough around rolling pin and gently unroll it onto 9-inch pie plate, letting excess dough hang over edge. Ease dough into plate by gently lifting edge of dough with your hand while pressing into plate bottom with your other hand.

2. Trim overhang to ½ inch beyond lip of plate. Tuck overhang under itself; folded edge should be flush with edge of plate. Crimp dough evenly around edge of plate using your fingers. Wrap dough-lined plate loosely in plastic wrap and freeze until dough is firm, about 15 minutes.

3. Line chilled pie shell with parchment paper or double layer of aluminum foil, covering edges to prevent burning, and fill with pie weights. Bake until edges are light golden brown, about 20 minutes, rotating plate halfway through baking. Remove parchment

The American Table
Monster Waves, Monster Pie

Long before Oahu's North Shore became the tourist haven it is today, it was a stretch of cow pastures known only to local ranchers and a small community of die-hard counterculture surfers, who considered the area's "monster" waves among the best in the world. It was here, just a few miles from the legendary Waimea Bay, that local farmer Takemitsu Nakamura, a second-generation American, opened the Sunset Beach Store with his wife, Eva, in 1956. The modest shop functioned as a general store in the sparsely populated area.

Thirty years later, Nakamura's son Ted integrated a bakery into the store, fueling those brave (some would say foolhardy) surfers with an appropriately caloric diet of doughnuts, breads, and cakes.

Ted's Bakery soon became the most profitable piece of the family business. He added pies to the menu—macadamia cream pie, *lilikoi* (passion fruit) pie, and chocolate haupia pie. At first the bakers produced 20 pies a day to sell on site, but once local restaurants caught wind of how good they were, Ted's began taking commercial orders. Before long, Ted's Bakery was baking more than 15,000 pies a week for restaurants all over the island. Today, chocolate haupia pie is a popular dessert not only on any given Tuesday but for marquee holidays as well—many Hawaiian households now consider it an essential element of a Thanksgiving or Christmas spread.

Visit any Hawaiian island these days and you'll encounter versions of chocolate haupia pie at fancy restaurants and modest storefront bakeries alike. But pie purists, just like those intrepid surfers, still make the pilgrimage to the original Ted's Bakery, where they line up for slices of chocolate haupia pie even as monster waves crash onto Sunset Beach, just across the Kamehameha Highway.

Should You Buy a Cream Whipper?

There are few desserts that aren't improved by a swirl of fresh whipped cream. The easiest way to make it is to use a cream whipper, a pressurized canister powered by nitrous oxide. You simply fill the canister with heavy cream, twist on a single-use nitrous oxide charger, shake to distribute the gas, and press a lever to pipe out swirls and rosettes. But many cream whippers retail for upwards of $100.00. Are they worth the expense?

Eager to find out, we rounded up nine cream whippers, priced from $29.99 to $115.90, and used each to pipe a pint's worth of 2-inch whipped cream rosettes using every included decorating tip. We also had five testers—men and women, lefties and righties, pros and novices—use and evaluate each whipper.

Testers immediately zeroed in on the appearance of the whipped cream. Only a few models made swirls that were uniform, fluffy, and detailed; most produced misshapen, gloppy rosettes. The decorating tips weren't the problem; rather, we found that the unattractive, blobby rosettes were a result of testers having trouble gripping the

Rosettes are a good test of piping control.

canisters and using the dispensing mechanisms. Testers of all sizes preferred shorter canisters, which were easier to move and angle when dispensing the cream.

Testers struggled to control hard-to-grip, heavy, or sticky levers (one model with a button instead of a lever was immediately singled out as awkward); this lack of control resulted in blobby, unattractive rosettes. Top-performing products had smaller, more secure grips that allowed more leverage to dispense cream evenly and make perfect, detailed swirls. We also gave more points to whippers that felt sturdy and that were easy to load, charge with gas, change tips, empty, and clean.

We think the convenience of a good cream whipper is worth paying for. Our top two options are priced at $99.27 and $69.00 but produced flawless results (note that iSi also makes our lowest-rated whipper, so check the model numbers). Visit CooksCountry.com/jan17 for the full testing results. –LAUREN SAVOIE

KEY **Good ★★★** **Fair ★★** **Poor ★**

HIGHLY RECOMMENDED

		CRITERIA		TESTERS' NOTES
ISI Gourmet Whip **Model:** 1603 01 **Price:** $99.27 **Price of Chargers:** $31.97 for 50 branded chargers ($0.64 per charger) **Number of Tips:** 3 **Height:** 7.75 in **Distance to Reach Lever:** 3.6 in **Dishwasher-Safe:** Yes		Comfort Control Dispensing Ease of Setup	★★★ ★★★ ★★★ ★★★	Testers thought this whipper's shorter stature, rubber grip, and responsive lever made for effortless control, and both novices and pros easily piped uniform rosettes. Grips on the handle and neck made refilling and cleaning speedy.

RECOMMENDED

MOSA Professional Whipper 0.5 Liter **Model:** CSS2 **Price:** $69.00 **Price of Chargers:** $45.39 for 100 generic chargers ($0.45 per charger) **Number of Tips:** 3 **Height:** 8.3 in **Distance to Reach Lever:** 3.6 in **Dishwasher-Safe:** Yes		Comfort Control Dispensing Ease of Setup	★★★ ★★★ ★★ ★★★	This whipper's lever was easy to grasp, and testers praised its steady flow and attractive piping. Its wider decorating tips made rosettes that were perfectly fluffy. Our one gripe was that its narrowest tip produced a skinny, shaggy stream of cream.

and weights and continue to bake until crust is golden brown, 7 to 11 minutes longer. Let crust cool completely in plate on wire rack before proceeding with filling, about 45 minutes. (Baked, cooled crust can be wrapped in plastic wrap and stored at room temperature for up to 24 hours.)

4. FOR THE FILLING: Once crust has cooled completely, place chocolate in medium bowl; set aside. Whisk coconut milk, milk, sugar, cornstarch, and salt in medium saucepan until no lumps of cornstarch remain. Cook over medium heat, stirring and scraping saucepan corners constantly with rubber spatula, until mixture thickens to glue-like consistency and large bubbles break surface, about 6 minutes.

5. Quickly pour 1 cup coconut pudding over chocolate in bowl and whisk until smooth. Spread chocolate pudding evenly in cooled pie shell. Using clean, dry whisk, vigorously rewhisk remaining coconut pudding in saucepan, then gently pour on top of chocolate pudding and spread into even layer with rubber spatula. Refrigerate, uncovered, until set, at least 3 hours or up to 24 hours.

6. FOR THE TOPPING: Once pie is fully chilled, use stand mixer fitted with whisk attachment to whip cream and sugar on medium-low speed until foamy, about 1 minute. Increase speed to high and whip until stiff peaks form, 1 to 3 minutes. Transfer whipped cream to pastry bag fitted with medium open or closed star tip (about ½-inch diameter). Pipe whipped cream stars onto top of pie until completely covered. Serve.

TEST KITCHEN TECHNIQUE
Piping Whipped Cream

Fit a pastry bag with a medium (½-inch diameter) star pastry tip. An

open tip will give a soft appearance; a closed tip (pictured here) will make a tighter star with hard lines. Using gentle pressure and working in concentric

circles, pipe even-size stars over the top of the pie. (Alternatively, pipe stars in straight lines across the pie.)

INGREDIENT SPOTLIGHT
Coconut Milk

Coconut milk, not to be confused with coconut water, is made by steeping shredded coconut meat in water or milk. The meat is pressed or mashed to release as much liquid as possible and the liquid squeezed out and strained for a smooth texture.

In a test kitchen taste test, the winning **Chaokoh Coconut Milk** was voted the "creamiest" in the lineup.

Getting to Know Blue Cheese

While all blue cheeses get their flavor from harmless blue mold, different types vary wildly. Here's a guide to 12 funky blues.

BY CHRISTIE MORRISON

Danish Blue
GREAT DANE

"Boom! Pow! There's that blue cheese flavor," said one taster of this cheese. Danish Blue (or Danablu) is a powerful and complex cheese made from cow's milk and homogenized cream. It has a strong salty, tangy flavor with a slightly sweet finish. Its creamy yet crumbly semisoft texture is spotted with silvery blue pockets. It makes a great dessert cheese served with stone fruit or pears.

Roquefort
DEEP POCKETS

France's "cheese of kings and popes," once favored by Charlemagne, is a creamy, pungent sheep's-milk cheese produced in the Roquefort-sur-Soulzon region. Ivory-colored and pocketed with large clumps of dark green-blue mold (*Penicillium roqueforti*), Roquefort is "luxurious" and "supercreamy," with crystal-like granules that vary the texture. Its pungent flavor has a bit of sweetness and "a little sharpness that lingers at the back of the throat." Great for melting, it is also a star on a cheese plate.

Cashel Blue
ERIN GO BLUE

Cashel Blue cheese is a semisoft cow's-milk cheese that has been made in County Tipperary, Ireland since 1984. The cheese uses *Penicillium roqueforti*, but the mold spores are stirred into the warm milk rather than being injected into the cheese. This process results in the marble-like pattern of blue-green mold in the light-colored cheese. Tasters commented on the "buttery" flavor and "briny" notes as well as the creamy but "slightly granular" texture.

Cabrales
SPANISH GOLD

Cabrales is made in Asturias, Spain, from cow's milk or a mixture of cow's, sheep's, and goat's milk and is aged in limestone caves for two to four months. Cabrales is not injected with mold like other blue cheeses; humidity in the caves fosters the growth of a particular mold that cures from the outside of the cheese to the center. The cheese has a "spicy, peppery kick" and a semifirm, crumbly, chalky texture.

Stilton
BOLD BRIT

By law, this cow's-milk English cheese can be produced in only three counties—Derbyshire, Leicestershire, and Nottinghamshire. The distinctive blue lines are created by piercing the cheese with long needles to allow bacteria to infiltrate. Stilton is recognizable by its reddish-gold rind and its butter-colored interior. Our tasters praised its "tangy," "sharp" flavor and creamy, crumbly texture.

Gorgonzola
ITALIAN STAR

Produced in the Lombardy and Piedmont regions of Italy, Gorgonzola is a cow's-milk cheese available in two varieties: *dolce* (sweet) and *piccante* (also called naturale or mountain). The dolce version, which is more common in the United States, is aged for only two to three months versus piccante's six. Tasters loved dolce's ultracreamy texture, subtle spice, and "sweet finish." The mild blue flavor of Gorgonzola works well in our Cantaloupe and Blue Cheese Salad (**CooksCountry.com/cbcsalad**).

Saga Blue
BRIE BLEND

This mild blue cheese is actually a hybrid cross of blue cheese and Brie. Produced in Denmark from pasteurized cow's milk, the cheese is blue-veined and soft-ripened. Some tasters detected a slightly sharp, almost cheddar-like note and a "creamy but bracing bite." It is perfect on burgers or spread on crackers.

Cambozola
DEUTSCH BLAU

This German cow's-milk blue cheese is a cross between Camembert and Gorgonzola. Its triple-cream (at least 75 percent milk fat) base is Brie-like: creamy, soft, and buttery. In fact, it's often referred to as "blue Brie." The grayish-blue mold cuts through the richness, giving it a light funk on the finish. Tasters noted its nutty, mildly peppery flavor and slight tang.

Valdeon
ALL WRAPPED UP

This assertive, complex cheese, a blend of pasteurized cow's and goat's milks, hails from Castile-León in northwestern Spain. Valdeon is wrapped in sycamore leaves before being aged in caves for at least two months. This firm, crumbly cheese has a bluish-gray base color that is speckled with dots of blue mold. The full-flavored cheese is pleasantly "gamy" and slightly astringent. Serve it with fruit or preserves.

Bleu d'Auvergne
POWERFULLY PUNGENT

Some of the best cheeses are the stinkiest, and rich, funky, salty Bleu d'Auvergne is a prime example. Produced in the mountainous Massif Central region of France, it is made in the Roquefort style but uses cow's, rather than sheep's, milk (and is about half the price of Roquefort). Like Roquefort, it is soft and creamy, with pungent "blue" flavor and a strong aftertaste.

Stella Blue
CRUMBLY CHARACTER

This cow's-milk blue from Wisconsin is almost feta-like: firm, crumbly, mild, and salty. Because it is not relatively potent or complex, Stella is an excellent choice for a blue cheese salad dressing recipe; as a bonus, it crumbles readily and so is easy to work with. This mild cheese also works well in our Devils on Horseback (**CooksCountry.com/devils**).

ROASTED SALMON AND BROCCOLI RABE WITH PISTACHIO GREMOLATA

STIR-FRIED STEAK WITH SHIITAKE MUSHROOMS AND CABBAGE

CUMIN-CRUSTED CHICKEN THIGHS WITH CAULIFLOWER "COUSCOUS"

STEAK WITH LEMON-PARSLEY POTATO WEDGES AND BLUE-CHEESE SAUCE

STIR-FRIED STEAK WITH SHIITAKE MUSHROOMS AND CABBAGE Serves 4

✓ **WHY THIS RECIPE WORKS:** We stir-fry the mushrooms and cabbage together over high heat to help streamline the cooking process.

- 12 ounces flank steak, trimmed, cut lengthwise with grain into thirds, then sliced crosswise ⅛ inch thick
- ¼ cup oyster sauce
- 3 tablespoons vegetable oil
- 12 ounces shiitake mushrooms, stemmed and sliced thin
- 8 cups thinly sliced napa cabbage
- 4 garlic cloves, minced
- 1 tablespoon grated fresh ginger
- 3 scallions, sliced thin
- 1 tablespoon packed light brown sugar
- 1 teaspoon cornstarch, dissolved in 1 tablespoon water

1. Combine steak and 1 tablespoon oyster sauce in bowl. Heat 1½ teaspoons oil in 12-inch nonstick skillet over high heat until just smoking. Add half of steak in single layer and cook, without stirring it, for 1 minute. Stir and continue to cook until meat is no longer pink, about 30 seconds longer; transfer to clean bowl. Repeat with 1½ teaspoons oil and remaining steak.

2. Heat remaining 2 tablespoons oil in now-empty skillet over high heat until just smoking. Add mushrooms and cabbage and cook, stirring occasionally, until browned and cabbage is wilted, about 8 minutes.

3. Stir garlic, ginger, half of scallions, and steak into mushroom-cabbage mixture and cook until fragrant, about 1 minute. Stir in sugar, cornstarch mixture, and remaining 3 tablespoons oyster sauce and cook until thickened, about 30 seconds. Serve, sprinkled with remaining scallions.

ROASTED SALMON AND BROCCOLI RABE WITH PISTACHIO GREMOLATA Serves 4

✓ **WHY THIS RECIPE WORKS:** Using only one pan and the oven streamlines this dish and makes it an ideal (and healthy) weeknight dinner.

- ¼ cup shelled pistachios, toasted and chopped fine
- 2 tablespoons minced fresh parsley
- 1 teaspoon grated lemon zest
- 2 garlic cloves, minced
- 1 pound broccoli rabe, trimmed and cut into 1½-inch lengths
- 2 tablespoons plus 2 teaspoons extra-virgin olive oil
  Salt and pepper
  Pinch red pepper flakes
- 4 (6- to 8-ounce) center-cut skinless salmon fillets, 1 to 1½ inches thick

1. Adjust oven rack to middle position and heat oven to 450 degrees. Combine pistachios, parsley, lemon zest, and half of garlic in small bowl; set gremolata aside.

2. Toss broccoli rabe, 2 tablespoons oil, ¼ teaspoon salt, ¼ teaspoon pepper, pepper flakes, and remaining garlic together in bowl. Arrange on half of rimmed baking sheet. Pat salmon dry with paper towels, then rub all over with remaining 2 teaspoons oil and season with salt and pepper. Arrange salmon on empty half of sheet, skinned side down.

3. Roast until centers of fillets register 125 degrees (for medium-rare) and broccoli rabe is tender, about 10 minutes. Serve, sprinkled with gremolata.

TEST KITCHEN NOTE: Broccoli rabe is sometimes called rapini.

STEAK WITH LEMON-PARSLEY POTATO WEDGES AND BLUE-CHEESE SAUCE Serves 4

✓ **WHY THIS RECIPE WORKS:** Microwaving blue cheese and cream makes an incredibly easy and delicious sauce.

- 2 pounds russet potatoes, unpeeled, halved lengthwise and cut into 1-inch-thick wedges
- 3 tablespoons vegetable oil
  Salt and pepper
- 3 tablespoons minced fresh parsley
- 1 tablespoon grated lemon zest
- 2 (1-pound) boneless strip steaks, about 1 inch thick, trimmed and halved crosswise
- 4 ounces blue cheese, crumbled (1 cup)
- ½ cup heavy cream

1. Adjust oven rack to upper-middle position and heat oven to 475 degrees. Toss potatoes with 2 tablespoons oil, 1½ teaspoons salt, and ½ teaspoon pepper on rimmed baking sheet and arrange cut sides down in single layer. Roast until spotty brown and tender, about 25 minutes. Sprinkle with 2 tablespoons parsley and lemon zest.

2. Meanwhile, pat steaks dry with paper towels and season with salt and pepper. Heat remaining 1 tablespoon oil in 12-inch nonstick skillet over medium-high heat until just smoking. Add steaks and cook until well browned and meat registers 125 degrees (for medium-rare), 3 to 5 minutes per side. Let rest on wire rack.

3. Combine blue cheese and cream in bowl and microwave until blue cheese is melted and smooth, about 3 minutes. Slice steaks, sprinkle with remaining 1 tablespoon parsley, and serve with potatoes and blue cheese sauce.

CUMIN-CRUSTED CHICKEN THIGHS WITH CAULIFLOWER "COUSCOUS" Serves 4

✓ **WHY THIS RECIPE WORKS:** Sprinkling cumin over the chicken after browning and before roasting ensures pleasantly toasted seeds without any bitter burnt bite.

- 8 (5- to 7-ounce) bone-in chicken thighs
  Salt and pepper
- 1 tablespoon vegetable oil
- 4 teaspoons cumin seeds
- 1 head cauliflower (2 pounds), cored and cut into ½-inch pieces
- 1 teaspoon paprika
- ½ cup chopped fresh mint, plus 2 tablespoons torn mint leaves
- 1½ teaspoons grated lime zest, plus lime wedges for serving

1. Adjust oven rack to upper-middle position and heat oven to 375 degrees. Pat chicken dry with paper towels; season with salt and pepper. Heat oil in 12-inch nonstick skillet over medium-high heat until just smoking. Add chicken, skin side down, and cook until well browned, about 7 minutes. Transfer chicken, skin side up, to rimmed baking sheet (do not wipe out skillet) and sprinkle 2 teaspoons cumin seeds over top. Roast until chicken registers 175 degrees, about 15 minutes.

2. Meanwhile, working in 2 batches, pulse cauliflower in food processor to ¼- to ⅛-inch pieces, about 6 pulses. Heat fat remaining in skillet over medium-high heat until shimmering. Add cauliflower, paprika, ¾ teaspoon salt, ¾ teaspoon pepper, and remaining 2 teaspoons cumin seeds and cook until just tender, about 7 minutes. Off heat, stir in chopped mint and lime zest.

3. Serve chicken with cauliflower "couscous" and lime wedges, sprinkling torn mint leaves over top.

ITALIAN SAUSAGE WITH LENTILS AND KALE

FARFALLE WITH CRISPY PROSCIUTTO AND PEAS

**PEPPER AND ONION FRITTATA
WITH ARUGULA SALAD**

**APRICOT-GLAZED CHICKEN WITH
CHICKPEAS, CHORIZO, AND SPINACH**

FARFALLE WITH CRISPY PROSCIUTTO AND PEAS Serves 4

✓ **WHY THIS RECIPE WORKS:** Crisping the prosciutto not only develops its flavor but also creates a pleasing textural contrast in this dish.

- 12 ounces farfalle
- Salt and pepper
- 2 tablespoons extra-virgin olive oil, plus extra for drizzling
- 6 ounces thinly sliced prosciutto, cut into ½-inch pieces
- 1 onion, chopped
- ¼ teaspoon red pepper flakes
- 3 garlic cloves, minced
- 1 (28-ounce) can whole peeled tomatoes, drained and crushed by hand
- 1½ cups frozen peas
- 2 ounces Parmesan cheese, grated (1 cup)

1. Bring 4 quarts water to boil in large pot. Add pasta and 1 tablespoon salt and cook, stirring often, until al dente. Reserve ½ cup cooking water, then drain pasta and return it to pot.

2. Meanwhile, heat oil in 12-inch skillet over medium heat until shimmering. Add prosciutto and cook until crispy, about 10 minutes. Using slotted spoon, transfer prosciutto to paper towel–lined plate. Return skillet to medium heat; to fat left in skillet, add onion, pepper flakes, ⅛ teaspoon salt, and ½ teaspoon pepper. Cook until onion is softened, about 5 minutes. Add garlic and cook until fragrant, about 30 seconds. Add tomatoes and cook, stirring occasionally, until sauce is thickened, about 10 minutes.

3. Add peas, ¾ cup Parmesan, sauce, and ¼ cup reserved cooking water to pasta and toss to combine. Adjust consistency with remaining reserved cooking water as needed. Serve, sprinkled with prosciutto and remaining ¼ cup Parmesan and drizzled with extra oil.

TEST KITCHEN NOTE: Brighten up this dish with the addition of fresh basil.

ITALIAN SAUSAGE WITH LENTILS AND KALE Serves 4

✓ **WHY THIS RECIPE WORKS:** Cooking sausages on top of the lentil mixture infuses this one-skillet meal with rich, meaty flavor.

- 2 teaspoons extra-virgin olive oil
- 1½ pounds sweet Italian sausage
- 2 shallots, peeled, halved, and sliced thin
- 3 garlic cloves, minced
- 10 ounces kale, stemmed and chopped
- ¾ cup chicken broth
- Salt and pepper
- 1 (15-ounce) can lentils, rinsed
- 3 tablespoons plain yogurt
- 2 tablespoons whole-grain mustard
- 1 tablespoon water

1. Adjust oven rack to middle position and heat oven to 375 degrees. Heat oil in 12-inch skillet over medium-high heat until just smoking. Add sausage and cook until browned all over, about 5 minutes; transfer to plate.

2. Reduce heat to medium, add shallots and garlic to now-empty skillet, and cook until vegetables start to brown, about 3 minutes. Add kale, broth, ¼ teaspoon salt, and ¼ teaspoon pepper; cover and cook until wilted, about 5 minutes.

3. Stir in lentils. Arrange browned sausage on top of lentil mixture and transfer skillet to oven. Cook, uncovered, until sausage registers 160 degrees, about 12 minutes. Whisk yogurt, mustard, and water together in bowl; drizzle over top. Serve.

TEST KITCHEN NOTE: For a spicier kick, use hot Italian sausage. We prefer curly kale for this recipe, but other varieties will work.

APRICOT-GLAZED CHICKEN WITH CHICKPEAS, CHORIZO, AND SPINACH Serves 4

✓ **WHY THIS RECIPE WORKS:** Lemon zest and the mild spice of chorizo balance the sweetness of the apricot preserves.

- ¼ cup apricot preserves
- 2 teaspoons grated lemon zest
- Salt and pepper
- 4 (10- to 12-ounce) bone-in split chicken breasts, trimmed and halved crosswise
- 1 tablespoon vegetable oil
- 1 (15-ounce) can chickpeas, rinsed
- 6 ounces Spanish-style chorizo sausage, cut into ½-inch chunks
- 1 onion, chopped
- 1½ teaspoons smoked paprika
- 8 ounces (8 cups) baby spinach

1. Adjust oven rack to middle position and heat oven to 450 degrees. Combine preserves, lemon zest, ⅛ teaspoon salt, and ⅛ teaspoon pepper in bowl; set aside. Pat chicken dry with paper towels and season with salt and pepper.

2. Heat oil in 12-inch ovensafe skillet over medium-high heat until just smoking. Cook chicken, skin side down, until lightly browned, about 4 minutes. Transfer to plate, skin side up. Off heat, combine chickpeas, chorizo, onion, paprika, ⅛ teaspoon salt, and ⅛ teaspoon pepper in now-empty skillet.

3. Return chicken to skillet, skin side up, and brush apricot mixture over chicken. Bake until chicken registers 160 degrees, about 24 minutes. Transfer chicken to carving board. Return skillet to medium-high heat, add spinach, and cook until wilted, about 2 minutes. Serve.

PEPPER AND ONION FRITTATA WITH ARUGULA SALAD
Serves 4

✓ **WHY THIS RECIPE WORKS:** Adding a salad to this breakfast staple makes a well-rounded meal at any time, day or night.

- 12 large eggs
- 3 tablespoons half-and-half
- Salt and pepper
- 3½ tablespoons extra-virgin olive oil
- 2 red bell peppers, stemmed, seeded, and sliced thin
- 1 small onion, sliced thin
- 2 ounces (2 cups) baby arugula
- ¼ cup pitted kalamata olives, halved
- 2 teaspoons lemon juice
- 2 ounces goat cheese, crumbled (½ cup)

1. Adjust oven rack to upper-middle position and heat oven to 375 degrees. Whisk eggs, half-and-half, ½ teaspoon salt, and ¼ teaspoon pepper in large bowl until well combined.

2. Heat 1½ tablespoons oil in 12-inch nonstick skillet over medium-high heat until shimmering. Add bell peppers and onion and cook until spotty brown, about 8 minutes. Reduce heat to medium-low and stir in egg mixture. Cook, using spatula to scrape bottom of skillet, until large curds form but eggs are still very wet, about 2 minutes. Smooth egg mixture into even layer. Transfer skillet to oven and bake until surface is golden brown, 8 to 10 minutes. Slide frittata onto serving platter.

3. Toss arugula, olives, lemon juice, and remaining 2 tablespoons oil together in bowl. Season with salt and pepper to taste. Pile salad on top of frittata, sprinkle with goat cheese, and serve.

Holiday Eggnog

Grocery store eggnog doesn't hold a cup to the real stuff.

BY MORGAN BOLLING

F THE ONLY "eggnog" you've experienced is the prefab stuff you find in the dairy case around the holidays, you're forgiven for not liking it much. You're also forgiven for not knowing what it is. Most commercial eggnogs consist of milk pumped full of factory-produced stabilizers, yellow food coloring, and sweeteners. The U.S. Food and Drug Administration, in fact, requires just 1 percent of the drink to be actual egg yolk solids.

I long ago swore off eggnog, having never actually tried the real thing. So on a recent afternoon in the test kitchen, faced with the task of mixing up six existing eggnog recipes for a tasting, I didn't know what to expect. But I was happily surprised.

Real eggnog is made from a few simple ingredients: milk, eggs, sugar, nutmeg, and booze (rum, brandy, or bourbon). After sipping all six samples, my tasters and I decided to aim for an eggnog that would be just a touch sweet, creamy (but not too heavy), and fortified with a definite note of spirits. And while serious nogsters are split on whether to cook eggnog or whether to simply serve it raw, we settled on cooking the eggnog gently on the stovetop. Doing so gave us a slightly more nuanced flavor and also put to rest any safety concerns about serving uncooked eggs. I found that the best way to achieve a velvety texture with no scrambled eggs is to whisk together the egg yolks and sugar and pour heated milk over them, whisking constantly, before pouring the whole lot back into the pan and bringing it up, slowly, to 160 degrees—the safety zone.

My working formula consisted of 4½ cups of milk, 6 egg yolks (we preferred just yolks to whole eggs), and ½ cup of sugar, whisked until frothy and thick. We found this a bit sweet—one taster said it tasted like melted ice cream—so I cut back on the sugar and added a bit of salt to enhance the flavor. I was getting somewhere.

But a couple of longtime eggnog fans felt that the mixture was still a bit thin. So I ditched 1½ cups of the milk and replaced them with heavy cream: ¾ cup of cream whisked into the eggs and sugar and another ¾ cup frothed and folded in at the end.

About the booze: I settled on ½ cup of rum for 6 cups of nog—just enough

to give it a vigorous punch. For an alcohol-free version, I used root beer instead; it added some of the same caramel notes that come from rum.

To finish off my nog, I stirred in ¼ teaspoon of potent ground nutmeg, passing extra for those who wanted an additional dusting on top. My homemade eggnog was creamy, comforting, and festive. It's a shame I'll only have it once a year. Or will I?

EGGNOG Makes about 6 cups; serves 6 to 8

We prefer dark rum, but you can substitute brandy or bourbon, if desired.

- 1½ cups heavy cream
- 6 large egg yolks
- 6 tablespoons sugar
- 3 cups whole milk
- ¼ teaspoon salt
- ½ cup dark rum
- ¼ teaspoon ground nutmeg, plus extra for serving

1. Whisk ¾ cup cream, egg yolks, and sugar in medium bowl until thoroughly combined and pale yellow, about 30 seconds; set aside. Bring milk and salt to simmer in medium saucepan over medium-high heat, stirring occasionally.

2. When milk mixture comes to simmer, remove from heat and, whisking constantly, slowly pour into yolk mixture to temper. Return milk-yolk mixture to saucepan. Place over medium-low heat and cook, whisking constantly, until mixture reaches 160 degrees, 1 to 2 minutes.

3. Immediately pour eggnog into clean bowl. Stir in rum and nutmeg. Fill slightly larger bowl with ice and set eggnog bowl in ice bowl. Refrigerate until eggnog registers 40 degrees, 1 to 2 hours, stirring occasionally.

4. Just before serving, using stand mixer fitted with whisk attachment, whip remaining ¾ cup cream on medium-low speed until foamy, about 1 minute. Increase speed to high and whip until soft peaks form, 1 to 3 minutes. Whisk whipped cream into chilled eggnog. Serve, garnished with extra nutmeg. (Eggnog can be covered and refrigerated for up to 24 hours.)

NONALCOHOLIC EGGNOG

Reduce sugar to ¼ cup and substitute root beer for rum.

After trying brandy, bourbon, and rum, we settled on the potent, caramel-like flavor of rum.

The American Table
A Nog for the Road

We associate eggnog with the holiday season, but it wasn't always so. In colonial times, hardworking farm laborers and seafarers sucked it down during the day, and roadside inns and taverns served it as a fortifying drink for travelers. The basic makeup of eggnog has changed very little since then; as Isaac Weld wrote in his 1799 book *Travels Through the States of North America*: "The American travellers, before they pursued their journey, took a hearty draught each, according to custom, of egg-nog, a mixture composed of new milk, eggs, rum, and sugar, beat up together."

Boneless Rib Roast and Yorkshire Pudding

We wanted to bring these two classics together in one pan.

BY MORGAN BOLLING

A S OUR FRIENDS in the United Kingdom have known for generations, a crusty, custardy Yorkshire pudding is without peer as an accompaniment to a resplendent roast beef. It swabs up and soaks up all those drippings and gravy in the most rewarding way. This year I set out to create a foolproof recipe for both items—roast and pudding—that would have them ready for the table at the same time.

I started, naturally, with the beef. While I love the impressive stature of a bone-in standing rib roast, it can be tricky to carve at the table. So this year I opted for a boneless rib roast. Its rich marbling would guarantee plenty of beefy flavor, and searing and slicing the roast would be much easier.

To prepare it, I called upon the tried-and-true test kitchen method for bone-in rib roast. I salted the roast a day in advance to ensure complete seasoning. I then roasted it in a 250-degree oven until it hit 120 degrees (for medium-rare) and set it aside for an hour before searing the exterior in a piping-hot skillet. Next I made a quick sauce—a jus—with chopped onion, reduced beef broth, cornstarch for thickening, and a sprig of thyme. Even without the bones, this technique yielded a seasoned, crusty exterior enveloping a rosy, juicy interior.

While the roast was resting for an hour before its final sear, I set my sights on the slightly more complicated portion of my feast. Making a Yorkshire pudding—a savory pancake of milk (or water), flour, and eggs, similar to a Dutch baby or popover—can be a fraught process. It's all about texture: You want a custardy, moist interior with a contrasting crunchy exterior. The existing recipes I researched had a lot of folklore to wade through, often with "unbreakable" rules for success. I was skeptical.

Almost all British chefs agree that you need to use a preheated pan and a hot oven in order to get a better rise in your pudding. And despite my skepticism, this claim held true. After experimenting, I found that pouring the batter into a hot pan (and I mean really hot—preheated at 425 degrees until the fat was beginning to smoke) not only caused the pudding to achieve a towering height but also kept it from sticking to the pan. This was excellent news,

The beauty of a boneless rib roast is easy carving. Serve the end cuts to guests who prefer their meat more well-done.

as it meant I could use the same pan I roasted my beef in and thus take full advantage of those flavorful drippings.

Only one problem: There weren't enough drippings for my Yorkshire pudding. For a full, roasting-pan-size Yorkshire pudding, I'd need 6 tablespoons of fat, and my boneless roast was yielding less than half that. So for my next test, I chopped up the trimmings I'd removed from the roast's fat cap and placed about ¾ cup of them

in the roasting pan when the beef went in. This ensured that I'd have plenty of rendered fat for my pudding.

I was more doubtful about the existing recipes' call to stir together the batter and let it sit at room temperature before baking. Yet after a few tests, this rule, too, proved essential: I found that letting the batter sit at room temperature for 1 hour yielded a taller pudding. Why? Our science editor confirmed that the hour-long rest allowed time for the

gluten formed when mixing the batter to relax, so the pudding was able to rise more quickly in the oven.

With a succulent roast, a deeply savory jus, and my golden, gloriously tall Yorkshire pudding, all I needed was one final traditional condiment. I chose a sharp, bracing, supersimple stir-together horseradish sauce.

I was now ready for the holiday feast—and even my friends in the United Kingdom would be happy.

BONELESS RIB ROAST WITH YORKSHIRE PUDDING AND JUS
Serves 8 to 10

At the butcher counter, ask for a roast with an untrimmed fat cap, ideally ½ inch thick, in order to get enough trimmings to cook the pudding. Plan ahead: The roast must be salted and refrigerated for at least 24 hours before cooking. The roast and Yorkshire pudding can also be made separately from one another. To make only the roast, do not add the trimmed fat to the roasting pan. To make only the Yorkshire pudding, proceed with step 6, substituting 6 tablespoons of vegetable oil for the beef fat. Our winning roasting pan is the Calphalon Contemporary Stainless Roasting Pan with Rack. If you're using a dark, nonstick roasting pan, reduce the cooking time for the Yorkshire pudding by 5 minutes. Serve with Horseradish Sauce (recipe follows), if desired.

ROAST AND PUDDING
- 1 (5- to 5½-pound) first-cut boneless beef rib roast with ½-inch fat cap
  Kosher salt and pepper
- 2½ cups (12½ ounces) all-purpose flour
- 4 cups milk
- 4 large eggs
- 1 tablespoon vegetable oil, plus extra as needed

JUS
- 1 onion, chopped fine
- 1 teaspoon cornstarch
- 2½ cups beef broth
- 1 sprig fresh thyme

1. FOR THE ROAST AND PUDDING: Using sharp knife, trim roast's fat cap to even ¼-inch thickness and refrigerate trimmings for later use. Cut 1-inch crosshatch pattern in fat cap, being careful not to cut into meat. Rub 2 tablespoons salt over entire roast and into crosshatch. Transfer to large plate and refrigerate, uncovered, for at least 24 hours or up to 4 days.

2. Adjust oven rack to lower-middle position and heat oven to 250 degrees. Spray roasting pan with vegetable oil spray. Cut reserved trimmings into ½-inch pieces. Place 3 ounces (about ¾ cup) trimmings in bottom of prepared pan. Set V-rack over trimmings in pan.

3. Season roast with pepper and place fat side up on V-rack. Roast until meat registers 115 degrees for rare, 120 degrees for medium-rare, or 125 degrees for medium, 2½ to 3 hours.

4. Meanwhile, combine flour and 1 tablespoon salt in large bowl. Whisk milk and eggs in second bowl until fully combined. Slowly whisk milk mixture into flour mixture until smooth. Cover with plastic wrap and let rest at room temperature for 1 hour. (Batter can be covered and refrigerated for up to 24 hours. Let come to room temperature before proceeding with recipe.)

5. Transfer V-rack with roast to carving board, tent with aluminum foil, and let rest for 1 hour. Using fork, remove solids in pan, leaving liquid fat behind (there should be about 6 tablespoons; if not, supplement with extra vegetable oil). Increase oven temperature to 425 degrees.

6. When oven reaches 425 degrees, return pan to oven and heat until fat is just smoking, 3 to 5 minutes. Rewhisk batter and pour into center of pan. Bake until pudding is dark golden brown and edges are crisp, 40 to 45 minutes.

7. Meanwhile, pat roast dry with paper towels. Heat 1 tablespoon oil in 12-inch skillet over medium-high heat until just smoking. Sear roast on all sides until evenly browned, 5 to 7 minutes. Transfer roast to carving board.

8. FOR THE JUS: Return skillet to medium-high heat and add onion. Cook until onion is just softened, about 3 minutes, scraping up any browned bits. Whisk cornstarch into broth. Add broth mixture and thyme sprig to skillet and bring to boil. Reduce heat to medium-low and simmer until reduced by half and slightly thickened, about 7 minutes. Strain jus through fine-mesh strainer set over small saucepan; discard solids. Cover and keep warm.

9. Slice roast ¾ inch thick. Cut pudding into squares in roasting pan. Serve beef with Yorkshire pudding and jus.

The Ups (and Downs) of Yorkshire Pudding
Letting the batter rest for 1 hour and preheating the roasting pan in a hot oven for 3 to 5 minutes will help the Yorkshire pudding puff up during baking, and this is a good thing. But don't be disappointed when the pudding deflates shortly after it comes out of the oven or as you're slicing and serving it. That's supposed to happen. The custardy interior will be no less delicious, and people will still ask for seconds.

> ▶ A good roasting pan makes all the difference here. Go to **CooksCountry.com/roastingpans** to learn more about our favorite.

HORSERADISH SAUCE
Makes about 1 cup
Buy refrigerated prepared horseradish, not the shelf-stable kind, which contains preservatives and additives.

- ½ cup sour cream
- ½ cup prepared horseradish
- 1½ teaspoons kosher salt
- ⅛ teaspoon pepper

Combine all ingredients in bowl. Cover and refrigerate for at least 30 minutes to allow flavors to meld. (Sauce can be refrigerated for up to 2 days.)

TEST KITCHEN TECHNIQUE Trimming and Prepping the Fat Cap
Instead of scouring the meat case, we recommend asking the butcher directly for a first-cut boneless beef rib roast with an untrimmed fat cap, ideally ½ inch thick. You may have to call ahead and special-order this roast. Trust us: It's worth it.

1. TRIM
Using sharp knife, trim fat cap to even ¼-inch thickness. Refrigerate trimmings.

2. SCORE
Cut 1-inch crosshatch pattern into fat cap, being careful not to cut into meat.

3. RENDER
Place 3 ounces of reserved trimmings in roasting pan (rendered fat will be used for Yorkshire pudding).

Caesar Green Bean Salad

If Caesar dressing is good enough for lettuce, surely it's good enough for beans.

BY DIANE UNGER

IT'S HARD TO beat a classic Caesar salad: Bite-size pieces of torn Romaine lettuce leaves and crunchy croutons tossed in a salty, briny, sour, sweet, and savory dressing. For a twist, I wanted to take the things we love about Caesar salad and unleash them on a green bean salad that I could serve as a no-fuss holiday side.

I knew that I wanted the dressing to be thick enough to steadfastly cling to the green beans; to achieve this effect in the past, we've often turned to mayonnaise or mustard. Both condiments have proved useful in keeping dressings cohesive, so I made two dressings, employing mayonnaise in one and Dijon mustard in the other, along with lemon juice, Worcestershire sauce, garlic, and a few anchovies that I minced to a fine paste. I drizzled in 3 tablespoons of olive oil as I whisked, seasoned the mixture with pepper, and gathered my tasters for a side-by-side test. It was unanimous: We all preferred the lightly thickened emulsion created by the Dijon mustard.

For the green beans, most recipes I tried called for boiling them briefly before shocking them in ice water to stop the cooking (and help keep the beans bright green). While this method worked fine, the beans were a bit waterlogged. A colleague suggested boiling the green beans until tender, draining them, and transferring them directly to towels to dry, skipping the shocking step altogether. These beans had a deeper flavor, and any brightness I lost was minimal—and indiscernible once the beans were dressed. Plus, it was a lot easier than fussing with an ice bath.

A Caesar without croutons? Not on my watch. I took a nice crusty baguette and cut it up into ½-inch pieces (a 3-ounce piece of baguette gave me 3 cups of cubes). I tossed these with some olive oil and pepper (no salt, as I knew the dressing was highly seasoned) and toasted them in a skillet until they were golden brown and crispy all over, which took just 5 to 7 minutes.

I tossed the beans and croutons, along with an ounce of Parmesan cheese that I'd shaved with a vegetable peeler, with my dressing and transferred the lot to a holiday-worthy serving bowl. I topped it with more shaved Parmesan and gathered my crew. They loved this variation on the classic Caesar, and I loved how easy it was to put together.

CAESAR GREEN BEAN SALAD
Serves 4 to 6

For maximum crunch, use a good-quality baguette for the croutons. The dressing can be made up to 1 day in advance.

DRESSING AND GREEN BEANS

- 1½ tablespoons lemon juice
- 1 tablespoon Worcestershire sauce
- 1 tablespoon Dijon mustard
- 3 garlic cloves, minced
- 3 anchovy fillets, minced to paste
  Salt and pepper
- 3 tablespoons extra-virgin olive oil
- 1½ pounds green beans, trimmed
- 2 ounces Parmesan cheese, shaved with vegetable peeler

CROUTONS

- 3 ounces baguette, cut into ½-inch pieces
- 2 tablespoons extra-virgin olive oil
- ¼ teaspoon pepper

1. FOR THE DRESSING AND GREEN BEANS: Whisk lemon juice, Worcestershire, mustard, garlic, anchovies, ½ teaspoon pepper, and ¼ teaspoon salt in bowl until combined. Slowly whisk in oil until emulsified; set aside.

2. Line baking sheet with clean dish towel. Bring 4 quarts water to boil in large Dutch oven. Add green beans and 1½ teaspoons salt, return to boil, and cook until tender, 5 to 7 minutes. Drain green beans in colander and spread in even layer on prepared sheet. Let green beans cool completely.

3. FOR THE CROUTONS: Meanwhile, toss baguette, oil, and pepper in large bowl until baguette pieces are coated with oil. Transfer to 12-inch nonstick skillet (reserve bowl). Cook over medium-high heat, stirring occasionally, until golden brown and crispy, 5 to 7 minutes. Return croutons to reserved bowl.

4. Transfer dressing, green beans, and half of Parmesan to bowl with croutons and toss to combine. Season with salt and pepper to taste. Transfer to serving dish. Sprinkle with remaining Parmesan. Serve.

A mix of Worcestershire sauce, anchovies, and Parmesan makes this salad extra-savory.

TEST KITCHEN TECHNIQUES
Draining Green Beans

Instead of shocking the green beans in ice water to stop the cooking, we simply drain them and spread them onto a dish towel–lined baking sheet to cool.

Shaving Parmesan Cheese

Run a vegetable peeler over a block of Parmesan cheese to make paper-thin shavings.

Lighthouse Inn Potatoes

Back at the inn, this rich holiday side was made with leftover potatoes.
But for a dish this good, we didn't want to wait. BY ASHLEY MOORE

MY FAMILY HAS been making Lighthouse Inn Potatoes for parties and holiday dinners since I was a kid. Chunks of soft potatoes baked in a rich cream sauce and topped with golden bread crumbs—what's not to love?

The Lighthouse Inn was an iconic hotel and restaurant located in New London, a popular seaside town in southeastern Connecticut, for more than a century before it closed its doors in 2009. Executive chef Leon "Wally" Walden, who worked there for nearly 50 years before his 1992 death, was known for many of his dishes, but Lighthouse Inn Potatoes was perhaps his most beloved offering. After he died, the local newspaper, *The New London Day*, published his recipe in tribute.

The recipe that the newspaper published calls for leftover baked russet potatoes, so I followed suit, cutting up a few and baking them in a creamy sauce under a generous layer of butter-soaked bread crumbs. It was everything I remembered—the potatoes were tender, the sauce was silky and rich, and the topping was salty, crunchy, and satisfying.

But I didn't want to lean on leftovers. I wanted to start and eat my potatoes on the same day. Should be easy enough, right? I'd just have to precook the potatoes briefly before proceeding with the original recipe.

So I hit the kitchen, where I cut potatoes into chunks, boiled them in water until they were tender, immediately stirred them into the cream sauce, and slid them into the oven to bake. No dice: The sauce was thin and watery—not the smooth, silky texture I was looking for—and the potatoes weren't quite as tender.

After a conversation with our science editor, I realized what was happening to those leftover potatoes when they were resting overnight and why it mattered to the sauce. Because the potatoes were baked whole and only then cut into chunks, they weren't losing any of their starch along the way. But when I cut potatoes up and cooked them in water for a same-day dish, much of that valuable starch was sloughing off and being rinsed away.

After a few experiments, I found that if I cooked the potatoes in a heavy cream mixture and then dumped everything—cream included—into the baking dish before sliding it into the oven, the starch stayed in the sauce and left it rich and velvety.

But my dish was also a bit greasy. In pursuit of a lighter sauce, I tinkered with the amount of butter and also tried out both light cream and half-and-half. Tasters overwhelmingly preferred light cream, which stayed stable in the oven; half-and-half tended to curdle. To ensure a smooth, creamy sauce, I added just ⅛ teaspoon of baking soda to the mix; this tried-and-true test kitchen trick helped neutralize the very small amount of acidic tannin that came off the potatoes (this acid can lead to a curdled appearance) and kept things stable and silky.

As I dug into my final batch of creamy, savory, satisfying Lighthouse Inn Potatoes, I felt certain that, even though I'd tinkered with his recipe, Chef Wally would be happy enough to call them his own.

LIGHTHOUSE INN POTATOES
Serves 8 to 10
We prefer the texture of light cream for this recipe, but heavy cream will also work. Do not use half-and-half; It has a tendency to break. Grate the Parmesan on a rasp-style grater. Our favorite panko bread crumbs are from Ian's.

- 2 ounces Parmesan cheese, grated (1 cup)
- 1 cup panko bread crumbs
- 4 tablespoons unsalted butter, melted, plus 6 tablespoons cut into 6 pieces
  Salt and pepper
- 2½ pounds russet potatoes, peeled and cut into 1-inch chunks
- 3 cups light cream
- ⅛ teaspoon baking soda

1. Adjust oven rack to middle position and heat oven to 375 degrees. Combine Parmesan, panko, melted butter, and ¼ teaspoon salt in bowl; set aside.

2. Bring potatoes, 2½ cups cream, baking soda, 2 teaspoons salt, and 1 teaspoon pepper to boil in large saucepan over medium-high heat. Reduce heat to low and cook at bare simmer, stirring often, until paring knife slides easily into potatoes without them crumbling, 20 to 25 minutes.

Crunchy, buttery bread crumbs take this simple recipe right over the top.

3. Off heat, stir remaining ½ cup cream and remaining 6 tablespoons butter into potato mixture until butter has melted, about 1 minute. Transfer potato mixture to 13 by 9-inch baking dish. Sprinkle Parmesan-panko mixture over top. Bake, uncovered, until bubbling around edges and surface is golden brown, 15 to 20 minutes. Let cool for at least 15 minutes. Serve.

TO MAKE AHEAD
After potato mixture has been transferred to baking dish, let cool completely, cover with aluminum foil, and refrigerate for up to 24 hours. Before applying topping, bake, covered, until heated through, about 35 minutes. Apply topping and continue to bake, uncovered, 15 to 20 minutes longer.

The Lighthouse Inn

Locals claim that the Lighthouse Inn, originally a country house for a wealthy businessman before being turned into a resort, is haunted.

Soft and Chewy Gingerbread Cookies

Crisp gingerbread cookies can be great, but sometimes only soft and chewy will do.

BY KATIE LEAIRD

SLIDE A BATCH of gingerbread cookies into the oven and the aromas of cinnamon, nutmeg, and cloves swirl through the air. Everyone can agree that they smell wonderful. But ask them whether they prefer thin and crisp or soft and chewy and people pick sides.

I know this because I surveyed my fellow test cooks on a recent morning: Would you rather have a crisp cookie or a soft one? While many professed a preference for crisp cookies, soft and chewy cookies won the poll. A bit of research into the history of this holiday classic confirmed that this is no newfangled twist; fans of softer cookies have been around for generations.

Many of the gingerbread recipes I found had a low ratio of fat to flour, which made the dough easy to roll out and cut but meant that once baked, the cookies were too crunchy. I needed a dough that was firm enough to hold its shape in the oven (I wanted gingerbread people, not gingerbread amoebas) but that would stay soft and chewy after the cookies cooled; to get there, I'd need more fat. After a few tests, I arrived at 12 tablespoons of butter.

While recipes often call for a stand mixer for creaming the butter into the other ingredients, I opted for an even quicker path: the food processor. What's more, rather than waiting for butter to soften, I simply melted the butter gently in the microwave and allowed it to cool for just 5 minutes before adding it to the processor with the other ingredients (including a balanced blend of ground cinnamon, ginger, and cloves). The dough came together in just seconds, and nothing was lost for the lack of a creaming step. I turned my dough out onto a lightly oiled counter for a quick knead before wrapping it and refrigerating it for an hour.

After rolling out dozens of doughs, I learned that rolling to a ¼-inch thickness was ideal for soft and chewy cookies every time. Using parchment paper kept the mess to a minimum. I cut the cookies out right away (no need for a second visit to the fridge) and baked them until they were just set around the edges and slightly puffed in the center. As they cooled, the slightly puffed cookies settled into a sublime chewiness.

No gingerbread cookie should go undecorated, so I set to experimenting

One key to soft and chewy cookies is to roll the dough ¼ inch thick. Any thinner and you'll have crisp, brittle cookies.

with decorative icing. Basic icing made from confectioners' sugar and milk was too runny to achieve clearly defined decorating lines. Instead, I whipped egg whites and sugar into a stiffer mixture. The result was a structured frosting that was easy to apply, with a beautiful bright white gloss.

My simple soft and chewy gingerbread cookies boasted the full package: memory-sparking aroma, satisfying flavor, and festive decoration.

TEST KITCHEN TIP
When Are They Done?
Even professional bakers have trouble deciding when cookies that start out brown should come out of the oven. Our solution is to carefully observe them during baking and remove them when they are puffy and just set around the edges.

SOFT AND CHEWY GINGERBREAD COOKIES

Makes about 24 cookies

Let the melted butter cool before adding it in step 1, or the dough will be too sticky to work with. Because we roll the dough between sheets of parchment paper (no additional flour is added), the scraps can be rerolled and cut as many times as necessary. The cookies can be stored in a wide, shallow airtight container with a sheet of parchment or waxed paper between each layer for up to 3 days. Plan ahead: The dough needs to rest for at least an hour before rolling.

- 3 cups (15 ounces) all-purpose flour
- ¾ cup packed (5¼ ounces) dark brown sugar
- 1 tablespoon ground cinnamon
- 1 tablespoon ground ginger
- ¾ teaspoon baking soda
- ½ teaspoon ground cloves
- ½ teaspoon salt
- 12 tablespoons unsalted butter, melted and cooled
- ¾ cup molasses
- 2 tablespoons milk

1. Process flour, sugar, cinnamon, ginger, baking soda, cloves, and salt in food processor until combined, about 10 seconds. Add melted butter, molasses, and milk and process until soft dough forms and no streaks of flour remain, about 20 seconds, scraping down sides of bowl as needed.

2. Spray counter lightly with baking spray with flour, transfer dough to counter, and knead until dough forms cohesive ball, about 20 seconds. Divide dough in half. Form each half into 5-inch disk, wrap disks tightly in plastic wrap, and refrigerate for at least 1 hour or up to 24 hours.

3. Adjust oven racks to upper-middle and lower-middle positions and heat oven to 350 degrees. Line 2 rimmed baking sheets with parchment paper. Working with 1 disk of dough at a time, roll dough between 2 large sheets of parchment to ¼-inch thickness. (Keep second disk of dough refrigerated while rolling out first.) Peel off top parchment sheet and use 3½-inch cookie cutter to cut out cookies. Peel away scraps from around cookies and space cookies ¾ inch apart on prepared sheets. Repeat rolling and cutting steps with dough scraps. (Depending on your cookie cutter dimensions, all cookies may not fit on sheets and second round of baking may be required. If so, let sheets cool completely before proceeding.)

4. Bake until cookies are puffy and just set around edges, 9 to 11 minutes, switching and rotating sheets halfway through baking. Let cookies cool on sheets for 10 minutes, then transfer to wire rack and let cool completely before decorating and serving.

The American Table
Whose Gingerbread?

Common food lore attributes a famous gingerbread recipe to Martha Washington, wife of the first U.S. president George Washington, but according to the Donald W. Reynolds Museum and Education Center at Mount Vernon, no such recipe exists. There is, however, evidence that Martha loved the stuff—a bill of sale for 49 pounds of gingerbread cake, sent initially to the estate of Martha's first husband Daniel Custis, was chivalrously paid by her second husband, George.

The mistake is easy to understand because a recipe for gingerbread cake from Mary Ball Washington (below), George's mother, does exist. Besides the ample presence of spices, including cloves, allspice, cinnamon, and ginger, the elder Mrs. Washington added orange juice and orange zest, uncommon (and uncommonly expensive) ingredients at the time.

DECORATING ICING Makes 1⅓ cups

This recipe makes bright white icing. For colored icing, stir 1 to 2 drops of food coloring into the icing to achieve the desired color before transferring it to a pastry bag.

- 2 large egg whites
- 2⅔ cups (10⅔ ounces) confectioners' sugar

1. Using stand mixer fitted with whisk attachment, whip egg whites and sugar on medium-low speed until combined, about 1 minute. Increase speed to medium-high and whip until glossy, soft peaks form, 2 to 3 minutes, scraping down bowl as needed.

2. Transfer icing to pastry bag fitted with small round pastry tip. Decorate cookies and let icing harden before serving.

> Ground ginger gives our cookies subtle punch. Go to **CooksCountry.com/ginger** to read about our tasting of ground gingers.

Practice, practice . . . If you repeat similar designs, your results are likely to improve.

To get just the hue you're aiming for, mix food coloring into icing a little at a time.

TEST KITCHEN TIPS Decorating with Confidence

Decorating gingerbread cookies is easy—and fun—when you have a little know-how. Simple designs are often the most successful. After all, this type of cookie is a very small canvas.

Filling the Pastry Bag

Set a pastry bag fitted with a small round pastry tip in a liquid measuring cup or tall pint glass. Fold the bag over about halfway down into a cuff. Using a rubber spatula, load the frosting into the bag, packing tightly to eliminate air spaces. Twist tightly while again pushing on the frosting to squeeze out air.

No Pastry Bag?
Don't Let It Stop You

If you don't own a pastry bag, a zipper-lock bag makes a great stand-in. Load the bag with frosting, pushing it into one corner of the bag, and then make a very small snip in the corner (you can always make the cut larger if necessary).

Let 'em Cool

Frosting will liquefy if it's piped onto hot cookies. Let the gingerbread cookies cool completely on a wire rack before you start decorating them.

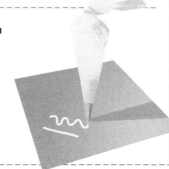

Hold the Bag Like a Pro, and Do a Test Run

Once your icing is loaded into the pastry bag, grab the bag at the base of the twist with one hand. Using your other hand as a guide, hold the tip at a 90-degree angle about ½ inch above the cookie and gently squeeze to decorate. Practice your design on a sheet of parchment paper—or on a sacrificial cookie—before you start decorating in earnest.

Cooking Class Easy Pound Cake

When it comes to flavor and texture, dessert doesn't get more straightforward than pound cake. But the classic recipe is notoriously fussy to make. Our version isn't. BY CHRISTIE MORRISON

EASY POUND CAKE Serves 8

The test kitchen's preferred loaf pan measures 8½ by 4½ inches; if you use a 9 by 5-inch pan, start checking for doneness 5 minutes early. To dress up the cake, try our Citrus Glaze (recipe follows).

- 1½ cups (6 ounces) cake flour
- 1 teaspoon baking powder
- ½ teaspoon salt
- 1¼ cups (8¾ ounces) sugar
- 4 large eggs, room temperature
- 1½ teaspoons vanilla extract
- 16 tablespoons unsalted butter, melted and hot

1. Adjust oven rack to middle position and heat oven to 350 degrees. Grease and flour 8½ by 4½-inch loaf pan. Whisk flour, baking powder, and salt together in bowl.

2. Process sugar, eggs, and vanilla in food processor until combined, about 10 seconds. With processor running, add melted butter in steady stream until incorporated. Pour mixture into large bowl.

3. Sift flour mixture over egg mixture in 3 additions, whisking to combine after each addition until few streaks of flour remain. Continue to whisk batter gently until almost no lumps remain.

4. Transfer batter to prepared pan and smooth top. Wipe any drops of batter off sides of pan and gently tap pan on counter to release air bubbles. Bake until toothpick inserted in center comes out with few moist crumbs attached, 50 minutes to 1 hour, rotating pan halfway through baking.

5. Let cake cool in pan on wire rack for 10 minutes. Run small knife around edge of cake to loosen, then flip cake out onto wire rack. Turn cake right side up and let cool completely, about 2 hours, before serving. (Cake can be wrapped in plastic wrap and stored at room temperature for up to 5 days. Wrapped cake can be placed in zipper-lock bag and frozen for up to 1 month.)

EASY LEMON POUND CAKE

Add 2 tablespoons grated lemon zest and 2 teaspoons lemon juice to food processor with sugar, eggs, and vanilla.

CITRUS GLAZE Makes about ¼ cup

To apply, spread glaze over the top of the cooled cake, allowing some to drip down the sides. Let the glaze set for at least 15 minutes before serving. This recipe makes enough glaze for one pound cake.

- ½ cup confectioners' sugar, sifted
- 1 tablespoon lemon, lime, or orange juice

Whisk confectioners' sugar and citrus juice in bowl until smooth.

▶ Go to **CooksCountry.com/jan17** for our recipes for Easy Almond, Easy Ginger, and Easy Orange Pound Cakes.

STEP BY STEP Easy Pound Cake

1. USE ROOM-TEMPERATURE EGGS
Let the eggs slowly come to room temperature, or put them in warm tap water for 5 minutes.
WHY? Room-temperature eggs whip into a loftier foam than cold eggs; aerated eggs help the cake rise.

2. GREASE AND FLOUR PAN
Coat 8½ by 4½-inch loaf pan with vegetable oil spray. Dust pan with several tablespoons of flour. Dump out excess flour.
WHY? A dusting of flour helps the pound cake climb the sides of the pan and prevents the edges from forming a hard, crusty lip.

3. ADD BAKING POWDER
Whisk 1 teaspoon baking powder with cake flour and salt in bowl.
WHY? Traditional pound cakes rely on beaten eggs alone for leavening. Adding a small amount of baking powder is extra insurance for a proper domed rise.

4. START BATTER IN FOOD PROCESSOR
Process sugar, eggs, and vanilla extract until combined, about 10 seconds.
WHY? The food processor ensures that the ingredients are thoroughly combined before the butter is incorporated.

5. ADD HOT MELTED BUTTER
With food processor running, pour butter through feed tube in steady stream until incorporated.
WHY? The temperature of hot melted butter and the processor's fast-moving blade emulsify the liquid ingredients more quickly and completely than a mixer.

How We Made it Easier

Most pound cake recipes require ingredients at precise temperatures and a finicky mixing method. Why? For a proper pound cake, the butter and eggs need to form a smooth emulsion that can then be aerated. If the butter or the eggs are too cold, the two never fully emulsify, and you end up with a curdled batter and a dense, heavy cake.

Our foolproof recipe calls for:

- a food processor (not a mixer) to create an ultrasmooth, aerated emulsion.
- using hot melted butter (instead of room-temperature butter) for quick emulsification.
- adding baking powder (instead of relying solely on beaten eggs) for lift.

Pan Size Matters

The two most common sizes of loaf pan are 8½ by 4½ inches and 9 by 5 inches. In the test kitchen, we use an 8½ by 4½-inch pan, and our pound cake emerges with a distinct dome. A 9 by 5-inch pan will produce a cake with a flatter top but an equally moist, tender, and flavorful interior.

FLAT TOP
If your loaf pan measures 9 by 5 inches, test for doneness about 5 minutes early.

Working with Flour and Eggs

Cake Flour versus All-Purpose Flour

Cake flour has a lower protein level (6 to 8 percent) than all-purpose flour (9 to 12 percent protein). Not all cakes require cake flour, and we call for it in only a few recipes where we feel it delivers decidedly better results than all-purpose flour. One such recipe is our Easy Pound Cake, where we prefer the fine, tender crumb that only cake flour can produce. In a pinch, replace the cake flour with 1⅓ cups of all-purpose flour mixed with 3 tablespoons of cornstarch.

1 ½ CUPS CAKE FLOUR	**1 ⅓ CUPS ALL-PURPOSE FLOUR**	**3 TABLESPOONS CORNSTARCH**

Baking with Cold versus Room-Temperature Eggs

Cake recipes often call for room-temperature eggs, which whip higher and give more lift than cold eggs. But is the difference between room-temperature and cold eggs so great that it could actually ruin a pound cake? To find out, we made pound cakes with both room-temperature and cold eggs. Cold eggs didn't whip as well as room-temperature eggs, so the batter didn't rise

SPEED IT UP
A 5-minute warm-water soak quickly brings eggs to room temperature.

properly, making the cake dense (the same held true for angel food and chiffon cakes). That said, we found that it's fine to use cold eggs in basic cake recipes that don't rely heavily on beaten eggs for lift.

The American Table
The Pound Cake Workout

In 16th-century England, sweet cakes enriched with eggs and/or butter were popular. These incredibly large, special-occasion affairs called for upwards of 20 pounds of ingredients leavened with yeast.

Over time, the dessert evolved into the aptly named pound cake, calling for just a pound each of butter, sugar, flour, and eggs. Yeast was no longer on the ingredient list; the cake was leavened solely by eggs and air (no chemical leaveners, either). Before the advent of the stand mixer, that meant so much mixing by hand that it's a wonder anyone ever attempted to make it. To wit: The earliest known published recipe for pound cake (in the 1747 cookbook *The Art of Cookery Made Plain and Easy* by Hannah Glasse) calls for beating the batter for an astounding full hour, all by hand.

6. SIFT IN DRY INGREDIENTS
Sift flour mixture over egg mixture in 3 additions. After each addition, whisk to combine.
WHY? Because overmixing will lead to a heavy, dense cake, sift the dry ingredients to aerate and break the ingredients into small particles that will mix in easily.

7. TAP PAN ON COUNTER
Transfer batter to prepared pan and smooth top. Tap pan on counter to release air bubbles.
WHY? Tapping the loaf pan releases large air bubbles from the batter that could cause tunneling (large holes) in the crumb of the finished cake.

8. ROTATE CAKE HALFWAY THROUGH BAKING
Bake until toothpick inserted in center comes out with few moist crumbs attached, rotating pan halfway through baking.
WHY? Rotating the cake as it bakes ensures even heating, even if your oven has hot spots.

9. LET COOL BRIEFLY IN PAN
Let cake cool in pan on wire rack for 10 minutes.
WHY? Letting the cake cool briefly in the pan allows it to firm up a little so it won't break apart when you remove it from the pan. (If you let it cool completely in the pan, it will be hard to remove.)

10. REMOVE CAKE FROM PAN AND LET COOL COMPLETELY
Run knife around edge, then flip cake onto rack. Turn cake right side up and let cool completely.
WHY? As the cake cools, the starches dry and firm up, making the cake easier to slice without tearing or crumbling.

Five Easy Ricotta Crostini

We want party snacks that are as easy to make as they are to enjoy. BY ASHLEY MOORE

WHEN I THINK of parties, I think of sparkling conversation, refreshing cocktails, and savory little pass-around party snacks like crostini. These little toasts (*crostini* actually means "little toasts" in Italian) provide an excellent blank canvas for a range of toppings, from cheese to meat to vegetables. Ideas flooded my brain and I couldn't wait to get started.

I knew that each of these stacked bites would need to deliver major flavor but also be easy to eat one-handed. (I'm presuming, of course, that the other hand will be grasping a glass of something refreshing.) So they needed to be sturdy, and they needed something to help the toppings stick.

For the toasted-bread platform, I chose a baguette. A thin slice of baguette is just the right size for finger food. I got the best results by brushing extra-virgin olive oil on one side of each slice of baguette and then baking the slices on a baking sheet until they were just crunchy enough.

For the sticky layer, I chose ricotta cheese. Its mild flavor would let the toppings shine, and its creamy texture is easy to work with and keeps toppings in place. Ricotta can sometimes be grainy, so I gave the cheese a quick whirl in the food processor with a little olive oil and some salt and pepper to smooth it out and thoroughly incorporate the seasonings.

For the toppings, I wanted to stick to bold pantry ingredients and fresh produce and herbs—no additional cooking required. I began with a simple, classic combination of tomatoes, basil, and garlic. For my first variation, I tossed together thinly sliced asparagus, peppery radishes, lemon juice, chives, and a bit of savory minced anchovy (trust me).

Next, I mixed chopped kalamata olives, sun-dried tomatoes, orange zest, and red wine vinegar and topped it all with crunchy chopped pine nuts. Thawed frozen peas with shallot, mint, and red wine vinegar made up the third variation. Finally, I swapped in sweet roasted peppers for the original tomatoes and combined them with minced capers, chopped parsley, and lemon zest.

Done. And with plenty of time left over to tidy up the kitchen and get ready for my guests.

RICOTTA CROSTINI WITH CHERRY TOMATOES AND BASIL
Makes 24 crostini

We prefer to use day-old bread for this recipe because it is easier to slice. The crostini are best topped shortly before serving. Our preferred whole-milk ricotta is BelGioioso Ricotta con Latte Whole Milk. A 12-inch demi-baguette will easily yield the 24 slices needed for this recipe.

- 24 (¼-inch-thick) slices baguette
- 6 tablespoons extra-virgin olive oil
- 6 ounces cherry tomatoes, quartered
- 1 small garlic clove, minced
- Salt and pepper
- 6 ounces (¾ cup) whole-milk ricotta cheese
- ¼ cup fresh basil leaves, torn

1. Adjust oven rack to middle position and heat oven to 400 degrees. Arrange baguette slices in single layer on rimmed baking sheet. Brush tops of slices with 2 tablespoons oil. Bake until golden brown and crispy, 8 to 10 minutes. Let cool completely on sheet, about 30 minutes.

2. Combine tomatoes, garlic, ¼ teaspoon salt, ¼ teaspoon pepper, and 2 tablespoons oil in bowl; set aside.

3. Process ricotta, ¼ teaspoon salt, and ¼ teaspoon pepper in food processor until smooth, about 10 seconds. With processor running, slowly add remaining 2 tablespoons oil until incorporated; transfer to bowl. Spread ricotta mixture evenly on toasted baguette slices. Spoon tomato mixture over ricotta and sprinkle with basil.

RICOTTA CROSTINI WITH ASPARAGUS AND RADISHES
Substitute 2 ounces asparagus, trimmed and sliced thin on bias, for tomatoes. Add 4 radishes, trimmed and sliced thin; ¼ cup minced fresh chives; 1 tablespoon lemon juice; and 1 minced anchovy fillet to asparagus mixture. Omit basil.

RICOTTA CROSTINI WITH OLIVES AND SUN-DRIED TOMATOES
Substitute ¾ cup pitted kalamata olives, chopped coarse, for tomatoes and ¼ cup toasted pine nuts, chopped, for basil. Add ½ cup oil-packed sun-dried tomatoes, patted dry and chopped coarse, and 1 teaspoon red wine vinegar to olive mixture. Process ½ teaspoon grated orange zest with ricotta mixture.

Don't overload your crostini: The last thing you want to do is spill on your party outfit.

RICOTTA CROSTINI WITH PEAS AND MINT
Substitute 1 cup thawed frozen peas for tomatoes, 1 minced small shallot for garlic, and torn fresh mint leaves for basil. Add 2 teaspoons red wine vinegar to pea mixture.

RICOTTA CROSTINI WITH ROASTED RED PEPPERS AND CAPERS
Substitute 1 cup jarred roasted red peppers, patted dry and chopped fine, for tomatoes. Reduce salt to ⅛ teaspoon and add ¼ cup chopped fresh parsley and 2 tablespoons capers, rinsed and minced, to red pepper mixture. Process ½ teaspoon grated lemon zest with ricotta mixture. Omit basil.

INGREDIENT SPOTLIGHT
Ricotta

Our winning ricotta—**BelGioioso Ricotta con Latte Whole Milk**—boasts a rich, dense consistency, in part because of the manufacturer's packaging method, which gently transfers the cheese to containers. Its slightly sweet flavor is ideal for crostini.

Slow Cooker Classic Butternut Squash Soup

Our aim: A simple squash soup that tastes deeply of (wait for it) squash. BY DIANE UNGER

BUTTERNUT SQUASH SOUP should be silky-smooth, deeply flavorful, and completely comforting. It should be light enough to serve in cups as an appetizer for a holiday dinner but substantial enough to serve in big bowls alongside hunks of crusty bread and a fresh salad for a modest weeknight supper.

But so many recipes cover up the earthy, slightly sweet flavor of the squash. Cooks add extras like sweet potatoes, leeks, potatoes, apple butter, or cider to the mix, and while many of them turn out a reasonable soup (we tried), the squash flavor seems to be an afterthought.

I wanted a soup that kept the focus on the squash, with room for garnishes to round things out. I wanted to make it in the slow cooker. And I wanted to make enough to have for supper tonight with plenty of leftovers to freeze and eat later in the week. A heady suite of challenges, but I was eager to take them on.

The first step is the toughest: peeling and cutting up a 3½-pound butternut squash. I used a vegetable peeler to remove that tough skin, halved the squash lengthwise, discarded the seeds, and cut the flesh into rough 1-inch pieces. This gave me about 9 cups of cut squash.

To build an aromatic base of flavor, I started with chopped onion. I zapped it in the microwave with butter until it softened (about 5 minutes) and then dropped it into the slow cooker. Next I tossed my squash chunks into the cooker, too, followed by 6 cups of water. I covered the cooker and let the soup cook on low for about 6 hours, until the squash was tender when I pierced it with a paring knife; I then pureed it right in the slow cooker using my immersion blender.

I had high hopes, but I soon found out that I'd sacrificed flavor by using water rather than a more flavorful liquid, like stock. What's more, the soup was thin and watery, not luxurious and creamy.

For my next experiment, I substituted flavorful chicken stock for the water. I also peeled, cored, and chopped a Golden Delicious apple to microwave with the onion. I added this to the slow cooker with the other ingredients and set it to cook. I also made another batch of the previous underwhelming soup (made with just

Pepitas (roasted pumpkin seeds) add crunch, chives add freshness, and sour cream adds tang.

Same Soup, New Flavor
Give leftovers a twist by topping them with inventive garnishes:

- crumbled blue cheese, toasted croutons, and crispy bits of bacon
- toasted sage leaves and drizzles of thinned sour cream
- dots of goat cheese and minced fresh parsley or tarragon

water and no apple) for comparison.

I set out both soups for my tasters. No contest: They strongly preferred the soup with the chicken stock and apple. This soup had a more complex and slightly brighter flavor (without tasting strongly of apple), and the pectin from

the apple gave the soup a slightly thicker texture, leaving it velvety and smooth.

Smooth soups are often finished with heavy cream, and I put that to the test in a four-way match-up: four soups with varying amounts of cream (1 cup, ½ cup, ¼ cup, and no cream at all) stirred in. Surprisingly, tasters nixed the cream completely in favor of the clean flavor and vibrant orange color of the unadulterated butternut.

For a final touch, I set out a range of garnishes for tasters to choose from. The most popular combination was sour cream, toasted pepitas, and chives, but simple buttery croutons, crumbled goat cheese or blue cheese, and minced fresh herbs (sage, parsley, and tarragon) also proved popular. Luckily, I had plenty of leftover soup with which to try them all.

SLOW-COOKER CLASSIC BUTTERNUT SQUASH SOUP
Serves 8

We prefer the flavor of whole squash for this recipe, but prepeeled and cut squash, available at some grocery stores, will also work. Our winning chicken broth is Swanson Chicken Stock.

- 1 onion, chopped
- 1 Golden Delicious apple, peeled, cored, and chopped
- 4 tablespoons unsalted butter, cut into 4 pieces
  Salt and pepper
- 3½ pounds butternut squash, peeled, seeded, and cut into 1-inch pieces (9 cups)
- 6 cups chicken broth
  Sour cream
  Roasted, salted pepitas
  Minced fresh chives

1. Combine onion, apple, butter, and 1 teaspoon salt in bowl and microwave, covered, until onion has softened, about 5 minutes. Transfer mixture to slow cooker and stir in squash and broth. Cover and cook until squash is tender, 6 to 8 hours on low or 4 to 6 hours on high.

2A. FOR A BLENDER: Working in batches, process soup in blender until smooth, 1 to 2 minutes. Transfer soup to Dutch oven. Rewarm over medium-low heat, about 2 minutes. Season with salt and pepper to taste.

2B. FOR AN IMMERSION BLENDER: Submerge blender in slow cooker and process soup until smooth, about 3 minutes. Season with salt and pepper to taste.

3. Serve soup, garnished with sour cream, pepitas, and chives.

Storing and Reheating Leftovers
The soup can be refrigerated in an airtight container for up to three days or frozen for up to two months. When you're ready to eat it, simply transfer the refrigerated soup to a saucepan and warm it over medium-low heat. A frozen portion of soup can be microwaved at 30 percent power to defrost it and then heated at full power until it's hot.

One-Pan Dinner Mediterranean Shrimp

The goal: a fresh, healthful weeknight supper without a sink full of pots and pans.

BY KATIE LEAIRD

IT'S COMMON TO see shrimp skewered on the grill, sizzling in butter in a hot skillet, or frying in a pool of hot oil in a Dutch oven. But an alternate option, a one-baking-sheet meal with shrimp as the centerpiece, calls for the oven.

The beauty of using shrimp for a speedy supper is that they cook through quickly when exposed to any sort of heat. And unlike other proteins that need direct contact with a hot surface or flame to achieve an appetizing sear, shrimp taste great without it.

But this is also the danger of shrimp—it's far too easy to overcook them. If they spend too long in the oven, their delicate flesh turns tough and rubbery. After a few initial tests, I discovered that 6 to 8 minutes in a 450-degree oven was perfect.

Finding vegetables that shared this short cooking time was a futile exercise—almost nothing I tried would cook through in that time frame. I knew I'd have to give the vegetables a good head start in the oven and then add the shrimp for just the final few minutes. Potatoes were easy enough to incorporate using this method. But what about something green?

I tried broccolini, an underused vegetable that I love, but it turned into an unappealing swampy mess on the baking sheet. Spinach just turned slimy. My breakthrough came when a coworker suggested I try fennel.

Though its pale color made it appear less vibrant than other green vegetables, the slightly sweet, licorice-like flavor of roasted fennel paired beautifully with the briny shrimp. By slicing the fennel bulb into wedges through the stem end, I was able to keep the layers intact as they cooked; plus, this thick cut provided more surface area for flavorful browning.

To liven things up and give the dish a Mediterranean flavor profile, I tossed the shrimp with oregano and lemon zest before adding them to the pan with crumbled feta and sliding it back into the oven. When the shrimp were cooked through, I scattered a handful of chopped kalamata olives over the top. A sprinkling of parsley and a squeeze of lemon put the final fresh touches on this satisfying, Mediterranean-style shrimp supper.

A spritz of juice from a lemon wedge lifts this light weeknight supper.

Roast Veggies First

Roast the longer-cooking potatoes and fennel until they are just tender. Then, flip the vegetables so their browned sides are facing up and scatter the oregano-and-lemon-scented shrimp and the feta on top to cook the shrimp. Sprinkle with parsley and kalamata olives before serving.

ONE-PAN MEDITERRANEAN SHRIMP
Serves 4 to 6

We prefer all-natural shrimp that aren't treated with sodium or preservatives. If buying frozen shrimp, the ingredient label should list only "shrimp."

- 1½ pounds Yukon Gold potatoes, peeled and sliced ½ inch thick
- 2 fennel bulbs, stalks discarded, bulbs halved lengthwise and cut into 1-inch-thick wedges through stem end
- 3 tablespoons extra-virgin olive oil, plus extra for drizzling
  Salt and pepper
- 2 pounds jumbo shrimp (16 to 20 per pound), peeled, deveined, and tails removed
- 2 teaspoons dried oregano
- 1 teaspoon grated lemon zest, plus lemon wedges for serving
- 4 ounces feta cheese, crumbled (1 cup)
- ½ cup pitted kalamata olives, halved
- 2 tablespoons chopped fresh parsley

1. Adjust oven rack to lower-middle position and heat oven to 450 degrees. Toss potatoes, fennel, 2 tablespoons oil, 1 teaspoon salt, and ¼ teaspoon pepper together in bowl. Spread vegetables in single layer on rimmed baking sheet and roast until just tender, about 25 minutes.

2. Pat shrimp dry with paper towels. Toss shrimp, oregano, lemon zest, remaining 1 tablespoon oil, ½ teaspoon salt, and ¼ teaspoon pepper together in bowl.

3. Using spatula, flip potatoes and fennel so browned sides are facing up. Scatter shrimp and feta over top. Return to oven and roast until shrimp are cooked through, 6 to 8 minutes. Sprinkle olives and parsley over top and drizzle with extra oil. Serve with lemon wedges.

INGREDIENT SPOTLIGHT Feta
Rich, tangy, and salty feta cheese never fully melts, maintaining some of its crumbly texture during baking. Our favorite—**Mt. Vikos Traditional Feta**—has a "funky" flavor and a "creamy, crumbly" consistency.

Cooking for Two Chicken Cacciatore

Syncing the sauce and the chicken made all the difference for this rustic supper.

BY CECELIA JENKINS

CACCIATORE, WHICH MEANS "hunter-style" in Italian, refers to a rustic dish of freshly caught game (usually rabbit), foraged mushrooms, and rosemary that's traditionally served after a hunt. It's since become a ubiquitous Italian American dish, with bone-in chicken substituting for rabbit and chunky tomatoes and peppers added to the saucy braise.

My biggest challenge was avoiding dry chicken and a too-thick or too-thin sauce. To leap over these hurdles, I had to find a way to sync the cooking of the chicken and the sauce so that everything finished at the same time. Nixing chicken breasts in favor of leg quarters fit the bill; dark meat stays moist in long braises, so the window of time for cooking them could be a bit more flexible than with white meat. Additionally, they cut a rustic figure in keeping with the style of the dish—not to mention that they're cheap.

After searing and setting aside the chicken legs, I sautéed cremini mushrooms, bell peppers, and onions in the same skillet. (Tasters greatly preferred the sweetness and brightness of red bell peppers to green.) Adding the tomato paste next gave it a chance to caramelize and develop complexity; garlic, rosemary, and pepper flakes contributed yet more flavor. Now for some liquid: I wanted something to balance the sweet tomatoes and peppers, and red wine was too heavy and earthy. Sharp, lighter white wine gave just enough acidity while broth added savoriness and diced tomatoes contributed a chunky texture. Scraping up the brown bits on the bottom of the pan ensured deep flavor.

I experimented with finishing the dish uncovered on the stovetop and in the oven. Both failed: The sauce from the stovetop sample, cooked over low heat, was overly thick and ketchup-like by the time the chicken was done, while the sauce from the oven resembled soup. I tried a hybrid method, covering my skillet on the stovetop until the chicken cooked through and then removing the lid for the last few minutes to let the sauce reduce. It worked beautifully—and since I was using forgiving leg quarters, I could leave them in the pan, as that extra time wouldn't affect their juiciness. With a sprinkling of fresh basil, I had chicken cacciatore for two in just an hour, no hunting required.

A few red pepper flakes lend a touch of heat to this dish; feel free to add more at the table.

CHICKEN CACCIATORE FOR TWO

Some leg quarters are sold with the backbone attached. Be sure to remove it before cooking to make serving easier. If serving with pasta, adjust sauce consistency with reserved pasta cooking water as needed.

- 2 (10-ounce) chicken leg quarters, trimmed
  Salt and pepper
- 2 teaspoons vegetable oil
- 6 ounces cremini mushrooms, trimmed and quartered
- 1 small onion, chopped
- ½ cup chopped red bell pepper
- 1 tablespoon tomato paste
- 2 garlic cloves, minced
- 1½ teaspoons minced fresh rosemary
- ⅛ teaspoon red pepper flakes
- ¼ cup white wine
- 1 (14.5-ounce) can diced tomatoes
- ½ cup chicken broth
- 1 tablespoon minced fresh basil

1. Pat chicken dry with paper towels and season with salt and pepper. Heat oil in 10-inch skillet over medium-high heat until just smoking. Add chicken and cook until browned, about 5 minutes per side. Transfer to plate, skin side up.

2. Pour off all but 1 tablespoon fat from skillet; heat fat over medium heat until shimmering. Add mushrooms, onion, bell pepper, ⅛ teaspoon salt, and ¼ teaspoon pepper and cook, uncovered, stirring occasionally, until vegetables are softened and browned, 8 to 10 minutes.

3. Stir in tomato paste, garlic, rosemary, and pepper flakes and cook until mixture is rust colored and fragrant, stirring frequently, about 2 minutes. Stir in wine and any accumulated chicken juices, scraping up any browned bits, and cook until liquid is evaporated, about 1 minute. Add tomatoes and their juice and broth and bring to boil.

4. Nestle chicken into sauce, skin side up. Reduce heat to medium-low, cover, and simmer until chicken registers 175 degrees, 22 to 25 minutes. Remove lid, increase heat to medium-high, and continue to cook until sauce is slightly thickened, about 5 minutes longer. Sprinkle with basil. Serve.

TEST KITCHEN TECHNIQUE
Prepping Leg Quarters
Cut off any large pockets of fat and then trim any skin that hangs off the leg quarter. If the backbone is still attached, cut through to remove it, along with any attached skin.

Our favorite Dutch oven costs $360. We needed a practical alternative. BY HANNAH CROWLEY

THE TEST KITCHEN GAUNTLET
7 Dutch Ovens, 8 Tests

We put each Dutch oven through the following battery of tests:

1. Time how long it takes to boil water
2. Cook one batch of White Rice
3. Fry 15 ounces of frozen French fries in 2 quarts of oil
4. Braise one batch of Beef Burgundy
5. Bake one loaf of Almost No-Knead Bread
6. Wash (five times) with abrasive sponge
7. Whack rim with metal spoon 50 times
8. Slam lid down onto its base 10 times

A DUTCH OVEN just might be the most versatile pot you can own. It can go on the stove and in the oven, which makes it ideal for braising meat; cooking soups, stews, and sauces; boiling water; frying; and even baking bread.

These pots come in all shapes, sizes, and materials. Over years of testing and using them daily in the test kitchen, we've determined that we like round Dutch ovens (oval ones hang off of burners) that hold a minimum of 6 quarts. And we like heavy pots made of enameled cast iron, which conducts and retains heat well and is easy to clean.

Our favorite, the Le Creuset 7¼ Round Dutch Oven, performs magnificently and, with proper care, should last a lifetime—but it costs $359.99. So we decided to try to find a great Dutch oven for a lot less money, setting a price cap of around $125.00. We chose seven challengers priced from $24.29 to $121.94 and put each one through a grueling battery of tests.

After weeks of rigorous testing, it was clear that all the pots can cook food acceptably, but we found three Dutch ovens we truly liked.

▶ To read the full testing results, go to CooksCountry.com/jan17

What traits mattered? First, material. We included two light aluminum pots in our lineup because we've heard complaints about how heavy enameled cast-iron Dutch ovens are. But cooking with these two light pots only reinforced our preference for those with cast-iron cores, as the aluminum pots were prone to scorching and dented easily.

Big, comfortable handles were a must for these heavy pots, and those with skimpy handles were downgraded accordingly. The interior color of the pots mattered, too. All of the cast-iron pots, save one, had a light interior that made it easy to monitor browning. The outlier had a dark nonstick finish that made it easy to clean but hard to see if the food was browning. Our testing also bore out a preference for pots with shorter sides, as tall sides made it more awkward to add food to hot oil in a safe, splash-free manner when frying.

But what really made some pots easier to use was their shape. Broad bases with straight sides were best. Two pots had rounded sides that curved in at the base, reducing some of their potential flat usable cooking surface. Larger cooking surfaces fit more food, so we could brown beef for stew in two batches versus three or four, a savings of up to 15 minutes. Aside from the time savings, prolonged browning can mean that the fond (the flavorful brown bits that form on the bottom on the pot) is more likely to burn, which can render your dinner inedible.

The Cuisinart 7 Qt. Round Covered Casserole performed like a champ in all of our cooking tests, and it costs just $121.94. It has the same advantageous shape and features as the Le Creuset—broad with straight, low sides; big comfortable handles; and a core made of cast iron. The trade-off? It's 3 pounds heavier than the Le Creuset, and it chipped cosmetically along its rim during our abuse testing. But it's a great pot and a great value.

HIGHLY RECOMMENDED

CUISINART 7 Qt. Round Covered Casserole

Model: CUI CI670-30CR **Price:** $121.94
Material: Enameled cast iron **Capacity:** 7 qt
Weight: 16.8 lb **Usable Cooking Surface Diameter:** 10 in

This model costs a third of what our favorite Le Creuset Dutch oven does and performed almost as well. With a very similar design—low, straight sides and a broad, off-white cooking surface—it allowed us to easily move food, sear in fewer batches, and monitor browning. The trade-offs: The Cuisinart pot is 3 pounds heavier and has slightly smaller handles than the Le Creuset pot, and its rim chipped during abuse testing.

WINNING TRAITS
- Enameled cast-iron construction
- Heats evenly and retains heat well
- **Easy-to-grip, comfortable handles**
- **Broad, squat shape**
- Heavy, but not too heavy
- Light-colored interior
- At least 6-quart capacity

Cooking	★★★
Capacity	★★★
Ease of Use	★★½
Durability	★★½

RECOMMENDED

CRITERIA

COOKING WITH CALPHALON
Enamel Cast Iron Red 7-Qt. Dutch Oven with Cover
Model: 1835758 **Price:** $111.30
Material: Enameled cast iron
Capacity: 7 qt **Weight:** 15.45 lb
Usable Cooking Surface Diameter: 9.5 in

Cooking	★★½
Capacity	★★★
Ease of Use	★★½
Durability	★★½

LODGE ENAMEL
7.5 Quart Dutch Oven
Model: EC7D43 **Price:** $84.99
Material: Enameled cast iron
Capacity: 7.5 qt **Weight:** 18.15 lb
Usable Cooking Surface Diameter: 8.5 in

Cooking	★★★
Capacity	★★
Ease of Use	★★
Durability	★★½

RECOMMENDED WITH RESERVATIONS

TRAMONTINA
6.5 Qt Round Cast Iron Dutch Oven
Model: 80131/076DS **Price:** $69.96
Material: Enameled cast iron
Capacity: 6.5 qt **Weight:** 13.45 lb
Usable Cooking Surface Diameter: 8.4 in

Cooking	★★★
Capacity	★★½
Ease of Use	★
Durability	★★½

LODGE ENAMEL
6 Quart Dutch Oven
Model: EC6D38 **Price:** $60.99
Material: Enameled cast iron
Capacity: 6 qt **Weight:** 13.85 lb
Usable Cooking Surface Diameter: 7.5 in

Cooking	★★★
Capacity	★★
Ease of Use	★
Durability	★★½

IMUSA
Cast Aluminum Caldero Dutch Oven with Natural Finish
Model: GAU-80506W **Price:** $24.29
Material: Cast aluminum
Capacity: 6.9 qt **Weight:** 3.7 lb
Usable Cooking Surface Diameter: 8.5 in

Cooking	★★½
Capacity	★★★
Ease of Use	★★
Durability	★

NOT RECOMMENDED

NORDIC WARE 6.5 Quart ProCast Traditions Dutch Oven
Model: 21624 **Price:** $60.00
Material: Cast aluminum
Capacity: 6.5 qt **Weight:** 5.95 lb
Usable Cooking Surface Diameter: 8 in

Cooking	★★½
Capacity	★★
Ease of Use	½
Durability	★

Taste Test Spiral-Sliced Ham

Spiral-sliced ham is an easy and elegant holiday centerpiece. But not all hams are created equal. BY JASON ALVAREZ

WHY DO SO many people serve ham for the holidays? A better question might be, why do people serve anything else? A salty-sweet spiral-sliced ham is pre-cooked (just heat, glaze if you like, and serve), sliced for easy carving, and feeds a crowd. These hams are big, easy, and delicious. But with so many products on the market, which one should you buy?

To answer this, we selected seven widely available varieties of bone-in spiral-sliced ham (a mix of shank-end and butt-end cuts; we tasted whichever was easier to find) and asked 21 editors and cooks to taste each one. We began by tasting slices of plain, oven-heated ham; we moved on to ham sandwiches stacked with never-heated, refrigerator-chilled slices, using a different ham from each manufacturer for each tasting.

None of the hams were awful, but some were definitely better than others. The flavors of four of the seven products were a little out of whack, with a single flavor—smokiness, saltiness, or sweetness—overwhelming the others. The lower-ranked hams also had textural issues, with the meat tending to be dry, chewy, or spongy. Conversely, three hams impressed our tasters with juicy, tender textures and smoky, salty, and sweet notes that were pronounced but never overly dominant. The key was balance: The best hams had it, but it was in short supply in the lower-ranked contenders.

What gives some hams better texture and balance of flavors than others? The manufacturers we spoke with refused to divulge their processing methods, so we turned to industry experts for answers. The first thing these experts told us was that the flavor of a ham is primarily the result of processing (and not of the pig's breed or diet), which explains why manufacturers didn't want to share their secrets. We learned that all of these hams are wet-cured; the curing turns the meat the classic pink color, removes water (and thus concentrates flavor and texture), and seasons the ham. Spiral-sliced hams are typically wet-cured by immersion in (and/or injection with) a brine made with water, curing salts, and some form of sweetener. Brine recipes vary and obviously have an effect on the texture and harmony of flavors (or lack thereof) in the finished product.

To get the brine to permeate, the hams are "massaged" in a mechanical tumbler, a contraption resembling an industrial-scale dryer where, as the name suggests, hams roll and tumble for anywhere from 2 to 24 hours. Not only does this help distribute the brine throughout the meat, but it also batters the hams against the tumbler's walls, tenderizing the meat by physical force. The constant pressure applied during tumbling also forces water out. So the length and force of tumbling is another carefully controlled variable that contributes to the success of the finished product.

After brining, hams are cooked to a temperature between 155 and 170 degrees and then smoked, usually with hickory wood. Methods and timing vary here, too, according to experts. Some manufacturers smoke their hams for as few as 2 hours, while others approach 24 hours. Add cooking and smoking to the factors that can make or break a ham.

In the end, we thought that all the hams were acceptable, but we did find three hams that were superior. With so many variables in the production process, it was clear that these three hams came from manufacturers with very carefully calibrated processes. Our winner, Johnston County Spiral-Sliced Ham, was tender and juicy, with the perfect balance of smoke, salt, sweetness, and fat. These hams are sold in stores and online as half hams, roughly 7.5 pounds each, with an average price of $64.95 per ham.

RECOMMENDED

TASTERS' NOTES

JOHNSTON COUNTY
Spiral-Sliced Smoked Ham
Price: $64.95
Salt: 940 mg **Sugar:** 2 g
Availability: In stores and online ($34.15 shipping fee)

Our winning ham scored highly for flavor and texture. Tasters noted its "nice smokiness" and said it had "just enough sweetness." This ham was "tender and moist" with the "classic ham flavor" our tasters wanted. "Awesome!" said one.

BURGERS' SMOKEHOUSE
Spiral-Sliced City Ham
Price: $66.50
Salt: 870 mg **Sugar:** 0 g
Availability: Online (free shipping)

This ham appealed to tasters who preferred "porky" hams with a "very smoky flavor" that was assertive but not over the top. This product was balanced, with a texture that was "moist" and "tender."

APPLEWOOD FARMS
Spiral-Sliced Ham
Price: $45.00
Salt: 910 mg **Sugar:** 2 g
Availability: Online ($19.95 shipping fee)

The flavors in this mellow, "pleasantly hammy," crowd-pleasing ham were nicely balanced. This ham appealed to those who preferred flavors more mellow than the bold "smoky sweetness" of the top two products.

RECOMMENDED WITH RESERVATIONS

COOK'S Spiral Sliced
Hickory Smoked Ham
Price: $24.40
Salt: 800 mg **Sugar:** 4 g
Availability: In stores

This one nailed that "classic" spiral-sliced ham flavor. Tasters were impressed by its combination of "smoky sweet" and "hammy, meaty" flavors. But it was downgraded slightly for a texture described as a bit "spongy."

CARANDO Hickory Smoked
Spiral Sliced Ham
Price: $24.50
Salt: 760 mg **Sugar:** 2 g
Availability: In stores

Tasters liked the "distinctly porky" and "mildly sweet and smoky" flavor of this ham. But their enthusiasm was tempered by a slightly "dry" and "chewy" texture.

HONEYBAKED HAM
Price: $75.95
Salt: 1,230 mg **Sugar:** 4 g
Availability: In stores and online ($9.95 to $39.95 shipping fee, varies by delivery day)

The original spiral-sliced ham, HoneyBaked strongly divided our tasters. Some found its sweet "honey" and "maple" flavors "delicious." Others found it "oddly sweet," verging on "candied," and overly salty (it has the most salt of any ham we tasted).

HICKORY FARMS
Spiral Sliced HoneyGold Ham
Price: $75.00
Salt: 750 mg **Sugar:** 4 g
Availability: Online ($10.00 shipping fee)

Tasters enjoyed this ham's "smoky," "meaty" flavor and "firm," "hearty" texture in sandwiches but found it "tough" and "leathery" when eaten plain. More than one taster noticed a faint "burnt" flavor.

Prices may be higher during holiday seasons. All nutritional information is per 3-ounce serving.

Cleaning a Stained Pot

Enameled Dutch ovens are prone to staining, and while we're not concerned with keeping our cookware pristine, staining can be problematic if the bottom of the pot darkens so much that we can't monitor browning. After testing various methods, we found that the best way to deep-clean a stained pot is to let it soak overnight in a solution of 1 part bleach to 3 parts water and then wash it thoroughly with soap and water.

A well-used pot before and after cleaning

Tips for Improved Longevity

Chipping is a common problem with enameled Dutch ovens, which makes sense since enamel is made from powdered glass. Le Creuset's enameled surface is very durable, but it's not completely impervious. Here are some tips for keeping your enamel intact:

1. Don't subject your pot to dramatic temperature changes, especially near moisture.
2. Don't clear food from utensils by whacking them on the pot's rim.
3. Don't scrape metal utensils—specifically, sharp ones—along the bottom.
4. Don't heat an empty pot; reserve high heat for boiling water or cooking dishes with plenty of liquid.

Heirloom Recipe

We're looking for recipes that have been handed down in your family for a generation or more and have earned a place in your heart. Visit CooksCountry.com/recipe_submission (or write to Heirloom Recipes, *Cook's Country*, P.O. Box 470739, Brookline, MA 02447) and tell us a little about the recipe. Include your name and mailing address. **If we print your recipe, you'll receive a free one-year subscription to *Cook's Country*.**

EASY MINCEMEAT FRUITCAKE

Makes 2 cakes

"Fruitcake has a bad reputation for being loaded with neon red and green candied fruit. This recipe that my mom always made uses jarred mincemeat and dried fruits."
–Janice Campbell, Reston, Va.

Mincemeat can be found in the baking section of most supermarkets. This recipe was tested using one 29-ounce jar of Robertson's Mincemeat Classic. The test kitchen's preferred loaf pan, the Williams-Sonoma Goldtouch Nonstick Loaf Pan, measures 8½ by 4½ inches; if you use 9 by 5-inch loaf pans, start checking for doneness 5 minutes earlier than advised in the recipe. Shred the apple on the large holes of a box grater.

- 1 cup golden raisins
- 1 cup dried cranberries
- 1 Granny Smith apple, peeled, shredded, and squeezed dry
- 6 tablespoons brandy, plus extra for brushing
- ⅓ cup finely chopped crystallized ginger
- 1 teaspoon grated orange zest
- 1 (29-ounce) jar prepared mincemeat (2½ cups)
- 1 (14-ounce) can sweetened condensed milk
- 6 tablespoons vegetable oil
- 2 large eggs, lightly beaten
- 2¾ cups (13¾ ounces) all-purpose flour
- 1 teaspoon baking soda
- ½ teaspoon salt
- 1 tablespoon confectioners' sugar

1. Adjust oven rack to middle position and heat oven to 300 degrees. Grease and flour two 8½ by 4½-inch nonstick loaf pans. Combine raisins, cranberries, apple, brandy, ginger, and orange zest in large bowl. Let sit for 15 minutes.

2. Stir mincemeat, condensed milk, oil, and eggs into fruit mixture until thoroughly combined. Whisk flour, baking soda, and salt together in separate bowl. Stir flour mixture into fruit mixture until thoroughly combined (batter will be very thick).

3. Divide batter between prepared pans, smoothing tops with spatula. Bake until toothpick inserted in center comes out clean, 1¼ hours to 1 hour 25 minutes, switching and rotating pans halfway through baking. Let cakes cool in pans on wire rack for 15 minutes. Invert cakes onto rack and let cool completely.

4. Brush tops and sides of cakes with extra brandy. Wrap cakes tightly in aluminum foil and store at room temperature for at least 24 hours or up to 3 days. To serve, dust with confectioners' sugar and slice with serrated knife.

FIND THE ROOSTER!

A tiny version of this rooster has been hidden in the pages of this issue. Write to us with its location and we'll enter you in a random drawing. The first correct entry drawn will win our winning inexpensive Dutch oven, and each of the next five will receive a free one-year subscription to *Cook's Country*. To enter, visit CooksCountry. com/rooster by January 31, 2017 or write to Rooster DJ17, *Cook's Country*, P.O. Box 470739, Brookline, MA 02447. Include your name and address. Jake Davis of Scappoose, Oregon, found the rooster in the August/September 2017 issue on page 6 and won our favorite dry measuring cups.

WEB EXTRAS

Free for 4 months online at CooksCountry.com

U.S. POSTAL SERVICE STATEMENT OF OWNERSHIP, MANAGEMENT, AND CIRCULATION

1. Publication Title: *Cook's Country*; 2. Publication No. 1552-1990; 3. Filing date: 10/01/16; 4. Issue frequency: Dec/Jan, Feb/Mar, Apr/May, Jun/Jul, Aug/Sept, Oct/Nov; 5. No. of issues published annually: 6; 6. Annual Subscription Price: $35.70; 7. Complete mailing address of known office of publication: 17 Station Street, Brookline, MA 02445; 8. Complete mailing address of headquarters or general business office of publisher: 17 Station Street, Brookline, MA 02445; 9. Full names and complete mailing addresses of publisher, editor, and managing editor. Publisher, David Nussbaum, 17 Station Street, Brookline, MA 02445, Editor, Jack Bishop, 17 Station Street, Brookline, MA 02445, Managing Editor, Todd Meier, 17 Station Street, Brookline, MA 02445; 10. Owner: America's Test Kitchen LP, 17 Station Street, Brookline, MA 02445; 11. Known bondholders, mortgages, and other securities: NONE; 12. Tax status: Has Not Changed During Preceding 12 Months; 13. Publication title: *Cook's Country*; 14. Issue date for circulation data below: August/September 2016; 15A. Total number of copies: Average number of copies each issue during the preceding 12 months: 398,963 (Aug/Sep 2016: 372,757); B. Paid circulation: 1. Mailed outside-county paid subscriptions. Average number of copies each issue during the preceding 12 months: 322,069 (Aug/Sep 2016: 309,389); 2. Mailed in-county paid subscriptions. Average number of copies each issue during the preceding 12 months: 0 (Aug/Sep 2016: 0); 3. Sales through dealers and carriers, street vendors and counter sales. Average number of copies each issue during the preceding 12 months: 17,473 (Aug/Sep 2016: 15,840); 4. Paid distribution through other classes mailed through the USPS. Average number of copies each issue during the preceding 12 months: 0 (Aug/Sep 2016: 0); C. Total paid distribution. Average number of copies each issue during the preceding 12 months: 339,542 (Aug/Sep 2016: 325,229); D. Free or nominal rate distribution (by mail and outside mail); 1. Free or nominal Outside-County. Average number of copies each issue during the preceding 12 months: 1,347 (Aug/Sep 2016: 1,116); 2. Free or nominal rate in-county copies. Average number of copies each issue during the preceding 12 months: 0 (Aug/Sep 2016: 0); 3. Free or nominal rate copies mailed at other Classes through the USPS. Average number of copies each issue during preceding 12 months: 0 (Aug/Sep 2016: 0); 4. Free or nominal rate distribution outside the mail. Average number of copies each issue during preceding 12 months: 515 (Aug/Sep 2016: 515); E. Total free or nominal rate distribution. Average number of copies each issue during the preceding 12 months: 1,862 (Aug/Sep 2016: 1,631); F. Total free distribution. Average number of copies each issue during preceding 12 months: 341,404 (Aug/Sep 2016: 326,860); G. Copies not Distributed. Average number of copies each issue during preceding 12 months: 57,559 (Aug/Sep 2016: 45,897); H. Total. Average number of copies each issue during preceding 12 months: 398,963 (Aug/Sep 2016: 372,757); I. Percent paid. Average percent of copies paid for the preceding 12 months: 99.45% (Aug/Sep 2016: 99.50%).

Chocolate-Pecan Torte

Don't let the simplicity of this cake fool you—it's pure decadence,
with a hefty portion of ground pecans and rum added to a rich chocolate torte.

TO MAKE THIS CAKE, YOU WILL NEED:

- **8 ounces bittersweet chocolate, chopped**
- **6 tablespoons unsalted butter, cut into 3 pieces**
- **1½ cups pecan halves, plus about 30 halves for decorating**
- **1 cup (5 ounces) all-purpose flour**
- **¾ teaspoon ground cinnamon**
- **½ teaspoon salt**
- **4 large eggs, separated**
- **1 cup packed (7 ounces) light brown sugar**
- **2 teaspoons vanilla extract**
- **⅓ cup spiced rum**
- **1½ cups Chocolate Glaze (recipe follows)**

FOR THE CAKE: Adjust oven rack to middle position and heat oven to 300 degrees. Grease 9-inch springform pan and line bottom with parchment paper. Microwave chocolate and butter in bowl at 50 percent power, stirring occasionally, until melted, 1 to 2 minutes; let cool slightly. Process 1½ cups pecans, flour, cinnamon, and salt in food processor until finely ground, about 30 seconds.

Using stand mixer fitted with whisk attachment, whip egg whites on medium-low speed until foamy, about 1 minute. Increase speed to medium-high and whip whites to soft, billowy mounds, about 1 minute. Gradually add ¼ cup sugar and whip until glossy, soft peaks form, 1 to 2 minutes.

Whisk egg yolks, vanilla, and remaining ¾ cup sugar in large bowl until pale and thick, about 30 seconds. Slowly whisk in chocolate mixture until combined. Slowly whisk in rum until combined. Using whisk, fold in one-third of whipped whites. Using rubber spatula, gently fold in half of pecan mixture. Repeat with half of remaining whites and remaining pecan mixture, finishing with remaining whites. Transfer batter to prepared pan and bake until toothpick inserted in center comes out clean, 45 to 50 minutes, rotating pan halfway through baking. Let cake cool completely in pan on wire rack.

TO ASSEMBLE: Remove sides and bottom of springform pan. Invert cake onto wire rack set over rimmed baking sheet; discard parchment. Pour glaze evenly over top and sides of cake. Refrigerate until set, about 30 minutes. Transfer cake to plate or pedestal and arrange pecan halves along bottom edge. Serve.

CHOCOLATE GLAZE

Makes 1½ cups

Plan to use the glaze immediately after making it.

- **8 ounces bittersweet chocolate, chopped**
- **¾ cup heavy cream**
- **2 tablespoons corn syrup**
- **Pinch salt**

Place chocolate in medium bowl. Heat cream in small saucepan over medium-high heat until just starting to simmer. Pour over chocolate and let sit for 5 minutes. Gently whisk mixture, starting in center and working outward, until melted and smooth. Gently stir in corn syrup and salt until combined. Use immediately.

Inside This Issue